ARNOLD READERS IN HISTORY

FORTHCOMING TITLES IN THE
ARNOLD READERS IN HISTORY SERIES

BRITISH POLITICS AND SOCIETY 1906–1951
Edited by John Stevenson

THE ENGLISH CIVIL WAR
Edited by Richard Cust and Ann Hughes

GENDER AND HISTORY IN WESTERN EUROPE
Edited by Bob Shoemaker and Mary Vincent

THE ORIGINS OF THE SECOND WORLD WAR
Edited by Patrick Finney

THE TUDOR MONARCHY
Edited by John Guy

WOMEN'S WORK: THE ENGLISH EXPERIENCE 1650–1914
Edited by Pamela Sharpe

THE FRENCH REVOLUTION

IN SOCIAL AND POLITICAL PERSPECTIVE

Edited by
PETER JONES
Professor of French History, University of Birmingham

A member of the Hodder Headline Group
LONDON • NEW YORK • SYDNEY • AUCKLAND

First published in Great Britain in 1996 by
Arnold, a member of the Hodder Headline Group
338 Euston Road, London NW1 3BH
175 Fifth Avenue, New York, NY 10010

Distributed exclusively in the USA by
St Martin's Press, Inc.,
175 Fifth Avenue, New York, NY 10010

British Library Cataloguing in Publication Data
A catalogue entry for this book is available from the British Library

Library of Congress Cataloging-in-Publication Data
Jones, Peter, 1949–
The French Revolution in social and political perspective / Peter Jones
p. cm. – (Arnold readers in history)
Includes bibliographical references and index.
1. France–Politics and government–1789–1799. 2. France–Cultural policy–History–
18th century. 3. France–History–Revolution, 1789–1799–Social aspects.
I. Title. II. Series.
DC148.J575   1996
944.04–dc20   96–10518
CIP

ISBN 0 340 65290 X (Pb)
ISBN 0 340 65291 8 (Hb)

Typeset in 10/12pt Sabon by J&L Composition Ltd, Filey, North Yorkshire.
Printed and bound in Great Britain by J. W. Arrowsmith, Bristol.

Contents

Preface

The French Revolution was a seminal moment in modern history. Its reverberations can still be felt in the choices which individuals make in their daily lives. States, too, seek to find themselves in the principles of 1789. No fewer than 39 sovereign nations were represented at the ceremonies held in Paris to mark the recent bicentenary of the French Revolution. How many events in the past can be said to have defied collective amnesia on such a scale?

For students the challenge posed by the Revolution is rather different, of course. Everyone has heard of it, most can locate it in time and place, but few have the opportunity to study it in depth. Those that do are apt to find the very open-endess of the event a source of confusion rather than contentment. There are two reasons for this state of affairs. As the years roll by, historians write more and more books and articles about the French Revolution. While some of this scholarship is reinforcing, even repetitious, much is intended to raise doubt where once there was certainty, to substitute tones of grey in the place of black and white. If the historiography of the Revolution is a problem for students, however, then so is its history. No doubt every generation contrives to define what are, or are not, the fit objects of study in its past, and, understandably enough, the choices made can be highly evocative of contemporary preoccupations. Yet what must strike even the most casual student of the French Revolution is the lack of definition attaching to his chosen subject. Indeed, the field of French Revolution Studies no longer possesses a predetermined shape. It has become a 'free for all' in which every craft specialism is represented and none enjoys uncontested superiority over the rest.

Those who seek a familiarity with the Revolution for short-term educational purposes have therefore to overcome two related problems. Compass and timer in hand, they need to find a pathway through an ever-expanding literature and, no less important, one which will guide them over the shifting historical terrain of the 1790s. The quantitative problem is the most immediate. 'What should I read on the French Revolution?' This is a question which perplexes course-leaders almost as frequently as students, especially when followed by the deflating query, '. . . and are the books/articles in the college library?' French history is big business, a fact which may have more to do with the delights of study in Paris than with the intrinsic merits of the subject. Be that as it may, each year sees the publication of many thousands of books, articles and scholarly theses. Thus, in the time which it has taken to assemble the present volume, the historiographical mountain has expanded to encompass hundreds, if not thousands, of additional items for study. Fortunately, not all of this writing is devoted to the French Revolution. Nevertheless, literature surveys have shown that the 10-year period of 1789–99 regularly accounts for some 10 per cent of historiographical output. Every year, that is to say, no fewer than 2000 items are published on the French Revolution, whether in French, English or other languages.[1] What to read when both time and language skills are in short supply – therein lies the quantitative problem.

Of course, the question of what to read is not as bleak as it sounds. For, as we all know, the answer is largely determined by how the subject is defined. Yet here the intending student of the French Revolution encounters what might be termed the qualitative problem. In recent years, historians of the Revolution have redefined the object of study in response to pressures of two types. Along with much of the profession, they have participated in a reordering of research priorities in tandem, perhaps, with the general slippage of philosophical and political assumptions in the Developed World over the post-Second World War decades. However, a more specific reassessment of the subject-matter of the Revolution has also taken place, in response to debates generated from within the community of French historians. These pressures are in many ways congruent, although the productive tensions which have aligned scholars against one another since the late 1960s have pushed the exercise in remapping the territory of the French Revolution further ahead than might otherwise have been the case.

Some indications of the global pressures acting upon the study of French history can be found in the analysis of published output undertaken by Thomas Schaeper.[2] While he underscores the trend towards contemporaneity with which all history teachers are familiar, the real significance of his findings lies in the qualitative domain. On the evidence of articles submitted with a view to publication in the *Journal of French Historical Studies*, interest in traditional political and diplomatic history waned fast in the 1970s and 1980s. No doubt the momentum which social history built up in the 1960s had something to do with this, but Schaeper observes that even the citadel of social history was far from secure. In the 1980s younger scholars quit the pastures of social and economic history where an older generation had happily grazed in droves. This migration tended to the benefit of intellectual and cultural history which increased exponentially in popularity. Rejuvenated by new methodologies, it also became something of a weapon of war against a social history constricted by Marxist and Annalist categories. These years also witnessed the rapid advance of gendered history which has been largely, if not exclusively, encapsulated within the parameters of cultural history. More women were entering the profession, and more were choosing to work on gender themes and concepts. By contrast, male scholars largely vacated this territory.

The debates current among specialist historians of the Revolution run parallel to these developments and contribute powerfully to the impression that the subject no longer possesses any defining contours. They are discussed more fully in the Introduction. However, it must be recognized that the fixity of the Revolution is largely illusory. Ever since historians first set out to explore the 1790s, there has been earnest disagreement as to what, or whom, can be considered a fit object of study. A glance at library back-shelves bearing portentous volumes of Court memoirs, parliamentary histories, studies of orators, of generals, of statesmen, makes this point sufficiently. It should not be forgotten, either, that when Georges Lefebvre[3] inserted the peasant into the picture (and Albert Soboul[4] the *sans-culottes*) there were complaints that these unscripted arrivals complicated the Revolutionary 'stage play'. We should not grumble too loudly, therefore, if, in more recent times, research into Counter-Revolution, into gendered behaviour, into political culture, and into discursive and symbolic practices, has temporarily muddied the waters; for the confusion surely is temporary. It issues from the old idea that for all practical and theoretical purposes the events of the 1790s can be described as a 'bourgeois revolution', or to be precise from the substantial number of objections that have now been raised against this proposition. With the clarity conferred by hindsight, it is apparent that Lefebvre and Soboul struck the first blows against the 'revolutionary bourgeoisie' as a viable concept. This is an old debate, however, which is no longer worth pursuing. The fact remains that modern-day students approach the French Revolution at a particularly parlous moment in its history/historiography. They are faced with some ruined buildings that could yet be patched up, a lot of rubble of no great value, and just the barest outline of foundation trenches hinting at an effect of reconstruction which has barely begun.

The purpose of this Reader is not to impose order where there is none. As yet, it is too early to do more than speculate on how an intellectually coherent vision of the French Revolution might be retrieved. Some indication of the most fruitful points of contact between scholars is offered at the end of the Introduction, but this is not to suggest that a convergence of ideas will necessarily take place. Rather, my purpose in assembling a collection of secondary writings on the Revolutionary period is to capture the range of activities taking place on the building-site. This approach tends inevitably to privilege the ongoing exertions of historians, rather than the sturdy constructions of the past that have now fallen into disrepair. I make no apology for adopting this approach. The classic statements on the French Revolution mostly address the question of origins and are still worth reading; but they have been gathered together in Readers before (*see* Glossary of Readers), and to include them would be to prejudice coverage of more recent research. In short, this volume looks to the future rather than the past. It tries to identify those books and articles which current and future generations of teachers may wish to recommend to students as benchmark texts. This involves a gamble on the future shape of French Revolution Studies as a curricular subject, of course. However, it is my judgement that intensive study patterned on the Special Subject courses offered by British universities will no longer provide the standard access route in the years to come. More likely, students will encounter the Revolution in a discrete form, that is to say packaged within thematic, comparative and interdisciplinary formats.

It would be disingenuous, nonetheless, to claim that this volume is no more than a cross-sectional guide to recent and current research. All selections presuppose the existence of organizing principles and these can be stated simply. I have angled the selection towards the 'social' and the 'political', although neither category is intended to set up barriers. The 'social', in my understanding, embraces all forms of cultural and intellectual history save those which radically deny human agency (*see* Introduction, p. 6), whereas the political makes full allowance for the significant enlargement of our understanding of the Revolution which has taken place under the rubric 'political culture'. As for chronological range, the materials chosen for inclusion delve into the final decades of the *ancien régime*, for it is precisely in this area that the conceptual tool of 'political culture' has proved most effective in highlighting the transition from absolute to constitutional monarchy. By contrast, coverage ceases with the familiar climax of power politics, that is to say with Thermidor, the dismantling of the Terror and the arduous task of laying to rest its legacy of violence.

With these parameters established, considerations of a more specific nature intervened. Accessibility and intelligibility come high on the agenda, for what is a Reader if not a book designed to accommodate the study needs of students. I have therefore excluded from this selection statements which appeared to me to lie beyond the intellectual resources of competent honours-level and graduate students. On occasion, this required the deletion of a text much praised by the scholarly community and its replacement with a similar, simpler statement by the same author. I have also made sparing use of the editorial power of abridgement, usually in order to achieve greater clarity, occasionally in order to save space. Such is the speed with which the corpus of writings on the French Revolution expands that the problem of duplication rarely arose, especially once the

decision to leave out the classic historiography had been taken. Getting the
balance of viewpoints right in what must of necessity be an English-language
publication was more troublesome. For a few French scholars still doubt
whether it is possible for 'Anglo-Saxons' to understand 'their' Revolution.
Hopefully, the inclusion of several pieces in translation will redress any
unintended bias towards an excessively Atlanticist interpretation.

Section 1 is designed to provide a point of entry. Without examining the
entrails of old debates, it furnishes the reader with enough information to
grasp the salient features of the neo-jacobin version of the Revolution, its
manifold deficiencies, and its blind spots. Several ways of rethinking the
question of origins are suggested, as is a means of working towards a fresh
consensus. The range of interpretive approaches made possible by the
removal of socio-economic structures from the explanatory equation is
the theme of Section 2. Gender issues and the use which Revolutionaries
made of body politic images feature next, in Section 3; whereas Section 4
attempts a broad sweep over the more conventional ground of the political
history of the Revolution. Section 5 extrapolates from that narrative in
order to dwell upon the pathology of Revolutionary politics. It explores
the ways historians have confronted the role of the crowd and their
attempts to reach an understanding of the Terror.

Notes to the Preface

1 Taking a 5-year average for the period 1989–1993 the figure is 2394. See
   *Bibliographie annuelle de l'histoire de France du cinquième siècle à 1958: année
   1993* (Paris, C.N.R.S. Editions, Paris, 1994), p.vii.
2 Thomas J. Schaeper, 'French History as Written on Both Sides of the Atlantic: A
   Comparative Analysis', *French Historical Studies*, 17(1991), 233–48.
3 *See* Georges Lefebvre, *Les Paysans du Nord pendant la Révolution française*
   (Paris, 1924, reprinted in a condensed version Bari, 1959). For a more accessible
   interpretation in English translation, *see* Georges Lefebvre, *The Coming of the
   French Revolution* (Princeton, N.J., Princeton University Press 1989).
4 *See* Albert Soboul, *Les Sans-culottes parisiens en l'an II: mouvement populaire
   et gouvernement révolutionnaire, 2 juin 1793 – 9 thermidor an II* (Paris, Librarie
   Clevreuil, 1958). For a condensed version in English translation, *see* Albert
   Soboul, *The Parisian Sans-Culottes and the French Revolution, 1793–4*
   (Oxford, Oxford University Press, 1964).

Acknowledgements

The inspiration for this book comes from my students; or, to be precise, it stems from their oft-repeated requests for guided reading on the subject of the French Revolution. However, the work of compilation would probably never have been undertaken had it not been for Christopher Wheeler. As the commissioning editor, Christopher persuaded me that the project was both worthwhile and viable from a publisher's point of view.

Unsure whether my advice on reading paralleled that given by other university and college teachers, I carried out extensive market research. Colleagues all round the world took time and trouble to reply to my questionnaire. Although the replies served mainly to demonstrate the immensity of the task (and the gaps in my own reading), I am grateful to all of my respondents. In particular, I would like to thank the following: Alan Forrest, Jean Boutier, Marianne Elliott, Gwynne Lewis, David Garrioch, John Bosher, Mike Sonenscher, Tip Ragan, Mike Fitzsimmons, Isser Woloch, Norman Hampson, Barrie Rose, Sarah Maza, Peter McPhee, Steven Reinhardt, Colin Lucas, Vivian Gruder, Don Sutherland, Jack Censer, Emmet Kennedy, Darline Levy, Clarke Garrett, Keith Baker, Michael Rapport, Patrice Higonnet, Robert Gildea, Martyn Lyons, Margaret Darrow, Lynn Hunt, Colin Heywood, Malcolm Crook, Tim Blanning, Colin Jones, Bill Doyle, Barry Shapiro, Frank Tallett, Douglas Johnson, James Figuglietti, Bill Murray, Mel Edelstein and Joan Landes.

The editor and the publisher would also like to thank the following for permission to use copyright material in this volume:

The New York Review of Books for Robert Darnton, 'What was Revolutionary about the French Revolution?', reprinted with permission from the *New York Review of Books*, Copyright © 1989 Nyrev, Inc; Cambridge University Press, Éditions Gallimard, and the author for François Furet, 'The French Revolution is Over', from François Furet, *Interpreting the French Revolution* (Cambridge, 1981), pp. 1–28; the author for Peter Jones, 'Georges Lefebvre and the Peasant Revolution:

Fifty Years On', *French Historical Studies* 16 (1990), pp. 545–63; Oxford University Press for Colin Jones, 'Bourgeois Revolution Revivified: 1789 and Social Change'. © Colin Jones 1991. Reprinted from *Rewriting the French Revolution: The Andrew Browning Lectures 1989* edited by Colin Lucas (1991) by permission of Oxford University Press; The University of Chicago Press and the author for Sarah Maza, 'Politics, Culture and the Origins of the French Revolution', *Journal of Modern History*, 61 (1989), pp. 703–23; Routledge for Gwynne Lewis, 'Rethinking the Debate', from Gwynne Lewis *The French Revolution: Rethinking the Debate* (1993), pp. 106–13, 121–22; University of California Press and the author for Keith Baker, 'Public Opinion as Political Invention', Jack R. Censer and J. D. Popkin, eds, *Press and Politics in Pre-Revolutionary France*, pp. 204–46, © 1987 The Regents of the University of California; Duke University Press for Roger Chartier, 'Do Books Make Revolutions?', from Roger Chartier, *The Cultural Origins of the French Revolution*, pp. 67–91, 207–10, reprinted with permission of Duke University Press, © Duke University Press, Durham, N.C., 1991; University of California Press and the author for James Leith, 'Ephemera: Civic Education Through Images', from R. Darnton and D. Roche, eds, *Revolution in Print: The Press in France, 1775–1800*, pp. 270–89, 347–48, © 1989 The New York Public Library, Astor, Lenox, and Tilden Foundations; Oxford University Press for Margaret Jacob, 'The Enlightenment Redefined', excerpted from Margaret Jacob, *Living the Enlightenment: Freemasonry and Politics in Eighteenth-Century Europe* (1991), pp. 215–24, 292–4, Copyright © 1991 Oxford University Press; The American Society for Eighteenth-Century Studies for Daniel Wick, 'The Court Nobility and the French Revolution: The Example of the Society of Thirty', *Eighteenth-Century Studies*, 13 (Spring 1980), pp. 263–84; The American Historical Association and the author for Jane Abray, 'Feminism in the French Revolution', *The American Historical Review*, 80 (1975), pp. 43–62; the author for Barrie Rose, 'Feminism, Women and the French Revolution', which first appeared in *The Australian Journal of Politics and History*, 40 (1994), pp. 173–86, and subsequently in *Historical Reflections/Réflexions Historiques*, vol. 21, no. 1 (Winter 1995), pp. 187–205; The Johns Hopkins University Press for Lynn Hunt, 'The Many Bodies of Marie-Antoinette: Political Pornography and the Problem of the Feminine in the French Revolution', from L. Hunt (ed.), *Eroticism and the Body Politic* (1991), pp. 108–30; the author for Olwen Hufton, 'Counter-Revolutionary Women', from Olwen Hufton, *Women and the Limits of Citizenship in the French Revolution* (1992), pp. 94–130; 168–74; The American Historical Association and the author for Timothy Tackett, 'Nobles and the Third Estate in the Revolutionary Dynamic of the National Assembly, 1789–1790', *The American Historical Review*, vol. 94, no. 2 (April 1989), pp. 271–301; Oxford University Press and the author for Claude Petitfrère, 'The Origins of the Civil War in the

Vendée', from *French History,* 2 (1988), pp. 187–207. Reprinted with permission of Oxford University Press; Elsevier Science for Alan Forrest, 'Federalism', from C. Lucas (ed.), *The French Revolution and the Creation of Modern Political Culture.* Vol. 2: *The Political Culture of the French Revolution* (Oxford, 1988), pp. 309–27. Reprinted with permission of Elsevier Science Ltd., Pergamon Imprint, Oxford, England; Blackwell Publishers for Norman Hampson, 'Saint-Just: the Military Commissar', from N. Hampson, *Saint-Just* (Oxford, 1991), pp. 140–60; Sage Publications for Martyn Lyons, 'The 9 Thermidor: Motives and Effects', *European Studies Review,* 15, pp. 123–46, © 1975 Sage Publications Ltd; Elsevier Science for Colin Lucas, 'The Crowd and Politics', from C. Lucas (ed.), *The French Revolution and the Creation of Modern Political Culture.* Vol. 2: *The Political Culture of the Revolution* (Oxford, 1988), pp. 259–85, reprinted with permission of Elsevier Science Ltd, Pergamon Imprint, Oxford, England; Harvard University Press for François Furet, 'Terror', from *A Critical Dictionary of the French Revolution* edited by F. Furet and M. Ozouf, Cambridge, Mass.: Harvard University Press, Copyright © 1989 by the President and Fellows of Harvard College. Reprinted by permission of the publishers. First published as *Dictionnaire Critique de la Révolution Française,* © 1988 by Flammarion; Oxford University Press for Richard Cobb, 'The Rise and Fall of a Provincial Terrorist' reprinted from Richard Cobb, *Reactions to the French Revolution* (1972) by permission of Oxford University Press. © 1972 Oxford University Press; Éditions Gallimard and Cambridge University Press for Bronislaw Baczko, 'The End of Year Two' reprinted from B. Baczko, *Ending the Terror: the French Revolution after Robespierre* (Cambridge, 1994).

Introduction

The major turning-point in the modern historiography of the French Revolution occurred in the late 1960s and early 1970s, for it was at this moment that the determinism of social and economic structures came under frontal attack. The challenge effectively relaunched the subject as a field of enquiry, making possible a series of advances in method and in knowledge. As a result, the decades of the 1980s and 1990s have registered sustained progress in our understanding of the socio-political, the socio-cultural and most recently the intellectual or ideological history of the *ancien régime* and the Revolution. The American historian George Taylor must bear a large responsibility for these developments. He it was who first dared to disconnect the Revolutionary dynamo from its socio-economic power-supply, declaring memorably that 1789 was 'essentially a political revolution with social consequences and not a social revolution with political consequences'.[1] Simultaneously, the British historian Richard Cobb, assisted by a swelling band of graduate students, was raising awkward questions for the received picture of the Revolution and its origins. Characteristically, though, Cobb's plea was for a better, empirically founded social history, rather than no social history at all. 'There are increasing signs', he wrote in 1970, 'that the study of the French Revolution is at last coming to terms with human beings; the Ice Age of Social Structures is over and the process of humanization is already under way, at least in England'.[2]

Taylor's conviction that a social, indeed socialist, interpretation was no longer essential for an understanding of the events of 1789 had been hardened by Alfred Cobban's determination to puncture some of the 'myths' surrounding the French Revolution.[3] By contrast, Cobb was grappling with the very recalcitrance of social history in times of civil turmoil, and in the process posing fundamental questions of method. 'How can anyone ever again write anything about the French Revolution on the national level when, apparently, every place is a law to itself and nothing is quite what it seemed to be at first sight?'[4]. Why American and British historians should have played such a prominent role in rejuvenating the study of the French Revolution is an interesting question, and one not easily answered. Detachment from all the interlocking myths of Jacobinism and latter-day Republicanism must count for something. Non-French scholars do not identify with the Revolution in the same way as do native historians. Once the conceptual breakthrough had been secured in the 1970s, many decided simply to steer clear of the 'quagmires'[5] of social interpretations altogether. Instead, they devoted their energies to opening up different lines of enquiry. However, it is no less true that academic study of the Revolution within France entered a barren period in the 1960s.

Overemphasis of social and economic structures ended up confining research, as the pages of the *Annales historiques de la Révolution française* (house-journal of Revolution scholars) bear witness. Moreover, the gathering strength of Braudel's Annales School tended to divert the best young historians away from French Revolution Studies, and to inhibit the renewal of mere *histoire événementielle*. As usual, Richard Cobb identified the culprit: 'the New Orthodoxy of the Sixième Section (Life, Death, Love, Passion, Envy, Rain, Water, Fear, Plague yes; human beings, no, never).'[6]

One major consequence of the faltering of neo-jacobin social history was the realization that a new explanation of origins would have to be found. Scholars on both sides of the Atlantic drew the conclusion that the answer must lie in the political history of the latter decades of the *ancien régime*. In France, progress in this direction was hindered by score settling, however. The more constructive features of the 'revisionist' critique mounted by François Furet and Denis Richet[7] only really began to attract attention in the late 1970s. The milestone publication which signalled the next stage in the development of French Revolution Studies was Furet's *Penser la Révolution française* (1978). It came out in English three years later (*see* Reading 2) and placed those still adhering to received wisdom in an untenable position. Course tutors could no longer afford to ignore the mounting number of historiographical discrepancies in the hope that the pieces would somehow fall into place over time. On the other hand, Furet could not at this stage offer a more convincing synthetic vision of the Revolution, although his rediscovery of the ideas of the nineteenth-century historian, Alexis de Tocqueville, promised a good deal. In any case, the most innovative research was now starting to come from the 'Anglo-Saxon' empirical school as American and British historians set about remapping the *ancien régime*.

A virtual *terra incognita* before the 1980s, our knowledge of the final decades of the *ancien régime* has been transformed. We have masterly biographies (Condorcet, Choiseul, Necker, Vergennes, Louis XVI), studies of the Court, of the professions (clergy, nobility, barristers) and of the institutions of state (monarchy, Church, *parlements*, Provincial Estates, Academies, salons, etc.). Although this research commenced with no fixed design (other than to escape the givens of Revolutionary historiography), it has proved enormously fertile in generating a new way of conceptualizing the political history of the late eighteenth century and in redefining a new, nonhegemonic social history. Both developments have occurred pretty much in tandem, but for the sake of clarity it is best to separate them out.

Political history, as traditionally understood, received scant attention from the scholars enquiring into the origins of the French Revolution for two reasons. First of all, the political history of the late *ancien régime* led nowhere, in as much as 1789 was deemed to have gouged an unbridgeable chasm between the old regime and the new. Second, political roles were derivative of the social, or so it was widely believed. This mechanistic view of political history scarcely encouraged fresh thinking about the parties involved in the collapse of absolutism. The privileged orders could be safely assumed to have had selfish interests and the Third Estate to have been fundamentally progressive in outlook, whereas the Bourbon monarchy plainly constituted a bastion of immobile conservatism. However, with the liberation of politics and its explosion as a category into an altogether more open-ended phenomenon dubbed 'political culture', hitherto undetected traits of modernity within the so-called old regime began to come to the fore. In the view of scholars like Keith Baker[8] and Lynn Hunt[9] the central innovation of these years was the growth of public opinion; understood not as the fickle temper of the masses but as a kind of rational counter-society of the educated which sat in judgement upon the contortions of Bourbon absolutism. Although it would be possible to root this critical community, both socially and institutionally, Keith Baker, at least, prefers to describe it as a political invention or rhetorical construct (*see* Reading 7) called into being during the jousts between the monarchy and the Parlement of Paris from the 1750s onwards.

Historians do not all agree on the significance to be attached to this rather disembodied depiction of public opinion (and its sociological projection in the form of a 'civil public sphere'[10]). Nonetheless, it has been enormously fruitful in stimulating research on the culture of the printed word, on the institutional forms of public life, on the construction of political vocabulary and on ministerial attempts to refashion the foundations of adminstrative élites. Twin conferences held at the universities of Chicago and Oxford in 1986–87 served to demonstrate the vigour with which study of the *ancien régime* was now being prosecuted, and they launched a succession of publications bearing the apt title: *The French Revolution and the Creation of Modern Political Culture*.[11] Critics were to point out that the revised reading of political history contained some strange omissions (Court politics, reforming absolutism, social conflict, women). The new agenda, that is to say, incurred the same suspicion of partisanship as the old; but at least the perspicacious student could now make a choice between rival approaches. Besides, some of the gaps and silences in the record were being plugged from other directions.

In the 1980s, social history shed its preoccupation with the lower orders and broadened to resemble something more akin to socio-cultural history. The convergence, it should be said, was aided by the willingness of cultural historians to abandon their exclusive preoccupation with the products of high art, literature and the theatre and to seek out subject-matter at less exalted social levels. Nothing captured this transition more vividly than the metamorphosis of the Enlightenment. In the hands of Robert Darnton[12] and subsequent practitioners, it ceased to resemble a movement of pure ideas by 20 or so 'great men' and became a branch of the social history of the *ancien régime*. As a result, the focus shifted from the *philosophes* to the *gens de lettres*, that is to say the literary intelligentsia who featured so prominently in the 'critical community' espied by political historians. The next shift will surely take the Enlightenment into closer alignment with government. For, as scholars reassess the achievements of Bourbon absolutism, it is becoming apparent that royal bureaucrats were one of the most potent forces driving reform-minded public opinion. A paradox? This approach certainly lays down a challenge to those who view the *philosophes* as a 'terrorist brigade'[13] bent on destroying the *ancien régime* from outside. Evidence is also accumulating, however, which argues for a relationship of complicity between the ideas of the Enlightenment and those in charge of the Bourbons' state-building mission in the 1770s and 1780s. Indeed, if historians could finally bring themselves to jettison the notion that absolutism functioned as a consistently conservative phenomenon, many of the subsisting tensions between political and social history and between the Enlightenment and the Revolution would be smoothed away.

As the unsung ranks of free thinkers have emerged from historiographical neglect, so have the institutions which gave their lives shape and meaning. We now know so much more about the business end of the Enlightenment, and about the vehicles that were created, or adapted, for the purpose of cultural diffusion. A case in point is freemasonry. Fearful lest they be accused of giving credence to conspiracy theories, social historians rarely mentioned the subject before the 1970s. Now the role performed by masonic lodges in the intellectual preparation of the Revolution is widely acknowledged (*see* Reading 10). Whether that role included the formulation of a rudimentary 'jacobin' ideology is a matter for discussion, but there can be no doubt that freemasonry massively extended both the geographical range and the social penetration of Enlightenment thought during the closing decades of the *ancien régime*. Academies and salons functioned at a more rarefied level. Nonetheless the latter, especially, have benefited from a major effort of re-interpretation, driven largely by the feminist critique of eighteenth-century historiography. Administering a corrective to older and very largely masculine statements about the Enlightenment, Dena Goodman reminds us that the salons provided a 'female-controlled discursive space'[14] and one located at the very nexus of cultural interchange.

The gender-based approach, indeed, was an early beneficiary of the meltdown of social structures and the rediscovery of human beings. It developed first as an adjunct to Cobb-style social history, that is to say as part and parcel of studies of the family, poverty and the crowd.[15] Even today, some 20 and 30 years after those pioneering attempts to capture the experiences of women caught up in the turmoil of Revolution, there remains a strong 'lived history' thread in the literature on women. However, somewhere along the way larger and more theoretical questions began to be asked, inspired no doubt by the publication in 1979 of an important document collection on *Women in Revolutionary Paris, 1789–1795*.[16] The underpinnings of this new research were avowedly feminist and the focus shifted away from the purely social. Since gender could now be deemed to constitute a 'founding category of modern politics, culture and ideology',[17] the objective was to interrogate the French Revolution, to find out why a liberating moment in the history of men did not confer equivalent benefits on women. This enquiry continues. It has produced re-readings of the role of women in the Enlightenment, and notably the suggestion already mentioned that the salons served as training facilities for female emancipation. It has shed some new light on the political mobilization of women after 1789 and the reasons why (male) revolutionaries did not welcome this incursion into the public arena. Finally, it has generated important research on the symbolic language of gender, on the revealing ways in which politicians used sexual and body metaphors in the cut and thrust of debate (*see* Reading 14).

Has a feminist reading of the Revolution now taken shape alongside the orthodox and the revisionist interpretations? The best offering of this type is Joan Landes' *Women in the Public Sphere in the Age of the French Revolution*, which was first published in 1988 and has been reprinted several times subsequently.[18] Paying scant attention to the nuanced colours in which social historians ply their trade, the author paints a picture of considerable freedom of action for women during the closing decades of the *ancien régime* followed by denial and exclusion at the hands of self-consciously masculine Revolutionaries. The universalistic rhetoric of 1789 should not be allowed to deceive, she warns, for the Republic was constructed with the deliberate intention of removing women from the public sphere. Objections have been raised against this scenario from several quarters (*see* Reading 13). However, its most vulnerable flank appears to be the suggestion that women, as a category, did not have a Revolution. This flies in the face of evidence accumulated by the other strand of the historiography on women, that is to say by scholars interested in the real-life experiences of individual women. Real-life Revolutionary women exercised formal and informal rights of citizenship in crowds, in village assemblies, in church congregations, in divorce petitions, in legal contracts and much else besides. In short, the challenging approach of Joan Landes and others like her raises a problem of perspective. It is certainly true that women were almost entirely excluded from the political public sphere by the end of 1793, but is that so surprising? More significant, perhaps, is the fact that women had enjoyed *any* freedom to mobilize and to participate in the political process.

The retreat of social and economic history, indeed the eclipse of social interpretations generally, gave fresh heart to those mainly interested in ideas. Intellectual historians had had a hard time defending their specialist viewpoint in the 1950s and 1960s. The determinism of deep structures, whether inspired by Marx or Braudel, tended to steamroller all that lay in its path. Even the research undertaken in the 1970s proved problematic. François Furet was tugging in the direction of a primarily ideological interpretation of the Revolution, but much of the work in progress on the Enlightenment tended to pull in the opposite direction, as we have seen. The breakthrough, for intellectual historians, was above all methodological. It took the form of borrowings from social anthropology and from contemporary literary theory which served jointly to propel scholars in search of inner meanings. Since the new breed of socio-cultural historians had already fastened attention on the printed word as the defining characteristic of eighteenth-century political culture, the quest for ideological explanations of the *ancien régime* and the Revolution soon settled into the study of language, or discourse.

This focus on discourse, and more especially upon the linguistic strategies employed by corporate groups, has been fruitful up to a point. Old-regime historians have been taught new ways of conceptualizing *parlementaire* resistance to the crown, and scholars of the Revolution now know better than to take the rhetoric of the *sans-culottes* at face value.[19] However, the risk inherent in this approach is that it tends to produce a slippage from people to ideas and from ideas to texts. That is to say the object of study becomes the emblematic text which is somehow deemed to express the essence of historical experience. Apologists for intellectual history point out, quite rightly, that language is not an epiphenomenon. It helps to fix and to define social and political reality. In practice, though, scholars like François Furet and Keith Baker are making larger claims which invite us to view language as the ultimate constituent of reality. How much attention should we pay to the human actors, therefore? Not much it would seem. According to Georges Lefebvre and Albert Soboul the masses made the Revolution, spurred on by a mix of socio-economic discontents. 'On the contrary', replies Keith Baker, 'the power of their actions depended upon a set of symbolic representations and cultural meanings that constituted the significance of their behaviour and gave it explosive force'.[20]

For such a potent force, this 'language' of symbolic representations and cultural meanings is worryingly opaque. Yet one thing is clear: it evacuates most forms of social history from the picture altogether. Instead, we are left with another version of the determinism of deep structures which satisfies some historians just as it frustrates others. The complexities of the old regime and the Revolution are reduced to ideological positions and then bracketed into language 'scripts'. According to the practitioners of the new intellectual history, the essential problem faced by the Revolutionaries was how to resolve the tension between Rousseauian notions of the General Will and a commitment to balanced powers and constitutional monarchy as enshrined in the thought of Montesquieu. That they failed to achieve a resolution and, as early as 1789, opted for the former rather than the latter (so it is suggested), more or less dictated the future course of the Revolution. Thus the Terror can be construed as a kind of intellectual nemesis. Its characteristic language (and therefore behaviour) was scripted from the moment of failure to establish a viable pluralistic monarchy at the very start of the Revolution (*see* Reading 22).

Many would dissent from this radical re-interpretation of the Terror. Indeed, the whole question of where we should locate the 'meaning' of the French Revolution remains a subject of intense debate. These issues, however, beg a larger question which will serve as a sobering final thought in our survey of recent literature. As some of the most eminent scholars of the Revolution part company with social and political history, of whatever vintage, it must be asked whether the phenomenon under study is not slipping out of the hands of the historians altogether. The craft of history-writing can only absorb so many new methodologies, and some of the latest arrivals seem to have had the effect of obscuring rather than illuminating how people behaved in the past.

This may prove to be a hasty and unnecessarily gloomy prognosis, however. For the political, the social and the intellectual histories of the French Revolution are not predestined to travel for ever along separate and divergent paths. Let us, instead, attempt a stocktaking of the current range of opinion. Such is the pace and the scope of ongoing research that few generalizations survive intact for long; indeed it is quite possible that some of the raw materials from which to construct a more consensual vision of the Revolution already exist. The problem of origins remains, to be sure. Many historians prefer to locate the forces that wrought the Revolution in the knowledge-based culture of the Enlightenment: 'its first cause was neither economic nor social, in the classic sense of either word. Its motor was instead the complicated cultural transformation of the country's possessing, administrative and educated élites in the preceding century.'[21] Probably no one, today, would dispute the need for a culturalist reading of the late *ancien régime*, but explanations couched in these terms are less adept at accounting for sudden and dramatic change. What is missing from such a generalization is some recognition of the element of conflict. Until socio-cultural historians acknowledge the role of conflict in generating and sustaining states of mind, it is unlikely that our understanding of the origins of the French Revolution will advance significantly. Yet the obstacle is surely more apparent than real, for a prudent acceptance that the *ancien régime* was also torn apart by uncontainable tensions is not to readmit class conflict by the back door.

Fear of slipping back into modes of thinking prevalent in the 1950s and 1960s inhibits dispassionate investigation of the 'bourgeois revolution' thesis, too. The difficulty stems, of course, from the materialist obsession which links the social formation of the bourgeoisie to the rise of capitalism. However, if we were to amputate the bourgeoisie from the economic history of the period and to insert it into the new cultural history of the *ancien régime*, a case could still be made for retaining a variant of the 'bourgeois revolution' hypothesis as a useful tool of analysis. After all, Jürgen Habermas' delineation of the 'civil public sphere' which has proved so fruitful in reinvigorating the study of eighteenth-century politics was originally conceived as a means of depicting the gestation and birth of a specifically bourgeois culture.[22] An argument for the reinstatement of the bourgeoisie which combines themes drawn from recent socio-economic historiography with evidence drawn from the perspective of political culture is included in this collection (*see* Reading 4). Nevertheless, it has to be admitted, many historians would still challenge any suggestion that the putative bourgeois culture should be described as liberal-individualist, let alone proto-capitalist or proto-revolutionary. For them George Taylor's model of a professional and landowning bourgeoisie sharing a corporatist and proprietary outlook continues to hold good.[23]

Maybe it would be more fruitful to search for historical agency elsewhere; in the realm of pure ideas, perhaps, or in the role of the state. Some discussion of the ways in which intellectual historians apprehend the Revolution has already been offered. It seems unlikely that a *rapprochement* will issue from this quarter. More promising, though, is the renewal of institutional history which is attracting many able social as well as political historians. Theda Skocpol's identification of the Bourbon state as a 'key actor'[24] in the process of Revolutionary change was crucial in this respect, for it introduced a new variable into arguments that had started to mark time. Who was largely responsible for the creation of public opinion and the moulding of the 'civil public sphere'? The Bourbons. What force supplied the momentum for the renovation of the social structures of the *ancien régime*? The Bourbon state machine. Whose activities contributed most to the dismantling of absolute monarchy? Those of Louis XVI and his reform ministers. There is a danger in viewing the state as an all-purpose *deus ex machina*, of course. Nonetheless, for one historian it provides a neat solution: 'the government itself generated such social origins of revolution as existed, first by consolidating the social bases of public opinion and of corporate or private opinion and then by rendering itself vulnerable (through fiscal exhaustion).'[25] Vulnerable, that is to say, to a combined assault by the privileged élites of the old society of orders.

Statist arguments of this type have obvious implications for how we should conceive the Revolution proper. Maybe Alexis de Tocqueville's verdict that the dynamo of the Revolution was simply a reincarnation of the *ancien régime* administrative state should be considered afresh, in which case the contemporary discourse buttressing the notion of 1789 as a radical break needs to be treated with care. Was its function in the minds and mouths of the Revolutionaries to provide a (self-deluding) illusion of change? At the level of pure ideas François Furet[26] and those who think like him doubt whether the transition did change anything in essence. The absolutism of Bourbon monarchs was re-embedded in the National Assembly in the form of the doctrine of sovereignty of the people. Thus, he argues, the Revolution can be described as Rousseauian and proto-republican in its fundamental characteristics from the very start, thereby blurring the distinction between 'liberal-constitutional' and 'jacobin-totalitarian' phases which he and other historians used to insist upon. The logic of this position also supposes that violence and terror were endemic from the beginning, as we have noted. However, the distillation of complex phenomena into logical essences raises awkward problems of an empirical nature, and at present it seems unlikely that the majority of scholars will be drawn far in this direction. The ongoing reappraisal of the *ancien régime* from a political culture perspective militates against glib statements to the effect that the Revolutionary legislatures inherited the absolutism of the old monarchy. How absolute was Bourbon political practice by 1789? A no less plausible argument could be made that the 1780s provided the theatre for the tortured birth of liberal constitutional monarchy which is what the deputies of the National Assembly would finally coax into life. Indeed research on the earliest phase of the Revolution is currently experiencing a revival, and the consensus view depicts those deputies not as instruments of the General Will but as cautious pragmatists committed to the politics of balance and compromise.[27]

It is by no means certain, then, that scholars will unite around a totalizing vision of the Revolution in the years ahead. The thread of discourse analysis is not strong enough to knit this wayward phenomenon together. However, if the Terror was not the product of a ready-scripted language, what was it? Richard Cobb supplied an answer to the question long before the current debate began (*see* Reading 23). The Terror, he concluded, emanated from the actions of fairly ordinary people who were taking decisions at the local, operational end of the Revolution. Many historians would still identify with this circumstantial, 'bottom up' viewpoint; but Cobb added an important rider – terror and Revolutionary violence can easily slip beyond the control of people and provide governments with an 'alibi for the absence of any coherent policy'.[28] In a sense, therefore, an historically specific language of the Terror did develop, but it sprang out of the descent into political violence after 1792. It did not drive the process. Where the ideological approach proves more useful is in exploring the painful disengagement from the characteristic rhetoric of Terror once its political *raison d'être* no longer obtained (*see* Reading 24). In truth, though, the primary question raised by these discussions relates not to the Terror as such, but to Revolutionary political culture. For an understanding of the part played by political violence in the events of 1789 and subsequent years seems to provide the historian with the clue that leads to a much greater prize: the secret of the political culture of the Revolution. Was it pluralist or totalitarian? Depending on the answer, what value judgement should we bestow upon the burgeoning political culture of the *ancien régime*?

It would be helpful for students, if not scholars who make their living by poking at the entrails of the Revolution, to end this introduction with the suggestion that a coherent interpretation is now in prospect. This is not the case, however. The chances of a new 'orthodoxy' emerging to replace the social interpretation fashioned by Lefebvre and Soboul are negligible. If the historiography of the French Revolution over the past 200 years teaches us anything, it is that 'orthodoxy' tends to be purchased at the price of reductionism and political correctness. Today, there are simply too many scholars working within too many traditions to produce the kind of alignment of opinion that characterized the post-Second World War decades. Nevertheless, it is both possible and permissible to speculate about the shape of French Revolution Studies in the years to come. For a start, the long-term viability of the new intellectual history pivoted on texts rather than context is open to question. As a discipline its place seems secure, but as a methodology applied to the study of the Revolution it has a number of drawbacks.

If, as appears probable, the well springs of intellectual history are not replenished, the most likely beneficiary will be the social history of the *ancien régime* and the Revolution. This shift will bring scant comfort to economic historians and historical materialists, however, for the replenishment of social history as an active category of research depends heavily on the vigour of culture and gender studies. Yet it is possible, as Gwynne Lewis[29] suggests (*see* Reading 6), that the best hope for a post-Revisionist meeting of minds lies down this road. If those historians whose professional training was broadly Marxist can accommodate an approach which grants considerable independence to ideas, culture and state formations (as now seems possible), then the historiography of the French Revolution has taken a major step forward. Yet it has to be matched among historians of culture, gender and, yes, language. They must recognize that real social and economic forces were at work in the years preceding 1789, and throughout the Revolutionary decade.

Notes to Introduction

1 George V. Taylor, 'Noncapitalist Wealth and the Origins of the French Revolution', *American Historical Review*, 72 (1967), p. 491.

2 *See* his unsigned review article in *Times Literary Supplement*, 29 January 1970, p. 109.

3 In his inaugural lecture as the newly appointed Professor of French History at the University of London in 1955. *The Myth of the French Revolution* is reprinted in Alfred Cobban, *Aspects of the French Revolution* (St Albans, Paladin), 90–112. The subsequent debate can be followed in William Doyle, *Origins of the French Revolution* (Oxford, Oxford University Press, 1980), pp. 7–40.

4 Richard C. Cobb, *Reactions to the French Revolution* (Oxford, Oxford University Press, 1972), p. 124.

5 The term is borrowed from Lynn Hunt, 'The French Revolution in Culture: New Approaches and Perspectives', *Eighteenth-Century Studies*, 22 (1989), p. 298.

6 Cobb, *Times Literary Supplement*, 29 January 1970, p. 109.

7 *See* their jointly authored *La Révolution française* (2 vols., Paris, Réalités-Hachette 1965; English translation London, Weidenfeld and Nicolson 1970).

8 Keith M. Baker, 'Public Opinion as Political Invention', in K.M. Baker, ed. *Inventing the French Revolution* (Cambridge, Cambridge University Press, 1990), pp. 167–72.

9 *See* introductory remarks of Hunt in 'The French Revolution in Culture: New Approaches and Perspectives', *Eighteenth-Century Studies*, 22 (1989), pp. 293–301.

10 The concept comes from Jürgen Habermas, *The Structural Transformation of the Public Sphere: an Enquiry into a Category of Bourgeois Society* (Cambridge, Polity Press, 1989. First published in German in 1962). For a discussion of its applicability to *ancien régime* and Revolutionary France, *see* Benjamin Nathans, 'Habermas's "Public Sphere" in the Era of the French Revolution', *French Historical Studies*, 16 (1990), pp. 620–44.

11 *See* Keith M. Baker ed. *The French Revolution and the Creation of Modern Political Culture*, vol. I: *The Political Culture of the Old Regime* (Oxford, Pergamon Press, 1987); Colin Lucas, ed. *The French Revolution and the Creation of Modern Political Culture*, vol. II: *The Political Culture of the French Revolution* (Oxford, 1988); François Furet and Mona Ozouf, eds *The French Revolution and the Creation of Modern Political Culture*, vol. III: *The Transformation of Political Culture, 1789–1848* (Oxford, Pergamon Press, 1990); Keith M. Baker, ed. *The French Revolution and the Creation of Modern Political Culture*, vol. IV: *The Terror* (Oxford, Pergamon Press, 1994).

12 *See* the collection of his essays published as *The Literary Underground of the Old Regime* (Cambridge, MA, Harvard University Press, 1982); also *The Great Cat Massacre and other Episodes in French Cultural History* (London, Allen Lane, 1984).

13 The image is used in Roy Porter, *The Enlightenment* (London, 1990), p. 7.

14 Dena Goodman, 'Governing the Republic of Letters: the Politics of Culture in the French Enlightenment', *History of European Ideas*, 13 (1991), p. 189.

15 *See* Olwen Hufton, 'Women in Revolution, 1789–1796, *Past and Present*, 53 (1971), pp. 90–108; 'Women and the Family Economy in Eighteenth-Century France', *French Historical Studies*, 9 (1975), pp. 1–22; Roderick Phillips, 'Women and Family Breakdown in Eighteenth-Century France: Rouen 1780–1800', *Social History*, 2 (1976), pp. 197–218.

16 *See* Darline G. Levy, Harriet B. Applewhite and Mary D. Johnson, *Women in Revolutionary Paris, 1789–1795* Urbana, ILL, University of Illinois Press, 1979).

17 *See* Sara E. Melzer and Leslie W. Rabine (eds), *Rebel Daughters: Women and the French Revolution* (New York, Oxford University Press, 1992), p. 7.

18 Joan B. Landes, *Women and the Public Sphere in the Age of the French Revolution* (Ithaca, Cornell University Press, 1988. Fourth printing 1993),

19 See, in particular, Dale K. Van Kley, *The Damiens Affair and the Unraveling of the Ancien Regime, 1750–1770* (Princeton, Princeton University Press, 1984); 'The Jansenist Constitutional Legacy in the French Revolution', in Baker, ed. *The French Revolution and the Creation of Modern Political Culture*, I, pp. 169–201; Michael Sonenscher, 'The Sans-Culottes of the Year II: Rethinking the Language of Labour in Revolutionary France', *Social History*, 9 (1984), 301–28; Richard M. Andrews, 'Social Structures, Political Elites and Ideology in Revolutionary Paris, 1792–94: A Critical Evaluation of Albert Soboul's *Les Sans-Culottes Parisiens en l'An II*', *Journal of Social History*, 9 (1985), pp. 71–112.

20 Keith M. Baker, 'Enlightenment and Revolution in France: Old Problems, Renewed Approaches', *Journal of Modern History*, 53 (1981), p. 303.

21 *See* P. Higonnet, 'Cultural Upheaval and Class Formation during the French Revolution', in Ferenc Fehér, ed. *The French Revolution and the Birth of Modernity* (Berkeley, University of California Press 1990), p. 69.

22 Habermas, *Structural Transformation*, pp. 14–26.

23 *See* George V. Taylor, 'Noncapitalist Wealth', pp. 469–96.

24 *See* Theda Skocpol, *States and Social Revolutions: a Comparative Analysis of France, Russia, and China* (Cambridge, Cambridge University Press, 1981), 14, pp. 24–33.

25 *See* Bailey Stone, *The Genesis of the French Revolution: a Global-Historical Interpretation* (Cambridge, Cambridge University Press, 1994), pp. 193–4.

26 François, Furet, *Interpreting the French Revolution* (Cambridge, Cambridge University Press, 1981), pp. 35–6, 38–9, 43, 48, 55, 78.

27 *See*, in particular, Barry M. Shapiro, *Revolutionary Justice in Paris, 1789–1790* (Cambridge, Cambridge University Press, 1993); Michael P. Fitzsimmons, *The Remaking of France: the National Assembly and the Constitution of 1791* (Cambridge, Cambridge University Press, 1994); Timothy Tackett, 'The Constituent Assembly and the Terror', in Keith M. Baker, ed. *The French Revolution and the Creation of Modern Political Culture*, vol. IV: *The Terror* (Oxford, Pergamon Press, 1984), 39–54; Peter M. Jones, *Reform and Revolution in France: the Politics of Transition, 1774–1791* (Cambridge, Cambridge University Press, 1995).

28 Richard C. Cobb, *The Police and the People: French Popular Protest, 1789–1820* (Oxford, Clarendon Press, 1970), p. 86.

29 Gwynne Lewis, *The French Revolution: Rethinking the Debate* (London and New York, Routledge, 1993), pp. 106–113.

SECTION

I

INTERPRETATIONS AND DEBATES

Presentation

Historians have always disagreed about the causes, course and consequences of the French Revolution. However, over time, the points of disagreement (and agreement) have shifted around a good deal. Issues which seemed cut-and-dried a generation ago now appear intensely problematic, and no doubt the reverse is true as well. The selection of essays, articles and book extracts brought together in this section makes no pretence at comprehensive coverage of a debate now more than 200 years in the making. Instead, it aims to provide a state-of-play account of the issues as defined by historians currently engaged in research. Of necessity this approach tends to tilt the agenda towards the 'political'. For the seminal work undertaken (or inspired) by François Furet in Paris and Keith Baker in Chicago during the 1970s and 1980s completely reshaped the discussion of origins and outcomes. Yet, in spite of some indications to the contrary, the flood tide of political culture has not carried all before it. Social history has not been evacuated from the debate, even if the determinism of social and economic structures no longer attracts many takers.

While it is perhaps too early to posit a fruitful exchange of ideas between two mutually suspicious traditions of scholarship, the materials reproduced here do enable us to identify several of the pivotal points in the debate. The challenge of objectivity in the face of an event of world-historical significance is one which every historian must address. For, as François Furet implies, the French Revolution is not yet 'over'. It continues to occupy our present as well as our past. Yet scholarly detachment is no more than preliminary mental exercise. We need to comprehend the Revolution as both event and process: that is to say as a dramatic moment of rupture embedded within a broader framework of continuity. This requires sensitive handling of evidence if we are to avoid talking down to the men and women of 1789; those participants in the drama who 'knew' that they were throwing off the shackles of history. Furthermore, the nature of our subject urges greater than usual caution in construing cause and effect. The French Revolution, it is suggested, cannot be measured in terms of its causes, however significant or insignificant these may have been. One of the characteristics of a world-historical event is to set its own agenda, which in turn renders suspect linear modes of argument linking outcomes to origins. If, however, at the subjective level, the Revolutionaries made their own choices, unbeholden and undaunted, a question is bound to arise: what forces helped to determine their actions? Contingent circumstance, perhaps, or the unfolding of an inner logic? The issue of political violence poses this question in a particularly stark form. Conventional explanations of the Terror emphasize the contingent, whereas historians committed to the political culture perspective detect in the Terror the playing-out of a logical process. Yet it is worth noting that such an approach tends to reassert the link between origins and outcomes in as much as the conditions that made possible the Terror were prefigured, or so it is claimed, in the political vacuum of absolute monarchy.

Issues such as these serve to articulate the ongoing debate. They encapsulate the differences among historians and enable us to put viewpoints into wider perspective. Attentive readers will not find it difficult to identify other points of sharp disagreement in the pages that follow. However, the first piece in this section is largely uncontroversial. Written for a lay readership on the occasion of the bicentenary, it tackles a deceptively simple question: what was so special about the French Revolution? The answer, Robert Darnton tells us, is that the events of 1789 triggered an enormous release of human energy, a mass mobilization of society against every institutional embodiment of authority. Few historians would dissent from this verdict, or the corollary proposition of an all-embracing politicization of everyday life. Yet Darnton confesses to feeling troubled by the collective savagery of the Revolution (in a way that the previous generation of historians was not). In this he signals his doubts about the Revolutionary Terror and the purely conjunctural arguments which served to explain (away) the phenomenon until recent times.

The Terror is only one of several targets in François Furet's sights. Penned in 1977 in response to the first signs of the intellectual crisis of Marxism, his essay begins with a passionate denunciation of 'commemorative' history. Historians who allow themselves to be co-opted to the task of preserving national myths end up writing bad history, he warns. Objectivity and the spirit of critical enquiry eventually give way to a 'pious rehashing' of the past. Yet his call for the Revolution to be laid to rest was bound to be premature. With the bicentenary of 1789 already in prospect, more commemorative prose seemed likely not less. In addition, the thrust of Furet's own research was scarcely exempt from *arrières pensées*, as soon became clear. Nonetheless, his essay provides a trenchant account of the ossification process, or what we would know better as the orthodox interpretation of the French Revolution. This is followed by some probing suggestions as to how the phenomenon of Revolution might be reconceptualized. The multidimensional thought of Alexis de Tocqueville bulks large in the rethinking exercise, with the result that we can glimpse in this essay most of the ideas from which the author would construct an alternative interpretation of the Revolution a decade or so later.

As François Furet readily concedes, the constant rehashing of Revolutionary historiography did not prevent significant scholarly progress from being made in a number of directions. After all, the criticism levelled at the so called neo-jacobin historians tended to query their frame of reference rather than their skills as researchers. The work of Georges Lefebvre is a case in point. Lefebvre was a consummate archival historian whose books and articles have withstood the attrition of revisionist scholarship in better shape than most. However, as the assessment offered by Peter Jones makes plain, his most durable achievements lie in the field of rural history, and peasant studies in particular. For all his uncritical jacobinism and sympathy for the socialist Left, Lefebvre was not a man to adjust his findings to suit prevailing theories. Thus, his discovery of a distinctive 'peasant revolution' contained a sting in the tail for party ideologues. The peasants, he concluded, neither consistently supported bourgeois Revolutionaries in their bid to found a new regime, nor shared in their supposed enthusiasm for capitalism. It should come as no surprise, therefore, that Lefebvre tends to be treated with condescension rather than outright hostility by those seeking to lay the ghost of commemorative history.

What about the 'bourgeois revolution'? Has the phrase lost all explanatory value now that its dialectical underpinnings have been removed; now that historians have separated out the throng of actors on the Revolutionary stage? On both counts Colin Jones enters a plea for the defence. In his view, this analytical tool is not dependent for its viability on the conceptual scaffolding of Marxism; on the other hand, it does demand that close attention be paid to the social history of the late *ancien régime* and the Revolution. Here, in the subtitle of his essay, lies the real thrust of his argument. Juxtaposed with Furet's piece, we find a starkly different assessment of the meaning of 1789.

The Revolution did have long term socio-economic origins after all. Notable among these, according to Colin Jones, was the growth of an increasingly urban and consumerist society which in turn triggered a mid-century shift of outlook in the direction of what might be loosely termed bourgeois values. Students familiar with the 'stagnationist' school of eighteenth-century economic history may feel that the picture of pulsating commercial capitalism has been overdrawn. Nonetheless, Jones's argument reaches firmer ground when he turns to the impact of the Enlightenment upon the professions. Service-sector personnel grew visibly in numbers and self-importance as the *ancien régime* wound to a climax. In the process they began to shed the particularist habits that had hitherto characterized occupational élites, and to develop a mentality of public-spiritedness which Jones dubs 'civic professionalism'. The concomitant expansion of opportunities for quasi-democratic social intercourse (whose institutional roots the political culture historians have done so much to uncover) tended to relay the new civic gospel between élites and enhance its impact. So far so good, but the argument loses some of its potency as we approach the threshold of 1789. For as Colin Jones concedes, the civic model of professionalism did not of necessity prevail. Enlightenment ethics notwithstanding, prototype bourgeois entered the Revolution burdened with corporatist hangovers and a preference for state service rather than buccaneering market behaviour.

Sarah Maza's contribution both complements and draws out the work discussed so far. She starts with a lucid outline of the successive revisionist assaults upon the received historiography of the Revolution, pausing only to dwell on the signal achievements of François Furet in the late 1970s (acknowledged above). That period of exceptional creativity established the intellectual framework for a major reinterpretation of the French Revolution, she declares, and the new Tocquevillian approach to 1789 received its accreditation at the Chicago 'political culture' conference hosted by Keith Baker in 1986. Indeed, the bulk of her essay comprises a critical review of the published proceedings of that conference. Maza conceives of the *French Revolution and the Creation of Modern Political Culture* (the first of the four volumes bearing this title) as a protracted attempt to test empirically hypotheses deriving from Tocqueville's study of the *ancien régime*. Almost immediately however, she detects flaws in the classic analysis, as well as raising doubts on other scores, too. Recent advances in urban social and fiscal history, for example, render Tocqueville's linear conception of state centralization decidedly problematic. More generally, she queries whether the vocation of politico-cultural history really lies in the area of text-based analysis. Linguistic and sociological theory is all very well, but it is apt to get caught on the sharp edges of empirical investigation.

Fittingly, the last item in this section is culled from Gwynne Lewis's own attempt to make sense of the polarized and increasingly fractionalized debate on the French Revolution. Rather than trumpet the virtues of one set of arguments over another, he explores the blurred frontiers of rival interpretations in search of middle ground. What does he find? Much evidence of hybrid social and economic structures, for a start. If neither feudalism nor capitalism dominated prior to 1789, an acceptable solution might be to label the late *ancien régime* a 'transitional' society. This would satisfy both empiricists and theoreticians, while, in the more immediate context, shedding light upon the paradoxical behaviour of Colin Jones's rising bourgeois. That leaves class conflict unaccounted for. Yet Lewis's commentary leaves the reader not entirely sure where to look for it, nor how to specify the manner in which it functioned. A variant of the 'stress zones' argument first put forward by Colin Lucas[1] seems to find favour; that is to say a vision of *ancien-régime* élites launched on converging trajectories only to be deflected by an unanticipated struggle for control of the state. Although the conflict took on political shape, the participants were in reality playing for high economic stakes – a verdict endorsed by fiscal and administrative historians. After a quarter of a century of intense debate, this compromise returns us to the state of play prevailing in the early 1970s. In the present climate of opinion, it looks unlikely that it will be bettered.

Note

1 *See* Colin Lucas, 'Nobles, Bourgeois and the Origins of the French Revolution', *Past and Present*, 60 (1973), pp. 84–126; reprinted in J.R. Censer, ed. *The French Revolution and Intellectual History* (Chicago, Dorsey Press, 1989), pp. 3–25; also in D. Johnson, ed. *French Society and the Revolution* (Cambridge, Cambridge University Press, 1976), pp. 88–131.

1

What was revolutionary about the French Revolution?

ROBERT DARNTON

I

What was so revolutionary about the French Revolution? The question might seem impertinent at a time like this, when all the world is congratulating France on the two hundredth anniversary of the storming of the Bastille, the destruction of feudalism, and the Declaration of the Rights of Man and of the Citizen. But the bicentennial fuss has little to do with what actually happened two centuries ago.

Historians have long pointed out that the Bastille was almost empty on July 14, 1789. Many of them argue that feudalism had already ceased to exist by the time it was abolished, and few would deny that the rights of man were swallowed up in the Terror only five years after they were first proclaimed. Does a sober view of the Revolution reveal nothing but misplaced violence and hollow proclamations – nothing more than a 'myth', to use a term favoured by the late Alfred Cobban, a sceptical English historian who had no use for guillotines and slogans?

One might reply that myths can move mountains. They can acquire a rock-like reality as solid as the Eiffel Tower, which the French built to celebrate the one hundredth anniversary of the Revolution in 1889. France will spend millions in 1989, erecting buildings, creating centres, producing concrete contemporary expressions of the force that burst loose on the world two hundred years ago. But what was it?

Although the spirit of '89 is no easier to fix in words than in mortar and brick, it could be characterized as energy – a will to build a new world from the ruins of the regime that fell apart in the summer of 1789. That energy permeated everything during the French Revolution. It transformed life, not only for the activists trying to channel it in directions of their own choosing but for ordinary persons going about their daily business.

The idea of a fundamental change in the tenor of everyday life may seem easy enough to accept in the abstract, but few of us can really assimilate it.

Reprinted in full from: *The New York Review of Books*, 19 January 1989. Reprinted with permission from *The New York Review of Books*. Copyright © 1989 Nyrev, Inc.

We take the world as it comes and cannot imagine it organized differently, unless we have experienced moments when things fall apart – a death perhaps, or a divorce, or the sudden obliteration of something that seemed immutable, like the roof over our heads or the ground under our feet.

Such shocks often dislodge individual lives, but they rarely traumatize societies. In 1789 the French had to confront the collapse of a whole social order – the world that they defined retrospectively as the Ancien Régime – and to find some new order in the chaos surrounding them. They experienced reality as something that could be destroyed and reconstructed, and they faced seemingly limitless possibilities, both for good and for evil, for raising a utopia and for falling back into tyranny.

To be sure, a few seismic upheavals had convulsed French society in earlier ages – the bubonic plague in the fourteenth century, for example, and the religious wars in the sixteenth century. But no one was ready for a revolution in 1789. The idea itself did not exist. If you look up 'revolution' in standard dictionaries from the eighteenth century, you find definitions that derive from the verb to revolve, such as 'the return of a planet or a star to the same point from which it started.'

The French did not have much of a political vocabulary before 1789, because politics took place at Versailles, in the remote world of the king's court. Once ordinary people began to participate in politics – in the elections to the Estates General, which were based on something approximating universal male suffrage, and in the insurrections of the streets – they needed to find words for what they had seen and done. They developed fundamental new categories, such as 'left' and 'right,' which derive from the seating plan of the National Assembly, and 'revolution' itself. The experience came first, the concept afterward. But what was that experience?

Only a small minority of activists joined the Jacobin clubs, but everyone was touched by the Revolution because the Revolution reached into everything. For example, it re-created time and space. According to the revolutionary calendar adopted in 1793 and used until 1805, time began when the old monarchy ended, on September 22, 1792 – the first of Vendémiaire, Year I.

By formal vote of the Convention, the revolutionaries divided time into units that they took to be rational and natural. There were ten days to a week, three weeks to a month, and twelve months to a year. The five days left over at the end became patriotic holidays, *jours sans-culottides*, given over to civic qualities: Virtue, Genius, Labour, Opinion, and Rewards.

Ordinary days received new names, which suggested mathematical regularity: *primidi, duodi, tridi*, and so on up to *décadi*. Each was dedicated to some aspect of rural life so that agronomy would displace the saints' days of the Christian calendar. Thus November 22, formerly devoted to Saint Cecilia, became the day of the turnip; November 25, formerly Saint Catherine's day, became the day of the pig; and November 30, once the day of Saint Andrew, became the day of the pick. The names of the new months also made time seem to conform to the natural rhythm of the seasons. January 1, 1989, for example, would be the twelfth of Nivôse, Year 197, Nivôse being the month of snow, located after the months of fog (Brumaire) and cold (Frimaire) and before the months of rain (Pluviôse) and wind (Ventôse).

The adoption of the metric system represented a similar attempt to impose a rational and natural organization on space. According to a decree of 1795, the meter was to be 'the unit of length equal to one ten-millionth part of the arc of the terrestrial meridian between the North Pole and the Equator.' Of course, ordinary citizens could not make much of such a definition. They were slow to adopt the meter and the gram, the corresponding new unit of weight, and few of them favoured the new week, which gave them one day of rest in ten instead of one in seven. But even where old habits remained, the revolutionaries stamped their ideas on contemporary consciousness by changing everything's name.

Fourteen hundred streets in Paris received new names, because the old ones contained some reference to a king, a queen, or a saint. The Place Louis XV, where the most spectacular guillotining took place, became the Place de la Révolution; and later, in an attempt to bury the hatchet, it acquired its present name, Place de la Concorde. The Church of Saint-Laurent became the Temple of Marriage and Fidelity; Notre Dame became the Temple of Reason; Montmartre became Mont Marat. Thirty towns took Marat's name – thirty of six thousand that tried to expunge their past by name changes. Montmorency became Emile, Saint-Malo became Victoire Montagnarde, and Coulanges became Cou Sans-Culottes (*anges* or angels being a sign of superstition).

The revolutionaries even renamed themselves. It wouldn't do, of course, to be called Louis in 1793 and 1794. The Louis called themselves Brutus or Spartacus. Last names like Le Roy or Lévêque, very common in France, became La Loi or Liberté. Children got all kinds of names foisted on them – some from nature (Pissenlit or Dandelion did nicely for girls, Rhubarb for boys) and some from current events (Fructidor, Constitution, The Tenth of August, Marat-Couthon-Pique). The foreign minister Pierre-Henri Lebrun named his daughter Civilisation-Jémappes-République.

Meanwhile, the queen bee became a 'laying bee' ('*abeille pondeuse*'); chess pieces were renamed, because a good revolutionary would not play with kings, queens, knights, and bishops; and the kings, queens, and jacks of playing cards became liberties, equalities, and fraternities. The revolutionaries set out to change everything: crockery, furniture, law codes, religion, the map of France itself, which was divided into departments –

that is, symmetrical units of equal size with names taken from rivers and mountains – in place of the irregular old provinces.

Before 1789, France was a crazy-quilt of overlapping and incompatible units, some fiscal, some judicial, some administrative, some economic, and some religious. After 1789, those segments were melted down into a single susbstance: the French nation. With its patriotic festivals, its tricolor flag, its hymns, its martyrs, its army, and its wars, the Revolution accomplished what had been impossible for Louis XIV and his successors: it united the disparate elements of the kingdom into a nation and conquered the rest of Europe. In doing so, the Revolution unleashed a new force, nationalism, which would mobilize millions and topple governments for the next two hundred years.

Of course, the nation-state did not sweep everything before it. It failed to impose the French language on the majority of the French people, who continued to speak all sorts of mutually incomprehensible dialects, despite a vigorous propaganda drive by the revolutionary Committee on Public Instruction. But in wiping out the intermediary bodies that separated the citizen from the state, the Revolution transformed the basic character of public life.

It went further: it extended the public into the private sphere, inserting itself into the most intimate relationships. Intimacy in French is conveyed by the pronoun *tu* as distinct from the *vous* employed in formal address. Although the French sometimes use *tu* quite casually today, under the Old Regime they reserved it for asymmetrical or intensely personal relations. Parents said *tu* to children, who replied with *vous*. The *tu* was used by superiors addressing inferiors, by humans commanding animals, and by lovers – after the first kiss, or exclusively between the sheets. When French mountain climbers reach a certain altitude, they still switch from the *vous* to the *tu*, as if all men become equal in the face of the enormousness of nature.

The French Revolution wanted to make everybody *tu*. Here is a resolution passed on 24 Brumaire, Year II (November 14, 1793), by the department of the Tarn, a poor, mountainous area in southern France:

> Considering that the eternal principles of equality forbid that a citizen say 'vous' to another citizen, who replies by calling him 'toi' . . . decrees that the word 'vous', when it is a question of the singular [rather than the plural, which takes *vous*], is from this moment banished from the language of the free French and will on all occasions be replaced by the word 'tu' or 'toi'.

A delegation of sans-culottes petitioned the National Convention in 1794 to abolish the *vous*, '. . . as a result of which there will be less pride, less discrimation, less social reserve, more open familiarity, a stronger leaning toward fraternity, and therefore more equality.' That may sound laughable today, but it was deadly serious to the revolutionaries: they wanted to build a new society based on new principles of social relations.

So they redesigned everything that smacked of the inequality built into the conventions of the Old Regime. They ended letters with a vigorous 'farewell and fraternity' ('*salut et fraternité*') in place of the deferential 'your most obedient and humble servant.' They susbstituted Citizen and Citizeness for Monsieur and Madame. And they changed their dress.

Dress often serves as a thermometer for measuring the political temperature. To designate a militant from the radical sections of Paris, the revolutionaries adopted a term from clothing: *sans-culotte*, one who wears trousers rather than breeches. In fact, workers did not generally take up trousers, which were mostly favoured by seamen, until the nineteenth century. Robespierre himself always dressed in the uniform of the Old Regime: culottes, waistcoat, and a powdered wig. But the model revolutionary, who appears on broadsides, posters, and crockery from 1793 to the present, wore trousers, an open shirt, a short jacket (the carmagnole), boots, and a liberty cap (Phrygian bonnet) over a 'natural' (that is, uncombed) crop of hair, which dropped down to his shoulders.

Women's dress on the eve of the Revolution had featured low necklines, basket skirts, and exotic hair styles, at least among the aristocracy. Hair dressed in the 'hedgehog' style ('*en hérisson*') rose two or more feet above the head and was decorated with elaborate props – as a fruit bowl or a flotilla or a zoo. One court coiffure was arranged as a pastoral scene with a pond, a duck hunter, a windmill (which turned), and a miller riding off to market on a mule while a monk seduced his wife.

After 1789, fashion came from below. Hair was flattened, skirts were deflated, necklines raised, and heels lowered. Still later, after the end of the Terror when the Thermidorian Reaction extinguished the Republic of Virtue, fast-moving society women like Mme. Tallien exposed their breasts, danced about in diaphanous gowns, and revived the wig. A true *merveilleuse* or fashionable lady would have a wig for every day of the *décade*; Mme. Tallien had thirty.

At the height of the Revolution, however, from mid-1792 to mid-1794, virtue was not merely a fashion but the central ingredient of a new political culture. It had a puritanical side, but it should not be confused with the Sunday-school variety preached in nineteenth-century America. To the revolutionaries, virtue was virile. It meant a willingness to fight for the fatherland and for the revolutionary trinity of liberty, equality, and fraternity.

At the same time, the cult of virtue produced a revalorization of family life. Taking their text from Rousseau, the revolutionaries sermonized on the sanctity of motherhood and the importance of breast-feeding. They treated reproduction as a civic duty and excoriated bachelors as unpatriotic. 'Citizenesses! Give the Fatherland Children!' proclaimed a banner in a patriotic parade. 'Now is the time to make a baby,' admonished a slogan painted on revolutionary pottery.

Saint-Just, the most extreme ideologist on the Committee of Public Safety, wrote in his notebook: 'The child, the citizen, belong to the fatherland. Common instruction is necessary. Children belong to their mother until the age of five, if she has [breast-]fed them, and to the Republic afterwards . . . until death.'

It would be anachronistic to read Hitlerism into such statements. With the collapse of the authority of the Church, the revolutionaries sought a new moral basis for family life. They turned to the state and passed laws that would have been unthinkable under the Old Regime. They made divorce possible; they accorded full legal status to illegitimate children; they abolished primogeniture. If, as the Declaration of the Rights of Man and of the Citizen proclaimed, all men are created free and equal in rights, shouldn't all men begin with an equal start in life? The Revolution tried to limit 'paternal despotism' by giving all children an equal share in inheritances. It abolished slavery and gave full civic rights to Protestants and Jews.

To be sure, one can spot loopholes and contradictions in the revolutionary legislation. Despite some heady phrasing in the so-called Ventôse Decrees about the appropriation of counterrevolutionaries' property, the legislators never envisaged anything like socialism. And Napoleon reversed the most democratic provisions of the laws on family life. Nevertheless, the main direction of revolutionary legislation is clear: it substituted the state for the Church as the ultimate authority in the conduct of private life, and it grounded the legitimacy of the state in the sovereignty of the people.

II

Popular sovereignty, civil liberty, equality before the law – the words fall so easily off the tongue today that we cannot begin to imagine their explosiveness in 1789. We cannot think ourselves back into a mental world like that of the Old Regime, where most people assumed that men were unequal, that inequality was a good thing, and that it conformed to the hierarchical order built into nature by God himself. To the French of the Old Regime, liberty meant privilege – that is, literally, 'private law' or a special prerogative to do something denied to other persons. The king, as the source of all law, dispensed privileges, and rightly so, for he had been anointed as the agent of God on earth. His power was spiritual as well as secular, so by his royal touch he could cure scrofula, the king's disease.

Throughout the eighteenth century, the philosophers of the Enlightenment challenged those assumptions, and pamphleteers in Grub Street succeeded in tarnishing the sacred aura of the crown. But it took violence to smash the mental frame of the Old Regime, and violence itself, the iconoclastic, world-destroying, revolutionary sort of violence, is also hard for us to conceive.

True, we treat traffic accidents and muggings as everyday occurrences. But compared with our ancestors, we live in a world where violence has been drained out of our daily experience. In the eighteenth century, Parisians commonly passed by corpses that had been fished out of the Seine and hung by their feet along the riverbank. They knew a '*mine patibulaire*' was a face that looked like one of the dismembered heads exposed on a fork by the public executioner. They had witnessed dismemberments of criminals at public executions. And they could not walk through the centre of the city without covering their shoes in blood.

Here is a description of the Paris butcheries, written by Louis-Sébastien Mercier a few years before the outbreak of the Revolution:

> They are in the middle of the city. Blood courses through the streets; it coagulates under your feet, and your shoes are red with it. In passing, you are suddenly struck with an agonized cry. A young steer is thrown to the ground, its horns tied down; a heavy mallet breaks its skull; a huge knife strikes deep into its throat; its steaming blood flows away with its life in a thick current. . . . Then bloodstained arms plunge into its smoking entrails; its members are hacked apart and hung up for sale. Sometimes the steer, dazed but not downed by the first blow, breaks its ropes and flees furiously from the scene, mowing down everyone in its paths. . . . And the butchers who run after their escaped victim are as dangerous as it is. . . . These butchers have a fierce and bloody appearance: naked arms, swollen necks, their eyes red, their legs filthy, their aprons covered with blood, they carry their massive clubs around with them always spoiling for a fight. The blood they spread seems to inflame their faces and their temperaments. . . . In streets near the butcheries, a cadaverous odor hangs heavy in the air; and vile prostitues – huge, fat, monstrous objects sitting in the streets – display their debauchery in public. These are the beauties that those men of blood find alluring.

A serious riot broke out in 1750 because a rumour spread through the working-class sections of Paris that the police were kidnapping children to provide a bloodbath for a prince of the royal blood. Such riots were known as 'popular emotions' eruptions of visceral passion touched off by some spark that burned within the collective imagination.

It would be nice if we could associate the Revolution exlusively with the Declaration of the Rights of Man and of the Citizen, but it was born in violence and it stamped its principles on a violent world. The conquerors of the Bastille did not merely destroy a symbol of royal despotism. One hundred and fifty of them were killed or injured in the assault on the prison; and when the survivors got hold of its governor, they cut off his head, and paraded it through Paris on the end of a pike.

A week later, in a paroxysm of fury over high bread prices and rumours about plots to starve the poor, a crowd lynched an official in the war ministry named Foulon, severed his head, and paraded it on a pike with hay stuffed in its mouth as a sign of complicity in the plotting. A band of rioters then seized Foulon's son-in-law, the intendant of Paris, Bertier de Sauvigny, and marched him through the streets with the head in front of him, chanting 'Kiss papa, kiss papa.' They murdered Bertier in front of the Hôtel de Ville, tore the heart out of his body, and threw it in the direction of the municipal government. Then they resumed their parade with his head beside Foulon's. 'That is how traitors are punished,' said an engraving of the scene.

Gracchus Babeuf, the future leftist conspirator, described the general delirium in a letter to his wife. Crowds applauded at the sight of the heads on the pikes, he wrote:

> Oh! That joy made me sick. I felt satisfied and displeased at the same time. I said, so much the better and so much the worse. I understood that the common people were taking justice into their own hands. I approve that justice . . . but could it not be cruel? Punishments of all kinds, drawing and quartering, torture, the wheel, the rack, the whip, the stake, hangmen proliferating everywhere have done such damage to our morals! Our masters . . . will sow what they have reaped.

It also would be nice if we could stop the story of the Revolution at the end of 1789, where the current French government wants to draw the line in its celebrating. But the whole story extends through the rest of the century – and of the following century, according to some historians. Whatever its stopping point, it certainly continued through 1794; so we must come to terms with the Terror.

III

We can find plenty of explanations for the official Terror, the Terror directed by the Committee of Public Safety and the Revolutionary Tribunal. By twentieth-century standards, it was not very devastating, if you make a body count of its victims and if you believe in measuring such things statistically. It took about 17,000 lives. There were fewer than twenty-five executions in half the departments of France, none at all in six of them. Seventy-one percent of the executions took place in regions where civil war was raging; three quarters of the guillotined were rebels captured with arms in their hands; and 85 percent were commoners – a statistic that is hard to digest for those who interpret the Revolution as a class war directed by bourgeois against aristocrats. Under the Terror the word 'aristocrat' could be applied to almost anyone deemed to be an enemy of the people.

But all such statistics stick in the throat. Any attempt to condemn a person by suppressing his individuality and by slotting him into abstract, ideological categories such as 'aristocrat' or 'bourgeois' is inherently inhuman. The Terror *was* terrible. It pointed the way toward totalitarianism. It was the trauma that scarred modern history at its birth.

Historians have succeeded in explaining much of it (not all, not the hideous last month of the 'Great Terror' when the killing increased while the threat of invasion receded) as a response to the extraordinary circumstances of 1793 and 1794: the invading armies about to overwhelm Paris; the counterrevolutionaries, some imaginary, many real, plotting to overthrow the government from within; the price of bread soaring out of control and driving the Parisian populace wild with hunger and despair; the civil war in the Vendée; the municipal rebellions in Lyons, Marseilles, and Bordeaux; and the factionalism within the National Convention, which threatened to paralyze every attempt to master the situation.

It would be the height of presumption for an American historian sitting in the comfort of his study to condemn the French for violence and to congratulate his countrymen for the relative bloodlessness of their own revolution, which took place in totally different conditions. Yet what is he to make of the September Massacres of 1792, an orgy of killing that took the lives of more than one thousand persons, many of them prostitutes and common criminals trapped in prisons like the Abbaye?

We don't know exactly what happened, because the documents were destroyed in the bombardment of the Paris Commune in 1871. But the sober assessment of the surviving evidence by Pierre Caron suggests that the massacres took on the character of a ritualistic, apocalyptic mass murder. Crowds of sans-culottes including men from the butcheries described by Mercier, stormed the prisons in order to extinguish what they believed to be a counterrevolutionary plot. They improvised a popular court in the prison of the Abbaye. One by one the prisoners were led out, accused, and summarily judged according to their demeanor. Fortitude was taken to be a sign of innocence, faltering as guilt. Stanislas Maillard, a conqueror of the Bastille, assumed the role of prosecutor; and the crowd, transported from the street to rows of benches, ratified his judgment with nods and acclamations. If declared innocent, the prisoner would be hugged, wept over, and carried triumphantly through the city. If guilty, he would be hacked to death in a gauntlet of pikes, clubs, and sabres. Then his body would be stripped and thrown on a heap of corpses or dismembered and paraded about on the end of a pike.

Throughout their bloody business, the people who committed the massacres talked about purging the earth of counterrevolution. They seemed to play parts in a secular version of the Last Judgement, as if the Revolution had released an undercurrent of popular millenarianism. But it is difficult to know what script was being performed in September 1792. We may never be able to fathom such violence or to get to the bottom of the other 'popular emotions' that determined the course of the Revolution: the Great Fear of the peasants in the early summer of 1789; the uprisings of July 14 and October 5–6 1789; and the revolutionary 'days' of August 10, 1792, May 31, 1793, 9 Thermidor, Year II (July 27, 1794), 12 Germinal, Year III (April 1, 1795), and 1–4 Prairial, Year III (May 20–23, 1795). In all of them the crowds cried for bread and blood, and the bloodshed passes the historian's understanding.

It is there, nonetheless. It will not go away, and it must be incorporated in any attempt to make sense of the Revolution. One could argue that violence was a necessary evil, because the Old Regime would not die peacefully and the new order could not survive without destroying the counterrevolution. Nearly all the violent 'days' were defensive – desperate attempts to stave off counterrevolutionary coups, which threatened to annihilate the Revolution from June 1789 until November 1799, when Bonaparte seized power. After the religious schism of 1791 and the war of 1792, any opposition could be made to look like treason, and no consensus could be reached on the principles of politics.

In short, circumstances account for most of the violent swings from extreme to extreme during the revolutionary decade. Most, but not all – certainly not the Slaughter of the Innocents in September 1792. The violence itself remains a mystery, the kind of phenomenon that may force one back into metahistorical explanations: original sin, unleashed libido, or the cunning of a dialectic. For my part, I confess myself incapable of explaining the ultimate cause of revolutionary violence, but I think I can make out some of its consequences. It cleared the way for the redesigning and rebuilding that I mentioned above. It struck down institutions from the Old Regime so suddenly and with such force that it made anything seem possible. It released utopian energy.

The sense of boundless possibility – 'possibilism' one could call it – was the bright side of popular emotion, and it was not restricted to millenarian outbursts in the streets. It could seize lawyers and men of letters sitting in the Legislative Assembly. On July 7, 1792, A.-A. Lamourette, a deputy from Rhône-et-Loire, told the Assembly's members that their troubles all arose from a single source: factionalism. They needed more fraternity. Whereupon the deputies, who had been at each other's throats a moment earlier rose to their feet and started hugging and kissing each other as if their political divisions could be swept away in a wave of brotherly love.

The 'kiss of Lamourette' has been passed over with a few indulgent smiles by historians who know that three days later the Assembly would fall apart before the bloody uprising of August 10. What children they were, those men of 1792, with their overblown oratory, their naive cult of virtue, their simple-minded sloganeering about liberty, equality, and fraternity!

But we may miss something if we condescend to people in the past. The popular emotion of fraternity, the strangest in the trinity of revolutionary values, swept through Paris with the force of a hurricane in 1792. We can barely imagine its power, because we inhabit a world organized according to other principles, such as tenure, take-home pay, bottom lines, and who reports to whom. We define ourselves as employers or employees, as teachers or students, as someone located somewhere in a web of intersecting roles. The Revolution at its most revolutionary tried to wipe out such distinctions. It really meant to legislate the brotherhood of man. It may not have succeeded any better than Christianity christianized, but it remodeled enough of the social landscape to alter the course of history.

How can we grasp those moments of madness, of suspended disbelief, when anything looked possible and the world appeared as a tabula rasa, wiped clean by a surge of popular emotion and ready to be redesigned? Such moments pass quickly. People cannot live for long in a state of epistemological exhilaration. Anxiety sets in – the need to fix things, to enforce borders, to sort out 'aristocrats' and patriots. Boundaries soon harden and the landscape assumes once more the aspect of immutability.

Today most of us inhabit a world that we take to be not the best but the only world possible. The French Revolution has faded into an almost imperceptible past, its bright light obscured by a distance of two hundred years, so far away that we may barely believe in it. For the Revolution defies belief. It seems incredible that an entire people could rise up and transform the conditions of everyday existence. To do so is to contradict the common working assumption that life must be fixed in the patterns of the common workaday world.

Have we never experienced anything that could shake that conviction? Consider the assassinations of John F. Kennedy, Robert Kennedy, and Martin Luther King, Jr. All of us who lived through those moments remember precisely where we were and what we were doing. We suddenly stopped in our tracks, and in the face of the enormity of the event we felt bound to everyone around us. For a few instants we ceased to see one another through our roles and perceived ourselves as equals, stripped down to the core of our common humanity. Like mountaineers high above the daily business of the world, we moved from *vous* to *tu*.

I think the French Revolution was a succession of such events, events so terrible that they shook mankind to its core. Out of the destruction, they created a new sense of possibility – not just of writing constitutions nor of legislating liberty and equality, but of living by the most difficult of revolutionary values, the brotherhood of man.

Of course, the notion of fraternity comes from the Revolution itself rather than from any higher wisdom among historians, and few historians, however wise, would assert that great events expose some bedrock reality underlying history. I would argue the opposite: great events make possible the social reconstruction of reality, the reordering of things-as-they-are so they are no longer experienced as given but rather as willed, in accordance with convictions about how things ought to be.

Possibilism against the givenness of things – those were the forces pitted against one another in France from 1789 to 1799. Not that other forces were absent, including something that might be called a 'bourgeoisie' battling something known as 'feudalism,' while a good deal of property changed hands and the poor extracted some bread from the rich. But all those conflicts were predicated on something greater than the sum of their parts – a conviction that the human condition is malleable, not fixed, and that ordinary people can make history instead of suffering it.

Two hundred years of experimentation with brave new worlds have made us sceptical about social engineering. In retrospect, the Wordsworthian moment can be made to look like a prelude to totalitarianism. The poet bayed at a blood moon. He barked, and the caravan passed, a line of generations linked together like a chain gang destined for the gulag.

Maybe. But too much hindsight can distort the view of 1789 and of 1793–1794. The French revolutionaries were not Stalinists. They were an assortment of unexceptional persons in exceptional circumstances. When things fell apart, they responded to an overwhelming need to make sense of things by ordering society according to new principles. Those principles still stand as an indictment of tyranny and injustice. What was the French Revolution all about? Liberty, equality, fraternity.

2
The French Revolution is over

FRANÇOIS FURET

I

Historians engaged in the study of the Merovingian Kings or the Hundred Years War are not asked at every turn to present their research permits. So long as they can give proof of having learned the techniques of the trade, society and the profession assume that they possess the virtues of patience and objectivity. The discussion of their findings is a matter for scholars and scholarship only.

The historian of the French Revolution, on the other hand, must produce more than proof of competence. He must show his colours. He must state from the outset where he comes from, what he thinks and what he is looking for; what he writes about the French Revolution is assigned a meaning and label even before he starts working: the writing is taken as his *opinion*, a form of judgment that is not required when dealing with the Merovingians but indispensable when it comes to treating 1789 or 1793. As soon as the historian states that opinion, the matter is settled; he is labelled a royalist, a liberal or a Jacobin. Once he has given the password his history has a specific meaning, a determined place and a claim to legitimacy.

What is surprising here is not that the history of the Revolution, like all histories, involves intellectual presuppositions. There is no such thing as 'innocent' historical interpretation, and written history is itself located in history, indeed *is* history, the product of an inherently unstable relationship between the present and the past, a merging of the particular mind with the vast field of its potential topics of study in the past. But if all history implies a choice, a preference within the range of what might be studied, it does not follow that such a choice always involves a preconceived opinion about the subject chosen. For that to happen, or to be assumed, the subject must arouse in the historian and his public a capacity for identifying with political or religious passions that have survived the passing of time.

The passing of time may weaken that sense of identification, or on the contrary preserve and even strengthen it, depending on whether the subject treated by the historian does or does not continue to express the issues of

Excerpt from Furet, *Interpreting the French Revolution* (Cambridge, Cambridge University Press, 1981), pp. 1–28.

his own times, his values and his choices. The theme of Clovis and the Frankish invasions was of burning interest in the eighteenth century because the historians of that era saw it as the key to the social structure of their own time. They thought that the Frankish invasions were the origin of the division between nobility and commoners, the conquerors being the progenitors of the nobility and the conquered those of the commoners. Today the Frankish invasions have lost all relevance, since we live in a society where nobility has ceased to act as a social principle. No longer serving as the mirror of an existing world, the Frankish invasions have lost the eminent place in historiography that that world once assigned to them, and have moved from the realm of social polemic to that of learned debate.

The fact is that beginning in 1789 the obsession with origins, the underlying thread of all national history, came to be centred precisely on the Revolutionary break. Just as the great invasions were the myth of a society dominated by the nobility, the saga of its origins, so 1789 became the birth date, the year zero of a new world founded on equality. The substitution of one birth date for another, in other words, the definition in time of a new national identity, is perhaps one of the *abbé* Sieyès's greatest strokes of genius, especially if one remembers that he anticipated the founding event by several months[1] and yet gave it its full meaning in advance:

> The Third Estate has nothing to fear from going back into the past. It will refer back to the year preceding the conquest; and since it is today strong enough not to be conquered, its resistance will no doubt be more effective. Why should it not send back to the forests of Franconia all those families who cling to the mad claim that they are descended from the race of conquerors and have inherited their rights? Thus purified, the nation will easily console itself, I believe, for no longer imagining itself composed only of the descendants of Gauls and Romans.[2]

These few lines tell us not only that the nobles' proprietary claims over the nation are fictitious, but also that, even if those claims were well founded, the Third Estate would have only to restore the social contract in force before the conquest or, rather, to found it by obliterating centuries of violent usurpation. In either instance it is a matter of constituting a 'true' origin for the nation by giving a legitimate date of birth to equality: that is what 1789 is all about.

But Revolutionary historiography has had the function of keeping alive that account of society's origins. Consider, for example, the manner in which studies are divided for the teaching of history in France. 'Modern' history ends in 1789 with what the Revolution christened the 'Ancien Régime', a period which, if it lacks a clearly marked birth-certificate, is thus given a duly signed death-certificate. Thereafter, the Revolution and the Empire form separate and autonomous fields of study, each with its own professorships, students, learned societies and journals, and the quarter-century separating the storming of the Bastille from the Battle of Waterloo is assigned a special place: it is both the end of the 'modern' era and the indispensable introduction to the 'contemporary' period, which begins in 1815; it is the period of transition that gives meaning to both, the watershed from which the history of France either flows back to its past or rushes toward its future. By remaining faithful to the conscious experience of the actors of the Revolution, despite all the intellectual absurdities implicit in such a chronological framework, our academic institutions have invested the French Revolution and the historian of that period with the mysteries of our national history. The year 1789 is the key to what lies both upstream and downstream. It separates those periods, and thereby defines and 'explains' them.

But it is not enough to say that the Revolution explains what lies downstream – the period beginning in 1815 that the Revolution is supposed to have created, made possible, inaugurated. The Revolution does not simply 'explain' our contemporary history; it *is* our contemporary history. And that is worth pondering over.

For the same reasons that the Ancien Régime is thought to have an end but no beginning, the Revolution has a birth but no end. For the one, seen negatively and lacking chronological definition, only its death is a certainty; the other contains a promise of such magnitude that it becomes boundlessly elastic. Even in the short term, it is not easy to 'date': depending on the significance the historian attributes to the main events, he may encapsulate the Revolution within the year 1789, seeing in it the year in which the essential features of the Revolution's final outcome were fixed, when the final page of the Ancien Régime was turned – or he may go up to 1794 and the execution of Robespierre, stressing the dictatorship of the Revolutionary committees and of the *sections*, the Jacobin saga and the egalitarian crusade of the Year II. Or he may use 18 Brumaire 1799 as the terminus, if he wants to acknowledge the extent to which Thermidorians had remained Jacobins, and include the government of the regicides and the war against the European monarchies. He may even integrate the Napoleonic adventure into the Revolution, perhaps to the end of the Consular period, or to Napoleon's Habsburg marriage, or even to the Hundred Days: a case can be made for any of these time frames.

One could also envisage a much longer history of the French Revolution, extending even farther downstream, and ending not before the late nineteenth or early twentieth century. For the entire history of nineteenth-century France can be seen as a struggle between Revolution and Restoration, passing through various episodes in 1815, 1830, 1848, 1851, 1870, the Commune and 16 May 1877. Only the victory of the republicans over the monarchists at the beginning of the Third Republic marked the definitive victory of the Revolution in the French countryside. The lay schoolteacher of Jules Ferry was a missionary for the values of 1789, and was more than an instrument; he was the embodiment of victory in that long battle. Integration of France's villages and peasant culture into the republican nation on the basis of the principles of 1789 was to take at least a century, and no doubt considerably longer in such regions as Brittany or the Southwest, which lagged in more than one respect. That recent history of the French countryside is still, for the most part, unwritten; yet it too constitutes a history of the Revolution. Republican Jacobinism, dictated for so long from Paris, won its victory only after it could count on the majority vote of rural France at the end of the nineteenth century.

But its electoral 'victory' did not mean that it was honoured or assimilated as a value, something so unanimously accepted as to be no longer debated. The celebration of the principles of 1789, the object of so much pedagogical solicitude, or the condemnation of the crimes of 1793, which usually serves as a screen for the rejection of those principles, has remained at the core of the set of notions that shaped French political life until the middle of the twentieth century. Fascism, by its explicit rejection of the values of the French Revolution, gave an international dimension to that conflict of ideas. But, interestingly enough, the Vichy régime, set up after the German victory, was less specifically fascist than traditionalist, and was obsessed with 1789. France in the 1940s was still a country whose citizens had to *sort out* their history, date the birth of their nation, choose between the Ancien Régime and the Revolution.

In that form, the reference to 1789 disappeared from French politics with the defeat of fascism. Today the discourse of both Right and Left celebrates liberty and equality, and the debate about the values of 1789 no longer involves any real political stakes or even strong psychological commitment. But if such unanimity exists, it is because the political debate has simply been transferred from one Revolution to the other, from the Revolution of the past to the one that is to come. By shifting the conflict to the future, it is possible to create an apparent consensus about the legacy of the past. But in fact that legacy, which is one of conflict, lives on by dominating the representations of the future, just as an old geological substratum, covered with later sedimentation, still moulds the features of the earth and the landscape. For the French Revolution is not only the Republic. It is also an unlimited promise of equality and a special form of change. One only has to see in it not a national institution but a matrix of universal history, in order to recapture its dynamic force and its fascinating appeal. The nineteenth century believed in the Republic. The twentieth century believes in *the* Revolution. The same founding event is present in both images.

And indeed, the socialists of the late nineteenth century conceived of their action as both coordinated with and distinct from that of the republicans. Coordinated, because they felt that the Republic was the prerequisite of socialism. Distinct, because they saw political democracy as a historical stage of social organisation that was destined to be superseded, and because they perceived 1789 not as the foundation of a stable State but as a movement whose logic required it to go beyond that first stage. The struggle for democracy and the struggle for socialism were the two successive forms assumed by a dynamic of equality originating in the French Revolution. Thus was formed a vision, a linear history of human emancipation whose first stage had been the maturing and the dissemination of the values of 1789, while the second stage was to fulfil the promise of 1789 by a new, and this time socialist, revolution. This two-pronged mechanism is implicit in Jaurès's socialist history of the Revolution, for example, but the great socialist authors were at first unable to give an account of the second stage; understandably so, since it was still in the future.

All that changed in 1917. Now that the socialist revolution had a face, the French Revolution ceased to be the model for a future that was possible, desirable, hoped for, but as yet devoid of content. Instead, it became the mother of a real, dated, and duly registered event: October 1917. As I [will go on to suggest] the Russian Bolsheviks never – before, during or after the Russian Revolution – lost sight of that filiation. But by the same token the historians of the French Revolution projected into the past their feelings or their judgments about 1917, and tended to highlight those features of the first revolution that seemed to presage or indeed anticipate those of the second. At the very moment when Russia – for better or worse – took the place of France as the nation in the vanguard of history, because it had inherited from France and from nineteenth-century thought the idea that a nation is *chosen* for revolution, the historiographical discourses about the two revolutions became fused and infected each other. The Bolsheviks were given Jacobin ancestors, and the Jacobins were made to anticipate the communists.

Thus, for almost two hundred years now, the history of the French Revolution has been a story of beginnings and so a discourse about identity. In the nineteenth century that history was virtually indistinguishable from the event it purported to retrace, for the drama begun in 1789 was played over and over, generation after generation, for the same stakes and around the same symbols, an unbroken memory that became an object of worship or of horror. Not only did the Revolution found the political culture that makes 'contemporary' France intelligible, but it also bequeathed to France conflicts between legitimacies and a virtually inexhaustible stock of political debates: 1830 was 1789 all over; 1848 re-enacted the First Republic; and the Commune echoed the Jacobin dream. It was not until the end of the century, with the spread of a republican consensus, first in the Parliament, then in the nation at large, and with the founding of the Third Republic, that the Revolution – at last, after a century – began to acquire academic respectability. Under pressure from the *Société d'histoire de la Révolution française*, founded in 1881 by a group of republican intellectuals, the Sorbonne offered in 1886 a 'course' in the history of the Revolution, taught by Alphonse Aulard. In 1891, that course became a 'chair'.

Did the Revolution, once it was officially taught, become national property, like the Republic? As in the case of the Republic, the answer is: yes and no. Yes, because in a sense, with the founding of the Republic on the vote of the people, and no longer on the Parisian insurrection, the French Revolution was finally 'over'; it had become a national institution, sanctioned by the legal and democratic consent of citizens. Yet, on the other hand, the republican consensus built on the political culture born in 1789 was conservative and obtained by default from the ruling classes, who could not agree on a king, and from the peasants and minor notables, who wanted a guarantee of security: indeed, it was the repression of the Commune that made the Republic acceptable in the provinces. However, a victorious French Revolution, finally accepted as a closed chapter of history, as a patrimony and a national institution, contradicted the image of change it implied, for that image involved a far more radical promise than lay schools and the separation of Church and State. Once the Revolution had succeeded in imposing the Republic, it became clear that it was much more than the Republic. It was a pledge that no event could fully redeem.

That is why, in the very last years of the nineteenth century, when the historiographical debate between royalists and republicans was still over what had been the political stakes of 1789, socialist thinking seized upon the notion of the Revolution as prefiguration. Aulard had criticised Taine for reconstructing the 'Origins of Contemporary France'. Jaurès saw the French Revolution as the beginning of a beginning, as a world that would give birth again: 'The least of its greatness is the present . . . Its prolongations are unlimited.'[3] The Russian Revolution of October 1917 seemed made to order to fulfil that expectation of a renewed beginning. Henceforth – as Mathiez made quite explicit[4] – the inventory of the Jacobin legacy was overlaid with an implicit discourse for or against Bolshevism, a development that hardly made for intellectual flexibility. In fact, the overlap of those two political debates extended the nineteenth into the twentieth century, and transferred onto communism and anticommunism the passions previously aroused by the king of France and by the Republic, *displacing* but not weakening them. Quite the contrary, for those passions were re-implanted in the present and given new political stakes to be

culled, like so many still indistinct promises, from the events of 1789 or
rather 1793. But in becoming the positive or negative prefiguration of an
authentically communist revolution, in which the famous 'bourgeoisie'
would not come to confiscate the victory of the people, the French
Revolution did not gain in meaning or in conceptual clarity. It simply
renewed its myth, which became the poorer for it.

I should like to avoid a misunderstanding here: that contamination of
the past by the present, that endless capacity for assimilation, which by
definition characterises a Revolution conceived as a starting point, does
not preclude partial progress in certain areas of scholarship. After all, the
Revolution has been an academic 'field' since the end of the nineteenth
century, and since then each generation of historians has had to do its
share of archival work. In that respect, the emphasis on the popular classes
and their action in the French Revolution has brought advances in our
knowledge of the rôle played by the peasants and the urban masses that it
would be absurd to ignore or underestimate. But those advances have not
appreciably modified the analysis of what we usually refer to as the 'French
Revolution' taken as a whole.

Take the problem of the peasantry, which has been studied and re-
evaluated in many works since the beginning of the century, from Loutch-
iski to Paul Bois, an area in which, it seems to me, Georges Lefebvre made
his main contribution to the historiography of the French Revolution.
From his analysis of the question and of peasant behaviour, Georges
Lefebvre came to two ideas: first, that, from the social point of view,
there were several revolutions within what is called *the* French Revolution; second, that the peasant revolution was not only largely autonomous
and distinct from the other revolutions (those of the aristocrats, the
bourgeois, and the *sans-culottes*, for example), but also anticapitalist,
that is, in his opinion, traditionalist and backward-looking.[5] Right off,
those two ideas are difficult to reconcile with a vision of the French
Revolution as a homogeneous social and political phenomenon opening
the way to a capitalist or bourgeois future that the 'Ancien Régime' had
blocked.

But there is more. Georges Lefebvre also noted that, in the rural history
of the Ancien Régime, capitalism was increasingly present, and that its
'spirit' had deeply penetrated the landed aristocracy. Consequently, as Paul
Bois showed later,[6] the same peasantry could successively come into conflict
with the seigneurs in 1789 and with the Republic in 1793 without the
'Revolution' having changed anything in the nature of the social pressures
exerted by the peasantry or the struggle in which it was engaged. As early as
1932, Georges Lefebvre could write: 'The Ancien Régime started the
agrarian history of France on the road to capitalism; the Revolution
abruptly completed the task that the Ancien Régime had begun.'[7] But
this conclusion, which sounds almost like Tocqueville, does not lead the

historian of Jacobin tradition, like his legitimist ancestor, to a critique of the very concept of revolution. He does not try to understand how one might reconcile the idea of radical change with that of an actual continuity. He simply juxtaposes, without attempting to make them compatible, an *analysis* of the peasant problem at the end of the eighteenth century and a contradictory *tradition* that consists in seeing the Revolution, through the eyes of its participants, as a break, an advent, a time both qualitatively new and different, as homogeneous as a brand-new fabric. It would not be difficult to show that the twentieth century's greatest university scholar of the French Revolution, the man who had a richer knowledge and a surer grasp of the period than anyone, based his synthetic vision of the immense event to which he devoted his life on nothing more than the convictions of a militant adherent of the *Cartel des Gauches* and the Popular Front.

The fact is that scholarship, although it may be stimulated by preoccupations stemming from the present, is never sufficient in itself to modify the conceptualisation of a problem or an event. In the case of the French Revolution, scholarship could, under the influence of Jaurès, 1917 and Marxism, take a turn toward social history and conquer new territories in the twentieth century. Yet it remains attached – indeed more closely than ever – to the old recital of origins, which was both renewed and made more rigid by deposits of socialist thinking. For the takeover of the history of the Revolution by social history, if it has opened new fields of research in specific areas, has only shifted elsewhere the question of origins: the advent of the bourgeoisie has been substituted for the advent of liberty, but it remains no less an advent. The durability of that notion is the more extraordinary since the idea of a radical rending of the social fabric of a nation is even more difficult to conceive of than the political break; in that sense, the historiographical shift from a political to a social emphasis shows the lasting power of the notion that the Revolution was an advent, precisely because such a shift is even more incompatible with 'revolution'. That intellectual contradiction is masked by the celebration of the beginnings. For in the twentieth century, more than ever before, the historian of the French Revolution commemorates the event he narrates or studies. The new materials he brings to bear are no more than supplementary ornaments offered up to his tradition. Lineages are perpetuated along with the debates: just as Aulard and Taine debated the Republic when writing about the French Revolution, so Mathiez and Gaxotte discussed the origins of communism.

This infinite capacity for commemoration, always an expression of national pride, explains why in France the Revolution has become a special field in historical studies. It was dignified as an academic specialty not because it contains demonstrably special problems, but because it allows the historian to identify with his heroes and 'his' event. The French Revolution therefore has its royalist, liberal, Jacobin, anarchist, or libertarian

histories, and this list is neither exclusive – for those tendencies do not
necessarily always contradict each other – nor above all restrictive. Mother
of the political culture into which all of us are born, the Revolution allows
everyone to look for filiations. But all those histories, which have bitterly
fought each other for the last two hundred years in the name of the origins of
their opposition, in fact share a common ground: they are all histories in
quest of identity. No Frenchman living in the second half of the twentieth
century can perceive the French Revolution *from the outside*. One cannot
practise ethnology in so familiar a landscape. The event is so fundamentally,
so tyrannically rooted in contemporary French political consciousness that
any attempt to consider it from an intellectual 'distance' is immediately seen
as hostility – as if identification, be it a claim to descent or rejection, were
inevitable.

Yet we must try to break the vicious circle of that commemorative
historiography. It has long been fashionable among people of my generation, who were brought up under the double influence of existentialism and
Marxism, to stress that the historian is rooted in his own times, his own
choices and his own constraints. By now the continued harping on those
truisms – however useful they may have been for combating the positivist
illusion that 'objectivity' is possible – is liable to perpetuate professions of
faith and polemics that have had their day. Today the historiography of the
Revolution is hampered, even more than by political ideology, by mental
laziness and pious rehashing. Surely, it is time to strip it of the elementary
significations it has bequeathed to its heirs, and to restore to it another
primum movens of the historian, namely, intellectual curiosity and the free
search for knowledge about the past. Moreover, a time will come when the
political beliefs that have sustained the disputes within our societies over
the last two centuries will seem as surprising to men as the inexhaustible
variety and violence of the religious conflicts in Europe between the
fifteenth and the seventeenth century seem to us. The very fact that the
study of the French Revolution could become a political arena will probably be seen as an explanatory factor and as a psychological commitment
of a bygone age.

But that 'cooling off' of the object 'French Revolution', to speak in Levi-
Straussian terms, is not to be expected from the mere passing of time. One
can define the conditions needed to bring it about, and even spot the first
signs of it, in our own time. I do not claim that those conditions will at last
provide us with historical *objectivity*; but they are already deeply modifying the relation between the historian of the French Revolution and his
subject, making less spontaneous and therefore less compelling the historian's identification with the actors, his commemoration of the founders, or
his execration of the deviants.

I can see two routes to that divestment, which I consider beneficial for
the renewal of the history of the Revolution. The first is emerging

gradually, belatedly, but ineluctably, from the contradictions between the myth of Revolution and the societies that have experienced it. The second is inherent in the mutations of historical knowledge.

The impact of the first, the contrast between myth and reality, is becoming increasingly clear. I am writing these lines in the spring of 1977, at a time when the criticism of Soviet totalitarianism, and more generally of all power claiming its source in Marxism, is no longer the monopoly, or near monopoly, of right-wing thought and has become a central theme in the reflections of the Left. What is important here, in referring to the historically related entities of Right and Left, is not that criticism from the Left, which has occupied a culturally dominant position in France since the end of the Second World War, carries more weight than criticism from the Right. Much more important is that in indicting the U.S.S.R. or China the Right has no need to adjust any part of its heritage and can simply stay within the bounds of counter-revolutionary thought. The Left, on the other hand, must face up to facts that compromise its beliefs, which are as old as those of the Right. That is why, for so long, the Left was loath to face up to such facts, and why, even today, it would often rather patch up the edifice of its convictions than look into the history of its tragedies. That will not matter in the long run. What does matter is that a left-wing culture, once it has made up its mind to think about the facts – namely, the disastrous experience of twentieth-century communism – in terms of its own values, has come to take a critical view of its own ideology, interpretations, hopes and rationalisations. It is in left-wing culture that the sense of distance between history and the Revolution is taking root, precisely because it was the Left that believed that all of history was contained in the promises of the Revolution.

The history of the French Left in relation to the Soviet Revolution remains to be written. It would show that Stalinism took root in a modified Jacobin tradition that consisted in grafting onto the Soviet phenomenon the ideas of a new beginning and of a nation in the vanguard of history. Moreover, it would show that during a long period by no means over, the notion of *deviation* from an unsullied beginning made it possible to salvage the pre-eminent value of revolution as an idea. But these two notions – of a new beginning and of a vanguard nation – are now giving way. Solzhenitsyn's work has become the basic historical reference for the Soviet experience, ineluctably locating the issue of the Gulag at the very core of the revolutionary endeavour. Once that happened the Russian example was bound to turn around, like a boomerang, to strike its French 'origin'. In 1920, Mathiez justified Bolshevik violence by the French precedent, in the name of comparable circumstances. Today the Gulag is leading to a rethinking of the Terror precisely because the two undertakings are seen as identical. The two revolutions remain connected; but while fifty years ago they were systematically absolved on the basis of excuses related to 'circumstances', that is, external phenomena that had nothing to do with the nature of the two revolutions, they are today, by contrast, accused of being, consubstantially, systems of meticulous constraint over men's bodies and minds.

Thus, the exorbitant privilege assigned to the idea of revolution, a privilege that placed it beyond the reach of internal criticism, is beginning to lose its standing as a self-evident fact. Academic historiography – in which the communists, almost as a matter of course, have taken over from the socialists and the radicals as the keepers of republican commemoration – still clings to that privilege and does not make light of its traditions. Holding on ever more closely to their short period of 'ancestral' history as if it were their social patrimony, those historians are not simply faced with the conceptual devaluation of their patrimony among intellectuals; they have trouble embracing, or even imagining, the intellectual changes that are indispensible to progress in the historiography of the Revolution.

In fact, this historiography should be made to show, not its colours, but its concepts. History in general has ceased to be a body of knowledge where the 'facts' are supposed to speak for themselves, once they have been established according to the rules. It must state the problem it seeks to analyse, the data it uses, its working hypotheses and the conclusions at which it arrives. If the history of the Revolution is the last one to adopt that method of *explicitness*, it is partly because all its traditions have drawn it, generation after generation, toward the myth of the beginnings; but, in addition, that myth has been taken over and canonised by a 'Marxist' rationalisation that does not change its character in any fundamental way but, on the contrary, consolidates the myth by making it appear a conceptual elaboration having the elemental power derived from its function as a new beginning.

I have explained my position [elsewhere:[8]] that rationalisation does not exist in Marx's writings, which do not include any systematic interpretation of the French Revolution; it is instead the product of a confused encounter between Bolshevism and Jacobinism, predicated upon a linear notion of human progress and punctuated by the two successive 'liberations', nested like a set of Russian dolls. The most hopelessly confused aspect of the 'Marxist' vulgate of the French Revolution is the juxtaposition of the old idea of the advent of a new age – the seminal idea of the French Revolution itself – with an enlargement of the field of history that is part of the very substance of Marxism. In fact Marxism – or perhaps one should say the kind of Marxism that penetrated the history of the French Revolution with Jaurès – has shifted the centre of gravity of the *problem* of the Revolution toward economic and social matters. It seeks to root in the progress of capitalism both the slow rise of the Third Estate (a theme dear to the historiography of the Restoration) and the apotheosis of 1789. In so doing, Marxism includes economic life and the fabric of society as a whole in the myth of a revolutionary break: before the Revolution, feudalism; after, capitalism; before, the nobility; after, the bourgeoisie. But since those propostitions are neither demonstrable, nor in fact even likely, and since, in any case, they shatter the accepted chronological framework, the Marxist approach amounts to no more than joining an analysis of causes carried out in the economic and social mode to a narrative of events written in the political and ideological mode.

At least that incoherence has the advantage of underscoring one of the essential problems of the historiography of the Revolution, which is how to fit the various levels of interpretation into the chronology of the event. If one is determined to preserve at any cost the idea of an objective break in the continuity of history, and to consider that break the alpha and omega of the history of the Revolution, one is indeed bound to end up with a number of absurdities, whatever the interpretation advanced. And those absurdities become the more inevitable as interpretation becomes more ambitious and encompasses more and more levels. One could say, for example, that between 1789 and 1794 the entire political system of France was radically transformed because the old monarchy then came to an end. But the idea that between those same dates the social or economic fabric of the nation was renewed from top to bottom is obviously much less plausible. The 'Revolution', then, is not a useful concept for making such assertions even if it is true that some of the causes of the Revolution were not exclusively political or intellectual.

In other words, any conceptualisation of the history of the Revolution must begin with a critique of the idea of revolution as experienced and perceived by its actors, and transmitted by their heirs, namely, the idea that it was a radical change and the origin of a new era. So long as that critique is absent from a history of the Revolution, superimposing a more social or more economic interpretation upon a purely political interpretation will not change what all those histories share, a fidelity to the revolutionary consciousness and experience of the nineteenth and twentieth centuries. Nonetheless, the social and economic deposits added by Marxism may have one advantage, for the absurdities to which they lead bring into sharp focus the dilemmas of any history of the Revolution that remains founded on the personal consciousness of those who made that history.

It is here that I encounter Tocqueville, and that I take the measure of his genius. At the very time when Michelet was working out the most penetrating of the histories of the Revolution written in the mode of personal identification – a history without concepts, made up of discoveries of the heart and marked by an intuitive grasp of men's souls and actors' motives – Tocqueville, and Tocqueville alone, envisaged the same history in the inverse mode of a sociological interpretation. It does not matter, therefore, that the Norman aristocrat did not hold the same *opinions* as the son of the Jacobin printer. Tocqueville, after all, did not write a more 'right-wing' history of the Revolution than Michelet. He wrote a *different* history of the Revolution, basing it upon a critique of revolutionary ideology and of what he saw as the French Revolution's illusion about itself.

Tocqueville's conceptual reversal of the accepted view of the French Revolution is not without analogies to the reversal that had marked his analysis of America. Before *Democracy in America*, European culture had conceived of America as the childhood of Europe, the image of its own beginnings and had dwelt on the process of settling and clearing, on man's conquest of untamed nature. Tocqueville's book, proceeding by deduction, as it were, from the central hypothesis about equality, turned that image inside out like a glove. America, he told the Europeans, is not your childhood, it is your future. There, freed from the constraints of an aristocratic past, is opening out the democracy that will *also* be the political and social future of old Europe. In the same way, although in reverse, Tocqueville renewed his paradox twenty years later in discussing the French Revolution, which had never – even and above all at the time of the American 'detour' – ceased to be his central concern. 'So you think that the French revolution is a sudden break in our national history?', he asked his contemporaries. In reality it is the fruition of our past. It has completed the work of the monarchy. Far from being a break, it can be understood only within and by historical continuity. It is the objective achievement of that continuity, even though it was experienced subjectively as a radical break.

Thus, Tocqueville developed a radical critique of any history of the French Revolution based only on the consciousness of the revolutionaries themselves. His critique is all the more penetrating as it remains within the political sphere – the relation between the French people and the governing power – which is precisely the sphere that *seems* to have been most profoundly transformed by the Revolution. Tocqueville is mainly concerned with the domination of local communities and civil society by the administrative power following the growth and extension of the centralised State. The takeover of society by the administrative State was more than the permanent feature linking the 'new' régime with the 'old', Bonaparte with Louis XIV. It also explained the developments by which 'democratic' (i.e. egalitarian) ideology penetrated throughout traditional French society. In other words, Tocqueville saw in the constitutive aspects of the 'Revolution', that is, an adminstrative State ruling a society informed by an egalitarian ideology, a work largely accomplished by the monarchy before it was completed by the Jacobins and the Empire. And what is called 'the French Revolution', an event later inventoried, dated, and magnified as a new dawn, was but the acceleration of a prior political and social trend. By destroying, not the aristocracy, but the aristocratic principle in society, the Revolution put an end to the legitimacy of social resistance against the central State. But it was Richelieu who set the example, and so did Louis XIV.

[I have analyzed elsewhere] the difficulties raised by that type of interpretation.[9] If Tocqueville never wrote a real history of the French Revolution it was, I believe, because he conceptualised only one aspect of that history, namely its continuity. He presented the Revolution in terms of its outcome, not as an event; as a process, not as a break. At the time of his death, he was working on his second volume and was confronting the problem of how to account for that break. But what remains fundamental in the work of this deductive and abstract mind, providentially wandering in a field suffused with the narrative method, is that it escaped the tyranny of the historical actors' own conception of their experience and the myth of origins. Tocqueville was not personally immersed in the choices that Necker, Louis XVI, Mirabeau or Robespierre had to make. He was a bystander. He was speaking of other things.

That is why his book is even more important for the method it suggests than for the thesis it advances. It seems to me that historians of the Revolution have, and always will have, to make a choice between Michelet and Tocqueville. By that I do not mean the choice between a republican and a conservative interpretation of the French Revolution, for those two kinds of history would still be linked together in a common definition of the problem, which is precisely what Tocqueville rejected. What separates Michelet and Tocqueville is something else: it is that Michelet brings the Revolution back to life from the inside, that he communes and commemorates, while Tocqueville constantly examines the discrepancy he discerns between the intentions of the actors and the historical rôle they played. Michelet installed himself in the visible or transparent Revolution; he celebrated the memorable coincidence between values, the people and men's action. Tocqueville not only questioned that transparency or coincidence, but felt that it actually masked the nearly unbridgeable gap between human action and its real meaning that characterised the French Revolution, owing to the rôle played by democratic ideology. For Tocqueville, there was a gulf between the Revolution's true outcome and the revolutionaries' intentions.

That is why, in my opinion, *L'Ancien Régime et la Révolution* remains the most important book of the entire historiography of the French Revolution. It is also why it has always been, for more than a century now, the stepchild of that historiography, more often cited than read, and more read than understood. Whether of the Right or of the Left, royalist or republican, conservative or Jacobin, the historians of the French Revolution have taken the revolutionary discourse at face value because they themselves have remained locked into that discourse. They keep putting on the Revolution the different faces assumed by the event itself in an unending commentary on a conflict whose meaning, so they think, the

Revolution itself has explained to us once and for all through the pronouncements of its heroes. They must therefore believe, since the Revolution says so, that it destroyed the nobility when it negated its principle; that the Revolution founded a new society when it asserted that it did; that the Revolution was a new beginning of history when it spoke of regenerating the human race. Into this game of mirrors, where the historian and the Revolution believe each other's words literally, and where the Revolution has become history's protagonist, the absolutely trustworthy Antigone of the new era, Tocqueville introduces a doubt that strikes at the very heart of the matter: what if that discourse about a radical break reflects no more than the illusion of change?

The answer to that question is not simple, nor would answering it take care of the whole history of the Revolution. Yet it is probably indispensable to a conceptualisation of that history. Its importance can be measured negatively: unless the historian comes to grips with it, he is bound to execrate or to celebrate, both of which are ways of commemorating.

II

If Tocqueville is a unique case in the historiography of the Revolution, it is because his book forces the reader to *take apart* the 'French Revolution' and try to conceptualise it. By means of explicit concepts, Tocqueville breaks up the chronological narrative: he treats a problem rather than a period. With him, the Revolution no longer speaks all by itself, in one sense or another, as if its meaning were clear from the outset and substantiated by the very course it took. Tocqueville, instead, subjects it to a systematic interpretation that isolates some of its elements, in particular, administrative centralisation during the Ancien Régime and its effect on what might be called the 'democratisation' of society. The very long time span studied by Tocqueville (he constantly calls upon, for example, the reign of Louis XIV to make his points) can be explained by the nature of the problem he has set for himself and by the interpretation he advances: the Revolution was in a direct line with the Ancien Régime.

I am not suggesting that every effort to conceptualise the 'French Revolution' must be set in a vast chronological framework. The two things are not connected, and the 'long term' is not the only analytical tool at the historian's disposal. I simply mean that every interpretation of the Revolution supposes some time frame, and that the historian who views the Revolution as continuity will naturally investigate a longer period than one who seeks to understand it as an 'event' or series of events. But the second approach is no less valid than the first, and equally conducive to a constructive interpretation. The only suspect approach is precisely that which characterises the historiography of the Revolution, and illustrates its analytical underdevelopment: writing the history of the same period over and over again, as if the story, being told, spoke for itself, regardless of the historian's implicit presuppositions.

Such a history could, of course, be explicitly conceived as a pure narrative designed to reconstruct the individual or collective experiences of the participants rather than to interpret the meaning or meanings of the events. However, I am not taking issue with Georges Lenôtre but with Mathiez. I am well aware that every history is implicitly, and in varying degrees, a mixture of narrative and analysis, and that 'scholarly' history is not exempt from that 'rule'. But what is peculiar to the historiography of the Revolution is the unvarying internal organisation of its discourse. The place of each genre within that history never changes. Analysis is restricted to the problem of 'origins' or causes, which are explanatory factors. Narative begins with the 'events', in 1787 or 1789, and runs through to the end of the 'story', until 9 Thermidor or 18 Brumaire, as if once the causes are set out, the play went on by itself, propelled by the initial upheaval.

That mingling of genres comes from confusing two objects of analysis: it fails to distinguish between the Revolution as a historical process, a set of causes and effects, and the Revolution as a mode of change, a specific dynamic of collective action. Those two objects cannot be dealt with in the same intellectual operation; even superficial examination shows that, for example, they involve two different chronological frames of reference. In examining the causes or the results of the Revolution, the observer must go back far beyond 1789 on the one hand, and far ahead beyond 1794 or 1799 on the other. Yet the 'story' of the Revolution is enclosed between 1789 and 1794 or 1799. If those who write it are not, in general, aware of those different levels of chronology, it is because they mentally telescope the different levels of analysis by resorting to the following implicit hypothesis: the course taken by the Revolution was inherent in its causes, since its participants had no choice but to do what they did namely, to destroy the Ancien Régime and to replace it with a new order. Whether that new order turned out to be democracy, as in Michelet, or capitalism, as in Mathiez, is irrelevant, for in both cases it is the consciousness of the participants that retrospectively shapes the analysis of their actions. The historian who wants to remain faithful to that consciousness without neglecting his duty to provide an explanation needs only to justify the advent of the new order in terms of necessity. If he does that, he actually has no need to concern himself with the outcome.

If it were true that objective reasons necessarily – and even inevitably – compelled men to take collective action to shatter the 'Ancien' régime and to install a new one, then there would be no need to distinguish between the problem of the origins of the Revolution and the nature of the event itself. For not only would historical necessity coincide with revolutionary action, but there would also be a perfect 'fit' [*transparence*] between that action and the general meaning attributed to it by the protagonists, who felt that they were breaking with the past and founding a new history.

The postulate that 'what actually happened' did so of necessity is a classic retrospective illusion of historical consciousness, which sees the past as a field of possibilities within which 'what actually happened' appears *ex post facto* as the only future for that past. But in the case of the French Revolution, that postulate overlaps a second one, from which it is inseparable: the illusion that 1789, or the period 1789–93, represents an absolute chronological break in the history of France. Before 1789, absolutism and the nobility held sway (as if those two features of the Ancien Régime went hand in hand). After 1789, liberty and the bourgeoisie came into their own. Lastly, hidden away in the sound and fury of the Revolution, were the promises of an early form of socialism. In keeping with what the protagonists of the revolutionary break had said, French history thus assumes the status of a new beginning, and the event itself becomes a kind of crucible in which the past was abolished, the present was constituted and the future was shaped. Not only was what happened fore-ordained; it also contained the seeds of the future.

Now the dominant 'concept' of today's historiography of the Revolution, 'bourgeois revolution', seems to me to be used less as a concept than as a mask concealing precisely these two presuppositions: that of the inevitability of the event and that of a radical break in time. And it is indeed an opportune 'concept' or mask, for it reconciles all levels of historical reality and every aspect of the French Revolution. After all, the events of 1789–94 are supposed to have given birth, simultaneously, to capitalism at the economic level, to the preponderance of the bourgeoisie in the social and political order, and to the ideological values that are assumed to go with those two developments. Moreover, those events betoken the fundamental rôle of the bourgeoisie as a class in the Revolution. Hence the confused notion of 'bourgeois revolution' inseparably designates both a historical content and a historical agent, arising together out of the fore-ordained explosion of the last few years of eighteenth century. The allegedly inevitable 'work' of the Revolution is thus given a perfectly suitable agent. In its systematic application of the idea that there was a radical break between 'before' and 'after', the 'social' interpretation of the French Revolution enthrones a metaphysical system of essence and fate. It is therefore much more than an interpretation of the Revolution: since it includes in its subject the whole problem of origins, that is, all of French society before 1789, it is also a retrospective vision of the 'Ancien Régime', which it defines *a contrario* by the new. Was the French Revolution indeed inevitable? In order to view it as such, all one has to do is reconstitute the flow of the movement toward it and that of the resistance it encountered and then set up, precisely in 1789, the shock that resolved the contradiction. On one side one places a stupid monarchy and an egotistical nobility, linked by common interests as well as by reactionary policies and ideologies. On the other, the rest of civil society, led, indeed carried along, by a rich, ambitious and frustrated bourgeoisie. The first set of forces functions not only as a factor of resistance to the historian's idea of evolution, but also as a dynamic counter-current: that is the rôle assigned to the 'feudal reaction' (or 'seigneurial' reaction, since the two terms seem to be used more or less interchangeably), as is well indicated by the term 'reaction', borrowed from mechanics. That reaction, which is supposed to have covered the second half of the eighteenth century, would account both for peasant violence in the summer of 1789 and for bourgeois resentment; in other words, for the conditions that united the Third Estate against the nobility. Impeded not simply by the natural inertia of tradition and of the State but by institutions and social classes that were actively and almost malevolently engaged in reconstructing the past, the forces of progress were reduced to a single and inevitable recourse: revolution.

In the general pattern of those two class fronts advancing from opposite directions towards each other as if to join battle, it is not difficult to recognise the view that the militants of the revolutionary years had of the events they were experiencing, and their interpretation of those events. They were expressing the logic of revolutionary consciousness, which, by its very nature, tends to promote a Manichaean explanation and to personify social phenomena. At this point the historian's occupational disease, which forever compels him to reduce the potential outcomes of a situation to a single one, since it alone occurred, is compounded by the intellectual simplifications that accompany and justify political violence in modern times. Hence the powerful attraction of single-cause explanations at every level of argument: victory of the Enlightenment over obscurantism, of liberty over oppression, of equality over privilege; or the advent of capitalism on the ruins of feudalism; or, finally, the synthesis of all these factors in a kind of logical balance-sheet, where they are lined up face to face in a systematic accounting of the past and the future. All these explanations employ the same logical mechanism. The Marxian synthesis enlarges the content while making it more rigid; but the mechanism itself has been at work since 1789, for it is a constitutive feature of the revolutionary ideology.

Integrated into a history whose every aspect it tends to incorporate, that mechanism spins its wheels in a vacuum and is more interesting for the contradictions it raises than for the problems it solves, as I have tried to show in a critique of the communist historiography of the Revolution.[10] Caricaturing the elementary traits of the revolutionary consciousness, carrying them to the absurdity of an illusory rigor presented as conceptualisation, this historiography illustrates the hopeless crisis of a tradition. It has lost the attractiveness of the epic story which it has placed in a strait-jacket without adding anything to its own power of explanation, since it reduces the story to nothing more than a disguise for the pre-suppositions underlying the narrative. Significantly, it is in one of the fields where the most notable progress has been made in recent years, the history of traditional French society, that that kind of historiography turns out to be most summary and most inexact. In the system of equivalences and opposites it has contrived in order to celebrate the inevitability of a new beginning, no feature stands up to scrutiny, whether it be the confusion between monarchical State and nobility, between nobility and feudalism or between bourgeoisie and capitalism, or the opposition between absolutism and reform, aristocracy and liberty, society of orders and Enlightenment thought.

I shall not enter here into the detail of my critique. However, it is necessary to add to it more general observation: the establishment of a logical (and almost always implicit) connection identifying the Revolution as an objective historical process with the Revolution as a set of events that 'actually happened' – the Revolution-as-content with the Revolution-as-mode – necessarily leads to deducing the first aspect from the second. Yet it seems to me that the wise thing to do is to see them separately, a course that is suggested not only by chronology but also, after all, by that old axiom – bourgeois as well as Marxist – that men make history but do not know the history they are making.

A phenomenon like the French Revolution cannot be reduced to a simple cause-and-effect schema. The mere fact that the Revolution had causes does not mean that they are all there is to its history. Let us assume for a moment that these causes are better understood than they actually are or that some day it will be possible to list them in a more functional order; the fact remains that the revolutionary event, *from the very outset*, totally transformed the existing situation and created a new mode of historical action that was not intrinsically a part of that situation. One could, for instance, explain the revolt of most of the deputies to the Estates General by the political crisis in the Ancien Régime; but the situation created in its wake by the vacancy of power and the ensuing insurrection added a totally unprecedented dimension to that crisis, with consequences that no one could have foreseen two months earlier. One could also explain the popular urban uprisings of June–July by the economic crisis, the price of bread, unemployment, the commercial treaty between England and France, and so forth; but that type of explanation does not account for the transition from the grain or tax riot – a relatively classic occurrence in towns under the Ancien Régime – to the revolutionary *journée*, governed by an altogether different dynamic. In other words, the debate about the causes of the Revolution does not cover the problem of the revolutionary phenomenon, which was largely independent of the situation that preceded it, and therefore had its own consequences. The main characteristics of the

Revolution as an *event* is a specific mode of historical action; it is a dynamic that one may call political, ideological or cultural, for its enhanced power to activate men and to shape events arose from the fact that it meant many things to many people.

Here again, Toqueville was the first to sense that central problem. For his approach centres on the examination of what I call the Revolution-as-process, in his case a process of continuity. Tocqueville contends that the Revolution extended, consolidated and brought to perfection the administrative State and the egalitarian society whose development was the main achievement of the old monarchy. Hence, he finds an absolute incompatibility between the objective history of the Revolution – its 'meaning' or end result – and the meaning attributed to their own actions by the revolutionaries. . . . Setting out from Tocqueville's present – the Revolution's outcome – *L' Ancien Régime* goes on to analyse the origins of the Revolution. There the central rôle was played by the administrative monarchy, which had emptied the society of orders of its living substance and opened the way less to equality of condition than to egalitarianism as a value. But between the origins and the end result, between Louis XIV and Bonaparte, there is a blank page that Tocqueville never filled. It contains some questions that he raised but never clearly answered: why did the process of continuity between the old régime and the new involve a revolution? And what, in those circumstances, is the significance of the revolutionaries' political commitment?

It is true that Book 3 of *L'Ancien Régime* does contain some partial answers to those questions, such as the substitution of intellectuals for politicians in eighteenth-century France, or the spread to all classes of society of democratic attitudes. But the extaordinary vitality of egalitarian ideology between 1789 and 1793 remains for Tocqueville a kind of mystery of evil, a religion in reverse. Nowhere in his work does he establish a conceptual link between his theory of the French Revolution and revolutionary action as it was experienced by contemporaries and expressed in such characteristic phenomena of the period as Jacobinism. Tocqueville makes us wonder whether one can even establish such a link; he forces us to separate, at least temporarily, the two parts of the confused amalgam called the 'history of the Revolution', and to stop juxtaposing the analysis of causes with the description of events as if the two techniques were part of one homogeneous discourse, and as if one could be deduced from the other.

These 'events', being political and even ideological in nature, invalidate by definition a causal analysis based on economic and social 'contradictions'; moreover, such an analysis, even when it deals with the political system and its legitimacy, does not take into account the radically new dimension added by revolutionary momentum. There is something in the concept of revolution (used in the latter, 'radical' sense) that corresponds to its 'experienced' historical reality, and is not subservient to the logical sequence of cause and effect: the appearance on the stage of history of a practical and ideological mode of social action totally unrelated to anything that came before. A specific type of political crisis made it possible, but not inevitable; and revolt was not its model, since revolt was by definition a part of the old political and cultural system.

The French Revolution is thus the matrix of a new type of historical action and consciousness, related to, but not defined by, a specific situation. One must take stock of that entire complex in order to propose an interpretation, instead of proceeding as if revolutionary consciousness were the normal result of legitimate grievances and a perfectly natural phenomenon in human history. The Marxist vulgate of the French Revolution actually turns the world upside down: it makes the revolutionary break a matter of economic and social change, whereas nothing resembled French society under Louis XVI more than French society under Louis-Philippe. And since it fails to take any distance from the revolutionary consciousness whose illusions and values it shares, it is incapable of realising that it treats the most radically new and the most mysterious aspect of the French Revolution as no more than the normal result of circumstances and as a natural occurrence in the history of the oppressed. After all, neither capitalism nor the bourgeoisie needed revolutions to appear in and dominate the history of the major European nations in the nineteenth century. But France was the country that, through the Revolution, invented democratic culture, and revealed to the world one of the basic forms of historical consciousness of action.

Let us first consider the impact of the circumstances, not of misery or oppression but of society's independence from politics. If the Revolution invented new structures and upset the old ones, if it set in motion enough new forces to transform the traditional mechanisms of politics, it was because it took over an empty space, or, rather, proliferated within that once forbidden sphere of power that it so suddenly invaded. In the dialogue between societies and their States that is part of the underlying texture of history, the Revolution tipped the scales against the State and in favour of society. For the Revolution mobilized society and disarmed the State; it was an exceptional situation, which provided society with a space for development to which it does not normally have access. From 1787, the kingdom of France had been a society without a State. Louis XVI continued to rally the consensus of his subjects round himself, but behind that traditional façade lay panic and disorder; while royal authority was nominally still respected, its legitimacy no longer extended to the agents of the crown. The king, it was said, had bad ministers, perfidious advisers and nefarious *intendants*; but as yet no one realised that this old monarchist refrain for difficult times had ceased to exalt the authority to whom the people could turn as an ultimate recourse, and had become instead a call for citizen control. In other words, civil society, where examples filter down from top to bottom, was ridding itself of the symbolic power of the State, along with the rules it imposed.

Then came 1789. Affecting everyone, from the noblest of nobles to the humblest of peasants, the 'revolution' was born of the convergence of very different series of events, since an economic crisis (a complex phenomenon in itself, involving agricultural, 'industrial', meteorological and social factors) took its place alongside the political crisis that had begun in 1787. This convergence of several heterogeneous series, surely a fortuitous situation, was to be transformed as early as the spring of 1789 by a retrospective illusion in which it was seen as the inevitable consequence of bad government and as the central issue in the struggle between patriots and aristocrats. For the revolutionary situation was not only characterised by the power vacuum that was filled by a rush of new forces and by the 'free' activity of society. It was also bound up with a kind of hypertrophy of historical consciousness and with a system of symbolic representations shared by the social actors. The revolutionary consciousness, from 1789 on, was informed by the illusion of defeating a State that had already ceased to exist, in the name of a coalition of good intentions and of forces that foreshadowed the future. From the very beginning it was ever ready to place ideas above actual history, as if it were called upon to restructure a fragmented society by means of its own concepts. Repression became intolerable only when it became ineffectual. The Revolution was the historical space that separated two powers, the embodiment of the idea that history is shaped by human action rather than by the combination of existing institutions and forces.

In that unforseeable and accelerated drift, the idea of human action patterned its goals on the exact opposite of the traditional principles underlying the social order. The Ancien Régime had been in the hands of the king; the Revolution was the people's achievement. France had been a kingdom of subjects; it was now a nation of citizens. The old society had been based on privilege; the Revolution established equality. Thus was created the ideology of a radical break with the past, a tremendous cultural drive for equality. Henceforth everything – the economy, society and politics – yielded to the force of ideology and to the militants who embodied it; no coalition nor any institution could last under the onslaught of that torrential advance.

Here I am using the term ideology to designate the two sets of beliefs that to my mind, constitute the very bedrock of revolutionary consciousness. The first is that all personal problems and all moral or intellectual matters have become political; that there is no human misfortune not amenable to a political solution. The second is that, since everything can be known and changed, there is a perfect fit between action, knowledge and morality. That is why the revolutionary militants identified their private lives with their public ones and with the defence of their ideas. It was a formidable logic, which, in a laicised form, reproduced the psychological commitment that springs from religious beliefs. When politics becomes the realm of truth and falsehood, of good and evil, and when it is politics that separates the good from the wicked, we find ourselves in a historical universe whose dynamic is entirely new. As Marx realised in his early writings, the Revolution was the very incarnation of the *illusion of politics*: it transformed mere experience into conscious acts. It inaugurated a world that attributes every social change to known, classified and living forces; like mythical thought, it peoples the objective universe with subjective volitions, that is, as the case may be, with responsible leaders or scapegoats. In such a world, human action no longer encounters obstacles or limits, only adversaries, preferably traitors. The recurrence of that notion is a telling feature of the moral universe in which the revolutionary explosion took place.

No longer held together by the State, nor by the constraints that had been imposed by power and had masked its disintegration, society thus recomposed itself through ideology. Peopled by active volitions and recognising only faithful followers or adversaries, that new world had an incomparable capacity to integrate. It was the beginning of what has ever since been called 'politics', that is, a common yet contradictory language of debate and action around the central issue of power. The French Revolution, of course, did not 'invent' politics as an autonomous area of knowledge; to speak only of Christian Europe, the theory of political action as such dates back to Machiavelli, and the scholarly debate about the origin of society as an institution was well under way by the seventeenth century. But the example of the English Revolution shows that when it came to collective involvement and action, the fundamental frame of intellectual reference was still of a religious nature. What the French brought into being at the end of the eighteenth century was not politics as a laicised and distinct area of critical reflection but democratic politics as a national ideology. The secret of the success of 1789, its message and its lasting influence lie in that invention, which was unprecedented and whose legacy was to be so widespread. The English and French revolutions, though separated by more than a century, have many traits in common, none of which, however, was sufficient to bestow on the first rôle of universal model that the second has played ever since it appeared on the stage of history. The reason is that Cromwell's Republic was too preoccupied with religious concerns and too intent upon its return to origins to develop the one notion that made Robespierre's language the prophecy of a new era: that democratic politics had come to decide the fate of individuals and peoples.

The term 'democratic politics' does not refer here to a set of rules or procedures designed to organise, on the basis of election results, the functioning of authority. Rather, it designates a system of beliefs that constitutes the new legitimacy born of the Revolution, and according to which the 'people', in order to establish the liberty and equality that are the objectives of collective action, must break its enemies' resistance. Having become the supreme means of putting values into action and the inevitable test of 'right' or 'wrong' will, politics could have only a public spokesman, in total harmony with those values, and enemies who remained concealed, since their designs could not be publicly admitted. The 'people' were defined by their aspirations, and as an indistinct aggregate of individual 'right' wills. By that expedient, which precluded representation, the revolutionary consciousness was able to reconstruct an imaginary social cohesion in the name and on the basis of individual wills. That was its way of resolving the eighteenth century's great dilemma, that of conceptualising society in terms of the individual. If indeed the individual was defined in his every aspect by the aims of his political action, a set of goals as simple as a moral code would permit the Revolution to found a new language as well as a new society. Or, rather, to found a new society through a new language: today we would call that a nation; at the time it was celebrated in the *fête de la Fédération*.

This type of analysis has the two-fold advantage of restoring to the French Revolution its most obvious dimension, the political one, and of focusing attention on the true break in continuity it wrought between 'before' and 'after', that is, a change in the ways of legitimating and representing hisorical action. The action of the *sans-culottes* of 1793 is important not because it involved a 'popular' social group (impossible, by the way, to define in socio-economic terms) but because it expresses in its chemically pure form, as it were, such revolutionary notions of political action as obsession with treason and plot, the refusal to be represented, the will to punish, and so forth. And there is no way, nor will there ever be one, to explain those notions by a social situation fraught with conflicting interests. The first task of the historiography of the French Revolution must be to rediscover the analysis of its political dimension. But the price to pay is two-fold: not only must we stop regarding revolutionary consciousness as a more or less 'natural' result of oppression and discontent; we must also develop a conceptual understanding of this strange offspring of '*philosophie*' (its offspring, at least, in a chronological sense).

Notes

1 *Qu'est-ce que le Tiers Etat?* was written at the end of 1788 and published in January 1789.
2 *Qu'est-ce que le Tiers Etat?*, ed. Edme Champion (Paris: Société d'histoire de la Révolution française, 1888), ch. 11, p. 32.

3 Jean Jaurès, *Histoire socialiste de la Révolution française* (Paris: Éditions Sociales, 1968); preface by Ernest Labrousse, p. 14.

4 A. Mathiez, *Le Bolchevisme et le Jacobinisme* (Paris, Librairie de 'L'Humanité', 1920).

5 Georges Lefebvre, 'La Révolution française et les paysans' (1932), in *Études sur la Révolution française* (Paris, P.U.F., 1954; 2nd edn, introduction by Albert Soboul, 1963).

6 Paul Bois, *Les Paysans de l'Ouest* (Paris and The Hague, Mouton, 1960).

7 Lefebvre, 'La Révolution française et les paysans', p. 263.

8 F. Furet, 'Le Catechisme révolutionnaire', *Annales: Economies, Sociétés, Civilisations*, 27 (1971), pp. 255–89.

9 *See* F. Furet, *Interpreting the French Revolution* (Cambridge and Paris, 1981), pp. 132–63.

10 See above, note 8.

3

Georges Lefebvre and the peasant revolution: fifty years on

PETER JONES

Among historians, the name Georges Lefebvre needs no introduction. Anyone who has studied the French Revolution, whether at school or at a university, will have come across his books. They are plentiful, accessible, and apparently authoritative. At the last count, his text book histories of the Revolution had been translated into a dozen languages. With the two-hundredth anniversary of that event upon us, an evaluation of Georges Lefebvre's writings seems especially timely. Bicentenaries are hollow occasions unless accompanied by critical reflection, a function most effectively performed by the historian.

Georges Lefebvre was the 'Grand Old Man' of French Revolutionary historiography. He achieved this feat by living a very long time, by publishing frequently, and by endless indefatigable research in the archives. By the time of his death in 1959, he was acknowledged as the outstanding scholar of his generation; probably the outstanding Revolutionary scholar of *any* generation. This was quite an achievement when we consider the calibre of the men who launched the academic study of the French Revolution: Alphonse Aulard, Jean Jaurès, Philippe Sagnac, and Albert Mathiez. Lefebvre was a master of his craft: a diplomatic historian, a historian of

Reprinted in full from: *French Historical Studies 16 (1990), pp. 545–63.*

power, a quantifier, a psycho-historian, and a social historian all rolled into one. But it was in the guise of a socio-political historian, of a student of the French peasantry, that he showed the greatest prowess.

It should also be said that Lefebvre was a man of the Left who identified instinctively with what the revolutionaries were trying to achieve, and by the same token detested the counterrevolution and all its works. He could be dogmatic and was sometimes accused of writing dogmatic history. Alfred Cobban, one of his earliest critics, once accused him of putting 'almost too much meaning' into the history of the French Revolution.[1] Yet such a comment seems more revealing of the Anglo-Saxon historiographical tradition than of Lefebvre's purpose. Of course he identified with the Revolution; of course he could be dogmatic, but it was a dogmatism tempered by a scrupulously scientific methodology. There was, as we shall see, a certain tension between Lefebvre the scholar and Lefebvre the political animal. In a BBC radio broadcast some years ago, Richard Cobb once described Lefebvre as a 'Jacobin,' and I think that this label captures the essence of the man. He could be a fierce egalitarian (notwithstanding a keen awareness of his status as a professor at the Sorbonne); he had some blind spots even as a historian, but he rarely flinched from the task of modifying received wisdom and doctrine when it ran counter to the evidence of his researches.

I

Lefebvre's death in 1959 left peasant studies denuded; there was no rising generation of young scholars waiting in the wings to carry on his work. Research interests had changed, and his few pupils were busy conquering other territories. Albert Soboul[2] and George Rudé[3] had just made their mark with seminal works on the Paris crowd during the Revolution, and Richard Cobb would shortly produce a definitive study of the *armées révolutionnaires*.[4] Only Alun Davies, as far as I know, continued Lefebvre's work on the peasantry, but he published little after 1964.[5] The master's synthesis remained intact — scarcely challenged, but scarcely added to either.

But what was that synthesis exactly? Put in a nutshell, Lefebvre 'discovered' the peasant revolution; or to be more precise, he rescued the peasantry from historiographical neglect. In a series of books, articles, and editions published between 1924 and 1957, Lefebvre assembled a new and much more complex interpretation of the Revolution than had hitherto prevailed among historians. It rested on three interlocking propositions:

1 that country dwellers actively, massively, and purposefully participated in the Revolution, at least until 1793;

2 that their participation was independent in the sense that it was not, of necessity, geared to the actions and the reactions of the Revolutionary bourgeoisie;

3 that the majority of peasants shared an anticapitalist mentality which tinctured their participation in the events of the 1790s.

The peasant revolution, he declared, was 'autonomous in terms of its origins, its proceedings, its crises, and its tendencies.'[6] Moreover, the peasantry were dubious about the main capitalist thrust of the Revolution. Despite appearances, their intervention may be described as 'conservative as much as revolutionary; they destroyed the feudal regime but consolidated the agrarian structure of France.'[7]

Until comparatively recent times, none of this has seemed the least bit contentious, which is a measure of Lefebvre's achievement in rewriting the history of the Revolution. 'Rewriting' is perhaps too strong a verb; nevertheless, he modified the classic interpretation of the Revolution in several respects. None of his predecessors nor his contemporaries had entirely neglected the role of the peasantry, but their writings made few concessions in this direction. They depicted a Revolution which was basically a knock-out contest between the aristocracy and the bourgeoisie. The peasantry made a brief appearance in the ring, but as auxiliaries of the bourgeoisie and not as a third force. Lefebvre changed all this. By pushing the peasantry into the center of the stage he turned the Revolution into a much more complex social interaction, and by suggesting that the peasantry and not the bourgeoisie might have set the political agenda, he conjured forth an interpretation of events in the 1790s that was much less coherent in the ideological sense. His contention that the instincts of the peasant masses were diametrically opposed to those of bourgeois revolutionaries intimated the same.

II

Georges Lefebvre's earliest critics fastened on this point. Even before his death, Alfred Cobban accused Lefebvre of wanting to 'have his cake and eat it too.' That is to say, he accused Lefebvre of solemnly preaching that 1789 was a 'bourgeois revolution' while simultaneously subverting the notion with his discovery of an 'autonomous peasant revolution.' There are signs that Albert Soboul, too, found the reformulation rather disturbing in its implications. In his early articles and text books he rallied faithfully to Lefebvre's new perspective, but he took pains to emphasize that, in his view, the peasant revolution 'developed within the framework of the bourgeois revolution and did not surpass it.'[8] Of course, Soboul's own researches, as a result of which he uncovered the 'autonomous revolution of the *sans-culottes*,' had similar theoretical implications.

Cobban also criticized Lefebvre's system of social classification, with particular reference to his concept of a 'rural bourgeoisie.' This is a point that many historians have raised subsequently, not least Albert Soboul and Roland Mousnier. If I remember correctly, the concept of a 'rural bourgeoisie' was first employed by the Russian agrarian historian Karéiew, but it needs to be tied down firmly to a time and a place if it is to have any meaning. Lefebvre liked to describe the prosperous upper echelons of the peasantry as a 'rural bourgeoisie,' but to apply the term 'bourgeois' to *laboureurs* seems contrived, and Cobban, ever on the alert for too much 'meaning,' suspected a rhetorical device. Whatever validity Lefebvre's model may possess for the Northeast of France, it corresponds poorly with perceived social and economic realities elsewhere. Most historians would nowadays exclude the 'laborious' element from the 'rural bourgeoisie.' In the Centre, the South, and the Southwest, where the spectrum of wealth and opportunity among the peasantry was much more compact, the 'rural bourgeoisie' consisted of village intellectuals, professionals, and non-noble landowners living off rent. Nonetheless, the significance which Lefebvre attached to this group is well taken: in 1787 and 1788 they emerged as the pacemakers of the Revolution at the grass roots.

III

Recalling the legacy of Georges Lefebvre in 1969, Marc Bouloiseau remarked: 'Scarcely a congress, colloquium, or encounter devoted to the eighteenth century, the Revolution, or the Empire takes place at which his name is not mentioned.'[9] And yet he went on to suggest that the vigour which Lefebvre brought to Revolutionary scholarship had ebbed somewhat. There is an important truth here. Lacking a band of disciples committed to the advancement of peasant studies, Lefebvre's legacy stagnated in the 1960s. To be sure, Alfred Cobban had launched a series of broadsides between 1954 and 1964, but Cobban was a brilliant critic adept at picking holes in other people's theories rather than at producing watertight ones of his own. Besides, he was no match for Lefebvre as an agrarian historian and he died in 1968. The modern age of peasant studies only really began in the mid-1970s, but it rapidly developed a scholarly momentum that carried it beyond the stage of criticizing and reworking the precepts which Lefebvre had enunciated in his celebrated article, 'Les Paysans et la Révolution française,'[10] over forty years earlier.

If we set aside the new perspectives opened into comparative and *longue durée* history during the 1970s, it is possible to detect movement on three broad fronts: (1) continued testing of the Lefebvre synthesis, conducted, for the most part, in the tradition of Alfred Cobban; (2) scholarly attempts to view the actions of the peasantry during the Revolution from a non-Lefebvrian viewpoint; and (3) exploration of areas of peasant involvement with the Revolution which Lefebvre did little more than reconnoiter, or which he entirely neglected.

None of these developments occurred in isolation, of course. Nearly all the scholars currently engaged in rethinking the peasant revolution have acknowledged their debt to Lefebvre; critical appraisal, reformulation, and refocusing are, of necessity, overlapping exercises. Nevertheless, it is helpful to separate the issues if we are to appreciate the directions in which peasant studies have been pushed since the death of the master. The issues which have provoked most discussion in recent years are in rough sequential order

seigneurialism
the crisis of the ancien régime
the commons and collective rights
agrarian capitalism
Jacobinism and the peasantry
counterrevolution and the peasantry
state-making and the peasantry

Each of these topics will be explored in the following pages.

IV

Seigneurialism. The idea among historians that the Revolution owed its origins and found its early purpose in resistance to something known variously as 'seigneurialism' or 'the feudal regime' was not unique to Lefebvre; it goes back to a book by Henri Doniol,[11] and even earlier. Nevertheless, Lefebvre refined contemporary wisdom on the subject of feudalism and documented the mechanisms of seigneurial lordship as they applied still in the eighteenth century. He professed, moreover, to believe in some kind of 'feudal reaction,' or intensification of feudal impositions that occurred in the decades immediately preceding the Revolution, and which he described in his seminal article of 1933 as an 'intensification of the feudal regime that appears incontestable in the eighteenth century, especially in the second half.'[12] Even so, he must have had some doubts about the phenomenon, because six years later, on the occasion of the 150th anniversary of the Revolution, he proposed as a topic for research to discover whether 'feudal dues were collected more scrupulously in the years down to 1789, whether, therefore, that which we call the "feudal reaction" was a reality.'[13]

Cobban, needless to say, objected strenuously to the suggestion that relationships could still be termed 'feudal' in the eighteenth century. He clearly viewed the term as another rhetorical device to prop up Lefebvre's Marxist, or neo-Marxist, interpretation of the Revolution. Yet Cobban did not reject the reality of seigneurial surplus extraction, nor the likelihood that it was becoming more burdensome as the ancien régime drew to a close. Instead, he substituted the notion of a commercial reaction taking place in the countryside, or rather a process wherein new business techniques were applied to old relationships. Lefebvre, I feel sure, would have disagreed with none of this, while insisting that it was only part of the picture. He had, after all, been one of the first historians to note the growth of agrarian capitalism 'under the cover of feudal dues.'[14] What Cobban's criticism seems to amount to – on this point – is a quibble about labels and not much else.

However, an American historian, G. V. Taylor,[15] was moved (by Cobban?) to take a firmer line. His researches led him to the conclusion that the historical profession's obsession with the ramifications of feudalism/seigneurialism on the eve of the Revolution was misplaced. Even the peasantry showed little interest in the issue; no doubt, he infers, because seigneurial surplus extraction was negligible. This view shows signs of hardening into a new orthodoxy, at least among Anglo-American historians, but it is one that I believe to be mistaken. Even on Taylor's own evidence drawn from the *cahiers de doléances*, it is difficult to sustain the assertion that the peasantry were not hostile to the emanations of seigneurialism. Furthermore, there now exists additional research that testifies to a widespread popular inclination to challenge the institutions of seigneurialism in the 1770s and the 1780s. Admittedly, the case for a global 'feudal reaction' has yet to be made with conviction, but there are grounds for supposing that these decades, in particular, witnessed discrete 'mini-reactions' in a wide scatter of districts and localities.

V

The crisis of the ancien régime. This explanatory concept is closely linked to that of 'seigneurialism,' and it is a concept that nearly all Revolutionary historians find useful in one form or another. If Lefebvre did not invent it, he was the first to set down the details in *Les Paysans du Nord* (1924), and his conviction that the Revolution was first and foremost the product of a crisis in the rural economy was powerfully supported by Ernest Labrousse.[16] Labrousse supplied the most celebrated statistic of French Revolutionary historiography: an index of the purchasing power of the urban and rural poor. Taking the years 1726–41 as the baseline, he calculated that the average price of essential consumer goods had risen by 45 percent when compared with the period 1771–89. If the period 1785–89 is isolated, the rise works out to 65 percent. By comparison, nominal wages rose by only 22 percent over the period 1726–89. Therefore, in the course of five decades the purchasing power of wage earners declined by up to a quarter. What this analysis leaves out of account, though, is any sense of 1787–89 as a political revolt, and it is from this direction that a challenge to the Lefebvre-Labrousse thesis has arisen in recent years. G. V. Taylor has expressed his opinion quite succinctly: '1789,' he declares, was 'essentially a political revolution with social consequences and not a social revolution with political consequences.'[17] This is also the view shared by William Doyle, a lucid English critic of received wisdom on the subject of the pre-Revolutionary crisis when he writes: 'Down to the spring of 1789, the forces pushing France toward Revolution were almost entirely political. There was no underlying social crisis; it seems unlikely that such discontents as surfaced in the *cahiers* would have done so without the stimulus provided by the constitutional wranglings that followed the collapse of the government.'[18] The difficulty posed by such an extreme denial of Lefebvre's scenario is that it simply leaves out of account the accumulating evidence of peasant discontent (in Gascony, the Toulousain, the southern Massif Central, Burgundy) during the two and three decades before the Revolution.[19]

No one, it seems, disputes the fact that there was a sharp economic and social crisis in 1788 and 1789, but the case for concentrating on the 'political' at the expense of the 'socio-economic' fails to convince. The seeds of Lefebvre's 'autonomous peasant revolution' had been sown in the 1770s and 1780s, and it is worth remembering that in several parts of the kingdom country dwellers were in an insurrectionary mood several months *before* the meeting of the Estates General.

VI

The commons and collective rights. Georges Lefebvre always believed that the great mass of the French peasantry were motivated by collectivist instincts. Since the majority of country dwellers possessed little freehold property, they set much store by use-rights on the land of others. He implies that even when the prospect of small plots of land materialized in 1793, the poorer peasantry hesitated. They ended up clinging to their use- and access-rights and thereby forced liberal revolutionaries into a posture of compromise.

This vision of the rationally minded plotfarmer opting to retain grazing rights rather than to risk a general partition of common lands has much to recommend it. A recent study of peasant farming in Uganda demonstrated that the wherewithal to keep a cow could virtually double a poor family's standard of living; on the other hand, a plot could produce food. But freehold plots attracted taxes and might swiftly become economic liabilities in the absence of a regular supply of animal manure. Not surprisingly, there has been a great deal of debate over Lefebvre's attribution of anti-capitalist 'instincts' to the poor peasantry. Cobban, as usual, was the first in the field, and he challenged Lefebvre's conclusions on the grounds of evidence: the depiction of a rural community consisting of wealthy peasants who were anxious to abolish free grazing and to partition the commons and of poor peasants who wished to preserve both the commons and collective rights did not add up. Citing in his support petitions and addresses to the Revolutionary Assemblies, Cobban maintained that 'it was patently the poorer inhabitants of the country who were in favour of the *partage* of the commons and the better-off ones who were against it.'[20] Lefebvre's suspect concept of the 'rural bourgeoisie' is the villain of the piece, it seems. According to Cobban's reformulation, the 'rural bourgeoisie' behaved in an unbourgeois manner and conspired to impede the consolidation of freehold property.

I suspect that the truth of the matter will not be found in schematic statements. Nor will it be found in any single source of documents, such as the petitions filed away by the Committee of Agriculture. The peasantry spoke with many voices on the subject of the commons and collective rights, and it is futile to search for positions applicable at all times and in all places. So much depended upon the agricultural balance in a given locality, the incidence of stock raising, market opportunities, the extent and quality of common land, and so on. Free grazing on village stubble could serve the interests of the poor, but it could serve the interests of the prosperous elite and those of nonresident landowners too. Likewise the commons: historians have supposed that the issue was simply whether or not to divide. But, in reality, the issue was less the question of *partage* than that of the *mode de partage*. During the course of the Revolution partition in proportion to landholding, partition in inverse proportion to landholding, partition by household, and partition by head were all mooted at various times. Peasant reactions varied accordingly: wealthy *laboureurs* saw much to be gained from a censitary partition, much less from a 'division par tête d'habitant.'[21] As for the poor, they remained ambivalent about the exercise. A *partage* that was financially onerous, sacrificed the village pasture, and produced a random scatter of exiguous strips was not necessarily a blessing.

VII

Agrarian capitalism. Alfred Cobban's reluctance to adhere to Lefebvre's socioeconomic analysis of the peasantry opens up some interesting theoretical perspectives. If, in reality, the defence of common rights was waged by the better-off farmers, whereas the poor peasantry evinced a firm attachment to individualism and egalitarianism, this surely implies some revision of Lefebvre's characterization of the peasant revolution as anti-capitalist. Perhaps the 'instincts' of the poor peasantry were not as obdurately collectivist as we have been led to believe. Such thoughts clearly surfaced in the mind of Anatoli Ado,[22] who in 1971 published the first full-length study of the peasantry during the Revolution to have appeared since Lefebvre's death. Ado's book is a major contribution to the debate on the peasantry, and its repercussions are likely to endure for some time to come. Published originally in Russian, it still has not been translated into English, nor, as far as I know, into French. As a result, Ado's message has taken some time to permeate. On the other hand, the lack of a translation may have conferred upon the book a prestige that is unwarranted. Scholars are fairly familiar with Ado's conclusions, but are unable (unless they read Russian) to check his arguments.

What are these conclusions? Broadly speaking, Ado resolved the dilemma into which Lefebvre plunged the quasi-Jacobin and quasi-Marxist orthodox interpretation of 1789. He suggested that bourgeois and peasant revolutions did, after all, proceed hand-in-hand, and he insisted that the anticapitalist instincts of the peasant masses which Lefebvre had chronicled were more apparant than real. Instead, he substituted a vision of peasant-led agrarian capitalism (sometimes referred to by the phrase *la voie paysanne*, as opposed to *la voie anglaise* or the route toward capitalism pioneered by improving landlords). As a result, Lefebvre's peasant revolution loses much of its specificity; it is no longer out of step and it is no longer at logger-heads with the guiding spirit of the (bourgeois) Revolution. A more ideologically coherent and, in a sense, pre-Lefebvrian interpretation of events is offered instead.

Ado's revisionism carries implications for nineteenth- and twentieth-century history, too. If capitalism failed to materialize in the post-Revolutionary countryside, it was not for want of zeal among the peasantry, so we are told, but because successive Revolutionary legislatures did little to help the peasantry break up the large landed estates. Ultimately, therefore, it was the survival of the world of *rente* with its obstinately feudal mentality, rather than the persistence of the rural community and the supposedly regressive instincts of the peasant masses, that held back the agrarian development of modern France.

Quickly, and perhaps with a sense of relief, French historians swung behind the new interpretation in the 1970s. Albert Soboul, for instance, largely abandoned his mentor's perspective on the peasant revolution, although not without expressing some misgivings. Ado's thesis, he remarked in a generally favourable review, tended to oscillate between 'erudite analysis and cavalier overview.'[23] Amid a general revival of interest in peasant studies, he set a number of postgraduate students to work on the points at issue between Lefebvre and Ado. Meanwhile, in 1977, Florence Gauthier published a book which applied the new theoretical perspective to the agrarian history of Picardy.[24]

Such studies are welcome, for it is only by dint of laborious burrowing in local archives that the relevant merits of the two positions can be tested. No doubt, research currently in progress will resolve the issue, but my own preliminary investigations have failed to find much of a basis for *la voie paysanne* thesis. Lefebvre does seem to have minimized the extent to which the poor peasantry were prepared to pursue the dream of freehold property. And a recent historian has taken him to task for underestimating the intensity of popular pressure for land reform on the cereal plains around Paris.[25] That said, however, Anatoli Ado's pioneer class of 'petty peasant producers' endowed with land as a result of the Revolution is exceedingly difficult to identify. Arguably, most poor peasants did *not* press for the division of the commons; and whether they did or did not, most commons survived unscathed in any case. The point holds for *émigré* estates, too. Laws requiring the subdivision of biens nationaux evoked a patchy response at best. No doubt, the Revolution did liberate the productive energies of a fraction of the poor peasantry in some localities, but there exists little evidence to suggest that this energy helped nurture the spirit of capitalism in the countryside. Petty proprietors did not abandon their attachment to collective rights just because they had clambered up one rung of the property-owning ladder. For all the self-deceiving talk in the Convention about creating a property-owning democracy, the *partage* laws of 1793 utterly failed to reshape the social pyramid in the countryside. For every peasant proletarian who kept his slice of common land and made it fruitful, a dozen more gave up in disgust or pledged their plots in settlement of debts.

VIII

Jacobinism and the peasantry. Ado also launched an assault on Lefebvre's characterization of Montagnard agrarian policy. Unlike Mathiez, Lefebvre doubted whether Robespierre and his associates possessed an original and audacious programme for social reform. More specifically, he rejected out of hand the suggestion that the Convention appealed for peasant support with coherent proposals to redress agrarian grievances. The Montagnards were all bourgeois individualists who distrusted radical schemes for land redistribution and who positively repudiated communism. They conceptualized peasants as 'citizens of the countryside,' thereby closing their minds to the possibility that there might have existed specifically agrarian discontents. Ado, by contrast, sees more purpose – even premeditation –

behind the Convention's dealings with the peasantry. The natural constituency of Jacobinism in the countryside consisted of poor peasant farmers,
agricultural labourers, and artisans, or so he claims, but Jacobin rhetoric
and Jacobin political practice never quite measured up. Initially, in the early
summer of 1793, the Mountain pandered to the '40 sous' section of the rural
community with laws permitting the partition of the commons and a free
distribution of land drawn from *émigré* estates. Thereafter, considerations
of national efficiency and productivity became paramount, and the
committees increasingly geared their policies to the interests of the
property-owning peasantry.

   This is a more meaningful scenario than that envisaged by Georges
Lefebvre, but the net result is pretty much the same: the Montagnards
found themselves caught on the horns of a dilemma. They sought to
reassure proprietors worried at the prospect of the *loi agraire* while
simultaneously endeavouring to placate peasant proletarians who were
demanding the *loi agraire*. Whether the objects of Jacobin social policy
can be separated out as neatly as Ado suggests is a matter for discussion
among historians. My impression is that Jacobin relish for socially levelling legislation (decrees of 3 June and 10 June 1793, 13 September 1793,
and that of 22 October 1793 tackling some of the grievances of share-
croppers) actually increased as the Year Two wore on. Nevertheless, Ado
has performed a service in drawing attention to the tensions within the
peasantry. More important, he has triggered a further round of research
into the nature and extent of agrarian radicalism – a subject which
Georges Lefebvre never fully probed. My own researches on the Seine-et-
Oise (not yet published), those of Guy Ikni[26] on the Oise, and those of
Florence Gauthier[27] on the Somme add a new dimension to the standard
accounts of land hunger in the royal parks and on the cereal plains
surrounding the capital.

                                    IX

Counterrevolution and the peasantry. The 'discovery' of the counterrevolution is probably the greatest achievement of French Revolutionary
historiography since Lefebvre's death. From a position on the periphery
of academic history writing, it has steadily moved into the foreground,
even the centre ground; so much, indeed, that the most recent text book
history of the Revolution to be written in English bears the title *France
1789–1815: Revolution and Counterrevolution*. In it Donald Sutherland
argues that 'the history of the entire period can be understood as the
struggle against a counterrevolution that was not so much aristocratic as
massive, extensive, durable and popular.'[28] 'Massive, extensive, durable
and popular' – these words would have shocked Georges Lefebvre and

most of the historians of his generation, who had been raised in the Jacobin historiographical tradition according to which a 'popular counterrevolution' was a contradiction in terms. Perusal of Lefebvre's thousand-page study of the peasantry in the Nord department will uncover just thirty-six pages devoted to the subject of the counterrevolution. And this, despite the fact that the Nord experienced invasion by the Austrians and an official counterrevolution in 1793–94. As for his survey article entitled 'La Révolution française et les paysans' it makes no mention of counterrevolution at all.

In retrospect, the absence of the counterrevolution from Lefebvre's *œuvre* does appear a glaring omission. It seems to me undeniable that there was a peasant dimension to the counterrevolution. The hostilities in the West, and more particularly in the Vendée, involved large numbers of peasants and rural artisans in armed defiance of the Republic, as Claude Petitfrère has demonstrated.[29] In the South, peasant commitment to the bloody politics of counterrevolution was more measured, but unmistakable nonetheless. Thanks to the work of such historians as Paul Bois,[30] Charles Tilly,[31] Tim Le Goff,[32] Donald Sutherland,[33] and Roger Dupuy[34] on the West, and Richard Cobb,[35] Gwynne Lewis,[36] and Colin Lucas[37] on the South, it is no longer possible to dismiss the counterrevolution as a historiographical footnote. But the counterrevolution has proved a happy hunting ground for those interested in peasant studies in another sense, too. It has provided a laboratory in which to test the dynamics of peasant politicization. Charles Tilly's recourse to modernization theory in a bid to uncover the well-springs of the Vendée revolt is the best-known example, but more recently two Canadian historians have used their extensive knowledge of revolution and counterrevolution in Brittany to launch a major reinterpretation of the political history of the 1790s.

According to Tim Le Goff and Donald Sutherland,[38] the real reason why some parts of France rallied to the Republic while others succumbed to the counterrevolution has little to do with political leadership, patchy modernization, religion, or any other standard variable. Instead, it has a lot to do with property structures and modes of tenure. Support for the Revolution, they argue, can be correlated with the incidence and density of peasant proprietors within the general mass of country dwellers, whereas sympathy for the counterrevolution flourished most vigorously in regions dominated by tenant farming and sharecropping. The rationale that crystallized opinion at the grass roots was, they believe, the uneven distribution of the material benefits arising out of the reforms of 1789–93. This sensitivity to the differential impact of the Revolution is very impressive: Le Goff and Sutherland restore to prominence issues such as tax reform and the shabby dealings over the tithe which have been neglected by historians for decades. Whether their thesis offers a global explanation of the political geography of France in the 1790s seems more doubtful. I think that it does not, mainly because the thesis appears flawed in its very conception (can rural society be divided into teams of proprietors and teams of tenants/sharecroppers?). It is worth noting that Roger Dupuy expresses similar reservations in his recently submitted thesis on the Breton *chouannerie*.[39] He also doubts whether cost/benefit analysis of the Revolution would necessarily work out in favour of the proprietors. Many peasant landowners were grindingly poor, whereas a proportion of the tenantry were affluent and well able to turn the Revolution to good account. Tenurial distinctions disguised socioeconomic distinctions, he suggests, and it is these latter that we should concentrate upon if we want to understand how rural communities polarized.

X

State-making and the peasantry. Alexis de Tocqueville once observed that the Revolution began with Calonne's administrative reforms of 1787, yet few historians of the peasantry have thought it necessary to familiarize themselves with the administrative history of the ancien-régime monarchy. Marc Bloch drew attention to the agrarian reforms sponsored by a coterie of royal bureaucrats in the 1760s and 1770s,[40] but his work was not followed up, nor was de Tocqueville's reminder of the destabilizing effect of the local government initiative of 1787. My own work on the southern Massif Central contains, so far as I am aware, the only recent assessment of the impact of Calonne's reforms on the rural community.[41]

This is now starting to change. Awareness is growing among rural historians that the crisis of the late ancien régime possessed a statemaking dimension that penetrated to the very roots of French society. That restless energy which absolute monarchy displayed during the gladiatorial confrontations of the Pre-Revolution was not the beginning but the culmination of a modernizing offensive that dated back to the 1760s. While presiding over a body politic formally divided into estates, the Bourbons were busily subverting the notion of a three-tiered society, and they were subverting it in a way that was bound to have repercussions upon the peasantry. The competition between monarchy and seigneurie to extract the lion's share of peasant surplus was, perhaps, the most dramatic symptom of state muscle-flexing in the countryside. As the Third Estate of the *bailliage* of Nemours put it in the *cahier* which they addressed to their monarch: 'If you are going to take what remains of our income, at least dispense us from paying what we owe to our seigneurs because we must have something left.'[42]

Such thoughts are brought into sharper focus on reading Hilton Root's recent book which probes what he terms the 'agrarian foundations of French absolutism.'[43] Root manages to make much more sense of pre-

Revolutionary tensions in the Burgundian countryside than had been done hitherto by pointing out that the intendants were active participants in disputes between villages and their seigneurs. Increasingly, the intendants and their subordinates posed as guardians of the community interest, intervening where necessary to protect the peasantry from seigneurial excesses. Although fiscal motives were no doubt paramount, royal officials were not above shaping government policy in accordance with their own estimate of how best to maintain the solvency and stability of the rural community. Thus, officialdom, at the provincial and the local level, conspired with the rural community to block the government's agrarian reforms.

The appeal of this mode of argument is the fact that it fits in with what seems to have been happening in the Auvergne, Upper Guyenne, and Lower Normandy. It also makes better sense of the aggressive litigiousness of Burgundian villages on the eve of the Revolution – a phenomenon which Robert Forster noted in the Duchy of Saulx-Tavanes but could not completely explain.[44] However, there is a danger in Root's methodological approach: it reduces each and every aspect of agrarian history to a matter of state *dirigisme*. The autonomy of the peasantry – as vindicated by Georges Lefebvre – is here reduced to nothing. The state shaped the peasantry, but not vice versa. This is an interesting, if arguable, proposition when applied to the ancien régime, but it is then grafted onto the agrarian history of the Revolution in a way that fails to convince. Clearly, Hilton Root has little sympathy for Lefebvre's complex vision of the peasantry, and his suggestion that 'peasant unrest might have had little influence on the course of agrarian reform during the Revolution' underlies this fact.[45]

In 1964 Alfred Cobban pleaded against what he perceived as 'a radical misinterpretation of French agrarian history at the time of the revolution.'[46] In 1987 an American essayist, Ferenc Fehér, expressed similar misgivings: 'The term the "peasants" revolution' warrants caution and has but limited relevance,' he concluded.[47] Does this mean that Georges Lefebvre's model of a distinctive peasant revolution, 'autonomous in terms of its origins, its proceedings, its crises, and its tendencies' has outlived its usefulness?[48] I think not. Much of the research that I have discussed in this article has served to validate Lefebvre's insight. Some has produced complementary or corroborative evidence, and some, it is true, has served to blur the specific character attributed to the peasant revolution. Yet few, if any, of the historians mentioned in these pages would argue that Lefebvre's interpretation is totally misconceived.

The debate continues over what significance we should attach to seigneurialism; yet evidence of its relevance to daily life continues to accumulate, whereas evidence in support of the contrary proposition does not. In consequence, it would seem perverse to deny that the Revolution sprang, in large measure, from a crisis of the rural economy. Whether the resulting peasant revolution should be defined as regressive and anti-capitalist in character is a question that offers scope for a more genuine debate. I would rally to Lefebvre's point of view on this issue, if only because his analysis of the property instincts of the poor peasantry seems most subtle and flexible. 'The rural masses,' he wrote to the conclusion to *Les Paysans du Nord*, 'were not hostile to the principle of individual property, but they limited it strictly and remained very attached to customary ideas.'[49] By contrast, the exponents of *la voie paysanne* thesis tend to aggregate all fractions of the peasantry under a progressive and petty-bourgeois banner. Lefebvre's formulation opens the door to a range of possible reactions, Ado's seems to close it.

Whether the Mountain's agrarian 'policy' amounted to very much leaves me undecided for the moment. Ado construes it in such a way as to extract maximum meaning, whereas Lefebvre seems to go to the other extreme. More research into the conditions governing policy formulation under the Revolutionary Government will be required before this issue can be satisfactorily resolved. The same cannot be said of the counterrevolution, which has absorbed the major share of research and public interest in recent years. Georges Lefebvre died a staunch Jacobin-socialist, little suspecting that the counterrevolution might have had a popular base. The findings of recent research in this area would have been an unwelcome revelation to him. And so too would the findings of an opinion survey commissioned by a weekly magazine on the eve of the bicentenary. It revealed that the majority of his compatriots held Marie-Antoinette in higher esteem than they did Danton, Robespierre, Saint-Just, or Marat. When asked the question: 'Do you sympathize more with the armies of the Revolution, or with the armies of the Vendeans or *chouans* who fought against the Revolution?,' some 38 percent of respondents declared in favour of the Revolution, but 30 percent – not many fewer – voted for the Vendeans.[50] Georges Lefebvre, interred at Père Lachaise, must have turned in his grave.

Notes

1 A. Cobban, *The Social Interpretation of the French Revolution* (Cambridge, 1964), p. 9.
2 A. Soboul, *Les Sans-culottes parisiens en l'an II* (Paris, 1958).
3 G. Rudé, *The Crowd in the French Revolution* (Oxford, 1959).
4 R. C. Cobb, *Les Armées révolutionnaires: Instrument de la Terreur dans les départements, avril 1793 – floréal an II* (2 vols., Paris, 1961–63).
5 A. Davies, 'The New Agriculture in Lower Normandy, 1750–1789,' *Transac-*

tions of the Royal Historical Society, 8 (1958), pp. 129–46; 'The Origins of the French Peasant Revolution of 1789,' *History,* 49 (1964), pp. 24–41.

6 G. Lefebvre, '*La Révolution française et les paysans,*' reprinted in *Etudes sur la Révolution française* (Paris, 1954), p. 249.

7 Lefebvre, 'La Révolution française et les paysans,' p. 257.

8 A. Soboul, 'Classes et luttes de classes sous la Révolution,' *La Pensée,* 53 (1954), reprinted in A. Soboul, *Comprendre la Révolution: Problèmes politiques de la Révolution française, 1789–1797* (Paris, 1981), p. 47.

9 M. Bouloiseau, 'Présence de Georges Lefebvre,' *Annales historiques de la Révolution française,* 41 (1969), pp. 557.

10 Reprinted in G. Lefebvre, *Etudes sur la Révolution française,* pp. 246–68.

11 H. Doniol, *La Révolution française et la féodalité (Paris, 1874).*

12 G. Lefebvre, *Etudes sur la Révolution française,* p. 256.

13 *See Commission de recherche et de publication des documents relatifs à la vie économique de la Révolution. Assemblée générale de la commission centrale et des comités départementaux, 1939. Vol. 1, La Bourgeoisie française, de la fin de l'ancien régime à la Révolution; l'Exploitation seigneuriale au XVIIIe siècle d'après les terriers; la Condition des ouvriers* (Besançon, 1942), p. 17.

14 G. Lefebvre, *Etudes sur la Révolution française,* p. 256.

15 G. V. Taylor, 'Revolutionary and Nonrevolutionary Content in the Cahiers of 1789: An Interim Report,' *French Historical Studies,* 7 (1972), pp. 479–502.

16 C. E. Labrousse, *Esquisse du mouvement des prix et des revenus en France au XVIIIe siècle,* 2 vols. (Paris, 1933). *See also* Labrousse, *La Crise de l'économie française à la fin de l'Ancien Régime et au début de la Révolution* (Paris, 1944).

17 G. V. Taylor, 'Noncapitalist Wealth and the Origins of the French Revolution,' *American Historical Review,* 72 (1967), p. 491.

18 W. Doyle, *Origins of the French Revolution* (Oxford, 1980; 2nd ed. 1988), p. 158.

19 *See* P. M. Jones, *The Peasantry in the French Revolution* (Cambridge, 1988), pp. 30–59.

20 A. Cobban, *The Social Interpretation of the French Revolution,* p. 114.

21 Decree of 10 June 1793, section II, article 1.

22 A. Ado, *The Peasant Movement in France during the Great Bourgeois Revolution of the End of the Eighteenth Century* (Moscow, 1971; 2nd edition 1987). In Russian.

23 A Soboul, 'Sur le mouvement paysan dans la Révolution française,' *La Pensée,* 168 (1973), p. 105.

24 F. Gauthier, *La Voie paysanne dans la Révolution française: L'Exemple de la Picardie* (Paris, 1977).

25 *See* G.-R. Ikni, 'La Critique paysanne radicale et le libéralisme économique pendant la Révolution française,' unpublished paper read at *La Révolution française et le monde rural,* Colloquium, Paris, October 1987. *See also* F. Gauthier and G.-R. Ikni, 'Le Mouvement paysan en Picardie: Meneurs, pratiques, maturation et signification historique d'un programme (1775–1794),' in E. P. Thompson et al., *La Guerre du blé au XVIIIe siècle. La Critique populaire contre le libéralisme économique au XVIIIe siècle. Etudes rassemblées et présentées par Florence Gauthier et Guy-Robert Ikni* (Paris, 1988), pp. 187–203.

26 G.-R. Ikni, 'Recherches sur la propriété foncière: Problèmes théoriques et de méthode,' *Annales historiques de la Révolution française,* 52 (1980), pp. 390–424; 'Documents sur la loi agraire dans l'Oise pendant la Révolution française,' *Annales historiques compiégnoises,* 19 (1982), pp. 18–26.

27 F. Gauthier, 'Formes d'évolution du système agraire communautaire en Picardie (fin XVIIIe – debut XIXe siècle),' *Annales historiques de la Révolution française*, 52 (1980), pp. 181–204.

28 D. M. G. Sutherland, *France 1789–1815: Revolution and Counterrevolution* (London, 1985).

29 C. Petitfrère, 'Les Grandes Composantes sociales des armées Vendéennes d'Anjou,' *Annales historiques de la Révolution française*, 45 (1973), pp. 1–20.

30 P. Bois, *Paysans de l'Ouest: Des structures économiques et sociales aux options politiques depuis l'époque révolutionnaire dans la Sarthe* (Le Mans, 1960).

31 C. Tilly, *The Vendée* (London, 1964).

32 T. J. A. Le Goff, *Vannes and its Region: A Study of Town and Country in Eighteenth-Century France* (Oxford, 1981).

33 D. M. G. Sutherland, *The Chouans: The Social Origins of Popular Counter-Revolution in Upper Brittany, 1770–1796* (Oxford, 1982).

34 R. Dupuy, 'Aux Origines de la chouannerie en Bretagne, 1788–1794: Société rurale et contre-révolution' (University of Rennes, Thèse pour le doctorat d'état, 2 vols., 1986).

35 R. C. Cobb, *The Police and the People: French Popular Protest, 1789–1820* (Oxford, 1970); *Reactions to the French Revolution* (Oxford, 1972).

36 G. Lewis, *The Second Vendée: The Continuity of Counter-Revolution in the Department of the Gard, 1789–1815* (Oxford, 1978).

37 C. Lucas, 'The Problem of the Midi in the French Revolution,' *Transactions of the Royal Historical Society*, 28 (1978), pp. 1–25; 'Résistances populaires à la Révolution dans le sud-est,' in J. Nicolas, ed. *Mouvements populaires et conscience sociale. Colloque de l'Université de Paris VII, Paris, 24–26 mai 1984*, (Paris, 1985), pp. 473–85.

38 T. J. A. Le Goff and D. M. G. Sutherland, 'The Social Origins of Counter-Revolution in Western France,' *Past and Present*, 99 (1983), pp. 65–87; 'Religion and Rural Revolt in the French Revolution: An Overview,' in J. M. Bak and G. Benecke, ed. *Religion and Rural Revolt: Papers presented to the Fourth Interdisciplinary Workshop on Peasant Studies, University of British Columbia, 1982*, (Manchester, 1984), pp. 123–45.

39 R. Dupuy, 'Aux Origines de la chouannerie en Bretagne,' 2, pp. 775–95.

40 M. Bloch, 'La Lutte pour l'individualisme agraire dans la France du XVIIIe siècle: L'oeuvre des pouvoirs d'ancien régime,' *Annales d'histoire économique et sociale* 2 (1930), pp. 329–81, reprinted in M. Bloch, *Mélanges historiques*, 2 vols. (SEVPEN, 1963), 2, pp. 593–637.

41 P. M. Jones, *Politics and Rural Society in the Southern Massif Central, c. 1750–1880* (Cambridge, 1985), pp. 178–86.

42 *Archives parlementaires de 1787 à 1860. Recueil complet des débats législatifs et politiques des chambres françaises (première série, 1787–99)*, 92 vols. (Paris, 1862–1980), 4, pp. 196.

43 Hilton, L. Root, *Peasants and King in Burgundy: Agrarian Foundations of French Absolutism* (Berkeley, 1987).

44 R. Forster, *The House of Saulx-Tavanes: Versailles and Burgundy, 1700–1830* (Baltimore, 1871).

45 Hilton Root, *Peasants and King in Burgundy*, 19. See also Root, 'The Case against Georges Lefebvre's Peasant Revolution', *History Workshop*, 28 (1989), pp. 88–102.

46 A. Cobban, *The Social Interpretation of the French Revolution*, p. 146.

47 F. Fehér, *The Frozen Revolution: An Essay on Jacobinism* (Cambridge and Paris, 1987), p. 14.

48 G. Lefebvre, 'La Révolution française et les paysans,' p. 249.
49 G. Lefebvre, *Les Paysans du Nord pendant la Révolution française* (Bari, 1959; first published in Paris, 1924), p. 908.
50. Le Figaro Magazine, 23 January 1988.

4

Bourgeois revolution revivified: 1789 and social change

COLIN JONES

The decision on July 16, 1789 to demolish the Bastille presented a wonderful opportunity to Pierre-François Palloy. The 34-year-old building contractor, who – so he said – had helped to storm the Bastille on 14 July, took on the job of demolition. The grim medieval fortress was soon a building site, offering much-needed employment to about 1000 hungry Parisian labourers and providing a diverting and edifying spectacle for the leisured élite. The famous Latude, who had made his name by publishing an account of his imprisonment in the state fortress, was on hand to act as tourist guide to the site. Latude's publishers rushed out extra editions of his work, and Bastille commemorative volumes were soon among the bestsellers. A further wave of popular interest accompanied the discovery by Palloy's workmen in early 1790 of subterranean cells filled with chains and skeletons. This was not the Man in the Iron Mask, but it was something.

Palloy, however, was attracting some unwanted attention. When he presented accounts to the National Assembly in October 1790, certain right-wing deputies suggested that he had made a huge profit from the whole enterprise. Bertrand Barère, the future colleague of Robespierre in the great Committee of Public Safety, sprang to Palloy's defence. 'Ce n'est pas un marché qu'on a fait . . . C'est une destruction politique; c'est un acte vraiment révolutionnaire . . . Ainsi la démolition de la Bastille tourne au profit de la Nation et à l'honneur de la liberté.'[1] Fine words and flattery: but Palloy's books seem not to have balanced. Although he managed to avoid investigation, he seems to have made a considerable profit from merely selling off the stones of the Bastille; many went, for example, into the construction of the Pont de la Concorde. He went further than this, moreover, setting up a manufactory in his home in which huge numbers of the stones were carved into little replicas of the Bastille.

Reprinted in full, except for notes, from: C. Lucas, ed. *Rewriting the French Revolution. The Andrew Browning Lectures 1989* (Oxford, Clarendon Press, 1991), pp. 69–118.

Chains and irons found on the site were created into similar memorabilia:
medals, dice-boxes, paperweights, snuff-boxes, inkpots, and the like.
Palloy enrolled a host of fellow *vainqueurs de la Bastille* to act as his
travelling salesmen – he called them his *apôtres de la liberté* – taking
stocks around the departments to meet what was clearly a great demand.
Three parcels of Bastille memorabilia were presented gratis to each of
France's eighty-three departments – though the latter did pay the transport costs, which allowed a profit to be made, and doubtless further
stimulated local demand.

As he protests at his stone Bastille models being undercut by cheap
plaster imitations, we should perhaps tiptoe quietly away from this interesting entrepreneurial figure who clearly awaits his Samuel Smiles – or
better still, his Richard Cobb. From the vantage-point of the Bicentenary in
1989, with its chocolate guillotines and Bastille boxer shorts, his story
nevertheless neatly demonstrates that the commercialization of the French
Revolution is as old as the Revolution itself. The character sketch does,
moreover, illustrate some of the themes I wish to develop here: namely, the
Revolution and economic opportunities; bourgeois entrepreneuralism;
consumerism and fashion; civic sensibilities; the interlocking of business
and rhetoric.

To bring a bourgeois to the centre of the stage may, however, appear
gloriously *dépassé*. After all, 1989 marked not just the bicentenary of
the Revolution, but also the twenty-fifth anniversary of the publication,
in 1964, of Alfred Cobban's *Social Interpretation of the French Revolution*,
the classic text of the Revolutionist school which has come to dominate
French Revolutionary historiography. Over the last quarter of a century,
the Revisionist current has virtually swept from the board what is now
identified as the Orthodox Marxist view. The idea, almost axiomatic to
the historians whom Cobban attacked – Mathiez, Lefebvre, Soboul – that
the Revolution marked a key episode in the passage from feudalism to
capitalism is now either widely discounted or else viewed as a *question mal
posée*. And the idea – regarded as a truism before the 1960s – that the
Revolution was a bourgeois revolution is now held up to ridicule. Indeed,
George V. Taylor, one of the Grand Old Men of Revisionism, recently
warned off historians from using the term 'bourgeois' which is, he contends, 'freighted with too many ambiguities to serve in research as a
general analytical tool or operational category'.[2]

In the place of the old Marxist orthodoxy – the Revisionists always talk
of the Marxist interpretation in the singular, as if Marxists never disagreed, or else robotically took their cue from the Politburo – a New
Revisionist Orthodoxy has gradually sprung up, which by now has permeated into general interpretations and views, in much of French publishing as well as in English and American scholarship. The New Orthodoxy

will have little truck with social interpretations in general, and the bourgeois revolution in particular. Far from being the heroic, world-historical, almost transcendental force which Karl Marx had seen him as, the bourgeois now cuts a shabby figure. Revisionist historians viewed him as pathetically insecure, anaemic, transitional – zombie-esque, in the view of Simon Schama.

The Old Regime bourgeoisie, so the New Orthodoxy goes, burnt its candle at both ends. At the top, merchants and manufacturers who built up sufficient wealth were swift to disinvest from productive activities and sink their capital in land, seigneuries, and venal office. Their propensity to ape their social betters was exemplified by their wish to achieve noble status, and indeed many former traders and manufacturers referred to themselves as *bourgeois vivant noblement*. The preference for status over profit which this behaviour is alleged to exemplify can be dated back centuries, as Colin Lucas and William Doyle have reminded us, and may thus be dubbed, as George Taylor would have it, atavistic. At its bottom end, the Revisionists tell us, the bourgeoisie was equally undynamic. Peasants who might have enriched themselves by production for the market preferred risk-avoidance and subsistence strategies, and coralled themselves away from their bourgeois betters in the ghetto of a 'popular culture' they shared with guild-dominated, and equally 'traditionalist' urban workers.

This was a bourgeoisie more deeply riven by internal schisms than by class antagonisms – and indeed the Revisionists reserve some of their sharpest barbs for those starry-eyed 'Marxist' idealists who retain some attachment to the concept of class struggle. Indeed, the New Orthodoxy has it that there was less unity shown by the bourgeoisie as a class than, for example, by the inter-class élite of upper bourgeois and nobles. One must admire the Revisionists' sleight of hand, for the Old Regime nobility, normally portrayed (they tell us) as monolithically parasitic and feudal in its outlook, are nowadays viewed as hyper-dynamic and entrepreneurial. The nobility dominated the key sectors of the economy, Guy Chaussinand-Nogaret assures us, exercised overwhelming cultural hegemony, and generously held out a co-operative hand to those awestricken bourgeois wishing to enter France's social élite. Once viewed as the agents of a 'feudal reaction' which shut out talented commoners, the nobility is now seen as the leading partner in an enlightened élite, entry into which through venal office was still surprisingly easy. The term 'open élite' is now being used less in regard to eighteenth-century England, following the broadsides of Lawrence and Jeanne Stone, than to Old Regime France. The Revolution's persecution of this enlightened noble-dominated group can only, in its injustice, its economic irrationality, and its lack of humanity, be compared to anti-Semitism (the comparison is Chaussinand-Nogaret's). Yet the nobility would have the last laugh, for once the Revolution was over, they formed the backbone of the class of landowning and professional notables which dominated nineteenth-century France.

The idea that France's late eighteenth- and nineteenth-century history essentially concerns the formation of an élite of notables (the latter, incidentally, every bit as much a portmanteau term as that of 'bourgeois', against whose vagueness Cobban inveighed), with the Revolution as an unwelcome intrusion or even an irrelevant footnote, has become a keystone of the New Revisionist Orthodoxy. It fits in very snugly with the systematic disparagement of the economic significance of the Revolution. Far from marking the passage from feudalism to capitalism, the Revolution could not even transform the economic structures and shortcomings of the economy: agrarian productivity only registered progress, Michel Morineau tells us, after 1840, and industrial capitalism had generally to await the railway age. Late eighteenth-century France was in any case only just emerging from *l'histoire immobile*, Emmanuel Le Roy Ladurie's description of a kind of neo-Malthusian prison-camp in which French society had been interned since the fourteenth century. The Revolution thus becomes little more than a minor fold in the flowing fabric of that *longue durée* so beloved of the *Annales* school.

This tendency within the Revisionist camp to minimize the social changes associated with the Revolution has led to most recent historiographical running being made by historians of politics and culture. Lynn Hunt has chided social historians for concentrating their interest on mere 'origins and outcomes',[3] and for failing to recognize that the revolutionary character of the 1790s resides in the fabrication of a new political culture. The outstanding work of Keith Baker, and the 1987 Chicago conference proceedings, *The Political Culture of the Old Régime*, which have been published under his direction, buttresses that view.[4] In the Brave New Revisionist World, discourse reigns supreme and social factors bulk exceeding small. It often seems, for example, as if the new political culture had no long-term social roots, but emerged in a process of inspired and semi-spontaneous politico-cultural *bricolage* in 1788–9. François Furet, for example, the veritable pope of contemporary Revisionism, sees 1789 as ushering in a political logic and a proto-totalitarian discourse which lead in unilinear fashion to the Terror. The idea that the Revolution's shift to the left in the early 1790s might have something to do with the counter-revolution is roundly dismissed: the revolutionaries are diagnosed as suffering from a plot psychosis predating any real threat to their work. The Revolution was on the track to Terror from the summer of 1789, socio-political circumstances notwithstanding.

François Furet has been a devastating critic of the unreflective sociologism of the old Marxist approach as exemplified in some of the writings of Albert Soboul. The pendulum has now swung to the other extreme, however, and many Revisionists seem to wish to reduce the history of the

Revolution to political history with society left out. A typical recent example of the way in which discourse analysis and high politics override the social angle is the treatment which a number of recent authors have given to the famous Night of August 4, 1789, when the National Assembly issued a decree formally abolishing feudalism. Overlooking or discounting evidence about the blatant fixing of this session, ignoring the ridiculously high rates of compensation for losses of feudal rights the deputies awarded, turning a blind eye to stories of violent peasant revolution which, magnified by rumour, were pouring into Paris and Versailles at the time, William Doyle, Norman Hampson, Michael Fitzsimmons, and Simon Schama all view the explanation of the behaviour of the deputies as lying in the altruism of the old 'enlightened' élite. One of the key moments in the social transformation of France, the zenith of peasant influence on the course of events, thus merely becomes a vacuous chapter in group psychology, with the Assembly acting as if hermetically sealed from out-side social influences. What Simon Schama characterizes as a 'patriotic rhapsody' becomes for Michael Fitzsimmons a kind of beautific vision, a Close Encounter of the 4 August Kind, in which the deputies self-denyingly pledged themselves to 'the sublimity of the Nation'. The Revolution as a whole thus becomes 'the reaction of groups and individuals to the imposi-tion by the National Assembly of its new vision of France',[5] an approach congruent with George Taylor's famous characterization of the Revolution as a 'political revolution with social consequences rather than a social revolution with political consequences'.[6]

This denigration of the popular and collectivist aspects of the Revolu-tion and the downplaying of social origins to the political crisis of 1789 keys in with some other recent accounts, moreover, which view French society as largely the opponent or the victim of the new political culture. From Donald Sutherland's account, for example, one gains the impression that nine-tenths of French society in the 1790s was objectively counter-revolutionary. (This, incidentally, is a view which calls into question François Furet's diagnosis of plot psychosis.) If there was a popular revolution at all, Douglas Johnson tells us, it was the Counter-Revolu-tion. From evacuating the Revolution of all positive social content to viewing the repression of counter-revolution as 'genocide' by a 'totalitar-ian' power is only a short step – and one which certain historians have not been afraid to take.

Perhaps we are wrong to judge the views of the New Revisionist Orthodoxy by the uses to which they are being put by the political Right; after all, the Old Marxist Orthodoxy was shamelessly exploited by the Left. What is, however, worrying for a social historian is the extent to which social change is disparaged in or omitted from the New Revisio-nist Orthodoxy. It is not my intention to pose as King Canute, vainly bidding the Revisionist wave to recede. On the contrary, I would contend that a great deal of Revisionist research being done in fact subverts the main, rather brittle assumptions around which the New Revisionist Orthodoxy has hardened. In this essay, I would like to mine that seam in a way which suggests that we need to rethink our attitudes towards some of the key problems associated with the relationship of the Revolution to social change. While many may prefer cosily to relax in the platitudes of the New Revisionist Orthodoxy, we may in fact be moving towards a situation in which new research allows us to relate afresh to some of the problems of causation which concerned Marxist French Revolutionary historiography. This may come as a shock to many Revisionists, who tend to relate to that historiographical tradition by presenting a knockabout pastiche of the views of the alleged Old Marxist Orthodoxy, a kind of pantomime in which a succession of Revisionist Prince Charmings rescue Marianne from the clutches of a wicked, mean-spirited old Stalinist Baron – a part reserved in most scripts for the late Albert Soboul. Using the research of both Revisionist and Marxist scholars, I am going to be foolhardy enough to suggest that the Revolution did have long-term social origins. I will go on to suggest that these related directly to the development of capitalism and indeed that the much-disparaged term 'bourgeois revolution' retains much of its force and utility.

One of the cardinal tenets of the New Revisionist Orthodoxy is that eighteenth-century France was – with the possible exception of the enlightened élite – 'traditionalist', preferring a flight from capitalism rather than its warm embrace. Much of the force of this view has in the past resided in unfavourable comparisons made with the allegedly more mature capitalist economy of Great Britain, undergoing in the period from 1780 the classic Rostovian 'take-off' into self-sustained economic growth. Against this, the argument runs, the French economy can only seem 'backward' or 'retarded'.

One has only to scratch the surface of this approach today to realize that it lies in tatters. The work of François Crouzet, Nicholas Crafts, Patrick O'Brien and others have pointed up the buoyancy of French economic performance over the eighteenth century, and shown that in many respects it even may have outdistanced Great Britain. Annual averages of both agricultural and industrial growth were higher in France than in Great Britain. If we are to believe Patrick O'Brien and Caglar Keyder, a broad comparability between the British and the French economies continued into the early twentieth century. France's per capita physical product tripled between the early nineteenth and early twentieth centuries, and the authors see this as part of a development which stretches back into the eighteenth century. Perhaps Britain's priority in emergence as First Industrial Nation owed less to her economic performance over the eighteenth century than to factors which predated 1700 –

the stability of Britain's financial institutions grounded in the establishment of the Bank of England in 1694, and Britain's early switch to mineral fuel, which stimulated the emergence of a coal-fuel technology which would contribute importantly to the industrialization process. But rather than talk in terms of retardation or backwardness, perhaps we should just accept that there is more than one way towards industrialization, and that the British route, though first – or perhaps because it was first – was not necessarily the most appropriate for others. France did not have the sudden spurt in industrial performance which England enjoyed, but her more balanced and drawn-out pathway to industrialization was no less effective in the longer term, and may indeed be particularly deserving of attention in that it avoided many of the direst social costs which accompanied Britain's Industrial Revolution.

Clearly, there are dangers in comparing the economic performance of England and France on the basis of hypothesized aggregate data, not least because the unit of economic growth in the eighteenth century was the region rather than the nation-state. Yet historians such as Herbert Lüthy miss the point when they draw attention to the fact that France's economic performance in the eighteenth century hid a disparity between more progressive port cities and their hinterlands on one hand, and the more backward, traditionalist economies of the remainder of France. For even Britain had its Dorsets and its Rutlands – to say nothing of its Sligos, Denbighshires, and Ross and Cromartys – as well as its Lancashires and Birminghams. Moreover, many regional and urban historians of France now emphasize the extent of rural penetration achieved by dynamic urban centres. The eighteenth century saw an increase in intensity of urban domination over surrounding provisioning areas.

If we start to accept that France's industrialization process was not inferior to Britain's, but merely different, then we can acknowledge that much of the French economic performance was a valid response to its situation in terms of resource-levels, geographical configuration, markets, and so on. Although France had achieved by 1789, in global terms, important levels of industrialization and urbanization, it is unhelpful merely to mark these down as a second-best to those of a Britain, whose pattern of industrialization was anyway highly specific. Thus, for example, it is not necessarily a major drawback that France's manufacturing sector was to a considerable degree situated in the countryside and took the form of rural industry rather than factory concentration. Despite the late and startlingly dynamic appearance of cotton production in France in the late eighteenth century, France's industries tended to be traditional, artisanal, and rural-based. Luxury and semi-luxury goods, consumption and production of which were stimulated by the Bourbon court, played a much more important role too in the industrial sector than in Hanoverian England. More concentrated forms of manufacturing – cotton production, coal, minerals – made up a minority of the total output, and it is significant that relatively few of those nobles involved in industry – a small minority, it should be noted, of the total noble order – were engaged in the traditional sector which accounted for the bulk of French manufacturing production. The prevalence of rural industry, moreover, helps account for the high rural population density levels achieved in many regions. Between 80 and 85 per cent of France's population was still based in the countryside in 1789. Far from retarding the economy, it may be that the peasant orientation of the rural economy acted as a kind of holding operation, circumventing a massive rural exodus which the urban economy might not have been able to exploit, and which might have landed France in a classic Malthusian trap.

Clearly, one should not whitewash France's manufacturing sector in the eighteenth century. Serious problems existed, and these became particularly acute in the last two decades of the Old Regime, which saw a recession in all branches of the economy. Even before British manufactures benefitting from precocious mechanization had wiped the floor with the more traditional sectors of textile production after 1786, the woollen and silk industries were in deep trouble, following the loss of markets in the Levant and in Spanish possessions. In reviewing the reasons for this situation, French manufacturers could be forgiven for not blaming themselves for lack of enterprise so much as laying the blame at the door of the state, whose fiscal policy seemed to inhibit growth, whose armed forces were signally failing to secure French industry the world outlets it required, and whose economic policies were too erratic, too favourable to the nobility, and too little attuned to the commercial interest.

Economic historians are also kinder these days on the agrarian sector of the Old Regime economy than was that celebrated chauvinist Arthur Young. Young's well-known critique of French agriculture on the eve of the Revolution has cast a long shadow. It is not simply that Young constantly disparaged any rural trait which did not seem to fit into the English ideal type of agrarian change – hence his attacks on small farms, sharecropping, absentee landlords, peasant collective practices, and so on. In addition it has to be borne in mind that he was often comparing French general practice with English best practice. It would be fairer to compare, shall we say, the efficiency of a Gascon small farmer with that of a Scottish crofter, a Welsh hill-farmer, or an Irish potato-eating peasant than with a prosperous Suffolk tenant-farmer. Notwithstanding Young's strictures – wholly predicated on the inherent merits of the 'English way' – we should not denigrate the overall performance levels of France's agrarian sector prior to 1789: population grew from 21.5 million in 1700 to 28.6 million in 1789 – an increase of a third. These extra mouths had to be fed; fed they were, an achievement all the more remarkable for being made without the kind of technological breakthroughs current in English farming. If French peasants in 1789 were hungry and turbulent, at least they were not starving and comatose as they had been in 1709–10, the last great famine in French history. The additional food supply did not come to any marked degree from improved agricultural techniques – although there were some attempts, particularly on the open-field seigneuries of northern France, to follow in England's footsteps in technique. In general terms, food supply to cope with population growth was achieved through a combination of incremental improvements and changes: more marginal land brought under the plough, better storage, more scientific milling, better marketing. Though at times of bad harvest it might still seem that grain was a prisoner, as Ernest Labrousse has put it, 'immobilisé sur place faute de moyens d'évasion [et] gardé par des foules anxieuses, pire que geôliers',[7] in fact massive markets in grain operated throughout the course of the eighteenth century. This allowed regions to make a choice of agrarian vocation: areas of more fertile farmland could specialize in grain, while other regions could develop non-subsistence production, whether agrarian or industrial. Languedoc provides a good example of the kind of regional division of labour which might result: in many areas of Upper Languedoc, as Georges Frêche has shown, grain was king, and landowners specialized in its production in the knowledge that surpluses could be marketed via the excellent river basin of the Garonne, extended now by the road system and the Canal du Midi which made even the normally loquacious Arthur Young gasp in admiration. Lower Languedoc, in contrast, its food supply assured, specialized increasingly in wine production and domestic industry. The results were impressive: using only traditional agricultural methods, grain production in the area of the Midi-Pyrénées as a whole studied by Frêche rose by some 15 per cent down to 1789, but population increased by between 45 and 55 per cent on average. Better marketing was the key to this disparity.

There is in fact an increasingly strong-looking case for arguing that the French peasantry overall was more market-orientated than historians have often allowed. Since the times of Marc Bloch and Georges Lefebvre, there has been a virtual consensus among historians that the communal practices of the 'traditionalist' peasantry – common land, grazing rights, gleaning rights, and so on – inhibited that 'agrarian individualism' allegedly integral to rural capitalism. The brilliant work of Olwen Hufton on the poor has helped consolidate this view, for the distinct impression has emerged that the majority of France's population were less concerned with market forces than with crude biological survival. With peasants unwilling or unable to display the required 'modernizing' attitudes, it was left to the domain agriculture of seigneurs in north-eastern France to provide the leading edge of agrarian revolution. The so-called seigneurial reaction, as Cobban originally suggested and as Le Roy Ladurie has documented, should thus be seen, it is generally suggested, as the diffusion of more businesslike, capitalistic methods of estate management. The revival of long-obsolete feudal dues goes hand in hand with encroachment on the commons, more rational surveillance and collection of dues and innovations in farming technology as part of a noble-inspired capitalistic development. Perhaps. A number of recent studies have, however, suggested that this was not the only route to capitalism in the countryside, and that there was a peasant way. Road haulage and marketing provided a valuable supplement for the middling and wealthier peasant. In Pont-Saint-Pierre in Normandy, the subject of a fine recent monograph by Jonathan Dewald, the peasant on the make in the eighteenth century was the peasant with a horse and cart, who could benefit from increased demand for food and higher prices by activities as a haulier as well as a producer. Moreover, the recent work of Hilton Root has shown that the communal practices usually viewed as the bane of rural capitalism could in fact coexist with commercialism: he demonstrates how village communities in Burgundy exploited their communal rights over woodland by marketing firewood, a precious commodity in eighteenth-century France. He also shows how richer peasants upheld the commons on which their large herds – whose produce was also marketed – could graze. Just how far this peasant model applies to other regions is open to question. There is a certain amount of supporting evidence from other localities, while the findings of the Soviet scholar Ado on peasant revolts point in much the same direction.

What is particularly interesting about Hilton Root's work is that it allows us to reconceptualize relations between peasants and seigneurs in ways which relate to the specific forms in which commercial capitalism emerged in France. It was not so much that seigneurs were more 'feudalistic' in their demands – though many may have been. Rather, the demands that they did make were now seen through the eyes of a more market-conscious peasantry. The archaic feudal due of *guet et garde*, for example, which had in an earlier age been viewed as some kind of quid pro quo for the seigneur's services of protection, justice, and charity, looked archaic and oppressive in the eighteenth century when peasants preferred royal to seigneurial courts and when the need for protection had long passed – and indeed when fortified *châteaux forts* were being replaced by elegant country houses. The sense of injustice and unfairness which this created in the peasantry seems to have been heightened by the commercial nexus in which they increasingly found themselves. Peasants were not slow, moreover, to take their issues and their arguments to royal courts, where they found lawyers to articulate their grievances in the language of natural rights. The 'moral economy' of the Burgundian peasantry at least seems less paternalistic and pre-capitalist than it is usually accounted, and more consonant with commercial values. As Peter Jones has demonstrated – contrary to one of the hallowed myths of Revisionism, namely that there was no social crisis prior to 1788–9 – a great many rural areas were gripped by severe social conflict in the decades leading up to the Revolution. It is becoming increasingly apparent, moreover, that the last half-century of the Old Regime was in addition a Golden Age of Peasant Litigiousness throughout France. Perhaps, indeed, to misquote Clausewitz, we should see the peasant revolution of 1789 as litigation by other means.

These examples, and the development of regional economic specialization, stand as testimony to a society characterized as much by circulation, mobility, and innovation as by the traditionalism, subsistence farming, and cultural stagnation which feature so strongly on the litany of the New Revisionist Orthodoxy. Perhaps over four million French men, women, and children were dependent for their living on viticulture in 1789, as well as endless hundreds of thousands involved in domestic industry. These individuals had little choice but to embrace the market. They might begrudge it; but they did not flee from it. It is significant in this respect too that road improvements were bringing distance times sharply down in the last decades of the Old Regime: the state road system, now under the care of an increasingly professionalized Ponts et Chaussées service, cut overall distance times from Paris by between 40 and 60 per cent on average. The better articulation of the market was witnessed too by the relative decline of the great periodic regional fairs which had lumberingly animated economic life hitherto: regular urban markets now provided the necessary stimuli. The overall volume of French trade quintupled between the death of Louis XIV and the Revolution, and between three-quarters and four-fifths of this took place within the home market. Although the retailing network lacked the sophistication of that of England, a great many localities witnessed 'the rise of the shopkeeper'. The new primacy of exchange and circulation was nicely symbolized by the movement to knock down urban ramparts. Indeed *circulation* (now of goods and persons as well as of the blood) was one of the buzz-words in the general vocabulary of the late Enlightenment, and a host of others related either to transmission and circulation (*commerçant, commercial, baromètre, oscillation, fluctuation, conversion, électriser*, etc.) or to consumption (*consommation, consommateurs, commodité*, etc.) This is the language of an increasingly commercial society. Jean-Claude Perrot, in his study of Caen in the Old Regime, has compared job descriptions as they feature in municipal tax rolls in 1666 and 1792. What is particularly striking is the appearance by the later date of a whole range of terms which characterize a commercial and a consumer-orientated society. Consider for example (running the two fields together): *commissionnaire, directeur de postes, commis des postes, directeur des messageries, banquier, ingénieur des ponts, râpeur de tabac, maître du jeu de boule, maître du jeu de billard, musicien, directeur de spectacles, professeur d'équitation, marchand de modes*, and *marchand de parapluies*.[8]

I would like to stick with *parapluies* a little longer. A good deal of research is going on at the moment on post-mortem inventories. I have been surprised at the extent to which objects like umbrellas – whose relationship to subsistence, traditionalism, and even popular culture seems obscure or tangential – are found even in the homes of the relatively humble. Daniel Roche's work on the *People of Paris* has underlined the extent to which Parisians underwent a mini-consumer revolution in the eighteenth century: furnishings and room space in the dwellings of the popular classes show greater functional differentiation and more aware-ness of fashion, with, for example, showy pieces of furniture such as writing-tables, card-tables and coat-stands becoming more common; wall-paper, wall-hangings, mirrors, snuff-boxes, teapots, razors, chamberpots, and clocks are found in greater abundance; people spend more money on clothes, and these in turn become more showy and more responsive to changes in fashion; and the humble umbrella makes its appearance. Recent, unpublished work by Cissie Fairchilds bears out this general picture. Cheap versions of cultural artefacts formerly categorized as the luxuries of the well-to-do – Fairchilds calls them 'populuxe products' – are increasingly widely dispersed: umbrellas, porcelain plates, clocks, mirrors, and so forth. Books and other reading matter might also be included in the list. Doubtless servants played a crucial role in all this as cultural inter-mediaries between the élites and the masses. The tendency is very wide-spread in the urban milieu – even the poorest immigrant stonecutter from the Limousin or impoverished Lyonnais weaver had his Sunday best. It seems to have been disproportionately prevalent among women, who were more attuned to fashion than men and who may also have been seen as objects of conspicuous consumption. In many rural settings, too, pocket-watches and silver, gold, and enamelled buttons increasingly bestudded the Sunday waistcoats of peasant farmers. Perhaps, in her way, Charlotte Corday was trying to bring this new consumerism to the attention of historians, for she took care to murder the hapless Marat in that highly fashionable populuxe product, a zinc bathtub.

The widespread diffusion of populuxe products in late eighteenth-century France is matched by a similar consumerism in diet and in leisure habits. Perhaps historians overemphasize the bipolarity within Old Regime society. A great deal of evidence suggests that between Olwen Hufton's poor and Guy Chaussinand-Nogaret's élite of notables, there were sub-stantial middling and even lower-middling groups who were doing quite nicely for much of the eighteenth century. Bread may have been the major item of the popular budget, but wine used up much family income, as the boom in the drinks trade attested. The consumption of sugar, tea, coffee, and chocolate rose dramatically and this was not simply a reflection of increased élite use; for *café au lait* was well on its way to becoming the breakfast of the urban labouring classes, and was probably penetrating the countryside as well. The fact, for example, that snuff-boxes and hats had become barometers of social status reflects changing social criteria, as does the wide diffusion of tobacco, which had become a prime necessity for many. We should see the mass growth of prostitution in the cities of Old Regime France as another area of burgeoning male consumer demand. The emergence of 'red-light districts' in many towns is moreover only part of a general reshaping of urban space which testifies to new cultural tastes: the century saw a boom in pleasure-gardens, coffee-houses, billiard-halls, theatres, libraries, malls. Enthusiasm for urban improvement and 'environmental engineering' (public health measures, drainage, ventilation, etc.), to which J. C. Riley has recently drawn attention, owed much to the wish to open up spaces for pleasure and public consumption.

The consumer market, particularly in the urban setting, then, seems to have been far larger and more buoyant than historians have been usually willing to admit. The tendency has been to write off French towns, in which this new consumerism was centred, as a polarized mixture of, as one contemporary put it, 'richesse et gueuserie, faste et mendicité, magnificence et saleté',[9] which strikes a poor contrast with middle-class England allegedly undergoing the 'first consumer revolution'. Yet while doubtless in consumer terms England led the field – one had only to see those swooning tourists agog in the West End shops – it also had its problems. Living standards of the English working classes were stagnating in the late eighteenth century, a period at which England's rate of economic growth may also have been slowing down. While the intensity of consumerism was probably still more marked in England than in France (if only because a higher proportion of England's population inhabited towns), the actual scale of the market was probably similar. After all, France's population grew by 7.1 million in the eighteenth century – twice England's population increase of 3.6 million. London, with nearly a million inhabitants, clearly outgunned Paris, with its 650,000. But the number of city-dwellers in France as a whole rose by over 40 per cent between 1725 and 1789, and the 5.3 million French town-dwellers in 1789 comfortably exceeded Britain's urban population of 2.3 million by the later date. Even were we to accept that per capita disposable income was much higher in England than in France, the total demand generated by a very large number of even quite poor people is considerable, so that the scale of demand on France's colossal home market was still pretty impressive.

In urban centres in both France and England, moreover, one of the liveliest and most dynamic of periodical publications was the advertiser, the branch of the media most attuned to a consumerist society. For too long overlooked by cultural historians, who have concentrated their interest on the enlightened culture of the élite on one hand and the purportedly timeless demotic escapism of the *Bibliothèque bleue* on the other, advertiser-like *Affiches* were established in most major French cities over the

eighteenth century. In 1789, there were forty-four in existence, and they
tended to prosper in administrative centres where the liberal professions
and the tertiary sector were particularly strong. Aimed at providing for 'le
plaisir . . . et l'utilité du public',[10] and filled to the brim with small-ads
and advertisements for every conceivable need from cosmetics to piano-
tuners, these periodicals testify not only to the existence of a sizeable
audience of consumers, but also to the lively spirit of exchange and
consumerism which animated them.

Every society makes its cultural heroes in its own image, and it therefore
seems particularly significant that one of the great popular heroes of
eighteenth-century France was the smuggler Mandrin, usually portrayed
Robin Hood-like distributing consumer goods (tobacco, light textiles, salt)
at a fair price to the poor and needy. If Mandrin was a consumerist hero
for a consumerist and increasingly materialistic age, by the same token the
century's hate figures were the officials of the General Farm, the collectors
of indirect taxes who were widely viewed as leeches, privileged blood-
suckers on the body social. The state perhaps attracted a certain amount
of flak from popular consumers. No one took the old sumptuary legislation seriously: the last measure, in 1720, had forbidden commoners wearing of jewellery save with the written permission of the king. But
government tolls and taxes inhibited consumerism – and perhaps a certain
amount of naked consumer envy was canalized away from the wealthy
towards the state, which could be be blamed for conspiring to put populuxe products and new consumer needs out of the reach of many. If this
was a 'moral economy', it was one attuned to novelty and individualistic
materialism as well as subsistence and community values.

I have thus far portrayed eighteenth-century France as a more and more
commercial society, increasingly sensitive to the market, very different
from the stagnating, traditionalist society encountered in the New Revisionist Orthodoxy. Seen from this viewpoint, it seems clear that the main
intermediaries and beneficiaries of this growing commercialization were
the allegedly 'traditional' bourgeoisie. Merchants, artisans, shopkeepers,
and the *paysannerie marchande* were in the fore, with only a sprinkling of
the nobility. The size of the bourgeoisie grew over the century from 700,000
or 800,000 individuals in 1700 to perhaps 2.3 million in 1789 – getting on
for 10 per cent of the global population. The New Revisionist Orthodoxy
that bourgeoisie and nobility were somehow identical in economic terms
thus seems rather wide of the mark: even were we to take all of the 120,000
nobles Chaussinand-Nogaret claims to have been in existence in 1789 as
engaged in entrepreneurial activity – a hypothesis very far from the mark,
as Chaussinand-Nogaret would admit – they would still be sinking without trace in a bourgeois sea. Entrepreneurial nobles were anyway more
likely to be involved in monopoly capitalist ventures or financial dealing

than in the more humdrum bread-and-butter mercantile and manufacturing activities which were the staple of French commercial capitalism.

The exact timing and the character of the commercialization of French society inevitably varied from region to region and from class to class. But it may well be feasible to link it with the great change in *mentalités* observable from roughly the middle of the century. I do not wish to get embroiled in the religious significance of the move away from baroque piety which Michel Vovelle, Pierre Chaunu, Philippe Ariès, and others have detected in wills and other socio-religious documents: was it dechristianization or anticlericalism? was it a shift towards a more sincere, internalized spirituality? Yet however the mutation is interpreted, it is clear that something important was happening from that time to the most basic attitudes towards death, life, and material possessions. Evidence from wills also suggests that the comportment of nobles and bourgeois was relatively distinct. The diffusion of coitus interruptus – 'le toboggan contraceptif', as Jean-Pierre Bardet[11] has picturesquely put it – even in rural areas also supports the view that a seismic shift in *mentalités* was in process in the latter half of the eighteenth century. Overall, it thus seems fair at least to hypothesize that changes in *mentalités* and the commercialization of society are connected phenomena.

This hypothesis is strengthened by the fact that the commercialization of Old Regime society did not simply relate to the provision of material goods, but covered the provision of services more generally and was indeed tantamount to the development of a more consumerist outlook on everyday life. The service sector of the French economy – in social terms overwhelmingly in non-noble hands – remains the great unknown for economic historians, who usually leave it out of their aggregate calculations. It seems likely that it was doing extremely well, and that the mercantile developments of the century had stimulated a concomitant expansion in both the numbers and the wealth of individuals involved in transport, domestic service, the provision of legal, medical, and other general services. The range of what we might loosely call the 'professions' also rose: to the 'profession of arms', and the three classical liberal careers of theology, law, and medicine, were added over the course of the century a host of related or analogous occupations: schoolteacher, estate manager or *feudiste*, scientist, and civil engineer are just a few that spring to mind.

In the New Revisionist Orthodoxy, the professions are usually patronizingly labelled the 'traditional élites', the assumption being that they remained locked in the rigidities of the 'society of orders' until August 4, 1789. In fact they were in a state of institutional and intellectual ferment in the eighteenth century. Each seems to have undergone important institutional changes over the century, and developed in self-esteem, self-definition, and commitment. This was accompanied by a certain consumerism –

one might say a bourgeoisification – in their lifestyles which reflects the extent to which they were adjusting to the inroads and the potentialities of commercial capitalism.

To look at any one of the professions in the late eighteenth century is to uncover a welter of ongoing debates – grounded, I would contend, in the changing size and nature of demand – on the nature of professionalism. In these debates, issues fundamental to the role of the service sector in a capitalist economy – the provision of services, rational organization, public accountability, market forces, quality control, and so on – were addressed. These are matters which we can as yet glimpse only darkly, and on whose exact nature we can at this stage only hazard guesses. To make an outrageously bald generalization, however, it seems helpful to classify the arguments utilized into two broad camps. On the one hand there were arguments for professionalization which adopted a corporative framework, and which sought changes on a 'vertical', internalist, and hierarchical basis. Expertise, internal discipline, and segregation from the wider society was the key. On the other hand, there were arguments which adopted a civic dimension, where the framework for professionalism was transcorporative, egalitarian, 'horizontal'. The profession should be opened up on to the wider society. Both sets of arguments utilized the same kinds of language, though if proponents of the corporative professionalism tended to think in terms of 'subjects' of the 'state' (sometimes even personalized still as 'the king') the civic professionalizers referred to 'citizens' and the 'Nation' or, sometimes, 'the public'. It is a language which in its most democratic and egalitarian formulations prefigured the debates in the National Assembly in the summer of 1789.

Let us take the profession of arms as an example. David Bien, in a brilliant Revisionist article, has familiarized us with the notion of the professionalization of the army officer corps. This took the form of measures aimed to produce an effective army, Spartan in its virtues (though Prussia was the real blueprint), operating within more bureaucratic and hierarchical structures, and enjoying more efficient training and a more articulated career structure. Even the infamous Ségur ordinance of 1781 which limited high command to officers enjoying four quarters of nobility can be regarded as a professionalizing measure. The aim of the ordinance was to exclude not commoners so much as recently ennobled bourgeois who had bought their way into the corps through the system of venal office and were thought to lack the sense of inbred honour which only dynasties of military nobility could produce in young recruits. What has tended to be seen as a flagrant instance of feudal reaction thus takes on the more anodyne colours of military professionalization; privilege is legitimized by service, high birth by social utility. Unfortunately, this is only half of the story. Though Bien does not tell us so, in fact there was more than one way of construing professionalization. The corporative model of the old nobility was matched by a very different, civic model, reflected and furthered by the writings of Rousseau, but transcending any narrow lineages of literary influences. Embraced by many younger officers, this model was grounded in the belief that professionalism could best be achieved through opening up the army on the wider society. The military man was a citizen before he was a soldier: this basic message comes through in a whole host of writings from the 1770s onwards, rising in a crescendo, as one might expect, with the American War of Independence. Guibert's *Essai de tactique* (dedicated *A ma patrie*) (1772) and Joseph Servan's *Le soldat citoyen* (1780) may serve as instances of the genre. Consider in this respect too the early career of Lazare Carnot, the 'Organizer of Victory' in Year II, and a military engineer in the last years of the Old Regime. Carnot's prize-winning 'Éloge de Vauban' (1784) is a fine example of civic professionalism. Writing self-proclaimedly as a *militaire philosophe et citoyen*, Carnot praises the technical skills of Vauban as a servant, but he also sees him as a friend of the people, whose professional artistry was intended to defend *la Nation* from the sufferings of war. In this civic version, the professional ethic was combined with a critique of Ségur-style privilege, and the corporative pofessionalism which camouflaged it.

Antagonistic strands of civic and corporative professionalism are to be found in the secular clergy prior to 1789 too, as Timothy Tackett has shown. The corporative model owed much to the continuing post-Tridentine reforms of the Catholic hierarchy, which aimed to make of parish priests spiritual gendarmes working obediently under their bishops. Intensive training, through seminaries and apprenticeship as *vicaires*, bade fair to make the Catholic clergy a force quite as disciplined, quite as *pur et dur* as the professionalized army corps. The equation of professionalism with the wearing of the clerical cassock highlighted the congruity. This conception of the parish priest had increasingly to compete, however, with a more civic view which stressed the duties the clergy owed to the Nation. The citizen-clergy, often fuelled by Richerist ideas, resented the overly hierarchical and disciplinarian character of the Church, as well as its social dominance by the high nobility; practised the virtues of charity and consolation to their fellow citizens; and invoked the rights of the Nation. Their lifestyle as well as their outlook became increasingly bourgeois: the watches, clocks, mirrors, books, and other decorative bric-à-brac found in their homes revealed them as very much part of the new consumer culture. The large number of civic-minded lower clergy elected to the Estates-General were to play a crucial role in helping to win the political initiative for their bourgeois fellow deputies in the Third Estate.

Schoolteachers – very largely within the aegis of the church – were a group amongst which this civic ideology made a particular mark. The pedagogy of the last decades of the Old Regime was thoroughly infused with civic values. Schoolteachers included some of the most eloquent and persuasive members of the revolutionary assemblies: Lanjuinais, Fouché, Billaud-Varenne, Daunou, François de Neufchâteau, Manuel, and Lakanal are a representative crop.

There was to be a good admixture of medical men among the deputies of the revolutionary assemblies too, the good doctor Guillotin not least. Debates over professionalism in the world of medicine were complicated by the traditional split between unviersity-trained physicians and the more artisanal surgeons. Medicine was a jungle: the physicians cordially despised the surgeons, and the major medical faculties were perennially at daggers drawn. Over the course of the century, however, important changes took place. Surgeons hoisted up their prestige, wealth, and status: a liberal education came to be required for a surgical career. A growing professionalization on their part, grounded in their highly cen-tralized organization – the King's First Surgeon was effectively 'King of Surgery' throughout France – was helped by their proven utility in their service of the royal armies. As the century wore on, many physicians also tried to transcend the corporative petty-mindedness for which they were famous, and to stress the public benefits of medical professionalism. The foundation of the Royal Society of Medicine in 1776 was viewed as an attempt to give some corporative structure to the straggling bands of physicians throughout France; but it also made a great play of its mission as recorder and diagnostician of epidemics and as information network on disease and the environment. Above all, it stood as the scourge of medical 'charlatanism', and argued that social utility and public health required the enforcement of a monopoly of medical services by trained physicians. Even before 1789, medical eulogists were portraying the dedicated physician as a bastion of citizenship, a cross between an altruistic notable and a secular saint devoted to his ailing flock.

The legal profession seems in many respects to have been the least professionalized of the traditional professions prior to 1789. The training of lawyers was almost scandalously routine, and though there was an insistence that graduates should do an apprenticeship before they prac-tised independently – four years in Paris after 1751 – the profession had little hierarchical and disciplined character. Yet, as Bailey Stone has argued, the magistrates of the Parlement held a highly elevated conception of their professional competence, and this led them strongly to support not only the corporative rights of their caste and the 'fundamental laws of the kingdom' but also the prerogatives of the Nation. A highly vocal minority of barristers and attorneys, moreover, generated many of the ideas of civic professionalism we have noted in the other professions. Free legal advice centres established by Boucher d'Argis in Paris in 1783 and in Toulouse by Bertrand Barère in 1787 exemplified this. Lawyers in a number of jurisdic-tions in eastern France – and possibly elsewhere – also developed a new style of argument over seigneurial duties heavily impregnated with civic values. Responding to peasant feelings that seigneurial dues were effectively unfair exchange – as I suggested earlier – lawyers argued that archaic feudal dues infringed natural freedom and justice. It was a dispute over *guet et garde*, plus the Parlement of Besançon's refusal to register the royal decree of 1780 abolishing mortmain, which detached many laywers in the region from their formerly emphatic solidarity with their parlementary colleagues. These civic values thus articulated the antiseigneurial grievances of the peasantry as well as the professional ethic of the law, and laid the foundations of the cultural hegemony of Natural Rights in 1789.

Though riddled with corruption and the object of tremendous popular hostility, as the *cahiers* were to make clear in 1789, legal practitioners still maintained a high estimation of their constitutional importance. They sometimes claimed to comprise a kind of Fourth Estate, for example, a position which clearly chimed in with the constitutional pretensions of the Parlements. As Sarah Maza and Keith Baker have shown, many legal practitioners came to exploit civil and criminal cases so as to develop significant civic and political arguments, which were widely followed by the literate public – as well as by others not so literate. The Calas affair is only one example – there are many – in which a contentious lawsuit led to an outpouring of pamphlets and polemical writings, normally the work of lawyers or attorneys, which invoked *l'opinion publique* as a kind of supreme arbiter. The sociological supports of this powerful concept clearly lay in the growing market for cultural products and services over the eighteenth century which I have already described. Be that as it may, 'public concern' in the mouths of prerevolutionary lawyers and polemicists predicated a feel for natural justice soon to receive more famous embodiment in the Rights of Man and the Nation, promulgated by a National Assembly in which were to sit some 151 lawyers. The 'tas de bavards, avocats, procureurs, notaires, huissiers et d'autres semblables vermines' who, in the charmingly unlovely language of the *Père Duchesne*,[12] dominated every subsequent revolutionary assembly owed much to their exposure before 1789 to the problems inherent in exercising their profession in a fast-changing commercial society whose service sector was being transformed.

The debate over professionalism, civic and corporative, is particularly interesting to follow in the state bureaucracy, where it is complicated by the system of venal office. Classic Weberian reforms were increasingly introduced over the last decades of the Old Regime, to limit the rampant patrimonialism which characterized the service generally. The most hated branch of the service, the General Farm, was most advanced in its corporative professionalism, having introduced a wide range of rational bureaucratic procedures, and also having installed a career structure for employees which included a contributory pensions fund. Elsewhere, there was a reaction against the prevalence of venal office. The latter was widely blamed for, as one critic put it, 'cette séparation injurieuse qui règne entre l'administration et la Nation'.[13] Venality was in fact reduced or abolished in a number of services in the last decades of the Old Regime, including the *maréchaussée*, the postal system, and the saltpetre service. Necker attempted to centralize the multiple treasuries of the financial bureaucracy. There were some valiantly civic-minded administrators who endeavoured to move the popular imagination into believing them citizens as well as Crown servants. But bureaucrats continued to be seen essentially as *vendeurs d'espérance et de protection, de petits despotes, d'insolents roitelets*, the very embodiment of privilege, without any social utility or public benefit.[14] One can understand why the revolutionary assemblies would desire to debureaucratize French society – a familiar phantasm.

Showing an awareness of the interpenetration of political and economic factors which is in itself an object-lesson to historians, many critics of venal office in the late Old Regime attacked the way in which such posts could entail what might be seen as unfair market advantage. This whole question of venal office has been reopened in recent years by a number of important Revisionist articles. In an article in the *Historical Journal* in 1984, for example, William Doyle demonstrated that the market for venal office was more buoyant than Marxists and indeed many Revisionists had held. The price of some offices falls, but far more rise, and Doyle concludes in general that overall the price of office was rising; he ascribes this to the traditionalism of the Old Regime bourgeoisie, who were failing to give up their secular preference for status over profit.

Before this view finds its niche within the canon of the New Revisionist Orthodoxy, however, let us consider how this rise in the value of venal office might relate to the growth of the market for services. The post of court physician (*médecin du roi*), on which I have done some research, is an interesting starting-point. In 1720, only seventeen physicians could claim this title, while in 1789, eighty-eight, to whom might be added quite as many *chirurgiens du roi* and *apothecaires du roi*. The price of these posts seems to have been pretty buoyant. As only a handful of the individuals who could style themselves *médecin du roi* came near the person of the monarch, or even resided at Versailles, it might be concluded that here was a title that meant prestige and little else. In fact, this was far from the case. The purchase of a post was a means of circumventing the monopoly which the Paris Medical Faculty had on medical services within the capital. One has only to remember the wild enthusiasm of Parisians for every medical fad and fancy in the eighteenth century to see how valuable that access could be: Paris rocked to, and *médecins du roi* made money out of, the crazes for vapours, male *accoucheurs*, smallpox inoculation, Mesmerism, and a good many forms of treatment for venereal disease – the most exotic of which must surely have been Lefebvre de Saint-Ildephont's anti-venereal chocolate drops. This particular court physician claimed that one could medicate one's wife against venereal infection by providing her with an unending supply of boxes of chocolates.

Crudely put, purchase of a post within the royal medical Household was a means of cashing in on medical consumerism. It represented a headlong rush towards a market – even an entrepreneurial interest in stimulating it – rather than a flight from it. One wonders whether there are similar stories to tell about many of the other venal offices. Indeed, if we turn again to William Doyle's list of venal offices for which prices were rising, we find that a good number of them – attorneys, notaries, legal clerks, auctioneers, and wigmakers – do indeed relate to expanding markets for professional services or fashionable lifestyle. Venal office (and perhaps a similar case might be mounted for land purchase) begins to look less like an option for status than a shrewd investment aimed to give the purchaser access to a market or edge within it. Money bought privilege within this market as well as within the polity and within the social hierarchy.

Attacked by their co-professionals as the embodiment of privilege and social inutility, many venal officers themselves grew progressively disenchanted by their posts. The advantages of market edge plus the returns on the initial investment palled as the monarchy, increasingly beset by financial problems, came to interfere with the venal office market in a number of ways. The value of the investment was reduced by a series of injudicious decisions by the monarch to levy forced loans, for example (on the *corps* of financial officials in particular), to increase the number of offices in a particular *corps*, or to reduce wages. The downturn in the economy from the 1770s may also have diminished the buoyancy of many markets for services. Economies in the state bureaucracy – pursued by all controllers-general in the last years of the Old Regime, but with no greater vigour than by Loménie de Brienne in 1787–8 – must have helped venal officers to see the writing on the wall. In any event, with state bankruptcy on the horizon, it was a pretty shrewd move, on the Night of August 4, 1789, to agree to the abolition of all venal offices. For the abolition was agreed on the basis of compensation which, it was hoped, would be financially more advantageous than forcible expropriation or sale in depressed market conditions. So much for the 'patriotic rhapsodies' of altruism!

In the question of venal office were encapsulated many of the problems of the absolute monarchy. The state operated the most extraordinarily ornate system whereby it sold offices which thereby became the private property of their owners. The holders could not be bought out *en bloc* – the expense was too colossal; so kings turned disadvantage to advantage by levying forced loans on the main bodies of venal office-holders to help it in its financial difficulties. The king was thereby to a certain extent digging his own grave, in that these loans ran up the National Debt to colossal proportions. In addition, the royal demands amplified the corporate awareness of the bodies of venal office-holders. This was particularly marked in the case of the towns, as Gail Bossenga has recently shown. Venal municipal offices, constantly chopped and changed over the course of the century, bred discontent both within the charmed circle of municipal officials, and outside in sectional groups wanting to get in. This provided a seed-plot in which – over all sorts of issues, from street lighting to local taxes – could grow a civic awareness quite as cogent as that developing within the professions.

A growing sensitivity to civic issues is found elsewhere in Old Regime society too. Even at village level, Hilton Root finds Burgundian peasants deciding on local matters utilizing, in pretty sophisticated fashion, the concept of the General Will long before the latter term was dreamed up by Jean-Jacques Rousseau. Urban guilds were often too the micro-sites for similar exercises in political education and the exercise of political democracy. They too, like Hilton Root's peasants, utilized the courts as means of redress, with lawyers playing the part of cultural intermediary between legal form and social issues. If we suspend the New Revisionist Orthodoxy's certainty that modern political culture was born in 1789, we can glimpse within Old Regime society, even at these lowly levels supposedly locked away into the bromides of a 'popular culture', a vibrant and developing political sensibility which cries out to be inventoried, classified, and understood.

Although what came to be at issue often had far wider ramifications, these burgeoning debates within the professions and other corporative cells of the Society of Orders were at first often localized and sectional. The courts and, by way of the press, the notion of 'public opinion' provided a conduit along which civic sensibilities could penetrate the body social, as we have seen. A number of other institutions came to act as a crucible in which these fragmented disputes were fused into a supra-corporative consciousness. The Enlightenment Academies were a case in point. Their internally democratic practices favoured such fusion, for the niceties of the social hierarchy were normally not observed within them, and bourgeois rubbed shoulders with noble, as well as doctor with lawyer. To be frank, the Academies were often dominated by local nobles and dignitaries, and consequently stuffy, if worthy, in their procedures. The egalitarian, meritocratic sharing of experience which they embodied was doubtless important for some. Even more important, however, were the Masonic lodges. The cult of Masonry had its adepts throughout the social pyramid; yet the numerical predominance among the body of 50,000 French Masons was clearly with the professional classes and with their social equivalents. Businessmen – often excluded from Academies for being lacking in tone and breeding – were here in massive numbers: they represented 36 per cent of members in major cities, and the proportion was often well over 50 per cent in numerous localities. Soldiers were the main professional category, although lawyers, administrators, and doctors – if few priests – were also there in bulk. The same elements – in a slightly different mix – were found in *sociétés de lecture, chambres littéraires* and their like.

These new forums for egalitarian mixing and discussion were as much organs of sociability as anything else. In his recent work on Masonry, Ran Halévi has dubbed this a 'democratic sociability'. Halévi, like his close collaborator François Furet, is in fact particularly interested in the lodges as lineal ancestors of the Jacobin Clubs, and so chooses a narrowly political term. I prefer the term 'civic sociability', which I think expresses rather better the urban and wider cultural implications of this form of social mixing, and has the additional merit of making explicit the clear affinities it has with the civic ideologies and practices exuded by the professional and corporative institutions of the Old Regime.

In the light of the previous discussion, we can now revisit the debate on the social origins of the Revolution of 1789. Given the development of commercial capitalism in eighteenth-century France, the spread of a consumer society, the development of professionalization within the service sector of the economy which this helped to spawn, and the appearance of associated forms of civic sociability, it no longer looks realistic to disparage the vitality nor indeed the ideological autonomy of the Old Regime bourgeoisie. Far from the social structure of Old Regime France being locked remorselessly into 'traditional' 'pre-capitalist', 'archaic' forms, the progress of commercialization and the spread of a consumer society suggests a relative 'bourgeoisification' of Old Regime society. Far from an élite of 'notables' melding harmoniously and cosily together in the last years of the Old Regime, moreover, conflict over the role of privilege and the implications of citizenship was endemic and established an explosive agenda beneath the surface calm of the Society of Orders. Yet though civic sociability had achieved much, it had signally failed to capture control of the state apparatus. This was to be the achievement of the men of 1789.

Who, then, were the 'revolutionary bourgeoisie' (if we can now assume there was one)? Alfred Cobban characterized it as a mixture of land-owners, venal officers, and professional men. To a certain degree he was correct. Yet he saw both the professions and the venal office-holders as declining, inferiority-complexed classes, so many shrinking violets easily written off as 'traditional élites'. What I have argued here is that the professions and indeed a great many venal office-holders, far from being sectional and 'traditionalist' in their orientation and outlook, were in fact responding to and very much part of the development of capitalism in the Old Regime. These groups were more genuinely bourgeois than ever before, and exuded a new civic professionalism which had its roots in a developing 'market-consciousness' and which clashed with the corporative values espoused by many of their fellows. They shared the vision and the reflexes of the commercial bourgeoisie of the Old Regime in a far more direct way than has hitherto been recognized. Moreover, although they thought through these problems at first perhaps largely through the corporative framework, the ongoing debts on professionalization nurtured widening perspectives. Masonic lodges, *sociétés de pensée*, and the like further elaborated and refined the debate and also opened it up so that it included sections of the economic bourgeoisie in the years leading up to 1789. Professionalization was thus not simply a part of the noble reaction, as David Bien might have us believe. In its civic form, professionalism legitimated the attack on privilege, even when the latter was defended by corporative values. It stimulated a conception of the state as something which was not so much embodied in the dynast as present in the 'Nation', an ideological construct which developed *pari passu* with the growth and elaboration of the market. The organs of civic sociability, finally, provided forums in which new ideas of equality, democracy, and civic concern could take material form among an increasingly homogeneous bourgeoisie and their allies among the liberal aristocracy.

In his notorious *Qu'est-ce que le Tiers État?*, Sieyès showed himself very much the apologist for this new civic consciousness. He argued that the 'Nation' was composed of useful classes and groups which with great lucidity he itemized as including agriculture, industry, the mercantile interest, services 'pleasant to the person', and the public services of the army, the law, the Church, and the bureaucracy.[15] His thinking was not as much the early appearance of a revolutionary ideology which sprang out fully developed from the political context, as the Revisionists are prone to argue. Rather, as the list of groups suggests, the new ideology of the Third Estate was in essence the ideology of prerevolutionary civic professionalism. Its presence in one of the cardinal texts of the Revolution of 1789 indicates something of the contribution this new and increasingly aggressive civic ideology made to the downfall of the Old Regime. The civic sociability which had developed among this fraction of the bourgeoisie in the last decades of the Old Regime was corrosive of the deferentialism and hierarchical structures of the Society of Orders.

The ability of the Old Regime state to provide social and political conditions free from privilege and corporatism was in question long before its financial shipwreck in 1787–8. In the decades which preceded 1789, successive ministers had found themselves trying to float public loans by appeals to a general public increasingly impregnated with civic consciousness. The mercantile and professional bourgeoisie – together with the liberal fraction of the noble class – were, however, loath to go on extending moral or financial credit to a state which continued to conjugate public interest with the entrenched privileges of the aristocracy. As a social force, public opinion stretched out and reached every corner of this

increasingly commercialized society. As an intellectual construct, moreover, 'public opinion' was too closely tied into the cultural hegemony
established by the professions and the new organs of civic sociability to
be plausibly invoked by a monarch who seemed to be indissolubly wedded
to the maintenance of the institutions of privilege. The Nation, credit,
public opinion, professionalism, and civic sociability had become woven
into a spider's web in which privilege became helplessly stuck – and was
then devoured. Far from the financial crisis of 1789 being, as the
Revisionists contend, somehow extrinsic to earlier social developments,
it was in many ways the apotheosis of the social, political, and cultural
developments I have been outlining.

The influence of the professional classes upon the Revolution was not
only at the level of cultural hegemony. When one looks at political
participation in 1789 and in the following revolutionary decade, what
strikes one at once is the importance of the professional classes at every
level and their interpenetration with other branches of the bourgeoisie.
Cobban's original perception that declining venal officers and liberal
professions dominated the Constituent Assembly is at least a starting-
point, though his analysis is misguided: venal officer-holders were not
necessarily a declining group; and anyway further research has shown
that their representation in later revolutionary assemblies fell drastically,
while that of professional men (including, increasingly, what one might call
career or professional politicians) stayed consistently high. Moreover, as
Lynn Hunt has brilliantly shown, local administration was very much in
the hands of lawyers, physicians, notaries, and local bureaucrats, often
with a good admixture of the merchants and manufacturers found only
rather rarely at national level. In 1793 and 1794, a bigger input of petty
bourgeois elements – shopkeepers, artisans, and minor clerks – is often
visible, and in the countryside wealthier peasants got a look in. But this
really only underlines the bourgeois and professional orientation. Recent
work on Parisian local politics confirms the general picture: the districts of
1789–90, as R. B. Rose has shown, were a fairly representative bourgeois
cross-section; while incisive work on the Parisian sansculottes of Year II,
conducted by Richard Cobb and others in his wake, has revealed the more
solidly bourgeois backgrounds of many militants who, for reasons of
political expediency, deflated their social rank in the democratic
atmosphere of the Terror.

The analysis of Edmund Burke, cited by Lynn Hunt, that the Revolution
was the work of 'moneyed men, merchants, principal tradesmen and men
of letters' thus seems pretty accurate, as a description of both the key
participants in the political process after 1789 and many of the major
proponents of 'civic sociability' before that date. It is important, in the
light of my earlier arguments, however, to view Burke's 'men of letters'
not as an autonomous, free-standing group, but rather as the vocal

representatives of the professions. This interpretation clashes, I am aware, with Robert Darnton's fine studies of men of letters as a significant influence on the revolutionary process. However, to classify men of letters as an autonomous group seems to distort and to underplay the professional and corporative framework within which such men had done – and maybe continued to do – their thinking. Clearly the concept had an important role in revolutionary ideology and myth-making. In particular, there is a brand of counter-revolutionary interpretation which rejoices at seeing the Revolution allegedly in the hands of an anomic pack of Grub Street low-life, seedy intellectuals cut off from any experience of real-life political problems, and consequently wild and utopian in their aims. The professional prism puts quite a different, more solid, more pragmatic, more market-orientated view on the revolutionary bourgeoisie. The latter is no more synonymous with Darnton's riff-raff intelligentsia than Old Regime professionals are with David Bien's reactionary army officers.

I have suggested that there was a far closer, organic link between the development of capitalism in the eighteenth century and the emergence of more 'market-conscious', and public-spirited intellectual élites than historians have normally allowed. The attractiveness of this hypothesis is amplified when we look at much of the social and economic legislation carried out by successive revolutionary assemblies which would do so much to shape nineteenth-century France. If one assumes that the liberal professionals who made up such an important constitutive part of the assemblies are socially autonomous from the economic bourgeoisie, then reforms as classically capitalistic in their character as the formation of a national market, the abolition of guilds, the introduction of uniform weights and measures, the removal of seigneurial excrescences, the redefinition of property rights come to be seen as the product of conspiracy, accident, or a hidden hand. The impregnation of the bourgeoisie with market values, the 'bourgeoisification' of the professions, and the organic links developing between the professions and mercantile groups prior to 1789, on the other hand, help to provide a more viable political and cultural framework for understanding why such reforms were introduced. These phenomena constitute a 'silent bourgeois revolution' which was the essential precursor of the noisier, messier, and better-known events of 1789.[16] They also help to explain why one of the most durable and toughest legislative legacies of the revolutionary years should be the so-called 'career open to talents', a principle which was indeed tailored to the career interests and civic sense of the liberal professions by, precisely, the members of the liberal professions who dominated the assemblies.

A great deal more work still needs to be done on relations between the different branches of the bourgeoisie – the different types of professionals, the landed and commercial bourgeoisie, and so on – as well as what Colin

Lucas has called the 'stress zones' between them. These relationships, moreover, shifted, sometimes radically as a result of the revolutionary experience. The quotation by Barère with which I began is symptomatic of the problem: Barère attacks commerce and speculation from a political viewpoint; yet, on the other hand, his rhetoric connives in a good commercial operation. We need to know more about how the Revolution affected the professions, and the arguments about professional standards, quality control, educational requirements, and public interest which had percolated within them throughout the late Enlightenment. The events of 1789 moved these debates which had gripped the professions under the Old Regime on to a new level, and their subsequent history highlighted the mixed and sometimes contradictory legacy of the revolutionary experience.

There was to be, it seems, no single trajectory for the professions in the 1790s, nor any common destiny for their members. The abolition of venal office on 4 August and the enunciation of the principle of the career open to talent in the Declaration of the Rights of Man on August 26, 1789 left a great deal of room for debate and disagreement of how professionalism should be conjugated with the exigencies of citizenship. The response of each of the professions differed, and new fault-lines emerged out of the process. The furore within the army is relatively well-known. How far did the rights of soldiers as citizens entitle them to political activities which, in the opinion of many of their supporters, nullified professional *esprit de corps*? The path towards the patriotic citizen-soldier of Year II passed by way of the Nancy mutiny and its repression and the emigration of 60 per cent of the putatively 'professional' noble officer corps. The late 1790s and the Napoleonic period were to see the reassertion of a more corporative version of professionalism, with the sacrifice of many of the more democratic procedures of Year II, such as election of officers.

The experience of the clergy was rather different. The Civil Constitution of the Clergy may in many respects be viewed as the charter of a professionalized secular clergy, establishing as it did democratic procedures, rational hierarchies, and a well-founded career structure. Yet civic professionalism fell foul of corporative professionalism: many priests found it difficult to accept the loss of their monopoly of spiritual services consequent on the enunciation of the principle of freedom of conscience, and jibbed at National Assembly's failure to consult either the Church as a corporate entity or its hierarchical head, the Pope. The 1790s was to prove an often tragic backcloth against which the clergy rethought their attitudes towards ecclesiastical hierarchy, conscience, and civic responsibility.

A similar reassessment was necessary for the medical and legal professions and for the state bureaucracy. The career open to talents and the attack on privilege within corporate hierarchies justified the attack on the Old Regime bureaucracy, the abolition of many of its services (such as the

General Farm, probably the most corporatively professionalized of all state services), the closure of legal and medical faculties, and the dissolution of first attorneys, then barristers. By the late 1790s, however, a barrage of complaints emerged from all quarters which highlighted how the opening up of a free field for medical and legal practice had damaged public interest and (so it was said) standards of professional competence. The public was, it was argued, prey to medical charlatans, legal sharks, and corrupt and ill-trained clerks. The reassertion of a corporative hierarchy and the reintroduction of better training methods under the Thermidorian Convention, the Directory, and the Consulate attested to a reworking of the relationship between profession, state, and public.

There is much about the civic-inspired deregulation of many of the professions in the 1790s and their corporative reprofessionalization later in the decade which remains obscure. Certainly the professions were transformed in the Revolutionary decade – a fact palpable in the disappearance of many pre-revolutionary titles such as *procureur, avocat, chirurgien,* and so on. After the perils of the 'free field' had been exposed, it looked as though for most the best guarantee of professional success after 1789 was state utility. Hence the unrivalled prestige of the armed forces from the late 1790s; hence the formidable strengthening of the state bureaucracy; hence the emergence of a prestigious scientific profession, very much under the wing of the state; hence too the arguments of state utility advanced by doctors and lawyers in their attempts to win government support. The civic and corporative models of professionalization which had emerged in the Ancien Régime were transformed by the experience of the 1790s; but in broad terms, it was something akin to the corporative model which often prevailed, while maintaining the career open to talent which the civic model had required. The Revolution had changed both the context of and the protagonists in the debate over professionalism. And the transformed professions were to make a massive and well-documented contribution to the character of nineteenth-century France.

The professions remained after 1800, finally, still very much tributary to the market for their services. Though the state was often a valued client, most depended very considerably on the overall situation of the economy. As the Revisionists have pointed out with an often wearisome frequency, the Revolution did not mark a transition to industrialism in the French economy. (Actually, Georges Lefebvre and Albert Soboul seem to have been pretty much aware of that fact too, as their balanced assessments of the sometimes contradictory social and economic legacy of the Revolution should make clear.) France's economy was still in the commercial mould, and the professions inevitably reflected that fact. *Pace* many Revisionists, however, the French economy was not irredeemably traditionalist nor stagnatingly precapitalist. France continued its measured and balanced way towards industrialization. Indeed growth in the early nineteenth century, even before the creation of a national rail network, is now being recognized as having been far stronger than has often been thought. In that progress, the Revolution had been perhaps a less heroic and dramatic episode than the Old Marxist Orthodoxy would maintain; though it certainly had far more importance, and positive influence, than the New Revolutionist Orthodoxy would allow. The legislative achievement of successive Revolutionary assemblies and the eradication of Old Regime privilege provided a more appropriate environment for commercial capitalism in general to develop, and the bourgeoisie in particular to prosper. France moved slowly towards its industrializing goal at the end of a bourgeois nineteenth century for which the stage had been set by a bourgeois revolution, Revisionist reports of whose sad demise I persist in finding greatly exaggerated.

Notes

1 *Archives parlementaires de 1787 à 1860*, 1st ser., 19 (1884), 433 (session 4 Oct. 1790).

2 G. V. Taylor, 'Bourgeoisie', in B. Rothaus and S. F. Scott, *Historical Dictionary of the French Revolution*, 2 vols. (Westport, Conn., 1985), i. p. 122.

3 L. Hunt, *Politics, Culture and Class in the French Revolution* (London, 1986) p. 9.

4 K. M. Baker, ed. *The French Revolution and the Creation of Modern Political Culture*, i. *The Political Culture of the Old Regime* (Oxford, 1987).

5 M. Fitzsimmons, *the Parisian Order of Barristers and the French Revolution* (Cambridge, Mass., 1987), p. 197.

6 G. V. Taylor, 'Noncapitalist Wealth and the Origins of the French Revolution', *American Historical Review*, 72 (1967), p. 491.

7 F. Braudel and E. Labrousse, *Histoire économique et sociale de la France, ii, 1660–1789* (Paris, 1970), p. 416.

8 J. C. Perrot, *Genèse d'une ville moderne: Caen au XVIIIe siècle*, 2 vols. (Paris, 1975), i. p. 260–2.

9 Citation from Marchand, 1769, quoted by E. Le Roy Ladurie in G. Duby, ed. *Histoire de la France urbaine, iii, La Ville classique (De la Renaissance aux Révolutions)* (Paris, 1981), p. 289.

10 G. Feyel, 'La Presse provinciale au XVIIIe siècle: géographie d'un réseau', *Revue historique*, 272 (1984), p. 368.

11 J.-P. Bardet, *Rouen aux XVIIe et XVIIIe siècles: Les Mutations d'un espace social* (Paris, 1983), p. 269.

12 Cited in F. Brunot, *Histoire de la langue française des origines à nos jours*, ix (Paris, 1967), pp. 944–5.

13 V. Azimi, '1789: L'Echo des employés, ou le nouveau discours administratif', *XVIIIe Siècle*, 21 (1989), p. 134.

14 Azimi, '1789: L'Echo des employés ou le nouveau discours administratif', p. 134.

15 E. J. Sieyès, *Qu'est-ce que le Tiers Etat?* ed. S. E. Finer (Chicago, 1963), pp. 63–4.

16 The phrase 'silent bourgeois revolution' comes from D. Blackbourn and G.
   Eley, *The Peculiarities of German History: Bourgeois Society and Politics in
   Nineteenth-Century Germany* (Oxford, 1982).

5

Politics, culture and the origins of the French Revolution

SARAH MAZA

'Revisionist' interpretations of the French Revolution and its causes no
longer deserve that label. In the quarter of a century since Alfred Cobban
published *The Social Interpretation of the French Revolution*, the rejection
of Marxian categories and, in most cases, of any socioeconomic explanation of the upheaval that began in 1789 has become the new orthodoxy.[1]
The overhaul of the field that occurred in the wake of Cobban's challenge
to the rise-of-the-bourgeoisie model has been likened to a Kuhnian scientific revolution. Before the early 1960s, the explanatory power of a class-
struggle model for the Revolution seemed as commonsensically obvious to
historians as the sun's motion around the earth did to pre-Copernicans. In
both cases, however, the established, 'normal' paradigm eventually collapsed under the pressure of an accumulated mass of new empirical
evidence that contradicted it.

It is no doubt easier for humanity to survive temporarily without a
coherent view of the causes of the French Revolution than without a
satisfactory explanation of the cosmos, although lecturers in Western
civilization classes and graduate students facing their orals have at times
been inclined to doubt this. In fact, the search for a new paradigm got
underway as soon as the old one was challenged. But innovators are often
reluctant to recognize the ultimate implications of their challenge to
orthodoxy: in the same way that Tycho Brahe attempted to use Coperni-
can astronomy while clinging to the idea of a fixed earth and a moving sun,
the post-Cobban years witnessed several attempts at formulating a non-
Marxian but still primarily social explanation of the French Revolution.

Cobban himself saw the Revolution as essentially a political struggle,
but one that was fuelled by social conflicts as an heterogeneous 'bourgeoisie' of landowners, *rentiers*, and office-holders reasserted its dominance over the growing ranks of the propertyless. In a classic article
published in 1973, Colin Lucas located social tensions more precisely,

Reprinted in full, except for notes, from: *Journal of Modern History,* 61 (1989), pp. 703–23.

and higher up on the social scale: it was demographic pressure on traditional channels of social promotion (the army, administration, and law courts), he argued, that created social bottlenecks in a previously fluid process of upward social mobility. The Third Estate, made up of the frustrated central and lower sections of the elite, came naturally to construe its political revolt as a broader struggle of talent against privilege. Demographic pressure and thwarted upward mobility were also invoked by another scholar as explanations of the genesis of revolutionary ideology. In an equally influential piece, Robert Darnton argued that the virulence of prerevolutionary and revolutionary pamphleteering was shaped by the experiences of growing numbers of ambitious young writers embittered by their exclusion from the closed world of literary patronage.

Neither Cobban's nor Lucas's theses, nor any other of what one might term the 'soft revisionist' persuasion, flourished as *the* satisfactory alternative to Marxian orthodoxy, no doubt because they lacked the all-encompassing coherence of the latter. It could be argued, after all, that most societies harbour their share of disgruntled social climbers and bitter would-be intellectuals and that it requires more than a population boom to transform social frustration into revolution. Cut loose from economic determinism, such social tensions seem a poor predictor of the upheaval that began in 1789. But while some historians were still trying to reinterpret the tensions of eighteenth-century French society, others were beginning to ponder the most radical implications of the revisionist position as they had been formulated as early as 1967 by an American scholar, George Taylor. Taylor's research on eighteenth-century economic and financial history had led him to an early rejection of the entire Marxist paradigm. Eschewing the search for an alternative social explanation, he bluntly concluded, in a much-quoted phrase, that the French Revolution 'was essentially a political revolution with social consequences and not a social revolution with political consequences.'[2]

It has taken the last two decades for scholars in the field to come to terms with the methodological consequences of Taylor's (and others') 'hard revisionism.' At first the dominant tone was one of gleeful negativism, as leading scholars in the field devoted much of their energy to demonstrating how utterly wrong – at least on the conceptual level – every hallowed Marxist account had been. By the late 1970s, however, the need for a more constructive approach began to push the field in new directions: if the crisis that came to a head in 1789 was in essence political, then the key that would unlock the meaning of the Revolution lay in the political history of the Old Regime, and especially in that of its final decades. In 1980, the first results of this historiographical revolution were given elegant synthetic expression in William Doyle's *Origins of the French Revolution*.

The very organization of Doyle's overview forced readers to come to terms with the magnitude of the change that had taken place in the field. Gone were the obligatory first chapters taking stock of social and economic conditions and reviewing the long-term causes of the Revolution; instead, Doyle devoted the first half of his book to the political collapse of the French Monarchy and the transformation of political life that accompanied it. Only in the second half of the book, which covers the period just before and after the convening of the Estates-General, does Doyle devote several chapters to the conventionally defined groups making up eighteenth-century society – nobility, bourgeoisie, and peasantry – each of which appears in turn on the scene as an adjunct or a catalyst in the political maelstrom of 1788–89. In the opening section of Doyle's overview the emphasis falls heavily on contingency, on the failures of intelligence and will of the rulers and ministers who presided over the debacle of the monarchy. Louis XV and his successor showed ineptitude in their choice of advisers and allowed disgraced ministers to organize factions that disrupted the conduct of affairs of state; they and their ministers caved in all too easily to the pressure of political opposition from the Parlement of Paris, which could easily have been resisted; and the ultimate effort at reform, the convening of an Assembly of Notables in 1787, was undermined by Calonne's miscalculations and his high-handed treatment of the body he himself had assembled. In short, Doyle's authoritative synthesis drew from a range of recent work in the field the conclusion that there was nothing preordained about the crisis that broke out in 1789, that the drift to revolution was the result of an accidental convergence of causes, most of them (in the broad sense) political.

For most historians writing in the 1980s, of course, 'politics' can no longer be narrowly defined as a jockeying for power played out in the highest spheres of government. For all Doyle's emphasis on contingency and personality, his account devotes a substantial amount of attention to what Jürgen Habermas called 'structural change in the public sphere.'[3] His opening chapters do not chronicle the rise and fall of Turgot, Necker, and Calonne; they address such topics as 'The System of Government,' 'Opposition,' and 'Public Opinion.' The organizing principle of Doyle's synthesis (taken here as the standard 'revisionist' account) seems to be that the nature of political life was slowly but profoundly altered in the decades between 1750 and 1789. A series of ill-timed bankruptcies destroyed what was left of the government's financial credit; religious struggles over Jansenism and the expulsion of the Jesuits, as well as the humiliating setbacks of the Seven Years' War, undermined the monarchy's moral credit and damaged what was left of the king's aura of sacrality. At the same time, the Parlement's protracted struggles with the monarchy impressed upon the minds of many subjects such notions as the necessity of constitutional government and the legitimacy of political opposition. Most important, the spread of literacy, the influence wielded by dissenting men of letters, and the ever-increasing volume of propaganda churned out by all parties in pamphlet form all contributed to the rise of a new locus of power, that of 'public opinion.' The failure of the last two monarchs and their ministers can mainly be chalked up to their inability to adapt to the changing conditions in which power had to be exercised after 1750. More than a 'political crisis,' the French Revolution can be seen as the culmination of a 'crisis of the public sphere.'

This new focus on the public sphere was given its most important theoretical expression a decade ago in a brilliantly iconoclastic piece by the French scholar François Furet. In the early 1960s Furet had coauthored with Denis Richet the only major revisionist account of the Revolution to come out of France, and in subsequent years he pursued, in the form of articles, a sort of guerrilla warfare against the French Marxist establishment in the field. In 1978, Furet's polemical pieces against what he termed the Marxist 'catechism' were reprinted as *Penser la Révolution Française*, along with the new and much longer essay provocatively entitled 'The French Revolution Is Over.' [*See* Reading 2.] The title of this, Furet's most famous piece, alludes to his contention that, since Michelet and Jaurès, orthodox accounts of the Revolution, be they Socialist or Left-Republican, had been flawed by a complete lack of distance from the event. For ideological reasons, such historians had taken the words of the revolutionaries at face value and in doing so condemned themselves to writing 'commemorative history,' to an endless reproduction of 'the French Revolution's illusion about itself.'[4]

The conceptual framework for Furet's reexamination of the meaning of revolutionary language came from the work of Alexis de Tocqueville, whose writings on the French Revolution had been up to then mostly ignored by French scholars in the field. Furet, however, took seriously Tocqueville's argument that the French Revolution left the nation's social and economic structures largely untouched and that where administrative matters were concerned it reinforced and accelerated a process of centralization that had been underway for at least a century. But Tocqueville had stopped short of spelling out the implications of his paradox where the revolutionary process itself was concerned: if the real story was one of continuity, Furet asked, then why the *perception of change*? Why such insistent proclamation in speech and symbol of the idea of a complete break with the past? The object of Furet's theoretical investigation was precisely this disjuncture between reality and perception. Drawing implicitly on the textual preoccupations of poststructuralist thinkers such as Jacques Derrida, Furet insisted that the meaning of the Revolution lay precisely in its language, its paradoxical 'discourse of rupture.' In Lynn Hunt's vivid formulation, Furet offered a vision of the French Revolution as 'a great talking machine whose grinding gears drowned out the insidious truth of administrative continuity.'[5]

The logic of Furet's argument (and his ideological purpose) led to a highlighting of the Jacobin dictatorship and the Reign of Terror: this was no accidental escalation of events, he maintained, no regrettable response to an emergency situation, but the most characteristic and pristine expression of the divorce between the objective and subjective meanings of the Revolution. Here again Furet's argument extended and completed Tocqueville's. The triumph of the highly abstract and Manichaean ideology of 1793 with its glorification of unbounded state power could be traced back, ironically, to the high-handed administrative practices of the Old Regime monarchy; devoid of political experience and denied access to positions of administrative responsibility, educated Frenchmen fell all too easily under the sway of men of letters before the Revolution. After 1789, the power vacuum left gaping by the collapse of traditional authority was quickly filled by the political 'illusions' peddled by inexperienced ideologues. Entirely removed from sociopolitical realities, as before the Revolution, the rhetoric of political innovation nonetheless invested the very centre of political life and became a force unto itself: 'a network of signs completely dominated political life.'[6] But even as they claimed to speak for 'the people,' to articulate the irresistible will of 'the Nation,' Robespierre and his colleagues did nothing more than resurrect and reinforce, under another guise, the ideological structures of administrative absolutism. This was Tocquevillian irony with a vengeance.

Furet's controversial but undeniably creative approach to the political culture of the French Revolution was shaped by two major currents in contemporary French intellectual life, whose coupling would have been unlikely in the English-speaking world. On the one hand, his ideas grew out of militantly antitotalitarian (mostly anti-Marxist) concerns, the rearguard settling of intellectual scores with the French Communist party known locally as *libéralisme*; on the other hand, his approach drew much of its innovative strength from the intellectual radicalism of deconstruction, with its emphasis on the autonomy of textual dynamics.

This explains, perhaps, the discomfort with which Furet's ideas have often been received in the Anglo-American world where historians sympathetic to the former would be likely to resist the latter, and vice versa. Nonetheless, the publication of *Penser la Révolution française* represented the most important turning point in the recent historiography of the French Revolution, the most coherent (if extreme) statement of a new position since the eclipse of the Marxist paradigm. Anglo-American revisionists had tended to argue, as did Furet himself earlier in his career, that the genesis and subsequent course of the Revolution were a matter of contingency, of historical 'accident'; Furet's new work suggested a structural logic to the process that culminated in 1793, a logic that had to do with culture and politics (and specifically the culture *of* politics) rather than social and economic forces. In the process, it contributed mightily to restoring Tocqueville's classic analysis as the central paradigm to be reckoned with by historians in the field.

The voluminous collection of essays entitled *The Political Culture of the Old Regime*, edited by Keith Michael Baker, is the first major product of the Tocquevillian revival triggered by the work of Furet. The volume grew out of a conference held in Chicago in 1986, in which Furet himself played a major role as one of the organizers; it is the first of three such collections in a broader project entitled *The French Revolution and the Creation of Modern Political Culture*, the next two volumes of which are to be based on conferences held in Oxford and Paris in 1987 and 1988, respectively. This is a prestigious enterprise designed to coincide with the Revolution's bicentennial: the first volume has been lavishly (and expensively) produced by Pergamon Press, and most of its twenty-seven contributors are established leaders in the field from American, French, and British universities. This volume contains essays that extend back in time to encompass the entire early modern period, and it is divided into clusters of topics covering the ideology and culture of the Old Regime state, its relations with society, political and intellectual dissent, the prerevolutionary crisis, and the genesis of new political concepts.

The choice of specific themes (which were assigned to the participants) amounts to what could be seen as an ambitious effort to test empirically the three major hypotheses that make up Tocqueville's argument in *The Old Regime and the French Revolution*. First, Tocqueville traces the origins of the revolutionary crisis back to the centralizing efforts of the monarchical administration, which asserted itself starting in the seventeenth century at the expense of local and corporate bodies; second, he argues that the social fragmentation and political immaturity that resulted from the state's predatory behaviour allowed the triumph of highly abstract and politically irresponsible forms of ideological dissent; finally, in a brilliantly ironic twist, Tocqueville suggests that the monarchy and its servants were sufficiently affected by those very dissenting ideologies to embark on the belated efforts at reform that precipitated the political crisis. The levelling of corporate society, the triumph of ideological abstraction, the political suicide of the monarchy: it is the welding of these themes that makes for the beauty and force of Tocqueville's argument. But can each of these in turn withstand the test of empirical evidence?

It is Tocqueville's first (and most fundamental) thesis, the extension of state power at the expense of corporate bodies, that is most drastically called into question by some of the essays in this volume. A synoptic view of the evolution of the French monarchy seems initially to confirm the Tocquevillian pattern. Michel Antoine's opening essay offers an elegantly erudite version of a classic case. The French monarchy, he argues, originally defined itself and behaved as a judicial power whose primary function was to arbitrate between lesser judicial bodies; it was the pressure of circumstances such as the Wars of Religion that led the state to assert its control by increasing its administrative powers. This evolution from *monarchie judiciaire* to *monarchie administrative* was reflected, as Antoine astutely remarks, in the linguistic shift whereby such verbs as *gouverner* and *administrer* came to be used intransitively: one no longer governed a province; one governed, period.

This long-term shift in the functions and very meaning of the monarchical institution affected the rituals of power as well as its language. Ralph Giesey's contribution charts the seventeenth-century migration of royal pomp from 'state ceremonials' to 'court ritual.' The former, including royal funerals, coronations, ceremonial *entrées*, and *lits de justice*, occurred at irregular intervals in variable locations and enshrined both the perpetuity of royal power and the king's function as judicial mediator. In the second half of his reign, Louis XIV ceased entirely to perform such ceremonies, opting instead for the sedentary and quotidian rituals of court etiquette. This bespoke a de facto extension and bureaucratization of royal power, which was now understood 'as operating normally and civilly, rather than remotely and capriciously.'[7] The paradox inherent in Giesey's and Antoine's essays, taken together, is that the more closely royal power centred upon the person and dwelling of the king, the more impersonal and bureaucratic it in fact became.

The increasing powers taken on by the royal administration would seem to entail a corresponding decrease in the authority wielded by other groups; some of the material offered here does indeed support such a contention. Dominique Julia, for instance, chronicles the collapse, after 1750, of the traditional political cooperation between the monarch and his higher clergy. A onetime partner in the government by virtue of the theory *des deux puissances*, the clergy found itself repeatedly opposed and silenced by the monarchy on a succession of important issues: the civil rights of Jansenists and Protestants, the expulsion of the Jesuits, the circulation of heretical books. Politically browbeaten and internally divided, the clergy gradually retreated into the conduct of its own affairs. Professional corporations and artisanal guilds, including the powerful Six-Corps of Paris, were no more able to assert themselves politically than was the clergy, or so at least argues Jacques Revel. Turgot's attempted suppression of the guilds in 1776, Revel argues, briefly provoked a defensive political furor that exaggerated the importance of such institutions; from their partial restoration in the fall of 1776 until their final demise in 1791, corporations and guilds remained as quiescent as they had been before the crisis. And yet the Tocquevillian vision of a society cowed into servile 'equality' by a top-heavy state is belied by what we know of the realities of eighteenth-century French urban life, with its conspicuous displays of hierarchical pomp and loud assertions of corporate pride.

It has long been a commonplace to remark that royal power in France somehow depended on the existence of a highly corporate society; in a pathbreaking article, and arguably the single most innovative contribution to this volume, David Bien exposes the nuts-and-bolts reasons why this was, and continued to be, the case. The eighteenth-century French state, as is well known, lurched from one financial crisis to the next, bedevilled by a staggering national debt, costly military expenditures, rising taxes, and a general loss of public confidence. Given its poor and ever-deteriorating credit standing, Bien asks, how did the state manage to secure from its subjects the long-term loans it so desperately needed? The answer to this puzzle, as Bien explains it, resides in the existence of a two-tiered system of credit that drew upon and reinforced the values and structure of local societies.

Over the two centuries preceding the Revolution, French kings had found an important source of periodic revenue in the sale of offices: in return for their capital investment, office-holders acquired a paid public function, a small but regular income from the state, and, most important, the compound of fiscal advantages and intangible social benefits known as 'privilege.' The capital garnered from the sale of offices amounted, in effect, to a sort of perpetual debt secured by the monarch, since office-holders could not reclaim their investment – nor, in all likelihood, would they ever wish to do so. For the monarchs this was a never-ending source of revenue: not only were new offices constantly created and sold, but if the value of an office increased (if, for instance, the non-state income it generated grew appreciably), the state could swoop down and demand its share of capital gains in an operation euphemistically labelled an *augmentation de gages.* But how could large numbers of office-buyers, not all of whom were prodigiously wealthy, secure the capital necessary to invest in an office in the first place, or to retain it if its market value increased? The answer is that an office-buyer or holder usually enjoyed very good personal credit locally and that such an individual almost invariably belonged to one of the many *corps* making up the urban elite. Given the local statute of these corporate bodies, and the fact that their debts were collectively assumed and therefore a good risk, they could easily and quickly borrow money from fellow-townsmen at an interest rate of 5 per cent. For local lenders, this represented a much safer, more convenient, and more profitable investment than long-term state bonds, which barely yielded 1 or 2 per cent. The crown was able in this way to overcome its poor credit by borrowing money indirectly (and efficiently) via the confidence enjoyed locally by corporate bodies; it was financially dependent on the existence of a system of corporate power and privilege.

The two fine essays contributed by Gail Bossenga and Hilton Root are grist for this mill: Bossenga shows that in urban power struggles the crown

tended to throw its weight behind whichever groups were best able to help
it to secure revenues, while Root makes a case for the royal administration's dependence, for fiscal purposes, on rural communal institutions and
on corporate methods of tax collection. In political as well as fiscal
matters, the reality was often one of pragmatic collusion between the
royal administration and powerful privileged bodies. Historians have
been mesmerized, William Doyle argues, by the appearance of a toe-to-
toe struggle between king and Parlement, by the magistrates' noisy claims
to power and Louis XV's no less shrill assertions of authority; these
clashes have drawn attention away from the more mundane functioning
(at least until 1771) of a stable system of quasi-constitutional government
based on cooperation between the two parties. The informed arguments
advanced by Bien, Bossenga, Root, and Doyle should lead us to rethink the
accepted notion that the eighteenth-century state tried to ride roughshod
over traditional governing bodies: it could not, in several respects, afford to
do so.

And yet the quiet hum of daily administration was drowned out by the
loud clatter of ideological dissent, by the voices of philosophes flailing out
at *l'infâme*, of physiocrats denouncing the evils of the guild system, of
magistrates excoriating despotic government. 'Thus,' wrote Tocqueville,
'alongside the traditional and confused, not to say chaotic, social system of
the day there was gradually built up in men's minds an imaginary ideal
society in which all was simple, uniform, coherent, equitable, and rational
in the full sense of the term.' This development, he argued, grew out of the
anomalous authority wielded by men of letters who, precisely *because* they
lacked political experience, could hold sway over a nation equally innocent
of the pragmatic realities of government and become 'the leading politicians of the age.'[8] How dangerously naive were, in fact, the dissenting
political ideologies that circulated in late eighteenth-century France? And
to what extent can oppositional ideas and propaganda of any sort be
attributed to the influence of 'men of letters' estranged from the political
process?

Among the several essays in the volume that deal with the history of
ideas, those by Lucien Jaume and (to a lesser degree) Pierre Rosanvallon
come closest to adhering to a strictly Tocquevillian line. Jaume's purpose
is to establish the continuity between the French idea of 'subject' and that
of 'citizen' by linking the 'absolutist' traditions represented by Hobbes
and Rousseau to the political ideologies of the prerevolution and revolution. He argues that both notions implied subjection to an omnipotent
sovereign; that in both cases that sovereign was construed as an external
entity rather than an emanation of the bonds between individuals; that
monarchical and revolutionary 'absolutism' rested on a similar if at times
implicit, repression of individual political and economic liberties.
Rosanvallon's essay sketches out a fundamental opposition between the

ideas of France's foremost utilitarian thinker, Helvetius, and the English tradition represented by Mandeville, Hume, Bentham, and Smith: the upshot is a critique of the French utilitarian tradition for its failure to articulate the congruence between private and public interest, with Helvétius relegated in the end to the dubious company of Rousseau, Sieyès, and Saint-Just. If some of the conclusions reached in these essays are undoubtedly valid, their relentless negativism (and their lionizing of the *tradition libérale*) is troubling; one is left with the uncomfortable suspicion that they tell us more about French intellectual life in the 1980s than in the 1780s.

Much more balanced is Mona Ozouf's stimulating discussion of the birth of the notion of 'public opinion.' Ozouf traces the gradual allocation of moral and political authority to an abstraction, the 'tribunal' of public opinion, whose anonymous but public judgements were invoked rhetorically, long before the Revolution, by servants of the monarchy such as Malesherbes and Necker. The idea of public opinion emerged just as the transcendent, sacral qualities of royal authority were being called into question and served as its functional replacement. But whereas the physiocrats argued that 'opinion' could be equated with self-evident reason, and was therefore unitary and infallible, other writers like Mably, Garat, and Suard wrestled with the problems inherent in deducing 'opinion' from a multiplicity of conflicting interests and judgements. Ozouf concludes that the Revolution at different stages embodied both of these definitions of 'public opinion': the archaic-authoritarian and the modern-democratic.

The conclusions that can be reached from a reading of the texts alone are often ambiguous, and at worst tedentious. Socially grounded approaches to eighteenth-century literary life – in the form of individual or group biographies, histories of intellectual institutions, or the social history of ideas – should yield more decisive answers to the question of whether Tocqueville was right in his assessment of the influence wielded by prerevolutionary literati. Robert Darnton's essay provides solid evidence of the growing importance of writers and writing in the second half of the eighteenth century. Whereas in 1757 the almanac *La France littéraire* listed 1187 writers, some three decades later 2819 individuals were counted as such. Darnton's sociological analysis of the group, however, hardly suggests alienation: a majority of these writers lived in the more prosperous and culturally advanced areas of northern France; with their average age hovering around fifty they hardly qualified as young rebels; and most of them belonged by birth to the traditional Old Regime elites of the nobility, clergy, and urban professionals. But Darnton's view of the eighteenth-century literary world has long been that of a community sharply divided between academic mandarins and Grub Street hacks; he concludes here with a reiteration of that view, a lively contrast between the conservative

Rivarol's cruel satire of penniless scribblers, *Les Gens de lettres*, and a prerevolutionary play to the glory of Grub Street written by future Jacobin Fabre d'Eglantine.

If Darnton's paper explicitly confirms Tocqueville's argument by pointing to the growing importance of *gens de lettres*, and, in certain sectors at least, to their growing anomie, Daniel Roche's essay on the politics of national and provincial academies no less explicitly challenges it. Literary and scientific academies, Roche insists, showed no signs of alienation from social and political power structures, but neither were they subservient to the monarchy. Rather, they collaborated in vital ways with the monarchical administration, providing it with counsellors and technicians and with informed and enlightened forums in which the pressing social and scientific issues of the day were debated; in the process, they 'broke their way into the political arena,' bridging the gap between states and society.[9]

Where, then, are we to locate the 'political Enlightenment'? In the polite, earnestly progressive debates of the academies, or in the venom that flowed from garrets and underground presses? And was the chasm between those two universes really as wide as Darnton insists it was? One of Roche's arguments suggests the beginnings of an answer to this quandary. The *sociabilité culturelle* of the academies, he says, brought together on the local level members of the nobility with the bourgeoisie of merit and talent; the academies represented, in this respect, a blueprint for the more open political life of the revolutionary decade. The argument could be extended to many other forms of less institutionalized intellectual exchange: the Republic of Letters as a whole may have served, as Habermas and others have argued, as a prototype for the politics of the republican public sphere, and this regardless of the exact message delivered by any given individual or group.

Ideological dissent and propaganda did indeed pervade the public sphere in the second half of the eighteenth century, and they flowed, as we are now discovering, from a much broader array of groups than just 'men of letters.' The systematic character assassination of Chancellor Maupeou carried out in instalments in Pidansat de Mairobert's *Journal historique*, for example, or the provocations regularly dished out by the renegade lawyer Nicolas Linguet in his London-based *Annales Politiques* hardly qualify as conventional literary or political texts; and yet these men and others, as Jeremy Popkin demonstrates, pioneered in the 1770s and 1780s all of the characteristic techniques of revolutionary journalism, including mudslinging, sloganeering, and the hammering out of explicitly partisan positions. They invented a form of expression that redefined politics, for as Popkin points out journalism was uniquely suited to highlighting the temporal instability of the established order: 'It alone was a medium suited to a politics of constant change.'

Mairobert and Linguet were of course maverick types who could hardly be expected, given the marginal nature of their enterprises, to glorify the status quo. More startling, no doubt, is the discovery that antiestablishment propaganda was produced in massive quantities by the establishment itself. The Parlement of Paris has long enjoyed the reputation of having been the realm's chief troublemaker, although it was assumed that the magistrates' activism served the selfish political interests of the nobility. Of late, however, the Parlement's stock has been rising again, thanks in particular to the work of Dale Van Kley. Religion, Van Kley has forcefully reminded us, was no peripheral concern in the Age of Enlightenment; opposition to the monarchy often crystallized at mid-century around the deathbeds of devout Jansenists who were denied the last rites for refusing to bow to the dictates of the royally backed Church hierarchy. The Parlement of Paris's role as the main champion (and theorist) of Jansenist resistance had a direct impact on popular political consciousness: as Van Kley has elsewhere demonstrated, the half-crazed domestic servant Robert-François Damiens, who in 1757 stabbed and nearly killed Louis XV, had absorbed much of his political bitterness from masters who were magistrates in the Parlement.

By the 1780s, of course, the Augustinian heresy was no longer explicitly a political issue. But the concepts and terms familiar to embattled Jansenism, Van Kley argues here, survived into the 1770s and 1780s, merging easily with the Parlement's political resistance to ministerial 'despotism': the radical ecclesiology that gave pride of place to laymen like the magistrates, the conciliarism that recast the king as a 'minister' or 'mandatory,' the Gallicanism that shaded easily into nationalism, the glorification of the law as 'testimony' or 'truth.'[10] Such was the force and success of the Parlement's *jansénisant* constitutional rhetoric that the crown began to respond in kind, hiring its own pamphleteers to hammer out the opposing view that the monarchy was the true champion of the people (and specifically of the 'most numerous and useful' portion thereof) against the 'feudal aristocracy' in the courts.

Although the suggestion that royalist and ministerial pamphleteers churned out rhetoric that fanned the flames of class war may seem surprising, it is confirmed by Vivian Gruder's exhaustive study of the pamphlet literature of the late 1780s. In a bid to recapture the lead in public opinion, defenders of royal policies turned increasingly in 1787 and 1788 to denunciations not only of the *parlementaire* magistracy but also of the high nobility and clergy, and indeed of the wealthy in general. Van Kley concludes, in an important insight, that the explosive political rhetoric of 1789, as represented most famously by Sieyès's *What Is the Third Estate?* can be read as 'a sort of Hegelian synthesis between the *parlementaire* thesis of national sovereignty and the ministerial antithesis of the ahistorical nation as Third Estate.'[11]

We are a long way from Tocqueville's attribution of ideological dissent to the abstract musings of naive intellectuals. If we are to ascribe the political ferment of the prerevolutionary decades to the influence of 'men of letters,' we will have to broaden that category to include anyone who could hold a pen long enough to deliver himself of a pamphlet – and owing to the prestige and declining cost of the printed word in late eighteenth-century France, this included just about everyone from ministers to paid hacks. One can still plausibly argue that the invasion of the public arena by this multiplicity of competing discourses must have been intimately linked to the weakness and self-contradictions of the monarchy. Did the French monarchy, then, unwittingly clear the ground for its opponents by commit-ting political suicide in its last years?

None of the essays in the volume deal with the state's ill-fated reform attempts prior to the crisis of 1787–89 and their effects upon popular and elite political consciousness. In general, it seems clear that in the second half of the century the monarchy was not endearing itself to most of its subjects. But although both Roger Chartier and Michel Vovelle make valiant efforts in their papers at documenting the deterioration of the royal image in the popular mind, we still have surprisingly little reliable information about popular political attitudes prior to the revolution. The emphasis here is less on the monarchy's long-term political misjudgements, however, than on the short-term decisions in the late 1780s that amounted to a process of ideological, or conceptual, self-obliteration.

The king himself was open to reforming arguments in those final months, and he responded positively to appeals to his humanity and sense of justice. On those grounds, as Vivian Gruder shows, he granted the doubling of the Third Estate and even after the Commons' rebellion, on June 23, 1789, acquiesced to important fiscal and administrative reforms. In the course of that same royal session, however, the royal administration adamantly upheld the principle of three separate orders, less out of a concern to defend the traditional social order, Gruder argues, than as a means of reasserting and buttressing its own political authority. The crown, which had first relied on privilege for fiscal purposes and then denounced it via its pamphleteers, was now using it as a rampart against constitutional change. This hardly made for coherent policy, and by the summer of 1789 the monarchy was reaping the whirlwind it had (partially) sown.

The same sort of incoherence had afflicted the administration's orga-nization of the elections to the Estates-General. The ambiguities that marked the electoral process are hardly surprising given the fact that, as Keith Baker shows us, the definition of 'representation' was very much up for grabs in the late eighteenth century. Few people, perhaps, still held to the absolutist notion that the multiplicity of orders and estates could only be embodied in the single person of the monarch. The Parlements, how-ever, clung to the idea that they 'represented' the king and the people to one another via the judicial process, while the physiocrats sketched out a 'social' definition of representation grounded in property ownership. Although Rousseau repudiated the notion altogether, Sieyès hammered out a workable definition of representation by conflating the Rousseauian General Will with the social categories of the physiocrats. In the winter and spring of 1789, the king and his ministers were forced to improvise an electoral process within the context of this tangle of competing definitions.

Both François Furet and Ran Halévi have chosen to highlight the elections of 1789 for the explicit purpose of illustrating and defending the Tocquevillian thesis of continuity between the Old Regime and the Revolution: 'The question that [the electoral period] poses to the historian,' writes Furet, 'is not that of understanding the break between the Old Regime and the Revolution, but [that] of the manner in which the Old Regime produced the Revolution via the Estates-General.'[12] Furet proceeds to demonstrate that the electoral procedures were a Janus-like compound of 'aristocratic' and 'democratic' elements: they preserved the traditional distinctions between orders yet established a system of numerically proportional representation based (except within the clergy) on fiscal and residential, rather than corporate, criteria. Halévi takes a closer look at the actual implementation of these procedures; drawing on the work of Augustin Cochin as well as his own research, he suggests that the elections were prematurely democratic, artifically separating as they did the nobility from its 'natural sphere of influence' and suddenly promoting 'new, specialized, anonymous and powerful [political] personnel.' He concludes with the ominous remark that the Old Regime in its death throes may have organized in this fashion 'the very first purge of the French Revolution.'[13]

Furet and Halévi are intent on demonstrating that the monarchy should be credited with introducing at least the principles of electoral democracy to the nation, however unwittingly or unwillingly. '[The monarchy] bequeathed democracy to the Revolution,' Furet concludes, 'while offering it its scapegoat.'[14] They are right in insisting that the elections of 1789 have not received the attention they deserve (as opposed to the more archaic *cahiers de doléances*) and that this episode has much to teach us. But their use of the subject for polemical purposes has a strawman quality to it: no serious historian of any persuasion would argue against the general idea that political mobilization of a proto-democratic sort began at least as early as the convening of the Estates-General, and that this was a direct result of governmental decisions. There are better ways of arguing for Tocquevillian continuity. But do these and other papers confirm Tocqueville's other proposition that well-intentioned reforms were the chief precipitant of the Revolution and that 'the most perilous moment for a bad government is one when it seeks to mend its ways'?[15] It might be more accurate to conclude, following Vivian Gruder, that the crown reacted to the pressure of events with self-defeating ambivalence. Faced with serious challenges to its authority, the monarchy responded by hitting the gas pedal and the brakes simultaneously: no wonder it soon skidded out of control and crashed.

'If we are to grasp its nature, then,' writes Keith Baker in his introduction to the volume, 'we must approach the French Revolution not simply as the repudiation of the Old Regime but as its creation.'[16] The wealth of new information and insights generated by this approach in *The Political Culture of the Old Regime* amply vindicates its adoption – although readers may quarrel with the collection's methodological bias or object to its (more or less explicit) ideological implications. At first sight it also seems that this collective testing of the Tocquevillian paradigm, with its emphasis on the relationship between the state and society and on themes of continuity, makes for a great deal more coherence than is usually to be found in collections of this sort. But an overall assessment of the conclusions assembled here brings to light a profound rift among the contributors with regard to precisely this issue of continuity.

Many of the conference participants – especially those dealing with the history of ideas, and/or those adhering most closely to the Tocqueville-Furet paradigm – have highlighted here the structural continuity between old regime, revolutionary, and postrevolutionary political 'modernity.' In its most extreme version, this sort of argument suggests the following conclusion: had the peculiarly Gallic monster of 'absolutist' republicanism not reared its ugly head in the early 1790s, the nation could have enjoyed a more gradual English-style transition from the new political culture of the 1770s and 1780s to *juste-milieu* constitutional politics, averting in the process some of the revolutionary blood-baths and imperial dictatorships that marked nineteenth-century history. Although David Bien, Gail Bossenga, and Hilton Root fully acknowledge their debt to the Tocquevillian argument, theirs is a significantly different conclusion. In towns and villages all over the realm, they argue, the state was bound by the chains of fiscal necessity to a hierarchical corporate society whose survival it continued to promote. Breaking those chains would require no less than a profound sociopolitical upheaval. David Bien pointedly concludes that 'within the existing framework reform was never a real alternative to revolution.'[17]

In spite, or perhaps because, of this divergence at its core, the volume represents a milestone in the historiography of the origins of the French Revolution; it should also provoke questions and debates around the definition of the increasingly popular but ever-elusive term 'political culture.' Readers will find little solace in Keith Baker's introductory definition of the term, which is overly long and abstract – in his attempt, perhaps, to accommodate all of the conference participants, Baker has offered us too much of a good thing. In practice, however, it can be noted that although many of the essays concern political behaviour, the emphasis here is heavily textual, and those texts at the core of the discussion are explicitly political. At least half of the contributions centre on legal and administrative texts, printed propaganda, and political theory; a disproportionate number of essays, it seems, are devoted to detailing the finer points of the thought of Rousseau, Mably, Sieyès, or the obscure but apparently ubiquitous Jacob-Nicolas Moreau.

This makes for a certain amount of monotony, which could have been avoided had the concept of political culture or the notion of what constitutes a political text been approached in a more eclectic and less conventional fashion. Beyond Ralph Giesey's essay, for instance, no attention at all is paid to the tangible, visual, iconic dimensions of political culture, not all of which by any means were confined to Versailles. The eighteenth-century state did not just sign edicts and pay its publicists; it also organized royal weddings and funerals, quashed riots, sent up balloons, and had a hand in the erection of public buildings and the opening of artistic salons. Especially if one is to trace continuities into the revolutionary period, such visible public manifestations of power should be given pride of place.

Even if one is to remain within the realm of the written word, a broader range both of texts and of questions could be brought to bear upon the subject. Regardless of the symptomatic importance of Rousseau's *Social Contract* or of Adrien Le Paige's *Lettres historiques sur le parlement*, relatively few eighteenth-century French men or women were able to come to terms with such arduously abstract works. But can we not read as political texts such works of fiction as *La Nouvelle Héloïse* or *The Marriage of Figaro*, whose impact on readers and spectators is abundantly documented? And what can we say of a five-hundred-page volume on prerevolutionary French political culture that has not one word to say about the paintings of Jacques-Louis David? Some serious consideration of such works of imagination and attention to the ideological implications of artistic and narrative styles and structures could diversify and enrich our understanding of 'political culture': if 'politics' can be approached as a cultural form, it is no less true that 'culture' can be read for its political message.

Some such broader approach might also generate an important new set of questions. It is unquestionably the case that, as this volume has forcefully reminded us, the intellectual ferment of the prerevolutionary decades allowed for the genesis or redefinition of an important set of political concepts such as public opinion, constitutional government, representation, and the like. It is no less true, however, that this period created a set of *social* categories and images: while on the one hand theatrical melodrama and sentimental painting construed, starting in the 1760s, the image of the virtuous middle-class family, on the other hand libertine novels, pornography, and political propaganda set up its antithesis in the person of the 'aristocrat' as sexual and political predator. One need not believe in a social interpretation of the French Revolution to be convinced of the mobilizing force of such images. If the French Revolution created a political vocabulary, it also bequeathed to the modern world a no less enduring and important social mythology whose roots can also be traced back to the prerevolutionary period. As the Revolution itself was to demonstrate, French men and women ill-equipped to deal with the subtleties of constitutional argument could nonetheless be politically aroused by the threat of an 'aristocratic conspiracy.' We need to know more, in short, about the ways in which political messages were inscribed within social images even prior to the Revolution.

Finally, the most conspicuous absence here is that of any discussion of the gendered dimension of the transition from Old Regime to revolutionary political culture. The symbolic dichotomy of male and female is, after all, hardly peripheral to the subject: the late eighteenth century in France witnessed the transition from a political culture based on court society, in which women were highly visible (whatever their actual role) as royal wives, relatives, and mistresses, to a polity that was incarnated in all-male assemblies. This conscious and explicit exclusion of women from the public sphere of the French Revolution was prefigured in the 1750s and 1760s by the writings of Rousseau, and in the 1770s and 1780s by the public outcry against the likes of Madame Du Barry and Marie-Antoinette; it was followed, ironically, by the allegorization of the Republic in a female form. A definition of 'political culture' which excludes such developments is, to say the least, restrictive.

As Keith Baker himself candidly tells his readers, objections were raised at the conference by participants who feared that the neo-Tocquevillian approach it promoted would result in a devaluation of social-historical or materialist approaches to the question. It seems safe to predict, however, that in the long run such divisions will be ironed out by the pendulum swings of historiography: once the textual-political trend inaugurated by Furet has exhausted its innovative force, the mainstream of the field will be back to doing social history again. In fact, some of the essays in this volume point to the shape that a renewal of social-historical approaches to the question might take. If modes of production did not by and large determine social relations in late eighteenth-century France, fiscal and administrative concerns often did. As Gail Bossenga surmises, 'Perhaps the search for the social origins of the French Revolution should be redirected towards analyzing what groups were embedded in the Old Regime's institutional and financial network of power.'[18] Therein may lie the basis for a new consensus.

Divisions will probably endure, however, between historians who look to the Revolution as a creative force and those who deplore its disruptive excesses as 'accidents' within an otherwise continuous historical evolution. Continuity was given the lion's share here, but it is, after all, only half of the story: Lynn Hunt's was the only essay to remind us that, even before the Estates-General, one of the central themes in political discourse was the rejection of the historical precedent and indeed the wholesale repudiation of the past. This is the sort of rhetoric that Furet would label 'illusion,' but much in this case rests upon one's choice of words: one person's delusion is, after all, another's creative imagination. The actors in the great political drama of 1789 and beyond, and many of those whose ideas laid the groundwork for the Revolution, insisted that theirs was a wholly unprecedented enterprise, that they were making a clean break with the past, and one for the better: at the risk of writing 'commemorative history,' we should continue to take seriously that claim.

Notes

1 The work reviewed in this essay is Keith Michael Baker, ed., *The French Revolution and the Creation of Modern Political Culture*, volume 1: *The Political Culture of the Old Regime* (Oxford: Pergamon Press, 1987).
2 George Taylor, 'Noncapitalist Wealth and the Origins of the French Revolution,' *American Historical Review*, 72 (January 1967), p. 491.
3 J. Habermas, *The Structural Transformation of the Public Sphere: an Enquiry into a Category of Bourgeois Society* (Cambridge, 1989. First published in German in 1962).
4 F. Furet, *Interpreting the French Revolution* (Cambridge, 1981), p. 14.
5 Lynn Hunt, review of *Penser la Révolution française*, *History and Theory*, 20 (1981), p. 318.
6 Furet, *Interpreting the French Revolution*, p. 48.
7 R. Giesey, 'The King Imagined', in Baker, ed., p. 56.
8 A. de Tocqueville, *The Old Regime and the French Revolution* (New York, 1955), pp. 146; 139–41.
9 D. Roche, 'Académies et politique au siècle des lumières: les enjeux pratiques de l'immortalité', in Baker, ed., pp. 342–3.
10 Dale Van Kley, 'The Jansenist Constitutional Legacy in the French Prerevolution,' in Baker, ed., pp. 169–201.
11 Van Kley, 'The Jansenist Constitutional Legacy in the French Revolution', p. 196.
12 François Furet, 'La monarchie et le règlement électoral de 1789,' in Baker, ed., p. 375.
13 R. Halévi, 'La Monarchie et les élections: position des problèmes', in Baker, ed., pp. 399–400.
14 Furet, 'La monarchie et le règlement électoral de 1789,' p. 385.
15 Tocqueville, *The Old Regime*, p. 177.
16 Keith Michael Baker, 'Introduction,' p.xi.
17 D. Bien, 'Offices, Corps and a System of State Credit: the Uses of Privilege under the Ancien Régime', in Baker, ed., p. 111.
18 G. Bossenga, 'City and State: an Urban Perspective on the Origins of the French Revolution', in Baker, ed., p. 136.

6

Rethinking the debate

GWYNNE LEWIS

The French Revolution is the historical event which has launched a thousand *colloques*. Contemporaries knew that it would. For William Wordsworth, recalling his visit to France in 1791–2:

> The land all swarmed with passion, like a Plain
> Devour'd by locusts, Carra, Gorsas, add
> A hundred other names, forgotten now,
> Nor to be heard of more, yet were they Powers,
> Like earthquakes, shocks repeated day by day,
> And felt through every nook of town and field.[1]

At the height of the Terror, Maximilien Robespierre expressed the opinion that 'The French people appear to have outstripped the rest of the human race by two thousand years'.[2] Karl Marx was not wholly convinced, criticizing the tendency of the French bourgeoisie to go back 2000 years and dress up in Roman togas, but then Karl Marx was German, not French. None the less, the Marxist interpretation of history, which placed the French Revolution in a dynamic, world-historical perspective, helps to explain the continued fascination – and repulsion – of the revolutionary period for generations of historians. Immanuel Wallerstein argues that 'the French Revolution and its Napoleonic continuation catalyzed the ideological transformation of the capitalist world-economy *as a world-system*'.[3] Even revisionist historians, who deny the transforming power of the Revolution in the process of capitalist change, agree that, from a political and cultural angle of vision, the events of the Revolution 'have since become the basic script for the modern drama of "revolution" still central to the meaning of politics in our own century'.[4]

Marxisant historians have prioritized the socio-economic interpretation of the Revolution, revisionists the politico-cultural; there appears to be little chance of a meeting of minds. But before we hazard a few opinions on the possible emergence of a 'post-revisionist' consensus, let us examine, perforce very briefly, divisions *within* the ranks of *marxisant* and revisionist historians in an attempt to establish the fact that what divides the two

Reprinted in full from: G. Lewis, *The French Revolution: Rethinking the Debate* (London, Routledge 1993), pp. 106–13; 121–22.

camps *may* not be as important as that which unites them. Let us begin with the central issues of capitalism and class.

One of Professor Cobban's principal objections to the Marxist 'social' interpretation of the Revolution was that if '1789' was a 'bourgeois revolution', it was certainly not precipitated by an industrial, capitalist bourgeoisie, since capitalism before 1789 was still, in the main, commercial and proprietary. Most revisionist historians have followed this lead – if '1789' was a 'bourgeois revolution', it was certainly not a *capitalist*, bourgeois revolution, one which laid the foundations of a modern, industrialized society. France was predominantly an agrarian society; factories were few and far between; traditional, *commercial*, not industrial, capitalism held sway, and so on. However, agreement on this central issue is certainly not unanimous amongst the revisionists. It was a leading revisionist historian, Guy Chaussinand-Nogaret, who argued that France, *before 1789*, experienced an industrial 'take-off', 'an industrialised France would be born from the old regime experiments that Le Creusot or the cotton industries managed to keep going'.[5] Not all revisionists, therefore, are obsessed by rhetoric and semiotics; a few offer important, new interpretations concerning the development of modern capitalism. Nor should it be thought that all *marxisant* historians favour the idea of a fully fledged, industrial, capitalist bourgeoisie precipitating a revolutionary crisis. For example, it is somewhat ironic that Albert Soboul, a constant target of revisionist historians, condemned out of hand as a 'Marxist-Leninist' ideologue, should have painted a far less rosy picture of industrial growth in France before the Revolution than did Chaussinand-Nogaret, repeatedly reminding us that 'Capitalism [before 1789] was still essentially commercial.'[6] For Soboul, as for many other Marxist historians, the real crisis of the *ancien régime* concerns the *retardation* of modern forms of capitalist production, blocked by the structures and *mentalités* of an aristocratic society. The significance of 1789 was that many, though not all, of these blockages were removed.

There remains, however, a fundamental difference in approach, indeed, I would argue, *the* fundamental difference in approach between *marxisant* and revisionist historians. This concerns questions of class and revolution, the role of *necessary*, possibly violent, class struggle in the process of historical change. Was an 'elite' of bourgeois and nobles responsible for promoting capitalist growth, or was there a necessary, predetermined, historic clash between a 'capitalist' bourgeois class and a 'feudal' noble class? For Chaussinand-Nogaret capitalism was associated with an elite, an elite led, however, by the nobility, not the bourgeoisie. For Albert Soboul, on the other hand, the link between the bourgeoisie and the evolution of modern capitalism is central to his *social*, class, interpretation of history. The opening sentence of his impressive general work on the Revolution is uncompromising: 'The Revolution of 1789–94 marked the

arrival of modern bourgeois capitalist society in the history of France.'[7]
For Soboul, for what he termed 'the classic historiographical tradition' (i.e.
marxisant) of the French Revolution, '1789' was a necessary stage in the
development of a modern, bourgeois, capitalist society, just as 1917 and
1949 represented stages in the realization of the Marxist utopia of a
communist, then classless society. The conservative culture of the 1970s
and 1980s in America and Britain, the fall of Stalinist, communist regimes
in Europe altered the historical agenda, creating more politico-cultural
space for revisionist approaches to the Revolution, and to history in
general.

But, to return to this possibility of the emergence of a post-revisionist
consensus, it should be noted that, long before the fall of the Berlin Wall,
marxisant historians were moving to accommodate the valid criticisms of
revisionists concerned about too determinist, too structuralist an approach
to the study of history. Edward Thompson's aptly titled work, *The Poverty
of Theory*, a powerful indictment of Althusserian, ahistorical structural-
ism, containing a few side-swipes at Marx himself (no wonder Thompson
has often been regarded by true believers as more of an English Whig
historian than a Marxist!) was published as early as 1978. Eight years
before this, Régine Robin produced a study of the social structure of
Semur-en-Auxois which argued, *inter alia*, that the period we are dealing
with should be seen as a 'transitional' one in the process of change
between a feudal and capitalist society.[8] For Robin, the actions and
attitudes of the pre-revolutionary bourgeoisie were conditioned by their
place in a post-feudal society, a unique, transitional society, but one in
which capitalism was undermining the old feudal structures. Robin's thesis
posits a less rigid separation between a 'capitalist' and a 'feudal' mode of
production, thus satisfying part, at least, of the revisionist case. It knocks
a big hole in the more rigid, class-conflict theories of historical change. As
Tim Blanning explains: 'Such a pattern is entirely compatible with Marxist
theory and, ironically, can accommodate without strain the empirical
research of revisionists seeking to deny the validity of that theory.'[9] I
should like to see more research conducted along the lines suggested by
Robin, and more particularly by Christopher Johnson concentrating, in
particular, on the relationship between proto-industrialization, changing
patterns of work, and the social consequences of these changes.[10] If
eighteenth-century French society was a transitional, *unique* form of
society, the essential bridge to the fully developed capitalist society of
the nineteenth century, then proto-industrial structures, which could and
did accommodate seigneurial interests, may be said to have provided the
central arches.

More recently, George Comninel produced an interesting and provocative book entitled *Rethinking the French Revolution: Marxism and the
Revisionist Challenge*, which went much further than Robin's in its

acceptance – very uncritically in places – of the revisionist argument concerning the lack of modern capitalist development before 1789, but endeavouring to retain an 'historical materialist' approach to the problems this posed for a *marxisant* sociologist. Comninel's book is long on theory and short on facts, but it illustrates the lengths to which, in this post-modern, post-communist age, Marxist thinkers are prepared to go to meet the revisionist challenge. For Comninel, as for Edward Thompson to a certain extent, Marx himself was long on theory and short on facts. He argues with some conviction, that Marx never really studied the pre-revolutionary period in France; he simply borrowed the notion of the 'bourgeois revolution' from the French early nineteenth-century historians such as François Guizot. There can be no doubt that the identification between the 'triumph of the bourgeoisie' and the French Revolution had been made long before Marx. Sieyès and Barnave had laid the foundations for the thesis during the Revolution itself, whilst it was François Mignet, not Karl Marx, who wrote: 'The Fourteenth of July had been the triumph of the middle class.'[11]

However, according to Comninel, the Barnaves, the Guizots and the Mignets were wrong, and hence so was Marx, since he did little more than borrow the idea from them. Anyway, for historians like Mignet and Guizot, history was certainly not a process; it stopped with the arrival of the all-conquering bourgeoisie in 1830. Interesting that the American revisionist Francis Fukuyama should have convinced himself that the 'The End of History' should be dated from America's victory over the Soviet Union in the 1980s – yet another attempt to suggest that liberal capitalism is the answer to western Europe's prayers. Comninel is convinced that the revolutionary bourgeoisie did not simply represent 'a capitalist class'; furthermore, that there was 'no fundamental social division between the forms of property and economic interests of the bourgeoisie and the nobility'.[12] Here surely is another bridge across the troubled waters of *marxisant* and revisionist historiography. There was no 'class struggle' related to the growth of modern forms of capitalism before, or indeed during, the Revolution; there was, instead, conflict within a ruling elite.

Is the similarity, however, more apparent than real? Was 'the Revolution simply a political contest between rival factions of a single "elite"', Comninel asks. His answer, an unequivocal 'Of course not', suggests that the two sides are continuing to shout at each other over a pretty wide chasm. For Comninel, after all, 'The French Revolution was a specific product of the class relations of the ancien régime.' 'Class struggle' is very much back on the agenda. In pre-revolutionary France, peasants, among other social groups, were being exploited, and 'Recognition of the funda-mental exploitative relationship is necessarily also recognition of class struggle.' However, it should be noted that these class struggles are not related directly to the existence of modern forms of capitalism before 1789, nor to the exploitation of a non-existent 'proletariat', nor to the 'feudal' exploitation of the peasantry, since 'feudalism' too was, in Comninel's mistaken view, the fiction of vulgar Marxist historians. The class struggles of the *ancien régime* were created out of the conflict between 'bourgeois' and 'aristocrat' over the spoils (surplus-value in Marxist parlance) to be acquired from the State which, following the line taken by de Tocqueville, had become the supreme arbitrator of power, social and political. For Comninel, class exploitation is as much political as it is economic. Stripped of its Marxist rhetoric, there is surely much in Comninel's interpretation which reminds one of the influential article published by Colin Lucas in 1973, 'Nobles, bourgeois and the origins of the French Revolution',[13] including the idea of a 'section of the ruling class', and 'an intra-class conflict over basic political relations' with an aristocratic elite elbowing aside an aspiring but thwarted bourgeoisie 'interested in a state administration open to talent'.

There is a final point concerning the possibility, if not – dare I phrase it thus? – of a synthesis emerging from the dialectical struggle between *marxisant* and revisionist historians, then of some measure of agreement (only totalitarian ideologues would ask for more!) over the meaning of the Revolution two hundred years on. It is interesting, for example, that two historians, approaching the same problem from very different methodological perspectives, should both conclude that not enough emphasis has been placed on the importance of the State when studying both the causes and the course of the French Revolution. For Comninel, aspiring bourgeois and the higher echelons of the aristocracy were competing for power which was mediated through the State. The *political* crisis of 1787–9, when the bourgeoisie realized that the aristocracy was intent on seizing greater control over the State and, in consequence, made a take-over bid for *la nation*, was also economic, since the State was 'intimately involved', through legal and political channels, in the process of economic exploitation: 'not only will the state be the "arbiter" of normal class struggle, and the primary opponent of class insurrection, but it may itself become directly implicated as the *object* of struggle between the classes'.[14] John Bosher, in his recent textbook on the Revolution, argues that 'A new Leviathan was born during the French Revolution', the modern French State. Certainly Bosher's approach differs significantly from that of a *marxisant* sociologist like George Comninel, but, to take just two areas spotlighted by Bosher, the massive expansion, indeed the very idea, of salaried civil servants, and the 'grand scale' of the Directory's dealings with war-suppliers and bankers, both underline the importance of the State as the dispenser of economic and political power.[15] Again, it was Karl Marx who wrote that 'The task of the first French Revolution was to destroy all separate local, territorial, urban and provincial powers in order to create the civil unity of the nation.'[16] Marx's interpretation of the

Revolution has as much to do with the creation of the modern State as it has with the development of modern capitalism; the two were, of course, inter-dependent for him. William Doyle, again coming from the anti-Marxist camp, has also stressed the fundamental importance, when considering the birth of the modern French State, of the abolition, following the decrees of August 1789, of 'the whole structure of provincial, local, and municipal government'.[17]

These few examples may be interpreted as a plea for a non-determinist, but not necessarily a non-ideological, approach to the study of the Revolution, premised upon the conviction that historical truth is relative rather than absolute. For if the Marxist interpretation of history, supercharged with alarming nonsense like the 'dictatorship of the proletariat', has taken a severe drubbing over the past two decades, the revisionist onslaught, with its equally disturbing teleological, and ahistorical nonsense about Rousseau and Robespierre being the intellectual and philosophical forebears of Pol Pot, has failed to win a convincing majority. As Colin Jones has phrased it: 'The Revisionist vulgate is a very negative one, more united in opposition to the old orthodoxy than in anything else.'[18] There is an intellectual sense of déjà-vu about sections of this particular Vulgate, a kind of 'L'année dernière à Ferney'. But, if any real meeting of minds is to be achieved, *marxisant* historians, or, at least, some of them, need to accept a more Thompsonian, yes, a more cultural 'history-as-process' approach, whilst revisionists need to remind themselves that social history is not, of necessity, the history of structurally determined, pre-ordained social classes.

My principal criticism of the contribution made by revisionists over the past two decades, and it is one shared by many British historians of the Revolution, Marxist *and* non-Marxist, concerns the way in which they have ignored or down-graded the importance of the social question during the 1790s. Deeply engaged in the ideological and intellectual struggle against Marxism as some leading revisionists have been, one can readily understand why this should have happened: like the more politically charged Marxist, they have allowed their ideological commitment or anti-Marxist methodology to light their way to their libraries. Maybe this is not always a bad thing. The antagonisms, personal and political, between a Mathiez and an Aulard, or a Soboul and a Furet, have produced good historical fruit, even if they tasted rather bitter at times. It should always be remembered, however, that for the leaders of the Revolution, heirs of those applied social scientists, the *philosophes*, the social question remained at the top of the political agenda, at least until 1795, after which French society became increasingly bureaucratized and militarized. And, as Richard Cobb's brilliant forays into the field of history have shown, one does not have to wear a red, or even pink, tie to show a proper historical concern for the ordinary people who were the main sufferers of the revolutionary upheaval.

It *was* the involvement of peasants, artisans and shopkeepers which provided the main dynamic of the Revolution *during its early years*. Tim Blanning, as close to true revisionism as a good English empiricist historian can possibly be, informs us that: 'If the bourgeois had had their way, the Revolution would have been closed down by 1791 at the latest. It was only insistent pressure from below which drove them on to destroy feudalism in its entirety.'[19] Throughout the 1790s, fear of 'popular despotism' fashioned the immediate political responses of politicians as well as the subsequent ideology of the liberal bourgeoisie. One should not dismiss this involvement, direct and indirect, of millions of French men and women as the actions of 'the chaotic people', or 'the arbitrary brutalities of the mob'.[20] There is a vast amount of work still to be completed on the social history of the Revolution. Let us give the last word to Ferenc Fehér, a revisionist historian who expressed his agreement with François Furet when the latter, in a recent lecture, expressed the desire for 'an act of reconciliation' – on the historiographical and political fronts – if modern democracy was to be successfully defended: 'I am in complete agreement with Furet's postulate, but I deem it feasible only on the basis of creating a legitimate space for the constant renegotiation of "the social question" on the basis of political freedom as an absolute precondition.'[21]

Notes

1 W. Wordsworth, *The Prelude*, ed. E. de Seligman (Oxford, Oxford University Press, 1970) Book IX, II. pp. 178–83.
2 G. Rudé ed., *Robespierre* (New Jersey, Prentice-Hall, 1967), p. 69.
3 I. Wallerstein, 'The French Revolution as a World-Historical Event', F. Fehér ed., *The French Revolution and the Birth of Modernity* (Berkeley, University of California Press, 1990) p. 122.
4 'Introduction', in K. Baker, ed., *The Political Culture of the Old Regime* (Oxford, Pergamon Press, 1987) p. xxiii.
5 G. Chaussinand-Nogaret, *The French Nobility in the Eighteenth Century*, trans. W. Doyle (Cambridge, Cambridge University Press, 1986) p. 106.
6 A. Soboul, *Comprendre la Révolution: problèmes politiques de la Révolution française* (Paris, Maspero, 1976).
7 A. Soboul, *The French Revolution, 1787–1799* (London, Unwin Hyman, 1989) p. 3.
8 E. Thompson, *The Poverty of Theory and Other Essays* (London, Merlin Press, 1978). R. Robin, *La Société française en 1789: Semur-en-Auxois* (Paris, 1970).
9 T. C. Blanning, *The French Revolution: Aristocrats versus Bourgeois?* (London, Macmillan, 1989) p. 16.
10 See, for example, C. Johnson, 'Artisans versus Fabricants: urban protoindustrialisation and the evolution of work culture in Lodève and Bédarieux, 1740–1830', European University Institute (Florence) Working Paper, no. 85/137, n.d.

11 G. Comninel, *Rethinking the French Revolution: Marxism and the Revisionist Challenge* (London, Verso Books, 1987).

12 For the remainder of this section of the argument see Comninel, *Rethinking the French Revolution*, pp. 196–200.

13 See *Past and Present* 60 (1973), 84–126.

14 G. Comninel, *Rethinking the French Revolution*, p. 172.

15 J. F. Bosher, *The French Revolution* (London, Weidenfeld & Nicolson, 1989), see chapter 11.

16 G. Comninel, *Rethinking the French Revolution*, p. 203.

17 W. Doyle, *The Oxford History of the French Revolution* (Oxford, Oxford University Press, 1989) p. 117.

18 C. Jones, 'Revisionism, post-revisionism, and new perspectives on the French Revolution', in C. Jones ed., *The French Revolution in Perspective* (Nottingham, University of Nottingham Press, 1989) p. iii.

19 Blanning, *The French Revolution*, p. 3.

20 S. Schama, *Citizens: a Chronicle of the French Revolution* (London, Viking Press, 1989) pp. 748 and 648.

21 Fehér, *The Birth of Modernity*, p. 7.

SECTION

II

SOCIO-CULTURAL APPROACHES

Presentation

The five readings comprising this section have been chosen in order to illustrate the range of socio-cultural approaches that have flourished following the revision of the social history agenda. The significant expansion of gender-based research (covered in Section 3) also bears witness to this development. However, it is immediately apparent that most of the pieces reproduced here focus on the Enlightenment and its articulation to the Revolution. This is the area in which the new cultural and intellectual history has raised the most substantial challenge to conventional thinking. In effect, practitioners have relaunched the *ancien régime* as a fit object of study – as a period of history in its own right, and as a period able to provide clues towards a fuller understanding of the direction subsequently taken by the Revolution. The Tocquevillian thrust of much modern scholarship surfaces once again.

However, the real breakthrough was achieved by the Annales historians in the mid-1970s.[1] Equipped with the methods of quantitative analysis and a brisk disregard for élite conceptions of cultural history, they more or less recharted the landscape of the Enlightenment. That process implied the retrieval of the Enlightenment from the clutches of literary historians and its re-embedding in the fabric of the eighteenth century. The study of emblematic texts retreated in the face of an expanded definition of literary production and consumption; 'high' art encountered the 'low' art of votive painters, graphic illustrators and caricaturists; *philosophes* met penny satirists and pornographers, and very nearly on equal terms. In short, the Enlightenment lost some of its status and integrity to become, instead, another eddy in the long-term history of mentalities.

More recent researchers, whose work is represented here, tend to approach the Enlightenment and its relationship to the Revolution from the perspective of political culture. As such, they generally acknowledge and exploit the bridgehead established by the Annales historians, while pulling back from some of their more advanced positions. For instance, the process of embedding the Enlightenment continues apace. As a result, we now have a greatly extended knowledge of the politics of the old regime which is directly applicable to the aetiology of the Revolution. The emphasis on mentalities and long-term cultural shifts has also proved helpful in enhancing our understanding of the growth of the 'civil public sphere' and its concomitant, a definably 'public' opinion. On the other hand, the protagonists of the political-culture approach display a diminished interest in the socio-economic underpinnings of cultural change and, in some cases, a methodological preference for the 'explanatory' text which is reminiscent of the old, scriptural school of Enlightenment scholarship.

Keith Baker's cogent analysis of the emergence of public opinion displays all of these characteristics. While concerned primarily with the construction of public opinion as a rhetorical device, his essay provides a useful schematization of how modern, contestatory politics started to take shape in the interstices of the *ancien régime*. In theory, if not in practice, the political culture of absolutism allowed no room for dissent, for differences of opinion, outside the immediate vicinity of the monarch. Yet everything began to change in the 1750s with the growth of a 'public' politics that threatened to shatter the absolutist mould. Within two and three decades the *de facto* existence of a pluralist polity was universally recognized. Everyone – monarchs, ministers, disgruntled courtiers – competed for the approbation of public opinion, conceived now as a stable, rational and univocal presence in society. Yet, in Baker's account, the new, freestanding politics hovered uncertainly between the approved models of enlightened absolutism and the turbulent, divisive practices of constitutional opposition on the English pattern. In consequence, he dubs the final decades of Bourbon absolutism a period of transition characterized by a specific, but fundamentally unstable, form of politics. After 1789, the unanimist politics of the 'general will' would prevail.

As a reading of the political history of the *ancien régime*, Keith Baker's essay carries a large measure of conviction. Some historians might question the chronology of retreat from the hallowed practices of absolutism, but the stress which he lays upon the changes taking place in the 1770s and 1780s is to be welcomed. In recognizing the shifting character of political practice under the later Bourbons, he demonstrates the potential of the political-culture approach and its capacity to make statements that reach across the Revolutionary watershed. However, his conceptualization of public opinion seems less secure. An analysis rooted in emblematic texts ascribes a unity of operation to public opinion that it may not have possessed in practice, at least not until the establishment of quasi-representative institutions to focus and channel opinion at the very end of the *ancien régime*. We need to bear in mind, too, that Baker's presentation deliberately leaves the social dimension of public opinion out of account. A social interpretation would probably blur chronologies further, and also challenge the fixity of the phenomenon in question. After all, the Sun King (Louis XIV) himself was not above playing to the gallery of public opinion when the occasion demanded. A social interpretation might also readmit a version of the 'bourgeois revolution' thesis via the back door.

Roger Chartier writes as the master synthesizer of Enlightenment studies. He brings the qualitative preoccupations of the political culture historians to bear upon the quantitative achievements of the Annalists. From a position of nearly unrivalled knowledge of the book trade in eighteenth-century France, he asks the crucial question: what does this evidence tell us about the causes of the Revolution? The answer is not quite as simple as we have been led to believe. The well-documented fact of the ready availability of subversive literature does not, in itself, explain the erosion of respect for traditional society. Indeed, he warns against the tendency to reify the Enlightenment, suggesting that its status and authority as a precursor may have more to do with the Revolutionaries' own search for origins and legitimacy. Instead, he urges on historians the importance of measuring the *impact* of reading. This is the point at which the 'quantitative' and the 'qualitative' are bound to part company. Using forensic skills, he presses the case not for probing the ideological stance of texts so much as investigating how they were received, and how shifting habits of reading may have encouraged critical styles of thinking and modes of behaviour. The case can scarcely be described as conclusive, Chartier readily concedes, but it gains in plausibility when placed alongside other 'detaching' processes, such as Dechristianization, about which we know very much more.

If the precise impact of the printed word remains an issue for discussion among scholars, few would doubt the potency of icons and images, whether painted or printed. Even allowing for a substantial retreat of literacy in the course of the eighteenth century, a significant proportion of the urban poor and a vast population of country-dwellers still could not decipher everyday printed matter. The Revolutionaries recognized as much, of course, and their attempts to communicate by other means provide the material for James Leith's article on civic imagery. Leith directs our attention to what is sometimes rather dismissively labelled an 'ephemeral' art form: that is to say engraved symbols and allegorical representations appearing on letterheads, proclamations, certificates, identity cards and so forth. These were not stylistic adornments but elaborate devices for the transmission of primary messages about the Revolution. They were mass-produced and instantly accessible to the illiterate or the semi-literate. Whether the ignorant shared the conventional Enlightenment belief in the moulding capacity of such images is another matter. Leith, however, demonstrates both the ingenuity and the tenacity with which all sections of educated opinion pursued the goal of regeneration through the medium of graphic art.

Margaret Jacob's contribution retraces some of the ground covered in the previous readings and invites us to pause and take stock. Appropriately, it comes from the conclusion to her pan-European study of eighteenth-century freemasonry. She applauds the creative vigour with which investigators are now unpackaging the Enlightenment, but urges scholars interested primarily in linguistic modes of analysis not to mistake the dynamism of the phenomenon under study. In her view, that dynamism must ultimately be explained in social and institutional terms. In other words, the classic statements of the Enlightenment derived their force from the social and institutional constituencies that received and transmitted them. The notion that 'texts' can be treated as independent actors is disturbing and methodologically suspect, she feels. The real actors in the cultural drama of the Enlightenment were user bodies such as the masonic lodges which could be found in towns large and small by the end of the *ancien régime*. Yet the many thousands of freemasons were not just passive consumers; they brought to bear upon the Enlightenment an ideology of civic zeal. In the process, they helped to fashion what would become the egalitarian culture of the Revolution, while still embedded within the social hierarchies of corporate society.

The ambiguities of social station and political outlook as the *ancien régime* entered its final crisis are thrown into stark relief by Daniel Wick's study of the behaviour of the courtier nobility. Written in 1980, this article served initially to advance the debate about the social origins of the French Revolution. However, since the refocusing of historians' interests, it is now better read as a pioneer investigation of the formal politics of Bourbon absolutism. The author contends that the Court still functioned as the centre of politics in the 1780s, but successful power-broking in the antechambers of the palace of Versailles demanded skilled management of the patronage system. Neither Louis XVI nor Marie-Antoinette understood the concept of 'divide and rule'; indeed, Louis showed signs of wishing to remove power from the hands of courtiers altogether. At any event, by the time Controller General Calonne unveiled his plans for root-and-branch reform, a powerful faction of 'liberal' nobles had come into being, with neither a material nor a political stake in the continuation of the *status quo*. Wick's study thus uncovers another dimension of the erosion of support for the monarchy. Using his evidence, we also gain a better understanding of the fluid character of late *ancien-régime* political culture as dissatisfied courtier families sought to influence the verdict of public opinion by circulating discreditable brochures about the queen.

Note

1 Named after the journal *Annales: Economies, Sociétés, Civilisations*, which was founded by Marc Bloch and Lucien Febvre and continued by Fernand Braudel.

7
Public opinion as political invention
KEITH BAKER

The theme of this essay can be presented quite simply. Turn to the eleventh volume of the *Encyclopédie*, published in 1765. Look up the article 'Opinion.' There you will find the traditional rationalist distinction between rational knowledge and uncertain opinion vividly illustrated by a metaphor contrasting the full, clear light of the midday sun with the flickering, feeble glow of a torch in the darkness. 'Rational knowledge [*la science*] is a full and entire light, which reveals things clearly, shedding demonstrable certainty upon them; opinion is but a feeble and imperfect light, which reveals things only by conjecture and leaves them always in uncertainty and doubt.'[1] Appearing as it does in a work constructed along

Reprinted in full, except for notes, from K. M. Baker, ed. *Inventing the French Revolution: Essays on French Political Culture in the Eighteenth Century* (Cambridge, Cambridge University Press, 1990), pp. 167–99, 337–45.

the fault lines in the rationalist theory of knowledge upon which the traditional distinction between knowledge and opinion depended, this article surprises only by its utter conventionality. In fact, its conception of opinion is precisely the same as that underlying the vast compendium of conventional wisdom on the matter compiled in 1735 by the marquis de Saint Aubin under the title *Traité de l'opinion, ou Mémoires pour servir à l'histoire de l'esprit humain*, a treatise which concludes its contemplation of the variability of opinion, predictably enough, with a Hobbesian argument for absolute monarchy.

The matter becomes more interesting, though, if one turns to the *Encyclopédie méthodique* and again looks up the term *opinion*. The first thing one finds is that the original article has simply disappeared. There is no entry at all for *opinion* in the section entitled 'Logique, métaphysique & morale,' nor is it to be found in the section entitled 'Philosophie.' Instead, the term shows up not in the philosophical sections of the *Encyclopédie méthodique* but in the political sections – in the sections concerning *finances* and *police* – where it now appears not as mere *opinion*, but as *opinion publique*. Even more remarkable, in migrating from the philosophical to the political sections of the work and accepting its designation as 'public', 'opinion' has also taken on a radically different character. Whereas before its principal characteristics were flux, subjectivity, and uncertainty, now they are universality, objectivity, and rationality. Within the space of a generation, the flickering lamp of 'opinion' has been transformed into the unremitting light of 'public opinion,' the light of the universal tribunal before which citizens and governments alike must now appear.

How do we explain the sudden mutation of 'opinion' into 'public opinion,' so dramatically exemplified by this comparison between the *Encyclopédie* and the *Encyclopédie méthodique*? What were its implications for the nature of French political culture at the end of the Old Regime? Many studies of the idea of public opinion assume the existence of some corresponding social referent as a residual fact of common life in any society – a kind of perpetual noise in the system which must in some way be taken account of, whether or not its existence is formally acknowledged by political actors or explicitly designated under the rubric of 'public opinion.' Others see it as a specific phenomenon of modern societies, brought into being by long-term changes in literacy, by the growth of capitalism and the commercial expansion of the press, by the bureaucratic transformation of particularistic social orders into more integrated national (and now international) communities. Without denying the importance of these latter developments, I wish to insist on the significance of public opinion as a political invention, rather than as a sociological function. The term *opinion publique* was not entirely unknown before the last decades of the Old Regime. But in the course of these decades, it suddenly emerged as a central rhetorical figure in a new kind of politics. Suddenly it designated a new source of authority, the supreme tribunal to which the absolute monarchy, no less than its critics, was compelled to appeal.

A politics of contestation

To understand this phenomenon is to recognize the importance of the profound transformation in French political culture that began to occur in the mid-eighteenth century and was already well under way on the eve of the French Revolution. From the 1750s on, a politics of contestation became an increasingly marked feature of French public life. Appropriately enough, it erupted first in the course of a conflict over religious matters: the quarrel over the refusal of sacraments to Jansenist dissenters, most fully studied in recent years by Dale Van Kley and D. Carrol Joynes. Since the time of the Wars of Religion, as Hobbes and Bossuet had each emphasized, in their very different ways, it had been the fundamental responsibility – and the principal justification – of absolute authority to contain the ideological potential of religious disputes to disturb political order. In the 1750s, however, the French monarchy found itself dramatically unable to perform this function. Every assertion of authority places that same authority at risk. And the absolute monarchy, unable to impose peace upon the church hierarchy and the parlements (the contending parties in the bitter dispute over the civil rights of recalcitrant Jansenists) – unable even to enforce their respect for the law of silence in this matter that it was driven in desperation to proclaim in 1754 – suddenly found the very nature of its own authority at issue in the new patterns of political contestation to which the quarrel over the refusal of sacraments gave rise. Absolute authority was at issue not only in the bold contentions to be found in the repeated *remontrances* presented by the parlementary magistrates to the king and in the stubborn refusal of the magistrates to abandon their position even in the face of exile. It was also at issue in the illegal and clandestine circulation of the parlementary *remontrances* and in the assiduity with which they were bought – in dramatic numbers – by members of the literate public. It was at issue in the proliferation of pamphlets that marked the rhythm of the dispute over the refusal of sacraments and extended its politicizing effects on French public life. It was at issue in the seditious murmurs – the *mauvais discours* – heard among the Parisian populace. And it was at issue, too, in the space that a journal such as the *Gazette de Leyde* devoted to this dispute, in that journal's ability to enlarge the circle of readers following its course, and in the editors' claim to announce the views of 'the public' in such a contested matter.

Strictly speaking, of course, none of these political practices was consistent with the theory of royal absolutism. That theory depended on a view of the monarch as the only public person: the source and principle of unity in a particularistic society of orders and Estates. If politics is defined as the process by which competing claims and policies are transformed into authoritative definitions of the general good, then absolutist politics occurs, in ideal terms, only in the mind and person of the king. To save absolute authority from the taint of arbitrariness, the monarch must take counsel from others, and he may also seek advice at will; conversely, individuals and corporate bodies may make their own representations to the monarch, urging their particularistic claims and policies upon him. Authorized institutional channels existed under the Old Regime to maintain these practices of counsel and representation (the royal council, the parlements, the right of individual and corporate petition), and the king could create others, should he feel the need to do so. There were also informal channels (the court, personal networks that could reach the king's ear, patterns of clientage and influence) that shaped royal decision making by means of personal intrigue. But there was no reason why the process of seeking counsel or offering representations should be made public beyond the particular (and particularistic) circles of actors directly involved, simply because there was no other public person to address apart from the king – no other person or entity or institutional process whose legitimate function it was to decide questions on behalf of the community as a whole. Hence the notion, frequently invoked, of government as the *secret du roi*. Hence the principle, fundamental to the politics of absolutism, that parlementary *remontrances* (since in theory they represented the counsel of the officers of a particular royal court before the throne) should never be made public or even circulated by one parlement among the others. Hence the illegality of open discussion, by unauthorized persons without explicit permission, of matters pertaining to governmental policy or public order. The politics of absolutism was not a public politics.

Yet, first in the case of the disputes over the refusal of sacraments in the 1750s, then in the course of the institutional conflicts over the liberalization of the grain trade in the 1760s, and finally in the context of a campaign against the fiscal practices and arbitrary procedures of the administrative monarchy that grew throughout the decades preceding the Maupeou coup, French politics broke out of the absolutist mould. The reign of silence imposed by an absolute monarch could no longer contain debates and contestations that made increasingly explicit appeal to a world of public opinion beyond the traditional circle of institutional actors. Frustrated in its efforts to prevent open debate of religious politics in the 1750s, the royal government fought a rearguard campaign, in the following decade, to limit public discussion of financial administration. Obliged to solicit proposals for fiscal reform directly from the parlements and other courts in 1763, for example, the crown took fright when the ensuing discussion spilled beyond its constituted channels. A royal declaration of 1764 insisted on the dangers of 'memoirs and projects formed by persons without standing [*sans caractère*], who take the liberty of making [these writings] public, instead of submitting them to those persons destined by their position to judge them.' To remedy such an 'excess of license,' the crown prohibited the printing, sale, or hawking of any writings 'concerning the reform of our finances, or their past, present, or future administration.'[2]

But these were 'vain precautions,' as one contemporary writer on administrative matters was subsequently to exclaim: 'as if the greed of the foreign presses did not rush to publish everything and, too often, to distort everything.'[3] The most immediate effect of the royal order was to provoke a dramatic response of the parlement of Dijon (drafted in effect by Dupont de Nemours) denouncing the generality of the prohibition, insisting on the impossibility of stemming the tide of brochures by such means, and arguing for the importance of public discussion of administrative questions. Despite its scope, the royal declaration of 1764 failed to contain the skirmishing of public political discussion that, by the time of the Maupeou coup, had expanded once again into a full-scale pamphlet war. For observers of Mme d'Epinay's persuasion, this escalation of political debate represented 'an irremediable evil', threatening the essence of the state. Questions regarding the fundamental constitution of the realm could not be publicly discussed in this way without risk that 'the knowledge the peoples acquire must, a little sooner, a little later, produce revolutions.'[4] Unable to stifle these processes of political contestation, however, the government found itself under increasing pressure to participate in them, as Moreau had been urging since the 1750s, by appropriating the ideological strategies of the opposition for its own purposes. In the course of subsequent decades, the preambles to important decrees grew longer and more explicit in their explanations and justifications of government policies; ministers proved adept in the strategic proliferation of pamphlets and anonymous brochures; apologists for absolute government sought to deploy the ideological resources of the monarchy in its own defense. Reluctantly, inconsistently, yet with an increasing sense of urgency as successive pre-revolutionary crises became more acute, agents of the monarchy found themselves presenting their briefs before the tribunal of the public.

The fundamental importance of this notion of public opinion as a political tribunal has been emphasized by Jürgen Habermas in an indispensable work.[5] In his analysis, however, the concept emerged in the mid-eighteenth century primarily to mediate the tension between the state and civil society: It served as the device by which bourgeois society sought to limit and transform the power of the absolute state. In contrast, I wish to emphasize the extent to which the concept took on meaning in France in the context of a political crisis of absolute authority (neglected by Habermas, who underestimates the potential for political opposition under the Old Regime), as the crown and its opponents within the traditional political system invented and appealed to a principle of legitimacy beyond that system in order to press their competing claims. From this perspective, we should resist the temptation (frequently encountered) to think of 'the public' simply in sociological terms, reducing it to a putative social referent among specific groups and classes. Beyond the fact that the notion implied access to the printed word, the social composition of 'the public' remained relatively ill defined in the last decades of the Old Regime, until clarification was forced by the political processes set in train by the calling of the Estates General. 'Public opinion' took form as a political or ideological construct, rather than as a discrete sociological referent. It emerged in eighteenth-century political discourse as an abstract category, invoked by actors in a new kind of politics to secure the legitimacy of claims that could no longer be made binding in the terms (and within the traditional institutional circuit) of an absolutist political order. The result was an implicit new system of authority, in which the government and its opponents competed to appeal to 'the public' and to claim the judgement of 'public opinion' on their behalf.

There is a revealing parallel to be drawn here between the mid-eighteenth century appeal to 'the public' in French domestic affairs and the similar appeal (at the very beginning of the century) to 'the public' in European international affairs. Both appeals implied a subversion of previously accepted principles of authority. In the latter case, the idea emerged of an international public as a tribunal to which warring states referred their claims by means of printed propaganda. The concept functioned, in effect, as an abstract authority, invoked at a point when older principles of hierarchy and order in the international domain had lost their power to constrain political actors: The hierarchical universal order of Christendom had been dissolved into 'Europe,' understood as a dynamic secular system of competing powers.

In the case of the French monarchy under Louis XIV, however, there remained a fundamental conflict between the monarchy's need to appeal its claims openly to an international public tribunal and the consequent risk of submitting its policies to the judgement of a domestic one. By the end of Louis XV's reign, the monarchy no longer seemed to have a choice in the matter. The logic of the new political situation required that the government address its claims to a domestic 'public,' deploying pamphlets and other devices of political contestation in internal affairs with as much energy as it had previously done in the international arena. It also required that the government tolerate (and attempt to use to its advantage) the circulation within French borders of relatively independent newspapers such as the *Gazette de Leyde*, which in turn advanced their own competing claims to define the nature and content of public opinion. But by accepting the logic of a politics of contestation in this way, the royal government unwittingly conspired with its opposition to foster the transfer of ultimate authority from the public person of the sovereign to the sovereign person of the public.

The English model

How did the French think about the eruption of this new politics of contestation within their theoretically 'absolute' monarchy? What did they think of its implications for social and political order? One way to approach these questions is to consider their attitudes toward the most obvious eighteenth-century example of a politics of contestation, that to be found across the Channel. It was not an example that the French found altogether reassuring. Many, like the editors of the *Courrier d'Avignon*, found the English spectacle of party divisions and opposition politics both bizarre and profoundly threatening, even after the efforts made by Montesquieu to explain this phenomenon to his compatriots in *De l'esprit des lois*.[6] Nor was Montesquieu himself perhaps as unambiguous in his evaluation of English politics as his current reputation as the founder of the modern liberal interpretation of the British constitution would suggest. His adumbration of a theory of the separation and balance of powers, understood as the essential condition of English liberty, did not entirely erase from his work the evidence of hesitations and ambivalences in the face of the English system of government. To many of his contemporaries, he still seemed to be describing an ambiguous, disturbing, and even dangerous phenomenon – a phenomenon to be understood and marvelled at – rather than a model to be imitated.

In this respect, the second of Montesquieu's famous chapters discussing English politics is particularly revealing. In the first and most celebrated – Chapter 6 of Book 11, entitled 'Of the English constitution' – he had outlined, in relatively formal terms, his theory of the separation of powers. In the second – Chapter 27 of Book 19, entitled 'How the laws can contribute to the formation of the customs, the manners, and the character of a nation' – he turned to an analysis of the political practices and passions deriving from the nature of the English constitution – that is to say, to the character of English political culture more generally. This chapter opens with a theoretical explanation of the formation of political parties, followed by an extremely allusive interpretation of the Glorious Revolution of 1688. But the terms of this essay in political sociology are striking.

Montesquieu begins by pointing out that since there would be two prominent powers in the state he discussed in Book 11, and since each of its citizens would be free to act independently, according to his will, the majority of them would support one of these powers or the other. Moreover, since the executive power had positions and employments at its disposal, people who hoped to obtain its patronage would gravitate toward it, whereas those who could hope for nothing from this source would attack it. This division between the 'ins' and 'outs' would give rise to a constant play of political passions:

> All the passions being free there, hate, envy, jealousy, the desire to enrich and distinguish oneself would appear in all their extent; and if it were otherwise, the state would appear like a man stricken by illness, who would have no passions because he had no strength.
>
> The hate that would exist between the two parties would last, because it would always be powerless.
>
> The parties being composed of free men, if one of them became dominant, the effect of liberty would be that it would be brought down, while the citizens, as hands helping the body, would come to raise up the other.
>
> Since each individual, always independent, would follow his caprices and his fantasies a great deal, there would be frequent changes of party; an individual would abandon the party in which all his friends would be left, in order to join another in which he would find all his enemies; and often, in this nation, one would forget the laws of friendship and those of hate.
>
> The monarch would be in the same situation as private persons; and, contrary to the ordinary maxims of prudence, he would often be obliged to give his confidence to those who would have offered him the most and to disgrace those who would have best served him, thereby doing by necessity what other princes do by choice.[7]

This analysis hardly seems to present to French readers a version of a stable and orderly political process. Instead, Montesquieu portrays English public life as dominated by egoistic passions, played out in a world in which the relationships among political actors are constantly shifting, according to the necessities – or the contingencies – of party conflicts. But hate, envy, jealousy, and so on, are not the only passions to appear in this strange political culture of the English. Montesquieu also finds the English moved by fear. This is not the heavy, silent fear of a people enslaved under the yoke of despotism. It is the unpredictable, anxious fear – Montesquieu uses the term *terreurs* – of a people always 'uneasy about its situation,' a people that would believe itself constantly in danger, 'even at times when it is most secure.'

This would be all the more the case because those who would oppose the executive power most energetically, being unable to acknowledge the self-interested motives for their opposition, would increase the terrors of the people, which would never know exactly whether it was in danger or not. But that indeed would help enable it to avoid the true perils to which it could subsequently be exposed.[8]

Thus Montesquieu portrays the English as a free people, but a people thrown by its very liberty into a constant state of insecurity. It is true that the legislative body, more enlightened than the people whose confidence it has received, can calm these movements of popular agitation. This fact is, for Montesquieu, one of the great advantages of representative government over the direct democracy of the ancients, in which popular agitations were translated immediately into legislative effects. But it is also true that the fear and insecurity he is describing seem to emerge as the virtual principle of English government (in Montesquieu's sense of that term – namely, the passion that makes a polity function). Indeed, it is in the operation of this passion that Montesquieu appears to find his explanation of the Glorious Revolution.

Since this explanation contains a number of bizarre elements, it will be well to quote the relevant paragraphs in full:

Thus, when the terrors imprinted [in the popular consciousness] had no certain object, they would produce only vain clamors and insults. And they would even have this good effect, that they would tighten all springs of government and make all the citizens attentive. But if they occurred on the occasion of a reversal of the fundamental laws, they would be silent, deadly, atrocious, and produce catastrophes.

Soon there would be a dreadful calm, during which everyone would unite against the power violating the laws.

If, in the case where the anxieties have no certain object, some foreign power threatened the state and endangered its fortune or its glory, then the lesser interests would yield to the greater, and everyone would unite in support of the executive power.

But if the disputes were formed on the occasion of a violation of the fundamental laws and a foreign power appeared, there would be a revolution that would change neither the form of the government nor its constitution. For the revolutions shaped by liberty are only a confirmation of liberty.

A free nation can have a liberator; a subject nation can only have another oppressor.[9]

It seems legitimate to find a reference to the events of 1688 in this discussion of the coincidence of a violation of the fundamental laws and the appearance of a foreign power. But there are, nevertheless, many rather odd aspects to the analysis that Montesquieu presents. How do we explain, for example, his introduction of quite particular facts – the appearance of 'a foreign power,' with its clear reference to William of Orange, for example – without even identifying them? How do we account for the fact that, here and throughout this chapter of *De l'esprit des lois*, Montesquieu speaks of England without ever explicitly mentioning the country by name (at the beginning of the chapter, the nation considered is identified simply as the 'free people' about which the author has already spoken in Book 11), even though he introduces into his discussion the particulars of its history, its geography, its commerce, its internal and external politics? How do we explain the fact that this entire chapter is written in the conditional mood, even when it refers to well-established aspects of English society (we find, for example, such 'conditionals' as 'if this nation inhabited an island . . . '; 'if this nation were situated toward the north . . . '; 'if this nation established distant colonies . . .')?

In response to such questions, I would propose two possible hypotheses, which are not necessarily mutually exclusive. The first points to Montesquieu's announced intention to be 'more attentive to the order of things than to things in themselves.'[10] From this perspective, his use of the conditional mood allows him to analyze the essential functioning of English politics in an abstract and theoretical manner, as involving a series of logical consequences of certain given conditions, and to introduce into a sort of mental experiment the particularities of English history and geography. The result is an explanation of the phenomenon of English politics that is presented as completely logical and necessary, once the details of the English situation are taken into account. Here, as elsewhere throughout *De l'esprit des lois*, Montesquieu's most profound impulse is to subordinate particular facts to the more general relations of a theoretical order of things. But that impulse is not always expressed in the conditional mood, use of which is quite rare, for example, in the early theoretical chapters of the book explaining the typology of the three principal forms of government. Why should it be employed so overwhelmingly in the particular discussion of England?

This question suggests a second hypothesis. Does the conditional form of Montesquieu's analysis of English politics serve to underline the profound strangeness of the political and social order he is trying to understand and explain to his French audience? Among the English, as we have already seen, the passions are always at play, and the laws of love and hate (to say nothing of the principle of honour) are constantly forgotten in the manoeuvering among parties. This is a nation in which the partisan interests of the opposition nourish the terrors of the people, where the vain clamours that result from a kind of false political consciousness become the safeguard of liberty. This is a nation 'always in the heat of excitement,' which can therefore be 'more easily led by its passions than its reason,' a nation in which 'it would be easy for those who govern to engage it in enterprises against its natural interests.'[11] Yet it is also a nation in which 'it could happen that it would undertake things beyond its natural strength, yet mobilize against its enemies immense fictional riches, which the confidence and the nature of its government would render real.'[12] One of the effects of Montesquieu's reiterated use of the conditional mood in describing such a society is to foster an understanding of England as a singular, even fantastic phenomenon: a society in which the traditional boundaries between the true and the false, between stability and disorder, between the real and the possible, seem no longer to obtain.

How then to explain such a phenomenon? To explain is to classify. But it is immediately evident that Montesquieu was unable to situate the English political system within the tripartite classification of the forms of government developed in the first books of *De l'esprit des lois*. It was clearly not a republic of the classical variety, for the individualistic, self-interested, unpredictable political behaviour of the English was far from the civic virtue of the ideal republic. Neither was it a despotism, for there was a world of difference between the floating political terrors of a free people and the fear of a people subject to the arbitrary will of a despot. But neither was it a monarchy constituted by fundamental laws and sustained by the existence of intermediary bodies: The principle of honour was not to be found among the springs of English political action. Thus, the English political system existed outside the primordial classification initially announced by Montesquieu. It was 'a nation in which the republic is hidden under the form of monarchy,'[13] a kind of political mutation different from all other forms of government in that it had liberty itself as its object. From this point of view, then, Montesquieu's tendency to discuss the government of England simply as one of a 'free people,' without explicitly identifying the country by name, suggests an effort not simply to describe English politics but to conceptualize it in more abstract terms as a type – indeed, as an entirely new type – of polity.

It is therefore possible to discern in *De l'esprit des lois* the elements of a new classification of the forms of government, which emerges as the work develops. In this classification, based on a new distinction between the ancient republics and modern commercial states, England becomes the very type of the modern state, free and individualistic, whereas the traditional French monarchy remains in the middle – the sentiment of honour being, in effect, the middle term between the civic virtue of the ancients and the egoistic individualism of the moderns. Thus a new classificatory schema – republic/monarchy/England – is superimposed upon the old one – republic/monarchy/despotism – in the course of Montesquieu's argument. The first two terms are identical in both classifications; only the third term is transformed, as 'despotism' gives way to 'England.' Is there any significance to be found in this relationship of substitutability? What is it that England may have in common with despotic regimes?

Montesquieu offers the elements of a fascinating response to this question in a well-known passage of his description of the nature of monarchy:

> There are people in some states of Europe who have thought to abolish all seigneurial jurisdictions. They have not understood that they are trying to do what the English parliament has done. Abolish in a monarchy the prerogatives of the seigneurs, of the clergy, of the nobility, and of the towns; you would soon have a popular state, or else a despotic state. . . .
>
> The English, to foster liberty, have eliminated all the intermediary powers that formed their monarchy. They have good reason to preserve this liberty; if they were ever to lose it, they would be one of the most enslaved peoples on earth.[14]

Marvelling at the results of the English experiment with political liberty, Montesquieu seems, in some moods, to have regarded it as a risky experiment that has created a polity precariously close to despotism. It was not an experiment to be urged upon the French. This is perhaps the reason why he proceeds, in this discussion of the nature of monarchy, to offer an allusion to John Law, promoter in France of a financial system on the English model:

> Mr. Law, owing to his ignorance equally of the republican and the monarchical constitution, was one of the greatest promoters of despotism that Europe has ever seen. Besides the changes he made that were so abrupt, so extraordinary, so unprecedented, he wished to eliminate intermediary ranks and annihilate political bodies: he dissolved the monarchy by his chimerical reimbursements and seemed to want to buy back the constitution itself.[15]

What should we conclude from this argument? If I have insisted on some ambiguities and ambivalences in Montesquieu's thinking about English politics, I have not done so to deny his evident admiration for that 'republic . . . hidden under the form of monarchy.' But it is as well in this context to remember the strong sense of the term 'admire,' which implies wonder and amazement rather than mere approbation. Montesquieu presented his readers with a kind of political prodigy: a bizarre, disturbing, even dangerous phenomenon, not one that was necessarily to be imitated. As he concluded at the end of his chapter analyzing the English constitution, there was something unnervingly *extreme* about the English political experience.

> I do not mean by all this to diminish other governments or to say that this extreme political liberty must mortify those who enjoy only a

moderate liberty. How could I say this, I who believe that the excess even of reason is not always desirable and that men almost always adapt better to the mean than to the extremes?[16]

'A government stormy and bizarre'

Once we recognize Montesquieu's hesitations in the face of English politics, it becomes easier to understand how writers who wished to contest the model of the English constitution could turn his arguments against him. This was the strategy adopted in 1753 by one of his earliest critics, François Véron de Forbonnais, in an essay entitled 'Du gouvernement d'Angleterre, comparé par l'auteur de *l'Esprit des lois* au gouvernement de France.' Véron de Forbonnais had relatively little to say about Montesquieu's discussion of the balance of powers in Book 11 of *De l'esprit des lois*, except to insist that he found only 'principles of disunity in all this fine system.'[17] It was, rather, the description of English politics in Book 19 that attracted his attention. The play of passions depicted as evidence of political vitality in that analysis seemed to Véron de Forbonnais to be very far from the behaviour normally expected in a healthy political regime:

> On the contrary, I would regard this state of agitation as that of a sick man, to whom a raging fever had given an unnatural force, capable of killing him. . . .
> What? This nation that is so superior to all the others only ever acts by the agitation of the passions and is not capable of taking reason as its guide? Is this praise that the legislator wants to bestow upon it?[18]

Nor was Véron de Forbonnais convinced by Montesquieu's explanation that the 'terrors' imprinted on English popular consciousness served to safeguard public liberty. In his view, such an explanation seemed to suggest that 'the state of calm is for England the most dreadful state. Terror is the principle of movement in England.'[19] Little wonder, then, that the English had been subjected to frequent and dangerous revolutions, which had brought them to the brink of destruction and cost them rivers of blood: 'Was there ever a more chimerical good than a liberty that destroys me?'[20] According to Véron de Forbonnais, there was no alternative but to conclude from the analysis presented in *De l'esprit des lois* that England's vaunted liberty was illusory:

> It is free only in appearance because, if its happiness does not depend on a king, what is more frightening is that its happiness depends on the revolutions whose germ lives constantly within its bosom and

permits no tranquillity to this state, because the most profound peace is followed in an instant by the most dangerous storm.[21]

Véron de Forbonnais was not alone in drawing such conclusions. Many were the works that denounced the instability of English government and the turbulence of its history. Numerous were the writers who thundered against the example of this 'government stormy and bizarre.' Among the most zealous was the abbé Dubois de Launay, author of a *Coup d'oeil sur le gouvernement anglais*, published in 1786, whose phrase this is.[22] Entering the lists against the 'Anglomania' he saw subverting traditional values of order and authority, Dubois de Launay offered a whole repertoire of the vices of English government, the most fundamental of which was its constant instability. Not that this phenomenon was in his view at all surprising. Quite the contrary. 'It would be astonishing,' he insisted, 'if a government established on so uncertain and shaky a basis were stable, constant, and uniform; it must necessarily totter and waver incessantly, bend before *every wind of doctrine*, and be as changeable as the empire of opinion.'[23]

In Dubois de Launay's view, there were several reasons for the continual disorder found in English history and politics. The most important was the fatal ascendancy of the people within the English political system. *Tumultum ex tumultu, bellum ex bello ferunt*: Brandishing a tag from Sallust to clinch his point, Dubois insisted that there was no system of government more stormy than the exercise of popular power.

> It is impossible for the people, once it has made itself master, to put an end to one disorder except by another, to one revolt except by another even more deplorable than the first; with the result that, whenever this abuse prevails, the remedy for public misfortunes is still more disastrous than what it is meant to cure.[24]

But there was more to be found in England than dreamed of by the ancient political authorities. There, the age-old tendency of the people to remain in a permanent state of agitation was aggravated by such new developments as the liberty of the press and the system of political parties supported by it. 'This liberty to grumble and complain about the established governments is an inexhaustible source of trouble and revolutions,' Dubois maintained. It led necessarily to 'those sudden and unexpected movements, those violent commotions that disturb and sometimes overthrow states.'

> England has had this deplorable experience a hundred times. The history of English revolutions is almost the entire and complete history of the English. Why? Because in that country a combat reigns constantly between two parties, the party of the government and that of the *opposition*. . . . From these continual debates are

born the innumerable revolutions of which England has been the theater and which have made so much blood run.[25]

It goes virtually without saying that Dubois de Launay was an enraged apologist for absolute monarchy, a form of government that he defended in language that appears to turn Hobbes back upon Rousseau. 'Only in monarchies is everyone truly free,' he insisted. 'The will of all being submitted and united to the will of one, what each wills, everyone wills; what everyone wills, each wills: and that is liberty. Any other constitution will have the appearance of liberty; this one alone has the reality.'[26] But it was not necessary to be as conservative as Dubois to find oneself uneasy in the face of the political contestations, the party conflicts, and the constant disorders of English government. The comprehensive studies of eighteenth-century French attitudes toward the English constitution carried out by Gabriel Bonno and Frances Acomb offer numerous examples of a similar unease, even among the most enlightened thinkers. Acomb finds two clear strands within enlightened thinking critical of the English political model. For republican writers inspired by Rousseau and frequently sharing his distrust of representation, on the one hand, the existence of party political conflicts in England demonstrated that liberty was still far from fully established in that country. For the physiocrats, on the other hand, the same pattern of political contestation demonstrated how far the English were from the social tranquillity to be assured by rational acceptance of the necessary and essential order of society. Currents of Anglomania notwithstanding, there was clearly a strong – perhaps even a dominant – tendency within eighteenth-century French opinion to regard the English political model as turbulent and dangerous. And the crisis of English government during the 1760s and 1770s, from the Wilkes affair to the Gordon Riots, offered abundant evidence to confirm such a view of English political life.

It is not surprising, then, to find English politics figuring prominently under the entry 'Anarchie' in the *Dictionnaire de jurisprudence* of Prost de Royer, published between 1781 and 1788, or to rediscover it in the article 'Administration,' under the rubric 'Esprit de corps. Discorde. Opposition. Corruption. Influence. Probité. Justice.' A moderate and enlightened spirit, a partisan of administrative reform and publicity in matters of administration, Prost de Royer followed English political events with great interest and wrote of them frequently. He had read *De l'esprit des lois*, Sir William Blackstone's *Commentaries*, and the influential *Constitution d'Angleterre* by Jean-Louis Delolme. But despite the arguments of these works and his own admiration for the openness of English government, he found many unhealthy aspects of English politics. 'This system of opposition is considered the shield of the English constitution,' he maintained in his article 'Administration.' 'But what is this violent remedy that acts only by disturbing the whole body, irritating the nerves, affecting the head, burning the entrails? Can this violent regime be durable?'[27] The same fear of the politics of constitutional contestation found its expression in the article 'Anarchie':

> What is, in effect, a government composed of three powers, which ceaselessly spy on one another, accuse one another, impinge upon one another, erode one another? . . .
>
> What is this *opposition* to the *influence* of the throne and to the activity and secret of administration? . . .
>
> What is this *coalition*, by turns extolled as virtuous and decried as shameful? . . .
>
> Either patriotism and virtue are the soul of this government, or they are not. In the first case, all these devices, all these words are dishonorable and useless. In the second case, they are still useless, and despite the efforts of genius, patriotism, and individual virtue, fundamental and constitutional *anarchy* will always reappear.[28]

The dictionary of Prost de Royer may seem a relatively obscure example of the characteristic uneasiness of the French in the face of the disorder of English political life. But his work is revealing in yet another respect. The discussion of English politics in his article 'Anarchie' is followed immediately by a discussion of the problem of anarchy in a monarchical government such as France and, in particular, of the conflicts between the parlements and the crown that he describes as 'l'anarchie judiciaire.' In this context, he cites with approbation the discourse pronounced by Lamoignon de Malesherbes on 21 November 1774, at the time of the restoration of the parlements by Louis XVI:

> Let us never forget that the gravest attack upon a nation is to sow the seed of intestine divisions . . . and that the greatest benefit of the monarch [who is] today so dear to his people is to have appeared as a peacemaker in the temple of justice. Let us crown the work that he has so gloriously begun, let us succeed in confounding the authors of public calamities by uprooting from our hearts all the seeds of discord and by ushering in – after the storms – the light of the purest, calmest, and most serene day.[29]

A fine hope indeed, although one not long to be realized. The patterns of political and constitutional conflict that had culminated in the Maupeou 'revolution' of 1771 soon reasserted themselves to bring about the new crisis that prepared the revolution of 1789. But by assimilating party conflicts in England to practices of parlementary opposition in France in this way, Prost de Royer was pointing to a growing similarity between English and French politics at the end of the Old Regime. It was a comparison favoured increasingly by his compatriots. In the 1750s the abbé Mably in his *Droits et devoirs du citoyen* and the marquis d'Argenson in his journal had both detected a political wind blowing from across the Channel. Their perception was shared by Moreau, who found the growing political challenge of the French magistrates even more threatening to the exercise of monarchical authority than the power of Parliament in England. Such a view would have surprised an English visitor like Horace Walpole, who deprecated the efforts of his friends among the parlementary magistrates, during the 1760s, to represent themselves as the constitutional equivalent of members of Parliament. But it was a comparison upon which ministerial propaganda was also to insist a decade later in the pamphlet war over the Maupeou coup.

Consider, for example, the argument of a pamphlet published in the form of a letter purportedly sent from London in May 1771, in which the putative English author reproaches the French for the drift toward English practices he detects in their political culture:

> I revert to your facility in copying others' fashions, but permit me to tell you that you have pushed this talent to an unexpected point. It is true that this has happened by degrees, but they have been more rapid than one would have hoped for: I refer to the multiplicity of remonstrances of your different parlements or other courts, in opposition to what your king or his council have demanded. . . . We, your old neighbors and rivals, have long been acquainted with the birth, growth, successes, reverses, and pretensions of your parlements. But finally, I hear, you have in recent years formed a party of opposition, as we have done in England. . . . What! You wish also to liken yourselves to us in this respect and submit yourselves, with your frivolous heads, to all our political convulsions? Is it possible that you have so quickly forgotten the history of your former troubles, which have been described in every living language in order to leave to posterity a record of the evils that fanaticism, anarchy, disunity in government, and the influence of a few factious spirits caused in one of the finest parts of Europe?[30]

The rhetorical argument of this pamphlet may seem transparent in its efforts to mobilize against the parlements the profound French fear of civil strife inherited from the sixteenth century, a fear that had long sustained the appeal of absolute monarchy. But it was a shrewd move to link this fear to the example of English political instability by assimilating the magistrates' resistance to parliamentary opposition. Indeed, the tendency to cast the magistrates in the role of a political opposition in the English manner – helped as it was by the willingness of a journal such as the *Gazette de Leyde* to report the magistrates' actions and deliberations in precisely this light – seems to have become increasingly explicit as the Revolution approached. By 1787, for example, reports from the British embassy in

Paris could describe the antiministerial tactics within the parlement of Paris quite simply as the work of 'what they now style here, in the language of England, the side of opposition.'[31]

In fact, the British diplomats (whose dispatches analyzed the development of the prerevolutionary political crisis in France with considerable insight) frequently reflected on the nature of the changes in the political culture of the French that had 'brought them nearer to the English than they had ever been before.'[32] One of them, Daniel Hailes, ascribed this transformation in large part to French contact with revolutionary America. But he also argued for the impact of the foreign, and particularly the British, press in fostering public political interest. Reporting to his government from Paris in 1786, he concluded that 'the almost unrestrained introduction of our daily publications (tolerated indeed by the Government from the conviction of the impossibility of preventing it) having attracted the attention of the people more towards the freedom and advantages of our constitution, has also infused into them a spirit of discussion of public matters which did not exist before.'[33] In the light of such developments, the vehemence of Dubois de Launay's *Coup d'oeil sur le gouvernement anglais* is scarcely surprising. His denunciations of the dismal, destabilizing effects of public debate and party conflicts in England became the more immediate in their point as the French found their own public life transformed by similar processes of political contestation.

Nor is it surprising that, in the final confrontation between the parlements and the crown in 1788, the specter of English anarchy again figured in prominsterial pamphlets as a rhetorical weapon against parlementary claims. One such pamphlet derided the magistrates for efforts to introduce the English constitution into France just as others had introduced English fashions. Such efforts, the pamphleteer argued, were misplaced: 'One can certainly dress and get drunk like an Englishman from one moment to the next, but one cannot give the English national spirit to the French nation.'[34] They were also dangerous. They conjured up images of the execution of Charles I – 'the most execrable crime that could ever stain human memory' – and threatened France once again with a 'horrible anarchy, [which] after having delivered over the citizens to all the cruelties of civil war, would inevitably bring about the ruin of the state.'[35]

The English themes were played upon even more dramatically during the last months of the Old Regime by that master of the new political journalism, and most impassioned enemy of the parlements, Linguet. His vitriolic pamphlet, *La France plus qu'anglaise*, launched a powerful attack on the deliberations of the restored parlement of Paris on 25 September, 1788, which included the magistrates' celebrated declaration calling for the convocation of the Estates General according to the forms of 1614. The burden of Linguet's pamphlet was that parlementary resistance was propelling France well beyond anything the English had achieved in the domain of disorder.

> In *hats*, in *frock-coats*, in *jockeys*, in *whiskies*, in seditious *gatherings* and turbulent and dangerous *rejoicings*, the French people has only been able to imitate the English, taking up their forms of behavior as it took up their dress. But in republican audacity – or rather, in anarchic license – the king's councillors among the Gauls have found means of far outdistancing the inhabitants of the banks of the Thames.[36]

In the wake of the May Edicts, Linguet insisted, resistance to government authority had reached a degree of license, fury, and publicity exceeding anything witnessed in England. The parlements' new demands for the punishment of the ministers Brienne and Lamoignon, which Linguet compared in detail with the trial procedures that brought the earl of Strafford to the scaffold and paved the way for the execution of his royal master, were simply declarations of revolt. If they imitated English turbulence in their license, they lacked the English sense of proper procedure in such matters.

> England is the example they constantly cite to us, the model they pretend to take. It is from this idol of Montesquieu's that his fellow magistrates want to receive the *antiministerial* sword – a blade stained with the blood of kings even more than with that of ministers. Yet what do we see in this *England* but the most solemn reproof of the actions and procedures of the parlements in *France*? There we find an almost superstitious respect for rules that are constantly being violated in *Paris* in the name of a desire to imitate *London*.[37]

Absurd and inconsistent in themselves, Linguet argued, the efforts of the parlementaires to transplant the English constitution to France were nevertheless profoundly dangerous.

But Linguet offered another, no less serious indictment of the political claims of the parlements in *La France plus qu'anglaise*. Not only were the magistrates threatening the state with the evils of anarchy and aristocratic despotism, but they were succeeding in 'passing off their excesses as the result of *public opinion* and then wresting a solemn legitimation of them from the throne.'[38] Addressing himself directly to Louis XVI, Linguet repudiated this appropriation of the public voice – which he himself had struggled so vigorously to articulate through the radical journalism of his *Annales politiques, civiles, et littéraires* – in the defense of aristocratic interests. 'Your majesty,' he insisted, '. . . should not allow himself to be alarmed or disheartened by this phantom of PUBLIC OPINION so artificially displayed on all the standards of the confederations that league together against his rights. No, sire, the true *public opinion* is not against you, nor against your authority.'[39] From the perspective of Linguet's pamphlet, then, the significance of the parlementary declaration of 25 September was clear. It presented the challenge of a yet more intense period of political contestation, characterized by an explicit competition to invoke the new authority of *public opinion* and to define and control its true expression. It is to the nature of the concept of 'public opinion' that I now wish to turn.

'Public opinion'

So far in this essay I have sought to pursue two parallel themes. First, I have sketched the appearance within the context of the Old Regime of a politics of contestation, the terms of which compelled competing actors — whether they were engaged on behalf of the government or in opposition to it — to appeal beyond the traditional forms of absolutist politics to the tribunal of 'the public.' Sociologically, the nature of this entity remained ill defined: Indeed, one can understand the conflicts of the Pre-Revolution as a series of struggles to fix the sociological referent of the concept in favour of one or another competing group. But politically, and more critically, the notion of the 'public' came to function as the foundation for a new system of authority, the abstract source of legitimacy in a transformed political culture. As a result, French politics came increasingly to resemble English politics, with its open contestations and factional divisions played out in a constant competition to claim public support. With that development in mind, I have therefore suggested a second theme: the unease with which many French political writers regarded the passions and disorders, the perpetual conflicts and instabilities, that they found in the English political system. To the extent that English government exemplified the principles and practices of a politics of contestation, the attitudes of the French toward it suggest fundamental anxieties about a transformation that was introducing similar phenomena into their own political culture. The problem was to imagine a form of political practice that would acknowledge the new authority of 'the public,' on the one hand, while avoiding the conflicts and instabilities of a politics of contestation, on the other.

It is illuminating to address, from this point of view, the nature and meaning of the notion of 'public opinion' itself. A comprehensive analysis of the significance of that concept in eighteenth-century French political culture remains to be written. But it seems clear that the meaning of the term underwent considerable elaboration between its appearance in Rousseau's *First Discourse*, in 1750, and the outbreak of the French Revolution. For Rousseau, who used the term in a number of his works, 'public opinion' was the 'opinion of others in society':[40] the collective expression of the moral and social values of a people, the shared sentiments and convictions embodied in a nation's customs and manners and applied in its judgments of individual actions. It was the source of reputation and esteem among men, the judge of character and beauty, the customary sanction against immoral and improper actions. Its principal characteristic, in this sense, was the complexity of its resistance to conscious attempts at change, a point Rousseau liked to illustrate with reference to the history of dueling in France. 'Neither reason nor virtue nor the laws will subjugate public opinion, so long as one has not discovered the art of changing it,' he argued as he developed this theme in his *Lettre à M. d'Alembert*.[41] Public opinion was therefore a social rather than a political category in Rousseau's thinking, a challenge to the legislator's art rather than an expression of political will. Hence its appearance in *Du contrat social* in the chapter praising the Roman censorship as a means of preserving a people's mores:

> As the declaration of the general will is made by law, so the declaration of the public judgment is made by censure; public opinion is the kind of law of which the censor is the minister and which (like the prince) he merely applies to particular cases.
>
> Far from the tribunal of the censorship being the arbiter of the people's opinion, it is only the declaration; and as soon as it diverges from that opinion, its decisions are empty and without effect.[42]

This general social meaning of 'public opinion' as a collective judgment in matters of morality, reputation, and taste seems to have been the most familiar one in French usage, particularly in the period from 1750 to 1780. Examples can be found in the works of such writers as Duclos, the marquis de Mirabeau, Helvétius, d'Alembert, Mercier de la Rivière, Mably, Beaumarchais, and Holbach. From about 1770, however, the term begins also to take on connotations of the Enlightenment and to acquire a more explicitly political resonance. This shift is announced in the 1767 edition of the *Considérations sur les moeurs*, to which Duclos added a new paragraph elaborating upon his discussion of the role of men of letters. 'Of all empires,' he argued, 'that of *gens d'esprit*, without being visible, is the most extensive. The powerful command, but the *gens d'espirt* govern, because in the long run they form public opinion, which sooner or later subjugates or overthrows every kind of despotism.'[43] Raynal, in turn, made the political implications of such an argument more explicit in the *Histoire philosophique et politique des . . . deux Indes* (1770). 'In a nation that thinks and talks,' he insisted, 'public opinion is the rule of government, and government must never act against it without giving public reasons nor thwart it without disabusing it.' A government in which neither public opinion nor the general will was consulted, he argued in condemning the unrepresentative character of the English House of Commons with respect to the colonies, would therefore be an instrument of slavery.[44]

But the idea of the emergence of enlightened public opinion as a political force was perhaps put most succinctly a few years later by that remarkably informative observer of French political culture at the end of the Old Regime, Louis-Sébastien Mercier. 'In the last thirty years alone,' he argued in the *Tableau de Paris* in 1782, 'a great and important revolution has occurred in our ideas. Today, public opinion has a preponderant force in Europe that cannot be resisted. Thus in assessing the progress of enlightenment and the change it must bring about, we may hope that it will bring the greatest good to the world and that tyrants of all stripes will tremble before this universal cry that continuously rings out to fill and awaken Europe.'[45] For Mercier, this revolution was the achievement of writers who had raised their voices against political vices and dangerous stupidities: 'They have asserted the rights of reason, from the Menippean satire to the latest political pamphlet; and recently, in very important crises, they have decided public opinion. On their account, it has the greatest influence on events. They seem at last to be forming the national spirit.'[46]

Among the recent crises Mercier probably had in mind, the events of the Maupeou coup had been the most dramatic and the most powerful in fostering French political consciousness in the face of arbitrary government. Thus when Malesherbes insisted, in the celebrated *remontrances* written in 1775 on behalf of the magistrates of the restored Cour des Aides, that all the agents of the sovereign power 'must be subject to three sorts of restraints: the laws, recourse to higher authority, and public opinion,'[47] the definition of public opinion he had in mind was not simply the generalized social practice of the nation's customs and values invoked by Rousseau. On the contrary, public opinion was to be the enlightened expression of active and open discussion of all political matters, the free exercise of the public voice regarding the daily conduct of affairs, the institutional remedy for the administrative secrecy and arbitrariness that was threatening France with despotism. This new role of the public in political matters had been made possible in a great nation, Malesherbes maintained, by the invention of printing and the growth of literacy.

> The art of printing has thus given writing the same publicity that the spoken word possessed in the midst of the assemblies of the nation during the first age. But it has taken many centuries for the discovery of this art to have its full effect upon men. It has required that the entire nation gain the taste and habit of informing itself by reading. And it has required that enough men become skilled in the art of writing to lend their ministry to the entire public, taking the place of those gifted with natural eloquence who made themselves heard by our forefathers on the Champs de Mars or in the public judicial hearings.[48]

With the press as its forum, the printed word as its medium of persuasion, and writers as its ministers, the new tribunal of the public offered the possibility of achieving a functional modern equivalent of the primitive democracy of the Franks when they first appeared in Gaul. Reminding the young monarch of 'the example of those early kings who did not feel their authority threatened by the liberty they gave their subjects to implore their justice in the presence of the assembled nation,' Malesherbes invited Louis XVI to 'imitate in this matter the conduct of Charlemagne . . . [and] reign at the head of a nation whose entire body will be your council.'[49]

A similar vision of a king restored to communication with his people motivated the ideas for the reform of local government that Turgot developed in 1775 in the wake of the Maupeou coup. As described by Condorcet, in his *Vie de M. Turgot* (1786), the hierarchy of local assemblies envisaged by the reforming minister were intended to substitute free, open, and rational discussion of administrative matters for 'that public opinion [which is] a kind of obstacle common to all absolute governments in the conduct of affairs, the resistance of which is less constant, but also less tranquil, often as powerful, sometimes harmful, and always dangerous.' In the eyes of this mathematical theorist of public decision making, 'opinion' had not yet lost all its negative connotations of instability and irrationality by virtue of becoming 'public.' But once habits of rational participation in the conduct of local affairs had 'subjugated public opinion' to the rule of reason, he argued, the conditions would be established for informed consent in an assembly at the national level.[50]

Although Turgot's ideas for public participation in government were never formally presented to Louis XVI during his ministry, we know that the monarch's later reactions to the published version of the *Mémoire sur les municipalités* were negative. Nor was the king willing to accept the role of Charlemagne, as Malesherbes held it out to him in the *remontrances* of the Cour des Aides. Although the king ordered these *remontrances* stricken from that court's registers, he could not long prevent their appearance in print before the tribunal that Malesherbes praised as 'independent of all powers and respected by all powers . . . that tribunal of the public . . . the sovereign judge of all the judges of the earth.'[51] There were to be many other appeals to that same tribunal in the years that followed, and from many different sides. It was the court of last resort – 'that supreme judge to which the most absolute tribunals are subordinated, *public opinion*' – to which Linguet appealed from exile when he was disbarred from the practice of the law he had done so much to make the focus of public political attention.[52] It was the public consciousness that the younger Mirabeau insisted on his right to 'arouse' in 1779 in condemning his father's arbitrary use of *lettres de cachet* to confine him in the prison of Vincennes.[53] It was the tribunal to which Necker addressed himself so loquaciously in the 1780s, explaining and defending his conduct of financial affairs, and which his great rival Calonne invoked in condemning abuses before the notables in 1787. As we have seen, the parlements proclaimed the force of 'public opinion' in 1788, in justifying their resistance to ministerial authority, and Linguet acknowledged its power in denouncing the magistrates' claim to popular support. A few months later, Sieyès could also be found appealing to the progress of 'public opinion' in asserting the right of the Third Estate to constitute the nation and transform its constitution.

Finally, even the dogged Moreau, defending the monarchical constitution to the last, attested to the new power of the concept of public opinion in the waning months of the Old Regime. He had long urged the government to seize the ideological initiative in appealing to the public against the parlements. His *Exposition et défense de notre constitution monarchique française* was a now desperate effort to contest demands for revolutionary change being made in its name. 'Allow me merely to observe,' he argued, 'that if the pamphlets are without number, their authors can still be counted, and neither their opinions nor mine will ever form what one means by the term 'public opinion' – unless one agrees that there can be an immense difference, in every sense, between public opinion and the unanimous wish of the nation.[54] In attempting to deny the authority of public opinion to demands for a new constitution, Moreau not only underlined the significance of the concept on the eve of the meeting of the Estates General: He was also obliged to uphold the legitimacy of a new political meaning of the term, defined as the unanimous will of the nation.

What, then, was the meaning and significance of the concept of public opinion on the eve of the French Revolution? How had it developed in the decades of increasingly intense political contestation that ushered out the Old Regime? For a preliminary answer to these questions, we cannot do better than to turn to the two most systematic and extended discussions of the idea to appear in France during this period. The first consists of the reflections on the subject offered by a political actor particularly well placed to understand the nature of French government at the end of the Old Regime: the minister Jacques Necker. The second is the lengthy essay on the relationship of enlightenment and public administration with which the editor Jacques Peuchet introduced the volumes of the *Encyclopédie méthodique* devoted to *police*.

Between liberty and despotism

Necker's roller-coaster political career amply reveals the new dimensions of political contestation in French public life in the last years before the revolution. The pamphlets circulated by his opponents toward the end of his first ministry subjected him to open and personal vilification of a kind more familiar to English ministers than to French; unprecedented public support, assiduously cultivated during the years out of power, forced his recall in 1788 to preside over a regeneration of French national life, the political dynamics of which he was quite unable to control; his dismissal in July 1789 sparked the popular insurrection that brought the monarchy to political defeat. Necker's admiration for English government was well known; his reverence for 'public opinion' no less explicit. Mme de Staël, reverting to the old topos *vox populi, vox dei*, said of her father that public opinion 'had something of the divine for him.'[55] Whether or not this was the case, the controversial minister certainly made the appeal to public opinion a cardinal principle of his political practice. Necker's view of the problems facing French government was sketched out for the king in a memorandum on the creation of provincial assemblies, written in 1778 and made public by his political enemies (to the minister's embarrassment) in 1781. Convinced that monarchical government could not indefinitely tolerate the pattern of political contestations producing 'all these continual shocks, in which authority loses when it is not completely victorious,'[56] he argued for a systematic political strategy that would contain the power of the parlements to disturb the conduct of public affairs. Such a strategy, he insisted, must necessarily recognize that the parlements would remain a threat as long as they believed themselves 'supported by public opinion.' It was essential 'either to deprive them of this support or to prepare for repeated conflicts that will trouble the tranquillity of your majesty's reign and eventually lead either to a degradation of authority or to extreme actions, whose consequences cannot be precisely measured.[57]

But how was this campaign to wean the public from the parlements to be achieved? Necker proposed two modes of action. The first consisted of the creation of provincial assemblies with administrative responsibilities, institutions with which Necker began experimenting in Berry in 1778 and Haute Guyenne in 1779. Establishments of this kind, he argued, would eliminate the administrative abuses and fiscal evils that fed parlementary ambitions to intervene in political affairs. The second mode of action consisted of the introduction of publicity into all matters relating to government finances. As a banker, Necker was well aware of the importance of *la confiance publique* in financial affairs and understood the manner in which that confidence was maintained, across the Channel, by regular governmental accounting. By 1781 he had already moved the French government in this direction with the publication of the famous *Compte rendu*, envisaged as the first of a continuing series of published financial accounts. The unprecedented success of the *Compte rendu* is well known: three thousand copies were said to have been sold the first day of its publication, with perhaps as many as ten thousand a week in the period thereafter. And although the veracity of the accounting that Necker offered as controller general still remains a matter of debate, this should not blind us to the most revolutionary aspect of the publication of the *Compte rendu*, the fact that it opened the financial condition of the monarchy to public discussion.

The implications of Necker's decision for the political practice of the Old Regime were perhaps best described by the minister of foreign affairs, Vergennes, in a celebrated letter written to Louis XVI in 1781. According to Vergennes, Necker's Anglomania had led him to forget the fundamental principle of monarchical government: 'The monarch speaks; all others belong to the people and obey [*le monarque parle: tout est peuple et tout obéit*].'[58] Nothing was more dangerous for the political order of the Old Regime, then, than to attempt to introduce the English practice of publicity:

> The example of England, which publishes its accounts, is taken from a people that is restless, calculating, egoistic. Its application to France is an insult to the [French] national character, which is sentimental, trusting, and entirely devoted to its kings. Everything is lost in France, sire, if your majesty permits his ministers to invoke the English system of administration, for which your majesty's predecessors have shown such frequent and justified aversion.[59]

As Vergennes rightly emphasized (without acknowledging how far his own political reliance upon the press to foster the French alliance with the rebellious American colonies tended in the same direction), Necker was teaching strange new doctrines and attributing a revolutionary significance to 'the party that he calls "public opinion."' Ascribing the disorders of the Wars of Religion, the Fronde, and the Regency to the baleful influence of foreigners, Vergennes insisted that Necker was, in his turn, endangering the French monarchy through his ignorance of its fundamental principles. 'His *compte rendu* is, in the last result, a pure appeal to the people, the pernicious effects of which for the monarchy cannot yet be appreciated or foreseen.'[60] But Necker, for his part, regarded the initiative taken in the publication of the *Compte rendu* as quite simply involving the recognition, now unavoidable, of the appearance of a new force in politics. He argued for the importance of this force at greater length in his *De l'administration des finances de la France*, the public defence of his ministerial conduct, the very appearance of which, in 1784, offered yet another challenge to the secrecy of absolutist politics. And in so doing, he offered a series of characterizations of public opinion that are of particular interest in relationship to the growth of political contestation in eighteenth-century France, on the one hand, and the fears of the politics of contestation exhibited in contemporaneous views of English government on the other.

These characterizations were taken up and amplified in a striking manner in the extended historical, philosophical, and sociological analysis of the nature and meaning of public opinion presented by Jacques Peuchet, in the *Encyclopédie méthodique* in 1789.[61] As a writer on *police*

– the theory and practice of public administration – Peuchet offered a fascinating reworking of the principles of absolute government within the framework of a comprehensive discussion of the relationship between reason and authority in a progressively more enlightened society. His lengthy essay, informed by a broad familiarity with the classics of eighteenth-century political science and a keen interest in contemporary developments within French political life, is one of the most fascinating expressions of enlightened political culture to appear at the very end of the Old Regime.

Taken together, then, the views of the minister and the theorist elaborate in relatively systematic terms the meaning of the notion of public opinion as a central feature in the theory and practice of politics on the eve of the French Revolution. The nature and significance of the concept may best be suggested by a summary listing of the characteristics upon which their definitions converged.

1 'Public opinion,' Necker argued, is the 'spirit of society,' the fruit of the continual communication among men.[62] Peuchet gave this theme a more extended treatment by placing his discussion of public opinion within the framework of a general account of the progress of European society, an account explicitly inspired by William Robertson's *History of the Reign of Charles V* (translated by J.-B.-A. Suard in 1771) and suggestive in many respects of Condorcet's later *Esquisse d'un tableau historique des progrès de l'esprit humain*. Social progress, he argued, had made the enlightened eighteenth century very different from the world of the ancients, among whom the phenomenon of public opinion was unknown. 'Public opinion may thus be regarded as a social production of our century.'[63]

2 As a social phenomenon and the expression of society itself, public opinion possesses none of the institutionalized power, none of the financial or military resources, of the state. It nevertheless represents a force far greater than any formal agency of political constraint. In Necker's words, it is 'an invisible power that, without treasury, guard, or army, gives its laws to the city, the court, and even the palaces of kings.'[64] It is 'a tribunal before which all men who attract attention are obliged to appear: There, public opinion, as if from the height of a throne, awards prizes and honors, makes and unmakes reputations.'[65] The same emphasis on public opinion as an enlightened court of last resort appears in Peuchet's definition of the term: 'This word designates in a general manner the sum of all social knowledge [*lumières sociales*], or rather the result of this knowledge, considered as grounds for the judgments made by a nation on the matters submitted to its tribunal. Its influence is today the most powerful motive for praiseworthy actions.'[66]

3 Public opinion is therefore a court. As such, its authority is universal; its

sway extends to all estates and conditions of men. In insisting on this
point, in fact, Peuchet found that he could do no better than to quote
directly from Necker's *De l'administration des finances*. 'It reigns over
all minds, and princes themselves respect it whenever they are not
carried away by excessive passions: Some willingly take it into
account, moved by their ambition for public favor, and others, less
docile, are still unwittingly subject to it as a result of the influence of
those around them.'[67]

4 Public opinion is peaceful. It is incompatible with divisions and factions.
Consequently, it is the characteristic expression of the politically tranquil eighteenth century. 'This authority of opinion was unknown,'
Necker argued, 'so long as internal troubles exhausted all sentiments,
occupied all thoughts. Spirits divided by factions according to which one
could only love or hate were incapable of uniting under the more
tranquil banners of esteem and public opinion.'[68] Elaborating upon
the same theme in slightly different terms, Peuchet represented the
growth of public opinion as a cause, rather than simply a consequence, of eighteenth-century political stability: 'It has extended the
sphere of useful and beneficent principles, repressed a host of abuses,
declared an implacable war against all the systems of persecution and
intolerance; finally, it has become our firmest support for order, the
guide and the guardian of *police* and of manners.'[69]

5 As a basis for social order, public opinion is stable and durable. There is
nothing ephemeral in its operation. 'Very slow to take form,' as Peuchet
insists, it alone 'can oppose a dike to the torrent of disorders.'[70] Long
synonymous with fickleness, flux, and subjectivity, the very notion of
'opinion' has now been stabilized by its conjunction with the term
'public,' thereby taking on the universality and objectivity of *la chose
publique* in absolutist discourse. Necker made this point emphatically:

> It is necessary to avoid confusing public opinion, as I have
> described it here, with those ephemeral movements that often
> pertain only to certain societies and certain circumstances. It is
> not before such judgments that the man capable of conducting a
> great administration should prostrate himself. On the contrary, it
> is necessary to know how to disdain them, in order to remain
> faithful to that public opinion whose characteristics are all author-
> itative [*imposants*] and which reason, time, and the universality of
> sentiments alone have the right to consecrate.[71]

6 The universality and objectivity of public opinion are constituted by
reason. Its force therefore derives from 'the progress of enlightenment,'
which Necker invoked and Peuchet analyzed at considerable length. This
is why 'there will never be a powerful safeguard against errors and false
systems, so long as public opinion is feeble in its judgments, uncertain in

its knowledge, and distracted in its attention.'[72] For Necker, it followed from the power of language in human affairs that the monarch was under an obligation to enlighten the public by explaining his actions and giving the preambles to his laws 'that imprint of truth that is so easy to recognize.'[73] Peuchet drew a more radical conclusion. He claimed that true legislative authority had already passed from the monarch to the enlightened elite, whose public function it was to lead the nation toward greater knowledge and rationality. 'Public opinion has its source in the opinion of the enlightened, whence it gains partisans and becomes the general conviction [*le voeu général*],' he argued. 'The most important revolutions have been accomplished by public writings, by more or less dogmatic works. Writers have become the true legislators of peoples. . . . They have laid hold of public opinion, making it the universal instrument and determining cause of all the movements that occur in the state of peoples.'[74]

In Peuchet's view, moreover, the emergence of the periodical press was a particularly important aspect of the process by which enlightened writers had displaced the public authority of rulers. Journals and newspapers, 'these means of universal communication,' had become 'the nourishment, the support, and the weapon of philosophy.' Through their agency, 'an entire sect, an entire nation, the whole of Europe, is called to pronounce judgment upon a host of objects regarding which, previously, only despotism or the interest of particular individuals had the right to make themselves heard. From this gathering of ideas, from this concentration of enlightenment, a new power has formed that, in the hands of public opinion, governs the world and gives laws to the civilized nations.'[75]

7 The power of publicity in political affairs was particularly visible among the English, whose practices in this respect both Necker and Peuchet admired. But they also agreed that 'the authority exercised in France by public opinion'[76] was a specially important phenomenon. 'This power of public opinion is infinitely more feeble in other countries and under different forms of government,' Necker argued. Among enslaved peoples, everything depends upon the will of the monarch. Republican regimes, on the contrary, 'know only popular support or the ascendancy of eloquence in the national assemblies. Moreover, liberty, which forms the essence of such governments, inspires in men more confidence in their own judgments, and one could even say that, jealous of every kind of empire, they cherish their own opinions to the point of independence and take a secret pleasure in diverging from the opinions of others.'[77] In explaining why 'public opinion' must be a particularly important phenomenon in France, these considerations suggest a broader conclusion. They imply, in effect, that public opinion expresses the political sociability of a nation that is neither enslaved nor truly free.

Necker invited this conclusion somewhat obliquely by insisting on the remarkable effects of this 'spirit of society' when it 'reigns in all its force in the midst of a sensitive people, which loves equally to judge and be judged, which is neither distracted by political interests nor enfeebled by despotism nor dominated by too seething passions.'[78] But the point was made quite explicit by Peuchet. 'Public opinion,' he insisted, 'differs from both the spirit of obedience that must reign in a despotic state and the popular opinions that prevail in republican deliberations. It is composed of a mass of ideas that human experience and the progress of enlightenment have successively introduced into a state whose government does not permit expression of the energetic character of national liberty, but where the security of the citizens is respected. . . . It is the weapon that an enlightened people collectively opposes to the precipitous operations of an ambitious minister or a misguided administration. Its slow action would be little suited to a free people, and slaves would not have the force to direct it against the undertakings of an irascible and powerful master.'[79]

Taken together, then, the characteristics imputed to 'public opinion' by Necker and Peuchet present an image of a political system in remarkable contrast not only to the traditional politics of French absolutism but to the politics of contestation often exemplified in contemporary French discussion by the English model. 'The ascendancy of public opinion, more than any other consideration, often opposes obstacles in France to the abuse of authority,' Necker argued. 'It is uniquely this opinion and the esteem in which it is held that preserves a sort of influence for the nation by giving it the power to reward and punish by praise or disdain.'[80] Public opinion therefore functions, in effect, as a mean between despotism and extreme liberty. It serves as a barrier against arbitrary will and the abuse of power, yet it implies none of the divisions, factions, passions, or political conflicts of a completely free government – phenomena that presented so alarming a spectacle to many French observers looking across the Channel. Public opinion, in other words, implies acceptance of an open, public politics. But, at the same time, it suggests a politics without passions, a politics without factions, a politics without conflicts, a politics without fear. One could even say that it represents a politics without politics.

Rather than suggesting a politics of contestation, the concept of public opinion therefore constitutes an image of a politics of rational consensus, untroubled by the passions of willful human action. In this context, once again, Montesquieu's reflections on the nature of English political life seem suggestive. 'In a free nation,' he argued, 'it is very often a matter of indifference whether individuals reason well or badly; it is enough that they reason: From this ensues liberty, which guarantees the effects of this reasoning. Similarly, in a despotic government, it is equally pernicious to reason well or badly; that one reasons is enough for the principle of the government to be shaken.'[81] According to this logic, the difference between reasoning well and reasoning badly matters neither to those who are free nor to those who are enslaved. But to those who are neither enslaved nor fully free, the difference must matter a great deal. The explications of the notion of public opinion offered by Necker and Peuchet suggest that the concept took form precisely in this intermediate space between liberty and despotism. It offered an abstract court of appeal to a monarchy anxious to put an end to several decades of political contestation. And it held out the ideal of a tranquil expression of public reason to a people who, in wishing for responsible government, remained nonetheless horrified by the spectacle (and haunted by the memory) of the play of divisive political passions.

Conclusion

In his *Mémoires historiques sur la vie de M. Suard*, Dominique-Joseph Garat recalled a conversation between Jean-Baptiste-Antoine Suard and John Wilkes regarding the endless conflicts generated by English practices of political opposition. Wilkes defended perpetual contestation as essential to the defense of liberty, on the grounds that those who hold power will constantly abuse it if they are not constrained by fear of the truth and threatened by the possible loss of their position. The tactics of parliamentary opposition, he insisted, compelled the government not only to act rationally but to give good reasons for its actions to the nation as a whole. 'The freest of nations is never sure enough of its liberty, which is a fortress constantly under siege: The ramparts must be manned, even when the firing has stopped.'[82]

Suard disagreed: 'Convinced that it is good for a people to be constantly alert and enlightened,' Garat recalled, 'he could not persuade himself that a state of war was the true social state.' Did freedom really require 'alarms where there are neither dangers, storms, nor clouds?', Suard demanded of Wilkes. 'The agreement of opinions alone gives the springs of public order a mild and easy force. Once this agreement is found, obedience anticipates the law, and the political spheres are subject to harmony, just like the celestial spheres.' For Wilkes's metaphor of a constant battle for liberty, Garat preferred to substitute the more tranquil image of a peaceful and rational search for public opinion, an endeavour to which party divisions were as antithetical as they were to the solution of a mathematical problem.

> What does the term 'representation' mean? What can the representatives represent, if not public opinion? Let debates occur, then, and let them continue as long as this opinion is uncertain; that is good

and inevitable, and however long and animated the debates are, the gallery of the nation will follow them with an attention too concentrated to be tumultuous. We do not divide into parties over a game of chess, or over two solutions of the same mathematical problem. Why? Because, even for those who know neither the rules of the game, nor the rules of mathematical solutions, the solution and the outcome of the game become facts which only have to be attested. For that, *parties* are totally unnecessary. Could it be possible, could it be true, that in all these discussions there is only one dispute: that the ministry is really at issue when it is a question (and one speaks the language) of the interests of the country and of humanity?[83]

The dispute between Wilkes and Suard illustrates well the profound paradox implicit in the concept of public opinion as it took form in France at the end of the Old Regime. In practice, that concept was invoked with increasing frequency in the course of the open political contestations which transformed the nature of French public life in the second half of the century, making French politics more similar to the unstable politics of the English than many French observers were willing to admit. Yet, in theory, public opinion was consistently depoliticized. As the image of a rational consensus untroubled by the passions of willful human action, it was conceived, on the one hand, as the very antithesis of the dangerous play of political passions that many French observers saw across the Channel, and contrasted, on the other, with the direct exercise of political will in the ancient republics. Construed as rational, universal, impersonal, unitary, it took on many of the attributes of the absolute monarchical authority it was replacing, just as it prefigured many ambiguities of the revolutionary will to which it in turn gave way. The idea of party divisions and conflicting political interests was as antithetical to the rationalist conception of a unitary public opinion as it was to be to the voluntarist conception of a unitary general will.

Conceived in this way, public opinion can be seen as functioning historically as a kind of liminal concept between absolute authority and revolutionary will. If it had a relatively fleeting place in the history of French political discourse – for its hegemony lasted barely a quarter-century – it is nevertheless of central importance for our understanding of the transition from the Old Regime to the French Revolution. The political culture of absolutism had already been transformed in its last decades by changes that brought a new political space into existence well before 1789. If the press was the medium of this political space, 'public opinion' was its ultimate principle of authority. That the crown had already implicitly accepted the legitimacy of this alternate authority can be seen, for example, in its willingness to open up the question of the forms of the convocation of the Estates General to public investigation and debate by the declaration of July 5, 1788 – an action that Tocqueville shrewdly compared to announcing the nature of the French constitution as a topic for the kind of prize-essay competition that was so favoured a form in the Enlightenment. And that subjects of the crown were no less willing, in their turn, to appeal to the court of public opinion seems clear from the thousands of briefs presented before that court in the last months of 1788. 'Public opinion' had become the articulating concept of a new political space with a legitimacy and authority apart from that of the crown: a public space in which the nation could reclaim its rights against the crown. Within this space, the French Revolution became thinkable.

Notes

1 *Encyclopédie, ou Dictionnaire raisonné des sciences, des arts et des métiers, par une société de gens de lettres . . .*, 17 vols. (Paris, 1751–65), 11:507, s.v. *opinion*.
2 *Déclaration du roi, qui fait défenses d'imprimer, débiter, ou colporter aucuns écrits, ouvrages ou projets concernant la réforme ou l'administration des finances: Donnée à Versailles le 28 mars 1764.*
3 Antoine François Prost de Royer, *Dictionnaire de jurisprudence et des arrêts, ou Nouvelle édition du Dictionnaire de Brillon, connu sous le titre de Dictionnaire des arrêts et jurisprudence universelle des parlements de France et autres tribunaux . . .*, 7 vols. (Lyons, 1781–8), 2:838 (s.v. *administration*).
4 Ferdinando Galiani, *Correspondance avec Mme d'Epinay, Mme Necker, . . . etc.*, ed. Lucien Percy and Gaston Maugras, 2 vols. (Paris, 1881–2), I, p. 375.
5 Jürgen Habermas, *Strukturwandel der Oeffentlichkeit* (Neuwied, 1962). An English translation of that work has now appeared as Habermas, *The Structural Transformation of the Public Sphere*, tr. Thomas Burger and Frederick Lawrence (Cambridge, Mass., 1989).
6 Charles-Louis de Secondat, baron de Montesquieu, *De l'esprit de lois*, ed. J. Brèthe de la Gressaye, 4 vols. (Paris, 1950–61).
7 de Secondat, *De l'esprit de lois* 3, p. 28.
8 de Secondat, *De l'esprit de lois* 3, p. 29.
9 de Secondat, *De l'esprit de lois* 3, p. 30.
10 de Secondat, *De l'esprit de lois* 3, p. 5.
11 de Secondat, *De l'esprit de lois* 3, p. 30–1.
12 de Secondat, *De l'esprit de lois* 3, p. 31.
13 de Secondat, *De l'esprit de lois* 1, p. 133.
14 de Secondat, *De l'esprit de lois* 1, p. 45.
15 de Secondat, *De l'esprit de lois* 1, p. 47.
16 de Secondat, *De l'esprit de lois* 2, p. 76.
17 François Véron de Forbonnais, 'Du gouvernement d'Angleterre, comparé par l'auteur de *l'Esprit des lois* au gouvernement de France' in *Opuscules de M. F . . .* [Fréron], vol. 3., *Contenant un extrait chapitre par chapitre du livre de l'Esprit des lois, des observations sur quelques endroits particuliers de ce livre, une idée de toutes les critiques qui en ont été faites, avec quelques remarques de l'éditeur* (Amsterdam, 1753), p. 179.
18 de Forbonnais 'Du gouvernement d'Angleterre, comparé par l'auteur de *l'Esprit des lois* au gouvernement de France, pp. 179–81.

19 de Forbonnais 'Du gouvernement d'Angleterre, comparé par l'auteur de *l'Esprit des lois* au gouvernement de France, p. 182.

20 de Forbonnais 'Du gouvernement d'Angleterre, comparé par l'auteur de *l'Esprit des lois* au gouvernement de France, p. 185.

21 de Forbonnais 'Du gouvernement d'Angleterre, comparé par l'auteur de *l'Esprit des lois* au gouvernement de France, pp. 212–13.

22 Henri Dubois de Launay, *Coup d'oeil sur le gouvernement anglais* (n.p., 1786).

23 de Launay, *Coup d'oeil sur le gouvernement anglais*, p. 26.

24 de Launay, *Coup d'oeil sur le gouvernement anglais*, pp. 132–3.

25 de Launay, *Coup d'oeil sur le gouvernement anglais*, pp. 168–70.

26 de Launay, *Coup d'oeil sur le gouvernement anglais*, p. 193.

27 Prost de Royer, *Dictionnaire de jurisprudence et des arrêts*, 2, p. 866.

28 de Royer, *Dictionnaire de jurisprudence et des arrêts*, 4, p. 763.

29 de Royer, *Dictionnaire de jurisprudence et des arrêts*, 4, p. 764.

30 *Extrait d'une lettre, en date de Londres, du 3 mai 1771* (n.p., n.d.), pp. 4–5.

31 Oscar Browning, ed., *Despatches from Paris, 1784–1790* (London, 1909–10), 1, p. 221.

32 Browning, *Despatches from Paris, 1784–1790*, 1, p. 148.

33 Browning, *Despatches from Paris, 1784–1790*.

34 *Songe d'un bon français, suivi de la lettre d'un anglais* (London, 1788), 37. The *lettre d'un anglais* is dated '15 July 1788.'

35 *Songe d'un bon français, suivi de la lettre d'un anglais*, 29, 26.

36 [S.-N.-H. Linguet], *La France plus qu'anglaise, ou Comparaison entre la procédure entamé à Paris le 25 septembre 1788 contre les ministres du roi de France et le procès intenté à Londres en 1640, au comte de Strafford, principal ministre de Charles premier, roi d'Angleterre; avec des réflexions sur le danger imminent dont les entreprises de la robe menacent la nation, et les particuliers* (Brussels, 1788), 26.

37 [S.-N.-H. Linguet], *La France plus qu'anglaise, ou Comparaison entre la procédure entamé à Paris le 25 septembre 1788 contre les ministres du roi de France et le procès intenté à Londres en 1640, au comte de Strafford, principal ministre de Charles premier, roi d'Angleterre; avec des réflexions sur le danger imminent dont les entreprises de la robe menacent la nation, et les particuliers* (Brussels, 1788), 82.

38 [S.-N.-H. Linguet], *La France plus qu'anglaise, ou Comparaison entre la procédure entamé à Paris le 25 septembre 1788 contre les ministres du roi de France et le procès intenté à Londres en 1640, au comte de Strafford, principal ministre de Charles premier, roi d'Angleterre; avec des réflexions sur le danger imminent dont les entreprises de la robe menacent la nation, et les particuliers* (Brussels, 1788), 45–6.

39 [S.-N.-H. Linguet], *La France plus qu'anglaise, ou Comparaison entre la procédure entamé à Paris le 25 septembre 1788 contre les ministres du roi de France et le procès intenté à Londres en 1640, au comte de Strafford, principal ministre de Charles premier, roi d'Angleterre; avec des réflexions sur le danger imminent dont les entreprises de la robe menacent la nation, et les particuliers* (Brussels, 1788), 12.

40 Jean-Jacques Rousseau, *Lettre à M. d'Alembert sur les spectacles*, ed. M. Fuchs (Geneva, 1948), 89–90.

41 Rousseau, *Lettre à M. d'Alembert sur les spectacles*, p. 93. For Rousseau's discussion of dueling in relationship to public opinion, see Rousseau, *Lettre à M. d'Alembert sur les spectacles*, 90–9, and *Du contrat social*, ed. Maurice Halbwachs (Paris, 1943), p. 408.

42 Rousseau, *Du contrat social*, p. 407.

43 Charles Pinot Duclos, *Considérations sur les moeurs*, 5th ed. ([Paris], 1767), pp. 270–1.

44 Guillaume Thomas François Raynal, *Histoire philosophique et politique des . . . deux Indes*, 6 vols. (Amsterdam, 1770), 6, pp. 391–2; 415.

45 Mercier, *Tableau de Paris*, 4, p. 289.

46 Mercier, *Tableau de Paris*, 8, p. 109.

47 [Chrétien-Guillaume Lamoignon de Malesherbes], *Très Humbles et Très Respectueuses Remontrances que présentent au roi notre très honoré et souverain seigneur les gens tenants sa Cour des aides* (6 May 1775), in *Les 'remontrances' de Malesherbes, 1771–1775*, ed. Elisabeth Badinter (Paris, 1978), p. 204.

48 [Chrétien-Guillaume Lamoignon de Malesherbes], *Très Humbles et Très Respectueuses Remontrances que présentent au roi notre très honoré et souverain seigneur les gens tenants sa Cour des aides* (6 May 1775), in *Les 'remontrances' de Malesherbes, 1771–1775*, ed. Elisabeth Badinter (Paris, 1978), p. 273.

49 [Chrétien-Guillaume Lamoignon de Malesherbes], *Très Humbles et Très Respectueuses Remontrances que présentent au roi notre très honoré et souverain seigneur les gens tenants sa Cour des aides* (6 May 1775), in *Les 'remontrances' de Malesherbes, 1771–1775*, ed. Elisabeth Badinter (Paris, 1978), p. 275.

50 M-J.-A.-N. Caritat, marquis de Condorcet, *Oeuvres*, ed. A. Condorcet-O'Connor and F. Arago, 12 vols. (Paris, 1847–9), 5:123–4.

51 Chrétien-Guillaume Lamoignon de Malesherbes, 'Discours de réception à l'Académie français' (16 February 1775), in *Oeuvres inédites de . . . Malesherbes*, ed. N. L. Pissot (Paris, 1808), 151. The *remontrances* of 6 May 1775 appeared in print in 1779 in [Dionis du Séjour], *Mémoires pour servir à l'histoire du droit public de la France en matière d'impôts . . .* (Brussels, 1779).

52 S.-N.-H. Linguet, *Appel à la posterité, ou Recueil des mémoires et plaidoyers de M. Linguet pour lui-même, contre la communauté des avocats du Parlement de Paris* (n.p., 1779), 372.

53 Honoré Gabriel Riqueti, comte de Mirabeau, *Lettres originales de Mirabeau, écrites du donjon de Vincennes pendant les années 1777, 78, 79, et 80 . . .*, 4 vols. (Paris, 1792), 3, p. 202.

54 Jacob-Nicolas Moreau, *Exposition et défense de notre constitution monarchique française*, 2 vols. (Paris, 1789), 1, p. xvii.

55 Anne Louise Germaine, baronne de Staël-Holstein, *Considérations sur les principaux événements de la Révolution française*, as quoted in Egret, *Necker*, 61.

56 Jacques Necker, 'Mémoire au roi, sur l'établissement des administrations provinciales,' in *Oeuvres complètes*, ed. A.-L. de Staël-Holstein, 15 vols. (Paris, 1820–21) (henceforth cited as *OC*), 3, p. 347.

57 Necker, 'Memoire au roi, sur l'etablissement des administrations provinciales', 3, p. 365.

58 Soulavie, *Mémoires historiques*, 4, p. 153; cited in Egret, *Necker*, pp. 177–8.

59 Soulavie, *Mémoires historiques*, 4, p. 158.

60 Soulavie, *Mémoires historiques*, 4, pp. 159; 155.

61 Jacques Peuchet, 'Discours préliminaire,' in *Encyclopédie méthodique: Jurisprudence*, vol. 9, *Police et municipalités*, i–clx. This first of the two volumes on *police*, edited by Peuchet for the *Encyclopédie méthodique*, was published in Paris in 1789; a second appeared in 1791.

62　*OC*, 4, pp. 47, 51.
63　Peuchet, 'Discours préliminaire,' x.
64　*OC*, 4, p. 50.
65　*OC*, 4, p. 47.
66　Peuchet, 'Discours préliminaire,' ix.
67　Peuchet, 'Discours préliminaire,' quoting *OC*, 4, p. 49.
68　*OC*, 4, pp. 47–8.
69　Peuchet, 'Discours préliminaire,' ix.
70　Peuchet, 'Discours préliminaire,' lxxx–lxxxi.
71　*OC*, 4, p. 56. This passage reappeared in the article on public opinion in the section of the *Encyclopédie méthodique* devoted to '*finances*,' an article that is basically a compilation of excerpts from Necker's discussion of the subject. See *Encyclopédie méthodique: Finances*, 3 vols. (Paris, 1784–7), 3, pp. 262–4.
72　*OC*, 5, p. 613.
73　*OC*, 4, p. 59.
74　Peuchet, 'Discours préliminaire,' p. x, li.
75　Peuchet, 'Discours préliminaire,' p. lxxxvi.
76　*OC*, 4, p. 50.
77　*OC*, 4, pp. 49–50.
78　*OC*, 4, pp. 50–1.
79　Peuchet, 'Discours préliminaire,' pp. ix–x.
80　*OC*, 4, pp. 52–3.
81　Montesquieu, *De l'esprit des lois*, 3, p. 38.
82　Dominique-Joseph Garat, *Mémoires historiques sur la vie de M. Suard, sur ses écrits, et sur le XVIIIᵉ siècle*, 2 vols. (Paris, 1820), 2, p. 94.
83　Garat, *Mémoires historiques sur la vie de M. Suard, sur ses écrits, et sur le XVIIIᵉ siècle*, pp. 94–5.

8

Do books make revolutions?

ROGER CHARTIER

[Three authors whose ideas have been discussed elsewhere] had a ready answer to this question. They can speak for themselves.

Alexis de Tocqueville:

Never before had the entire political education of a great nation been the work of its men of letters, and it was this peculiarity that perhaps did most to give the French Revolution its exceptional character and the régime that followed it the form we are familiar with. Our men of letters did not merely impart their revolutionary ideas to the French

Reprinted in full, except for notes, from R. Chartier, *The Cultural Origins of the French Revolution* (Durham, N.C., Duke University Press, 1991), pp. 67–91, 207–10.

nation; they also shaped the national temperament and outlook on life. In the long process of moulding men's minds to their ideal pattern their task was all the easier since the French had no training in the field of politics, and they thus had a clear field. The result was that our writers ended up by giving the Frenchman the instincts, the turn of mind, the tastes, and even the eccentricities of the literary man. And when the time came for action, these literary propensities were imported into the political arena.[1]

Hippolyte Taine:

Philosophy winds through and overflows all channels public and private, by manuals of impiety, like the 'Théologies portatives,' and in the lascivious novels circulated secretly, through epigrams and songs, through daily novelties, through the amusements of fairs and the harangues of the Academy, through tragedy and the opera, from the beginning to the end of the century, from the 'Oedipe' of Voltaire to the 'Tarare' of Beaumarchais. It seems as if there was nothing else in the world. At least it is found everywhere and it floods all literary efforts; nobody cares whether it deforms them, content in making them serve as a conduit.[2]

Daniel Mornet:

Philosophy made it possible for those who chose to take up politics to discourse about it. Political pamphlets doubtless circulated at all times during the Old Regime, even when censorship was most severe and most effective, but they were fairly rare and they circulated with some difficulty. After 1770, however, and particularly after 1780, the freedom to write that the Philosophes had demanded was nearly total in fact. . . . That is why the hundreds of libels published with not the least philosophical intent and utterly anodyne treatises were among the causes that had the strongest effect upon opinion: they displayed political problems before it and gave it a taste for reflection on [political matters].[3]

A common idea underlies these three statements: reading is endowed with such power that it is capable of totally transforming readers and making them into what the texts envisage. Thus these three authors, each in his own way, understood the shaping of opinion in prerevolutionary France as a process of internalization, on the part of more and more readers as the century progressed, of ways of thinking proposed by the philosophical texts. Borne by the printed word, the new ideas conquered people's minds, moulded their ways of being, and elicited questions. If the French of the late eighteenth century fashioned the Revolution, it is because they had in turn been fashioned by books. Furthermore, those books provided an abstract discourse remote from the practice of daily affairs and a criticism of tradition destructive to authority. This is my working hypothesis, although I reserve the right to express a few doubts along the way.

Increased readership

Figures show – to begin with the most massive set of data – that booksellers offered a more numerous and increasingly avid reading public a profoundly transformed product. As far as the readers are concerned, the most important point here is perhaps not so much the overall rise in literacy (the rate rose from 29 percent to 47 percent for men and from 14 percent to 27 percent for women between 1686–90 and 1786–90) as it is the increasing evidence of printed matter in social milieux in which people had formerly owned few books. During the course of the century, in fact, there was an increase in both the proportion of the population that owned books (particularly among craftsmen and shopkeepers) and the size of their libraries. In Paris, books, which at the beginning of the century appeared in only 30 percent of inventories after death for domestic servants and 13 per cent for journeymen workers, figured in 40 percent and 35 percent, respectively, of such inventories in 1780. In the towns and cities of western France, the proportion of inventories after death that mention printed works rose, between the end of the seventeenth century and the middle of the eighteenth century, from 10 percent to 25 percent in estates evaluated at less than 500 livres; from less than 30 percent to more than 40 percent in estates worth between 500 and 1000 livres; from 30 per cent to 55 percent in those between 1500 and 2000 livres; and from 50 percent to 75 percent in those evaluated at more than 2000 livres. The size of the collections grew as well: between the end of the seventeenth century and the 1780s, the mode in libraries belonging to the *bourgeoisie à talents* shifted from a bracket of 1–20 volumes to one of 20–100 volumes; among the clergy the modal number of books owned increased from 20–50 volumes to 100–300 volumes; in the libraries of nobles and men in the legal professions the mode increased from between 20 and 50 volumes to more than 300 volumes. Although not all those who had achieved literacy could be counted as potential purchasers of books (especially in rural areas, where printed works were still only rarely found in peddlers' stocks), in the towns, at least, the market for books had grown and a larger number of readers demanded a larger number of texts.

New commercial formulas arose to satisfy the demands of these readers (which often exceeded their means), such as the *cabinets de lecture* opened by booksellers after 1760 and book lenders' shops and stalls that enabled people to read without buying. Subscribers to the *cabinets de lecture* paid an annual fee of from ten to twenty livres in exchange for the right to read or borrow works that they might not be able to acquire themselves: gazettes and newspapers (which had a high subscription price), larger reference works such as dictionaries, encyclopedias, and almanacs, and the latest literary and philosophical works. The *cabinets de lecture* enabled subscribers to read extensively while spending little and made prohibited titles discreetly available. They were successful both in Paris and in the provinces and attracted a large clientele from among members of the liberal professions, the merchant classes, students, and professors, and even among the better-off craftsmen. The book lenders, for their part, made books available to Parisians by the day or even by the hour. As Louis-Sébastien Mercier wrote in his *Tableau de Paris* (a work that will often serve as our guide in this chapter), 'There are works that excite such a ferment that the bookseller is obliged to cut the volume in three parts in order to be able to satisfy the pressing demands of many readers; in this case you pay not by the day but by the hour.'[4] Installed in small shops or working from stalls in the open, these *bouquinistes* probably reached the readers who were lowest on the social scale and who devoured novelties and political pamphlets in the public areas of France's major city. Thus, even though the private libraries revealed in the notaries' inventories increased in both number and size during the last decades of the Old Regime, they are insufficient to measure the hunger for reading matter that tormented even the humblest city dwellers.

A transformed product

The eighteenth-century book industry offered this proliferation of readers a totally transformed product. The most spectacular change in the book trade, as reflected in the requests for *permissions publiques* (both *privilèges* and simple permissions to publish), was the decline – first slight, then precipitous – of religious books. Religious titles, all categories included, accounted for one-half of the production of Paris printers at the end of the seventeenth century and still made up one-third of their output in the 1720s, but they accounted for only one-fourth of book production early in the 1750s and only one-tenth in the 1780s. Since the other general bibliographical categories (law, history, belles-lettres) remained fairly stable throughout the century, it was the arts and sciences, whose proportional share doubled between 1720 and 1780, that benefited the most from the decline in books of liturgy and piety. This shift is even more pronounced where tacit permissions were concerned and where works in the arts and sciences claimed the largest share. Although such works accounted for only a quarter of the requests for tacit permissions in the 1750s, following belles-lettres, toward the beginning of the 1780s they headed the list, with more than 40 percent of requests. With the sciences leading the field as far as official permissions – *permissions du sceau* – were concerned, and with political works heading the list in requests for tacit permissions, the arts and sciences advanced irresistibly, offering readers the opportunity to inventory and enlarge their knowledge, but proffering works of criticism and reform as well.

Works published with a permission – 'public' or tacit – nevertheless constituted only a part of what was available to the French reading public of the eighteenth century. A large number of books that the book trade designated 'philosophical' were also in circulation. Printed by typographical societies situated beyond the confines of the kingdom (in Switzerland or in the German principalities), imported clandestinely, sold 'under the cloak,' and prohibited and actively pursued by the royal authorities, the works characterized in commercial correspondence and secret catalogues as 'philosophical' were a mixed bag. First, there were philosophical texts in the general sense of the term: works that held up morality and politics, beliefs and authority, to critical examination. Second, there was a pornographic literature that relied upon the classics of the genre but also included new titles. Third, there was an entire assortment of satires, libels (*libelles*), and scandalmongering narratives (*chroniques scandaleuses*) – sensational texts often spiced with salacious passages that denounced the highhandedness and corruption of the powerful. 'Philosophical' books, known to the police as 'bad books,' were a dangerous commodity. Those who transported, stocked, or distributed them ran heavy risks: confiscation, the Bastille, the galleys. And even though printing houses outside the kingdom were beyond the reach of the officers of the king of France, they could on occasion arouse the fury of the Protestant powers who governed them. This meant that discretion was needed to circumvent surveillance (or to corrupt the authorities); it also meant that 'philosophical' books usually commanded a price twice that of other books.

The magnitude of the output of prohibited works has long been underestimated in studies that attempt a quantitative analysis of book circulation on the basis of administrative archives (in this case, the registers listing permissions to print) or notarial inventories of libraries drawn up for estate appraisals. Permission registers lack the many titles for which the bookseller-printers would never have dreamed of requesting a permission (even a tacit permission), so sure were they that the authorities would turn them down. Estate inventories generally fail to mention the titles that zealous heirs spirited away, before the inventory was drawn up, in the interest of protecting the memory of the dear departed. Mercier corroborated this practice when he described the *huissiers-priseurs*, court functionaries who seized and appraised confiscated goods and presided over public auctions: 'The licentious books and the obscene prints are put aside by the *huissier-priseur* and are not sold publicly, but the heirs divide them up and have no scruples about selling their father's bed, his shirts, and his suits of clothing.[5]

Thus the titles listed in the public permissions registers indicate only a part of what Old Regime readers might have read. Taking the year 1764 as an example, we can see that the proportion of total book production that failed to figure in the official registers is considerable. Out of the 1548 titles that were published in French that year and that exist today, only 40 percent figure among the requests for permissions addressed to the director of the book trade. Close to two-thirds of the books printed were thus produced either with a secret and purely verbal authorization, with no authorization at all, or in violation of a prohibition. The bookseller-printers based outside the kingdom captured the better part of the market for books that lacked public permissions. Mercier noted as much in his virulent criticism of the royal censors:

> These are the men most useful to the foreign presses. They enrich Holland, Switzerland, the Low Countries, etc. They are so hesitant, so pusillanimous, and so punctilious that they dare give their approval only for *insignificant* works. And who could blame them for it, since they are personally responsible for what they have approved? It would mean running a danger without glory to act otherwise. Since they add weight, in spite of themselves, to a yoke that is already incommodious, the manuscript flies off to seek a country of reason and wise liberty.[6]

Mercier's remark is not just an often-repeated commonplace; it states an essential truth about publishing. As Robert Darnton wrote, 'it is possible that the majority of French books produced during the second half of the century came from presses situated outside France.'[7]

Pirated and prohibited books

We must distinguish clearly between the two groups of books – prohibited books and pirated books – that made up this illicit commerce. When the two sorts of works were seized on entering the capital, they received very different treatment, both from the corporate authorities of the book trade and from the police. Prohibited books were confiscated and marked for destruction. Pirated titles (that is, as the *Encyclopédie* defines them, works 'printed by someone who does not hold the right to do so, to the prejudice of the person who holds [that right] through the ownership the author has ceded to him; [an] ownership rendered public and authentic by the King's Privilege or by other equivalent letters of the [king's] Seal') were either returned to the sender or turned over to the bookseller who held the *privilège* for the title, who could then sell the copies and pocket the proceeds. Everyone involved in the book trade was acutely aware of the difference. Foreign publishers prepared two catalogues of their offerings: a public one for pirated editions and a secret one for 'philosophical' books, and clandestine book smugglers were quite aware that the risks they ran were not the same for the two sorts of merchandise.

Pirated books were a fundamental part of the book trade, and they fuelled the activities of both the provincial presses (notably in Lyons and Rouen) and foreign presses (in Avignon, Switzerland, and Holland). They formed the basis of the publishing strategies of foreign typographical societies, which were always on the lookout – through their literary agents, travelling salesmen, and corresponding booksellers – for titles in high demand that would make good reprints. They accounted for a large part of the booksellers' business, as attested by the large number of pirated books that emerged from the stockrooms when, in application of a decree in August 1777 concerning the book trade, there was a two-month grace period during which such works could be authorized by the application of an official stamp. Records of the stamping process are extant for eight of the twenty *chambres syndicales* of the book trade, and these indicate that 387 209 copies were legally put back onto the market in this manner. The decree stipulated rigorous penalties for editions pirated after the grace period – 'a fine of six thousand livres for the first infraction, an equal fine and abrogation of licence (*déchéance d'état*) in case of a repeated offence,' to which might be added damages and interest that the owner of the infringed *privilège* could obtain through the courts from the publisher of the pirated edition.

The king's 'act of indulgence' (as the preamble to the edict termed it), which accorded the two-month grace period for the legalization of pirated books in circulation, reflects two things. First, it recognized the broad scope of a commerce that concerned not only provincial booksellers but their colleagues in the capital. Panckoucke, for example, ordered foreign pirated editions of his own publications and of titles that he sold for the royal presses (the Imprimerie royale), preferring their low cost to the expense of financing a new edition himself. Second, it is clear from the king's clemency that although pirating books was a commercial offence and a violation of the *privilège*, it was not a threat to political or religious authority because, by definition, the pirated titles had all been granted a public permission. Thus the act, through illicit commerce, increased the circulation of legally authorized works – which perhaps explains why some bookseller-printers' names and addresses appear in the works they pirated.

The same was not true of the *libelles contre la morale* so vigorously attacked by Mercier (whose own *L'An Deux Mille Quatre Cent Quarante* and *Tableau de Paris*, ironically, figured among the 'best-sellers' of the clandestine book trade):

[As for] the books that have that odious nature, it is better to put them to the pulper – that is, to mash them in a machine made for that purpose, which transforms these scandalous pages into useful cardboard boxes. They make up the tobacco boxes that everyone carries in his pocket. The impious and obscene work, pulped and varnished, is in the hands of the prelate: he plays and fiddles with the object of his former anathemas; he takes snuff from what formerly composed *Le Portier des Chartreux*.[8]

The circulation of 'philosophical' books

But was the corpus of prohibited books that flooded the kingdom principally made up of such *libelles contre la morale*, now totally forgotten, or of the texts that tradition considers the very expression of the philosophy of the Enlightenment? This question can be answered only partially and provisionally until such time as Robert Darnton publishes his promised study of the 720 titles most frequently mentioned in police archives and in the records of the typographical societies. In the meantime, three lists of prohibited books, taken as examples rather than as necessarily representative, can shed some light on the matter. The first is a listing of the works seized from a Parisian bookseller, Roch Moureau, on July 31, 1777. On the order of Lieutenant General Lenoir of the Paris police, sixteen titles (there were fifty-nine copies in all) were sent to the Bastille for storage before they could be pulped. What sorts of works were they? Five titles were pornographic works: some were classics of the genre (the *Académie des dames ou les entretiens galans d'Aloysia* of Nicolas Chorier, the Latin original of which dates from 1678); others were more recent titles (*La Fille de joye*, translated from the English in 1751, and *L'Arétin* of Du Laurens [1763]). Equal in number to the erotic repertory were political libels and scandal-mongering narratives, among them two texts by Pidansat de Mairobert (the *Anecdotes sur la comtesse Du Barri* [1775] and the *Correspondance secrète et familière de M. de Maupeou* [1772]) and *L'Espion chinois*, by Ange Goudar (1764). Finally, there were the philosophes: Voltaire (with three titles: *La Pucelle d'Orléans*, *La Bible enfin expliquée*, and the *Histoire du Parlement de Paris*), d'Holbach (*La Morale universelle, ou les devoirs de l'homme fondés sur la nature*), and Mercier (well represented with eleven copies of his *L'An Deux Mille Quatre Cent Quarante*).

The order that the *marchand forain* Noël Gille, based in Montargis, sent to the Société Typographique de Neuchâtel on July 30, 1777 covers the same repertory, though it is weighted differently. Although pornography is still much in evidence (with *L'Histoire de dom B****, portier des Chartreux, Margot la ravaudeuse*, and *Thérèse philosophe*, attributed to the marquis d'Argens, joining the *Académie des dames* and *La Fille de joye*), the philosophes account for most of the 23 titles. Gille the book peddler ordered 6 titles by d'Holbach, 5 works by Voltaire (aside from *La Bible enfin expliquée*, the *Lettres philosophiques*, the *Evangile de la raison, Dieu et les hommes; oeuvre théologique mais raisonnable*, and the *Questions sur l'Encyclopédie*), the complete works of Helvétius, and various works of Jean-Jacques Rousseau. Only one libel is included in his order, but it is an extremely violent one: Le Gazetier cuirassé, *ou Anecdotes scandaleuses de la cour de France*, by Théveneau de Morande. It was published in London in 1771 but declared itself 'printed a hundred leagues from the Bastille, at the sign of Liberty.' Noël Gille used the societé's secret catalogue to write out his order (which, incidentally, was not filled by the Société Typographique de Neuchâtel, which was not eager to do business with those whom it suspected – with reason – of being bad business risks). It seems clear that he had access to their catalogue, since the better part of the titles he requested (15 of 23) figure on a handwritten list of 110 titles headed *Livres philosophiques*, made up in 1775, that Robert Darnton found among the archives of the Société Typographique. Using idiosyncratic spelling, phonetic except for the word *philosophique*, which was rewritten correctly, as if it were copied, the peddler requested that similar lists be sent to him regularly in the future:

> Sit vous voulet trete avec moi vous pouve manvoier votre cathalo sur tout les livres [filo] philosophique duquelle je poures vous faires eun debis au condisions que vous merranderrer les marchandise fran de porre jusqualion. [If you would like to do business with me you can send me your catalogue of all the philosophical books, from which I can give you an order, on the condition that you send me the merchandise prepaid to Lyons.][9]

In Troyes, the titles ordered and received between 1781 and 1784 by Bruzard de Mauvelain, a bookseller who dealt in works that circulated 'under the cloak,' show yet another picture. Out of a total of 120 works that he requested, 48 were ordered at least three times (996 book copies out of a total of 1528 copies ordered). Three genres dominate in this corpus of prohibited books: libels and political pamphlets (314 copies), pornographic works (206 copies), and scandalmongering narratives (178 copies). There are fewer philosophical treatises (only 107 copies), and the category includes neither Voltaire nor Rousseau, inclining instead toward the materialists (La Mettrie, Helvétius, d'Holbach) and the popularizers of the Enlightenment (Mercier, with his two titles, and Raynal, with *L'Histoire philosophique et politique des établissemens et du commerce des Européens dans les deux Indes* [1770]).

Reorders show which sorts of clandestine literature were most avidly consumed. Heading the list, ordered eleven times for a total of eighty-four copies, was a libel attacking the depravity of the late king, *Les Fastes de*

Louis XV, published in 1782. Next came a pornographic work, *Les Muses du foyer de l'Opéra* (five orders, forty-six copies), a chronicle describing the shocking mores of the great; *La Chronique scandaleuse, ou Mémoires pour servir à l'histoire des moeurs de la génération présente* written by Guillaume Imbert de Boudeaux and printed in 1783 'in Paris, in a corner from where one sees everything' (five orders, forty-five copies); and a licentious anticlerical poem of Charles Bordes published in 1777, *La Papesse Jeanne* (six orders, forty-four copies). Furthermore, pamphlets denouncing the despotism of the monarchy (*lettres de cachet* and the state prison in particular) were sure sellers. The *Mémoires sur la Bastille* of Linguet, *Des lettres de cachet et des prisons d'Etat* of Mirabeau, the *Remarques historiques et anecdotes sur le château de la Bastille* of Brossays du Perray, and the *Mémoire sur les maisons de force* accounted for eighty-seven copies. Mauvelain's orders, unlike those of Noël Gille, eschewed the canonical texts of the Enlightenment in favour of a denunciatory literature aimed at the aristocracy, the court, and, ultimately, the king.

Philosophy and 'low literature'

Does this change in reading material show the effect of a radicalization of people's minds during the 1780s? Or does it show only that Mauvelain's specialized commerce in Troyes left the classics of the Enlightenment to other book dealers? It is difficult to know for sure. It is certain, in any event, that until the end of the Old Regime philosophical treatises and politico-pornographic *libelles* were linked in both the practical dealings of the book trade and the mechanisms of repression. The catalogue titled *Livres philosophiques* distributed by the Société Typographique de Neuchâtel in 1775 stands as proof of this. The 110 titles it contains quite naturally include a good number of works of the genre that Mauvelain's clients found most to their liking: licentious works and political pamphlets and chronicles. Fifteen pornographic titles are offered, including all the classics of the genre, ancient and modern, from *La Putain errante*, a translation of Aretino, to *Thérèse philosophe*, from the *Vénus dans le cloître, ou la religieuse en chemise* to the *Histoire de dom B*****, portier des Chartreux* and its companion volume, the *Histoire de la tourière des carmélites*. In the category of political denunciation, libels like the *Mémoires authentiques de Mme la comtesse Du Barry* (London, 1772) accompany multivolume series such as *L'Espion chinois* (six volumes) and the *Journal historique de la révolution opérée dans la constitution de la monarchie française par M. de Maupeou* of Pidansat de Mairobert and Mouffle d'Angerville (seven volumes in all, three of which had appeared when the catalogue was drawn up).

What is most striking in the secret catalogue of the Société Typographique de Neuchâtel, however, is the massive presence of the philosophes. The foundations of the new thought are represented by Fontenelle (if indeed the work given as *La République des incrédules* is his posthumous *La République des philosophes*), Boulainvilliers, Hobbes (d'Holbach's translation of *Human Nature*), and Bayle (through an *Analyse raisonnée* of his works in eight volumes by François-Marie de Marsy and Jean-Baptiste-René Robinet). Also represented are Diderot (with the *Lettre sur les aveugles*, the *Lettre sur les sourds et muets*, and the *Bijoux indiscrets*), Rousseau (*Le Contrat social* and the *Oeuvres diverses*), the popularizers of the Enlightenment (Raynal, Du Laurens, Mercier, Bordes), and the materialist current (four titles of Helvétius, *De l'Esprit* among them, the *Oeuvres philosophiques* of La Mettrie, and, above all, fourteen works written or translated by d'Holbach). But the author who dominates the catalogue is Voltaire, with thirty-one titles that range from the *Lettres philosophiques* of 1734 to the *Romans et contes philosophiques* and the *Questions sur l'Encyclopédie*, published in the early 1770s.

Voltaire is also the author best represented in the second document I cite here: a catalogue drawn up between June and September 1790 by the Parisian bookseller Poinçot, who had been given the responsibility of inventorying the confiscated books stored in the Bastille in 1785 in the last campaign for the destruction of dangerous books of the Old Regime. Poinçot had received this commission after he had volunteered that it 'was possible to make use, to the profit of the City, of the great mass of printed matter heaped up pell-mell and without order, which would be lost in the humidity and the dust if haste were not made to rescue it.[10] The list, which covers books confiscated during the five years preceding the Revolution, is divided into four inventories and includes 564 items, which correspond to 393 different titles. It mentions a certain number of new titles along with the works already cited. In the pornographic repertory, for example, we find *La Foutromanie, poème lubrique*, by Sénac de Meilhan (à Sardanapolis, 1775), the *Errotika Biblion* of Mirabeau (à Rome de l'Imprimerie du Vatican, 1783), and *Le Rideau levé, ou l'éducation de Laure* (à Cythère, 1786). The pamphlets include libels directed at the queen (*Les Amours de Charlot et de Toinette* [1779] and the *Essais historiques sur la vie de Marie-Antoinette d'Autriche, reine de France* [1781]).

In the storerooms of the Bastille, as in the warehouses of the Société Typographique de Neuchâtel, the works of the philosophes shared the fate of the *chroniques scandaleuses*. The two listings even show similar results: Voltaire heads the list of books in the Bastille in 1790 with eighteen works. Next comes d'Holbach (eight titles), then Rousseau (four titles, including *Du Contrat social*, the *Discours sur l'origine et les fondements de l'inégalité parmi les hommes*, and *Emile*), and, with one or two titles each, Helvétius, Diderot, Condorcet, Raynal, and Mercier. Although only seven prisoners were inmates in the state prison on July 14, 1789, all the classics of the Enlightenment were there, victims of censorship and the king's police along with the pamphlets that Mercier so scorned:

> A totally flat, totally atrocious, totally calumnious libel appears under the cloak; it is immediately bid up. People pay a crazy price for it; the peddler, who does not know how to read and is only trying to earn bread for his poor family, is arrested. He is thrown into the Bicêtre [prison], where his fate is predictable. The more the pamphlet is prohibited, the more avid people are for it. When you read it and you see that nothing compensates for its base temerity, you are covered with shame for having run after it. You hardly dare say, 'I have read it.' It is the scum of the basest literature, and what thing has not its scum?[11]

Thus the fundamental dichotomy dividing the literary field – we need only recall Voltaire's diatribes – into authors worthy of the name and *folliculaires* belonging to the 'unhappy class who write in order to live' established no radical break between what the two groups wrote. Admittedly, the distinction justified strategies that made scorn for *la basse littérature* the essential sign of quality in a writer. As Mercier's *Tableau de Paris* tells us: 'Among the ancients public consideration was alive; our glory is dim in comparison with the honors paid for services rendered to humankind. To slough off the burden of gratitude among us, people cry at every hand, "The number of authors is immense!" Yes – of those who usurp that name or who have produced one lone tract in their lives. But in fact there are in France no more than thirty writers constantly pursuing their art.' Mercier went on in a note to draw a distinction between writers 'worthy of the name' who deserved to share 'public consideration' (and its retributions) and 'compilers, journalists, translators at so much the page' who failed to merit that honour.[12] It is not difficult to guess in which category the author of the text implicitly placed himself. When the writers excluded from the Republic of Letters internalized the distinction themselves, the opposition between the 'High Enlightenment' and the 'Low-Life of Literature' (the terms are Robert Darnton's), between the established philosophes and the 'gutter Rousseaus' (*les Rousseau des ruisseaux*), lent structure to literary rivalries, pitting the frustrated ambitions of the 'low-lifers' against the well-endowed positions monopolized by the 'High Enlightenment' writers.

Still, in both the commercialization and the repression of 'philosophical' books, both sorts of writers knew a common fate, in fortune and misfortune alike. Defined as one specific corpus within all book production, such works may perhaps have shared a horizon of reading that responded to expectations arising from the attraction of prohibition and the seductions of irreverence or transgression. The coherence of this set of extremely heterogeneous works was not a matter exclusively of how they were viewed by the bookseller, the police, or the reader; it was rooted in the authors' writing practices as well. For one time, even the best-known authors did not hesitate to use the forms most common to low literature. Thus Voltaire was a past master in both the use and the subversion of the defamatory *libelle*, the anti-religious satire, and the political pamphlet, all the while juggling pseudonyms, false attributions, and parodic signatures. Second, genres were by no means clearly separated. Not only did philosophic discourse often invade pornographic texts (at times even infiltrating titles, as with *Thérèse philosophe, ou Mémoires pour servir à l'histoire du P. Dirrag et de Mlle Eradice*); the philosophes themselves indulged in the licentious genre (as in Voltaire's *La Pucelle d'Orléans* or Diderot's *Bijoux indiscrets*, published in 'Monomotapa' in 1748). This free circulation of forms and motifs doubtless reinforced the perception of 'philosophical' books as a unified set of texts. Does this mean that they should be taken as the torches that set the Revolution ablaze?

From reading to belief

Most assuredly yes, according to Robert Darnton, who has little doubt that the large-scale diffusion of this critical and denunciatory literature, which increased in both its flow and its virulence during the two final decades of the Old Regime, profoundly transformed the representation of the monarchy by undermining its founding myths, by ridiculing the rituals through which it was expressed, and by accustoming the French to think of themselves as the victims of an arbitrary and decadent state. Thus 'philosophical' books, whatever their intent, produced a veritable 'ideological erosion' that may have made the revolutionary rupture inevitable. According to Darnton,

> The political tracts worked a dozen variations on a single theme: the monarchy had degenerated into despotism. They did not call for a revolution or foresee 1789 or even provide much discussion of the deeper social and political issues that were to make the destruction of the monarchy possible. Inadvertently, however, they prepared for that event by desanctifying the symbols and deflating the myths that had made the monarchy appear legitimate in the eyes of its subjects.[13]

Thus there was a close connection between the deep penetration of corrosive and profanatory prohibited works and the exhaustion of systems of belief that guaranteed the king the respect and love of his people.

But does this view perhaps invest reading with a force and an efficacy that it may not have had? Let us return to Mercier for a moment. In his eyes, several things seriously diminished the force of persuasion of denunciatory works. First, the social sphere in which they circulated was much more restricted than for licentious works:

> Much criticism has been leveled at philosophical books, read by a small number of men, and which the multitude is totally unable to understand. The indecent engraving triumphs publicly. Every eye is struck by it; [the eye] of innocence is troubled, and modesty blushes. It is time for severe relegation to within the merchant's folders of what they have the impudence to display even outside their shops. Think of it: maidens and honest women also pass by in the streets![14]

Next, Mercier argued, interest in denunciatory literature was ephemeral: 'Where is the libel that, after fifteen days, has not been flayed by public opinion and abandoned to its own infamy?'[15] Finally, he argued the public's incredulity: 'Formerly it was fairly common to find a number of critical posters on the affairs of the day. . . . Caricatures of this sort are no longer affixed to walls; they have passed into pamphlets distributed on the sly. . . . Satirical thrusts are now found only in pamphlets [and] the fashionable world finds them amusing without giving them too much credit.'[16] Louis-Sébastien Mercier was far from postulating that the readers of 'philosophical' works gave full credence to the representations that the texts attempted to impose. His description of the way they were read recalls the characterization of popular reading by the English sociologist Richard Hoggart, who spoke of 'an oblique way' of receiving a text that involves 'scepticism,' 'unbelief,' and 'silent resistance.'[17] The images in the libels and the topical pamphlets were not graven into the soft wax of their readers' minds, and reading did not necessarily lead to belief. If a connection existed between the massive distribution of an aggressively disrespectful pamphlet literature and the destruction of the image of the monarchy, it was doubtless neither direct nor ineluctable.

Shared books and contradictory choices

Another proof of the need for caution in linking philosophical books and revolutionary thought is the presence of the same philosophical reading matter (in all senses of the term) among readers who made highly contradictory choices in the face of the revolutionary event. This happened in the case of Rousseau's work, which was known and loved among the common people. In his *Journal of My Life* the journeyman glazier Jacques-Louis Ménétra mentioned only six works, and three of them were by Rousseau (the *Contrat Social*, *Emile*, and *La Nouvelle Héloïse*). He claimed to have been on familiar terms with the author when Rousseau was in Paris for the last time, between 1770 and 1778: 'We went into the café de la Régence He asked for a pitcher of beer He asked me if I knew how to play chess I said no He asked me if I knew how to play checkers I said a little He joked He said that was right for my age We played I lost I listened and I heard people all around who kept saying But that is Rousseau that's surely his brother.'[18] The ardent Rousseauism of Parisian *sans culottes*, fueled by Jacobin discourse, the radical newspapers, and Rousseau's promotion to the Pantheon, was rooted in the reading preferences of the most 'popular' readers of the Old Regime.

At the other end of the social scale, aristocratic readers were also devotees of Rousseau. One indication of this is the number of nobles (court nobles, provincial nobility, men ennobled through service to the crown) among Rousseau's correspondents; at 36 percent of all correspondents, they are as numerous as members of the Third Estate. Another sign is the cult of Rousseau's memory in the gardens of Ermenonville, where, at the invitation of the marquis de Girardin, the great names of the aristocracy came on pilgrimage. Yet another indication is the longstanding attachment, the Revolution notwithstanding, of counterrevolutionary émigrés to both the man and his work (*Social Contract* excepted).

Rousseau not only provided reading matter for both plebeians and aristocrats; he was also the favourite author of some members of the commercial middle class, who took him for their *maître à penser*. This is evident in the letters that Jean Ranson, a La Rochelle merchant, addressed to Ostervald, one of the directors of the Société Typographique de Neuchâtel. For Ranson, Rousseau was a veritable mentor: 'Everything that *l'Ami* Jean-Jacques has written about the duties of husbands and wives, of mothers and fathers, has had a profound effect on me, and I confess to you that it will serve me as a rule in any of those estates that I should occupy.' Rousseau's death deeply affected him: 'So, Monsieur, we lost the sublime Jean-Jacques. How it pains me never to have seen or heard him. I acquired the most extraordinary admiration for him by reading his books. If some day I should travel near Ermenonville, I shall not fail to visit his grave and perhaps to shed some tears on it.'[19] One point of reference – the work and, even more, the person of Rousseau, the guarantor of the truth of his statements – thus inspired different and even contradictory interpretations, just as it prompted contradictory allegiances.

The same is true concerning the *Encyclopédie*. Where its subscribers can be identified (as in Besançon and in the Franche-Comté for the quarto edition of Neuchâtel), there are two lessons to be drawn. First, it is clear that because of its high price (even when the cost was lowered by a smaller format), the *Encyclopédie* could be purchased only by notables. Even more than the great merchants (a minority among subscribers), it was the society of the traditional elites (clergy, military nobles, members of the Parlement, men of the law and of the liberal professions) who made up the work's true public. Second, although some of those who acquired the *Encyclopédie* were dedicated to the revolutionary cause, the majority was doubtless indifferent or hostile to it. Subscribing to the work emblematic of the Enlightenment thus implied no commonality of choice or of action among its readers, any more than its massive presence in the milieux most closely tied to the Old Regime state signified a radical rupture with traditional ways of conceiving of society.

Finally, the books owned by émigrés and condemned persons that were confiscated by the revolutionary authorities after 1792 attest to the strong and durable attachment to the philosophical corpus on the part of victims or enemies of the Revolution. What they read was not fundamentally different from the reading matter of the most deeply committed revolutionaries. Thus Buffon and the *Encyclopédie* accompanied Maréchal de Broglie to prison, and in the Temple Louis XVI read Montesquieu and Voltaire along with Corneille and La Fontaine. These facts, which confirm Tocqueville's intuition ('basically, all who ranked above the common herd were of a muchness; they had the same ideas, the same habits, the same tastes, the same kinds of amusements; *read the same books* and spoke in the same way'),[20] make it impossible to attribute too direct a role to books. The new representations that they proposed did not become imprinted on the readers' minds, and in all cases they were open to varied use and multiple interpretations. It is thus perhaps risky to credit the incontestable success of philosophical works with the increase in distance between French society and the monarchy.

That distance was not necessarily the result of an intellectual operation, but it may easily have been set up in the immediacy of ordinary practices, actions taken without deliberation, and words that had become commonplaces. Mercier astutely pinpointed such spontaneous downshifts, which were all the more profound for being unconscious. They were discernible in ready-made formulas downgrading royalty by use of the expression *à la royale*: 'A vulgar expression and frequently employed. Beef *à la royale*, cakes *à la royale*, boot scrapers *à la royale*) the cooked meats man puts the word in golden letters over his shop door; the pork products vendor sells hams and sausages *à la royale*; one sees nothing but *fleurs de lys* crowning stewing hens, gloves, boots, and ladies' shoes, and the teas vendor cries, *A la royale!*' No hostility toward the monarchy was implied in all this. To the contrary, as Mercier noted, '*à la royale* means, in the figurative sense, *good, excellent, most excellent*, because the common people do not suppose that the mediocre, in any form, could have the temerity to draw near to the court.'[21] Still, common usage desacralized the attributes and symbols of royalty, depriving it of all transcendent significance. Elsewhere, Mercier noted:

> Among the iron-mongers of the quai de la Mégisserie there are storehouses of *old shop signs* appropriate for decorating the

entrance of all the taverns and smokers' dens of the faubourgs and the suburbs of Paris. There all the kings of the earth sleep together: Louis XVI and George III exchange fraternal embraces; the king of Prussia lies with the empress of Russia; the emperor is level with his electors; there, finally, the [papal] tiara and the turban mingle. A tavern owner arrives, pokes all these crowned heads with his foot, examines them, and picks at random the likeness of the king of Poland; he bears it away, hangs it up, and writes underneath, *au Grand Vainqueur.*[22]

The scene – and it matters little whether it was actual or imaginary – indicates that the image of royal majesty demanded no particular reverence and evoked no fear. This suggests another relationship between the shifts in sensibility and the large-scale circulation of texts undermining royal authority. Why could not the infatuation with philosophical books have been made possible only because a previous symbolic and affective disinvestment had worked to make them acceptable, comprehensible, and a matter of course? In this case philosophical books, far from producing a rupture, would result *from* a rupture.

There is in this notion a first reason to question the efficacy so often supposed for the philosophical text. There is a second reason also, however. Although the texts, and most particularly the political libels, were indeed mechanisms intended to produce desired effects, the techniques they used were always deciphered through expectations, interpretive tools, and levels of comprehension that varied from one reader to another or that could lead any one reader to lend a different and even contradictory status to a given work at a later point in time. Reading the philosophical literature backward, starting from the revolutionary event, runs the risk of attributing to it a univocal denunciatory and persuasive meaning. Eighteenth-century readers did not necessarily believe in the truth of what they were given to read (for example, on the arbitrary acts of a monarchy become despotic or on the depravity of the sovereign and his court), but their incredulity in no way diminished their avid appetite for forbidden books.

The pornographic *libelles* that focused on the great, the royal favourites, the queen, and the king serve to illustrate this point. Such texts operated on several levels and lent themselves to a plural reading. First, they followed the traditional conventions of the erotic genre: they used a codified vocabulary to express sexual pleasure; they played with the literary forms of the age and invested them with an unexpected content; they usually contained one character whose gaze stood in for the reader's. With the political libel, however, although these mechanisms are still recognizable as such, they are put to the service of an overriding purpose. Still, their message is not immediately perceptible. This is clear in the earliest pamphlets attacking Marie-Antoinette (the *Amours de Charlot et de Toinette* or the *Essais historiques sur la vie de Marie-Antoinette d'Autriche, reine de France*). Like the *mazarinades* more than a century earlier, these texts did not necessarily aim at making people believe that the queen truly was as she was pictured; rather, they attempted to justify her adversaries in the court by disqualifying her. Readers aware of the struggles among the various courtly coteries understood that the meaning of such texts was not literal but lay in the effects they had on court politics. Other, more easily manipulated, readers might believe the accusations levelled against a queen described as governed by her senses and unfaithful to her duty. Thus a set of themes was put into place (amplified after 1789 by the revolutionary pamphleteers) that unflaggingly associated the image of a ravenous, bloodthirsty queen with the image of a lascivious and dissolute woman. These varying horizons of reading, which accorded a variety of statuses to any one text, were to some extent determined by the way in which the 'philosophical' books themselves were organized, with over-lapping genres, crisscrossing motifs, and the blending of levels of discourse such as political denunciation, pornographic description, and philosophical reflection. This very plurality, inscribed in the texts themselves, makes it impossible to conclude that they were read in an identical manner by all their readers or that their interpretation could be reduced to any one simple ideological statement.

Did the Revolution construct the Enlightenment?

Should not the terms of our initial question perhaps be reversed to sustain the idea that it was the Revolution that made the books and philosophy – that is, that it was on the basis of the revolutionary event that a corpus of works was constituted and authors selected who were held to have prepared and announced it? The ways and means of this retrospective construction of the Enlightenment by the Revolution are many. Election to the Pantheon was the most spectacular of these but also the most selective, since only two writers from past centuries – Voltaire and Rousseau – were glorified as *grands hommes*, all others proposed (Descartes, Fénelon, Buffon, Mably) having been rejected by the revolutionary assemblies. Thus those two authors were recognized as true precursors of the Revolution. This is implicit in the inscriptions engraved on the sarcophagus containing Voltaire's mortal remains when they were transferred to the Pantheon on July 11, 1791, in a moment of unanimous national sentiment and alliance between the Revolution and the constitutional church. On one side the inscription reads:

> He combatted atheists and fanatics
> He demanded the rights of man against the
> servitude of feudalism;

The other side reads:

> Poet Historian Philosopher
> He enlarged the human spirit and taught it
> that it must be free.[23]

This is similar to what Robespierre said of Rousseau in his discourse 'Sur les rapports des idées religieuses et morales' of May 7, 1794 (which, incidentally, lashed out at the materialist 'sect' of the encyclopedists):

> Among those who, in the times I speak of, stood out in the career of letters and philosophy, one man [Rousseau], by the elevation of his soul and by the grandeur of his character, showed himself worthy of the ministry as preceptor of humankind. . . . Ah! if he had been witness to this revolution whose precursor he was and that bore him to the Pantheon [on October 12, 1793], who can doubt that his generous soul would have embraced with transport the cause of justice and equality![24]

The canon for precursors was not limited to the two authors elected to the Pantheon. It also included a variety of genres, such as the anthologies, or *florilèges*, published in the almanacs and the literary journals, and works of extracts that offered selections from one author or a group of authors. Véron's political catechism, *Au peuple. Des vérités terribles, mais indispensables, tirées de J.-J. Rousseau, Mably, Raynal, etc. et de tous les philosophes amis des principes de l'égalité*, belongs to the second genre, while the poem 'Les philosophes,' which appeared in *L'Almanach des Muses* for 1794 and celebrated Fontenelle, Voltaire, Diderot, Franklin, and Rousseau, belongs to the first. In political celebrations in the year II, busts of the philosophes and the martyrs for liberty also figured in this retrospective quest for legitimacy. Thus in Roye, Picardy, ceremonial honours were paid to Voltaire, Rousseau, Buffon, Benjamin Franklin, Marat, and Lepeletier de Saint-Fargeau, and their praises were sung in 'civic couplets.'[25] The same was true of a number of widely circulated printed objects such as decks of cards (in the year II, the printer Gayant replaced the kings with 'philosophers' – Voltaire and Rousseau, but also Molière and La Fontaine), revolutionary almanacs, ABCs, and catechisms. The *Alphabet des sans culottes, ou premiers éléments d'éducation répub-licaine*, also of the year II, offered the following exchange:

Q: Who are the men who by their writings prepared the revolution?
A: Helvétius, Mably, J. J. Rousseau, Voltaire, and Franklin.
Q: What do you call these great men?

A: Philosophers.
Q: What does that word mean?
A: Sage, friend of humanity.[26]

In one sense, then, it was the Revolution that 'made' the books, and not the other way around, since it was the Revolution that gave a premonitory and programatic meaning to certain works, constituted, after the fact, as its origin.

From the book to reading: desacralized reading

That fact, however, does not invalidate our first question, which we can now formulate thus: What place should one accord to the circulation of printed matter in the intellectual and affective transformations that rendered the sudden and radical break with absolute monarchy and a corporatively organized society thinkable, admissible, and decipherable? Even more than the critical and denunciatory representations massively proposed by the 'philosophical' books, in all their diversity, should we not emphasize the transformations that profoundly modified the ways people read? The hypothesis of a *Leserevolution* has been advanced for Germany of the latter half of the eighteenth century. According to this hypothesis, the new style of reading showed several characteristics that distinguished it from traditional practices: the reader's increased mobility before more numerous and less durable texts; the individualization of reading when, in essence, it became a silent and individual act taking place in privacy; the religious disinvestment of reading, which lost its charge of sacrality. A communitarian and respectful relation to the book, made up of reverence and obedience, gave way to a freer, more casual, and more critical way of reading.

Debatable and much debated, this hypothesis nonetheless accounts adequately for the transformation of reading practices in eighteenth-century France. With the tripling or quadrupling of book production between the beginning of the century and the 1780s, the multiplication of institutions that enabled clients to read without having to buy, and the increasing flood of ephemeral print pieces (the periodical, the libel, the topical pamphlet), a new way of reading, which no longer took the book as authoritative, became widespread. The motif, so often chosen by late-eighteenth-century writers and painters, of patriarchal, biblical reading at the *veillée*, when the head of the peasant household read out loud to the assembled family, was one way of expressing regret for a lost manner of reading. In the representation of an idealized peasant world dear to the lettered elite, communitarian reading signified a world in which the book was revered and authority was respected. Use of this mythic figure is an obvious criticism of the way city people read – typically insatiably, negligently, and sceptically.

One last time Louis-Sébastien Mercier comes to our aid to define a cultural change – or, what is just as important, belief in such a change. His judgment appears contradictory. On the one hand, he deplored the loss of a diligent, attentive, and patient manner of reading: 'In Paris hardly anyone reads any work that has more than two volumes. . . . Our worthy forebears read novels in sixteen volumes, and still they were not too long for their evenings. They followed with transport the manners, the virtues, [and] the combats of ancient chivalry. As for us, soon we will be reading only from [decorated fire-] screens.'[27] On the other hand, Mercier noted that reading had invaded all social practices and that since it had become the commonest of habits it had obliged the book to change form:

> The mania for *small formats* has replaced the one for the immense margins that were all the rage fifteen years ago. Then one had to turn the page at every instant; all you bought was white paper, but it pleased [book] lovers. . . . Fashion has changed: no one looks for anything but *small formats*; in this way, all our pretty poets have been reprinted. These little books have the advantage of being able to be pocketed to furnish relaxation during a walk, or to ward off the boredom of travel, but at the same time, one must carry a magnifying glass, for the print is so fine that it requires good eyes.[28]

In the long run, Mercier's seemingly contradictory remarks converge in a common notion: when reading penetrated the most ordinary circumstances of daily life and avidly consumed texts that were soon abandoned, it lost the religious reference that had long inhabited it. In this way, a new relationship between reader and text was forged; it was disrespectful of authorities, in turn seduced and disillusioned by novelty, and, above all, little inclined to belief and adherence. The new manner of reading was accompanied by the exercise – both on a large scale and in the immediacy of practice – of Kant's 'public use of one's reason' on the part of 'private persons.'[29] Thus the crux of the matter is not the content of 'philosophical' books, which quite possibly did not have the persuasive impact generously attributed to them, but rather a new mode of reading that, even when the texts it took on were in total conformity with religious and political order, developed a critical attitude freed from the ties of dependence and obedience that underlay earlier representations. In that sense, transformations in reading practices were part of a larger-scale change in which historians have been wont to discern a process of dechristianization.

Notes

1 Alexis de Tocqueville, *L'Ancien Régime et la Révolution* (Paris: Gallimard, 1967), pp. 239–40, quoted from *The Old Regime and the French Revolution*, trans. Stuart Gilbert (Garden City, N.Y.: Doubleday, 1955), pp. 146–47.

2 Hippolyte Taine, *L'Ancien Régime* (Paris: Robert Laffont, 1966), vol. I, *Les Origines de la France Contemporaine*, p. 205, quoted from *The Ancient Regime*, new rev. ed., trans. John Durand (New York: H. Holt, 1896), pp. 274–75.

3 Daniel Mornet, *Les Origines intellectuelles de la Révolution français 1715–1787* (Paris: Armand Colin, 1933, 1967), p. 432.

4 Louis-Sébastien Mercier, *Tableau de Paris. Nouvelle édition corrigée et augmentée*, 8 vols. (Amsterdam, 1782–83), 'Loueurs de livres,' 5, 61–66, quotation pp. 61–62.

5 Mercier, *Tableau de Paris*, 'Huissiers-priseurs,' 5, 337–45, quotation p. 341.

6 Mercier, *Tableau de Paris*, 12 vols (Amsterdam, 1783–88), 'Censeurs royaux,' 11, 51–52.

7 Robert Darnton, 'Le livre prohibé aux frontières: Neuchâtel,' in H. J. Martin and R. Chartier, *Histoire de l'Edition français* (4 vols., Paris 1982–6), 2, 342–59, quotation p. 343.

8 Mercier, *Tableau*, 'Saisies,' 7, 183–88, quotation pp. 187–88.

9 Robert Darnton, 'Un colporteur sous l'Ancien Régime,' in *Censures. De la Bible aux Larmes d'Eros* (Paris: Editions du Centre Georges Pompidou, 1987), pp. 130–39.

10 Report addressed to the mayor of Paris on October 19, 1790, quoted from Frantz Funck-Brentano, *Archives de la Bastille, la formation du dépôt* (Dole: C. Blind, 1890), p. xiv.

11 Mercier, *Tableau*, 'Libelles,' 7, 22–28, quotation p. 22.

12 Mercier, *Tableau*, 'Trente Ecrivains en France, pas davantage,' 8, 106–14, quotation pp. 106–7.

13 Robert Darnton, 'A Clandestine Bookseller in the Provinces,' in his *The Literary Underground of the Old Regime* (Cambridge, Mass., 1982), p. 147.

14 Mercier, *Tableau*, 'Estampes licencieuses,' 6, 92–94, quotation p. 94.

15 Mercier, *Tableau*, 'Libelles,' 7, 22–28, quotation pp. 22–23.

16 Mercier, *Tableau*, 'Placards,' 6, 85–89.

17 Richard Hoggart, *The Uses of Literacy: Changing Patterns in English Mass Culture* (Fairlawn N. J.: Essential Books, 1957), pp. 197, 224, 228, 230.

18 *Journal de ma vie. Jacques-Louis Ménétra, compagnon vitrier au 18e siècle*, ed. Daniel Roche (Paris: Montalba, 1982), pp. 218–22, 300, quoted from Ménétra, *Journal of My Life*, trans. Arthur Goldhammer (New York: Columbia University Press, 1986), p. 182.

19 Robert Darnton, 'Readers Respond to Rousseau: The Fabrication of Romantic Sensitivity,' in his *The Great Cat Massacre and Other Episodes in French Cultural History* (New York: Basic Books, 1984), pp. 214–56, quotations pp. 236 and 237.

20 Tocqueville, *L'Ancien Régime et la Révolution*, p. 158, quoted from *The Old Régime and the French Revolution*, p. 81, emphasis added.

21 Mercier, *Tableau*, 'A la Royale,' 5, 148–49.

22 Mercier, *Tableau*, 'Vieilles enseignes,' 5, 123–26, quotation p. 123.

23 James Leith, 'Les trois apothéoses de Voltaire,' *Annales Historiques de la Révolution Française* 34 (1979): 161–209, quotation p. 200.

24 Robespierre, 'Sur les rapports des idées religieuses et morales avec les principes
   républicains et sur les fêtes nationales,' in his *Textes choisis*, 3 vols. (Paris:
   Editions Sociales, 1958; 1974), vol. 3 (*November 1793–juillet 1794*), pp. 155–80,
   quotation pp. 171–72.
25 Leith, 'Les trois apothéoses de Voltaire,' p. 207.
26 Quoted from Hans Ulrich Gumbrecht and Rolf Reichardt, 'Philosophe,
   Philosophie,' in *Handbuch politisch-sozialer Grundbegriffe in Frankreich
   1680–1820*, 10 vols., ed. Rolf Reichardt and Eberhard Schmitt (Munich: R.
   Oldenbourg Verlag, 1985–), 3, 7–88, quotation p. 64.
27 Mercier, *Tableau*, 'Bouquiniste,' 2, 128–32, quotation pp. 131–32.
28 Mercier, *Tableau*, 'Petits formats,' 4, 80–84, quotation pp. 80–81.
29 Immanuel Kant, 'Beantwortung der Frage: Was Ist Aufklärung?' in his *Berli-
   nische Monatsschrift* (1784), quoted from 'What Is Enlightenment?' in *Foundations of the Metaphysics of Morals and What is Enlightenment*, trans. Lewis
   W. Beck (Indianapolis: Bobbs-Merrill, 1959, 1975), p. 87.

9

Ephemera: civic education through images

JAMES LEITH

In his *Gutenberg Galaxy: The Making of Typographic Man* (Toronto,
1962) the guru of the mass media, Marshall McLuhan, argued that, as
the earliest example of mass production, the printing press produced a
flood of identical copies of a text that vastly surpassed anything scribes
could produce by hand. McLuhan was right to emphasize the impact of the
printed word on modern culture, but his analysis failed to emphasize that
the printing press also made possible a proliferation of images through
engravings on a scale unprecedented in human history. We can consider the
outpouring in France of engraved images from the great collections that
were established as a result of the law issued under Louis XIV requiring
that two copies of every engraving be deposited in the Bibliothèque royale,
now the Bibliothèque Nationale. The vast collections of engravings from
the Old Regime and the Revolution attest to the flood of images as well as
words that issued from the printing press.

The decade of the Revolution itself produced thousands of printed
images. In addition to larger engravings such as allegorical composi-
tions, political caricatures, scenes of contemporary events, portraits of

Reprinted in full, except for illustrations and notes, from R. Darnton and D. Roche, eds.
Revolution in Print: The Press in France, 1775–1800 (Berkeley, University of California Press
in collaboration with the New York Public Library, 1989), pp. 270–89, 347–48.

leaders, and even wallpaper, smaller images proliferated everywhere – on certificates given to the conquerors of the Bastille, on paper money, on official letterheads, on legal headings and stamps, on membership cards of political clubs or sectional committees, on copies of the Rights of Man, on the new calendar, on lists of republican adages, on children's games, playing cards, ladies' fans, tops for little boxes, and frontispieces and vignettes in civic manuals. These images, especially those on a small scale, are sometimes called 'ephemera,' but this underrates their importance. Because they were sometimes produced in tens of thousands of copies, these images reached large numbers of people who might not have been reached by newspapers, pamphlets, or books. In any case, as heirs to the sensationalist psychology of the Enlightenment, the revolutionaries had great faith in the power of images to make a lasting impression on the minds of the citizenry. Above all, they believed images could arouse emotions in a way printed words could not.

Early in the Revolution the certificates given to the conquerors of the Bastille and to members of the new National Guard were decorated with emblems of the new order. In June 1790 the National Assembly decided to accord special recognition to citizens who had distinguished themselves in the attack on the old prison-fortress. At the top of the certificate, in an oval formed by oak branches, appear the names of a trinity representative of this phase of the Revolution – the National Assembly, the Law, and the King (*see* figure 9.1). As we shall see, the Revolution produced a succession of trinities, mostly short-lived. On one copy of this certificate in the Bibliothèque Nationale, someone has stroked out the word 'King.' On the left, atop a column, is a figure of Hercules, the demigod who was already becoming associated with popular power. On the right, atop an identical column, is Mercury, bearing a copy of the new constitution. In a cartouche underneath is a scene of the attack on the Bastille, surmounted by a French cock and surrounded by cannon. Broken chains lie on the ground. Later, Hercules appears again on the certificate of membership in the new National Guard, once again associated with the capture of the Bastille, along with the slogan 'Live free or die.' On the other side is a figure of Justice with the inscription 'Men are equal under the law' (*see* figure 9.2).

The new paper money became a major medium for diffusing revolutionary slogans, allegorical figures, and symbols. Originally the *assignats*, as they were called, were bonds backed by confiscated church property, but they quickly developed into the basic currency of the country. At first they bore the likeness of Louis XVI as he had appeared on coins before the Revolution, but revolutionary symbols were soon added and eventually took his place. Most interesting was the use of the equilateral triangle on the *assignat* of ten sous issued in 1792. The equilateral triangle had been used in the past as a symbol of the Trinity for Christians or of the Supreme

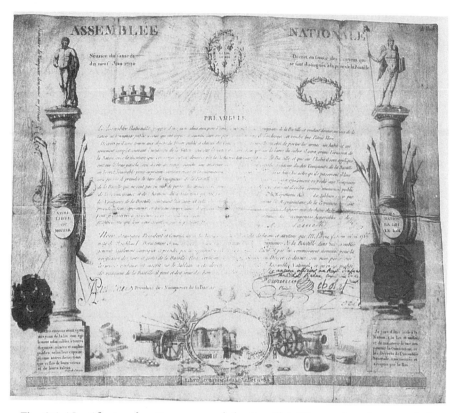

Fig. 9.1 'Certificate of a Conqueror of the Bastille' ('Brevet de vainqueur de la Bastille . . .). N.d. Engraving. Bibliothèque Nationale, Cabinet des Estampes, Collection de Vinck.

Being for Masons. The Masonic version appears on the back of U.S. one-dollar bills. From early in the Revolution this triangle was used to consecrate various ideals – the so-called three good kings: Louis XII, Henry IV, and Louis XVI; the union of the three estates, now all equal; or the three-fold ideals of the constitutional monarchy – the Nation, the Law, and the King, as it appears on this *assignat*. Like the others, this trinity did not survive for long and was soon replaced by another threesome: Liberty, Equality, and Security.

Soon after August 10, 1792 the figure of Liberty replaced the image of the king. An ancient allegorical figure going back to classical antiquity, Liberty is usually attired in a flowing gown, holding a rod capped with a bonnet. The rod reminded the viewer of the one a Roman magistrate had used to touch and thereby emancipate a slave; the bonnet stood for those worn by former slaves as a sign of freedom. Sometimes Liberty is accom-

Fig. 9.2 'Certificate of the National Guard.' [1793]. Engraving. Bibliothèque
Nationale, Cabinet des Estampes (cat. no. 2).

panied by a broken yoke, and occasionally by a cat, another age-old
symbol of freedom. The image of Liberty had become more prominent
in France at the time of the American War of Independence. There had
been engravings showing Franklin leading her to America or being
crowned by her atop a globe with the rebel colonies in the centre. With
the outbreak of the Revolution in France, Liberty became an increasingly
familiar figure, at first in the company of the King, then frequently
standing by herself. At the time of the overthrow of the monarchy she
was ready to move over to become the central symbol of the Republic.
Already she dominates the *assignat* of fifty livres issued in December 1792,
where she appears holding the rudder of state in one hand, a civic crown in
the other. A French cock stands at her side atop a pedestal, which in turn is
decorated with a fasces and a Liberty bonnet (*see* figure 9.3).

At the peak of the Revolution, Liberty also dominated the letterheads of
the multitude of government bodies – various ministries, committees, commissions, and units of the army. Her characterizations depended on the
function of the particular government bodies. In the vignettes on stationery
for generals, Liberty (or the Republic) was usually accompanied by weapons,

Fig. 9.3 *Assignats* of 1792: 50 livres, série 4127. Musée de l'Imprimerie et de la Banque, Lyon, France (photo: Studio Dussouillez, Rutter).

whereas on that of the Committee of Public Instruction she appears reading a book. Especially interesting is the letterhead of the Committee of Public Safety, where Liberty appears holding a pike surmounted by a Liberty bonnet in one hand, and in the other fasces – symbol of national unity and state authority. In the background are other symbols of power: a club, lightning bolts, a warship, a cannon, a sword, the scales of Justice, and a volcanic mountain. The latter was an obvious allusion to the radicals who sat on the high benches of the Convention, earning them the nickname *la Montagne*, and who dominated the revolutionary government during the Terror. Overhead was an All-Seeing Eye, no longer so much a symbol of the Supreme Being as of the ubiquitous surveillance of the committee and its agents. This version of Liberty was altogether too militant, too closely associated with the dreaded committee to survive the end of the Terror.

The headings of laws were probably seen by more people than the letterheads on official stationery. In December 1793 the Convention decided to publish a bulletin in order to disseminate laws in a readily available form throughout the Republic. Called the *Bulletin des lois*, the first number did not appear until the following May. In the centre of the parallelogram that formed the heading was Liberty, sitting enthroned like the kings of the Old Regime and holding a fasces in her right hand (*see* figure 9.8). Later an axe was added to the centre of the fasces, suggesting even greater power (in ancient Rome it meant a magistrate could impose

Fig. 9.4 Identity card, Commissioner to the Central Bureau. Musée de la Revolution Française, Vizille, France.

the death sentence), and an equilateral triangle was placed in her left hand. Two other equilateral triangles balanced each other at the ends of the heading, one resembling the old symbol of the Divinity with an All-Seeing Eye in the centre, and the other in the form of a carpenter's level, the usual symbol of equality. There were thus three mystical triangles altogether. At the end of each *Bulletin* was a stamp, a sort of printed seal, portraying the French People in the guise of Hercules trampling on broken monarchical symbols. In his right hand he supports Liberty and Equality with their usual emblems, suggesting that with the support of the people the ideals they represent would triumph over the world (*see* figure 9.9).

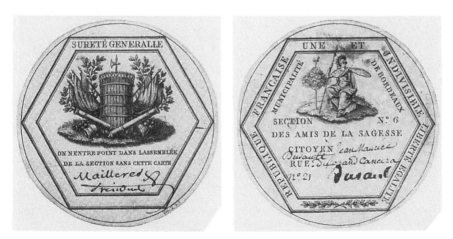

Fig. 9.5 Identity card, Friends of Wisdom. Bordeaux: (left) obverse: 'General Security – No Admission to the Assembly without This Card'; (right) reverse: Municipality of Bordeaux. Section of the Friends of Wisdom. Musée de la Revolution Française, Vizille, France.

Fig. 9.6 Deputy's badge to the National Assembly. Department of Sarthe: (left) obverse; (right) reverse. Musée de la Révolution Française, Vizille, France.

Fig. 9.7 Identity card, Franklin Section. Bordeaux: (left) obverse; (right) reverse. Musée de la Révolution Française, Vizille, France.

The original heading and stamp on the *Bulletin des lois* survived longer than one would expect. Following the overthrow of Robespierre and his colleagues and the subsequent reaction against the excesses of the Terror, the Convention approved a more conservative constitution than the one

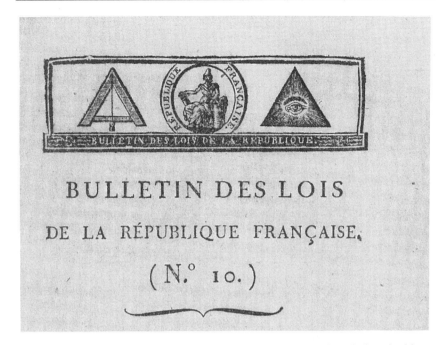

Fig 9.8 'Law bulletin of the French Republic' (*Bulletin des lois de la République française*...). [Paris]: Imp. Nationale des Lois, 11 messidor, an II (June 29, 1794). The New York Public Library, General Research Division.

proclaimed in 1793 but never implemented. The Constitution of Year III (1795), which established the Directory, was accompanied by a declaration that emphasized duties as well as rights. In 1797 the heading and the stamp were finally revised to reflect the more conservative Republic. In the centre of the heading, instead of Liberty enthroned, appeared an octagon enclosing the number of the publication. In place of the triangles at either end were figures of Law and Justice. The radical Level of Equality was still there, but shrunken in size and almost lost among the other symbols (*see* figure 9.10). Even more significant was the change in the stamp at the end. The People – Hercules gave way to tablets of the law, radiating light and resting on a winged thunderbolt, symbol of swift execution. All this was encircled by a serpent biting its tail, a traditional sign for eternity. The message was clear: The rule of law was to replace the awesome power of the people.

Just as printed laws were indispensable for informing citizens of new legislation, so printed versions of the Declaration of the Rights of Man were essential for acquainting them with the underlying principles of the new regime. Because each phase of the Revolution produced a new version of the Declaration – 1789, 1793, and 1795 – there were three waves of

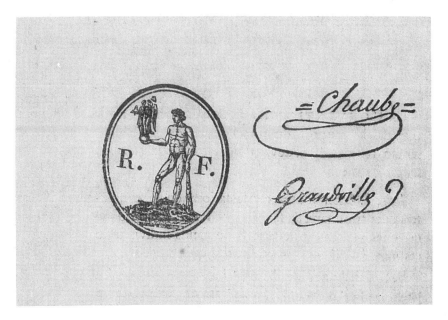

Fig. 9.9 'Law bulletin of the French Republic' (*Bulletin des lois de la République française* . . .). [Paris]: Imp. Nationale des Lois, [1794]. The New York Public Library, General Research Division.

publication of their texts. Usually these were handsomely decorated so that they could be mounted on citizens' walls. A fine example is a version of the Declaration of 1789 dedicated to the free French and their friends by a Helvetian. The Feudal Monster has been toppled from his pedestal, leaving only his boots in place. Little *putti* celebrate his downfall around a musket, capped with the Liberty bonnet, which rises from where the Monster had once stood. On one side a pelican feeds her young with her own flesh and blood, an ancient symbol of self-sacrifice, while on the other side lightning and an eagle emerge from clouds. The seventeen clauses of the Declaration are engraved on tablets leaning against the pedestal, probably evoking the tablets of Moses. To the left Hercules tramples on a hydra on whose various heads are visible a tiara, a cardinal's hat, a bishop's mitre labelled 'inconstitutionnel,' and the mortarboard of a *parlementaire*. Little details are eloquent: a dog urinates on the fallen Monster while children play among the debris; in the background on the upper-left, peasants chase a deer, exercising their new freedom to hunt; and in the sky, Renown trumpets, 'Ah, ça ira, ça ira,' the popular refrain of the period. Later on, copies of the republican Declaration of 1793 were decorated with fasces, Mountains, and busts of republican martyrs.

In order to spread revolutionary principles and create a new civic

BULLETIN DES LOIS DE LA RÉPUBLIQUE

N.º

127.

AU NOM DE LA RÉPUBLIQUE FRANÇAISE.

(N.º 1225.) *ARRÊTÉ du Directoire exécutif, contenant rectification d'erreurs dans le texte d'une édition originale de la Constitution française.*

Du 14 Prairial, an V de la République une et indivisible.

LE DIRECTOIRE EXÉCUTIF, vu, 1.º une édition originale de l'acte constitutionnel imprimé à l'imprimerie de la République, portant, article 216 :

« Tous les cinq ans, on procède à l'élection de tous » les *membres* du tribunal.

« Les juges peuvent toujours être réélus. »

2.º Une autre édition également originale de la Constitution imprimée à l'imprimerie nationale, où cette disposition de l'article 216 est ainsi transcrite :

« Tous les cinq ans, on procède à l'élection de tous » les *juges* du tribunal.

« Ils peuvent toujours être réélus. »

3.º Les extraits délivrés, collationnés et certifiés conformes par le citoyen *Camus*, garde des archives de la République, tant de la minute originale authentique de l'acte constitutionnel, déposée aux archives de la République, que de celle du procès-verbal de la Convention nationale, du 5 fructidor an III ; desquels il résulte que le véritable texte de l'article 216 de l'acte constitutionnel

3.   A

Fig. 9.10 'Law bulletin of the French Republic' (*Bulletin des lois de la République française . . .*). [Paris]: Imp. Nationale des Lois, 14 prairial, an V (June 12, 1797). The New York Public Library, General Research Division.

Fig. 9.11 'Rights of Man and of the Citizen,' in *Collection complète des tableaux historiques de la Révolution française*, vol. 3. An VI (1797–98). The New York Public Library, The Miriam and Ira D. Wallach Division of Art, Prints and Photographs.

morality, leaders encouraged publication of numerous manuals and catechisms, many of them designed for the rising generation (*see* figure 9.12).
Some of these were richly illustrated, for example *L'Ami des jeunes
patriotes, ou catéchisme révolutionnaire*, by Chemin fils, a little hand-
book approved by the Commune of Paris and accepted by the Convention. The frontispiece depicted the martyrdom of Bara (which is spelled

Institutrice républicaine

Fig. 9.12 'Republican schoolteacher.' [1793]. Engraving. Bibliothèque Nationale,
Cabinet des Estampes (cat. no. 149).

'Barra'), a thirteen-year-old boy who had attached himself to the republican army fighting counterrevolutionaries in the Vendée. When captured, he was killed, the story goes, when he refused to cry 'Vive le Roi,' and cried out instead 'Vive la République!' Underneath were pictures of two other young heroes, Richer and Pajot. Other plates were interspersed among the text. Some dealt with writing letters, but one depicted the attack on the Tuileries Palace on August 10, 1792, and others portrayed the principal allegorical figures of the Revolution – Equality holding a level and a fasces, Liberty holding a cannonball and a club, and the Sovereign People in the guise of Hercules. Other plates illustrated the need for public security and respect for private property. Besides some lessons in reading, writing, and arithmetic, the text recounted the story of young Bara and explained the Declaration of Rights and the Constitution of 1793.

Another medium for inculcating the new civic ideals consisted of lists of adages and maxims that could be mounted on walls. These, too, were sometimes richly decorated; for example, the list entitled *Maximes du jeune républicain* embellished by the well-known engraver François-Marie Quéverdo. In the centre of the heading is a medallion featuring the Republic, who is wearing the luminous eye of Reason as a pendant and is holding the Book of Destinies. In the background is a Temple of Immortality atop a mountain. Over her head is the equilateral triangle denoting the Divinity, along with the injunction 'Adore the Eternal.' On either side of the medallion stand infant *genii*, one holding doves, the other holding a club like Hercules. The latter, along with a French cock, stands on a defeated hydra. The medallion on the left shows Equality, accompanied by Nature with two rows of breasts to suggest bountifulness. The medallion on the right frames Liberty, holding an orb in one hand and a fasces in the other. The thirty-eight republican maxims appear below in two columns divided by a pike entwined with branches, a tricolor banner, and images of four republican martyrs – Lepelletier, Marat, Chalier, and Bara – the models of ultimate self-sacrifice, with a ring of stars over their heads suggesting immortality. On the banner is the inscription from the facade of the Panthéon, 'To Great Men, the Grateful Fatherland.' At the bottom is a beehive, a symbol of community, and, once again, the pelican feeding her young with her own flesh and blood.

The republican calendar adopted by the Convention in September 1793 strikes many people today as very odd, but in fact it embodied a new view of history. The Convention had chosen to number years from the declaration of the Republic on September 22, 1792 instead of from the birth of Christ, implying a new start in history. Because the beginning of the Republic coincided with the autumnal equinox, the revolutionaries interpreted this to signify that the heavens were in favour of equality. The fact that the sun also moves from dominating one hemisphere to dominating the other was taken to augur the course of the Revolution around the world. The new names of the months not only jettisoned the names of ancient gods and a couple of Roman emperors but also were supposedly based on nature and on the changing seasons (ignoring the fact that they described the climate only in the north of France). Moreover, the new ten-day week, like the projected ten-hour day, represented the drive to metricize everything. At the same time it purposely make it difficult to keep track of Sundays, saints' days, and other Christian holy days. Like the new laws and the Declaration of Rights, this new calendar had to be impressed on the minds of the citizenry. Publishers responded to this challenge with lavishly decorated versions suitable for hanging in homes, usually in two parts, one covering fall through winter, the other spring through summer. Once again, these calendars were laden with symbolic Mountains, figures of Liberty and Equality, and images of republican martyrs.

Games, too, were used to communicate the meaning of the Revolution to the masses, especially to children. 'How then can one move hearts and arouse love of the fatherland and its laws?' Rousseau had asked before the Revolution. 'Dare I say it? By children's games.'[1] After 1789 the ancient *jeu de l'oie*, the goose game, was adapted to revolutionary ends. In the game players toss dice to determine how far they advance along squares toward the goal. In the seventeenth century the goal had been to move from squares showing Roman emperors through those with early French monarchs to those depicting the reign of Louis XIV. Early in the Revolution updated versions of the goose game appeared in which players progress from the storming of the Bastille through major events of the Revolution to the National Assembly, 'The Palladium of Liberty.' The squares, each depicting an important event or achievement in miniature, provided children an illustrated history of the Revolution. The lucky squares, bearing images of geese, each represented one of the old parlements, now discredited as strongholds of reaction. The player landing on a square depicting bridled geese was allowed to move forward the same number of squares again. Some versions of this game presented an even longer view of history, beginning before civilization, in the 'state of nature,' tracing the growth of abuses, and moving finally through the Enlightenment to the Revolution.

The effort to mobilize all the available media to convey the revolutionary message reached its peak in Year II of the Republic (1793–94). 'Actually everything ought to have a moral purpose among a republican people,' argued one of the reports of the Popular and Republican Art Association; 'they ought to meet with lessons even in their diversions.'[2] In line with this objective, even playing cards were brought into conformity. The old symbols on cards and their names were no longer tolerable because they recalled despotism and inequality: *Lois* (Aces), *Rois* (Kings), *Dames* (Queens), and *Valets* (Jacks); 'Valet' especially suggested social subordination. One pair of publishers had the idea of printing new cards that would constitute a civic manual on the Revolution by confronting the player only with images of Liberty and Equality. For Kings they substituted Genii of War, Peace, Arts, and Commerce; for Queens they substituted Liberties of Religion, Marriage, the Press, and the Professions; and for Jacks they substituted Equalities of Duties, Rights, Ranks, and Colours. With their new cards they published a little brochure explaining the new images. Other printers produced packs of cards bearing images of philosophes, republican soldiers, and sans-culottes.

These are only some of the ways in which printed revolutionary images were conveyed to the French people. Space does not allow us to deal with all the other places where printed images appeared, but we have enough examples to see that the revolutionaries came close to realizing an ideal of some of the thinkers of the Enlightenment. When Helvétius had declared, 'Education can do everything,'[3] he did not mean that instruction in school alone could shape individuals; he meant that if all the influences that impinge on individuals from birth onward could be coordinated, then one could mould any kind of citizenry one desired. This was what the revolutionaries sought to do. They believed that, combined with republican schooling, printed words in various formats, revolutionary music, didactic plays, civic festivals, and public monuments, the flood of images could contribute to an educational environment which could create a *nouvel homme* for the new society.

Notes

1 J.-J. Rousseau, *Oeuvres Complètes*, 3 vols. (Paris: Pléiade, 1964), 3, p. 955.
2 Athanase Détournelle, *Aux armes et aux arts! Peinture, sculpture, architecture, gravure. Journal de la Société républicaine des arts séant au Louvre* (Paris: Détournelle, n.d.), pp. 155–57.
3 C.-A. Helvétius, *De l'homme, de ses facultés intellectuelles et de son éducation*, 2 vols. (London 1771), in *Oeuvres complètes* (Paris: P. Didot l'aîné, 1795), 12:71 (sec. 10, chap. 1).

10
The Enlightenment redefined
MARGARET JACOB

Historians once understood the Enlightenment as the work of about twenty men, the great philosophes and their followers. The study of Voltaire, Diderot, Hume, Franklin, and the rest remains a thriving industry, particularly in English-language scholarship. It may be described as analogous to the historiographic emphasis that was once placed upon the great magisterial leaders and theologians of the sixteenth-century Protestant Reformation, Luther, Calvin, Zwingli, and so on. But in contemporary scholarship, the Reformation is now seen as a vast cultural upheaval, a social and popular movement, textured and rich because of its diversity. So too we must now begin to understand the Enlightenment.

The call for a textured social and political history of the Enlightenment was first made many years ago by the late Franco Venturi speaking at the Trevelyan Lectures.[1] Historians working in the French Enlightenment, and especially in the Dutch, and occasionally in the Scottish Enlightenment, have gone part of the way toward answering his call (as had Venturi himself) and have done so by arriving at a more social and cultural understanding of the historical era where modern thought begins. We now know a great deal about the new enclaves of enlightened sociability, about the reading societies, salons, scientific academies, and philosophical societies; so too do we know a great deal more about the disseminators and even the buyers of books which they, and we, would classify as enlightened.

Yet even more knowledge is required before Venturi's call can be satisfactorily answered. To date, and quite recently, historians of political culture in England, The Netherlands, and Germany display the greatest vitality in the project of texturing the Enlightenment. This has required innovation in both theory and research. We have now begun to see eighteenth-century political culture, despite its ancien régime qualities, as being capable of revealing the sources of modernity. We have focused upon nonparliamentary, ostensibly civic forms of behaviour, and discerned in them a nascent political consciousness. Most remarkably, historians of culture find in the new zone of voluntary associations the makings of civil society. We find this nascent process in radically different sets of

Reprinted in full, except for notes, from M. C. Jacob, *Living the Enlightenment: Freemasonry and Politics in Eighteenth-Century Europe* (New York, Oxford, Oxford University Press, 1991), pp. 215–24, 292–94.

national circumstances. Some historians detect a noticeably modern civic consciousness in voluntary associations in midcentury Britain, in clubs to promote the 'useful' in the Dutch Republic, and similarly in secret societies (of both left and right) in the absolutist German states. These insights depend upon a more subtle understanding of politics than is normally found in traditional political history with its emphasis on the formal institutions of government.

Very slowly we are beginning to assess the civic meaning of the new secular culture found throughout western Europe. By searching amid the enclaves of masonic fraternizing in a variety of national histories, this book has sought to enhance the social and political tendency within Enlightenment scholarship. It has sought to demonstrate, at least in western Europe, the universal character of the Enlightenment's concern for the civic and the ideological, for contemporary issues of power, for expanding the definition of the public, both its space and who shall have access to it.

In each national setting western European elites of the eighteenth century, from minor aristocrats to merchants and literate professionals, created new forms of political consciousness that looked away from the passivity of the subject, toward the activity of the citizen, away from absolutism and oligarchy, toward more representative forms of government. The vehicle for that transition can be found in the zone of civil society created not simply in the theories of the philosophes but also in social practices, and in almost every European country from the early 1700s onward. Freemasonry, as I have attempted to show, was only the most overtly civic of the many new voluntary societies, and all the more important as a result. Its importance, especially in western Europe, was nowhere greater than in the French Enlightenment.

Two trends are observable in the recent historiography of the French Enlightenment. The first trend, and it is not unique to French history, is the turn toward the linguistic; the second, largely confined to French historiography, is known as the work of the Annales school. We shall return to its efforts to quantify the Enlightenment and to locate its adherents and promoters – the readers and publishers of enlightened books. It seems important to say something first about the turn toward the linguistic, in part because it is more recent and hence innovative, and more problematic. The search for the languages of the past, for discourse, or discourses embedded in texts – now seen by some historians as the essence of the historical experience (as best it can be reconstituted) – has many intelligent advocates and practitioners. Clearly language has a great deal to do with the enterprise of the cultural historian, or for that matter any historian. Language, however, is spoken by people, and therefore its meaning is socially negotiated. The problem presented but not resolved by the turn toward language lies in our being able to distinguish among and between languages. If all is language, then the importance of language assumes the importance of any other absolute, for instance, the material interests postulated by Marxist historians. The determination of which language, or which material interest, achieved dominance cannot be brought any closer to understanding simply by postulating the one, or the other, as supremely important, as the medium through which, and because of which, human beings practice and negotiate power and authority.

Perhaps we need to acknowledge that all aspects of the human condition to which we give importance receive the assignment as the result of a social negotiation. This negotiation occurs over physical objects, for instance, over land and food; it also occurs over words. If the meaning of a word becomes the determinant of human action and motivation, then we must recognize that the agreement to make any set of words important is a social negotiation, that is, not a magical process and hence ultimately unknowable, but rather a process to which human speakers of language bring all that they value. Even the agreement to designate paper cut in uniform sizes and sewn together with black letters on its 'pages' as a book requires a social process that engages the whole human being, as speaker, crafter, thinker, buyer, and seller.

Once so designated, of course, the book becomes a 'text' by a similar, yet even more complex, process of negotiation. Once it has occurred, linguistically inclined historians get awfully interested. Texts, they intelligently argue, have a life of their own. Recently historians of the Enlightenment such as Dena Goodman have laid emphasis upon the texts of the great philosophes as dynamic entities: 'I would like to know how writers might change the world through the writing of texts,' she writes.[2] The political texts she analyzes are treated as actors in themselves, with both a form and content intended to transform the reader. Her analysis rightly presumes that people changed their thinking on fundamental issues in the course of the eighteenth century: 'The citizens of the eighteenth century Republic of Letters were the first to see themselves in both the literary and political terms that the name of their community implies.'[3] Clearly the texts of the great philosophes played a fundamental role in creating the new citizens.

Yet in placing emphasis on the enlightened text as dynamic in and of itself, how different is this from Cassirer's approach to the Enlightenment first published in 1932? In a classic work he explicated the Enlightenment's definition of reason as empirically grounded and inherently critical of orthodoxy, and he embraced it as the metaphysical reality of reason. As a true believer, Cassirer defined reason as dynamic in relation to the historical process, as 'the original intellectual force which guides the discovery and determination of truth.' He then analyzed the power of reason 'to bind and to dissolve' in the Enlightenment.[4] For Cassirer reason became in the eighteenth century 'a kind of energy, a force . . . [that] dissolves everything believed on the evidence of revelation, tradition

and authority.' We may wish texts to possess a similar and independent
ontological existence – just what Cassirer wanted for the rationality he
saw embodied in them and proclaimed by the Enlightenment. We may
want the text to exist as a historical force explanatory in itself. But do
texts in fact possess such an ontological standing?

Texts can be regarded as entities only if they are simultaneously understood as speech acts. Senders and receivers of speech acts (i.e., people) are
not indifferent; rather, the message they give and receive 'derives from its
use in a determinate situation and, more precisely, in a socially structured
interaction.'[5] What we are doing for the Enlightenment by returning to the
enclaves of sociability is attempting to recreate one of the situations of its
texts, in this instance the speech acts of hundreds of fraternal speakers and
listeners. But the critic may say that there are so few 'great' texts being sent
out or received in the [masonic] lodges that we cannot any longer locate
Cassirer's Enlightenment. Indeed, the critic may wish to pretend that
speech acts bear no relation to texts crafted in the isolation of the study,
that writing has little if anything to do with any community of sociability.
This seems a facile distinction, without merit in relation to how and when
people think, and how seamless a process thinking, speaking, and writing
appear to be. The discourse of an age consists in countless speech acts
delivered with greater or lesser formality or spontaneity, imbued with
greater or lesser originality, or none at all, but at the actual moment of
speaking or writing no more or less privileged. The status of the act, as
well as the longevity of its impact, is the result both of the intention of its
originator and of how and by whom it is received.

Clearly the many and varied voices found in the zone of the new civil
society are only part of the story of the Enlightenment, one locus of
enlightened acts of speech. Introducing them into the historiographic
discussion, however, has the effect of enriching it. We move the discussion
beyond the idealism of Cassirer, as well as beyond the proclivity toward
static objectivism present in modern language theory.

The great strength of Cassirer's approach to the Enlightenment (and by
analogy the methods of the historian of language) is also its weakness. The
map he gave us is still useful, but it floats above the terrain, pinpointing
only the tallest buildings, all the texts of the major philosophes, ignoring
the many architects, master builders, and artisans who helped to create
them as texts and then in new social enclaves gave them various and
distinctive meanings. In Cassirer's hands the Enlightenment became rei-
fied, its texts scriptural. Asserting the independence of the text for reasons
drawn from language theory may be done with the intention of avoiding
the platonizing of Cassirer, but it also inhibits the creation of the master
narrative that moves from text to text. This was the major strength of
Cassirer's approach. Since language has its own rules, or so the most
extreme exposition of the theory goes, it no longer becomes interesting

to recapture the dialogue among and between texts. Cassirer, and many of the historians from the 1930s to the 1960s who wrote so convincingly about the Enlightenment, at least managed to map out its overall development, the influence of text upon text, of science upon social thought, and so forth. By contrast it is not clear what in the end binds the linguistically self-contained texts currently being postulated to a coherent and dynamic cultural movement.

In the 1960s Peter Gay gave us a magisterial synthesis of the thought of the magistrates of the Enlightenment, those twenty or so philosophes. It may prove to have been the last and best example of a genre of historical writing that is closer to Cassirer than it is to Venturi.[6] From the historiographic tradition represented by Cassirer and later and more subtly by Gay, we get the best litmus test yet devised for assessing participation in the European Enlightenment, whether conservative, moderate, or radical, namely, the willingness to accept the new science, particularly in its Newtonian form. Not least, out of the genre of what I shall call the magisterial historiography of the Enlightenment, came the sense of the philosophe as embattled, as being what Gay calls the 'party of humanity.'

If the texts of the great philosophes were forces hurled into space, the ultimate gravitational force that gave them a trajectory and brought them back to earth lay in the combined energy of some men and a few women brought together in the new enclaves of sociability. In the philosophical societies, the scientific academies, the salons, and, as I have argued here, most especially in the masonic lodges, the context for the text was created, discussed, and reformed, just as members were simultaneously moulded, instructed, disciplined, censured, and complimented as the result of their interaction. The shared sense of the importance of their activity, reinforced by dues, ceremonies, ornaments, and decorations, as well as by libraries purchased and lectures attended, or, in the scientific academies, by nature observed and thus engaged in ways that promised control – this made some men and a few women different.

Because brought together by their cultural interests, and not by their religion or occupation or social status, sociable people were forced to negotiate as individuals. But rather than imagining them as atoms in a void, we need instead to imagine a plenum filled with atoms disguised by size, shape, colour – in other words by beliefs, values, affectations, virtues, vices, and most especially by elaborately encoded marks of social and economic status. The negotiations into which sociable participants had forced themselves by virtue of their interest in finding fraternity, or conviviality, or knowledge, required rather considerable self-restraint and discipline, not to mention in the masonic case an elaborate ideology that incessantly repeated certain words: brotherhood, equality, virtue, and so on. But the words dealt with, or perhaps sought to reconcile, other social negotiations. As we have seen [. . .] many brothers did not like other brothers for reasons that were more than characterological, that had to do with power and interests, with the deep social and economic divisions of the European anciens régimes.

Once we enter into the realm of powers and interests we are face to face with the political. Thus in all the new social spaces of the eighteenth century, even in the officially sponsored French academies, historians have looked and found political language. The societies, lodges, and academies inevitably created their own internal politics. They were also places where political values and ideologies from the larger society could be negotiated, discussed, and refined. In the examples we have seen from the masonic lodges the membrane between private politics and public politics could be remarkably porous. In the lodges the attentions of men were focused self-consciously on constitutions, on governance, legality, legitimacy, social order, self-improvement, and harmony. I have argued here that focusing on the civic in private and in ways that were empowering made more likely its being focused upon in the public realm.

The constitutional practices employed by the freemasons were derived from seventeenth-century England. English Whigs (as well as a few Jacobites) transmitted those practices onto the Continent. The lodges thus became one link in the chain that connects English political culture, and in particular its revolutions, to the late eighteenth-century democratic revolutions on the Continent. In the lodges from Amsterdam, Nijmegen, Liège, Paris, or Strasbourg, the old order was acutely mirrored while it was being transformed. Everything men knew about society and government through their life experiences was brought to the 'work' of the lodge. Some of what they knew came from sources very old, from humanistic and classical education, but some of their knowledge also came from the philosophes. Into the mental universe of the lodge also came debates about the constitution or about despotism or about privilege, the terms of which varied from country to country and employed a multiplicity of languages. In England political discourse could be court or country, in France it could be parlementaire or monarchist, Jansenist or Rousseauian, in The Netherlands it could be patriot or Orangist. In all places in western Europe it could be republican with a strong indebtedness to the English Commonwealth tradition. Indeed, so many political vocabularies could be spoken in eighteenth-century culture that one historian has wittily labelled the process 'ideo-linguistic promiscuity.'[7] The lodges, like some of the other philosophical societies, brought legitimacy to these many conversations.

In addition, the greater or lesser exclusivity of all the new societies when combined with their search for wisdom or knowledge allowed their members to imagine themselves as enlightened, as completely modern, up on the latest learning or just news. The experience of private sociability acted as a counterweight, even a rival, to the experience of the court, the church or corporation, guild or confraternity. But those experiences were also important in the political culture that took shape in the eighteenth century. For one thing the older forms of socializing made the new secular sociability of the eighteenth century happen more easily. We can see this most clearly in England, where Protestants long schooled in the discipline of sermon attending helped to create the audience for the scientific lecture, one so large that by midcentury dozens of lecturers were able to make a living doing nothing else. Under certain circumstances traditionally religious communities could also possess political postures and articulate opposition to authoritarian or established governments or elites. Methodists and Unitarians in Britain, Mennonites in the Dutch Republic, and especially Jansenists in France could and did speak politically.

Yet sometimes the older forms of fraternizing and community were hostile to the new rivals, which by the 1770s would replace them as the locus for discontent and dynamic change. Science was suspect in many religious quarters throughout much of the seventeenth and even into the eighteenth century. Whereas Unitarians and Mennonites fostered the new science, Methodists were known to attack Newton as a symbol of a social order they distrusted. Eighteenth-century Jansenists showed no particular interest in promoting the new science. Yet they were better about it than the Jesuits, their great and bitter rivals. The French Jesuits, who attacked freemasonry in their schools, never taught Newtonian science until the 1750s. By then the fathers of the young men in their charge could have been meeting under the auspices of the Grand Architect of the Universe, the new version of the deity invoked by the lodges and made possible by science.

In one sense enlightened sociability should be seen as an inevitable response to the economic and commercial development of the West. Western European towns and cities were oftentimes much bigger by the middle of the eighteenth century, and more prosperous. European mastery of the world through trade, colonization, and enslavement had an impact upon the cities, and hence their cultural lives. Sociability was a refuge from the anonymous; the lodges were familiar places for merchant travellers far from home. They were also signs of surplus money, of consumption and prosperity among the upper layers of European society. The printed word in all its forms had also vastly expanded by the middle of the century, and it brought news of distant worlds with peoples of vastly different beliefs and values. At least one historian believes that the origin of atheism as a systematic way of thinking has to be understood in relation to the jolt international trade inflicted upon Western theology and its self-perpetuating insistence that everyone by nature believed in God. Any early eighteenth-century reader of travel literature about exotic people could tell that the claim was nonsense.

The printing press and the literature it spawned far and wide cannot be separated from sociability; indeed, the first literary and philosophical societies in Britain met around gatherings of readers of *The Spectator*, a witty journal filled with the latest news from London. By the middle of the century, again, just about any heresy or critique of established authority could be printed in one of the main western European languages (French, English, and Dutch), especially if printer or author or both were prepared to be anonymous or clandestine. If worse came to worse, they circulated manuscript copies from hand to hand, often to be discussed in the Parisian salons run by women. A manuscript put into circulation around 1719 (and printed then in a very limited edition) said that Jesus, Moses, and Mohammed were the three great impostors. Our masonic master Rousset de Missy concocted the edition from a variety of sources, not least Spinoza and his own imagination, and now almost every major European library has a copy of it.[8] The manuscript had been copied over and over and circulated in every country. Eventually it was reprinted during the French Revolution complete with a new treatise showing how corrupted the old religions had been, prior to the establishment of the republic and its cult of the Supreme Being.

We now know more about the printed word, its physical production, its cost, its circulation, the backgrounds of its authors and readers than did the generation of historians who wrote about the Enlightenment up until the mid-1970s. Again the most innovative work has been done by students of the French Enlightenment, for example, Robert Darnton and Daniel Roche, although some of the methods of the Annales school were anticipated by Daniel Mornet in his classic *Origines intellectuelles de la Révolution française* (Paris, 1933). *Living the Enlightenment* would have been easier to write for an English-speaking audience if Mornet's book had ever been translated. All would then be familiar with the importance that he attached to the masonic lodges and the care with which he handled the subject of their role in the French Revolution. Most important he actually read the masonic records available to him; he saw the importance of the text. He did that in the early 1930s at a time when paranoia about the Jewish-Masonic conspiracy was rife in Europe, and would in the end engulf large portions of it.

Sometime between 1945 and now, freemasonry largely dropped out of serious scholarship, with some important exceptions. [. . .] The reasons for the subject's neglect in English-language scholarship are complex: the topic has been dominated by devotees and opponents, none of them very careful in their use of evidence; secrecy has been seen to be irrational and hence freemasonry can be lumped by some with the 'lunatic fringe.' Not least, the lodges have ceased, at least in the United States and Britain, to be enclaves of the liberal and progressive as they were in nineteenth-century Europe. As a result, the quantitative scholarship of what is called the Annales school of Enlightenment studies has focused on the lodges in quantitative ways – in that Halévi's work is superb – but paid little attention to the content of masonic discourse or to the meaning of masonic practices. In not addressing the masonic text historians of the Enlightenment have missed the one movement of the century that embraced its progressive aspects, was quantitatively much larger in membership than the academies, and provided one of the few forums where philosophes and their followers met with men of commerce, government, and the professions. However distant from the salons of Paris, brothers consistently imagined themselves as among 'the enlightened.'

As a result of the impact of Annales scholarship we are left at the moment with what Aram Vartanian has described as 'two Enlightenments [which] evolved, side by side, in eighteenth-century France: the intellectual one that is the subject of common knowledge [i.e., the Enlightenment of the philosophes], and a popular, essentially non-intellectual analogue, about which as yet little is known.'[9] The quantitative work of the Annales historians of the French Enlightenment – and we should not leave out Michel Vovelle, who documented the decline of traditional religiosity through the study of last wills and testaments – has cracked open the door to seeing the Enlightenment as a social movement with political implications. Here I have attempted to open it more. As Vartanian observed, having these two Enlightenments is not exactly the happiest historiographic place to be. For surely they must bear relation one to the other. He reckons that there were probably no more than fifty thousand individuals in France, 'most of them probably coming from the middle and upper bourgeoisie, a sizeable number from the nobility,' who had their secularized religiosity formed through exposure to the writings of the philosophes. I think the estimate is a bit low; there had been perhaps thirty-five thousand men, and possibly over a thousand women, in French lodges by the 1780s. But how do we get at the thinking of even a few thousand of them; where do we find the bridge between these two Enlightenments, the Enlightenment of the philosophe and the popular Enlightenment?

The Annales school has suggested that we look at the French provincial academies with about twenty-five hundred academicians in any one year as one rather narrow bridge between the two Enlightenments. Clearly, as Vartanian notes, the academies display aspects of what I call civil society. They voted, discussed, and debated, and they regarded knowledge and rhetoric as important enough to be shared and as instruments of power. These participants in the new civil society were for the most part neither major philosophes (the Royal Society in London even denied Diderot membership because of his materialism; the Dutch academy of science in Haarlem went after Joseph Priestley for similar reasons) nor the purveyors of heresy and irreligion. They were, however, progressive in relation to the material order, wanting nature studied, in some places fostering engineering projects, and they embraced the ideology of reason, order, and harmony as essential to the natural and human order.

Yet particularly in France there was an official quality to the academies.

They were closely linked to the state, so closely in fact that in the Revolution they were mercilessly purged. Although one historical sociologist has tried to see the Enlightenment as a state-sponsored phenomenon, the opinion does not meet the test of historical scholarship and would have been almost laughable to many a philosophe who did time in the Bastille for what he had written, fled from the censors, often to the Dutch Republic, or just chose to live near a border.[10] The sociologist based his argument partly on the findings of the Annales school and the attention it has rightly focused on the provincial academies. The lodges, by contrast, could not even be remotely described as state sponsored. However identified they could be with king or oligarch, they occupied a space between the official and the officially suspect. In the lodges local intellectuals – with publishers as remarkably front and center in the lodges often as their orators – mixed with merchants and professionals, and these are the groups where we can find wills being dechristianized, books bought, and official institutions castigated for their backwardness. Think of the brothers in Amsterdam listening to the exiled abbé Yvon, their orator, and imagining themselves in the very presence of Diderot and his circle. With such an image in mind the Enlightenment breaks out of the circles of the philosophes, out of the provincial academies, and enters a wide spectrum of literate male, and occasionally female, society.

It also crosses every national border. France was not the only locus of the new culture of Enlightenment. One of the great strengths of the older historiography about the philosophes (master practitioners being Peter Gay, earlier Ernst Cassirer, Carl Becker, Paul Hazard, and Daniel Mornet) was their knowledge of cultures other than France. They could traverse the Atlantic, as well as the Channel, not to mention the borders through the Low Countries and of course Germany. The international perspective they brought to the study of eighteenth-century culture was in turn built upon by R. R. Palmer, who gave us a model of the late eighteenth-century revolutions in the American colonies, the Low Countries, France, Germany, Ireland, and the Austrian lands. We may grow impatient with the tidiness of the international model, with all that it leaves out, with its built-in assumption that Enlightenment and Revolution universally equal progress. But surely it is a more profound historiography that writes about the late eighteenth-century revolutions from a perspective both international and sympathetic rather than one of barely concealed dislike. At the moment a few historians who write about early modern revolutions do not much like revolutions. They argue that the principles articulated in 1789 led to the Terror. Arguments such as these leave the historiography of the Enlightenment with basically two choices: Detach the Enlightenment from those revolutions, in particular the French Revolution, or adopt the posture of extremists and condemn the Enlightenment.

For better or for worse we are the children of both Enlightenment and Revolution. Many in the postwar generation who now write history would not have been so privileged had it not been for the democratic principles first articulated in the English Revolution, both in the 1640s and again in 1689, affirmed and vastly transformed by the late eighteenth-century revolutions. One of the extraordinary achievements of the early nineteenth century in western Europe was the vast expansion of educational opportunities deeper into society, intended for both girls and boys. That expansion which we can witness from Amsterdam to Paris cannot be understood apart from the legacy of enlightened political culture as it sought to create from the 1790s on, in each country, a universal national culture. In that endeavor are present elements of the utopianism that masonic discourse could so readily express. Before the utopian elements in enlightened discourse could be transformed into the thinkable, one great break with the past had to occur. It was the French Revolution that self-consciously broke away and in the process invented modern politics. The eighteenth-century antecedents of our politics and of democratic discourse must be acknowledged, and these antecedents are more readily located in the lodges than in any other form of Continental sociability.

In the final analysis freemasonry, for all of its exclusivity, secrecy, and gender bias, transmitted and textured the Enlightenment, translated all the cultural vocabularies of its members into a shared and common experience that was civil and hence political. Rather than imagining the Enlightenment as represented by the politics of Voltaire, or Gibbon, or even Rousseau, or worse as being incapable of politics, we might just as fruitfully look to the lodges for a nascent political modernity. In them discourses both civic and enlightened merged and old words like fraternity and equality took on new meanings, with which in 1789 the whole of the West became suddenly familiar. Perhaps we can now better understand why opponents of the French Revolution thought they knew which of their enemies, among their many enlightened foes, was most obviously to blame for what had happened.

Notes

1 Franco Venturi, *Utopia and Reform in the Enlightenment* (Cambridge: Cambridge University Press, 1971) introduction.
2 Dena Goodman, *Criticism in Action. Enlightenment Experiments in Political Writing* (Ithaca, N.Y.: Cornell University Press, 1989), p. 2.
3 Goodman, *Criticism in Action. Enlightenment Experiments in Political Writing*, p. 3.
4 Ernst Cassirer, *The Philosophy of the Enlightenment*, trans. Fritz C. A. Koelln and James P. Pettegrove (Boston: Beacon Press, 1951), p. 13.

5 Pierre Bourdieu, *Outline of a Theory of Practice*, trans. Richard Nice (Cambridge: Cambridge University Press, 1977), p. 25.

6 Peter Gay, *The Enlightenment: An Interpretation* (New York: Random House, 1967).

7 The phrase belongs to Dale van Kley, 'The Jansenist Constitutional Legacy in the French Prerevolution,' in Keith M. Baker, ed. *The French Revolution and the Creation of Modern Political Culture*, vol. 1: *The Political Culture of the Old Regime* (Oxford: Pergamon Press, 1987), p. 180.

8 *Traité des trois imposteurs, des religions dominantes et du culte, D'après l'analyse conforme à l'histoire: contenant Nombre d'observations morales, analogues à celles mises à l'ordre du jour pour l'affermissement de la République* . . . , Paris, 1796.

9 Aram Vartanian, 'The *Annales* School and the Enlightenment,' in O. M. Brack, Jr., ed. *Studies in Eighteenth-Century Culture*, vol. 13 (Madison: University of Wisconsin Press, 1984), p. 237.

10 For that interpretation see Robert Wuthnow, *Communities of Discourse: Ideology and Social Structure in the Reformation, the Enlightenment, and European Socialism* (Cambridge: Cambridge University Press, 1989).

11

The court nobility and the French Revolution: the example of the Society of Thirty

DANIEL WICK

One of the most remarkable features of the early years of the French Revolution was the prominence of members of the French nobility among the Revolutionary leadership. Historians wishing to maintain the thesis of the 'bourgeois' Revolution have either ignored these noble revolutionaries altogether or dismissed their presence as irrelevant to the true nature of the class struggle of 1789. Georges Lefebvre, for example, acknowledged that there were nobles in the forefront of the movement for constitutional reform in 1788–89. 'But they were only a minority; otherwise the Revolution would have taken place by common accord.'[1] Perhaps so. But Lefebvre and other historians of the French Revolution have failed to address satisfactorily the question: Why did some nobles become revolutionaries while others did not? Was it simply that some nobles had read more of Voltaire and Rousseau than others? Or were noble revolutionaries merely

Reprinted in full, except for notes, from *Eighteenth-Century Studies*, 13 (Spring 1980), pp. 263–84.

bourgeois in disguise, whose titles of nobility were freshly minted during the final years of the *ancien régime*? Each of these two answers has its scholarly adherents. Whether taken separately or together, however, neither answer has proved persuasive to most historians of the French Revolution. This problem of the noble revolutionary is most acute if we restrict our considerations to the nobility of the Sword. Many members of the nobility, after all, may be susceptible to inclusion in Guy Chaussinand-Nogaret's rather generous definition of a noble as 'a bourgeois who has succeeded.'[2] But surely Sword nobles, provided their noble origins are well-documented, cannot be classified as bourgeois, successful or otherwise.

According to Georges Lefebvre the most important and influential group of liberal nobles in France during the period 1788–89 was the Society of Thirty. Meeting in Paris from November 1788 to May 1789, the members of this Society directed the activities of the Patriot Party which triumphed in the elections to the Estates General. Yet a prosopographical analysis of these liberal nobles reveals that nearly half of them belonged to the nobility of the Sword. Moreover, the twenty-three Sword nobles in the Society of Thirty belonged, in general, to families that had traditionally been attached to the Court at Versailles. Parisian Robe nobles had a long history of resistance to royal authority. But what of the nobility of the Sword?

The families of these twenty-three members of the *noblesse d'épée* were for the most part, prominent in the highest circles of Parisian Society.

Twenty-one of the twenty-three Sword nobles in the Society of Thirty were members of the *noblesse de cour*, the most prestigious class of French nobles. Of the nineteen families to which these nobles belonged, twelve could prove noble origins before 1300, six between 1300 and 1500, and one (Mirabeau) between 1500 and 1600.[3] Seventeen of the nineteen families had been admitted to the Honors of the Court, which meant that they possessed the much coveted distinction of having been presented to the king and queen in a formal ceremony which permitted them to take part in social functions at Court. Such nobles were called *présenté*, a category which distinguished them from other members of the *noblesse d'épée* who were described by the genealogists of the king as *non-présenté* nobles. The two Sword nobles of the Society of Thirty in this category were Condorcet and Mirabeau. That these seventeen families had been admitted to the Honors of the Court does not necessarily mean that they belonged to the Court nobility. But if all *présenté* nobles were not Court nobles, all Court nobles necessarily had to be *présenté* nobles. According to François Bluche, the Honors of the Court were essential prerequisites to '. . . the right to take part in the "cercles de la Cour", to assist at balls and at receptions . . .' and, especially under Louis XV, 'to be invited to intimate suppers.'[4] Nevertheless, although their participation in Court activities varied considerably, the twenty-one *présenté* nobles in the Society of Thirty

must be considered Court nobles. Their families represented their interests
at Court even if they were not personally in attendance. The extent to
which they benefited from the influence of their families at Court is
another question, one that will be examined in due course.

That twelve out of seventeen or seventy percent of these Court families
could trace their noble affiliations to the year 1400 or earlier meant that
they belonged to the most distinguished category of the *noblesse de cour*,
the *ancienne noblesse*. The Court nobles in the Society of Thirty, therefore,
were not marginal figures. On the contrary, they occupied a position at the
very summit of the social hierarchy of eighteenth-century French society. In
order to understand why such men withdrew their support from the *ancien
régime* and, as members of the Society of Thirty, embarked on an active
campaign to change its traditional institutions, it is necessary to examine
the role played by the Court in the political and social life of prerevolutionary France. What forces were at work in the eighteenth century that
contributed to the disaffection of these members of the Court nobility
from the very source of their power and prestige?

The political importance of high society during the *ancien régime* has
been generally underestimated by historians. The memoirs that detail its
activities have the appearance of superannuated gossip, unfit for the
solemnities of historical analysis. Talleyrand was more perceptive. 'In
countries where the constitution is lost in the clouds of history,' he
observed, 'the influence of society must be immense.'[5] Political power
was not exercised solely through formal institutions such as the royal
bureaucracy and the parlements. There existed a vast informal network
of political influence dominated by the great noble families. Indeed, upon
close examination, Parisian high society in the eighteenth century appears
to have less the aspect of a collection of separate individuals striving for
recognition than it does of a complex of family alliances in which noble
dynasties competed with one another for social, economic, and political
power. Rivalries among the great families revolved largely around who was
to receive and dispense the largesse of the Court, what families would be in
line for offices of wealth or power, and what factions would conduct the
affairs of state. For the high nobility everything depended upon whether or
not one had the ear of the king or one of the king's favorites. Court
factions were divided between the 'ins' and the 'outs.' The 'ins,' whoever
they may have been at any given time, were vociferously loyal to the
monarchy and vigorous supporters of the status quo from which they
benefited so handsomely. The 'outs,' on the other hand, also claimed
loyalty to the Crown, but muttered darkly about 'ministerial despotism,'
cabals, and unsavory intrigues while busying themselves with complicated
projects designed to get the 'ins' out. Court intrigue and family rivalry
were, of course, traditional features of political life in the *ancien régime*.
The fiscal and constitutional crisis of the late 1780s, however, was accom-

panied by a crisis in the politics of the French Court, a crisis in which the Court nobles who joined the Society of Thirty played an important role.

The apparently trivial and empty existence that men and women led at Versailles has caused historians to assume that superficiality of appearance should be equated with superficiality of substance. Yet from the time of Henri IV to the end of the *ancien régime* the French Court was the centre of the political life of the kingdom. The growth in power of the French monarchy was reflected in the evolution of Court society. In the words of Norbert Elias, 'the sociology of the Court is at the same time the sociology of monarchy.'[6]

The creation of the Court at Versailles was designed to extend the king's power over the recalcitrant nobility by making it increasingly dependent on the monarchy for income and privileges. The organization of living space at Versailles with its hundreds of tiny, uncomfortable apartments forced nobles to live together in an interdependence that reflected their ultimate dependence on the king. Since the king was the ultimate source of power, it follows that nobles were constantly competing with one another for the king's favor. Nobles combined into factions centered around individuals thought to have influence with the king. There were factions that attached themselves to the royal mistresses, for example, or to the princes of the blood, or to powerful ministers of state such as Colbert. Louis XIV never permitted one faction to dominate over the others for any extended period of time. To do so would encourage the other factions to forget their differences and unite against him. He based his power on the rational manipulation of rivalries at Court, a policy that required him constantly to change the distribution of power among the factions so that final power was retained in his own hands. It may seem paradoxical that the atmosphere of jealousy, rivalry, and intrigue at Versailles should contribute to social and political equilibrium but there is no doubt that it did so. Saint-Simon may have complained grumpily about the 'vile reign of the bourgeoisie' under Louis XIV but he also knew very well that his own position, and that of the other members of the old nobility, depended on the king.[7] As long as the men and women of the Court remained preoccupied with undermining one another's influence, they were incapable of diminishing the power of absolutist monarchy. As Le Roy Ladurie has pointed out, the significance of the politics of the Court did not stem from the fact that the Court was all-powerful, for it was not. 'But it was in the bosom of the Court where one could most effectively bear on the levers of power.'[8]

Louis XV recognized the importance of maintaining political equilibrium by acting as the ultimate mediator among rival factions at Court but he was far less skilled than Louis XIV at such manipulations. Assailed by attacks of religious guilt, Louis XV often permitted the *dévot* party, which was powerfully represented by the queen, the dauphin, and the king's daughters, to influence his decisions. Opposed to the *dévot* faction was what may be called the 'party of ideas,' represented by Madame de Pompadour and the duc de Choiseul. The rivalry between these two major factions was intense and Louis XV vacillated between favoring one faction over the other. Throughout Louis XV's reign an uneasy balance was maintained between the two chief factions at Court, a balance that was to be destroyed by Louis XVI and Marie Antoinette.

Throughout the seventeenth and eighteenth centuries, until the death of Louis XV, the politics of the Court had revolved around the members of the royal family and the chief mistresses of the king. The royal family had always been represented by at least two generations of its members, a fact which provided the nobility of the Court with several avenues of access to the monarch. With the accession of Louis XVI, however, this was no longer true. The new king and queen were very young and the king's brothers were even younger. There was no member of the royal family around whom it was possible to form an effective faction. Moreover, Louis XVI, who detested his grandfather's moral laxity, declined to have a mistress. Thus the possibility of influencing the king through someone like Madame de Pompadour was eliminated. The consequence was that the primary means of access to the king was through Marie Antoinette, whose influence over Louis XVI was to increase enormously throughout his reign. Unfortunately for them, neither Louis XVI nor Marie Antoinette understood how the politics of the Court functioned. Maria Theresa had warned her daughter: 'Do not change anything. Let matters go on as they are. Otherwise chaos and court intrigue will become too much for you both.'[9] Instead of maintaining the shaky equilibrium of the status quo, however, Marie Antoinette proceeded to alienate the Court nobility and isolate herself within a tiny circle of friends and admirers.

The queen began her reign by dismissing the comtesse de Noailles from her position as principal lady in waiting and insulting the older women of the Court by remarking, 'I do not know how any woman past thirty dares· appear at Court.' Marie Antoinette regarded the comtesse de Noailles, whom she called 'Madame l'Étiquette,' as a stuffy disciplinarian and she was tired of the somber, elderly women of the Court. This might have been dismissed as mere youthful enthusiasm in anyone who did not occupy such a high position. For the queen to be so unmindful of political and social realities, however, was disastrous. As Maria Theresa warned her daughter: 'To please five or six young ladies or cavaliers, you are losing all the others.'[10]

Furthermore, the queen liked to meddle in politics. Turgot's ultimate dismissal was due as much to Court intrigue as to the supposed failures of his economic policy. By letting it be known that she belonged to the anti-Turgot faction, Marie Antoinette alienated a number of powerful families: the Aiguillons, the La Rochefoucaulds, and the Noailles, who were supporters of Turgot. One of Marie Antoinette's chief deficiencies was that, unlike most previous queens of France, she never achieved a reconciliation with the families she alienated. Instead she did everything she could to make the separation between her circle and that of her supposed opponents as obvious and unpleasant as possible.

The structure of the Court under Marie Antoinette, therefore, operated in the direction of increasingly isolating the queen from many of the most powerful families at Court. Her tendency to withdraw into the little inner circle dominated by the Polignacs, the princesse de Lamballe, and the comte de Vaudreuil, and to exercise her influence only for her friends meant that those families who were out of favor with the queen found it increasingly difficult, if not impossible, to acquire the additional offices, pensions, and sinecures necessary for them to keep up their position at Court.

Nobles at Court usually maintained a house in Paris, an estate in the country, and an apartment at Versailles. Proximity to the Court aided nobles in receiving coveted government pensions. Income from their estates and from investments in real estate and securities represented only a portion of the revenues with which Court nobles financed the high cost of keeping up appearances and maintaining their social status in Paris and Versailles. Income from government pensions and sinecures was equally important. If we take into account the increasing cost of living, the general price rise, that was such a fundamental fact of the economy of eighteenth-century France, it is evident that income from all of these sources needed to be steadily increased by the Court nobility in order to maintain the traditional economic and social position of their families. Moreover, it was vitally important that Court patronage not only be maintained but increased. Income from sinecures was usually set at a fixed level. If a noble family had acquired a sinecure in 1715, for example, inflation would have seriously reduced the relative value of the office by the 1780s. The only way to compensate for this decline in income, as far as Court patronage was concerned, was to multiply the number of sinecures and offices that a noble family owned or controlled. With each great family at Court scrambling for control of the limited number of pensions, sinecures, and offices that the Crown had at its disposal, family rivalries and conflicts inevitably resulted. Under Marie Antoinette, however, Court patronage was increasingly dispensed to the members of her 'cercle.' The Polignacs, the princesse de Lamballe, the comte de Vaudreuil, and the other members of Marie Antoinette's coterie received a disproportionate share of the lucrative offices conferred on the Court nobility during Louis XVI's reign. This meant that the competition among the Court nobility for patronage grew more intense than under the previous reign because there were fewer available positions for which to compete. The effect of this competition upon the Court nobility was twofold. First, it aroused a general hatred among Court families for Marie Antoinette and her 'cercle.' Second, it meant that the economic and, therefore, the political ties of many nobles to the Court were increasingly weakened. As the Court came to be regarded as an undependable source of new income by Court nobles, its political significance was reduced. There was less point in playing the game of Court politics when the stakes were reduced, and Court nobility began more and more to shun Versailles, for it was becoming '. . . a provincial town which one visited with reluctance and left with alacrity.'[11]

How did the families of the Court nobles who joined the Society of Thirty fare in the distribution of Court patronage under Marie Antoinette and Louis XVI? An examination of the *Almanachs Royals* and the royal pension lists during the years of Louis XVI's reign demonstrates that these families were almost totally excluded from the dispensation of the 'favors of the Court.'

The *Almanach Royal* lists all the major positions at Court and includes, in addition to the *Maison du Roi* and the *Maison de la Reine*, the *Maisons* of the princes of the blood. In all, more than five hundred offices are listed that can be regarded as controlled directly by the Court. Not all of these offices, of course, were filled during the reign of Louis XVI, since many of the appointees of Louis XV were still alive. Moreover, some of the offices were hereditary, which meant that unless they were repurchased by the Crown they remained within the family of the original holder. Of those offices filled during the reign of Louis XVI, however, only two were bestowed upon members of the *families* of the Court nobles in the Society of Thirty and none at all was bestowed upon the individual nobles themselves. The duchesse de Luynes was made a *Dame du Palais* in 1775 and the same honour was given to the vicomtesse de Castellane in 1786. These two exceptions do not indicate that either the Albert de Luynes or the Castellane family was in favor with Marie Antoinette, since the two women were related to these families only by marriage. As an examination of the royal pension lists indicates, women were ordinarily listed as members of their father's family for the purpose of receiving offices and pensions. This was true, for example, of Marie-Anne-Julie Le Tonnellier de Breteuil, the comtesse de Clermont-Tonnerre, who received pensions totalling 16,000 livres annually. She received these pensions as a member of the Le Tonnellier de Breteuil family, not the family of Clermont-Tonnerre. Indeed, the royal pension lists substantiate the impression provided by the *Almanach Royal* that the families of members of the Society of Thirty were excluded from the 'favors of the Court' during the reign of Louis XVI. Out of the more than one thousand pensions which were granted by the *Maison du Roi*, the *Maison de la Reine*, the *Maison du Monsieur*, the *Maison du Comte d'Artois*, the *petite écurie*, and the *grande écurie* during Louis XVI's reign, none was given to the families of the Court nobles of the Society of Thirty. For these families, to be out of favor at Court was not merely injurious to social prestige, it was damaging to the pocketbook as well.

The social prestige and economic position of the Court nobility were undermined by the ill-advised actions of Marie Antoinette. The court over which she ruled which, for purposes of analytical convenience, may be called the Queen's Court, acquired a reputation for extravagance that was based largely on the fact that Marie Antoinette lavished favors on her few friends and withdrew them from her many enemies. The nickname of 'Madame Déficit' which the queen acquired was scarcely deserved, for the expenses of the Court only amounted to a mere six percent of the royal budget. It was not the amount of money that the queen spent but rather the way in which she spent it that aroused the hostility of the Court nobility, a hostility that was communicated to the citizens of Paris and to the country at large through the medium of the *libelles* subsidized by disgruntled nobles. The Aiguillon faction as well as the Rohan and Noailles factions circulated pamphlets against the queen which detailed imaginary love affairs and portrayed Louis XVI as a dim-witted cuckold. These *libelles* were regarded by many contemporary observers, including the comte de Vergennes and the Lieutenant General of Police, J.-C.-P. Lenoir, as one of the most important influences contributing to the erosion of public support for the monarchy. In addition to subsidizing the publication and distribution of *libelles*, disaffected nobles also made a point of disparaging the queen in the salons of Paris. Among the leading salons frequented by nobles who were *hors de cour* was that of Madame de Beauvau in the faubourg Saint-Honoré, the salon of the duchesse d'Enville, mother of the duc de La Rochefoucauld, where Lafayette, Liancourt, and Condorcet met frequently, and the homes of Madame de Sillery, Madame de Ségur, the marquise de Condorcet, and Madame de Flahaut among others. During the crucial summer and autumn of 1788, the homes and salons of disaffected nobles were turned into political clubs. Plans of action were formulated and carried out, the publication of pamphlets was planned and authorized, and a campaign of considerable vigor was conducted against the Court.

This outburst of anti-Court activity was only partially the result of Marie Antoinette's mismanagement of the Queen's Court. If the Queen's Court injured the social prestige and economic position of the Court nobility, the administration of the royal bureaucracy under Louis XVI diminished the political power of Court nobles. The vast administrative apparatus of the French state had as its center what may be called the King's Court, the high officials of the royal bureaucracy. Under Louis XIV diversification of recruitment into the royal bureaucracy had not removed the Court nobility from the center of power, and members of the high nobility continued to sit on the royal councils and advise the king on important matters of state. During the reign of Louis XV, however, the

Court nobility's prominence on the important royal councils diminished and its share of ministerial appointments was only modest. Louis XVI drastically reduced their presence in the royal administration by pursuing a policy of conscious and systematic discrimination in selecting royal officials and ministers of state. Moreover, he followed a parallel policy toward recruitment into the officer corps of the royal army.

The key to a career in the royal bureaucracy was the position of *Maître des requêtes*, for 'the king selected from the *maîtres des requêtes* his most powerful and trusted servants . . .' including the royal intendants, the councillors of state, and the ministers of state.[12] Of ninety-four *maîtres des requêtes* whose careers were examined by Vivian Gruder, sixty-six attained positions in the royal bureaucracy higher than that of provincial intendant and eleven of those rose to the highest posts in the royal government as secretaries and ministers of state. Yet the *maîtres des requêtes* were generally recruited from the provincial Robe nobility during the reign of Louis XVI. As Gruder has pointed out, the same pattern may be found in the recruitment of royal provincial intendants. Thus, diversification of recruitment under Louis XVI operated in the direction of the increasing exclusion of the Court nobility from the royal bureaucracy. As Gruder summarized the situation for the late eighteenth century, the servants of the Crown consisted of 'more new nobles, more newer members of the robe and pen; in short more 'new' men. . . . [13]

The exclusion of the Court nobility from the steppingstones to advancement within the royal bureaucracy was apparent in the social background of the men chosen by Louis XVI to serve him in the highest offices of the state. An overall view of the noble origins of the sixty-five ministers of state who held office between 1718 and 1789 reveals that only fifteen percent were of ancient extraction. Most of these, however, served under Louis XV. As John McManners has pointed out, of the thirty-six ministers who served under Louis XVI only three came from old feudal families. Louis XVI looked increasingly toward the provincial magistracy and the *Grand Conseil* for his ministers of state as well as for his *maîtres des requêtes* and intendants.

This policy of conscious discrimination was applied by the Crown to the military as well. The famous military reforms of 1781, which historians have argued excluded the bourgeoisie from rising to the higher ranks of the officer corps, were directed, not against the bourgeoisie, but against the court nobility: 'The purchase of officer's commissions favored the wealthy – the high bourgeoisie and especially the court nobility. . . . Such a policy as the one adopted by Louis XVI meant in fact to favor the provincial nobility, traditionally and loyally attached to the army, and secondarily the *roture* career soldiers who by long service gained the requisite knowledge and demonstrated their devotion.'[14] Jean Egret has summed the situation up by pointing out that the military reforms reduced the Court nobility's excessive monopoly over high military commands.

The Court nobility was even shorn of its influence on the King's Councils. Although it has been argued that the abortive experiment in noble government under the Regency known as the *polysynodie* eliminated the influence of the Court nobility in the royal government, Jean Labatut has recently pointed out that the high nobility continued to exercise important functions in the King's Councils. An examination of the makeup of the King's Councils from 1725 to 1788 demonstrates that the nobility of the Court were represented on the councils throughout the reign of Louis XV. At the accession of Louis XVI, however, their presence was almost entirely eliminated.

Louis XVI may have had good reasons for attempting to reduce the influence of the Court nobility in the royal bureaucracy, the army, and the King's Councils. His objective seems to have been greater professionalization. The politics of the Court militated against such professionalization because Court nobles were primarily interested in gaining lucrative positions for members of their families without regard for their merits or qualifications. This was certainly true in the army where, as David D. Bien has shown, Court nobles often paid little attention to their professional duties. It was also true in the royal bureaucracy where traditionally, according to J. F. Bosher, '. . . appointments and promotions were much affected, and often entirely made, by personal or family influence.'[15] Louis XVI apparently believed, probably correctly, that the most loyal servants of the Crown were to be found in the provinces. Like Louis XIV before him, he may have wanted to create an administrative and military elite that was dependent not on family influence or wealth but on the monarchy for its position. Unlike his distinguished predecessor, however, Louis XVI did not understand that the politics of the Court required the king to maintain social equilibrium by acting as mediator among the various competing interests at Court. By ignoring the interests of the great Court families, Louis XVI helped to create a dangerous and unstable situation.

If we view the operation of the King's Court and Queen's Court in conjunction, it is apparent that the reign of Louis XVI and Marie Antoinette marked an unprecedented assault on the traditional power and prerogatives of the Court nobility. The King's Court increasingly excluded members of the Court nobility from acquiring important and lucrative positions in the royal bureaucracy and the army. This policy probably affected all members of the Court nobility more or less equally. The Queen's Court, on the other hand, increased the competition among courtiers for pensions and sinecures and withdrew these financially rewarding marks of favor altogether from certain Court families. Although this development affected most members of the Court nobility, it had a special impact on those families that had incurred the queen's disfavor. The families in this category, therefore, found themselves in the unenviable position of being denied access to unimportant and important offices alike. These were the families that felt the full effects of the loss of income, prestige, and power that resulted from being 'out of favor at Court.' These were also the families that formed the core of the opposition to the 'Court party' among the nobility of the Sword. Representatives of these families were prominent among the Sword nobles who lent their support to the Patriot Party and became members of the Society of Thirty.

The socially most prominent members of the Society of Thirty were the dukes and peers. According to Jean Egret, it was the resistance of a number of peers in the *cour des pairs* to Calonne's reform programme that initiated the *révolte nobiliaire*. A coalition was formed between these *grands seigneurs* and the Paris Parlement which the royal government was unable to overcome. Among the nine men who held the title of 'duc' in 1788 and joined the Society of Thirty, five had been members of the *cour des pairs* in 1787 where they led the opposition to Calonne: Montmorency-Luxembourg, Luynes, Aumont, Béthune-Charost, and La Rochefoucauld. The duc de Fronsac acceded to the peerage in 1791 on the death of his father, the duc de Richelieu. Neither Aiguillon, Fronsac's cousin, nor Liancourt, the cousin of La Rochefoucauld, were members of the peerage. After the death of the duc de Biron on October 26, 1788, Lauzun took the title of duc de Biron but it was Lauzun's father, the duc de Gontaut, who joined the peerage. Whether they belonged to the peerage or not, the nine dukes in the Society of Thirty were certainly the bearers of old and distinguished names. Lauzun, it is true, had somewhat tarnished his reputation in the 1770s through a series of questionable financial transactions but he had partially rehabilitated his reputation (in Paris, if not at Court) through service in the American War of Independence.

As representatives of distinguished families these men had been active in aristocratic circles in Versailles and Paris. None was in favour at Court by 1788. Aiguillon was the son of the foreign minister whom Marie Antoinette hated for replacing Choiseul. As Aiguillon's cousin, Fronsac shared in his disgrace. Liancourt was a personal friend of Louis XVI but both he and his cousin La Rochefoucauld were disliked by the queen's circle because of their support of Turgot. Béthune-Charost had incurred the disfavor of the Court by writing tracts against the feudal system and by embarking on independent reforms on his own estates. Eight of these nine men belonged roughly to the same generation. The exception was Fronsac, twenty-two years old in 1788, who was by far the youngest of the group. Their median age in 1788 was forty-two. Aumont, Montmorency-Luxembourg, and Béthune-Charost were in their early fifties. Luynes, Liancourt, Lauzun, and La Rochefoucauld were in their early or mid forties and Aiguillon was thirty-eight. Although all nine men initially gave their support to the Patriot Party, they were not equally fervent in their devotion to the welfare of the Third Estate. Montmorency-Luxembourg and Aumont withdrew from the Society of Thirty in December 1788. Luynes and Fronsac favored a limited constitutional monarchy and became supporters of the *monarchiens* during the autumn of 1789. Montmorency-Luxembourg and Fronsac were early *émigrés* and Luynes, who emigrated after the flight to Varennes, joined the counterrevolution and became a secret agent of the comte d'Artois. Béthune-Charost played no significant political role during the Revolution. He remained in France and devoted himself to agricultural reform and to the building of charity hospitals. The most sympathetic supporters of the Patriot Party among these *grands seigneurs*, men who played an active part during the early years of the Revolution, were Lauzun (Biron), Aiguillon, La Rochefoucauld, and Liancourt.

Biron, friend of Talleyrand, Panchaud, and Mirabeau, veteran of the American War, and speculator on the Paris Bourse, played an active role in the Constituent Assembly as a moderate Patriot, somewhat to the left of the *monarchiens*. Aiguillon was a partisan of the left-wing Patriots led by Alexandre Lameth and Adrien Duport, and played a leading role in the events of the night of August 4, 1789, surrendering on behalf of the nobility most of the Second Estate's seigneurial and fiscal privileges. La Rochefoucauld was a friend of Lafayette, a patron of the arts and a supporter of humanitarian causes such as the abolition of slavery. As the son of the duchesse d'Enville who was a warm supporter of Turgot and the physiocrats, La Rochefoucauld had grown up in an atmosphere of 'enlightenment' and hostility to the Court. Liancourt was also a supporter of humanitarian causes, especially hospital reform. He was perhaps best known in 1788 as an agricultural reformer, in which capacity he received the English agriculturalist Arthur Young. Young was later able to return the favor when Liancourt fled France after the *journée* of August 10, 1792 and the murder of La Rochefoucauld by a mob (not a 'crowd') a few days later.

The political attitudes of these *grands seigneurs* spanned the spectrum of the Patriot Party of 1788. The older men were generally the most conservative. Exclusion from the 'favors of the Court' was enough to turn them temporarily against the monarchy, but when they began to believe their interests threatened, they rallied to the defense of the king. Biron and Aiguillon, who had felt the full force of the Court's displeasure, pursued a more liberal but nonetheless moderate political course. Liancourt and La Rochefoucauld, alienated from the Court, were the most radical; but this alienation only partially explains the political attitudes that they adopted. 'Our family,' Liancourt remarked, 'has always had an equal aversion to the state of domesticity and the state of intrigue.'[16] Liancourt and La Rochefoucauld regarded themselves as *philosophes* and humanitarians. Their dissatisfaction with the *ancien régime* was as much intellectual and emotional as it was economic and political. Nevertheless it cannot be said that being *hors de cour* had no effect on them whatsoever. Liancourt cordially detested Marie Antoinette and the Polignacs. Like many members of the *noblesse*, he believed that if the king were freed from the domination exercised over him by the Queen's Court, Louis XVI's naturally liberal and generous nature would come to the fore and France would be able to achieve constitutional government without bloodshed.

If opposition to the Court provided the initial reason for the revolt of these *grands seigneurs*, familiarity with the Court and an underlying emotional attachment to the monarchy were no doubt major reasons why their revolt did not go very far. Defense of privilege may be adduced to explain the relative conservatism of Montmorency-Luxembourg and Aumont. But for Aiguillon, Biron, La Rochefoucauld, and Liancourt, men who had willingly, even enthusiastically, renounced their privileges, this reason cannot account for their belated efforts to save the monarchy and the person of Louis XVI. Their tie to the Court, like their alienation from it, was, in many respects, quite personal. It was one thing for Robespierre, who had never known Louis XVI or Marie Antoinette, to demand their execution. It was quite another thing to expect old acquaintances to acquiesce to their slaughter.

Aside from the dukes and peers, the largest single contingent of Court nobles in the Society of Thirty were men who had served in the American War of Independence. The most famous of these men in 1788 was Lafayette. Lafayette's brother-in-law, the vicomte de Noailles, was also a member as were Lafayette's close friend, the comte de Latour-Maubourg, and his former comrades in arms, the three Lameth brothers. The median age of these six men in 1788 was thirty-one. They were all of the same generation. The youngest, Alexandre Lameth, was twenty-eight and the oldest, Noailles, was thirty-two. Much has been written about the impact of the American Revolution on Lafayette and his contemporaries. Louis Gottschalk maintains that Lafayette became a reformer and then a revolutionary largely as a result of his experience in America and his hero-worshipping reverence for George Washington. Lafayette was certainly the leader of the liberal nobility among veterans of the American War in 1788. It seems likely that most of these men picked up liberal ideas during their sojourns in the United States and that the political crisis of 1788–89 gave them an unparalleled opportunity to put some of these ideas into practice. Certainly this is part of the story. It is not, however, the entire story. Lafayette and the vicomte de Noailles were allied with the powerful House of Noailles as was Latour-Maubourg. The Noailles were bitter enemies of Marie Antoinette and her favorites, the Polignacs.

There is no doubt that the Noailles had been gloriously in favor at Court during the reign of Louis XV. One member of the family, the duc d'Ayen, claimed in 1747 that he did not have enough to live on and was promptly given an additional 20,000 livres in annual income. Another member of the Noailles family, the princesse de Carignan, accepted a huge sum of money from the king, and the maréchal de Noailles picked up an additional 150,000 livres to supplement his already handsome income. It has been estimated that the house of Noailles eventually came to receive about 1,800,000 livres annually in *rentes* and presents from the king. After the accession of Marie Antoinette and Louis XVI, the Polignacs ascended and the Noailles fell.

The Polignacs were a family of no particular distinction who were raised to prominence by Marie Antoinette. The duchesse de Polignac became the arbiter of the exclusive inner circle of friends with whom the queen retired to the Petit Trianon to play shepherdess. Marie Antoinette showered favors on the Polignacs who in return demonstrated a remarkable capacity for greed. Surviving on an income of 8,000 livres a year until 1774, the duc and duchesse de Polignac were the happy recipients of 500,000 livres a year by 1779. Scandals such as the affair of the 'alluvions de la Garonne' in which the Polignacs were accused of forming a company to dispossess the proprietors of the Médoc region of property worth a hundred million livres did little to add lustre to their reputation but they continued to enjoy the favors of the queen. During the years immediately preceding the Revolution, the Polignacs became the spokesmen for the extreme pro-Court party among the nobility. Opposed to even the mildest of reforms, the Polignacs were successful in blunting many of the feeble reform efforts of the monarchy. The Noailles, on the other hand, became leaders of the liberal nobility and rallied around them their friends and associates among the Court nobility who had also been left out in the cold by the Polignac ascendancy.

The Lameths were related to the Broglie house. In 1788 their grand-father, the duc de Broglie, refused to institute the military reforms of Guibert in the duc's regiment stationed at Metz. Broglie, joined by a number of other noble generals and marshals, in effect led a nationwide resistance among army officers to Guibert's reforms. The new reforms, which, among other things, called for the introduction of Prussian methods of discipline into the army, were designed to weaken further the hold of the Court nobility over major army appointments. These reforms were the logical continuation of Louis XVI's policy of opening up careers in the army to the provincial nobility. The reforms of 1788 were even more widely despised among officers connected to the Court nobility than the reforms of 1781 had been. The duc de Broglie proved himself to be a consistent opponent of the Crown. Along with the maréchal de Beauvau, he refused to take part in the Plenary Court as well. The comte de Castellane and the maréchal de Beauvau, both members of the Society of Thirty in 1788, regarded the military reforms and the establishment of the Plenary Court as evidence of a despotic tendency on the part of the Crown that must be checked. The Lameth brothers, all of whom were regimental colonels, joined their grandfather in this protest. By alienating a significant number of powerful and well-placed army officers in the midst of a political and financial crisis, the Crown had made a serious strategic error. The loyalty of the army, the ultimate mainstay of any government, was seriously undermined. Many of the army's leading officers gave their support first to the parlements and then to the Patriot Party.

The American War veterans in the Society of Thirty, younger and less personally attached to the king and the Court than the *grands seigneurs*, played a more radical role in the Revolution. Lafayette became the leader of the municipal party during the period from 1789 to 1792 and followed a political course that was radical chiefly in its rhetoric. The Lameths joined with Duport and helped to found the Jacobin Club. By the political standards of 1789, the Lameths were considered leaders of the left wing of the Patriot Party. Personal ambition rather than political principle divided the Lameths and Lafayette from 1789 to 1791. When the Lameths and Lafayette finally achieved a political rapprochement and attempted to save the monarchy from the radical forces that succeeded in capturing control of the popular societies and the Commune in 1791 and 1792, their efforts came too late. Like the other leaders of the Patriot Party in 1788 and 1789, these veterans of the American War were constitutional monarchists whose loyalty, in the final analysis, was directed to the king. Although the ideals and fundamental political principles of the Court nobles in the Society of Thirty changed very little from 1788 to 1792, the radical thrust of the French Revolution did change. Once in the vanguard of the Revolution these men became its reactionaries and, eventually, its victims. The Court nobles in the Society of Thirty did not fear the bourgeoisie. They possessed the kind of confidence in themselves that only high social position and youth can confer. Their self-confidence may have been misplaced but in 1788 these nobles saw only the cover of flowers, to use Ségur's famous metaphor, and not the abyss beneath.

The Court nobility in the Society of Thirty may have been loyal or at least sympathetic to Louis XVI, but they were not loyal or sympathetic to the *ancien régime*. During the years of Louis XVI's reign prior to the Revolution, a significant section of the Court nobility had been alienated from the Crown. The discriminatory (though laudable) recruitment policies of the royal government had deprived young Court nobles of the reasonable possibility of important careers in the royal bureaucracy and the army. The actions of Marie Antoinette and her coterie had alienated a number of powerful families from the Court and deprived those associated with these families of the possibility of obtaining the necessary patronage that enabled them to support their positions in society. The Court of Louis XIV had withdrawn power from the old Sword families and had given them patronage instead. The Court of Louis XVI withdrew both power and patronage. As it turned out, this was a fatal mistake.

Appendix

Table 11.1 Noble Origins of the Noblesse d'Epée in the Society of Thirty (P = Peer)

Name	Family	Year of Origin
Titles of Nobility Prior to 1300		
1. Aumont (P)	Aumont	1248
2. Beauvau	Beauvau-Craon	1265
3. Béthune-Charost (P)	Charost	1248
4. Castellane	Castellane	1089
5. Clermont-Tonnerre	Clermont-Tonnerre	1080
6. Lafayette	Motier	1250
7. La Rochefoucauld	La Rochefoucauld	1019
8. Lauzun	Gontaut de Biron	1223
9. Liancourt	La Rochefoucauld	1019
10. Luynes	Albert de Luynes	1298
11. Montmorency-Luxembourg (P)	Montmorency	955
12. Noailles	Noailles	1248
13. Talleyrand	Talleyrand	1245
Titles of Nobility Between 1300 and 1400		
14. Condorcet	Caritat	1320
15. Lally-Tollendal	Lally	1400 (Irish)
16. Lameth, A.	Lameth	1400
17. Lameth, C.	Lameth	1400
18. Lameth, T.	Lameth	1400
Titles of Nobility Between 1400 and 1500		
19. Aiguillon (P)	Vignerot-Duplessis	1461
20. Destutt de Tracy	Destutt de Tracy	1450 (Scottish)
21. Fronsac	Vignerot-Duplessis	1461
22. Latour-Maubourg	Latour	1480
Titles of Nobility After 1500		
23. Mirabeau	Riqueti	1584

Table 11.2 Membership of the Society of Thirty

| | Nobles | | Roturiers | |
	N	%	N	%
Sword	23	41.8	5	9
Robe	24	43.6		
Other*	3	5.6		
Totals	50	91.0	5	9

* Nobles of diverse origins: Letters Patent, Provincial Robe

Notes

1 Georges Lefebvre, *The Coming of the French Revolution*, trans. R. R. Palmer (New York: Random House, 1947), p. 33.

2 Guy Chaussinand-Nogaret, *La Noblesse au XVIIIe siècle* (Paris: Hachette, 1976), p. 54.

3 See Appendix, Table 11.1 for a list of the Sword nobles in the Society of Thirty. The only Robe noble in the Society of Thirty who was not a member of the Paris Parlement was Pierre-Louis Roederer who was a *conseiller* in the Parlement of Metz. See Appendix, Table 11.2.

4 Bluche, *Les Honneurs de la cour*, (Paris, 1957), preface.

5 Talleyrand, *Mémoires du prince du Talleyrand*, ed. the duc de Broglie (Paris, 1891), p. 49.

6 Norbert Elias, *La Société de cour* (Paris: Callman-Lévy, 1974), p. 18.

7 *See* E. Le Roy Ladurie, 'Système de la cour de Versailles,' *L'Arc*, 65 (1976), 21–35.

8 Ladurie, 'Système de la cour de Versailles', p. 34.

9 Alfred Cobban, *A History of Modern France, Vol. 1: 1715–1799* (London: Penguin, 1957), pp. 92–6).

10 *Correspondance secrète entre Marie-Thérèse et le comte de Mercy-Argentau*, ed. Alfred Arneth (Paris, 1875), II, 235; Jacques Levron, *La Vie quotidienne à la cour de Versailles aux XVIIe et XVIIIe siècles* (Paris: Hachette, 1965), p. 217; *Correspondance secrète*, II, p. 311.

11 The duc de Lévis, cited by Joseph Barry, *Passions and Politics: a Biography of Versailles* (Garden City, N.Y.: Doubleday, 1974), p. 298.

12 Vivian Gruder, *The Royal Provincial Intendants: A Governing Elite in Eighteenth-Century France* (Ithaca, N.Y.: Cornell Univ. Press, 1968), p. 202.

13 Gruder, *The Royal Provincial Intendants: A Governing Elite in Eighteenth-Century France*, p. 202.

14 Gruder, *The Royal Provincial Intendants*, pp. 223–24. See also David D. Bien, 'La Réaction aristocratique avant 1789: l'exemple de l'armée,' *Annales, E.S.C.*, 29 (1974), pp. 323–408, 505–34.

15 J. F. Bosher, *French Finances 1770–1795* (London: Cambridge Univ. Press, 1970), p. 61.

16 Ferdinand Dreyfus, *Un Philanthrope d'autrefois: La Rochefoucauld-Liancourt, 1747–1827* (Paris: Plon, 1903), p. 4.

GENDER IN THE PUBLIC SPHERE

Presentation

Research into the role played by women during the era of the French Revolution has come of age quite quickly. If, in the 1960s, all competent scholars were familiar with specific moments of female participation, there was no general awareness of the interconnections between these episodes; least of all of the potential for a fully gendered account of the Revolutionary climacteric. Even the pioneer work on the crowd undertaken by George Rudé did not really draw out the significance of female political activism. For example, his memorable portrait of Constance Evrard, the cook and Cordeliers militant caught up in the Champ de Mars affair (July 17, 1791), was drawn merely to illustrate the developing radicalism of 'many ordinary Parisians'.[1] In the 1960s and early 1970s, that is to say, social class rather than gender seemed to be the obvious line of enquiry to pursue.

Of course, it is also true that the post-war generation of French historians consisted overwhelmingly of men. This situation no longer obtains. Changes in the gender balance of the profession, combined with the retreat of class-bound social history, have facilitated the establishment of new research agendas. Women's history was an early beneficiary of these shifts, and the parallel growth of the women's movement ensured that it rapidly acquired academic breathing space. The question which students of the *ancien régime* and the Revolution need to address is whether gender can, indeed, be construed as a 'founding category'[2] for the purposes of analysis. After all, a sceptic might argue that women now occupy a place in Revolutionary historiography out of all proportion to the place they occupied in the Revolution proper. Penned largely by female researchers, the contributions brought together in this section provide a partial answer to this basic question. They demonstrate some of the strengths (but maybe also some of the shortcomings) of a gender-differentiated approach to the Revolution.

Gender-based analysis, however, raises problems of method that extend beyond those mundanely encountered in historical research. Foremost is the problem of definition. Is feminist history the object of enquiry, or is it the history of women? For as Barrie Rose points out, the two do not of necessity amount to the same thing (Reading 13). Jane Abray, whose article takes a lot for granted, assures us that all forms of collective female activity in a male-dominated society carry some kind of feminist charge (Reading 12). This proves less helpful than it might appear, however, when the empirically minded historian settles down to the task of elucidating the motivation behind the Revolutionary *journées*, or the reasoning behind the closure of female political clubs. Then, as always, there is the problem of discourse. Distinguishing the authentic voice of women Revolutionaries (and Counter-Revolutionaries) from the buzz and cackle of Jacobin politician – and administrator – speak calls for forensic skills of exceptional sensitivity. In fact Olwen Hufton wonders whether the potent rhetoric of Jacobin anti-feminism might actually have determined behaviour roles (Reading 15).

Commitment to the feminist research agenda in this domain can also lead to schematization. Fresh insights and interpretive advances are secured, but all too often at the cost of nuance, variety and a certain amount of awkward detail. The point holds for other single-issue approaches to the Revolution as well, of course. Even so, we need to stay on the lookout for two further methodological snares. The first is the problem of measurement over time; the second is the challenge to keep in view the wood as well as the trees. As Rose and, to a lesser extent, Abray and Hufton point out, evaluation of the gains made by women is heavily dependent on the timeframe adopted, for in matters to do with gender the Revolution was not a bloc. Neither should the mixed experiences of women in the 1790s be confused with their position after 1800, that is to say during the period of Napoleonic consolidation. Bold brush-stroke accounts that equate the triumph of 'bourgeois revolution' with the triumph of 'masculine power' have a mesmeric quality, but they incur the objection that the actual record of gender relations across the Revolutionary watershed does not lend itself to such neat packaging. Not the least of the difficulties inherent in this line of argument is the question of intentionality, for it leads directly to the final issue that needs to be addressed: the problem of perspective. Did Revolutionary politicians behave as 'bourgeois', as 'males', or as neutral enforcers of 'universal values'? A pragmatic answer would no doubt emphasize that they combined all of these roles, unevenly and according to circumstance. Yet even such a resolutely compromising answer demands acknowledgement of the libertarian revolution carried through by the 'men' of 1789. By massively enlarging the public sphere they enabled all manner of groups to organize and make claims, not least women. So, while it is undoubtedly significant that entirely female clubs came to be frowned upon during the Terror (for reasons that are not altogether clear), it is surely no less significant that women were able to mobilize at all. In short, students of the gender question, in particular, must guard against tunnel vision and the distorted sense of perspective that can result.

Many of the strictures mentioned above could be directed at the work of Joan Landes (see Introduction). However, all-embracing theories often bear their best fruit in the form of connections made and researches subsequently undertaken. So it is in this case. Landes' book has the great merit of demonstrating how the 'public/private sphere' paradigm can be employed to illuminate the history of women at the time of the French Revolution. That she uses Jürgen Habermas'[3] original enquiry into the formation of a 'civil public sphere' in a somewhat unorthodox fashion seems unimportant. Few historians have an unblemished record in this regard. Her longitudinal approach also has the virtue of widening the debate to include the 'public' role of women in eighteenth-century society. If some specialists believe that the potential for female emancipation before 1789 has been overstated, the approach still serves as a timely reminder of the need to build a gender dimension into discussions of political culture and the unravelling of the *ancien régime*. Male Revolutionaries of all stripes inherited from the Enlightenment and the drip-feed of the Court scandal press a profound belief that female sexuality and the wellbeing of the body politic were closely intertwined. The fears of degeneration that could result are explored by Lynn Hunt in her study of the multiple purposes served by the trial and execution of Marie-Antoinette (Reading 14).

In their separate and highly individual ways, the four pieces that make up this section show the modern historian of women at work. All four authors accept (albeit with varying degrees of confidence) that women did experience some form of empowerment during the Revolutionary decade, and that their fragile presence in the political arena, however inconsequential, did impact upon the behaviour of the dominant players. As the pioneer account of women's efforts to vindicate their claim to citizenship, Jane Abray's article is essential reading. What her study lacks in methodological sophistication is more than compensated for by its lucidity and chronological range. Written more than a decade before the main surge of research into women's history, Abray's article also enables us to gain a sense of how the subject has evolved. She explores the gender dimension of the Enlightenment and, taking into account some of the representational freedoms still enjoyed by women under the *ancien régime*, wonders whether the Revolution did not end up taking away more than it ever conferred upon the 'weaker' sex. She also tackles the issue of female political clubs, which has attracted much attention subsequently. However, her verdict on the enforced closure of the Société des républicaines révolutionnaires is notably more pragmatic than the fluent gender-driven readings which Lynn Hunt and others have penned.

Barrie Rose's article is a retort to the specifically feminist position on the French Revolution – or, at least, what he takes to be the considered opinion of feminist historians following the enthusiastic reception of Joan Landes' book (see Introduction). If the new Republic was constructed in such a way as to deny women access to the public sphere, the Revolution must be condemned – and on two counts. It neither delivered on the promise of liberty for humankind, nor did it safeguard the progress made by *salonnières* and other prominent women by the end of the *ancien régime*. Rose differs from this synopsis more in degree than anything else. He does not dispute that one of the endproducts of the Revolution was the thoroughgoing legal subjection of women, but argues that this outcome was not consciously willed by bourgeois/male Revolutionaries. Where others see ideological animus against women, he sees good intentions turned sour. Pragmatically, he also points to a not inconsiderable record of achievement in areas of direct concern to women, while also cutting down to size the inflated claims of female freedom of action under the *ancien régime*. In short, a reading of the events of the 1790s and 1800s which is not confined solely to legal and political issues suggests that women may indeed have experienced a revolution after all.

The essay penned by Lynn Hunt shifts the argument away from political rights demanded and denied. It is at once the most persuasively feminist and the most imaginative contribution included in this section. She takes the familiar episode of Queen Marie-Antoinette's trial, which merits a paragraph at most in the standard histories, and imbues it with a substantially new meaning. As depicted here, the trial brought out into the open a gender drama that had been playing in desultory fashion almost since the day of Marie-Antoinette's arrival in France. In the autumn of 1793, however, it reached a bloody climax as embattled Jacobin politicians sought to steady their nerves with a reaffirmation of what constituted male and female space. The trouble with Louis XVI's queen was that she appeared to blur gender distinctions at a time of national crisis. Indeed, as a whole corpus of pornographic literature dating back to 1774 bore witness, she symbolized the capacity of female sexuality to corrupt and betray the (masculine) body politic. Hunt decodes the trial transcripts in a way which makes this thesis seem, if not utterly convincing, at least entirely plausible. Where her gender-laden scenario falters, perhaps, is in the extension of the argument to embrace the hue-and-cry against women's political clubs. The ban on the Société des républicaines révolu-tionnaires intervened just two weeks after the removal of the threat posed by the queen, it is true; but nothing yet proves that anxiety over slipping gender roles was the overriding factor in the decision.

In contrast to Hunt, or for that matter Abray, Olwen Hufton is more interested in real women. That is to say the largely anonymous women of Revolutionary and Counter-Revolutionary crowds, rather than the emblematic, symbolic and sacrificial women of feminist historiography. She writes as a social historian for whom the credentials of women's history must be proved on the ground before the theoretical elaboration of gender roles can begin. What can this resolutely empirical approach tell us? First of all, she agrees with Rose that women did, quantitatively speaking, experience a revolution. Second, the chronology of that experience differed significantly from the generally accepted narrative account. Peasant women started to mobilize in late 1790 and 1791 when the disruptive consequences of the Civil Constitution of the Clergy became apparent at parish level. However, the climactic phase of their empowerment came later, in 1795 and the years beyond, when female country-dwellers strove almost single-handedly to re-establish a form of catholic worship. Employing contemporary administrative terminology, Hufton labels these initiatives the work of Counter-Revolutionary women, but this is apt to cause confusion. It also tends to diminish the significance of the phenomenon which she is describing – namely groups of women piloting their way through the political snares of the Revolution in a bid to restore some semblance of normality to a world turned upside-down. Nevertheless, her essay succeeds admirably in demonstrating how, notwithstanding the denial of full rights of citizenship, the mass of women could, and did, learn to manoeuvre in the public sphere.

Notes

1 G. Rudé, *The Crowd in the French Revolution* (Oxford, Oxford University Press, 1960), pp. 86–87.
2 *See* p. 5.
3 *See* Introduction, note 10.

12

Feminism in the French Revolution

JANE ABRAY

French feminism has a long history; its roots go back far beyond the tumult of new ideas that mark the Revolution. Since the Renaissance, indeed since the Middle Ages, French women – and men – had argued for equality of legal and political rights for the sexes. Woman's education, her economic position, and her relationship to her father and husband had all been worked over time after time. In the eighteenth century intellectuals carried on a desultory debate over the status of women. The discussion slowly grew more heated until, in the early years of the Revolution, a small group of bold thinkers demanded changes that, if effected, would have altered the character of French civilization far more than did the abolition of the monarchy.

Single or married, women had few rights in the law during the last decades of the *ancien régime*. Their testimony could be accepted in criminal and civil courts but not for notarized acts like wills. In some parts of France a single woman could enter into contractual relationships, but for the most part her rights – reasonably extensive as late as the thirteenth century – had atrophied. Generally speaking a single woman remained under her father's authority until she married; marriage transferred her to her husband's rule. Once married she generally had no control over her person or her property. Only the death of her husband could offer her some prospect of independence. As Robert Joseph Pothier, an eighteenth-century legal expert, explained, 'Our customary law has put women into such a condition of dependence on their husbands that they can do nothing valid, nothing that the civil law will recognize, unless they have been specifically authorized by their husbands to do it.'[1] Nor was the economic position of eighteenth-century women enviable. Although their earnings were vital to the survival of lower-class families, their wages were very low. The gild offices excluded women, and even the slight modernization of industry accomplished before the Revolution tended to worsen their condition. For the most part law and custom confined women to domestic service, heavy labor, and ill-paid labor-intensive industries like the lace trade. Surprisingly enough, French women did have some political rights. The regency was open to women. According to the king's summons of the

Reprinted in full, except for notes, from *The American Historical Review*, 80 (1975), pp. 43–62.

Estates-General women in religious orders and some noblewomen could send representatives to the Estates. A few women of the Third Estate, particularly widows, managed to participate in some of the primary assemblies.

This was the subordinate position that the eighteenth-century intellectuals debated. The great figures of the Enlightenment – Montesquieu, Voltaire, Rousseau, Condorcet, Diderot, and other *Encyclopédistes* – contributed to the discussion but were not its main speakers. From the middle of the century on a host of now-obscure writers took up the feminist case: Abbé Joseph-Antoine Toussaint Dinouart, Philippe Florent de Puisieux, Mlle Archambault, Pierre Joseph Caffieux, Pierre Joseph Boudier de Villemert, Mme Riccobini, [Antoine-Léonard?] Thomas, and Mme de Coicy. As advocates of social revolution this group must be accounted tame. Boudier de Villemert maintained that women ought to have 'a serious daily occupation' and recommended embroidery.[2] Potential feminists could have found sterner stuff in the *Journal des Dames*, a monthly magazine. Its editor in 1774, Mme de Montenclos, was an advocate of women's rights. She staunchly proclaimed, 'I am not out to draw attention to myself, but I swear I do want *to shatter our conventions* and guarantee women the justice that men refuse to them as if on a whim.'[3] Many of the opponents of these ambitions lurked in the vast literature on women's education. Restif de la Bretonne, following the path of Rousseau's *Emile*, ordered that all thought of equality between the sexes be suppressed. Women should be forbidden to learn reading and writing in order to limit them to useful domestic labour. Mme de Genlis urged that women's education be organized to prepare them 'for a monotonous and dependent life.'[4] While the supporters of feminism tended to exalt marriage and motherhood as a claim on society, the anti-feminists used this same 'natural vocation' to prove that women should be content to stay home and to obey their husbands.

By 1789 conventional wisdoms of all sorts, and even the image of the happy homemaker, had begun to quiver. For in the last years of the decade a more militant feminist theory had emerged in a spate of pamphlets. No longer content to make vague statements advocating equality, the partisans of women's emancipation got down to specific proposals about education, economics, and legal and political rights. Their brochures began to appear in 1787 and quickly multiplied. The general argument ran: human beings are naturally equal, therefore sexual discrimination is unnatural; husband and wife should be equal partners in marriage; women ought to have a better education and access to more, and higher-paid, jobs. Along with demands for marital and economic equality the new feminism laid claim to the vote.

The Marquis de Condorcet sounded the first blast of this trumpet in favor of the regiment of women. He reasoned that women, since they were not allowed to vote, were being taxed without representation and would be justified in refusing to pay their taxes. Moreover, said Condorcet, domestic authority should be shared and all positions and professions opened to both sexes. He observed that sexual inequality was a new state and not the traditional lot of women. A year later Condorcet insisted that women who met the property qualifications he proposed for the suffrage should vote. He also predicted that his ideas would get little support from women, as they were all too enamored of Jean-Jacques Rousseau to listen to him.

Most women ignored the feminists. Yet Condorcet found some allies. Two pamphlets, *Requête des femmes pour leur admission aux Etats-Generaux* and *Remontrances, plaintes et doléances des Dames Françaises*, called for political rights; the latter also criticized men for stultifying women's minds through a too-narrow education. Not all of these pamphlets were concerned primarily with political rights. 'We ask for enlightenment and jobs,' said the women of the Third Estate to the king, 'not to usurp men's authority, but to rise in their esteem and to have the means of living safe from misfortune.'[5]

One of the most important of these early pamphlets was *Cahier des doléances et réclamations des femmes, par Mme B . . . B . . . .* The anonymous author began by revealing her astonishment that women were not seizing the opportunity to make themselves heard. She described her own conversion to feminism – she had thought women weak and incompetent but now knew better – and asked whether men could continue to make women the victims of their pride and injustice at a time when the common people were entering into their political rights and when even the blacks were to be free. She insisted that just as a noble could not represent a *roturier* in the Assembly, so a man could not represent a woman. Mme B . . . B . . . then lashed out at the double standard of sexual morality, at the *droits d'ainesse* and at those of *masculinité*.[6] This pamphlet reappeared word for word as *Cahier des doléances et réclamations des Femmes du département de la Charente*.

Other pamphlets appeared along with a flurry of satires mocking the feminists' pretensions. Condorcet contributed another major statement in which he repeated his earlier arguments on behalf of women's suffrage and ridiculed one of the opposition's favourite arguments. 'Why should people prone to pregnancy and passing indispositions be barred from the exercise of rights no one would dream of denying those who have gout or catch cold easily?'[7]

A very few feminist proposals appeared in the *cahiers*. The most common of these was the appeal for improvements in the education of women. The Third Estate of Châtellerault (Poitou) made a unique suggestion. 'Let the assemblies be constituted according to an equitable procedure; accordingly let citizens of both sexes and of all ages have equal rights in participating in the debates of the assemblies and in the appointing of deputies.' Far more ordinary was their suggestion that paid midwives be provided for the countryside.[8] The drawing up of the *cahiers* also prompted comments from interested observers. One set of anonymous *Observations sur la rédaction des Cahiers de Paris* urged that men be forbidden to exercise 'women's professions,' thus assuring women the means of making their living and consequently keeping them from turning to prostitution. Henri Jabineau, a lawyer and abbé, sent thirty-two articles echoing these themes first to a Parisian electoral assembly and then to the Estates-General.[9]

Once the Estates had met and representative government had begun, the feminists changed their tactics. No longer did they rely on pamphlets and letters to the editor. Instead they took to sending delegations to the government and to using the political clubs as platforms. Representations to the National Assembly began very early. In November 1789 the Assembly received a series of 'Motions en faveur du sexe' that attacked the economic subordination of women and the evils of convent life.[10] This habit of addressing proposals directly to the government persisted at least until 1793. Mme Mouret went to the Assembly in 1790 to present a speech on the need for women's education. Early in 1792 several Parisians of both sexes requested the Assembly to pass a law against despotic paternal and marital power. In April of that year Etta Palm van Aelders, a Dutch feminist, petitioned the Assembly to provide education for girls, to guarantee women's legal majority at twenty-one, to give both sexes political freedom and equal rights, and to present divorce legislation. The following summer a woman from the Beaurepaire section [of Paris] addressed the Convention.

> Citizen legislators, you have given men a Constitution; now they enjoy all the rights of free beings, but women are very far from sharing these glories. Women count for nothing in the political system. We ask for primary assemblies and, as the Constitution is based on the Rights of Man, we now demand the full exercise of these rights for ourselves.[11]

The president congratulated her deputation for its zeal – and postponed discussion.

Such a discussion might have proved to be quite excited. The assemblies had their full complement of antifeminists, but they also contained a few advocates of women's emancipation. In 1792 Aubert-Dubayet of Isère spoke on the recording of vital statistics; he called women 'the victims of their fathers' despotism and of their husbands' perfidy' and warned that French law must not maintain women in a state of slavery.[12] In the spring of 1793 Pierre Guyomar, from the Côtes-du-Nord, presented the

Convention with his reflections on political equality. To him the only differences between men and women lay in their reproductive systems, and he could not understand why such physical differences should lead to differences before the law. Like many other contemporary feminists, Guyomar compared sexual to racial discrimination. He spoke, too, of 'une aristocratie formelle des hommes.'[13]

Supporters of women's rights did not completely abandon their old platforms. Letters to newspapers continued to appear. The founder of the *Journal des Droits de l'Homme*, a Cordelier named Labenette, defended the rights of women. A major feminist declaration arrived on the streets of Paris in 1791. Olympe de Gouges, having had enough of the 'rights of man,' announced the rights of women. Her text followed closely that of the declaration of August 1789.

> All women are born free and remain equal to men in rights. . . . The aim of all political associations is the preservation of the natural and inalienable rights of women and men. . . . The nation is the union of women and men. . . . Law is the expression of the general will: all female and male citizens have the right to participate personally, or through their representatives, in its formation.[14]

De Gouges also demanded equality of opportunity in public employment, the right to paternity suits, and an end to male tyranny generally. The following year Mary Wollstonecraft's *Vindication of the Rights of Women*, inspired in part by the Revolution, appeared in a French translation and created some stir.

Women also made their presence felt in the great revolutionary *journées* and in the army. While this activity was not, strictly speaking, feminist, any activity by women in a society that places a premium on female passivity has some feminist overtones. Nor were the implications of their actions lost on the women themselves. In 1789 the women of the Halles were singing:

> A Versail' comme des fanfarons
> J'avions amené nos canons: [*bis*]
> Falloit voir, quoi qu' j'étions qu'des femmes
> Un courage qui n'faut pas qu'l'on blâme.
>
> Nous faisions voir aux homm' de coeur
> Que tout comme eux j'n'avions pas peur: [*bis*]
> Fusil, musquetons sur l'épaule,
> J'allions comme Amadis de Gaule.[15]

The *Etrennes nationales des Dames*, a feminist newspaper begun in November 1789, used the same episode to threaten 'aristocratic husbands' that women could just as easily take up arms against them if they persisted in their pretensions. In January 1794, when the back of feminism had broken under the weight of public and governmental hostility, some women still remembered their old enthusiasms. A police spy reported on groups of women eager to see Reine Chapuy, a female cavalry soldier. The idea of her daring aroused several of these women to attack male cowardice and to exalt female courage.

Most of the people behind this agitation have left little trace. Some of their clubs can be pinned down; a few of the most flamboyant leaders survive as individuals. Of the Paris political clubs the Cercle Social was the first to advocate feminism. Its members began to hear radical ideas about women's place in society in October 1790; both Condorcet and Etta Palm used it as a forum. Several of the Parisian *sociétés populaires* accepted women: the Club des Indigents, Club des Halles, Club des Nomophiles, Club des Minimes, the Société Fraternelle des Jacobins, and that of the Carmes. Although the Société Fraternelle des Jacobins, for one, had female officers, there is no evidence that any of these clubs were directly involved in feminist activities. The same holds true of the provincial women's clubs in Besançon, Bordeaux, Dijon, Orléans, Strasbourg, and elsewhere. The provincial women's clubs attracted middle-class women, but in Paris the rank and file were usually from the lower classes. On the other hand the male feminists of whom we have record were generally fairly substantial citizens.

The feminist leaders about whom enough is known to permit biographical sketches were rather a curious crew. Olympe de Gouges – born Marie Gouze in 1748 – was a failed playwright whose royalism and opposition to Robespierre combined to bring her to the guillotine. She relied on brochures, posters, long letters to newspapers, and very unpopular plays to spread her message. She had little enough influence. As a police spy described the reaction to one of her placards, 'People stop a minute, then walk off saying, "Oh, it's just Olympe de Gouges!"'[16] There can be no doubt about the ardent feminism of the author of the *Droits de la Femme*. Although her execution in 1793 had obvious political causes, it was not without its significance as a gesture of repression toward the feminists. The semiofficial *Feuille du salut public* gloated, 'It seems the law has punished this conspirator for having forgotten the virtues that suit her sex.'[17]

Etta Palm, who like de Gouges glamorized her name by declaring herself the 'Baronne' d'Aelders, came to Paris from Holland in 1774. Palm urged the Constituent Assembly to form a company of amazons as 'a first blow to the prejudices that have been wrapped around our lives,' and she advocated 'a second revolution in our customs' to overthrow sexual tyranny.[18] She addressed to the general populace an *Appel aux Françaises sur la régénération des moeurs et nécessité de l'influence des femmes dans un gouvernement libre*. In 1791 she tried to organize a national federation of women's groups. Failure here did not stop her. She went on to address the Assembly, demanding equal employment and education, as well as political and legal equality. Its president replied ambiguously; the legislature would avoid taking any actions that might bring the citizens to regret and tears. Like de Gouges, Palm practised the wrong politics – she had, for example, invited the Princesse de Bourbon to be a patron to one of her charitable organizations. Unlike de Gouges she had the good sense to leave France before the government could arrest her.

Théroigne de Méricourt, whose real name seems to have been Anne Terwagne, is perhaps the best known of these three, largely because of the attacks her contemporaries made on her. She created a sensation in the early years of the Revolution, holding a salon, trying to form a women's club, participating in the attacks on the Tuileries, and striding about in riding clothes. Her feminism was something of a sideline, albeit sincere. In an autobiographical account she declared herself to be 'humiliated by the servitude and the prejudices in which male vanity keeps our oppressed sex.' She encouraged women to form a militia company because, she said, 'it is time for women to break out of the shameful incompetence in which men's ignorance, pride, and injustice have so long held us captive.'[19] Her attempts to found a women's club provoked Antoine-Joseph Santerre, the commander of the National Guard, to observe that the men of his section would rather find their homes in order when they came back after a hard day's work than be greeted by wives fresh from meetings where they did not always gain in sweetness. Like de Gouges and Palm, Théroigne was politically moderate, a friend to the Girondin deputies. The shock from a beating she received from a group of Jacobin women in the spring of 1793 seems to have turned her mind. After spending some time in an asylum she was released, only to be permanently recommitted in 1797.

Two other women deserve mention, the chocolate maker Pauline Léon and the actress Claire Lacombe, founders and presidents of the most famous of the women's clubs, the Citoyennes Républicaines Révolutionnaires. Founded in the spring of 1793, the club contributed to the fall of the Girondins, then drifted away from the Jacobins towards the *enragés*, a move that had much to do with its eventual suppression. The Républicaines were sans-culottes women, and their programme emphasized economic claims, notably cheap food, rather than strictly feminist demands. Nevertheless the Républicaines showed some sympathy for women's emancipation. Only two accounts of their meetings survive, and one shows the Républicaines discussing women's capacity to govern. At the first of these the *citoyenne* Monic concluded that women were certainly worthy to rule nations, perhaps even more so than were men. In June 1793 the Républicaines tried to put their ideas into practice by attempting to gain entry to the Conseil Général Révolutionnaire, newly set up in Paris.

The women of the Droits de l'Homme section had high praises for their activities.

> You have broken one of the links in the chain of prejudice: that one, which confined women to the narrow sphere of their households, making one half of the people into passive and isolated beings, no longer exists for you. You want to take your place in the social order; apathy offends and humiliates you.[20]

The feminist programme for educational, economic, political, and legal change developed piecemeal. To justify their goals the feminists used three major arguments. First, women were human beings who therefore shared in the natural rights of man, a conviction often explicitly expressed but also implicit in the borrowing of political terms like 'aristocracy' and 'despotism' to describe the old system. Feminists saw the women's struggle as parallel to and a continuation of the war of the Third Estate against the upper classes. Second, the feminists made use of women's biological role. As the mothers of all citizens women had a special claim on the state, for they guaranteed its survival. Unlike modern feminists, they made no attempt to define women as other than mothers and potential mothers. Third, once the Revolution was under way, feminists cited women's political contributions to the struggle for liberty and pointed to their continuing patriotism. Since they were fulfilling the duties of citizens women could not logically be denied the rights of citizens. The feminists felt they had solid grounds for their proposals, but one by one the revolutionary governments rejected them.

Education was the most important feminist rallying point. It was also the subject on which feminists and their opponents had managed some agreement before the Revolution. The conviction that women's education needed improvement had been fairly general before 1789. The revolutionary governments considered a multitude of educational projects from which some common principles can be extracted. Most projects followed Talleyrand's lead in declaring that both sexes must be educated and then sharply distinguishing between the kinds of education suitable to each. His 'Projet de décret' read in September 1791 sounded a note that would recur again and again. 'All the lessons taught in the public schools will aim particularly to train girls for the virtues of domestic life and to teach them the skills useful in raising a family.'[21] The *conventionnel* Alexandre Deleyre dismissed secondary education for women as unnecessary. Some of the less progressive legislators would have denied even primary education to girls, preferring to see them taught housekeeping at home. The Convention's Committee on Public Education did in fact vote to suppress girls' schools in the summer of 1795 but then changed its mind the following year. Since the revolutionary governments never succeeded in running a national educational system, it is difficult to evaluate their work and dangerous simply to assume that they neglected women. Yet is is clear that the government intended to reinforce and to perpetuate sexual differences through public education. It is also clear that the Revolution was unable to improve or even to expand women's education. On the other hand the secularization of education and the promise of an expanded primary school system held out some hope of employment to literate single women.

This was one of the few hopes the Revolution offered to women who had to earn their own living. The Committee of Public Safety and the Convention's education committee both flirted with the idea of training women to set type, but nothing came of it. Nor did the revolutionary governments make any effort to help the women injured by the collapse of luxury trades like silk and lace. The government established *ateliers nationaux* for men quite early in the Revolution, but it was reluctant to help women. Jean-Sylvain Bailly, the major of Paris, requested aid for them in January 1790, but it was almost two years before anything was done, and then action came from municipal, not national, authorities. Where women were admitted to the *ateliers* they were regularly paid less than men. In the Salpêtrière the administration relied in part on the profits of the unpaid labor of young girls to make ends meet. Small wonder women continued to complain.

Under the Old Regime women could sometimes vote and act as regents; during the Revolution they assumed their right to form political associations. Less than five years after the calling of the Estates-General this had all disappeared. The legislators barely considered female suffrage despite the heated arguments the feminists had put forward. Abbé Emmanuel-Joseph Sieyès voiced the general opinion as early as July 1789. 'Women, at least as things now stand, children, foreigners, in short those who contribute nothing to the public establishment, should have no direct influence on the government.'[22] The systematization of French electoral law eliminated the idiosyncrasies that had permitted women to vote; for the first time in centuries women were completely barred, as a group, from this aspect of the political process. Few people protested this exclusion. The women of Droits de l'Homme [section] in Paris and the Républicaines Révolutionnaires castigated the provisions of the Constitution of 1793, but only by making speeches in the latter's club. Possibly the infrequency with which elections were held took the sting out of this exclusion; certainly at the level where politics really mattered, in the clubs and sections, women continued to vote for a time. Probably exclusion from the regency also mattered little, particularly when everyone was soon excluded by the abolition of the monarchy. The regency was not an important issue in itself, but it shows the ease with which the legislators could dismiss the idea of women participating in government.

Far more important to ordinary women than the vote or the regency was the issue of citizenship. Were women citizens enough to take the civic oath, one of the central means of demonstrating acceptance of the revolutionary ideals and of participating in communal life? In 1790, when the National Assembly swore the oath, the spectators, men and women, joined them. Within two months women's right to take the oath had become an issue. Brigent Baudouin, wife of a municipal officer in Lanion, wrote the Assembly on behalf of several women in her village. 'There is not a word about women in the Constitution, and I admit that they can take no part in government; nevertheless mothers can and should be citizens.' They should therefore, she continued, be permitted to swear the revolutionary oath before the municipal officers. Goupil de Préfeln, a member of the Cercle Social, moved that all married women of 'respectable conduct' be granted this honor. He added that mothers undoubtedly had more right to it than did childless women. The motion was tabled.[23] Swearing civic oaths became particularly important in the summer of 1790 during the Fêtes de la Fédération. In Beaune the National Guard invited eighty-four women to the ceremony, but the municipal authorities firmly refused to let them take part. In Toulouse the city officials, momentarily forgetting *la galanterie française*, turned the fire hoses on the women present to disperse them. Examples could be found of women who did take the oath and who were invited to sign petitions and make other symbolic gestures – for example, at the Champs de Mars in 1791 – but the whole issue of women's citizenship remained clouded. With no sure rule to which to appeal, women had to depend on the good will of local authorities. Even at this low, but symbolically vital, level women's political status continued to be a matter of privileges not rights. The Committee of Public Safety and the Directory would both find themselves dealing with the consequences. A representative on mission, J. -B. Jérôme Bô, wrote the committee in 1794 to advise exemplary punishment of troublemakers, especially of those women who claimed that the law could not touch them because they had not taken the civic oath. In 1796 some factions used women to create disorder; since the government did not take them seriously, women could get away with subversive speeches for which men could be jailed.

The revolutionary governments had at one time taken women's activities quite seriously, but only long enough to outlaw their clubs. Apparently article 7 of the second Declaration of Rights, guaranteeing the rights of free speech and assembly, no more applied to women than did article 5, which promised equal access to public office for all citizens. The Mountain sent the women's clubs crashing down in the fall of 1793. The ostensible cause was the unrevolutionary conduct of the Républicaines Révolutionnaires, a charge that could be supported in fact by the admiration of Claire Lacombe and Pauline Léon for Jacques Roux, Théophile Leclerc, and the *enragés*. The campaign against the Républicaines began in the Jacobin club on a strictly political note. A member announced that the women had taken up with Leclerc; François Chabot, Claude Basire, and Taschereau spoke against Lacombe's new political line. 'I do not doubt that she is a tool of the counterrevolution,' said Chabot sagely.[24] At this point the campaign against the Républicaines was specifically political and focused on them alone. Yet how soon the campaign changed! A month later a deputation of women from several sections came to the Convention to protest the activities of the Républicaines; one of them requested the abolition of their club. The Convention forwarded their complaint to the Committee of General Security. Fabre d'Eglantine made good use of this opportunity to address the Convention. After the *bonnet rouge*, which the Républicaines wore during their meetings, comes the gun belt, then the gun, he warned. He reminded the Convention of the manner in which the women went after bread: like pigs at a trough. These were not good mothers and daughters but – significant although false characterization – 'des filles émancipées, des grenadiers femelles.' The members several times interrupted his speech with applause. A little later one of the women spectators came forward to demand the abolition of all women's clubs.[25]

The Convention must have been gratified by the report André Amar soon presented on behalf of the Committee of General Security. That committee, explained Amar, had considered two questions: should women exercise political rights and take part in government, and should women meet in political associations? From the specific case of the Républicaines Révolutionnaires the government had moved to consider the status of all French women. To both questions the committee replied in the negative. Women did not have the strength of character needed to govern; political meetings took them away from 'the more important concerns to which nature calls them.' Nature's imperious commands were not to be violated; women could have no political rights. Amar concluded:

> There is another aspect of women's associations that seems dangerous. If we take into account the fact that the political education of men is still at its very beginnings, that all the principles are not yet developed, and that we still stammer over the word 'liberty,' then how much less enlightened are women, whose moral education has been practically nonexistent. Their presence in the *sociétés populaires*, then, would give an active part in government to persons exposed to error and seduction even more than are men. And, let us add that women, by their constitution, are open to an exaltation which could be ominous in public life. The interests of the state would soon be sacrificed to all the kinds of disruption and disorder that hysteria can produce.[26]

Impressed, the Convention quickly voted to outlaw all women's clubs.

Had the government been content to close the Club des Citoyennes Républicaines Révolutionnaires without making these explanations its attitude would remain ambiguous. By expanding its target to include all women, of whatever political or apolitical stripe, the Committee of General Security and the Convention made it clear that political questions were merely a pretext. What they wanted to do was to exclude women, as a group, from public life. Anaxagoras Chaumette, the *procureur* of the Paris Commune, summed up the new order a fortnight later. Speaking in response to the arrival of a deputation of women at the Conseil Général of the Commune he lectured: 'So! Since when have people been allowed to renounce their sex? Since when has it been acceptable to see women abandon the *pious* duties of their households, their children's cradles, to appear in public, to take the floor and to make speeches, to come before the senate?'[27] The Committee of Public Safety drove the message home in an 'Avis aux Républicaines,' which appeared in the semiofficial *Feuille du Salut Public*. The committee began its admonition on a menacing note. It reminded women of the fate of Marie-Antoinette, de Gouges, and Mme Roland. The purpose of this reminder was strikingly clear in the choice of de Gouges. 'She wished to be a politician and it seems that the law has punished this conspirator for forgetting the virtues appropriate to her sex' – that is, not for the character of her opinions but for having had opinions. This lecture concluded by spelling out the virtuous life.

> Women! Do you want to be Republicans? . . . Be simple in your dress, hard-working in your homes, never go to the popular assemblies wanting to speak there. But let your occasional presence there encourage your children. Then *la Patrie* will bless you, for you will have done for it what it has a right to expect from you.[28]

Few people protested the suppression of the women's clubs. Lacombe brought a deputation of women to the Convention the following day; the deputies howled them down and hooted them out. In the provinces the clubs quietly dissolved. For a time the women in Paris could continue to participate in sectional assemblies and mixed clubs like the Société Fraternelle du Panthéon. Perhaps this softened the blow; in the capital at least women still had political outlets. Yet their status in the men's clubs was unclear. In the assembly of the Panthéon-français section a deputation from the Société des Amis de la République was warmly applauded when its spokesman asserted that the ban on women's clubs also forbade them to vote in other clubs. A member of the Paris Commune disagreed, and the matter was dropped. Vague reports of women's organizations crop up in records from later periods – a leader of a 'club des femmes jacobites' was arrested in May 1795; earlier the police had flushed out a 'nid des jacobines' – but these reports are too ambiguous to prove anything about women's political activities.

The suppression of the women's clubs effectively destroyed the feminists' political aspirations. It was not, however, the clearest statement on women's

rights the government made. After the *journée of Ier Prairial* of the Year III
(May 20, 1795), the Convention voted to exclude women from its meetings;
in future they would be allowed to watch only if they were accompanied by
a man carrying a citizen's card. Three days later the Convention placed all
Parisian women under a kind of house arrest. 'All women are to return to
their domiciles until otherwise ordered. Those found on the streets in
groups of more than five one hour after the posting of this order will be
dispersed by force and then held under arrest until public tranquillity is
restored in Paris.'[29] The progress of the Revolution had rendered the brave
hopes of the feminists of 1789–91 chimeric.

Only in regard to their legal status could feminists find some grati-
fication. The Revolution, so severe to women in public life, was kinder
to them in private life. Inheritance laws were changed to guarantee male
and female children equal rights. Women reached majority at twenty-one
under the new laws. Moreover they could contract debts and be witnesses in civil acts. Other legislation changed the laws concerning
women's property, giving them some voice in its administration, and
acknowledged the mother's part in decisions affecting her children.
Revolutionary divorce legislation treated both sexes equally. Yet some
inequalities remained. Women could not serve on juries; in practice they
were excluded from sitting on the Tribunaux de Famille, which
attempted to settle family quarrels from 1790 to 1796. Moreover the
gains were short-lived. The Napoleonic codes swept away almost every
advance the women had made, returning them to the status Pothier had
described in 1769.

The most important reason for the almost total failure of revolutionary
feminism was its narrow base. Feminism was and remained a minority
interest. The majority of French women – the logical constituency to which
the movement could hope to appeal – had no interest in changing their
social position. For the most part French women accepted the eighteenth-
century definition of femininity. Far more typical of their attitudes than
any of the feminist manifestoes is this speech made by the women of Épinal
to their men.

If our strength had equaled our courage we would, like you, have
hastened to take up weapons and would have shared with you the
glory of having won our freedom. But it took stronger arms than
ours to defeat the enemies of the Constitution; our weakness has
prevented us from taking part in this Revolution. We content ourselves with admiring your efforts.[30]

The feminist movement had been unable to reach these women. Neither its
words nor its action had made any sense to ordinary women. Feminism
never became part of the programme of the majority of the women's clubs.

Only the Besançon club considered urging the Convention to extend the suffrage to women, but faced with the mockery of local Jacobins it soon abandoned its project. At Orléans feminism never raised its head. One of the few lengthy series of *procès-verbaux* available from a women's club, that of Ruffec (Charente), shows not a hint of feminist attitudes in two years. The women's clubs were content to function as auxiliaries to male societies. The mixed clubs held themselves equally aloof, except for the short-lived efforts of the Cercle Social. If the various *sociétés fraternelles des deux sexes* approved of feminism, they kept the secret to themselves.

The prominent women of the Revolution are conspicuous by their absence. Mme Robert, coeditor of the *Mercure national*, belonged to the Société Fraternelle des Jacobins, but she was no feminist. She told her club, apropos of women inspectors for the public hospitals, that women could contribute greatly to the success of the inspections, but she went on to add, 'Their domestic duties, sacred duties important to the public order, prohibit their taking on any administrative functions, and I do not claim to draw them from their sphere.[31] Mme Roland, too, accepted the status quo. 'I am often annoyed to see women arguing over privileges that do not suit them; even the title of "author" seems ridiculous for a woman to me. However gifted they may be in these fields, they ought not to display their talents to the public.'[32] The Directory is often described as a woman-dominated regime and Mme Tallien cited as a leading example of women's power in this era. However she once wrote to the Convention, 'Woe indeed to those women who, scorning the glorious destiny to which they are called, express, in order to free themselves of their duties, the absurd ambition to take over men's responsibilities.'[33] Mme de Staël, perhaps the most important of the revolutionary women, seems to have had some feminist leanings, but she certainly cannot be brought forward as an activist. The pattern is clear: the most famous women of the period were careful to give the disreputable feminists a wide berth.

Nor did the supporters of women's rights capture the backing of the leading men of the Revolution. Condorcet was a real anomaly. Far more typical was Mirabeau, who gushed over the 'irresistible power of weakness,' warned that women's delicate constitutions limited them to the 'shy labors' of the home, and pondered whether they should ever be let out of the house.[34] Jacques-Réné Hébert, as one would expect, did not gush. Although he took some earthy shots at wife beaters – 'ces bougres de tyrans' – his sympathies were limited.[35] Robespierre's attitude remains enigmatic. Jacques Godechot asserts that he spoke in favor of votes for women in the Constituent Assembly, but other commentators place him in the opposite camp. The volumes of his *Oeuvres complètes* published to date shed no light. Louis-Antoine Saint-Just would go as far as agreeing that laws on adultery should be equal for both sexes but, like Mirabeau, he belonged to the 'faiblesse intéressante' school and urged that girls be educated at home, with due regard for the preservation of their chastity. For the rest, we can find clues in their newspapers. Louis Prudhomme's *Révolutions de Paris* reveled in misogyny. Jean-Paul Marat, Camille Desmoulins, and Gracchus Babeuf ignored the women's movement. Jacques Roux, like Condorcet, was an exception, but as a defender he was hardly an unmitigated blessing. The feminists, then, had been unable to win the backing of any of the important Revolutionary factions. Their following was confined to a few clubs and to isolated individuals, many of them political moderates whom the progress of the Revolution incidentally eliminated.

The characters of the feminist leaders were scarcely the sort to find favor with the respectable. Of those whose lives we know, only Condorcet was above reproach. The pretensions to gentility of de Gouges, Théroigne de Méricourt, and the 'Baronne' d'Aelders struck contemporaries as ludicrous, and this amusement carried over to their activities. The unsavory histories of Théroigne de Méricourt and Claire Lacombe did not help the movement any more than did Lacombe's and Léon's liaisons with the *enragé* Leclerc. While male revolutionaries might be forgiven their sexual peccadilloes, the women could count on no such toleration. Even as they protested the existence of a double standard it was at work against them. All of the feminist leaders were further compromised by their political convictions, whether moderate or extremist. Moreover the feminists were all held guilty for the acts of all other women – the émigrés, the *tricoteuses*, Marie-Antoinette, Charlotte Corday. Protest as they might, the feminists could never convince the public that the principle of collective responsibility should not be applied to the whole sex.

The feminists made tactical and strategic errors. Women's groups allowed themselves to be distracted too easily. The Républicaines Révolutionnaires let themselves become embroiled in street fights over the wearing of the *cocarde* and the *bonnet rouge*. All of the women's clubs suffered from their habit of putting other people's causes before their own. The provincial clubs settled meekly into ladies' aid societies, and even the fiery Républicaines were more interested in the price of bread than in women's wages. However commendable these positions may have been as expressions of largeness of spirit, they were sorely damaging to any attempt to work specific, radical change. The feminists showed other signs of political and managerial inexperience. They acted in isolation: individual leaders had no verifiable contacts with each other; the clubs proceeded independently, and the occasional attempts to set up a national organization came to nothing.

It would seem, too, that that vague entity, the spirit of the times, ran counter to the feminist revolution. One important aspect of this countercurrent was the ideal of the nuclear family. Time and again feminists tripped over the conviction that the changes they advocated were unnatural because women belonged in the home. This was the most frequent explanation given for refusing their requests. The idea of the family as a secure nest, maintained by the wife, to which the husband retired from his toil in the outside world, was a relatively recent development. It certainly did not reflect the reality of lower-class life, for lower-class women could not afford to spend all their time keeping house. It was the wealthy who developed a hagiographic tradition around the family. Once women were firmly confined to the home there was no 'need' for feminism, and the majority of middle-class politicians could only gaze upon it in blank astonishment. To their way of thinking, refusing the feminists' demands ought to have been counted as so many acts of kindness toward women, who were by nature too delicate for the dirty world into which the feminists tried to thrust them.

Revolutionary feminism began in a burst of enthusiasm. Its unpopularity, its own mistakes, and the blissful incomprehension and dogmatism of its opponents combined to obliterate it. While it lasted it was a very real phenomenon with a comprehensive programme for social change, perhaps the most far-reaching such programme of the Revolution. This very radicalism ensured that it would remain a minority movement, almost the preserve of crackpots. Influential contemporaries turned out speech after speech, newspaper after newspaper, report after report without ever acknowledging its existence. Despite its minority nature and its abject failure, revolutionary feminism is not without significance. It illustrates, as clearly as anything can, the changing seasons of the Revolutionary calendar and stands as striking proof of the essential social conservatism of this political upheaval.

Notes

1 Robert Joseph Pothier, *Traité de la puissance du mari* (1769), in his *Oeuvres complètes* (Paris, 1821), 10, p. 655.
2 Boudier de Villemert, *L'Ami des femmes*, pp. 51–4.
3 Quoted in Evelyne Sullerot, *Histoire de la presse féminine des origines à 1848* (Paris, 1966), p. 23, italics in original.
4 Mme de Genlis, *Adèle et Théodore ou Lettres sur l'éducation* (1782), in her *Oeuvres complètes* (Maestricht, 1782), 10, p. 30.
5 *Pétition des femmes du Tiers au roi, Ier janvier 1789*, extracts in Jeanne Bouvier, *Les femmes pendant la Révolution* (Paris, 1931), 249–50. Duhet compares this petition to *Cahier des doléances et réclamations des femmes, par Mme B . . . B . . . .' Les femmes et la Révolution*, pp. 32–9.
6 Bouvier, *Les femmes pendant la Révolution*, pp. 266–74.
7 Condorcet, 'Sur l'admission des femmes au droit de la cité,' published in the Cercle Social's *Journal de la société*, 1790, in Condorcet, *Oeuvres*, 10, pp. 119–30.
8 *Archives Parlementaires* (hereafter *AP*) (Paris, 1867–1972), 1789, vol. 2, pp. 691, 696. The government considered the need for midwives. See the meetings of July 31, Aug. 6, and Sept. 4, 1790, in *Procès-verbaux et rapports du comité de*

mendicité de la Constituante, 1790–91, ed. Camille Bloch and Alexandre Tuetey (Paris, 1911), pp. 104, 108, 168 n.1.

9 Charles-Louis Chassin, *Les élections et les cahiers de Paris en 1789* (Paris, 1888), 3, pp. 168, 384–86.

10 'Motions adressées à l'Assemblée nationale en faveur du sexe,' *Moniteur*, Nov. 29, 1789, reprinted in *Réimpression de l'Ancien Moniteur* (Paris, 1843–63), 2, pp. 262–3 (hereafter cited simply as *Moniteur*, with volume and page numbers of the reprint).

11 *AP*, July 4, 1793, vol. 68, p. 254.

12 *AP*, Aug. 30, 1792, vol. 49, p. 117.

13 *AP*, Apr. 29, 1793, vol. 63, pp. 591–99.

14 Olympe de Gouges, *Droits de la femme*, Sept. 1790, complete text in Bouvier, *Les femmes pendant la Révolution*, pp. 283–9.

15 Quoted in Cornwell B. Rogers, *The Spirit of Revolution in 1789* (Princeton, 1949), p. 182.

16 Report by Latour-Lamontagne, Sept. 21, 1793, in Caron, *Paris pendant la Terreur*, p. 155.

17 Quoted in Léopold Lacour, *Trois femmes de la Révolution* (Paris, 1900), 2. See also Charles Monselet, 'Olympe de Gouges,' in his *Les oubliés et les dédaignés* (Paris, 1859), 139–76; and the account of de Gouge's trial in Émile Campardon, *Le Tribunal révolutionnaire de Paris* (Paris, 1866), 1, pp. 164–5.

18 Quoted in *Bouche de fer*, Jan. 3, 1791, quoted in P. J. B. Buchez and P. C. Roux, *Histoire parlementaire de la Révolution française* (Paris, 1834–38), 8, pp. 424–7. There is no biographical study of Etta Palm. Episodes in her life are described in Aulard, 'Le féminisme pendant la Révolution française,' pp. 364–65; in Villiers, *Histoire des clubs de femmes*; and in Bourdin, *Les Sociétés populaires*, pp. 144–48, pp. 151, 160, 289. See also Marie Cerati, *Le club des citoyennes révolutionnaires* (Paris, 1966), pp. 19–21.

19 See Emma Adler, *Die Berühmten Frauen der französischen Revolution* (Vienna, 1906), 244–78. Her speech on the women's militia is quoted in Cerati, *Le club des citoyennes*, p. 18.

20 Quoted in Jeane Bouvier, *Les Femmes pendant la Révolution* (Paris, 1931), pp. 329–31.

21 *AP*, Sept. 10, 1791, vol. 30, pp. 449, 478–9, 499.

22 Sieyès's preliminary remarks on the constitution, July 10–21, 1789, *Recueil des pièces authentiques approuvées par l'Assemblée nationale de France* (Geneva, 1789), 1, pp. 193–9.

23 *Ibid.*, Mar. 29, 1790, vol. 12, pp. 402–3.

24 Meeting of Sept. 16, 1793, in *La Société des Jacobins: Recueil de documents*, ed. Alphonse Aulard (Paris, 1889–97), v.5, pp. 406–8. The Jacobins had earlier encouraged the Républicaines and granted them 'affiliation and correspondence.' Meetings of May 12 and Aug. 15, 1793, in *La Société des Jacobins*, p. 356. There is little doubt that it was the evolution of the women's politics to the left which drew the Jacobins' fire.

25 *AP*, Oct. 29, 1793, vol. 78, pp. 20–2.

26 *Moniteur*, Oct. 30, 1793, vol. 18, pp. 299–300.

27 *Moniteur*, Nov. 17, 1793, vol. 18, p. 450, italics in original.

28 *Moniteur*, Nov 17, 1793, vol. 18, p. 450.

29 Meeting of May 23, 1795, in *Procès-verbal de la Convention nationale* (Paris, 1792 – an IV), 62, p. 67.

30 'Compliment fait par les citoyennes d'Epinal à MM. les Députés arrivant de la

Confédération générale de Paris, le mercredi 28 juillet 1790,' *La Révolution dans les Vosges*, 17 (1929), p. 47.

31 Quoted in Marc de Villiers, *Histoire des clubs de femmes et des légions d'amazones* (Paris, 1910), p. 59.

32 Quoted in L. J. Larcher and P. J. Martin, *Les femmes peintes par elles-mêmes* (Brussels, 1858), pp. 68–9.

33 *AP*, Apr. 23, 1794, vol. 89, p. 215.

34 *AP*, Sept. 10, 1791, vol. 30, pp. 518–19.

35 Jacques-Réné Hébert, *Le Père Duchesne*, Dec. 6, 1790, no. 31, in *Le Père Duchesne d'Hébert*, ed. Fritz Braesch (Paris, 1938), p. 391.

13

Feminism, women and the French Revolution

BARRIE ROSE

I suppose the classic symbol of the involvement of women in the French Revolution is Madame Defarge, Charles Dickens' woman of the people from *A Tale of Two Cities*, who brought along her knitting to watch the guillotine at work, pausing only to cheer as an aristocratic head tumbled into the basket. Of this image we should note that Madame Defarge is above all here (though not elsewhere in the novel) a passive spectator. All the action, all the interesting activity is carried out by men. It is a man who pulls the lever: women sit and watch.

But of course the French Revolution was not altogether like that in practice. Another image of the women of the Revolutionary period also survives: the tough, militant women of Paris who marched out to Versailles on October 5, 1789 armed with murderous pikes, clubs and cutlasses, to capture the King and Queen and drag them back to Paris, thereby scotching the last-ditch royalist attempt at counter-revolution and firmly entrenching the Revolutionary victory of 1789.

The work of modern historians has emphasised and expanded this second image of the active, participating, revolutionary woman. In 1959 George Rudé, in *The Crowd in the French Revolution*, drew attention to the prominence of women in the many crowd actions between 1789 and 1795, especially in food riots, or more exactly, the intervention of crowds in the market place to force the lowering of food prices either by compelling the government to act, or by direct popular action. Many historians have

Reprinted in full, except for notes, from *The Australian Journal of Politics and History*, special issue, 40 (1994), pp. 173–86.

shown since that this kind of popular activism was not new in 1789, but had a long tradition behind it in France. During the Revolution itself such episodes as the food and grocery riots of February 1793 in Paris formed an essential part of the wider popular movement of the Sans-culottes that brought the Jacobins to power and compelled them to adopt official policies of price control and the repression of food hoarding and profiteering.

In my own study of *The Enragés*, published in 1965, I tried to show how the French Revolution also marked the beginnings of the organized participation of women in politics, particularly through the Society of Revolutionary Republican Women of 1793, and that while especially concerned with bread and butter questions – essentially the price of food – these women militants were centrally involved in the mainstream movement for political democracy and social equality, and had even begun to ask for equal rights for women.

The new emphasis on women's studies and the history of women which began to burgeon in the 1970s inevitably drew many historians to look again, more carefully, at the French Revolution period and to write women back into human history there, as in so many other eras and events. In 1975 appeared Jane Abray's study of 'Feminism in the French Revolution' in the *American Historical Review* [see Reading 12]; meanwhile Olwen Hufton, beginning with her article on 'Women in Revolution' in *Past and Present*, 1971, was turning her attention to the deeper questions of social history and women's role in the family and the workplace, and asking how far the Revolution changed things for women, and in which directions. Along with Professor Hufton's work probably the most important achievement in the field in the 1970s was the collection of documents edited by Darline Levy, Harriet Applewhite and Mary Johnson, *Women in Revolutionary Paris, 1789 to 1795*, which saw the light in 1979. I myself added a bit more to that topic in my book on *The Making of the Sans-culottes*, in 1983. I suppose the first thing we have learned from all this is how much still remains to be done. Despite Michael Kennedy's survey of provincial Jacobin clubs, there is nothing systematic yet on the activity of women in the provinces, outside Paris, for example. Again what happened in the history of women in France between 1795 and the 1830s? We have little idea.

The second thing we have learned is that we cannot always agree on what exactly we are trying to study. Is it feminist history or the history of women? For the two are not necessarily identical, as will become evident in the rest of this paper in which I propose to examine critically some feminist interpretations of the French Revolution in the light of what we know about the history of women in the Revolutionary period.

As a generalization I think it fair to say that feminists have found the history of the French Revolution profoundly dispiriting. Simone de Beauvoir, the founding sister, in a sense, of modern Feminism, set the tone in 1949 when she wrote in *The Second Sex*: 'It might well have been expected that the Revolution would change the lot of women. It did nothing of the sort. That bourgeois revolution was respectful of bourgeois institutions and values and it was accomplished almost exclusively by men.'[1]

Writing on France in 1974 in an American collection on 'new perspectives on the history of women,' under the title *Clio's Consciousness Raised*, Catherine Silver disposes of the French Revolution completely in the following paragraph:

> During the great revolution of 1789 – rhetorically dedicated to abstract equality – the women of France rioted, demonstrated and struggled in the cause. However apart from references to *citoyennes* – the female version of the new, universal social rank *citoyen* – women received no substantial benefit from the redistribution of rights after the destruction of the aristocracy. Such a pattern has long characterized the situation of women in France . . . .[2]

Finish. Nothing else except a footnote. This influential collection ran through several editions.

Jane Abray's article on feminism in the Revolution I mentioned earlier, concludes equally gloomily:

> Revolutionary feminism began in a burst of enthusiasm. Its unpopularity, its own mistakes, and the blissful incomprehension and dogmatism of its opponents combined to obliterate it. While it lasted it was a very real phenomenon with a comprehensive programme of social change, perhaps the most far-reaching such programme of the Revolution. This very radicalism ensured that it would remain a minority movement, almost the preserve of crackpots . . .

For Abray this tragic failure stands only 'as a striking proof of the essential social conservatism of this political upheaval' – that is to say, of the French Revolution.[3]

But even those who see themselves as historians of women before they are feminists surprise us with their negative sentiments at times. Thus Olwen Hufton's central interest is the history of the struggling poor and the working class, and she is forced to the conclusion that from their point of view the French Revolution, with its famines, wars, massacres, repressions and general disruption was an overwhelmingly negative experience.

'When the cards were down and the scores chalked up,' Hufton writes, 'what really was the experience of the working woman from 1789 to 1795? How else could she assess the Revolution except by examining her wrecked household, by reference to children aborted or born dead, by her own sterility . . . and what would her conclusion be except that the price paid for putative liberty had been far too high?'[4]

In fact, with a few exceptions, the French Revolution has received a generally bad press from feminist historians, over the last twenty years, just at a time when it has suffered an overwhelming assault from conservatives and revisionists.

The revisionist agenda, since the days of Alfred Cobban has been to destroy the inspirational signficance of the Revolution as a great movement of human liberation and progress, and reduce it to a useless and senseless bloodbath, which set back human civilization by a generation. For those of us who still struggle to defend the positive message of the French Revolution, the defection of the feminists is the unkindest cut of all, for we have always counted on support from that quarter. To our perhaps simplistic minds the Revolution stood for human freedom; women are human beings, and therefore the Revolution stood for the freedom of women.

But of course the problem is not really as simple as that. If we look at the French Revolution from the perspective of the end of the adventure – the overthrow of Napoleon in 1815, it is clear that the Revolution, taken in its widest interpretation, did not in fact give much to women. Indeed, as we shall see, there is once again a strong conviction, particularly among Marxist feminists, that its effects were wholly negative, that it was part of a general movement that made the condition of women in Europe substantially worse. That general movement is, of course, the 'bourgeois revolution.' There is a consensus that the triumph of the 'bourgeois revolution' meant the triumph of masculine power. Indeed it is a kind of syllogism: the French Revolution was a bourgeois revolution: the bourgeois revolution was a revolution for and by men: therefore the French Revolution was a revolution against women. As long ago as 1977 Margaret George, discussing the defeat of the most determined revolutionary thrust for political status by a woman's organization, in 1793, gave the French Revolution the Marxist thumbs down in *Science and Society*, even in its Jacobin and democratic phase.

'Sans-culotte is a male word' George writes, 'as the Revolution, the Convention, the Constitution and all positions of power were male . . . Jacobin revolutionaries, self-conscious architects of an egalitarian society, proudly engaged in remaking history towards the perfectibility of Man, consigned Women to civil nothingness, to a position more clearly inferior to that of the Catholic, feudal past, because now defined, cloaked and justified by the bourgeois deities of Reason and the laws of Nature.'[5]

The most sophisticated and powerful assault along these lines comes however from Joan Landes, a disciple of the Jürgen Habermas variant of Marxism. In 1988 Landes published her *Women in the Public Sphere in the Age of the French Revolution*, which has already gone through three reprints. Thus it appears to respond to a widespread need by feminists to re-evaluate the Revolution by an almost total rejection. The absolute nature of that re-evaluation can be gauged by a few quotations. 'The

Republic,' writes Landes, 'was constructed against women, not just without them.'[6] 'At the very least, the post-revolutionary identification of masculine speech with truth, objectivity, and reason has worked to devalue women's contribution to public life to a degree rarely matched in earlier periods . . . the structures of modern republican politics can be construed as part of an elaborate defense against women's power and public presence.'[7] Montesquieu's dream of the domestication of women was enacted by the male leadership of the French Revolution, and their post-revolutionary successors. Indeed the new symbolic order of nineteenth-century bourgeois society was predicated on the silence of public women.'[8] Finally Landes fiercely denounces what she calls the Revolution's 'phallic quality' – 'a product of the way political legitimacy and individual rights were predicated on the entitlement of men alone.'[9]

As a disciple of Habermas, Joan Landes argues that cultural history is central to interpretation of the past, and that what it is about is a struggle for access to and domination of a phenomenon described as 'the public sphere.' Before 1789, it seems, this 'public sphere' was an arena of conflict between the feudal classes and the rising bourgeoisie. In this epoch some women had a not inconsiderable access to the public sphere. Noble and wealthy women could exert an influence on public opinion, for example, through the salons or receptions over which they presided, attended by the leading thinkers of the age; salons such as those of Madame Du Deffand, Madame Geoffrin, the patroness of the *Encyclopedia*, the Princesse de Conti and the Duchesse de Choiseul. Madame de Pompadour, Louis XV's intellectually inclined mistress, managed to have Voltaire appointed Royal Historian at Versailles; prominent women frequently corresponded readily and effectively with the philosophes. Noblewomen and nuns even had some 'political space,' in the right to be represented, albeit by men, in the Estates General, the French national parliament.

The Revolution ushered in a period in which all that was lost. The public sphere was henceforth exclusively dominated by men, and women were relegated to a purely domestic role. The culprit was the bourgeois revolution, a masculine thing for which consciously aware women historians can hold no brief. 'Following the Revolution,' I quote Landes again, 'nearly three decades passed before feminists again achieved a public outlet. Beginning in the 1830s women organized collectively to demand redress from patriarchal institutions.'[10] However can we defend the French Revolution against such a devastating attack? Of course it would be easiest to simply follow the prevailing orthodoxy and declare that, whatever it was, the French Revolution was not a bourgeois revolution, and that therefore whatever it did for or to women had nothing to do with the rise of the bourgeoisie or with the new hegemony of the bourgeoisie in the public sphere. Landes' basic argument is thereby exploded even before it can be developed. But there may be some of us with lingering doubts about this 'prevailing orthodoxy.' Besides, even after throwing out the 'bourgeois revolution' as a sufficient explanation, we are still left with so many uncomfortable facts to account for.

For there is a great deal of truth in the arguments of feminists like Margaret George and Joan Landes. After all, the Revolution, taken *en bloc*, and including the Napoleonic consolidation, did leave women subordinated to a crushingly masculine state and society. And that subordination had begun even before Napoleon's rule.

The French Revolutionary Constitution of 1791 made women citizens of a kind, if only 'passive' citizens, unable to vote or stand for public office. The Jacobin Constitution of 1793 gave the vote to all men but to no women. The Constitution of the year III (1795) took the vote away from some of the men, and dropped the earlier notion of passive citizenship, and so women ceased to be citizens at all. Finally the Napoleonic law code of 1804 proclaimed a uniform regime of patriarchy which entrenched again most of the most oppressive features of the chaotic family law of the old regime. Wives must obey their husbands and live where they direct. Husbands may have their wives imprisoned for adultery, but not vice versa. Fathers may imprison their children for misconduct at will.

Control over women's property was placed squarely in masculine hands, since wives were made incapable of making contracts or of alienating or acquiring property or suing in the courts, without the formal consent of their husbands; all deliberately done, too, as one of the framers of the code, Portalis declared in introducing it: 'There has been no attempt to introduce dangerous novelties into the new legislation. All has been preserved from the old laws which can be reconciled with the present order of society; the stability of marriage has been upheld; wise rules for the government of families have been provided; the authority of fathers has been re-established; every way of assuring the submission of children has been brought back.'[11]

But take careful note of the language. This is not the bourgeois revolution speaking but the traditional French patriarchal society of the old regime reasserting itself after a period of public and domestic disorder.

Which brings me to one of the first points the defence will submit. Joan Landes appears to have fallen into the famous error attributed to Edmund Burke; to have pitied the plumage and forgotten the dying bird. It is true that for a few privileged women life before the Revolution was freer and more satisfying.

Yet even over the daughters of the nobility there hung, until the age of 25, the threat of arranged and indissoluble marriages, disinheritance through the rule of primogeniture, and forced relegation to the convent. For most working women, peasant women, and middle-class women the subordination codified by Napoleon was nothing new. A glance at Olwen Hufton's humane history of the *Poor of Eighteenth Century France* is enough to dispose of the notion of a vanished golden age for women destroyed by the bourgeois (read French) revolution.

No one sums up better the ceaseless struggle for survival in an economy of expedients punctuated by periodic dearth, war and unemployment: 'It needed only some everyday occurrence, a sickness of the main earner, his death, the drying up of domestic industry, the birth of a third or fourth child, to plunge the family into difficulties from which recovery was impossible.'[12]

It is in Hufton's own devastating chapter on 'Parent and Child' that we read that under the old regime 'A mother suffering from malnutrition often found it impossible to feed her child,' and that 'In certain parts of Britanny impoverished mothers did not even bother to toilet train their weaker children whose life span was hardly likely to merit the trouble.' The same chapter discusses 'the recourse to large doses of alcohol, sulphurous purgative and the rusty handle of a kitchen ladle' to end unwanted pregnancies, and the fate of the thousands of children of the poor who actually struggled into life: a death rate in the foundling hospitals of 60 per cent *a year.* Elsewhere, Hufton evokes a scene in which 'the women of the Auvergne . . . during the hard winter of 1786 . . . hammered, cold and hungry on the door of the *dépôt de mendicité,* and demanded to be arrested as beggars,' simply to avoid starvation.[13]

But to say that women's lot under the old regime was a harsh one hardly amounts to a satisfying rebuttal of the charges laid against the French Revolution.

Instead, I intend to fall back on 'good intentions' as a main line of defence: that the Revolutionary generation intended to make women's lot better in a great many respects, and, indeed, succeeded in a few.

Let me call my main witness for the defence. In 1980 James F. Traer published his study of *Marriage and the Family in Eighteenth Century France.* Traer begins by painting a grim picture of something he calls the 'traditional' family of 18th Century France before the Revolution. (He has idiosyncratic reasons for not calling it the patriarchal family as most other historians do, but that is what he means.)

Here is how it is defined:

> In the traditional marriage the husband and father exercised both legal and actual power over the person and property of his wife and children. He enjoyed management of their property and of the revenue it produced. The law permitted him to discipline his wife and children either by physical punishment or by confinement in a correctional institution. In short he was the ruler of his own small realm, similar to the monarch in his kingdom.[14]

Note that this 'traditional' family has nothing to do with the bourgeois revolution. In fact Traer does not notice any sign at all of a bourgeois revolution in eighteenth-century France. What he does see, instead, is a progressive cultural movement, the Enlightenment, in full spate, changing conceptions of human happiness and human relationships. Emerging from the matrix of the traditional family is a new phenomenon; 'a new and democratically organized modern family whose members were equal to one another and united by freedom of choice and love.'[15]

In Traer's own words 'In contrast to the "traditional" marriage and family, the "modern" family developed out of the literature and criticism of the French Enlightenment, translated into new laws and social realities during a massive political achievement.'[16] And what massive political achievement is this? The Revolution of 1789. 'The coming of the revolution in 1789' (I quote again) 'gave social critics and legislators the opportunity to implement a vast body of Enlightenment criticism and theory . . . Under the twin banners of liberty and equality they enacted legislation that they believed would create and foster a new pattern of marriage and family organization.'[17]

Well, so much for 'phallic revolutions'; let's hear it for liberty and equality! Especially since Traer brushes aside the Napoleonic code as a less than serious hindrance to the irresistible advance of the new model of marriage. His conclusion: 'The ideals of liberty and equality, together with romantic love and domesticity had created a modern conception of marriage and family that would become the norm for France, and indeed, for much of the Western world.'[18]

One of the more serious criticisms that may be laid at the door of James Traer is that he nowhere provides the evidence for the growth of the ideals of his 'modern' family by reference to specific figures or teachings of the Enlightenment.

On the other hand the concept of the transition from the patriarchal to the modern family is no stranger to historians. Lawrence Stone, for example, has coined the term 'affective individualism' for the guiding spirit of the 'modern' family. With the growth of affective individualism, to quote from Professor McManners' summary, the individual is recognized as unique and independent, entitled to his own ideas and to a degree of physical privacy; the child becomes the centre of family affection and grows up with the right to choose a marriage partner. The new 'closed domesticated nuclear' family is bound by ties of affection between husband and wife, parents and children, and recognizes the rights of its members to their individual pursuit of happiness. Stone is writing about the evolution of English society between 1500 and 1800, but in a chapter on 'Living, loving and dying' in his book *Death and the Enlightenment* McManners specifically applies the same analysis to France; focussing the change in attitudes on the eighteenth-century and discussing the positive influences of La Mettrie, Morelly, Helvétius and Holbach, of Diderot, Rousseau, and of course Condorcet, among others. Even Joan

Landes' arch-villain Montesquieu presented Roxane with sympathy in the *Persian Letters.*[19]

Unlike Joan Landes, James Traer has not enjoyed multiple reprints; clearly there are fewer people who want to know what *he* is saying. It will be obvious that I myself have doubts about the positive influence of the later stages of the French Revolution and of the Napoleonic Regime.

But I do think that what Traer has to say about the classic French Revolution, the revolution of 1789–1794, is worth a closer examination. Let us call an expert witness to the stand, therefore: Jacques Godechot on the Institutions of France under the Revolution and the Empire,[20] and try to find out some of the changes that the Revolution actually made in the life of Frenchwomen. First, take the case of the inheritance of property. In March 1790 the Constituent Assembly began by abolishing primogeniture for formerly noble property, at the same time as it abolished nobility itself. This meant that all the heirs of a property-owner could inherit, including daughters, and not just the eldest son or other male descendent, the previous practice. Two years later, in March 1793, the Convention extended equal inheritance rights to all kinds of property, and moreover this legislation was made retroactive to 1789. So that legally, brothers had to hand back a share of their property to their sisters; and many women exercised their rights, to the confusion of the courts.

Secondly, let us look at the institution of marriage. The Revolutionary Constitution of 1791 began by recognizing marriage as a civil contract between consenting partners. Since one can dissolve as well as make civil contracts, this opened the door to a tremendous upheaval in the social order, divorce. In Catholic France marriage was a sacrament and divorce impossible. The only possible way out of a bad marriage for a woman was a legal separation. But there all the cards were stacked for the husband. He retained control of the family property and of the children, and in some cases could have a troublesome wife shut away in a convent or even a prison. On September 20, 1792 the Legislative Assembly made divorce legal on a number of special grounds such as lunacy, desertion, injuries, condemnation as a criminal. But it also sanctioned divorce by mutual consent, or on the grounds of incompatibility by the application of either one of the parties. It left the younger girls with their mother and the boys with their father. Of course divorce for women is a double-edged weapon, as was evidenced when the Breton Municipality of Pont-Croix congratulated Citizen Allain, who had divorced 'a wife of sixty years of age, and had formed a new relationship with a young female companion in order to increase the number of defenders of liberty.' The municipality solicited a decree from the Convention to encourage the general spread of such patriotic conduct.[21]

On the other hand Roderick Phillips, in a careful examination of divorce statistics in the 1790s at Rouen in Normandy, shows that it was overwhelmingly women who made use of the new laws. Women petitioned for 71 per cent of unilateral divorces, and women were also the driving force in most divorces decreed by mutual consent.[22] As an aside it ought to be remarked that the Revolutionary debate on divorce reflected not despair at the breakdown of marriages, but an enthusiastic hope that allowing men and women to remarry who had been legally separated or mutually alienated would encourage the creation of new, loving marriages and happier families.

This attitude was consistent with the law of September 20, 1792 which lowered the age of parental consent to marriage to 21 from 30 for men and 25 for women. The Legislative Assembly also abolished the age-old right of parents to imprison their children for misconduct or disobedience.

I should like to tender here another piece of evidence from Godechot. On June 28, 1793 the Convention took into account the problem of the unmarried mother and ambitiously planned the provision of public maternity homes to accommodate them in every administrative District of France; on July 4 a network of orphanages to care for 'the natural children of the fatherland' up to the age of twelve was decreed, with provision for apprenticing them afterwards.[23] Unfortunately the Convention decreed a great many things that did not come to pass in a crisis era of national and civil war. Another such decree was the national provision of primary education for girls as well as boys. But again, the least we can say is that they had good intentions.

I submit that Godechot's evidence on only the two counts of inheritance and divorce is sufficient to vindicate James Traer's general argument and to refute Joan Landes. It is true that Napoleon made divorce very much more difficult to obtain for women, and that the restored Bourbon Monarchy abolished it altogether. It is also true that Napoleon partly abandoned the principle of equal inheritance by allowing one favoured heir, albeit under strict rules, to receive a larger share than the others, but the right of daughters to inherit a substantial portion of the parental estate survived both Napoleon and the Restoration.

What we have, in summation, therefore, is a Revolution inspired by the ideals of the Enlightenment which set out to make a better world for women, followed by a reaction, culminating in the Napoleonic code, that sought to force them back into the old patriarchal mode. To condemn the Revolution for the sins of the reaction seems to me to be illogical and unreasonable, and a flagrant case of throwing the baby out with the bathwater; a crime which, I regret to say, was almost as harshly punished after 1789 as under the ancien régime. I have to admit that I would have liked to have rounded out my argument by demonstrating that the French revolutionaries took a more humanitarian view of abortion and infanticide than the old regime.[24]

It now seems appropriate to turn to the much debated question of the 'abolition of feudalism' and its impact on French peasant families.

The Constituent Assembly announced the 'abolition of feudalism' on August 4, 1789, and shortly afterwards abolished church tithes also. Indeed, these reforms have traditionally been ranked among the major achievements of the Revolution in improving the living standards of the peasantry. Like all such achievements they have been recently exposed to critical scrutiny and their import has been downgraded. The most important so-called feudal or seigneurial dues were not officially abolished outright until 1793; in the meantime they had, legally, to be redeemed by the peasantry or continued to be paid. Where land was held on leasehold tenure the landlords were permitted to add the tithes to the rent *en bloc*, while in the long run competition for tenancies made possible higher rents which eroded gains resulting from the extinction of seigneurial dues. The successful imposition of new land taxes mopped up much of what remained.

However, millions of peasants who were not on leasehold but owned their own land obtained potentially massive advantages. How massive may be judged by the consideration of a few statistics.

Labrousse estimated that for France as a whole the combined burden of seigneurial dues and tithes amounted to a tenth of a peasant's gross harvest.[25] But there were many parts of France where much more was extracted from the peasants, as Peter Jones demonstrates in *The Peasantry in the French Revolution*. Thus in the Limousin the seigneurial dues amounted to a third and in Poitou to a quarter of the crop; the tithe, usually about a twelfth, was often an eighth in Gascony and a sixth in the Franche Comté. In 1780 the provincial assembly of Upper Guyenne complained that out of a dozen sheaves of corn 'the seigneur takes three, the tithe-owner one, while taxes absorb two more,' so that the peasant saved only a half of his gross harvest, after a third had been skimmed off by feudal exactions. Assuming an average grain yield of 5 or 6 to one (and it could be less) a further sixth needed to be set aside for seed grain leaving a net third of the gross harvest for domestic needs.

Thus there were parts of France where the landowning peasant regained a third of his gross harvest, and doubled his net, while an increase of net income by a fifth was fairly general. Consider the impact of such statistics on a family where the holding, under the old regime, had been barely large enough to sustain a family of two adults and three children. The inexorable logic is that, accidents of foreign and civil war notwithstanding, 'when the cards were down and the scores were chalked up,' while Olwen Hufton's desperate working woman certainly existed in 1795, by that same date peasant mothers could look back on an increase in the amount of food for domestic consumption and consequently an improvement in their own fertility, and the survival of an additional child or two whose early death would have been almost a foregone conclusion before 1789. And all this does not take into account peasant gains in the redistribution of land following the sell-off of church and some noble land, and the 1793 decree permitting the dividing up of the commons. By this decree incidentally, women were permitted to take part as equal voters in the crucial decision to partition, and were allocated equal shares. Nor does the assessment take into account a fairer distribution of taxes, or occasional 'tax holidays' when the collection mechanism broke down.

Thus far we have been looking, in a sense, only at the surface of history, at the conscious activities of reformers and legislators. But there are a number of more profound ways in which the Revolution benefited women in a lasting way.

For example, comparing the evolution of demographic statistics with the dates of political events produces some surprising and significant results. We have already been looking at divorce. Let us change tack and look at marriages instead. After all the vast majority of women expected and sought marriage as a normal completion of their lives. In 1966 Marcel Reinhard, a French historian who had a special interest in this field of studies, contributed an essay which summed up the demographic impact of the Revolution in two apparently contradictory conclusions.

The first:

> The most striking trend is the marked increase in the marriage rate. Comparing the annual mean with that of the two decades preceding and following 1789 the increase is often from twenty to twenty-five per cent, sometimes fifty and even sixty per cent or more, both in the rural areas and the towns . . . To sum up, the major effect of the Revolution was the increase in the number of marriages.[26]

But only a couple of pages later, in his general conclusion, Reinhard contradicts himself in a rather startling fashion: 'The major demographic effect of the Revolution is certainly the accentuation of the tendency to limit births. This is an extraordinary factor' Reinhard continues, 'as an increase in fecundity is evident in Belgium and England at the same time.'[27]

Let us forget the quibble about which was the *really* major demographic effect. We are still left with two of them.

The French Revolution coincided with a significant turning point in the experience of Frenchwomen: the marriage rate went up and the birth rate went down. Looking a bit further ahead we find these changes still operating strongly during the first years of the nineteenth century, for Louis Bergeron, the historian of the Napoleonic Empire tells us that while the marriage rate continued higher than before 1789, and while the population had grown by several millions, there were about ten per cent fewer births between 1811 and 1815 than between 1781 and 1784.

There is an obvious question that demands an answer here. More women are getting married earlier, and yet women are bearing significantly fewer children.

It is fashionable in some historical circles to jettison political history as the froth on the surface, and to concentrate instead on the deeper currents of social history, or 'real' history. I suggest that the study of the demographic impact of the French is an object lesson of the dangers of following this fashion too exclusively.

What then did the political event, the French Revolution, have to do with those almost equally revolutionary demographic effects?

The question of the rising marriage rate is the easiest to resolve; Reinhard answers it himself. In 1791 the Revolution abolished the guild system under which the trade guilds had compelled apprentices to remain bachelors throughout their training. Consequently many men, especially in the towns, became marriage prospects much earlier than under the old regime. At the same time as we have seen, the revolutionaries lowered the age of parental consent to marriage to 21 instead of 30 for men and 25 for women. The decline of the influence and power of the church was also of some importance; the Catholic Church had forbidden marriages during Advent and Lent.

All of these things played their part. But there was a final and clinching factor: conscription. During the Revolutionary and Napoleonic wars, whenever a major call-up threatened, a host of young men found that their minds underwent a sudden and salutary clarification. Bachelors were conscripted while married men were left at home; a series of marriage booms was the result.

There is less consensus on the Revolutionary connections of the falling birth-rate, partly because the beginnings of this trend were already in evidence in some parts of France well before 1789. Nevertheless there is good reason to believe that the French Revolution did play a significant role.

'Birth control became widespread in France earlier than in England and in other countries, both Catholic and Protestant of Western Europe,' comments another demographer, J. L. Flandrin. 'This has long been considered to have been an effect of the Revolution, with its dechristianising and egalitarian tendencies. The Revolution probably did accelerate the process, by liberating a part of the population of France from the prohibition the church had hurled against contraception and because the Revolutionary laws regarding succession ... obliged couples to limit their offspring in a draconian manner.'[28]

'In a little more than a generation' Louis Bergeron confirms in his history of the Empire, there was 'a massive break with the traditional conception of conjugal morality; a statistically significant introduction of contraception, inseparable, it seems, from a rupture, above all masculine, with the Catholic Church.'[29]

Jacques Dupâquier is even more precise in his general survey of the French population. 'One thing that seems certain' he writes, 'is that the "cultural revolution" of the years 1789 to 1794 created the appropriate conditions for the diffusion of a new family morality. In this short lapse of time millions of French people, pulled along by the dialectic of an irresistible movement, stripped off the traditional cloak.'[30]

We are dealing here with two delicate matters, what went on in the bedroom and what went on in the confessional, so we must tread carefully. First let us be clear that contraception in 1789 did not mean the use of chemical or mechanical devices. Condoms were certainly used by wealthy rakes to prevent disease, and prostitutes used crude tampons to prevent conception. But for the majority of French families, the experts conclude, family limitation was achieved by the practice of *coitus interruptus*, with abortion as a back-stop in case of accidents. Needless to say both these practices were fiercely condemned by the church and policed by the confessional. It is thus not without relevance that the French Revolution was marked by a general turning away from the church and by the collapse of the parochial system, and although Napoleon restored the Catholic Church in 1801, large parts of France remained, and remain to this day, dechristianised.

The next and significant question is: to what extent did women gain control over their own fertility as a consequence of the French Revolution? Olwen Hufton depicts the Revolutionary generation of women returning to the church almost en masse, scrubbing out the sanctuaries defiled by revolutionary vandalism.[31] But did they return as enthusiastically to obedience to all the Church's moral teachings? If so, how are we to explain the fact that while the population of countries as different as England and Russia virtually tripled in the nineteenth century, France's population increased by only about thirty per cent?

Of course, one possible answer is that it was men, not women, who gained control over family fertility. This certainly squares with a certain literary tradition of the France of peasants, small shopkeepers and petit-bourgeois generally: the men commit the sin, and the women go along to the priest to confess it. The men are staunchly anti-clerical, while the women are 'priest-ridden.'

My own guess in the face of a bedroom revolution so massive and continued, is that a substantial mass of French women were just as wicked as French men. Indeed Flandrin is convinced that, at least in the eighteenth century, it was the women who took the initiative and who persuaded the men to adopt conception control practices. The fact remains that one of the lasting legacies of the French Revolution to women was fewer pregnancies and smaller families. Many feminists, I imagine, would regard that as a major if unexpected improvement in women's conditions of existence. Ironically, it was one of the very last things that the men of the Revolutionary generation publicly advocated, planned or anticipated.

Notes

1 S. de Beauvoir, *Le Deuxième Sexe* (Paris, 1949), 2 vols. Vol. 1, p. 182.
2 C. B. Silver, 'Salon, Foyer, Bureau: Women and the Professions in France,' in M. Hartmann and C. W. Banner (eds), *Clio's Consciousness Raised* (New York, 1974), pp. 72–85.
3 *See* Reading 12, p. 251.
4 O. Hufton, 'Women in Revolution, 1789–1796', *Past and Present*, 53(1971), p. 108.
5 M. George, 'The "World Historical Defeat" of the Républicaines Révolutionnaires,' *Science and Society*, Vol. 40, No.4, Winter 1976–7, pp. 410–37, p. 411.
6 J. B. Landes, *Women and the Public Sphere in the Age of the French Revolution* (Ithaca, 1988), p. 12.
7 Landes, *Women and the Public Sphere in the Age of the French Revolution*, pp. 203–4.
8 Landes, *Women and the Public Sphere in the Age of the French Revolution*, p. 38.
9 Landes, *Women and the Public Sphere in the Age of the French Revolution*, p. 158.
10 Landes, *Women and the Public Sphere in the Age of the French Revolution*, p. 169. By an ironic contrast Simone de Beauvoir's original argument in 1949 was that 'It is important to underline that throughout all the Ancien Régime it was the women of the working classes (des classes travailleuses) who among their sex knew the most freedom': *Le Deuxième Sexe*, Vol. 1, pp. 182–3.
11 For a summary of the civil code, see H. A. L. Fisher, 'The Codes,' in *Cambridge Modern History* Vol. IX, pp. 148–79.
12 O. Hufton, 'Women and the Family Economy in Eighteenth Century France', *French Historical Studies*, Spring 1975, p. 22.
13 O. Hufton, *The Poor of Eighteenth Century France, 1755–1789* (Oxford, 1974), pp. 331–342.
14 T. F. Traer, *Marriage and the Family in Eighteenth-Century France* (Ithaca, 1980, p. 15.
15 Traer, *Marriage and the Family in Eighteenth-Century France*, p. 165.
16 Traer, *Marriage and the Family in Eighteenth-Century France*, p. 16.
17 Traer, *Marriage and the Family in Eighteenth-Century France*, p. 19.
18 Traer, *Marriage and the Family in Eighteenth-Century France*, p. 197.
19 J. McManners, *Death and the Enlightenment* (Oxford, 1981), pp. 444–65; see also R. Mauzi, *L'Idée du bonheur dans la littérature et la pensée françaises au XVIIIᵉ siècle* (Paris, 1960) for a general account of the humanising influence of the Enlightenment.
20 J. Godechot, *Les Institutions de la France sous la Révolution et l'Empire* (Paris, 1951).
21 T. Rodis, 'Marriage, Divorce, and the Status of Women during the Terror,' in M. Slavin and A. Smith (eds), *Bourgeois, Sans-culottes and Other Frenchmen, Essays on the French Revolution in Honor of John Hall Stewart* (Ontario, 1981), pp. 41–57; pp. 55–6.

22 R. Phillips, 'Women and family breakdown in eighteenth-century France: Rouen 1780–1800', *Social History*, No. 2, May 1976, pp. 197–218; p. 205; cf. p. 217: 'women petitioned for most divorces, even under the Napoleonic legislation.'

23 Godechot, *Institutions de la France*, pp. 379–80.

24 I am grateful to Dr. Alison Patrick for assuring me that the men of the Constituent Assembly did relent to the extent of replacing the death penalty for criminal abortion by twenty years in chains.

25 C. -E. Labrousse, 'The Evolution of Peasant Society in France from the Eighteenth Century to the Present,' in E. M. Acomb and M. L. Brown jr. (eds), *French Society and Culture since the Old Regime* (New York, 1966), pp. 43–64; p. 57.

26 M. Reinhard, 'Demography, the Economy and the French Revolution' in Acomb and Brown (eds), *French Society and Culture*, p. 20–42; p. 25.

27 Reinhard, '*Demography, the Economy and the French Revolution*', p. 28.

28 J. L. Flandrin, *Families in former times: Kinship, household and sexuality* (translated R. Southern, Cambridge, 1979), p. 238.

29 Bergeron, p. 121, citing E. Le Roy Ladurie, 'Démographie et funestes secrets: le Languedoc (fin XVIIIᵉ – debut XIXᵉ siècle), *Annales historiques de la Révolution française*, 1965, No. 4, pp. 385–400.

30 J. Dupâquier, *La population française au XVIIᵉ et XVIIIᵉ siècles* (Paris, 1979), p. 124.

31 O. Hufton, 'Women in Revolution, 1789–1796,' *Past and Present*, No. 53, 1971, pp. 107–8.

14

The many bodies of Marie-Antoinette: political pornography and the problem of the feminine in the French Revolution

LYNN HUNT

It has long been known that Marie Antoinette was the subject of a substantial erotic and pornographic literature in the last decades of the Old Regime and during the Revolution itself. Royal figures at many times and in many places have been the subject of such writing, but not all royal figures at all times. When royal bodies become the focus of such interest, we can be sure that something is at issue in the larger body politic. As Robert Darnton has shown, for example, the sexual sensationalism of Old Regime *libelles* was a choice means of attacking the entire 'establishment' – the court, the church, the aristocracy, the academies, the salons, and the

Reprinted in full, except for notes and figure, from L. Hunt, ed. *Eroticism and the Body Politic* (Baltimore and London, Johns Hopkins University Press, 1991), pp. 108–30.

monarchy itself. Marie Antoinette occupies a curious place in this literature; she was not only lampooned and demeaned in an increasingly
ferocious pornographic outpouring, but she was also tried and executed.

A few other women, such as Louis XV's notorious mistress Madame Du
Barry, suffered a similar fate during the Revolution, but no other trial
attracted the same attention or aired the same range of issues as that of the
ill-fated queen. The king's trial, in contrast, remained entirely restricted to
a consideration of his political crimes. As a consequence, the trial of the
queen, especially in its strange refractions of the pornographic literature,
offers a unique and fascinating perspective on the unselfconscious pre-
sumptions of the revolutionary political imagination. It makes manifest,
more perhaps than any other single event of the Revolution, the underlying
interconnections between pornography and politics.

When Marie Antoinette was finally brought to trial in October 1793,
the notorious public prosecutor, Antoine-Quentin Fouquier-Tinville, delivered an accusation against her that began with extraordinary language,
even for those inflamed times:

> In the manner of the Messalinas-Brunhildes, Fredegond and Médecis,
> whom one called in previous times queens of France, and whose
> names forever odious will not be effaced from the annals of his-
> tory, Marie Antoinette, widow of Louis Capet, has been since her
> time in France, the scourge and the bloodsucker of the French.

The bill of indictment then went on to detail the charges: before the
Revolution she had squandered the public monies of France on her
'disorderly pleasures' and on secret contributions to the Austrian emperor
(her brother); after the Revolution, she was the animating spirit of
counterrevolutionary conspiracies at the court. Since the former queen
was a woman, it was presumed that she could only achieve her perfidious
aims through the agency of men such as the king's brothers and Lafayette.
Most threatening, of course, was her influence on the king; she was
charged not only with the crime of having had perverse ministers named
to office but more significantly and generally with having taught the king
how to dissimulate – that is, how to promise one thing in public and plan
another in the shadows of the court. Finally, and to my mind most
strangely, the bill of indictment specifically claimed that

> the widow Capet, immoral in every way, new Agrippina, is so
> perverse and so familiar with all crimes that, forgetting her quality
> of mother and the demarcation prescribed by the laws of nature, she
> has not stopped short of indulging herself with Louis-Charles Capet,
> her son, and on the confession of this last, in indecencies whose idea
> and name make us shudder with horror.[1]

Incest was the final crime, whose very suggestion was cause for horror.

The trial of a queen, especially in a country whose fundamental laws specifically excluded women from ruling, must necessarily be unusual. There was not much in the way of precedent for it – the English, after all, had only tried their king, not his wife – and the relatively long gap between the trial of Louis (in December and January) and that of his queen ten months later seemed even to attenuate the necessary linkage between the two trials. Unlike her husband, Marie Antoinette was not tried by the Convention itself; she was brought before the Revolutionary Criminal Tribunal like all other suspects in Paris, and there her fate was decided by a male jury and nine male judges.

Because queens could never rule in France, except indirectly as regents for underage sons, they were not imagined as having the two bodies associated with kings. According to the 'mystic fiction of the "King's Two Bodies"' as analysed by Ernst Kantorowicz, kings in England and France had both a visible, corporeal, mortal body and an invisible, ideal 'body politic,' which never died. As the French churchman Bossuet explained in a sermon he gave with Louis XIV present in 1662: 'You are of the gods, even if you die, your authority never dies . . . The man dies, it is true, but the king, we say, never dies.'[2] It is questionable whether this doctrine still held for French kings by 1793, but it is certain that it never held for French queens. We might then ask why the destruction of the queen's mortal body could have had such interest for the French. What did her decidedly nonmystical body represent? In this essay, I argue that it represented many things; Marie Antoinette had, in a manner of speaking, many bodies. These many bodies, hydralike, to use one of the favorite revolutionary metaphors for counterrevolution, were each in turn attacked and destroyed because they represented the threats, conscious and unconscious, that could be posed to the Republic. These were not threats of just the ordinary sort, for the queen represented, not only the ultimate in counterrevolutionary conspiracy, but also the menace of the feminine and the effeminizing to republican notions of manhood and virility.

Most striking is the way in which the obsessive focus on the queen's sexualized body was carried over from the pamphlets and caricatures to the trial itself. In the trial there were frequent references to the 'orgies' held at Versailles, which were dated as beginning precisely in 1779 and continuing into 1789. In his closing statement Fouquier-Tinville collapsed sexual and political references in telling fashion when he denounced 'the perverse conduct of the former court,' Marie Antoinette's 'criminal and culpable liaisons' with unfriendly foreign powers, and her 'intimacies with a villainous faction.'[3] Herman, president of the court, then took up the baton in his summary of the charges against her: he too referred to 'her intimate liaisons with infamous ministers, perfidious generals, disloyal representatives of the people.' He denounced again the 'orgy' at the chateau of Versailles on October 1, 1789, when the queen had presumably encouraged the royal officers present to trample on the revolutionary tricolour cockade. In short, Marie Antoinette had used her sexual body to corrupt the body politic either through 'liaisons' or 'intimacies' with criminal politicians or through her ability to act sexually upon the king, his ministers, or his soldiers.

In Herman's long denunciation the queen's body was also held up for scrutiny for signs of interior intentions and motives. On her return from the flight to Varennes, people could observe on her face and her movements 'the most marked desire for vengeance.' Even when she was incarcerated in the Temple her jailers could 'always detect in Antoinette a tone of revolt against the sovereignty of the people.'[4] Capture, imprisonment, and the prospect of execution, it was hoped, were finally tearing the veil from the queen's threatening ability to hide her true feelings from the public. Note here, too, the way that Herman clearly juxtaposes the queen and the people as a public force; revelation of the queen's true motives and feelings came not from secrets uncovered in hidden correspondence but from the ability of the people or their representatives to 'read' her body.

The attention to the queen's body continued right up to the moment of her execution. At the moment of the announcement of her condemnation to death, she was reported to have kept 'a calm and assured countenance,' just as she had during the interrogation. On the road to the scaffold, she appeared indifferent to the large gathering of armed forces. 'One perceived neither despondency nor pride on her face.'[5] More radical newspapers read a different message in her demeanor, but they showed the same attention to her every move. The *Révolutions de Paris* claimed that at the feet of the statue of Liberty (where the guillotine was erected), she demonstrated her usual 'character of dissimulation and pride up to the last moment'. On the way there she had expressed 'surprise and indignation' when she realized that she would be taken to the guillotine in a simple cart rather than in a carriage.[6]

The queen's body, then, was of interest, not because of its connection to the sacred and divine, but because it represented the opposite principle – namely, the possible profanation of everything that the nation held sacred. But apparent too in all the concern with the queen's body was the fact that the queen could embody so much. The queen did not have a mystic body in the sense of the king's two bodies, but her body was mystical in the sense of mysteriously symbolic. It could mean so much; it could signify a wide range of threats. Dissimulation was an especially important motif in this regard. The ability to conceal one's true emotions, to act one way in public and another in private, was repeatedly denounced as the chief characteristic of court life and aristocratic manners in general. These relied above all on appearances – that is, on the disciplined and self-conscious use of the body as a mask. The republicans, consequently, valued transparency –

the unmediated expression of the heart – above all other personal qualities. Transparency was the perfect fit between public and private; transparency was a body that told no lies and kept no secrets. It was the definition of virtue, and as such it was imagined to be critical to the future of the Republic. Dissimulation, in contrast, threatened to undermine the Republic: it was the chief ingredient in every conspiracy; it lay at the heart of the counterrevolution. Thus, for example, to charge Marie Antoinette with teaching the king how to dissimulate was no minor accusation.

Dissimulation was also described in the eighteenth century as a characteristically feminine quality, not just an aristocratic one. According to both Montesquieu and Rousseau, it was women who taught men how to dissimulate, how to hide their true feelings in order to get what they wanted in the public arena. The salon was the most important site of this teaching, and it was also the one place where society women could enter the public sphere. In a sense, then, women in public (like prostitutes) were synonymous with dissimulation, with the gap between public and private. Virtue could only be restored if women returned to the private sphere. Rousseau had expressed this collection of attitudes best in his *Letter to M. d'Alembert on the Theatre* (1758): 'Meanly devoted to the wills of the sex which we ought to protect and not serve, we have learned to despise it in obeying it, to insult it by our derisive attentions; and every woman at Paris gathers in her apartment a harem of men more womanish than she, who know how to render all sorts of homage to beauty except that of the heart, which is her due.' And, as Rousseau warned ominously about women in the public sphere, 'no longer wishing to tolerate separation, unable to make themselves into men, the women make us into women.'[7] With her strategic position on the cusp between public and private, Marie Antoinette was emblematic of the much larger problem of the relations between women and the public sphere in the eighteenth century. The sexuality of women, when operating in the public sphere through dissimulation, threatened to effeminize men – that is, literally to transform men's bodies.

Central to the queen's profane and profaning body was the image of her as the bad mother. This might take many, even surprising forms, as in Fouquier-Tinville's charge that she was the calumniator of Paris – described in his closing statement as 'this city, mother and conservator of liberty.' The queen was the antonym of the nation, depicted by one witness in the trial as the 'generous nation that nurtured her as well as her husband and her family.'[8] The nation, Paris, and the Revolution were all good mothers; Marie Antoinette was the bad mother. It should be noted, however, that the nation, Paris, and the Revolution were motherly in a very abstract, even nonfeminine fashion (in comparison to Marie Antoinette).

The abstractness and nonsexual nature of these political figures of the mother reinforces what Carole Pateman has tellingly described as the characteristic modern Western social contract:

> The story of the original contract is perhaps the greatest tale of men's creation of new political life. But this time women are already defeated and declared procreatively and politically irrelevant. Now the father comes under attack. The original contract shows how his monopoly of politically creative power is seized and shared equally among men. In civil society all men, not just fathers, can generate political life and political right. Political creativity belongs not to paternity but masculinity.[9]

Thus, *La Nation* had no real feminine qualities; she was not a threatening effeminizing force and hence not incompatible with republicanism. *La Nation* was, in effect, a masculine mother, or a father capable of giving birth. Marie Antoinette's body stood in the way, almost literally, of this version of the social contract, since under the Old Regime she had given birth to potential new sovereigns herself.

Pateman is unusual among commentators on contract theory because she takes Freud seriously. As she notes, 'Freud's stories make explicit that power over women and not only freedom is at issue before the original agreement is made, and he also makes clear that two realms [the civil and the private, the political and the sexual] are created through the original pact.'[10] She is less successful, however, at explaining the preoccupation with incest in a case such as Marie Antoinette's.

The charge of incest in the trial was brought by the radical journalist Jacques-René Hébert, editor of the scabrous *Père Duchesne*, the most determinedly 'popular' newspaper of the time. Hébert appeared at the trial in his capacity as assistant city attorney for Paris, but his paper had been notorious for its continuing attacks on the queen. Hébert testified that he had been called to the Temple prison by Simon, the shoemaker who was assigned to look after Louis's son. Simon had surprised the eight-year-old masturbating ('indecent pollutions'), and when he questioned the boy about where he had learned such practices, Louis-Charles replied that his mother and his aunt (the king's sister) had taught him. The king's son was asked to repeat his accusations in the presence of the mayor and city attorney, which he did, claiming that the two women often made him sleep between them. Hébert concluded that

> There is reason to believe that this criminal enjoyment [*jouissance* in French, which has several meanings including pleasure, possession, and orgasm] was not at all dictated by pleasure, but rather by the political hope of enervating the physical health of this child, whom they continued to believe would occupy a throne, and on whom they

wished, by this maneuvre, to assure themselves of the right of ruling afterwards over his morals.[11]

The body of the child showed the effects of this incestuousness; one of his testicles had been injured and had to be bandaged. Since being separated from his mother, Hébert reported, the child's health had become much more robust and vigorous. What better emblem could there be of effeminization than the actual deterioration of the boy's genitals?

As sensational as the charge was, the court did not pursue it much further. When directly confronted with the accusation, the former queen refused to lower herself by responding 'to such a charge made against a mother.'[12] But there it was in the newspapers, and even the Jacobin Club briefly noted the 'shameful scenes between the mother, the aunt, and the son,' and denounced 'the virus that now runs through [the boy's] veins and which perhaps carries the germ of all sorts of accidents.'[13] Since it seems surprising that republican men should be so worried about the degeneration of the royal family, it is not farfetched to conclude that the incest charge had a wider, if largely unconscious, resonance. On the most explicit level, incest was simply another sign of the criminal nature of royalty. As Hébert complained rhetorically to the royalists: 'You immolate your brothers, and for what? For an old whore, who has neither faith nor respect for the law, who has made more than a million men die; you are the champions of murder, brigandage, adultery, and incest.'[14] Although incest can hardly be termed a major theme in revolutionary discourse, it did appear frequently in the political pornography of both the last decades of the Old Regime and the revolutionary decade itself. Perhaps the most striking example is the pornography of the marquis de Sade, which makes much of incest between fathers and daughters and brothers and sisters.

The official incest charge against the queen has to be set in the context provided by the longer history of pornographic and semi-pornographic pamphlets about the queen's private life. Although the charge itself was based on presumed activities that took place only after the incarceration of the royal family in the Temple prison, it was made more plausible by the scores of pamphlets that had appeared since the earliest days of the Revolution and that had, in fact, had their origins in the political pornography of the Old Regime itself. When the *Révolutions de Paris* exclaimed, 'Who could forget the scandalous morals of her private life,' or repeated the charges about 'her secret orgies with d'Artois [one of the king's brothers], Fersen, Coigny, etc.,' the newspaper was simply recalling to readers' minds what they had long imbibed in underground publications about the queen's promiscuity.

Attacks on the queen's morality had begun as early as 1774 (just four years after her arrival in France) with a satirical lampoon about her early morning promenades. Louis XV paid considerable sums in the same year to buy up existing copies in London and Amsterdam of a pamphlet that detailed the sexual impotence of his grandson, the future Louis XVI. Before long, the songs and 'little papers' had become frankly obscene, and the first of many long, detailed pamphlets had been published clandestinely. The foremost expert on the subject found 126 pamphlets he could classify in the genre of Marie Antoinette, libertine.[15] Even before the notorious Diamond Necklace Affair of 1785, and continuing long after it, the queen was the focus of an always-proliferating literature of derision preoccupied with her sexual body.

Although fewer than 10 per cent of the anti–Marie Antoinette pamphlets were published before 1789, they often provided the models for later publications. It is difficult to find out much about the publication (the precise dates or location) or authorship of the prerevolutionary pamphlets, since they were necessarily produced clandestinely. As Robert Darnton has vividly demonstrated, those authors who can be traced were from the French version of Grub Street. Men such as Théveneau de Morande and the count of Paradès worked sometimes for the French crown (as spies), sometimes for rival members of the court, sometimes for foreign printers, and always for themselves. The connection to members of the court is most significant, since it shows the intensity of the interlacing of social networks of communication under the Old Regime. The author of one of the best-known pamphlets, *Portefeuille d'un talon rouge*, made the connection explicit, tracing the circuit from courtiers to their valets, who passed the verses on in the market, where they were picked up by artisans and brought back to the courtiers, who then hypocritically professed surprise. The 'popular' images of the queen, then, had their origin in the court, not in the streets.

Politically pornographic pamphlets were often traced to London, Amsterdam, or Germany, where the most notorious of the French Grub Street types made their livings, and the French crown evidently spent large sums having such pamphlets bought up by its agents abroad and destroyed before they could reach France. Indeed, this new industry seems to have become a very lucrative one for those hack writers willing to live abroad, since large sums were paid to secret agents and printers, who were most likely in collusion with the writers themselves. In 1782 the *Mémoires secrets* described the government's reaction to the recently published *Essais historiques*:

> The dreadful *libelle* against the queen, of which I've spoken [in a previous entry], and others of the same genre, have determined the government to make an effort on this subject and to sacrifice money, which is very distasteful; with this help they have gotten to the source and asked for the assistance of foreign governments. They undertook searches in all of the suspect printing shops of Holland and Ger-

many; they took away everything that deserved to be, and they have even had the printer-booksellers arrested who have taken the chance of coming to France to introduce their merchandise; they have had them condemned to large fines.[16]

Needless to say, copies still made their way into France; in 1783, 534 copies of *Essais historiques sur la vie de Marie-Antoinette* were officially destroyed at the Bastille prison along with many other offensive productions.

Many of the major accusations against Marie Antoinette were already present in the pre-revolutionary pamphlets. The *Porte feuille d'un talon rouge* (also condemned in 1783) begins in classic eighteenth-century fashion with a preface from the presumed publisher announcing that someone had found a portfolio while crossing the Palais-Royal (the notorious den of prostitution and gambling that was also the residence of the king's cousin, the duke of Orleans, who was assumed to have paid for many of the pamphlets). In it was found a manuscript addressed to Monsieur de la H——— of the Académie française. It began, 'You are then out of your mind, my dear la H———! You want, they tell me, to write the history of tribades at Versailles.' In the text appeared the soon-to-be-standard allegation that Marie Antoinette was amorously involved with the duchesse de Polignac ('her Jules') and Madame Balbi. The comte d'Artois was supposedly the only man who interested her. These charges, as harshly delivered as they were, formed only part of the pamphlet's more general tirade against the court and ministers in general. Speaking of the courtiers, the author exclaimed, 'You are an abominable race. You get everything at once from your character as monkeys and as vipers.'[17]

The short and witty *Amours de Charlot et de Toinette* took up much the same themes, though in verse, but this time focused exclusively on the queen, the comte d'Artois, and the princesse de Lamballe (who would become the most famous victim of the September Massacres in 1792). Marie Antoinette was depicted as turning to lesbianism because of the impotence of the king. Then she discovers the delights of the king's brother.

The long 1789 edition (146 pages in the augmented French edition) of the *Essai historique sur la vie de Marie-Antoinette* (there had been many variations on the title since its first publication in 1781) already demonstrated the rising tone of personal hostility toward the queen that would characterize revolutionary pornographic pamphlets. In the most detailed of all the anti-Marie Antoinette exposés, it purported to give the queen's own view through the first person: 'My death is the object of the desires of an entire people that I oppressed with the greatest barbarism.' Marie Antoinette here describes herself as 'barbarous queen, adulterous spouse, woman without morals, polluted with crimes and debaucheries,' and she details all the charges that had accumulated against her in previous pamphlets. Now her lesbianism is traced back to the Austrian court, and all of the stories of amorous intrigues with princes and great nobles are given substance. Added to the charges is the new one that she herself had poisoned the young heir to the throne (who died in early 1789). Characteristic, too, of many of the later pamphlets will be the curious alternation between frankly pornographic staging – descriptions in the first person of her liaisons, complete with wildly beating hearts and barely stifled sighs of passion – and political moralizing and denunciation put into the mouth of the queen herself. The contrast with the king and his 'pure, sincere love, which I so often and so cruelly abused' was striking.[18] The queen may have been representative of the degenerate tendencies of the aristocracy, but she was not yet emblematic of royalty altogether.

With the coming of the Revolution in 1789, the floodgates opened, and the number of pamphlets attacking the queen rapidly rose in number. These took various forms, ranging from songs and fables to presumed biographies (such as the *Essai historique*), confessions, and plays. Sometimes, the writings were pornographic with little explicit political content; the 16-page pamphlet in verse called *Le Godmiché royal* (The royal dildo), for example, told the story of Junon (the queen) and Hébée (presumably either the duchesse de Polignac or the princesse de Lamballe). Junon complained of her inability to obtain satisfaction at home, while pulling a dildo out of her bag ('Happy invention that we owe to the monastery'). Her companion promises her penises of almost unimaginably delicious size.[19] In the much more elaborately pornographic *Fureurs utérines de Marie-Antoinette, femme de Louis XVI* of two years later, coloured engravings showed the king impotent and d'Artois and Polignac replacing him.

The Marie Antoinette pamphlets reflect a general tendency in the production of political pornography: the number of titles in this genre rose steadily from 1774 to 1788 and then took off after 1789. The queen was not the only target of hostility; a long series of 'private lives' attacked the conduct of courtiers before 1789 and revolutionary politicians from Lafayette to Robespierre afterwards. Aristocrats were shown as impotent, riddled with venereal disease, and given over to debauchery. Homosexuality functioned in a manner similar to impotence in this literature; it showed the decadence of the Old Regime in the person of its priests and aristocrats. Sexual degeneration went hand in hand with political corruption. This proliferation of pornographic pamphlets after 1789 shows that political pornography cannot be viewed simply as a supplement to a political culture that lacked 'real' political participation. Once participation increased dramatically, particularly with the explosion of uncensored newspapers and pamphlets, politics did not simply take the high road.

Marie Antoinette was without question the favorite target of such attacks. There were not only more pamphlets about her than about any other single figure, but they were also the most sustained in their viciousness. Henri d'Almeras claimed that the *Essais historiques* alone sold between twenty and thirty thousand copies. The year 1789 does appear to mark a turning point not only in the number of pamphlets produced but also in their tone. The pre-1789 pamphlets tell dirty stories in secret; after 1789 the rhetoric of the pamphlets begins self-consciously to solicit a wider audience. The public no longer 'hears' courtier rumours through the print medium; it now 'sees' degeneracy in action. The first-person rendition of the 1789 French edition of *Essai historique* is a good example of this technique.

Obscene engravings with first-person captions worked to the same effect. The engravings that accompanied the long *Vie de Marie-Antoinette d'Autriche, femme de Louis XVI, roi des français; Depuis la perte de son pucelage jusqu'au premier mai 1791*, which was followed by volumes 2 and 3, entitled *Vie privée, libertine, et scandaleuse de Marie-Antoinette d'Autriche, ci-devant reine des français*, are an interesting case in point. They showed Marie Antoinette in amorous embrace with just about everyone imaginable: her first supposed lover, a German officer; the aged Louis XV; Louis XVI impotent; the comte d'Artois; various women; various ménages à trois with two women and a man; the cardinal de Rohan of the Diamond Necklace Affair; Lafayette; Barnave, and so on. The captions are sometimes in the first person (with the princesse de Guéménée: 'Dieux! quels transports ah! mon ame s'envole, pour l'exprimer je n'ai plus de parole'), sometimes in the third (with the comte d'Artois: 'gémis Louis, ta vigueur inactive, outrage ici ta femme trop lascive'). The effect is the same: a theatricalization of the action so that the reader is made into voyeur and moral judge at the same time. The political effect of the pornography is apparent even in this most obscene of works. In volumes 2 and 3, the pornographic engravings are interspersed with political engravings of aristocratic conspiracy, the assault on the Tuileries palace, and even a curious print showing Louis XVI putting on a red cap of liberty and drinking to the health of the nation in front of the queen and his remaining son and heir.

That the pamphlets succeeded in attracting a public can be seen in the repetition of formulaic expressions in nonpornographic political pamphlets, 'popular' newspapers, petitions from 'popular societies,' and the trial record itself. The *Essai historique* of 1789 already included the soon-to-be-standard comparisons of Marie Antoinette to Catherine de Médecis, Agrippina, and Messalina. These comparisons were expanded at great length in a curious political tract called *Les Crimes des reines de France*, which was written by a woman, Louise de Keralio (though it was published under the name of the publisher, Louis Prudhomme). The 'corrected and augmented' edition dated 'an II' simply added material on the trial and execution to an already-long version of 1791. The tract is not pornographic; it simply refers to the 'turpitudes' committed by the queen as background for its more general political charges. Keralio reviews the history of the queens of France, emphasizing in particular the theme of dissimulation: 'The dangerous art of seducing and betraying, perfidious and intoxicating caresses, feigned tears, affected despair, insinuating prayers' (p. 2). These were the weapons of the queens of France (which had been identified as the arms of all women by Rousseau). When the author comes to the wife of Louis Capet, she lists many of the queen's presumed lovers, male and female, but insists upon passing rapidly over the 'private crimes' of the queen in favor of consideration of her public ones. Marie Antoinette 'was the soul of all the plots, the center of all the intrigues, the foyer of all these horrors' (p. 440). As a 'political tarantula,' the queen resembled that 'impure insect, which, in the darkness, weaves on the right and left fine threads where gnats without experience are caught and of whom she makes her prey' (pp. 445–46). On the next page, the queen is compared to a tigress who, once having tasted blood, can no longer be satisfied. All this to prove what the caption to the frontispiece asserts: 'A people is without honor and merits its chains / When it lowers itself beneath the scepter of queens.'[20]

The shorter, more occasional political pamphlets picked up the themes of the pornographic literature and used them for straightforward political purposes. A series of pamphlets appeared in 1792, for example, offering lists of political enemies who deserved immediate punishment. They had as their appendices lists of all the people with whom the queen had had 'relationships of debauchery.' In these pamphlets, the queen was routinely referred to as 'mauvaise fille, mauvaise épouse, mauvaise mère, mauvaise reine, monstre en tout' (bad daughter, bad wife, bad mother, bad queen, monster in everything).[21]

The movement from sexual misdemeanours to bestial metaphors was characteristic of much 'popular' commentary on the queen, especially in her last months. In the *Père Duchesne* Hébert had incorporated the Fredegond and Médecis comparisons by 1791, but still in a relatively innocent context. One of his favorite devices was to portray himself as meeting in person with the queen and trying to talk sense to her. By 1792 the queen had become 'Madame Veto,' and once the monarchy had been toppled, Hébert made frequent reference to the 'ménagerie royale.' In prison the former queen was depicted as a she-monkey ('la guenon d'Autriche'), the king as a pig. In one particularly fanciful scene, *Père Duchesne* presents himself in the queen's cell as the duchesse de Polignac ('cette tribade') thanks to the effect of a magic ring, whereupon the former queen throws herself into her friend's arms and reveals her fervent hopes for the success of the counterrevolution.[22] After her husband had been executed, the tone of hostility escalated, and Marie Antoinette became the she-wolf and the tigress of Austria. At the time of her trial, Hébert suggested that she be chopped up like meat for paté as recompense for all the bloodshed that she had caused.

Local militants picked up the same rhetoric. In a letter to the Convention congratulating it on the execution of the queen, the popular society of Rozoy (Seine-et-Marne department) referred to 'this tigress thirsty for the blood of the French . . . this other Messalina whose corrupt heart held the fertile germ of all crimes; may her loathsome memory perish forever.' The popular society of Garlin (Basses-Pyrénées department) denounced the 'ferocious panther who devoured the French, the female monster whose pores sweated the purest blood of the sans-culottes.'[23] Throughout these passages, it is possible to see the horrific transformations of the queen's body; the body that had once been denounced for its debauchery and disorderliness becomes in turn the dangerous beast, the cunning spider, the virtual vampire who sucks the blood of the French.

Explicit in some of the more extreme statements and implicit in many others was a pervasive anxiety about genealogy. For example, the post-1789 pamphlets demonstrated an obsession with determining the true fathers of the king's children (they were often attributed to his brother, the comte d'Artois). In a fascinating twist on this genealogical anxiety, *Père Duchesne* denounced a supposed plot by the queen to raise a young boy who resembled the heir to the throne to take the heir's place. The culminating charge, of course, was incest; in the trial, this was limited to the queen's son, but in the pamphlet literature, the charges of incest included the king's brother, the king's grandfather Louis XV, and her own father, who had taught her 'the passion of incest, the dirtiest of pleasures,' from which followed 'the hatred of the French, the aversion for the duties of spouse and mother, in short, all that reduces humanity to the level of ferocious beasts.'[24] Disorderly sexuality was linked to bestialization in the most intimate way.

Promiscuity, incest, poisoning of the heir to the throne, plots to replace the heir with a pliable substitute – all of these charges reflect a fundamental anxiety about queenship as the most extreme form of women invading the public sphere. Where Rousseau had warned that the salon women would turn their 'harem of men' into women 'more womanish than she,' the radical militant Louise de Keralio would warn her readers that 'a woman who becomes queen changes sex.'[25] The queen, then, was the emblem (and sacrificial victim) of the feared disintegration of gender boundaries that accompanied the Revolution. In his controversial study of ritual violence, René Girard argues that a sacrificial crisis (a crisis in the community that leads to the search for a scapegoat) entails the feared loss of sexual differentiation: 'one of the effects of the sacrificial crisis is a certain feminization of the men, accompanied by a masculinization of the women.'[26] A scapegoat is chosen in order to reinstitute the community's sense of boundaries. By invoking Girard, I do not mean to suggest that the

French Revolution followed his script of sacrificial crisis, or that I subscribe to the nuances of his argument. In fact, the Revolution did not single out a particular scapegoat in the moment of crisis; it was marked instead by a constant search for new victims, as if the community did not have a distinct enough sense of itself to settle upon just one (the king or the queen, for example). Nevertheless, Girard's suggestion that an intense crisis within a community is marked by fears of de-differentiation is very fruitful, for it helps make sense of the peculiar gender charge of the events of the fall of 1793.

The evidence for a feared loss of sexual differentiation in the Revolution is in fact quite extensive. Just two weeks after the execution of the queen (which took place on October 16, 1793), the Convention discussed the participation of women in politics, in particular the women's club called the Société des républicaines révolutionnaires. The Jacobin deputy Fabre d'Eglantine insisted that 'these clubs are not composed of mothers of families, daughters of families, sisters occupied with their younger brothers or sisters, but rather of adventuresses, knights-errant, emancipated women, amazons.'[27] The deputy Amar, speaking for the Committee on General Security of the Convention, laid out the official rationale for a separation of women from the public sphere:

> The private functions for which women are destined by their very nature are related to the general order of society; this social order results from the differences between man and woman. Each sex is called to the kind of occupation which is fitting for it . . . Man is strong, robust, born with great energy, audacity and courage . . . In general, women are ill suited for elevated thoughts and serious meditations, and if, among ancient peoples, their natural timidity and modesty did not allow them to appear outside their families, then in the French Republic do you want them to be seen coming into the gallery to political assemblies as men do?

To reestablish the 'natural order' and prevent the 'emancipation' of women from their familial identity, the deputies solemnly outlawed all women's clubs.

In response to a deputation of women wearing red caps that appeared before the Paris city council two weeks later, the well-known radical spokesman (and city official) Chaumette exclaimed:

> It is contrary to all the laws of nature for a woman to want to make herself a man. The Council must recall that some time ago these denatured women, these *viragos*, wandered through the markets with the red cap to sully that badge of liberty . . . Since when is it permitted to give up one's sex? Since when is it decent to see women abandoning the pious care of their households, the cribs of their

children, to come to public places, to harangues in the galleries, at
the bar of the senate?

Chaumette then reminded his audience of the recent fate of the 'impudent'
Olympe de Gouges and the 'haughty' Madame Roland, 'who thought
herself fit to govern the republic and who rushed to her downfall.'[28]

Marie Antoinette was certainly not in alliance with the women of the
Société des républicaines révolutionnaires, with Madame Roland or
Olympe de Gouges; they were political enemies. But even political enemies, as Louise de Keralio discovered, shared similar political restrictions
if they were women. Keralio herself was accused of being dominated by
those same 'uterine furies' that beset the queen; by publishing, Keralio too
was making herself public. Her detractors put this desire for notoriety
down to her ugliness and inability to attract men. As Dorinda Outram has
argued, women who wished to participate actively in the French Revolution
were caught in a discursive double bind; virtue was a two-edged sword that
bisected the sovereign into two different destinies, one male and one
female. Male virtue meant participation in the public world of politics;
female virtue meant withdrawal into the private world of the family. Even
the most prominent female figures of the time had to acquiesce in this
division. As Madame Roland recognized, 'I knew what role was suitable to
my sex and I never abandoned it.'[29] Of course, she paid with her life
because others did not think that she had so effectively restrained herself
from participating in the public sphere.

Read from this perspective on the difference between male and female
virtue, the writings and speeches about the queen reveal the fundamental
anxieties of republicans about the foundations of their rule. They were not
simply concerned to punish a leading counterrevolutionary. They wanted
to separate mothers from any public activity, as Carole Pateman argues,
and yet give birth by themselves to a new political organism. In order to
accomplish this, they had to destroy the Old Regime link between the
ruling family and the body politic, between the literal bodies of the rulers
and the mystic fiction of royalty. In short, they had to kill the patriarchal
father and also the mother.

Strikingly, however, the killing of the father was accompanied by little
personal vilification. Hébert's references to the pig, the ogre, or the drunk
were relatively isolated; calling the former king a cuckold ('tête de cocu')
hardly compared to the insistent denigration of Marie Antoinette. Officials
chose not to dwell on the king's execution itself. Newspaper accounts were
formal and restrained. On the day of the event, one of the regicide deputies
who spoke in the Jacobin Club captured the mood: 'Louis Capet has paid
his debt; let us speak of it no longer.' Most of the visual representations of
the execution (medals or engravings) came from outside of France and
were meant to serve the cause of counterrevolution.[30] The relative silence

about Louis among the revolutionaries reflects the conviction that he represented after all the masculinity of power and sovereignty. The aim was to kill the paternal source of power and yet retain its virility in the republican replacement.

The republican ideal of virtue was profoundly homosocial; it was based on a notion of fraternity between men in which women were relegated to the realm of domesticity. Public virtue required virility, which required in turn the violent rejection of aristocratic degeneracy and any intrusion of the feminine into the public. The many bodies of Marie Antoinette served a kind of triangulating function in this vision of the new world. Through their rejection of her and what she stood for, republican men could reinforce their bonds to one another; she was the negative version of the female icon of republican liberty but nonetheless iconic for the rejection. She was perhaps also an object lesson for other women who might wish to exercise through popular sovereignty the kind of rule that the queen had exercised through royal prerogative. The republican brothers who had overthrown the king and taken upon themselves his mantle did not want their sisters to follow their lead. In this implicit and often unconscious gender drama, the body of Marie Antoinette played a critical, if uncomfortable, role. The bodies of Marie Antoinette could never be sacred by French tradition, but they could certainly be powerful in their own fashion.

Notes

1 I have used the report on the session of October 14, 1793, in the *Moniteur Universel*, October 16, 1793.
2 As quoted in Ernst H. Kantorowicz, *The King's Two Bodies: A Study in Mediaeval Political Theology* (Princeton, Princeton University Press, 1957), p. 409 n. 319.
3 *Moniteur*, October 27, 1793, reporting on the trial session of October 14.
4 *Moniteur*, October 27, 1793.
5 *Moniteur*, October 27, 1793.
6 *Révolutions de Paris*, no. 212 (August 3–October 28, 1793).
7 Jean-Jacques Rousseau, *Politics and the Arts: Letter to M. d'Alembert on the Theatre*, trans. Allan Bloom (Ithaca, Cornell University Press, 1968), pp. 100–1.
8 Quotes from *Moniteur*, October 27, 1793, and October 18, 1793 (the latter the testimony of Roussillon, a barber-surgeon and cannoneer).
9 Carole Pateman, *The Sexual Contract* (Stanford, Stanford University Press, 1988), p. 36.
10 Pateman, *Sexual Contract*, p. 12.
11 *Moniteur*, October 18, 1793.
12 *Moniteur*, October 19, 1793.
13 *Moniteur*, October 20, 1793.
14 *Père Duchesne*, no. 298 (October 1793).
15 Hector Fleischmann, *Marie-Antoinette libertine: Bibliographique critique et analytique des pamphlets politiques, galants, et obscènes contre la reine.*

Précédé de la réimpression intégrale des quatre libelles rarissimes et d'une histoire des pamphlétaires du règne de Louis XVI (Paris, Bibliothèque des Curieux, 1911).

16 Henri D'Almeras, *Marie-Antoinette et les pamphlets royalistes et révolutionnaires: les amoureux de la Reine* (Paris, Librairie Mondiale, 1907), pp. 309–10.

17 *Portefeuille d'un talon rouge, contenant des anecdotes galantes et secrètes de la cour de France* (reprinted Paris, Bibliothèque des Curieux, 1911) p. 22.

18 Quotations from *Essai historique sur la vie de Marie-Antoinette, reine de France et de Navarre, née archiduchesse d'Autriche, le deux novembre 1755: Orné de son portrait, et rédigé sur plusieurs manuscrits de sa main* ('A Versailles, Chez La Montensier [one of her supposed female lovers], Hôtel des Courtisannes,' 1789), pp. 4, 8, 19–20.

19 *Le Godmiché royal* (Paris, 1789).

20 The full title of the edition I used is *Les Crimes des reines de France depuis le commencement de la monarchie jusqu'à la mort de Marie-Antoinette; avec les pièces justificatives de son procès* ('Publié par L. Prudhomme, avec Cinq gravures. Nouvelle édition corrigée et augmentée. Paris: au Bureau des Révolutions de Paris, an II').

21 *See*, for example, *Têtes à prix, suivi de la liste de toutes les personnes avec lesquelles la reine a eu des liaisons de débauches*, 2d ed. (Paris, 1792), 28 pp., and the nearly identical *Liste civile suivie des noms et qualités de ceux qui la composent, et la punition dûe à leurs crimes . . . et la liste des affidés de la ci-devant reine* (Paris, n.d., but Tourneux dates it 1792).

22 *Père Duchesne*, no. 194.

23 As quoted by Fleischmann, *Marie-Antoinette libertine*, p. 76.

24 *Vie privée, libertine et scandaleuse*, as reprinted in Fleischmann, *Marie-Antoinette libertine*, pp. 173–74.

25 [Keralio] *Les Crimes constitutionnels de France* (Paris, 1792), p. vii.

26 René Girard, *Violence and the Sacred*, trans. Patrick Gregory (Baltimore, Johns Hopkins University Press, 1977), p. 141.

27 *Réimpression de l'Ancien Moniteur*, 18: 290 (session of 8 Brumaire, year II, October 29, 1793).

28 Quotes from Darline Gay Levy, Harriet Branson Applewhite, and Mary Durham Johnson, *Women in Revolutionary Paris, 1789–1795* (Urbana, University of Illinois Press, 1979), pp. 215–6, 219–20.

29 Outram, '*Le Langage mâle de la vertu*: Women and the Discourse of the French Revolution', in *The Social History of Language*, ed. Peter Burke and Roy Porter (Cambridge, Cambridge University Press, 1987), p. 125, quotation from p. 126.

30 Lynn Hunt, 'The Sacred and the French Revolution,' in *Durkheimian Sociology: Cultural Studies*, ed. Jeffrey C. Alexander (Cambridge, Cambridge University Press, 1988), pp. 25–43, quotation from p. 32.

15

Counter-revolutionary women

OLWEN HUFTON

The Revolution[. . .]was not an optional experience to be embraced or rejected at will. Historians still search for the village which emerged totally unscathed by events. The bulk of French people were, of course, peasants. They lived in scattered hamlets or nuclear villages. They did not have the opportunity to participate in anything approaching a revolutionary *journée* but as taxpayers and suppliers of cannon fodder, they were called upon to defend the Revolution against its enemies. It was also unlikely that they would escape the excesses of Parisian or city revolutionary zeal. The peasant woman, however, has been somewhat neglected by historians of both sexes. This is unfortunate because, arguably, the response of this woman to the Revolution is critical.

We meet her only fleetingly in the history of the Revolution before 1795. She emerges here and there from as early as 1790–1 as the target of minor urban demonstrations in the market for her refusal to surrender milk, cheese, and eggs for assignats, in demonstrations to try to prevent the sale of common land and the abolition of traditional rights of gleaning and harvesting which were often an important part of the family economy of many peasant households. Above all, from 1791, she moves into the defence of traditional religion and its priesthood. In so doing, this woman is transformed little by little into a counter-revolutionary and in due course becomes part of the counter-revolution with a distinctive role to play.

During the bicentenary, an event which above all celebrated discourse and the use of terms, there was considerable debate on what should be considered counter-revolutionary and what anti-revolutionary. Such fine distinctions were not applied by contemporaries who used the term counter-revolutionary as they did aristocrat with a conspicuous generosity and contempt for precision. Even Jacques Roux, the militant of militants, was a counter-revolutionary in the mouths of the Jacobins. The women who are the concern here and were designated counter-revolutionary in the reports of police and government officials were not like the *chouans* those who took to the woods to make war on the Republic or who sought to establish an unmodified ancien régime or even those who in the cause of

Reprinted in full, except for notes, from O. Hufton, *Women and the Limits of Citizenship in the French Revolution* (Toronto, Buffalo, London, University of Toronto Press, 1992), pp. 94–130, 168–74.

the White Terror were ready to dismember the bodies of former Jacobin officials. They were more modest personnages who were prepared to turn their backs on the national line. Women who boycotted the mass of the constitutional priest, who in the hard years of 1793–4 organized clandestine masses, who continued to slap a cross on the forehead of the newborn, who placed a Marian girdle on the stomach of the parturient, and who gathered to say the rosary and taught their children their prayers were all committing counter-revolutionary offences. These women did not name their children after Marat. They continued to hallow a pantheon of saints in the way they had always done. If their husbands elected to buy favour by honouring a local official in the naming of their offspring, they slipped a saint's name on as well. They did not when they breast-fed their children reflect that they were endowing them with sound revolutionary principles and a hatred of aristocrats. They resented the décadi which destroyed traditional sociability patterns. They buried their relatives secretly at the dead of night. They probably encouraged their sons to defect and they certainly did not send their children to state schools. Unlike revolutionary woman who was a product of the big cities and the revolutionary *journées* and who had her heyday in 1793 and can be thought about as an architect of the Revolution and as deeply committed to the triumph of popular sovereignty, counter-revolutionary woman evolved slowly. She surfaced in the countryside, in some areas sooner than others, or in the small town which knew it was not a priority in the government's provisioning schemes. She began to win after 1795 though the victory was far from absolute or clear cut. Ultimately, however, she could claim to have made a significant contribution to the reversal of the national record. She nullified all attempts by the Directory to re-establish the rule of law by setting at nought its attempts to tolerate a Catholicism which would pronounce its loyalty to the state and by rendering null its attempts through a state-based civic education to create citizens in a patriotic mould, emancipated from the preconceptions of the past. Against change she posited tradition. She gave practical expression to a dicton existing in many provincial patois: 'Les hommes font les lois; les femmes les traditions.'[1]

This is the woman in Revolution whose spectre will haunt the politicians of the nineteenth century and serve to confirm them in their efforts to deny women the vote. Certainly, this woman has significance in the history of the Roman Catholic Church for it is her commitment to her religion which determines in the post-thermidorean period the re-emergence of the Catholic church on very particular terms, which included an express rejection of state attempts to control a priesthood and the form of public worship. Counter-revolutionary woman is therefore of consequence in the ongoing religious and political history of France.

Who was she and how does one find out about her? Richard Cobb was able to re-create the *sans-culotte* from his utterings and voluble disquisitions in the *sociétés populaires*, in the sections, and in police reports: a revolutionary man emerged clearly from his utterings. Such a direct re-creation of counter-revolutionary woman is impossible. When she speaks it is through the official who recounts her misdeeds and such officials, as Cobb reminded us in his study *The Police and the People*, were not dispassionate or innocent reporters. Cobb pointed out that an official report was written with an eye to impressing one's superiors if the official wanted to advance in state service. Objectivity was a low priority when promotion was the official's desideratum.[2] In short, any text we are proffered from this type of source needs careful scrutiny, not least when an official recounts his dealings with women and is conscious that his comportment may be judged according to different criteria from those used if he were dealing with men.

When officials encountered women and described their floutings of the law to their superiors, they might, in order to maintain their own image, proffer a distorted version to preserve their own reputation. For example, the description of a local response to the inauguration of the feast of the Supreme Being which ran: 'Quelques femmelettes ont fait des propos inciviques' (Some little women made uncivic remarks) might refer to several dozens of screaming women telling an official exactly what to do with the new deity. The allegation that in a small village of no more than two hundred inhabitants an official ceded the keys of the church in 1796 to several hundreds of fanatical women who threw him to the ground and tore his clothes might mean that the weary official was tired of standing his ground against reiterated insults and petitioning but needed to convince his superiors that he had ceded to *force majeure*. To cite a mere dozen might reveal him for a coward. Or, he might employ a series of euphemisms to cloak the truth. We need to have recourse to specific examples. 'La religion a semé la division dans les familles' (Religion has sown division in families) might be one way of saying that the men are loyal to the religious policy of the Republic but the women are not. What does one make of the Jacobin official who in the post-thermidor months found it needful to comment on the loyalty of his colleagues in the following way: 'il est bon patriot quoi qu'il envoie sa femme à la messe' (He is an excellent patriot although he *sends* his wife to mass)? Does this mean that the man had to seem to control his family if he was to hold an official position or does it mean that the Jacobin mayor had despaired of finding anyone whose wife did not go to mass to fill an official position?[3]

We also have to account for the evident scorn of officialdom in the heady days of the Jacobin dictatorship for what they interpreted as women's practices. When, in the year II, it was part of national policy to explain through the national agents *les bienfaits de la Révolution* to those villages and hamlets clearly less than 50 per cent committed to national policies, the rhetoric of persuasion stressed the following: first, that the Revolution represented a victory over political tyranny; second, that it achieved the equality of men; third, that it established the freedom of the individual; and fourth, that it secured the triumph of reason over 'fanatisme.' In this discourse, a model *homme/patriot, femme/fidèle aux prêtres* was allowed to surface. Officialdom clung to the notion that men would embrace the Revolution and that, in the natural order of things, women would in due course follow their husbands. It wallowed in an antifeminism which was indubitably latent in all politicians and which fed on the experience of resistance to its policies. It expected men to see the logic of its arguments. Young men must die for its principles; the rest must make personal sacrifices in the shape of money and goods and wage an unremitting war on the partisans of the old order, who were those who could not accept the crystal-clear logic of *civisme*, who did not respect the maximum, who made *propos inciviques*, or who behaved like women and went to church. It was in the course of this discourse that rural France heard perhaps for the first time the words *philosophie* and *raison* and that age-old practices were *superstition, momerie, fanatisme,* that peasants were the dupes of the enemies of the state. The discourse also made abundantly clear that peasants were considered idiots by the central authority but idiots who could be coaxed or bullied into acceptance of the official line, and the biggest idiots of all in their persistent irrationality were peasant women. When dealing with women, officialdom gave vent to its latent antifeminism in a vocabulary of abuse. Virtually unable to call a woman a woman, it used instead derisive derivatives like *femelles, femelettes, bigotes, bêtes, bêtes de laine, moutons, lentilles, légumineuses, fanatiques.*[4] These are merely a few of the more common nouns which were used in this discourse. The adjectives were still more graphic. Woolly-minded and with an intelligence equivalent to that of a farm animal, the peasant was seen as epitomizing ignorance and stupidity. The general questionnaire sent around in January 1794 to all the districts enquired very closely about local reactions to religious change. The rhetorical vocabulary involved transmits the flavour:

> *Question:* Has the sublime movement of the people against superstition encountered obstacles in its development?[5]
>
> *Answer:* The sublime movement of the people against superstition has met with very considerable obstacles in its development, [no prizes for saying yes]. We do not believe that these are produced by anything more than ancient prejudices which are always very difficult to overcome when one is dealing with the peasant mind because they are a product of ignorance.[6]

This questionnaire was sent out during the early phases of the dechristianizing campaign; within weeks, the peasant mind in official documents was to be presented not merely as ignorant but also as gendered. There was hope for re-educating the men, as far as officialdom was concerned; women were another matter.

Was the division of men and women in this way by officialdom consonant with the realities? Does available evidence show that officialdom based its analysis on hard evidence or deep-rooted antifeminism? In other words, did the discourse create the issue? Can one weed out fact from fantasy?

It is very obvious that the notion of irrational woman has a venerable history. It is as old as Greek medical treatises, was reaffirmed in renaissance thought, and persisted into modern times. The Enlightenment which immersed woman in nature and made her the creation of her reproductive organs was not prepared to put her on the same rational footing as men. Yet did the promotion of a contrast between manly commitment and female hostility to religious change justified by reference to the differential reasoning power of the two itself create a dichotomy of behaviour between the two? In other words, if the hostility of women is assumed in the rhetoric do women seize upon the role allotted to them? Did the origins of what French religious sociologists have called *le dimorphisme sexuel* (the differential attitude to religious practice between the sexes) conspicuous in the nineteenth and twentieth centuries spring from revolutionary discourse?

Michel Vovelle in his recent study *La Révolution contre l'Eglise* (Paris 1989) is prepared to give serious consideration to the notion that officialdom created the model of the superstitious priest who controlled woman in order to further his own ends and that this effort may have created new problems. He stresses that the *représentants en mission* and local patriots, when dealing with communities of a traditionally anticlerical disposition, might use gender difference to make a bid for the minds of men. To reinforce this notion one might add that whenever the overthrow of the Catholic faith was mooted the terms used assumed an explicitly masculine quality. In November 1793, for example the section of Gravilliers proclaimed to the Convention that it had closed its churches, which had served as lairs for filthy beasts who devoured wealth which should have fed young families and introduced desolation and division into the home. 'Leur enceinte à jamais consacré à la vérité, ne retentira plus que de la voix des Républicains qui instruiront leurs frères, que des mâles accents du patriotisme honorant la raison.'[7]

Some specialist studies of dechristianization show that in particular localities – the Seine et Oise provides the most striking instances – women shared with men in iconoclastic orgies. Yet, when they did so, as in Paris, there could often be considerable ambivalence. When, for example, Saint

Eustache in the middle of Les Halles was desecrated, two hundred or more women defended the baptismal chapel and their boast at the end of the day was that the altar cloth was still spotless. The presence of *sans-culotte* women at mass was not uncommon and many expressed unfaltering allegiance to a personage known as *la bonne petite mère*, no less than Mary, the suffering mother of God who also lost her son in a good cause. Such devotion, however, could and did coexist with considerable hatred for particular priests and the higher echelons of the ecclesiastical hierarchy.

In the century preceding the Revolution in most rural parishes a near totality of men and women observed, however perfunctorily, their religious obligations. Those who did not do so rarely accounted for more than 5–6 per cent of the parish and in the extreme west (the Vendée, Brittany, the Cotentin), the east (Alsace, Franche Comté and Lorraine), and Flanders, they were virtually non-existent. In a north to centre block (including the Ile de France, the Seine Valley, Champagne and Western Burgundy, the Auvergne and the Limousin) enclaves could be found with a mixed commitment to regular practice and a significant discrepancy *could* (though this was not necessarily the case) exist between the conformity of adult men and women in respect of Lenten confession and Sunday observance. For example, at Mennecy near Gonesse (Seine et Oise) 91 of 198 male householders, 149 of 198 married women, 28 of 66 bachelors over the age of 25, and a totality of widows and spinsters performed their Easter duties. As one moved further south to the Midi marked contrasts between localities occurred. There were pious mountains and impious garrigues, often *frontières de catholicité* (areas maintaining the faith against the onslaught of Protestantism in an earlier era) and villages of the plains and foothills which could be indifferent to religious demands, some of them perhaps former bastions of heresy which had been forced to express some conformity to Catholicism and which only had a very weak commitment.

The Revolution, however, seems at least in a majority of areas to have accentuated the difference in the commitment of men and women to regular religious practice though we need to make allowances for much local variation and in many cases the difference may only have been one of degree. After 1801 and the formal re-establishment of the Roman Catholic church in France, it was clear that there was a considerable difference in the degree of preparedness of both communities and individuals to return to regular religious worship. As the curé of Ars acknowledged, the battle for the minds of men – who had after all lacked religious instruction in youth or belonged to the revolutionary armies – was much harder to win. In the context of the Revolution the phenomenon of female commitment and male rejection became clearly visible though we must acknowledge significant regional variation.

From what point in the Revolution does the phenomenon manifest itself? Is there a point at which one can see women rather than men

contesting the dismantling of an institution which had been a conspicuous
point of reference in their lives? It had, after all, hallowed the great events
of life – birth, marriage, and death – as well as vaunted the virtues of
Catholic motherhood.

There is evidence, though it is much more striking in some areas than
others, of women demonstrating early hostility to 'intruder' priests in
1790–1 (those who replaced the nonjurors as parish clergy). Where the
incumbent in 1789 was popular and where he made a personal decision not
to accept the oath, then his decision could result in riotous incidents, when
officialdom read out the notification of legislation insisting that such an
oath be taken in front of the parish. At this stage, the principles involved in
the oath of loyalty to the constitution probably meant very little to the
women of the parish. Some priests held special meetings to explain their
decisions to their parishioners. The theological niceties involved when they
rejected the oath were then spelled out. Particularly pious spinsters or
widows who were often the main support of the parish priest and also
deeply involved in philanthropic work circulated anti-oath pamphlets and
in some towns, such as Strasbourg, actually organized petitions and
processions in protest against the obligatory nature of the oath. Perhaps
more often, however, the devotion of rural women was to an individual.
The spirit of the congregation at La Madeleine in Bayeux who yelled out to
the priest 'jurez ou ne jurez pas, cela ne nous fait rien du tout'[8] may be
totally representative. Where the local priest was prepared to take the oath,
as initially about half of them did, then friction was clearly postponed. The
nonjuror who found himself ousted from his presbytery used his firm
supports, notably widows and spinsters, to participate in an alternative
mass either in the parish church at an unseasonal hour or in a convent
chapel. Not only did such activity strip the juror of his congregation but it
also ensured that babies were not brought to him for baptism and he was
not sought to administer the last rites or burial services. These women did
not use the juror's confessional and they did not discourage their sons
from assaults on his property. Lacking any influence over village education
or control of charitable funds, the constitutional priest became a fervent
critic of the behaviour of the women of the parish and an active proponent
of a harsher line towards nonjurors. It is from this point that we have the
first written complaints from juring priests and administrators about
fanatical women who were exercising their influence over their husbands
or destroying domestic harmony or even leaving their husbands altogether.
Very occasionally in these reports the fear of the quasi-sexual power and
attraction of the parish priest over women exercised through the confessional surfaces as it had done under the old regime and would again do *ad
nauseam* in the second half of the nineteenth century. Such correspondence
embodied commentaries on the inherent female attachment to religion.

The juring clergy in their frustration fell back on Eve, declared this time to be influenced through a serpent called the nonjuror.

When in the summer of 1792, the nonjurors had to choose between flight or hiding, their parishioners did not necessarily flock back to their parish church to hear the juror. Some sought out a priest in hiding – though how many were able to do so is a matter of considerable speculation. Chanoine Flament identified about four hundred refractory priests performing services in the Orne, three hundred in the Haute Loire, and one hundred or more in the Sarthe throughout the Revolution.[9] Such figures, however, must be impressionistic and how frequently clandestine masses were held cannot even be guessed. Until the autumn of 1793 the juring clergy, their salary well in arrears and their future compromised by the dechristianizing surge emanating from the Paris sections, nonetheless continued to proffer their services.

After the spring of 1794, however, even the availability of a juror's mass was not to be taken for granted. The dechristianizing campaign had silenced the jurors and the marriage of priests and ceremonial burnings of *lettres de prêtrise* had destroyed whatever shred of credibility remained to the church created by the Constituent Assembly. Where a clandestine ceremony occurred, it was held in a private house or barn or illicit chapel and depended upon the complicity or ignorance of local officials and the energy of villagers in carrying out an exercise which could put them in danger of arrest. Such masses were celebrated with least risk in villages distant from prying urban officialdom or were held in a particular household by invitation from the individuals who were hiding the priest. Widows and former members of congregations emerged as those most likely to run the risk of priest sheltering.

Along with the disappearance of a regular mass went the silencing of the parish bell, which had not only been the most constant reminder of religious obligation but had also symbolized community solidarity and had warned of common dangers. On Fridays or Saturdays, it had been commonly rung to call the faithful to confession. Now such a spiritual exercise was rarely available and the habit of confession was generally lost. Nor was there any priest to administer the last rites or to offer catechetical instruction.

What is also abundantly documented is the attack on the old religion in the name of reason. Dechristianization began in Paris and was exported by officialdom, in some instances with an intensity befitting a witch hunt, which far exceeded anything sanctioned by the government. Sometimes, initiatives were local and emanated from the *sociétés populaires*. More often, an ambitious local official, anxious to make his reputation as a patriot and buttressed by an enthusiastic *représentant en mission* emanating from Paris, took initiatives. The *armées révolutionnaires* used iconoclasm and signs of rejection of the old religion as a test of revolutionary commitment.

Conscious of the antagonizing effect of the destruction of the traditional faith upon some of the rural communities, the Robespierrist response was to attempt a substitute devotion based on rationality. There followed from June 1794 a series of state cults – Liberty, Reason, the Supreme Being – all of them promoted as the worship of the rational.

It is pertinent at this point to consider the role played by religion in the lives of the rural masses and in particular to examine the attraction of reason as an abstract notion supplanting the belief in the supernatural in a traditional village. Just what, one might reasonably ask, is rational about life? Some are born crippled or blind, some sick; some get good husbands, some end up with a wife beater; some are fertile and some are barren. Rural society lived with the vagaries of the seasons, with drought, with hailstorms which could devastate a crop in an hour. It knew and was powerless against grain weevils or cattle pest. It still knew periodic visitations of epidemics from smallpox to viral pneumonia which could eliminate young and old. Some women died in childbirth; some found the exercise almost effortless. Viewed in this way, life was not rational but a grisly lottery in which the stakes were especially weighted against the poor.

To cope with ever imminent, if not inevitable, disaster, Europeans had over the centuries addressed a supreme if fitful orchestrator through the intercession of a priest who commanded knowledge of the relevant rites and practices. Christians also believed that the deity could be swayed by penitence and supplication to saints and above all to Mary. Marianism was by the eighteenth century perhaps strongest amongst women. Devotion to a woman who had been elected by this terrible god to bear his son in a stable and who had lost a son under terrible circumstances, who knew human suffering, and who, most of all, was prepared to mediate on behalf of suffering women with a male deity who could be manipulated – like most men – through his mother was an intrinsic part of the cult for women. As the Roman Catholic faith progressively became a fortress faith it was driven back into the home and hence largely into the hands of women. It became a faith based on the rosary with its ten Hail Marys for the one Our Father. The rosary was the perfect expression of a fortress faith. It offered the one means whereby the simple and illiterate, stripped of a priesthood and the familiar rituals of church ceremony, could maintain contact with their deity and could do so collectively. The congregation was replaced by the smaller unit of the family or the work group gathered, perhaps, for a *veillée* (evening get-together for work in a particular house, partly to economize on heat and light and partly for company). In some regions such as the lacemaking areas of the Velay or Lower Normandy, or areas characterized by high seasonal male migration like the Pyrénées or Savoy, or where male sociability patterns focused on the *cabaret* (tavern)

these meetings could be entirely female in composition. The recitation of
the rosary, for centuries encouraged by churchmen, now gained new
significance as the expression of a corporate faith. Many local officials
and even the emissaries of the Comité de Salut Public, the *représentants en
mission*, knew about but were prepared to turn a blind eye to such
practices. 'Let them have their rosaries,' wrote one *représentant* to the
Comité de Salut Publique, 'they will eventually weary of the ridiculous
practice and will give it up.'[10] Perhaps such tolerance emanated from the
uneasy realization that the wives and mothers of patriots were to be
counted amongst the bead tellers. Or, the exercise, when merely performed by women, was perceived to carry no threat. In short, and this
did not pass unacknowledged by authority, the faith feminized. It also
Marianized. The rosary was not the only expression of this Marianization.
The Mother of God herself appeared in woods and grottoes tearfully
denouncing the work of the Revolution and the assaults on her personage.

Unlike warm and familiar Mary, the official goddesses seemed ice
maidens, quite incapable of contributing anything to the business of living
or the business of dying. They commanded no hot line to the deity, no
proven record in the alleviation of labour pains or the extermination of
grain weevils. Frequently personified, if one could be found, by a young girl
whose virginity was deemed beyond question, the goddesses were earth-
bound, a religious travesty, a living testimony to the ridiculousness of a
religion based on reason.

The government knew women were not convinced by the changes just as
it was aware that women had most energetically opposed intruder priests
and had persistently boycotted the constitutional church. It knew too that
there existed rites and practices specific to women which were part of a
long process of acculturation. During parturition, for example, a Marian
girdle was placed on the mother's heaving stomach to help her in her
agony. In messidor of the year II, an article appeared in the *Moniteur*
which included the following statement: 'Under a good constitution and a
pure sky the parturient mother thinks of the constitution and feels no
pain.'[11] One wonders how many put this notion to the test. Very clearly,
however, the women's world of rituals impenetrable by the merely male
caused a disconcerting shudder, or perhaps no more than a transitory
sensation of impotence, amongst the politicians.

The central government did try to offer new ceremonies and festivals to
fill what it perceived to be a void. These were, however, largely confined to
the large towns. Some local authorities were more cognizant of the need to
provide an alternative sociability than others. The Société Populaire de
Charolles, for example, on 24 pluviôse an II commented on the dissatisfaction and riotous behaviour of women in communes where *les autels de
fanatisme* had been destroyed. A debate followed which asked the question:
why did women behave in this way? Was it because they had a greater taste

for mysticism than men? Of course not. What were the realities of Sunday? Old women walked to church and gossiped with other women and shared meals. This last was important for widows. Young girls went along enthusiastically to gape at the boys in a protected environment. On the décadi, in contrast, men went to the tavern which could never be a suitable place for women and consequently they were left grumbling at home. One solution proposed to win over the women was a dance every décadi which could be chaperoned by the old. This would provide women with an acceptable alternative social outlet and hence render the old religious practices redundant.

Such debates, however, did not solve the immediate problem of what was often a source of bitter contention between women in the parishes and officialdom, the issue of the closure of the church. The government and local officials, perhaps in default of alternative strategies, chose the immediate tactic of appealing to the men and hence attempting to isolate the women from them. Then, and perhaps more persistently from the mid-nineties, it also tried a policy designed to remould the acculturation of the French citizen.

Yet, in spite of knowing and becoming increasingly aware of women's resentment at the destruction of a conventional religion, in the year III when officialdom called upon men to stand up and be counted through oaths of loyalty and *certificats de civisme*, it made no such demands of women. It held that theirs was the private sphere and it was their husbands' job to exercise control. They were not citizens that is those partaking of the political, but citizenesses, owing first allegiance to the responsible citizen in the shape of husband or father. Their relationship to politics placed them at one remove. Let the citizen bring them to obedience.

Some clubs and *sociétés populaires* encouraged men to force their wives into gestures of contempt for the Catholic faith. For such efforts the officials were subsequently to pay dearly. The insistence of the *société populaire* at Arles, for example, that every male householder bring his wife to a ceremony where they could spit in unison upon the host to show that he was a patriot husband in control of his household may help to explain why these officials were so brutally murdered during the White Terror. Certainly, the attitude of the central government was that male obedience was the priority and that the obedience of irrational woman was of less significance. A woman's acts were in the first instance to be regulated by her husband. This existence at one remove from state control may have opened up some scope for subversive activity: the actions of women were to a degree condoned. This should not, however, be taken too far. Women died on the scaffold for their beliefs, if not as often as did men, and there is nothing, as Olympe de Gouges pointed out, apolitical about the guillotine.

The Terror not only demanded an appraisal of how one felt about the Revolution but also, by a new intrusiveness, applied the letter of revolutionary law with a new determination. It came forward with a new brand of officialdom prepared to push the law in some instances far beyond the intention of the Comité de salut public and this officialdom dominated departmental and local authorities and the *sociétés populaires*. This officialdom defined itself as the agent of reason, the disciple of philosophy. It took upon itself the function of converting the people, if need be through force and confrontation. It is from the pens of this officialdom that our version of counter-revolutionary woman emerges. It is not a neutral source, for this macho culture dreaded loss of face and sought scapegoats for its failures. Nevertheless, it did not invent counter-revolutionary women and though we need to be hypercritical of the evidence, it cannot be ignored.

The examples which will now be used are proffered to re-create the figure of the counter-revolutionary woman from the Haute Loire. We are fortunate to be able to draw on the maps of Michel Vovelle and Timothy Tacket to follow the ripples of the dechristianizing movement. The Haute Loire was not as tranquil as the Aube or the Pas de Calais but nor was it as immediately oppositional as the Vendée, Franche Comté, or the Lyonnais. It did not come out in open revolt like its neighbour, the Gévaudan and it worried the government less than did the contiguous Puy de Dôme. It is an area of impenetrable gorges, crags, with mountain streams and inadequate roads. It is not an easy place to penetrate and one might have thought it possible to live out one's life there relatively untroubled by the Revolution. Terror, after all, was without doubt at its most successful on flat land where communications were good and news of insubordination travelled easily. However, the area was to experience a group of ambitious local officials, the home-brewed equivalent of Maximilien de Robespierre, headed by Solon Reynaud, an ex-priest, one time mayor of Le Puy (1789), later in control of the department and Paris deputy, who chose to try to make his reputation in the area. He spoke of himself as the Couthon of the Haute Loire and hence was to confront the practices of the past in a particularly nasty and authoritarian manner. The department boasted the greatest number of guillotined priests in France. Moreover this was a region whose economy suffered particularly in the context of Revolution. It was a lacemaking economy directed and worked by women. These two factors allow us perhaps to paint a counter-revolutionary woman in very vivid oils rather than more delicate pastels. La Ponote [female inhabitant of Le Puy, *ed.*] and the woman of the Velay may not be totally typical but nor are they totally abnormal. There is no single model, perhaps, of counter-revolutionary woman but there are variations on a number of basic themes.

In this area, then, our counter-revolutionary woman was a lacemaker out of work because of the slump in luxury commodities. She lived in a hamlet, rather than a nuclear village. She had received her education at the hands of a *béate*, a local widow or spinster who lived in a house owned by the village in exchange for teaching girls to make lace and to recite the catechism and who in the evening organized work sessions in which lighting and heating were shared. The bell above her door punctuated the phases of the day and in winter when the snow fell and the church was unreachable, the *béate* replaced the priest and read a holy story and organized hymn singing. When the Catholic church became a schismatic church, she clung to the nonjuror and her premises became the locale of the clandestine church. In this way, though with progressive disenchantment both economically and socially, the villages of the Velay weathered the first three years of Revolution. The status quo, however, was to be dramatically challenged by the advent in the summer of 1793 of the conventionnel Reynaud who had political ambitions and wished to make his name at a national level. He identified religion as the disintegrant and disaffective factor in the relationship between the state and its citizenry. He took it upon himself, aided by a team of subordinates, to make war on a religion of royalism and women, the latter graphically described by him as *cette vermine malfaisante*.[12] His attack had a specific gender approach and it produced a specific gender response. His tactics could be thus summarized: first a more overt attack on the juring priesthood backed by the erection of a permanent guillotine at Le Puy; second, an attack on *les signes extérieures du culte*, bells, statues, crucifixes worn around the necks of women; third, the institution of the décadi, civil marriage and burial and penalties for non-observance. A particular eye was to be kept on women here because they were prone to ignore the décadi and he suggested some token arrests. The heaviest punitive action was of course against the priest. Lastly an end was to be put to the *béate* and her activities. She must be forced to take a civil oath in front of the women of the village or small town. This was in fact overstretching the law.

It was in response to this package that counter-revolutionary woman learned her techniques. The first was collective obstinacy – there was no room in this situation for individual heroism because an insurgent individual could be easily picked off whilst the women of an entire village acting together were much less vulnerable. The second technique was to use ridicule of an explicitly sexual or sexist variety. The spirit of such ridicule was in the vein of 'imagine grown men taking all this trouble with little us and see how we can embarrass you.' The third was to isolate an official recognized as weak or isolated in his devotion to the central line. The fourth was to vote with one's feet on issues where maternal authority mattered. These techniques, presently to be exemplified, were learned during the Terror and perfected under the Directory whose intent was to give the Revolution a second chance and this policy was to necessitate a second, if much emasculated, terror. This terror was in turn undermined by a war of attrition, much of it the work of women.

The first example of action by women is chosen to demonstrate the efficacy of standing one's ground in opposition to a particular issue and seeing how far obstinacy could go. We are in Montpigié, a small town with three sections in ventôse an III (February 1795) and Albitte, one of the *représentants en mission* boasting the most success as a dechristianizer, has arrived from Le Puy to receive the oath of loyalty from the *béates*. He has decided to make a holiday of the event and announces that the women of each section should gather separately in the Temple of Reason because it is important that the women should see their leader being brought into line: 'We summoned girls and women, female patriots, female aristocrats, the stupid, the *béates* [a play on the words *bêtes* and *béates*] without distinction to assemble in their section. I did not count on the fanatical hotheads presenting themselves. I was, overjoyed to see a large assembly of stupid little women.'

He took to the tribune and addressed them in terms designed to be understandable to the mentally retarded: 'I outlined the simplicity, the necessity and the importance of the oath they were asked to take: the bloody horrors of fanaticism and the belief of republicans in the existence of a gracious god who can only be worshipped by the practice of virtue and not by an exterior cult, full of theatricality and all for nothing.'[13]

He then asked for the handful of *béates* from Montpigié and the surrounding hamlets to take the oath. They stood up and announced themselves prepared to go to the guillotine rather than express loyalty to a pagan regime. Immediately all the other women present got to their feet and cheered resoundingly. These women, Albitte protested, were mothers of families and acting contrary to their husbands' wishes, the latter being absent. Seeing this, he said, he had no option but to dismiss the assembly and try again. The next day he had got a few guards to support him and tried another section of the town. This time, before he had had time to enter the tribune, a *béate* touched him on the arm and said she was ready for the guillotine now. The women of the village came to her support. Albitte's men moved in and rounded up about a hundred although the town did not have a really safe prison and this proved a considerable error. By evening the husbands of the married women facing household chores and coping with their children were demanding the release of their wives. The mayor's refusal to comply led to a gaol rising a few days later with a concerted effort from within and without. The *représentant en mission* released the married women and sent them home. They promptly mobilized the other women of the town. There was then a concentrated attack on the prison which resulted in the liberation of the *béates* and the incarceration of the mayor and the national agent.

It will be immediately apparent that no regime can support this kind of loss of face. At the same time, to move in the National Guard with its relatively heavy weaponry to confront rebellious but unarmed womanhood was not the answer to the problem. There were armed confrontations between guards and women with some loss of life on both sides but the guards were demeaned by such confrontation and not all were convinced of the need for an oath or by the dechristianizing campaign. Moreover, many of the protesting women were mothers or grandmothers who exercised their own kind of authority over the young guard and often used their first names. Authority was safest when it could pick off offenders one by one. Then there was less risk of loss of official dignity.

The most humiliating scenes for authority were without any doubt enacted less during the dechristianizing campaign than when authority sought to promote alternative deities – Reason, Liberty, the Supreme Being, who followed in quick succession in 1794. All of them were major disasters. One of the most graphic incidents occurred at Saint Vincent near Lavoûte sur Loire, former seat of the Polignacs and a place far from committed to the old regime or to the Revolution. The occasion was an instruction from Le Puy to read, on the décadi, in the Temple of Reason, a paean to the Supreme Being (June 1794). In the front row sat the local dignitaries, their wives and children. The unlucky celebrant began his patriotic oration when, at a sign from an old woman, the entire female audience rose, turned their backs on the altar of liberty, and raised their skirts to expose their bare buttocks and to express their feelings to the new deity. Confronted by the spectacle of serried rows of naked female back-sides the celebrant was reduced to gibberish. Officialdom departed in unseemly haste with aspersions on its manhood made from all sides. The humiliated celebrant wrote in anger to the department about his impotence before *ces gestes gigantesques et obscènes*.[14] News of this incident promoted its replication in the nearby bourgs of Lavoûte and across the hills at Saint Paulien. '*Montrer le cul aux gens* as an expression of female scorn has a long history in France even before Zola enshrined the practice in *Germinal*. It was emphatically a technique of the working classes. The middle-class or refined equivalent was simply to turn one's back or to sit on one's heels.

In two areas women could sabotage official policy and ideology virtually without effort. The control of birth and death were in the hands of women. The first was contained within the home; anyone could slap a cross on an infant brow. More disconcerting because it spilled over into the public domain was the preparation for death and the burial of the defunct.

Most people are attended in their final suffering by women. Hence, in the present context, their exit was in the hands of those likely to summon a clandestine priest or a female ex religious. The last could not pronounce absolution but she could urge the dying to repentence and reassure his or her relatives that they had fulfilled their spiritual obligations and opened

up the gates of paradise. The juring clergy had from 1791 faced a rejection
of their services to the dead and humiliating incidents such as the leaving
of the corpses of rotting animals in the parish church for burial. Such
gestures stripped the jurors of their hold over the populace. A priest who
did not have the keys to the kingdom of heaven could not be taken
seriously. Yet to obtain a Christian burial from a nonjuring priest was
progressively difficult after 1793 and so in the Haute Loire groups of
women undertook the burial, if need be at the dead of night. There is,
of course, good biblical precedent for the laying away of the dead by
faithful women. The contests which could emerge over the issue of burial
constitute my third illustrative tale.

The incidents occurred in Canton Vert, the revolutionary name for what
had been and is now Chaise Dieu. It is found in a series of letters written
by the municipal agent in the year VI. The letters, however, relate to
incidents stretching back over a longer period. The Directory was committed to freedom of worship provided the celebrant took an oath. To take
such an oath of loyalty to the Republic or indeed any oath required by the
government exposed any priest to rejection by the community. As in this
case, the community might attempt to run an alternative church using a
clandestine priest or someone who knew the liturgy.

The municipal agent of Canton Vert was also a constitutional priest
who had suffered imprisonment for failing to surrender his *lettres de
prêtrise* (the documents bestowing priesthood upon him). After the laws
of ventôse an III (February, 1795) he struggled to re-establish parochial
worship only to find himself frustrated by the women of the bourg who
found an effective leadership in a Sister of Saint Joseph du Puy who ran a
counter church, organized clandestine masses, and served as the agent for a
hidden nonjuror. Worse, she did all this from a house right opposite the
legally acceptable church presided over by the agent-priest.

His letters of protest to the department described body snatching. He
recounted how one Sister of Saint Joseph could gather together at any time
about thirty fanatical women (*fanatiques*) to help her but that she assumed
the role of director, orchestrating the event. The women would surround
the body and when the relatives tried to intervene and insist that it should
go to the church where the priest had taken an oath of loyalty, the thirty or
more 'furies and harridans' would attack the relatives and drive them away
by throwing stones. In the particular instance that the agent proceeded to
recount in some detail, the relatives were only ten in number and were
totally intimidated and retired leaving the disposal of the body to the
women. Next day there was an open clash on the issue between the priest
and the Sister of Saint Joseph. The slanging match is worth recounting
since it was done publicly and the priest/agent was humiliated. He called
her a *fanatique, druide, mégère, énergumène* (a fanatic, a druid, a vixen,
and a fury). She called him a *secteur de Calvin, philosophe*, a disciple of

the devil and its child the Republic. Her insults were lent force by a large crucifix which she was carrying when the altercation occurred and she advanced towards him waving it as if to exorcize the devil. As a *signe extérieure du culte*, the crucifix was quite illegal but it helped her to win the contest game, set, and match and she was cheered on by the onlookers. The curé appealed to the department: 'Rid us of these counter-revolutionary tricksters . . . The Sister of Saint Joseph du Puy as the chief of the fanatics should be pursued with all possible publicity [*avec éclat*] in order to deter the rest. Have the high priestess removed and overthrow her temple and her altar and place a prohibition on their re-establishment with a penalty for infraction . . . Frightened by the example made of their abbess, the other women will return to their duty.'[15]

Rentrer dans le devoir was exactly the consummation authority devoutly wished as its woman policy. To get the female population back into the home and obedient to husband and the law was summed up in this simple phrase.

The thermidoreans, confronted with the problems emanating from dearth and the general weariness of local officialdom after 1795 in face of the penury of funds and the hostility of the rural populace, were prepared to concede a great deal. The law of ventôse year III (21 February 1795) granted freedom of worship but precluded communes acquiring as a collectivity a church for community worship. It did not cede the parish church although it left to local authorities the option on offering such a building by auction. However, only individuals were allowed to bid and such individuals were then responsible before the law for what occurred within its walls. Resolutely, all exterior manifestations of religious affiliation were prohibited. There were to be no bells, no processions, no banners, no pilgrimages. If the Christian religion was celebrated within the church or elsewhere, only clergy who had taken a civil oath of loyalty might officiate. In short, and whilst explicitly committing itself to the official cults, the thermidoreans ceded something but it fell far short of what many communities wanted.

The policies of the thermidoreans were interpreted at the local level in very different ways. Some who took office in the aftermath of the Terror had overtly 'royalist,' that is to say anti-Jacobin, tendencies and were prepared to turn a blind eye to what was going on. Others adopted a much harder line. The government's decision to let Catholic worship occur provided it was contained within the framework outlined above was doomed to failure because by mid-1795 a religious revival was underway and in many, if not all regions, this revival was female orchestrated. The west, where religion fuelled civil war, and the east, where exiled clergy could return more easily and assume direction, provide strong exceptions to the more general picture. The pattern of the religious revival and the emotions which fuelled it varied between individuals and social groups, between villages, between town and country, and between one geographical location and another. It depended too upon how local officials were prepared to ignore much of what was happening. In some areas, the anarchy of the period allowed religion to resurface relatively unchecked. For women in large towns and cities, particularly in the Paris provisioning zone which formed a two-hundred-mile radius around the city and included cities like Rouen and Amiens, dearth prompted a desperate search for religious solace. Even in Paris, a police official commented on two queues, one at the baker's and one for mass.

For many urban women, there was more than a touch of guilt for a political past in which they had been very active collaborators, and the return of religion was by way of atonement. No such sense of personal guilt tinged the attitudes of rural women. In their view, what had happened was the fault of others. If the thermidoreans had hoped that their tolerance would bring peace, they were to be disillusioned.

To reconstruct the devotional patterns of the past, communities needed to take a number of basic steps. These were: the restoration of the church to its primitive usage; the procuring of sacred vessels and the means to summon the faithful to mass; the restitution of Sunday and the rejection of the décadi as the day of rest and the one on which an individual could fulfil his or her obligations and participate in a community ceremony. Then, at some stage, the decision had to be made of whom should be asked to officiate at the parish mass but this was seen as a secondary to securing the ancient locale for public worship.

Where local officialdom was prepared to hire out the church at auction and where such auctions have been carefully studied, as have those in Normandy by the Abbé Sévestre, then women, particularly widows, are seen to have been in the forefront. Even at impious Gonesse where some women had participated in the dechristianizing surge, 'les femmes menaient l'action.' At Mende, there was a curious contest for the honour of restoring the cathedral as parish church. Two women were rival contenders. One, Rose Bros, wife of a tailor and leader of a bread riot in 1789, proffered three hundred livres. Given the penury of her circumstances, it seems unlikely that the money was hers but rather that she was known as a courageous activist and was prepared to take the lead. Another woman, however, made a rival bid. She was Citoyenne Randon, wife of a former district official during the Terror. Her actions raise a string of questions. Was she distancing herself from her husband's past record? Was she seeking to save his skin from the fury of the populace in changing times? Was she anxious to wrench control from a troublemaker believing that she could direct the developing situation better? Did the women (largely, it would appear, widows with some means) generally act on their own behalf or on that of the community as a whole believing that the work of women would be shrugged off if reported to a timid set of officials?

There are occasional instances of husbands denouncing the activities of their wives but others may have been pleased enough to shelter behind their activities. However, what is clear is that in matters of religion in many of the villages and bourgs of provincial France, women dominated the public action. They did not sit obediently at home.

If no auctions were held, then very frequently riots occurred in which the doors of the church were forced and the community simply occupied the building, cleaned it up, and made it available for worship. News of a successful occupation in one community often encouraged surrounding ones to make a similar attempt. The riots had a distinctive form characteristic of female protest movements. The weaponry did not exceed stones and ashes. Women relied on their special status as women to promote their cause. Old and pregnant women were placed in the forefront and the rest, frequently bolstered by women from neighbouring parishes, brought up the rear with their aprons full of ashes to throw in the eyes of any opposition. If they succeeded in laying hold of the church, then they might move on to confront the official whom they thought to be guardian of religious vessels, or entire communities might rally to achieve the pealing of the bells. This act was the one encountering the most stubborn opposition from officialdom since a pealing bell pronounced to the outside world that republican law was ignored in the community. It pointed to their failure to control the situation in their parish, and it is the issue of the bells that provokes the most exaggerated accounts of women confronting unwilling officialdom. Often the seizure of the bell, followed by its rebellious peal, was used to symbolize local triumph over official policy and the angelus was tolled up to three times a day. In towns and larger villages, however, particularly those which were accessible, such activities brought out the National Guard and officials forced a more discreet religion upon the people. At Montpellier failure to gain control of the bells meant that those anxious to gather for parish worship had to fall back on the cowbell rung by small boys sent into the streets by their mothers.

Other issues were in their way decisive but took the citadel of republican authority by sap rather than direct confrontation. Amongst such issues was that of Sunday versus the décadi, the tenth day of rest decreed by the Jacobins when a republican calendar was inaugurated. Resented at the popular level as an evident reduction of leisure, to rural women, since the event was accompanied by no ritual or extended social contact, the laicized feast seemed a sham. The populace voted on this issue with its feet but the lead was frequently given by women giving their servants Sunday, not the décadi, as partial holiday.

Time off for the working man during the early nineties had come to mean drinking and for many men tavern sociability was a more than acceptable alternative to religious ritual. Under the ancien régime, this was a choice denied to many since the opening hours of the *cabaret* were limited on Sundays and *fêtes*. However, the removal of the curé as a check on the tavern keeper's business led to a burgeoning of tavern sociability. Associated also with local politics as the meeting place of the *société populaire*, the tavern became a more widely used place by men but not one for respectable women.

Frequently Sunday was hallowed by men lounging in the tavern whilst the women went to mass but the very indolence of the men on the sabbath was itself interpreted as an act of protest. Certainly, and this was particularly apparent in the years immediately after the Concordat before the church had mobilized itself anew to make a bid for the allegiance of men, the return of women to regular religious worship was far more conspicuous than was that of their menfolk.

It was very important that the renascent church should be served by personnel acceptable to the women. Where possible, this meant a nonjuror but such a personage could only operate illegally and hence much depended upon the compliance of the local authorities in turning a blind eye to his activities. Where a nonjuror could not be found, or where local circumstances were hostile to such illegal activity, women contented themselves with the services of a lay figure who knew the liturgy. Such a person could not offer communion but he satisfied the local need for a ceremony which was an expression of community solidarity. This practice disquieted churchmen and hostile lay authorities alike but it was well within the letter of the law.

The rejection of the juror by women caused the Abbé Grégoire extreme bitterness; his efforts to seize the initiative for the constitutional church in re-establishing Catholic worship were frustrated by what he termed *des femmes crapuleuses et séditieuses*.[16]

Perhaps, however, the *messes blanches*, or 'blind masses' as they were called, tell us a great deal about what women valorized in religion. They rejoiced in a safe expression of community sociability, the warmth and comfort of a religion with visible rituals, and those *signes extérieurs du culte* which both jurors and non-jurors were at pains to stress were of least spiritual significance to the Catholic faith. They were relatively indifferent to actual clerics themselves. Although there are instances of loyalty to one individual parish priest sustained throughout the Revolution, an uninterrupted relationship was rare. Driven underground and subjected often to considerable physical suffering in order to keep their identities secret from the authorities, many of the emergent nonjuring clergy were in very poor physical shape, and the lack of new recruits increasingly took its toll upon their numbers. This perhaps did not matter if rituals could be replicated. Their absence was then not noted.

The returning clerics wanted penitence. In the immediate context of famine, they got it but progressively after 1798 this spirit faltered. City women and men fell away and though the rural congregations remained large, the peasants did not expect to make financial sacrifices for their deity. The returning clergy claimed that interest in catechism classes and sending for the priest to perform the last rites were lost habits which no one was interested in reacquiring. They feared that they had lost control of the minds of an entire generation which had grown up without formal religious instruction other than that which the family could bestow.

The religious revival of the late 1790s occurred against a background of resolute opposition in the localities to government policies. If women's protest focused on reestablishing a church, that of young men took the form of draft dodging and desertion. By 1795, volunteers and conscripts no longer deserted in ones or twos but en masse, taking with them their weapons and effects. We hear of whole companies of soldiers in full uniform – which became progressively more bedraggled as the days wore on – walking the roads of France. One group crossed a half-dozen departments without being challenged. In order to survive, such gangs robbed the countryside mercilessly. Whilst some returned home, others lived in woods and mountainous areas known to their relatives, who helped to keep them provisioned. We hear most reports of desertion from the departments of the Massif Central, the Alps, and the Pyrénées and of course from the Vendée. There was no longer any emotive appeal to arms in defence of the Republic. The politicians tried to blame the English and 'emissaries of royalism.' Lacking the repressive forces necessary to round up the young men and fearful of the consequences of making desertion a capital offence lest still more defections occurred, authority lost control of the situation. Occasionally, it tried to stage a show trial as in the round-up of Jehu and his companions in the Haute Loire in 1798. This band, allegedly of several hundred young men, had gained an evil reputation for uncontrolled brigandage. To bring them to justice once captured, the Directory sanctioned a cordon around Le Puy lest a prison break should be attempted. Jehu, however, like Macheath in Gay's opera, won the heart of the prison warder's daughter who managed to get him out of jail, and the forces of authority suffered conspicuous loss of face. Other young men sought to get out of their military commitment by severing the fingers on their right hand so that they could not fire a rifle. In the Tarn the suggestion was made to dress such cowards in women's bonnets and march them round the town on the décadi, so that this parade might have the effect of drawing to the revolutionary spectacle 'a public utterly indifferent to republican institutions.'[17] Cobb and Forrest are insistent that desertion was one of the most effective means the common people had of expressing their hostility to a regime which had repressed and impoverished them and to which they felt no commitment.

For older men, those who did not have to go to war, there was a dangerous form of passive resistance which took the form of not paying taxes, idling in the tavern on a Sunday, and working in flagrant disrespect on the décadi. There was, however, in the Midi, a deadlier form of revenge on former terrorist supporters. Deserters played their part in flushing out republican strongholds but there was also a communal violence in which the adult males of a village or small town formed a gang of *égorgeurs* (throat slitters), who did not in fact do what their name suggested but beat up or threatened, insulted and humiliated, the households of men who were identified as former Jacobins, the supporters of Terror. Such violence was not the work of women but the latter could provide the incitement for action and contribute to the atmosphere of hostility by extending threats to the wives and children of those identified with Jacobin government. In part, we may be looking at a kind of squaring of the record in societies where the vendetta flourished and without this act of revenge for loved ones lost or families severed by the revolutionary record, normality could not be achieved.

However, such an interpretation must not obscure the violence or the anarchy of this period. The more one familiarizes oneself with the years 1796–1801, the more apparent it becomes that the attempt by women to establish a pattern of religious worship, and an expression of community solidarity which simultaneously hallowed the structure of family life, was the most constructive force one can determine at work in society. It was one which was working in the direction of normalization and a return to a structured lifestyle. Peacefully but purposefully, they sought to re-establish a pattern of life punctuated by a pealing bell and one in which rites of passage – birth, marriage, and death – were respected and hallowed. The state had intruded too far and women entered the public arena to push it back and won. It was one of the most resounding political statements to be made by the populace in the entire history of the Revolution.

Notes

1 The saying 'Men make laws, women customs' was often evoked in the nine-teenth century and interpreted as a reason for clerical influence.
2 R. C. Cobb, *The Police and the People*, pp. 50–2.
3 Examples taken from the Archives Départementales de la Haute Loire L430, 371, 1206.
4 'Females, little women, bigots, animals, woolly beasts, sheep, lentils, vegetables, fanatics.'
5 This was the official phrase for dechristianization.
6 An example of this questionnaire is found in J. Hardman, *French Revolution Documents* (Oxford, 1973), p. 173.
7 'These buildings will only contain the voices of republicans instructing their brothers and manly accents of patriotism honouring reason.' Section de Grav-illiers; cited in Hardman, *Documents*, 369–70. There seems to be little space here for sisters' or women's voices.

8 Archives Départementales Calvados Lv Liasse de Serments Bayeux. 'Take it or not, it doesn't bother us.'

9 Chanoine Pierre Flament, 'Recherche sur le ministre clandestin dans le département de l'Orne sous la Révolution,' *Bulletin de la Société historique et archéologique de l'Orne* xc (1972), pp. 45–74; E. Gonnet, *Essai sur l'histoire du diocèse du Puy en Velay,* p. 209; Charles Girault, *Le Clergé Sarthois face au serment constitutionnel*, pp. 31–3.

10 F. -A. Aulard, *Recueil des actes du Comité de Salut Public* (30 vols., Paris, 1889–1951), i, p. 353.

11 *Moniteur*, 19 Messidor an II.

12 More often this term was reserved for the *béates* (Archives Départementales, Conseil Général Le Puy 10 October 1793).

13 Rapport du 5 prairial an III, Archives Départementales Haute Loire LB14 (ancien cote).

14 Archives Départementales Haute Loire L376 ancien cote.

15 Archives Départementales Haute-Loire L802 ancien cote.

16 D. Woronoff, *La République bourgeoise de Thermidor à Brumaire*, pp. 143–4, gives a short account of Grégoire's efforts and frustrations. Blind masses have recently been interpreted by S. Desan, *Reclaiming the Sacred: Lay Religion and Popular Politics in Revolutionary France* (1990) as an attempt by women to create new rituals. I would prefer to see them as the resurrection of old rituals, as perfect in all details as possible except for the presence of a priest and, even here, the lay celebrant did not intrude upon the prerogatives of the real priesthood by giving communion.

17 Archives Nationales F9 316, Desertion, Tarn, Lautrec, 9 brumaire an VII.

SECTION

IV

REVOLUTIONARY
POLITICS

Presentation

When discussing the politics of the French Revolution, historians often resort to terms borrowed from the mechanical sciences. By common consent, the events of 1789 released a huge amount of pent-up energy which set in motion a 'dynamo' whose operation could be stilled only by the intervention of equivalent counter-vailing forces. If all would agree on the dynamic quality of Revolutionary politics, however, the debate over the specifics of the phenomenon is far from settled. Two issues in particular stand out: the problematic articulation of the politics of the *ancien régime* to that of the new; and the unresolved question of how properly Revolutionary politics should be characterized. Both of these issues beg the larger question, of course, which concerns the Revolution's self-image as a dramatic moment of rupture.

If (as now seems generally accepted) the latter decades of the *ancien régime* witnessed significant progress towards a new, pluralist political culture, it would seem reasonable to hypothesize a link to the energy-burst of Revolutionary politics in the years after 1789. However, specialists in old-regime political and cultural history seem reluctant to proceed far in this direction. Keith Baker, as has been noted already (Reading 7), prefers to confine the burgeoning politics of public opinion to an historical cul-de-sac. Revolutionary political action rested on very different assumptions, and it quickly abandoned any baggage carried over from the recent past. Many historians of the Revolution would agree with this conclusion. After all, both common sense and the weight of tradition dictate that the political experiences of the 1790s must be treated as generically different from what came before. However, the 1790s encompassed a long and tumultuous decade of radiating political practice and we should be careful with arguments that distil an essence labelled 'Revolutionary politics' and then project it back to Day One of the Revolution. As the opening contribution by Timothy Tackett makes plain (Reading 16), a transformist account of the issues and affiliations dividing deputies in the Estates General and the National Assembly can be highly instructive. Indeed, it is apparent that many contemporaries regarded the period from 1789 to 1791 as decidedly indeterminate and transitional. Only with the promulgation of a written constitution and the calling of a Legislative Assembly could Revolutionary politics begin in earnest.

Of course, the problem of ancestry rapidly turns into one of definition. How should the politics of the Revolution be characterized? There are several possibi-lities: we might wish to construct a political history around dominant personalities, around issues of policy or principle, or perhaps around the pursuit of power pure and simple. Alternatively, we might fathom an inner meaning which can be expressed in ideological terms. If all the actors in the Revolutionary stage-play were fired with a vision of Jean-Jacques Rousseau's 'general will', we can forget about mere individuals and political praxis. In this scenario the political culture of 1789 can indeed be differentiated from what came before; and, likewise, a 'logic' of political behaviour can be constructed which stretches from public debates in the Constituent Assembly to discussions behind closed doors in the Committee of Public Safety. Not surprisingly, such a radical denial of the relevance of Revolutionary politics finds scarcely an echo in the contributions comprising this section (unlike Section 5). Nevertheless, it can be useful to bear in mind the more philosophically informed approach when assessing the fragility of the representative institutions set up in 1790, and the manifest failure of the Revolutionaries to evolve a politics of give and take.

Unabashed empiricism aside, what else do the authors of the contributions gathered together here hold in common? Even at the mundane level, they display a reluctance to accept the rhetorical justifications of competing groups of Revolutionaries at face value. Tackett probes the posturing of France's first generation of elected representatives and finds clear evidence of the persistence of deep-seated socio-juridical cleavages, while Alan Forrest (Reading 18) strips away the propagandist rhetoric of Federalism to reveal a protean phenomenon beyond the reach of explanation in terms of a single political discourse. With the role of ideology muted, if not altogether excluded, several authors explore the power dimension of Revolutionary politics. Martyn Lyons, for instance, teases apart the various strands of opposition – personal, principled, and policy-driven – that contrived to bring about the fall of the Robespierrists (Reading 20). The materialist conception of political alignments is given a hearing, too; most notably by Claude Petitfrère (Reading 17), and more obliquely in the studies penned by Tackett and Forrest. As for the issues which our authors address, religion takes pride of place. For, on this evidence, nothing nourished political antagonisms more thoroughly than the tensions engendered by the religious policies of successive Revolutionary legislatures. The nemesis of those policies – in the shape of the Dechristianization Campaign – provided the final excuse for the repudiation of local power-broking in favour of a centralized model of authority. This is a theme which several of the contributors touch upon, but it is most effectively explored in Norman Hampson's study of the efforts of Saint-Just to galvanize the recalcitrant population of Alsace at a time of war emergency (Reading 19).

As befits a section which addresses the grand narrative of the Revolution, the five Readings are arranged in a chronological sequence. Timothy Tackett's essay spans the final months of the old regime and the opening months of the new. He brings a spotlight to bear upon a period familiar to economic and social-history specialists, but which, at the time of writing, was substantially neglected by political historians. If that omission has since been rectified, in part at least,[1] the very scope of Tackett's research continues to hold out the prospect of a major reassessment of the parliamentary history of the Revolution's earliest years. In this piece, however, the author contents himself with some trenchant comments on the initial apprenticeship of the deputies in the skills of electoral politics; on the shifting balance of parties, or rather factions, within the Constituent Assembly; and a well-supported analysis of the socio-cultural determinants of political allegiance during this period. Students will find the latter enquiry most rewarding. By mapping the contours of *ancien-régime* 'privilege' on to the terrain of political allegiance within the Constituent Assembly, Tackett effectively demonstrates the inadequacy of recent approaches to Revolutionary politics which emphasize ideological essences at the expense of social content.

Claude Petitfrère's article is a masterly synthesis of past and present knowledge about the Western uprising known as the War of the Vendée. Expertly translated by Malcolm Crook, it ranks among the clearest statements yet penned of what caused the revolt. Predictably enough, we learn that no single-factor explanation will suffice. The author confirms the accepted geography of the insurrection and, on the strength of his own researches, sharpens up its socio-economic contours. Viewed from this perspective, the rebellion reflected the mutual antagonisms of towns against villages, of peasants against bourgeois, and of losers against those who had done well out of the reforms of the Revolution. In consequence the subsequent civil war might easily be mistaken for a class struggle. However, Petitfrère is also alert to the intangibles in the equation: the cultural shock of the Civil Constitution of the Clergy; the regimenting effect of community pressure; and the under-representation of administrative and military authorities in the principal zones of insurrection. In short, the revolt was the product of a mix of frustrations in which mounting anger at the brusque enforcement of the Assembly's religious policy bulked large. The fact that it was allowed the time to develop into a full-scale war can be attributed to institutional weaknesses and the logistical shortcomings of Republican government throughout the region.

The War of the Vendée began in earnest just as a widespread disenchantment with the direction taken by the Revolution was coming to a head. This Federalist reflex (the term 'revolt' is a confusing misnomer) is the subject of Alan Forrest's contribution. At the simplest level, Federalism can be described as a campaign of civil disobedience waged for about three months during the summer of 1793 in which the local authorities of a large number of departments announced that they were no longer willing to accept the authority of central government. Ostensibly the justification for their action was the explusion from the National Convention of the Girondin deputies following the armed uprising of the Sections of Paris on 31 May to 2 June, but, as Forrest demonstrates, Federalism was largely a rhetorical invention of its enemies. It scarcely even amounted to the sum of its parts. In fact, he doubts whether a national, Girondist movement called Federalism ever existed (save perhaps in the minds of Bordeaux lawyers and merchants). So what was Federalism in reality? A reflex of political exasperation characteristic of sharply divided communities. Although indignation at the antics of Parisian demagogues supplied a veneer of unity, its origins were, in truth, local. Maybe this account defuses the threat posed by the Federalists to excess. After all, there was talk of relocating central government in a provincial town, and also some obstruction of the Republic's war effort. Nevertheless, Forrest's thoroughly researched paper provides a corrective to the standard, and still rather partisan, literature on the subject.

The pressures of war both simplified and complicated political life in frontier cities as the chapter drawn from Norman Hampson's biography of Saint-Just bears witness. Situated anywhere else but on the Rhine frontier, the Alsatians would have made ideal recruits to the Federalist cause (or worse heresies), but the presence of invading armies concentrated minds wonderfully. On the other hand, the conduct of political life beneath the all-seeing eye of the Committee of Public Safety brought its own problems. With powerful and determined *représentants-en-mission* billeted permanently in Strasbourg, none of the usual expedients employed by resident élites to deflect the attention of central government could be trusted to work. Indeed, Saint-Just and Le Bas soon dispensed with the services of local Jacobin administrators, preferring to rely on militants attracted from other parts of France. Yet there was also a price to be paid by central government in return for the services of the *représentants*. Overlapping jurisdictions, ill-defined powers, and delegated responsibilities all made for a perceptible loss of control. In this respect Hampson's focus on Saint-Just encapsulates the problems inherent in establishing Revolutionary Government during the autumn and winter of 1793. He brings out the frailties of policy formulation, and the haphazard manner in which change was implemented at the local level.

The activities of the *représentants* while on mission in the departments bulk large in the story of Thermidor as related by Martyn Lyons. Or to be precise, the activities of those *représentants* who were either slow or reluctant to acknowledge the shifting priorities of Revolutionary Government. Lyons is at pains to emphasize that the coup against Robespierre which was organized on 8 Thermidor and carried out the following day involved substantive issues of policy as well as personal fears and animosities. Some of the *représentants-en-mission*, like the Federalists before them, now appeared as symbolic obstacles on the path towards ever greater administrative centralization. However, the author is inclined to make more of policy disagreements on the subject of religion than have historians previously. Robespierre, it seems, was widely suspected of wishing to reinstate some form of quasi-catholic worship, notwithstanding the political risks that such a course of action would entail. At this juncture, Lyons brings the role of the Committee of General Security into the picture. He draws attention to the hefty contingent of anti-clericals in its midst, to the umbrella of police protection which it had extended to erstwhile *représentants-en-mission*, and to the well-known administrative tensions exacerbating relations with the Committee of Public Safety. All of these tensions, not to mention the excruciating build-up of individual resentments and misunderstandings, are closely analyzed. The final verdict – that the coup of 9 Thermidor was conceived by its chief architects as a blow from the Left – is persuasive. Yet it could have been made more so with further research into the roles played by Collot d'Herbois and Billaud-Varenne. Both of these conspirators had had close links with the Hebertists.

Note

1 *See* E. H. Lemay, *Dictionnaire des Constituants, 1789–1791* (2 vols., Oxford, Voltaire Foundation, and Paris, Universitas, 1991); B. M. Shapiro, *Revolutionary Justice in Paris, 1789–1790* (Cambridge, Cambridge University Press, 1993); M. P. Fitzsimmons, *The Remaking of France: The National Assembly and the Constitution of 1791* (Cambridge, Cambridge University Press, 1994).

16

Nobles and the Third Estate in the revolutionary dynamic of the National Assembly, 1789–1790

TIMOTHY TACKETT

For over two decades now, debate has raged between 'Marxists' and 'revisionists' over the question of the French Revolution. The outlines of this debate have become familiar even to historians with no particular expertise in eighteenth-century French studies. In place of the Marxist or Marxist-inspired vision of a revolution arising out of class conflict between nobility and bourgeoisie, most revisionists would stipulate a revolution 'caused' ultimately by the internal collapse of the monarchy. In this view, the nobles and the upper-class commoners were converging in the late eighteenth century into a single 'elite' group, bound by common economic interests and cultural experiences and by the substantial possibilities of social mobility into the nobility. When the two groups fell into conflict in 1789, it was either a kind of accidental aberration arising from misunderstandings, a difference in 'style,' or a failure of imagination and leadership.

Although most of the controversy to date has hinged on the question of revolutionary origins, François Furet, the leading French representative of revisionism, has also pushed a reconsideration of the revolutionary dynamic after the opening of the Estates General in May 1789. In his widely read and influential book, *Penser la Révolution*,[1] Furet argued that, once the revolution had begun, it was impelled forward through the workings not of a class struggle but of a power struggle [*see* Reading 2]. By June of 1789 and the creation of the National Assembly, the privileged orders, like the monarchy itself, had essentially 'capitulated,' and, by

Reprinted in full, except for notes and graph, from *The American Historical Review*, 94 (1989), pp. 271–301.

October, as Furet and Denis Richet wrote elsewhere, 'the battlefield had essentially been conquered, the fight was over: the revolution had been won.'[2] Thereafter, conflict within the National Assembly pitted various elements of the Third Estate against one another. The revolution was progressively democratized and radicalized as successive factions of Patriots each claimed to be the authentic voice of popular sovereignty, the true mouthpiece of the general will. Political struggle thus became a battle of rhetoric and of ideology – but with no class content. It also became a battle of denunciations, as each faction tried to outdo its opponents in its condemnations of 'aristocratic plots' and counterrevolutionary conspiracies. But, in Furet's view, these denunciations were largely contrived and the plots 'imaginary,' 'the figment of a frenzied pre-occupation with power,' and the indication also of an incipient terrorist mentality in evidence among the Patriots as early as 1789.[3]

But did the 'aristocrats' really capitulate and abandon the political struggle so soon? And were early revolutionary developments so totally devoid of social dimensions? I have no intention of considering Furet's complex and suggestive thesis in all its ramifications, or of attempting to treat every aspect of the revolution. Here, I would only present some of the results of recent research into factional organization and the revolutionary dynamic at the vital core of political life during the early revolution, the Constituent Assembly. In fact, despite the revisionist call for a return to politics – and despite the awesome number of studies devoted to this period in French history – the internal political life of France's first National Assembly is still rather poorly understood. This is true in part for historiographical reasons. Interest in the process and functioning of the Constituent Assembly has frequently been overshadowed by historians' tenacious fascination with the problem of the origins of the Republic and the Terror. But research has also been hampered by difficulties with sources. The official accounts of events within the assembly halls are often incomplete and tendentious. No minutes at all were maintained by the Third Estate through the second week in June, and, even after the appearance of official record keeping, minutes were commonly sanitized and abridged by the secretaries in power to promote a desired public impression of assembly activities. Moreover, the near absence of nominal roll-call votes – the principal meat of what once was called the 'new' history of parliamentary behavior – renders the careful quantitative assessment of deputy alignments all but impossible. Nevertheless, if it is not feasible to reconstitute voting records or follow the manifold, day-to-day fluctuations of every deputy, one can at least take note of such glimpses of collective behavior as revealed by the lists of adhesions to political clubs and the signatures on petitions. One can also make use of the incomplete records of the periodic elections of National Assembly officers – presidents, secretaries, and committee members. And, perhaps most important, one can examine the considerable number of accounts – many of them still only in manuscript – written by the deputies themselves in letters and memoirs to their families and home constituencies.

The earliest formation of political groupings within the Estates General will probably always remain somewhat uncertain. Yet the most important and influential of these could clearly trace their genealogies to the pre-revolutionary period. Within days of their arrival in Versailles, groups of liberal deputies of the second estate were regularly congregating at the residences of the Duc de La Rochefoucauld or the Marquis de Montesquiou or in the 'Viroflay Society' on the estates of the Duc de Piennes. A substantial number of the participants, perhaps the majority, were veterans of the Paris-based association of Patriots, the so-called Society of Thirty – from whose membership no fewer than twenty-six had successfully sought election to the Estates General [*see* Reading 11]. Most of these men were Parisians who had long known each other and who were linked through a dense network of association in masonic lodges, Mesmerist groups, and a variety of Enlightenment and philanthropic societies. Many nobles of the sword in the group were also bound together as outsiders to the clique of courtiers then in favor in Versailles. With considerable previous experience in political organization, young noblemen such as Adrien Duport, Charles and Alexandre de Lameth, the Marquis de Lafayette, and the Comte de Clermont-Tonnerre mapped the strategy that ultimately led to the secession of the liberal nobles from their order and their union with the Third Estate.

Several members of the 'Commoners' – Antoine Barnave, Jean-Paul Rabaut-Saint-Etienne, Abbé Emmanuel-Joseph Sieyès, for example – seem also to have attended meetings of the liberal noblemen. But the most celebrated and influential of the early Versailles clubs was in fact indigenous to the Third Estate. There is no need to repeat here the well-known history of the Breton Club. It should be emphasized, however, that many and perhaps most of the Breton deputies had previously participated in provincial estates or in the local committees that had coordinated opposition against the privileged orders and their attempts to dominate Breton affairs. Even before arriving in Versailles, the newly elected Third Estate delegations had met in Rennes to discuss strategy and many of the deputies then travelled to the capital together. After the opening of the Estates General, they followed a procedure apparently already practised during the last Estates of Brittany, debating important issues in a café each evening, arriving at a majority decision, deciding who would speak the next day in favor of that decision, and urging all participants to vote as a bloc. It was also the specific provincial context – coupled with the absence of all nobles and bishops from the delegation – that rendered the Breton representatives so exceptionally radical. From the earliest days of the

Estates General, they advocated a unilateral transformation of the Third
Estate into a 'salle nationale' or 'assemblée nationale' – anticipating by
some six weeks the famous motions by Abbé Sieyès to this effect.[4] Indeed,
for many in the Breton group, such a strategy was conceived not as a ploy
for forcing joint deliberation with the Nobles and Clergy but as the first
step in creating a constitution *without* the participation of the privileged
orders. They soon came to be identified with an unrestrained hatred of all
nobles: 'an extreme violence,' 'an implacable hatred of the nobility,' as two
of the more moderate deputies described it.[5]

Yet the Bretons' rapid rise to prominence in early June was by no means
inevitable and was rarely anticipated by contemporaries. Although the
Breton delegation began inviting representatives from other provinces to
participate in its meetings early on, many deputies expressed their aversion
and mistrust of the very idea of factions or 'cabals' or an 'esprit de parti,'
widely viewed as warping the representative process. The Lorraine landholder and sometime scholar Adrien Duquesnoy spoke harshly of the
Breton delegation as 'hotheads without measure and without moderation.' For the Bordeaux merchant Pierre-Paul Nairac, they were 'always
moving toward extreme positions,' while the Alsatian Etienne-François
Schwendt sharply criticized them for attempting to 'exercise a kind of
domination over all opinions.'[6] Others were clearly disconcerted by the
Bretons' abrasive attitude toward the nobility. In this, they reflected the
fears and ambiguities of men who were often socially and juridically at the
very frontier between noblemen and commoners. The majority had probably spent many years of their lives imitating aristocratic values and
patiently working within the aristocratic system. Whatever their views –
and perhaps rage – against the injustice or irrationality of such a society,
few had even dreamed that the system and its values could themselves be
changed. In any case, on May 18, the motion by the Breton Isaac-René-Guy
Le Chapelier, declaring that the deputies of the 'National Assembly' did
not represent specific orders but the whole nation, seems to have won the
support of only sixty-six deputies – of whom forty-three were from Le
Chapelier's own provincial delegation.

The spectacular success of the Bretons in early June was probably the
result of a number of factors. But, to believe the letters and diaries of the
deputies themselves, no single factor was more important than the growing
intransigence of the majority of the privileged deputies and their ultimate
refusal to consider compromise or reconciliation in any form over the
crucial question of voting procedure. For, in point of fact, the defenders
of privilege and tradition among the deputies, no less than the deputy-
Patriots, had also begun organizing in support of their positions. By the
end of May – and probably a good deal earlier – bishops in the first estate
were meeting with some regularity in the church of Notre-Dame in
Versailles. Many of the prelates had known one another for years and

were linked by ties of family as well as by a common educational experience at the seminary of Saint-Sulpice. They readily reactivated a miniature
version of the General Assembly of the Clergy – on which most of them
had long collaborated – and they were notably effective in countering the
activities of the more liberal curé-deputies, frustrating their efforts to unite
with the Third Estate until after the unilateral decision of that estate to
verify credentials in common.

Unlike the Clergy, the conservative and reactionary Nobles – the great
majority within the order – had no real institutional base on which to
build an effective organization. Nevertheless, a substantial number of the
Nobles undoubtedly knew one another prior to the convocation of the
Estates General. Historians have not previously noted that almost 40
percent of the Nobles were actually residents of Paris who had scattered
into the provinces to seek election in districts where their families owned
land and seigneuries. At least 78 percent of the Nobles had been educated
for the military and were or had previously been commissioned officers in
the army or navy. Close to two-thirds, moreover, could trace their families
back to at least the sixteenth century, while over half could apparently
prove lineage dating to the fourteenth century or earlier. They represented
most of the great families of France, and many were closely related to one
another – and to the equally aristocratic episcopal families – and had long
associated with one another at court and in Parisian societies. In short, the
Nobles of 1789 were an extraordinarily 'aristocratic' body in the full sense
of the word – considerably more so than their counterparts in the Estates
General of 1614. As a corps, they occupied a dramatically different sphere
of status and prestige – and probably of wealth – from that occupied by the
Third Estate. Although we know relatively few details about the political
workings of the Nobles during this period, the substantial blocs of votes
given to the winning candidates in the secret ballots for officers of the
order in June 1789 strongly suggest some measure of organization. Indeed,
the Marquis de Ferrières spoke of the 'club' of conservative noblemen, led
by Jean-Jacques Duval d'Eprémesnil – judge in Parlement and renegade ex-
associate of the Committee of Thirty – the Marquis de Bouthillier, and the
Vicomte de La Queuille. With the strong support and patronage of the
Comte d'Artois and the reactionary court faction, this group proved
remarkably successful through the end of June in maintaining the disciplined intransigence of the great majority of noble deputies. Indeed, several
of the originally 'liberal-leaning' noblemen, including some with statements of grievances (*cahiers de doléances*) mandating a vote by head in the
Estates General, are known to have been won over to the hard-line
position.

In any case, many of the Third Estate deputies became increasingly
convinced of the threat of such organization to the reforming desires of the
nation. The Breton deputy Jean-Pierre Boullé warned his constituents on

June 9 that the 'aristocratic committee' led by Eprémesnil was meeting daily to plot its strategy and that oganized action by the Patriots was necessary if the 'desires of the nation' were ever to triumph.[7] Even many of the normally moderate and prudent deputies – 'les hommes sages,' as they liked to call themselves – began commenting on the hopeless resistance to compromise on the part of the bishops and Nobles. With the 'aristocrats' of the first and second estates rejecting any form of conciliation, the Third ultimately had no choice, it was argued, but to pull together and go it alone. The self-consciously moderate Antoine Durand, a lawyer from Cahors, was outraged by the Nobles' statement of May 28, which accepted royal mediation but rejected in advance any discussion of a vote by head: the Nobles 'refuse to yield an inch of ground.' 'Those who have led the Nobles,' wrote the usually cautious judge Jean-Baptiste Grellet de Beauregard, 'have blocked all roads to compromise'; while his colleague from Toul, the *lieutenant général* Claude-Pierre Maillot, concluded that 'the violence of the Nobles' decisions have increased rather than weakened the determined resolution of the Third.' The wealthy landholder and mayor of Laon, Laurent de Visme, noted in his diary that under normal circumstances he would never have accepted Sieyès's motion of June 10, but now he was inclined to do so: 'The Nobles' actions have justified it.'[8]

The Breton Club probably reached the pinnacle of its ascendancy toward the middle and end of June. Boullé wrote on June 9 that 'during the last few days our salon has become the rallying point for all good citizens . .·. All the best citizens from all of the provinces are assembling there.' On that evening, the Breton group seems to have sent out delegates to argue its case within the individual *bureaux* – the small discussion groups into which the Assembly had recently divided itself – thus measurably contributing to the development of opinion in favor of the motion to be voted on the next day. To be sure, one should not underestimate the role played by the Abbé Sieyès himself, whose prestige and eloquent articulation of revolutionary objectives had an enormous impact on many of the deputies. But, in fact, each of Sieyès motions seems to have been discussed and debated in the Breton Club before being brought to the full assembly of the Third Estate, and the principles in question had been continuously advocated by the Breton delegation for well over a month. Once viewed with considerable mistrust by the majority of deputies, the Breton 'committee' now became the center of all political activity in the Third Estate. Impelled by the absolute intransigence of the Nobles and the apparent deadlock of the Clergy, buoyed and invigorated by the support of the Versailles crowds, the Third Estate achieved a remarkable consensus around the Tennis Court Oath and the revolutionary declarations of June 10, 17, and 23: a new definition of sovereignty and political legitimacy in open defiance of the monarchy that would probably have seemed impossible or unthinkable to most of the deputies just a few weeks earlier.

By all accounts, the period from late June to early August witnessed a substantial transformation of the political chemistry of the Assembly, a restructuring of many of the positions and alliances of the middle of June. Two developments in particular seem to have contributed to cracking the solidarity and apparent consensus of the nascent National Assembly. The first was the popular violence that exploded in the capital in mid-July but that continued in both Paris and the provinces well into August. In short order, the image of the 'people' held by many of the deputies – as revealed in their letters and diaries – was dramatically altered. The Rousseauist conception of the Common Man as repository of goodness and truth was frequently replaced, or at least strongly modified, by the image of the violent, unpredictable, and dangerous classes of July and August. To judge by the deputies' own writings, the most shocking event was usually not the storming of the Bastille on July 14 but the popular executions about a week later of the royal officials Joseph Foulon de Doué and Louis Berthier de Sauvigny, the details of which were luridly recounted in the Assembly by deputies who had witnessed them. Although several of the radicals revealed obvious sympathy for the past suffering of the people, and others were pushed by events toward a new, more expansive definition of the electorate they represented, the overall reaction was one of outrage and horror: 'barbarous and atrocious violence' (Visme), 'scenes of cruelty and horror' (the Third Estate deputies from Marseille), 'arbitrary ·executions that arouse horror' (Joseph Delaville Le Roulx from Brittany).[9] In any case, the July violence is known to have been a key factor in the movement of many deputies away from the more democratic vision of the new regime that had garnered increasing favor in June. It was certainly a major element in the changing position of the 'Monarchien' Jean-Joseph Mounier and his liberal noble ally, the Comte de Clermont-Tonnerre. Looking back on this event, Clermont-Tonnerre wrote in 1791: 'I feared that we were inciting atrocities; I remembered the St. Bartholomew's Day Massacre . . . and I sadly asked myself, 'Are we even worthy of being free?'[10]

The second development that contributed to breaking down the earlier consensus within the Third Estate was the entry of the privileged orders into the National Assembly. In point of fact, the process of integrating the first two estates into the Assembly was long and difficult. Even though a majority of the Clergy and a small minority of the Nobles came over to the Third of their own accord between June 22 and 26, the forced union of the remainder was nothing short of traumatic. Many of the recalcitrants were even ready to refuse the king's request for union on June 27, and it was only after receiving a warning from the Comte d'Artois that the king's life was in danger that they sullenly marched into the National Assembly, 'tears in their eyes, and rage and despair in their hearts.'[11] For the next three weeks, a significant minority of both the Nobles and the Clergy continued to boycott all votes and discussions and returned daily to their own meeting halls, frequently voting formal protests of decrees made in the Assembly. It was only after the Parisian insurrections of mid-July that the 'parti protestant' agreed to take part in the proceedings. 'Severed heads,' as one caustic deputy remarked, 'were frightfully instructive.'[12] But, even at that, it was early August before Jacques-Antoine-Marie de Cazalès and the Abbé Jean-Siffrein Maury and several other of the most conservative deputies who had fled – and, in many cases, been chased back by their own constituencies – formally announced their intention of participating in the National Assembly. Yet prolonged opposition of this kind was almost certainly not the norm. After the initial shock of June 27, the majority of the newly arrived clergy and noblemen seemed to adapt themselves to the situation with surprising grace. After a two-day break in late June, according to the Comte de La Gallissonnière, 'the deputies had calmed down a bit and were less frightened, and a new order of things seemed to appear.'[13] The Baron de Pinteville described the sharp reversal in sentiment of many of his colleagues who had long held back because of fear and pride and pressure from the reactionary 'party' but who were now swept by sentiments of patriotism and duty to the Nation: 'all was forgotten as they came forward with this act of self-sacrifice.'[14] For the Marquis de Ferrières, the experience was a revelation: nervous at first, he soon discovered that he was far more at ease with the commoners of the Third Estate than with the great court nobles, whom he had always detested. The Marquis de Guilhem-Clermont-Lodève, the Chevalier de Boufflers, Bishop Talleyrand, the bishop of Nancy, the archbishop of Aix, and numerous others made the transition with relative ease and were soon participating in the debates, some simply 'bending to the circumstances,' as Boufflers described it, others with a real measure of idealism and enthusiasm, convinced that 'the nobles . . . could be equally useful within the common hall of the Assembly.'[15]

It was not only these new recruits to the National Assembly who were affected. The entry of the privileged orders into their midst also had a profound effect on the deputies of the Third Estate. Numerous letters give expression to the explosion of joy and the feelings of fraternity with which the Third progressively welcomed the new arrivals. Whatever their rhetoric in late May and early June against the 'aristocrats,' the majority of the commoners were still awed by the great nobles and flattered that they might sit with them in the same assembly. Adrien Duquesnoy was effusive with praise for 'the finest names in the kingdom,' 'the most virtuous men in the kingdom,' who now gave the Assembly 'an aura of seriousness . . . that was previously lacking.' François-René-Pierre Ménard de la Groye, who had felt almost ashamed of his growing anger with the aristocrats in early June, again felt at ease when he dined with them and was delighted to observe 'a great deal of unity and cordiality among all the members of the Assembly.'[16]

Members of the Third Estate clearly went out of their way to encourage the participation of their new colleagues. The Vicomte de Malartic noted with evident satisfaction the deferential efforts of the commoners in his *bureau* to elicit his opinions on Saint-Domingue, where he had once lived. Félix Faulcon waxed poetic as he described the camaradarie of nobles and commoners spending the night together in the assembly hall during the mid-July crisis: 'These proud nobles, who once so greatly profited from their alleged privileges and the chance occurrence of their birth, now sleep or walk side by side with the commoners.'[17] The astute Ferrières rapidly sized up the new situation. 'The Upper Third will be flattered,' he wrote his sister, 'by the consideration shown them by the Nobles . . . Let the Nobles take a single step and the Third will take ten.'[18] Despite their suspicions of the 'aristocrats' and the latter's pretensions of social superiority and political dominance, the Commoners' ultimate desire at this stage in events was not to destroy the Nobles but to be treated by that body as equals. Indeed, this surge of fraternal sentiments among the orders should not be underestimated in evaluating the night of August 4, the dramatic session during which substantial portions of Old Regime institutions were swept away in the space of a few hours. Even though most interpretations of the event emphasize the behind-the-scenes manipulations of the Breton Club, it is doubtful that such tactics would have been effective without the short-lived atmosphere of brotherhood that permeated much of the Assembly in early August.

Only a few of the Third Estate deputies, several of them future Jacobins, seem to have viewed the situation with a more cynical eye. The Breton deputy Delaville Le Roulx despaired that the Assembly would be 'captivated by the seductive manners' of the Nobles and bishops and wondered how the Patriots might 'bring fresh energy to the Assembly and prevent it from slipping into error.' Maillot noted that the 'flattery and familiarity' of the privileged were more dangerous than their previous 'arrogance and pride.' And Jacques-Antoine Creuzé-Latouche, who had never wanted a union of the three orders in the first place, and who would have preferred that the Third Estate act on its own to write a constitution, saw only divisions ahead in the Assembly. 'Feeble individuals,' he wrote, previously brought into conformity with correct principles by the 'vigorous and virile' in the Assembly would now be won over by the nobles, and 'aristocratic and antipatriotic maxims' would become the order of the day.[19]

Creuzé's fears were probably not unfounded. After the heroic days of the early revolution, there is considerable evidence that the Breton Club's influence went into decline. Whether or not the number of adherents actually diminished, the entry of 600 new deputies into the National

Assembly – most of whom were clearly conservatives or moderates – invariably decreased the proportionate size of the radical contingent and reduced their hold on the large bloc of moderate Patriots within the Third Estate. In fact, by September, the 'comité breton' seems to have reverted to an exclusively provincial organization, no longer attended by deputies from other provinces. It was apparently badly divided over the issue of the royal veto and was meeting less frequently than before. Undoubtedly, the Patriots continued to meet to plan strategy in one way or another, but the meetings probably took place outside any formal organization. The Provencal deputy, Jacques-Athanase de Lombard-Taradeau, who openly aligned himself with the most advanced faction of the Patriots, never referred to the 'Breton Club' after July but only to 'what we call the "Palais royal" of the Assembly' or simply 'our party.' And his descriptions of the group's operations portray an extremely loose factional organization improvised on the spot, 'in the morning, before the beginning of the session, after much discussion among groups in the hall.' Indeed, if Lombard's accounts are at all typical, it seems likely that the lengthy hours passed in the National Assembly and in the various discussion groups and committees throughout the months of August and September, the sheer fatigue from the work involved, made nightly club meetings substantially more difficult.[20]

One indication of the decline in the Breton group's fortunes and the general movement of deputy opinion during this period comes – in the absence of roll-call records – from the various elections of officers to the National Assembly. The organizational regulations of the Assembly specified that every two weeks the deputies would meet in their *bureaux* – the thirty discussion groups, to which all members were assigned – to vote for a president and three secretaries. The president would serve for a two-week period and would be chosen in multiple ballots if necessary – in an effort to obtain a winner by absolute majority; the secretaries would be chosen by simple plurality on a single vote and would hold office for a month (so that there were always six secretaries in service at a given moment). Although a great deal depended on the personalities of the individuals holding the posts, all the officers had considerable potential power: the president to set the order of debate and designate – or reject – speakers, the secretaries to control the minutes of the meetings and to sort correspondence and decide which letters and petitions went to which committees. Since the votes were organized through the thirty individual *bureaux* – in isolation from the pressures of the galleries – and were apparently taken by secret ballot, they can be interpreted as a useful index of the evolution of deputy sentiment and perhaps also of the degree of organization of the various political factions.

The earliest elections seem generally to confirm the atmosphere of a united front previously identified for this period. To be sure, with the possible exception of the Abbé de Montesquiou, Agent-General of the Clergy, all fourteen of the individuals elected as officers between July 3 and August 3 had earlier reputations as Patriots. But while four of these – Le Chapelier, Sieyès, the Abbé Henri Grégoire, and Jérôme Pétion de Villeneuve – were probably considered radicals and later became members of the Jacobin Club, six others would undoubtedly have been classed as moderates, and four – Clermont-Tonnerre, Mounier, the Comte de Lally-Tollendal, and the Abbé de Montesquiou – soon embraced the more conservative 'Monarchiens' position. Perhaps equally significant, no less than ten of the fourteen were members of the privileged orders – though not all had actually been elected by their 'natural' estates. This marked preference for nobles and clergymen as assembly officers continued throughout the entire first year of the Constituent Assembly with nineteen of twenty-seven presidents and fifty-one of eighty-eight secretaries being drawn from members of the first two estates. The first three presidential contests were scarcely contests at all, with votes going overwhelmingly to the Duc d'Orléans (who declined), the archbishop of Vienne, and the Duc de Liancourt. The first and only Breton Club president, the Rennes lawyer Le Chapelier, obtained the post almost by accident in early August. In fact, he had come in third in the initial contest and was chosen in a second election only after the victor, the moderate Jacques-Guillaume Thouret, had resigned. And it was to be the last time a member of the Left would control the rostrum for almost seven months. Through the end of the year, the future Jacobins were largely an insignificant force in the presidential tallies, their candidates unable to muster more than 183 votes (out of over a thousand) in any of the elections for which voting totals are preserved. Indeed, to judge by the deputies elected to office from mid-August to mid-October, the best organized and most influential faction within the Assembly was not on the Left at all but on the Right.

Throughout the month of July, the organization of the recalcitrant privileged faction seems never entirely to have dissolved, despite the popular upheavals and the temporary flight of many of its adherents. Even after the meeting halls of the Nobles and the Clergy had been closed and converted into offices by Jacques Necker, director-general of finance, a core of the most conservative noblemen and bishops continued to meet in the homes of individuals. They were clearly acting as a corps on July 16 when they announced to the Assembly that they would henceforth join in the votes and the debates. It was most likely this same coalition that then coordinated the considerable deputy discipline involved in placing several of its numbers on the new Committee on Research at the end of July and in the election of Thouret to the presidency at the beginning of August. Significantly, it was toward the beginning of August that several Patriots first took note of the 'cabal' of nobles and clergy that was opposing them and voting as a bloc.

An initial turning point in the new evolution was undoubtedly the night of August 4. While in some respects this sweeping attack on privilege marked the ultimate fruition of the earlier flowering of fraternal generosity, it also carried with it the seeds of renewed factional strife. To judge by the reflections of the deputy letter writers, the suppression of seigneurial rights was accepted with resignation and sometimes with enthusiasm. 'If it leads to advantages for the public good,' wrote Ferrières to his wife, 'I will easily be able to console myself for my losses as a noble and as a seigneurial lord.' The chevalier Garron de la Bévière was more morose about the economic prospects of his order, but he, too, in a letter to his wife, accepted the inevitable: 'In the end, if it will promote general happiness, I have no regrets . . . One must yield to necessity.'[21] Yet large numbers of the clerical deputies were clearly upset by the suppression of the tithes without reimbursement and by the first proposals for the nationalization of church property. According to numerous witnesses, however, the key issue that united many of the nobles and clergymen as a solid and cohesive group was the debate two weeks later over including religious toleration in the Declaration of the Rights of Man and the Citizen and the counterproposal that Catholicism be made the state religion. In what were widely described as the most tumultuous debates to date, a number of deputies in all three estates seem to have dramatically crystallized their opposition to the revolution. Thus curé Emmanuel Barbotin, previously a strong supporter of the Third Estate, now became convinced that many Third Estate deputies were 'philosophers who have neither faith nor discipline'; while Guilluame Gontier de Biran, a chief *bailliage* magistrate from Bergerac, first came to perceive a dual menace to religion and the throne. For the Baron de Gauville – who had been irritated by the loss of his hunting rights on August 4 but who had generally accepted the abolition of seigneurial dues – it was precisely during these debates of late August that 'we began to recognize one another' and that he and his colleagues began sitting together consistently on the right side of the president's table.[22]

Nevertheless, the critical achievement in the organization of the Right was to be the work of a new coalition of more moderate conservatives, a number of them recruited from the Third Estate. The formation and general character of the 'Monarchiens' have been described in some detail by Jean Egret and, more recently, by Robert Griffiths. Unlike the extreme right of the recalcitrant Nobles and Clergy, who sought either a return to the Old Regime or a system of reforms based on the king's declaration of June 23, the Monarchiens sought to affirm the transformations of that summer but to ensure that ultimate sovereignty remained in the hands of the king as a buttress against the dangers of popular violence. Centered on the delegation from Dauphiné – the only provincial delegation that could match the Bretons in its cohesiveness and its tradition of group action – but also including important contingents from Auvergne and Normandy and a bevy of moderate nobles, the group resolved sometime in late July or early August to beat the Breton Club at its own game. In relatively short order, the Monarchiens had surpassed the Patriots in their level of factional organization. While the Breton Club had operated in an essentially democratic fashion, with relatively loose discipline and public debates in a café to which all were invited, the Monarchiens followed their more authoritarian and hierarchical penchant by establishing a small decision-making 'central committee,' which convened in private at one of the member's homes – and sometimes in the château of Versailles itself – and which then sent out directives through a system of subcommittees to all its potential adherents. Before votes in the *bureaux* for committee members or National Assembly officers, someone passed out notes listing the names that deputies were to inscribe on their ballots. On the floor of the National Assembly, Mounier's friend and colleague from Dauphiné, the Comte de Virieu, assumed the role of a veritable party whip: 'he can be seen in every corner of the hall, speaking, entreating, shouting, peering to see who will vote for or against.'[23] By early September, the progressively tighter coalition between moderate and extreme right was clearly in place, with Cazalès, Eprémesnil, and the Abbé Maury participating in the Monarchien central committee and speaking frequently in the Assembly in defence of Monarchien positions. On September 17, the radical printer-deputy from Lyon, Jean-André Périsse-Duluc, wrote that 'the coalition of nearly all of the Clergy and the Nobles, along with a lesser number of Commoners, has become so strong that the deputies involved never differ on their votes: without exception, all of them rise together or remain seated [in order to vote].'[24] Clearly, many of the 'aristocrats' were increasingly prepared to follow the rules of the game and work within the newly evolved parliamentary system, convinced of the real possibility of halting and perhaps reversing the revolution through political organization and majority votes.

The growing power of this new coalition was apparent in the choice of Assembly officers. After the middle of August, the Monarchiens not only won four successive presidential elections but also largely dominated the secretariat's table as well. In the election of August 31, they even obtained a clean sweep of the president – the bishop of Langres – and all three secretaries. Indeed, there is good evidence that the Monarchien coalition was the only group systematically organizing for elections during this period. The scraps of voting records remaining reveal that, in September, the Monarchien candidates alone received significant blocs of votes in every *bureau*, the remainder of the votes being spread out over an enormous range of individual deputies. 'For three weeks now,' wrote Virieu after the election of the bishop of Langres, 'the reasonable and upright deputies have quietly reclaimed the majority. The *enragés* have been beaten back on all fronts. In spite of their efforts, we have chosen the president and all three secretaries.'[25] The election in mid-September of the Monarchien Comte de Clermont-Tonnerre was perhaps even more galling to the Left in that, by the rotation procedure tacitly agreed on since July, the post should normally have gone to a member of the Third Estate.

To be sure, the coalition was frequently more successful in the electoral *bureaux* than on the floor of the Assembly itself, and it came up short on several of the key constitutional votes for which it militated with particular fervor – above all, the effort in early September to obtain a two-house legislature and an absolute royal veto on all legislation. Indeed, the alliance would seem to have broken down entirely on the issue of the number of chambers, with the extreme right apparently following a *politique du pire* and voting with the Patriots. But most of the deputies perceived the veto decision as a compromise vote between the Right's desire for an absolute veto and the Left's desire for no veto at all. And the Monarchiens and their allies won a considerable victory later in the month when it was decided that three successive legislatures would have to pass the same law in order to override a royal veto – a complication considered by some as tantamount to an absolute veto.

In any event, the deputies of the Left clearly believed themselves under siege from late August to early October. Lombard wrote home that 'our party is absolutely in the minority.' Louis-Prosper Lofficiel was convinced that, without the support of about forty clergymen and a hundred or so liberal nobles, 'we would certainly be defeated' on every vote. Périsse estimated that as many as two-thirds of all the deputies were influenced by the 'cabal' – although fortunately half of these were open-minded and could sometimes be won over.[26] For the celebrated writer, Constantin-François Chassebeuf de Volney, deputy from Anjou, the Assembly was now so divided and in danger of being won over by the aristocrats that it was necessary to elect a whole new assembly and a new set of deputies, chosen this time to represent the true social composition of the French population – notably, by eliminating most of the noble and clerical deputies. And after losing the vote on the manner of overriding a royal veto, the delegation from Brittany seriously discussed abandoning the Assembly altogether, an Assembly now deemed to be entirely dominated by the 'aristocrats'.

The political history of the Constituent Assembly after the dramatic events of October 5–6 – the march on Versailles that led to the transfer of both monarchy and Assembly to Paris – is generally less well known than the earlier period of the revolution. Many series of correspondence ended in the later half of 1789 or toward the beginning of the following year, as deputies found themselves burdened with ever-increasing demands on their time and as a growing national distribution of newspapers removed one of the principal *raisons d'être* for the letters home.

Nevertheless, it seems clear that the October Days did not mark the demise of the Right as a meaningful force in the National Assembly. The mass desertion of the conservative deputies – 300 are sometimes said to have taken out passports – is apparently a myth, altogether unsubstantiated by the evidence available. Although four of the Monarchien leaders did indeed leave the Assembly, Pierre-Victor Malouet, Clermont-Tonnerre, Virieu, and their associates continued their efforts on behalf of the Monarchien platform to the very end of the Constituent Assembly. Together, they formed first a 'Club des Impartiaux' and later a 'Club Monarchique.' Despite his initial despondency over the October events, Virieu ultimately repudiated the desertion of his friend Mounier and vowed to fight on: 'the sacred flame that burns within me is not yet extinguished, and is reviving . . . ' 'I will stay with the Assembly,' wrote Archbishop Boisgelin, 'and I will go with it [to Paris].' Gontier de Biran also affirmed his determination to stay on despite his anguish and disappointment over the events: 'I think that if it were not for the honour and desire of doing our duty, few of us would remain here.'[27]

For the next few months, the focus of power seemed to shift back toward the center of the political spectrum, with the unaligned 'Center' Patriots – Emmanuel-Marie Fréteau de Saint-Just, Armand-Gaston Camus, Thouret, and Jean-Nicolas Démeunier – picking up five of the six presidencies to the end of the year. Yet the factional organization, the very considerable coordinating capabilities created by the Monarchiens, seem to have been maintained. On occasion, the group was still able to elect its candidates as president: Boisgelin in November and the Abbé de Montesquiou in early January. Basking in his recent victory, the prelate congratulated himself for having rejected all the predictions of doom by Mounier and Lally-Tollendal and for having stayed on to fight. Where would he be now, he mused, 'if I had listened to the advice everyone was giving me?'[28] Like many other deputies, he was convinced that the decree of November 2 placing ecclesiastical lands 'at the disposal of the Nation' was actually a victory for his side. Everyone knew that some church lands would have to be sold, he wrote, but they had succeeded in simply admitting the principle without in any way turning all lands over to the state: 'They will perhaps be satisfied to sell off monastic property.'[29] The Monarchiens and their allies also continued to obtain election of their adherents to various committees, culminating in a dramatic vote in late November that gave them effective control of the powerful organ of investigation and repression, the Committee on Research.

Yet the October Days may well have marked the beginning of a certain shift within the Right coalition in favor of the more reactionary elements.

This evolution is particularly evident if one examines the breakdown of those deputies actually participating in Assembly debates – as suggested by entries in the index to the proceedings and debates of the Constituent Assembly. The frequency of participation of the Monarchiens dropped precipitously from September to March, continuing downward even after the departure of the four Monarchien leaders in October. During the same period, the most notable speakers of the extreme right were participating ever more frequently, so that from early 1790 to the end of the Constituent Assembly they had become the principal spokesmen for the Right. Unfortunately, much less is known of the factional organization of the extreme right during this period. But the religious issue, and particularly the question of church property seems increasingly to have become the central rallying point in binding together the most conservative elements of the Nobles, the Clergy, and the Commoners – or such, at least, was the opinion of the conservative Baron de Gauville.

Significantly – in the midst of the debates over ecclesiastical land and monastic vows – the group began holding its meetings in the Grands Augustins, in the same hall where the bishops had been accustomed to holding their *Assemblées générales* for generations. Here, according to the elderly Patriot lawyer René-Antoine-Hyacinthe Thibaudeau, 'They began by preparing in their committees the insidious measures that they then try to push through the Assembly.'[30] When the faction was forced to leave under the pressures of the Parisian crowds, they took refuge in the Capuchin monastery, which was directly attached to the assembly hall and which allowed the deputies to enter through a private passageway unseen by the crowds outside. It was here that the 'Capuchin Society' – as they came to be known – drew up their declaration of April 19, 1790, adhering to Dom Christophe-Antoine Gerle's motion six days earlier that Roman Catholicism be declared the state religion. Chased away once again by the Parisian crowds, the group seems to have continued its coordination in more secretive fashion through a series of small 'committees' that met in the homes of individuals, each committee delegating one of its members as liaison with a central steering committee. On occasion, they seem also to have met jointly with the Club des Impartiaux – confirming a continued loose alliance between the two alignments on the Right.

By the spring of 1790, there were already numerous signs of a shift of the Assembly's center of gravity in the direction of the Left. To believe the analysis of Visme, at the beginning of December the deputies were divided almost exactly into two equal parts. In the important vote of December 7, when the radicals attempted to revise the election laws to promote broader political participation, 'the Assembly divided into two almost equal parts sitting at opposite ends of the hall.'[31] And Périsse-Duluc noted the hesitancy of the Left to have any of its adherents sent out as *commissaires du roi* to organize the new local governments, for fear that the absence of even a few Patriots would tip the balance in favor of the Right. But, by late December and early January, a number of deputies from various points on the political spectrum were becoming aware of an evident erosion of the Right. By year's end, the Protestant banker from Lyon, Guillaume-Benoît Couderc, was convinced that 'the aristocratic influence in the hall is declining appreciably from day to day.' The Patriot curé Thomas Lindet concurred: 'The opposition party is diminishing . . . It is winning some small victories, but it is losing the major questions.' And Delaville, so pessimistic for the Left the previous September, now suggested, for the first time, that his 'party' was clearly in control of the situation: 'les hommes forts,' as he described them. 'Those who know anything of the Assembly' wrote Duquesnoy, 'cannot help but notice the progressive desertion and depopulation of that part of the hall where the Abbé Maury sits, and that there is no longer a sufficient number of seats at the other side of the hall.' By mid-January, the Assembly staff was having to install more benches on the Left to accommodate all the new arrivals.[32] To be sure, the Right retained a considerable residual strength through at least the middle of 1790 and was able to attract enough votes from the still rather volatile uncommitted deputies to win several presidential elections and a certain number of constitutional votes. Indeed, from late February through the middle of July, the elections suggest an Assembly more polarized than ever before. One might be tempted to speak of a veritable two-party system during this period, with nine of the eleven presidential victories going to either the Jacobin or the Capuchin candidates. But, by and large, the momentum and the initiative within the Assembly were increasingly passing to the left of hall.

The reasons for this evolution at this particular moment in the Assembly's history are not entirely clear. It was related in part, no doubt, to the increasing dominance within the Right of the most reactionary strand of conservatism, the strand associated in the minds of most deputies with the trio of Maury, Cazalès, and Eprémesnil. Many of the Monarchiens had built earlier reputations as patriots and reformist leaders. But the leaders of the opposition most in evidence by the end of 1789 had been identified from the beginning with a complete return to the Old Regime. As Duquesnoy suggested, far fewer people wanted to sit on the Right when the Abbé Maury became the central figure on his side of the hall. The situation was compounded in that the geography of the new meeting hall in Paris no longer provided any intermediate places in which to sit. The hall in Versailles had been essentially oval in its layout, while the long, narrow 'Manège,' divided in the middle by the speaker's platform and the president's table, forced every deputy to make a daily symbolic affirmation as to which side he was on.

Yet perhaps the single most important development in the resurgence of the Left was the formation in late November or early December of the

Jacobin Club and the rapid emergence of this association as a highly organized political force. In fact, the new *société* was not – as is often suggested – the simple continuation of the Breton Club, transferred from Versailles to Paris. By the end of the summer, the Breton group had already lost its character as the central rallying point for all Patriots. Once in Paris, the Bretons apparently continued their separate meetings for a time even after the creation of the Friends of the Constitution. Although a great many of the members of the new association had probably also been members of the earlier Breton Club, the Jacobins created a new kind of Patriot structure, more highly centralized and organized, patterned in many respects after the organization of the Right. Indeed, according to Louis-Marie de La Reveillière-Lépeaux, the initial formation of the Jacobin Club in late November was in direct response to the organizational offensive of the Right. Everyone knew, wrote La Reveillière, that 'the aristocratic party normally chose the Assembly officers because it held meetings in which it was decided in advance who was to be elected.' For this reason, the Left 'decided to hold meetings of their own so that they could ensure the Patriots' control of the *bureau*.'[33]

The details of this organization are still poorly known. It seems certain, however, that in addition to their general public meetings in the Dominican convent, the Jacobins created a central committee with prime responsibilities for guiding the general direction of the club and set up a far more efficient means of disciplining voting. But if, in many respects, they simply emulated the organization of the Monarchiens, the Jacobins also went beyond the Right in their efforts to systematically mobilize public opinion in favor of their initiatives through the creation of a correspondence committee as liaison with affiliated clubs in the provinces. It was almost certainly this new organization that allowed the Jacobins to increase their influence in the election of Assembly officers – first, from November onward, the secretaries and, by March 1790, the presidents as well. The same organization enabled the Left to begin systematically taking control of most of the committees. Thus, in the December election of the Committee on Research, the club engineered a dramatic turnabout, with the elimination of all the deputies on the Right and their replacement by twelve known Patriots, eight of whom were Jacobins. While in 1789 they obtained only a fourth of the committee assignments, in 1790 the Jacobin group was able to gain half of all new positions. Over the same period, the deputies on the Right saw their share of committee posts decline from one-fifth to less than one-tenth of all assignments.

By the early weeks of 1790, both outside observers and the deputies themselves were aware of the growing polarization of the National Assembly and of the extent to which developments in that assembly were increasingly dominated by two politicized and well-organized 'parties.'

As *L'Observateur* remarked, 'For the last month, two associations have existed in Paris. Each is composed of members of the National Assembly. The first . . . meets in the Jacobins of the *rue Saint-Honoré*; the second . . . meets in the *Grands-Augustins*. Both have a numerous membership; both are a source of uneasiness for Parisians from the influence they may have over the National Assembly.'[34] Lindet, in a letter to his brother, expressed it even more simply. 'A singular division reigns in the Assembly: the hall has become a battlefield where two enemy armies face one another.'[35]

But who were these two armies? What differences can one find in the character and composition of their respective contingents? Unfortunately, the participants in the Breton Club and the Monarchien group will probably never be known for certain. Membership in the Jacobin group can be generally reconstructed, however, through the research of Alphonse Aulard. Based on this source, 205 Constituent Assembly deputies would seem to have adhered to the 'Amis de la Constitution' in the months following December 1790. Although membership had undoubtedly varied somewhat since the club first formed in late 1789, this number is surprisingly close to the round figure of 200 who were supporting Jacobin candidates for committee assignments in April 1790. As for the 'Capuchins Society,' a substantial portion of its participation can be ascertained from the petition signed during the faction's meeting on April 19. Even though the specific object of the petition, the maintenance of Catholicism as the sole state religion, may have prevented the association of a few anticlerical conservatives – like the Marquis de Ferrières – the petition remains the best single record of factional adhesion to the Capuchins for the first half of 1790. In all, 292 deputies signed this document – suggesting an alignment on the Right significantly larger than the Jacobin group.

A preliminary analysis of the two groups of deputies suggests that the collective biographies of the Capuchins, on the one hand, and the Jacobins, on the other, were in certain respects dramatically different. Without a doubt, the most salient distinction was the remarkable alignment by Old Regime estate. More than eight out of ten Jacobins were deputies of the Third Estate, while more than nine out of ten Capuchins represented the two privileged orders. Indeed, among the handful of twenty-three Third Estate deputies belonging to the Capuchins, a third were actually nobles or clergymen who had been elected by the commoners. To be sure, the single largest contingent of Capuchins – slightly over half – were clergymen. They included almost all of the bishops, as well as some 40 percent of the parish priests in the Assembly. We have already noted the importance of opposition to the Constituent Assembly's religious policies in the general cohesion of the group. It is not surprising that the coalition soon came generally to be known as 'les noirs.' Yet if one includes the deputies from all three estates, some 54 percent of the Capuchins are found to have come from noble families. And of these, two-thirds were true 'aristocrats' who could trace back their lineage to the sixteenth century or earlier. Much can be made of the relatively modest family backgrounds of the three most visible leaders of the Right: Maury, Cazalès, and Eprémesnil – the first a commoner, the second two of first-generation nobility. Yet one should also not overlook the strong 'aristocratic' imprint on the Capuchins as a whole – aristocratic not only in the revolutionary meaning of 'conservative ideology' but with the older implication of ancient social or caste origins. Beyond Maury, Cazalès, and Eprémesnil, seven of the ten most common Capuchin speakers originated in families of this kind.

As for the Jacobins in the Assembly, the commoners among them – the vast majority – differed very little in their social contours from the Third Estate deputies as a whole. There was, however, a distinct over-representation of those calling themselves 'avocats' and a corresponding under-representation of the various categories of royal officeholders. Unfortunately, the socioeconomic position of the 'lawyers' in question is difficult to define and was almost certainly very diverse – from practising court lawyers to wealthy landowners who had never set foot in a court and whose law degrees were essentially symbols of status. The paucity of officeholders among the Jacobins is not insignificant, however, in that many of them – particularly the royal magistrates – occupied what was perhaps the highest status level of the entire Third Estate. They were also among those Commoners deputies with the greatest vested interests in the Old Regime. In all, only eleven clergymen and forty-two noblemen – representing any of the three estates – had thrown in their lots with the Jacobins. A few of the nobles – the Duc d'Aiguillon, the Vicomte de Noailles, the brothers Lameth, for example – were from among the greatest families of the kingdom. Of the central club leadership, both Alexandre Lameth and the parlementary magistrate Adrien Duport had been members of the second estate. It is significant, nevertheless, that this small group of Jacobin nobles was distinctly less 'aristocratic' than the large contingent of Capuchin nobles, with only a little over one-third holding titles dating before the seventeenth century. Indeed, almost half of all the newly ennobled Third Estate deputies – eighteen of thirty-eight – joined the Jacobins. Among the twelve most important leaders of the Constituent Assembly from the Jacobin deputies, those participating most frequently in National Assembly debates, only one – the Comte de Mirabeau – was an 'aristocrat' by birth.

Beyond the question of social differences, a preliminary prosopography would suggest two other ways in which the two political factions can be distinguished. In the first place, Capuchins and Jacobins would seem to have had somewhat differing residences. A full 26 percent of the Capuchins, compared to only 11 percent of the Jacobins, are known to have lived in Paris. Most of the Parisian Capuchins in question were in fact from great noble families who had won election in provincial *bailliages* by virtue of their names and status. Half of the Jacobins, by contrast – compared to only 30 percent of the Capuchins – came from small to medium-size provincial towns, with populations from 2,000 to 50,000 inhabitants. Among those Capuchins who did come from the provinces, however, a significantly larger proportion came from southern France – south of a line between La Rochelle and Geneva – and notably from the Massif Central and other interior provinces of the Midi, regions that were among the most isolated and economically backward in the kingdom.

In the second place, the Capuchins were distinctly older, on the average, than their opponents. Among those deputies for whom dates of birth are known, the Jacobins averaged 43.2 years old in 1790, three years younger than the average for all deputies, while the Capuchins averaged 49.5. Indeed, among the totality of the youngest deputies, those under thirty at the beginning of the revolution, no less than 40 percent adhered to the Jacobins – compared to 11 percent who associated with the Capuchins. Among those deputies over sixty-five at the opening of the Estates General, 28 percent became Capuchins and only 5 percent became Jacobins. Moreover, such differences cut across all three orders: the average ages of Jacobin clergymen, Jacobin noblemen, and Jacobin commoners were all lower than their respective counterparts within the rival faction. The differences were particularly dramatic among the small group of radical nobles, whose mean age was nearly ten years younger than that of their noble colleagues on the right side of the hall. A generational effect was clearly operational in the radicalism and conservatism of many of the deputies.

Factional confrontations between Left and Right continued as a characteristic feature of the Constituent Assembly to the very end of that body's existence in September 1791. Indeed, to judge by the [frequency of participation], the principal speakers on the Right were never more active than during the spring of 1791. Yet the political influence of the conservative coalition within the Assembly was ebbing sharply by the middle of 1790. Two extraordinary successes by the Patriots at the beginning of the summer undoubtedly contributed to breaking the momentum and the energy of the Capuchin–Impartial alliance: the formal suppression of the nobility on June 20 and the passage of the Civil Constitution of the Clergy three weeks later. Taken together, the two measures fostered a deep sense of fatalism and demoralization on the part of many of the deputies of the Clergy and the Nobles. The last president elected by the Right retired from office in the middle of July. From September of that year – after a succession of moderate Patriots – the Jacobins effectively came to dominate the presidency, as they already controlled the secretariat, through the end of the Constituent Assembly. By November, the Jacobin curé Lindet could write to his brother, 'The aristocracy no longer has an influence, it seems to me, on the choice of Assembly officers.'[36]

Yet the rise of the Jacobins to preeminence within the National Assembly had been neither rapid nor inevitable. Their triumph, if triumph it was, came not in 1789 – as it is usually suggested – but only in the second half of 1790. And the chronology is significant. Events during that first formative year of the revolution helped set the tone of the parliamentary process and establish many of the basic political presuppositions for years to come. Far from capitulating, the representatives of privilege and conservatism had asserted a dynamic presence within the Estates General and the National Assembly from the very beginning. Many of the reactionary deputies of the Clergy and the Nobles, whose initial intransigence had greatly contributed in crystallizing the revolutionary sentiment of June 1789, had eventually been won over by the successful organizational achievements of the Monarchiens and, rapidly adapting to circumstances, had set out in an alliance with the more moderate conservatives to exploit to their advantage the new system and its rules. Learning from the methods of the Breton Club, this coalition had soon taken the initiative, pioneering many of the electoral tactics usually attributed to the Jacobins, and playing a key role in the transformation of the more archaic Old Regime faction into a first sketch of the modern political party. In their heyday, their numbers closely matched – were actually somewhat superior to – those of the Jacobins, and they could feel justified in their ambition to win over a sufficient number of the nonaligned moderate majority to seize control of the Assembly. The Monarchien Malouet certainly believed this was possible, and he speculated, many years later, on what might have happened if a relatively small number of deputies on the Right had not decided to abandon the battle so early in the revolution. The Jacobin leader Alexandre Lameth made much the same argument, musing that the presence in the Estates General of deputies from the Breton nobility and upper clergy – groups that had boycotted the elections in the spring of 1789 – might have entirely transformed the situation.

Inevitably, the Patriots were intensely aware of the offensive of the Right and often, understandably, felt harried and besieged. They were also clearly conscious of the social composition of the group that opposed them at the other end of the hall. It was not a question of mere rhetoric, of the Jacobins concocting imaginary machinations by the aristocrats. In fact they faced genuine, genealogically certified aristocrats, swords at their sides, day after day in the Assembly itself: aristocrats who, for a time, were prominent elements in a highly organized political faction or alliance of factions, and who, for a time, could harbor the plausible hope of a 'legal' counterrevolution engineered through the Constituent Assembly itself. Little wonder that the Patriots on the Left soon felt compelled to match the organization of the Right with their own, highly centralized party organization. Little wonder that many deputies on the Left came to view all opposition parties as dangerous and illegal, and that the very concept of a 'loyal opposition' failed to develop in the early revolution. Obviously, a close 'internal' analysis of this kind does not answer all the questions about the dynamics of the revolution, or even about the dynamics of the National Assembly. A more general synthesis will have to take into account those exogenous factors – economic trends, crowd activities, international relations, and the pressures of newspapers, clubs, home constituencies, and Parisian assemblies – all those forces that exerted an overwhelming impact on revolutionary developments as a whole. A broader account will also have to confront the seemingly intractable problem of the influence of prerevolutionary ideologies on the men of 1789.

But the approach taken here does reveal the extent to which the political behavior of a significant and highly influential – if minority – segment of the National Assembly was associated with social divisions among the deputies. To be sure, the social divisions operative were not those of class. Most of the Nobles and most of the wealthy commoners who represented the Third Estate – as revisionist historians never tire of demonstrating – had basically similar relationships to the means of production. A Marxian analysis, whatever its utility for explaining other aspects of the revolution, is ultimately not very useful for the problems of the National Assembly. It seems likely that, for understanding social interaction within the Constituent Assembly, an analysis based on a complex of categories – such as wealth, status, education, and previous political experience – will prove far more helpful. In terms of the subjective element of status within the traditional value system – a value system with which the deputies, as revealed in their letters, long maintained an ambiguous relationship – there was clearly a world of difference between the majority of those individuals participating in the two major factional divisions of the Assembly. And it seems evident that the political-social dialectic between Left and Right, a dialectic whose origins can be traced to the earliest days of the Estates General and the National Assembly, would exert a major influence on the development of the new political culture of the French Revolution and of modern France.

Notes

1 François Furet, *Penser la Révolution* (Paris, 1978). In citations, I will use the English version, *Interpreting the Revolution*, trans. Elborg Forster (Cambridge, 1981).

2 Furet, *Interpreting the Revolution*, 46; François Furet and Denis Richet, *La Révolution française* (Paris, 1973), p. 99.

3 Furet, *Interpreting the Revolution*, p. 54.

4 Delaville Le Roulx, May 3 and 8, 1789, BB 12, AC, Lorient; Boullé, *Revue de la Révolution*, 10 (1887), 169, Sieyès had proposed an 'Assemblée nationale' the previous January. See his *Qu'est-ce que le Tiers Etat?*, ed. Edme Champion (Paris, 1889), p. 79.

5 Adrien Duquesnoy, *Journal d'Adrien Duquesnoy*, ed. R. de Crèvecoeur, 2 vols. (Paris, 1894), 1:13; Laurent de Visme, May 14, 1789, ms. 'Journal des Etats généraux,' Nouv. acq. fr. 12938, Bibliothèque Nationale.

6 Duquesnoy, *Journal*, 1:2; Pierre-Paul Nairac, May 19, 1789, ms. 'Journal,' 5 F 63, Archives Departementales de l'Eure; Etienne-François Schwendt in Rodolphe Reuss, ed., *L'Alsace pendant la Révolution française*, 2 vols, (Paris, 1880–94), 1, p. 108, *See also* Gaultier de Biauzat, *Correspondance*, 2:118; and Jean-Baptiste Poncet-Delpech, *La première année de la Révolution vue par un témoin*, ed. Daniel Ligou (Paris, 1961), pp. 11–12.

7 Boullé, *Revue de la Révolution*, 12 (1888), p. 50.

8 Durand, May 30, 1789, carton 5–56, Archives diocésaines de Cahors; Jean-Baptiste Grellet de Beauregard, 'Lettres de M. Grellet de Beauregard,' ed. Abbé Dardy, *Mémoires de la Société des sciences naturelles et archéologiques de la Creuse*, 2ᵉ sér., 7 (1899): July 10, 1789; Claude-Pierre Maillot to an unnamed municipal official of de Toul, June 3, 1789, JJ 7, Archives Communales de Toul (hereafter, AC, Toul); and Visme, 'Journal des Etats généraux,' May 26 and June 10, 1789. All four men were moderates who never joined the Jacobin Club. *See also* Pierre-Joseph Meifrund, June 10, 1789, ms. journal; copy in Institut de la Révolution française (Paris).

9 Visme, 'Journal des Etats Généraux,' July 22, 1789; letter of the deputies of Marseille, July 27, 1789, BB 361, Archives Communales de Marseille; Delaville Le Roulx, July 24, 1789, BB 12, AC Lorient. Numerous other examples could be given.

10 Du Bus, *Stanislas de Clermont-Tonnerre*, 123. See also Jean Egret, *La Révolution des notables Mounier et les monarchiens* (Paris, 1950), 92–103; and Montlosier, *Mémoires*, 1, p. 251.

11 August-Félix-Elizabeth Barin de La Gallissonnière, June 27, 1789, ms. journal, A4 LVI Archives de la Guerre; also Louis-Henri-Charles de Gauville, *Journal*, ed. Edouard de Barthélémy (Paris, 1864), 8. On the Nobles' initial refusal to obey the king, see Malartic, 'Journal,' June 27, 1789 MS. 21, BM, La Rochelle; and Jean-Baptiste de Cernon de Pinteville to his brother, undated letter of *ca.* June 27, J 2286, Archives Départementales de la Marne.

12 Maillot, July 18, 1789, JJ 7, AC, Toul. For a nobleman's interpretation, see Malartic, 'Journal,' July 16, 1789, MS. 21, BM, La Rochelle.

13 La Gallissonnière, ms. journal, A4 LVI, folio 154, Archives de la Guerre.

14 Pinteville, June 27, 1789, J 2286, Archives Départementales de la Marne.

15 La Gallissonnière, ms. journal, June 27, 1789, A4 LVI, Archives de la Guerre; also Ferrières, *Correspondance*, July 3, 1789; Guilhem-Clermont-Lodève, August 2, 1789, AA 23, Archives Communales d'Arles. Also Bernard de Brye, *Un évêque d'ancien régime à l'épreuve de la Révolution: Le cardinal A. L. H. de La Fare (1752–1829)* (Paris, 1985), pp. 249–59, Charles-Maurice de Talleyrand, *Mémoires*, ed. Duc de Broglie, 5 vols. (Paris, 1891–92), 1, pp. 123–4; Eugène Lavaquery, *Le Cardinal de Boisgelin, 1732–1804*, 2 vols. (Paris, 1920), 2, pp. 13–15.

16 Duquesnoy, *Journal*, June 26, 1789; Ménard de la Groye, July 7, 1789, 10 J 122, AD, Sarthe.

17 Faulcon, *Correspondance*, journal entry of 3 a.m., July 15, 1789, p. 69.

18 Marquis de Ferrières, *Mémoires*, 3 vols. (Paris, 1825), August 10, 1789.

19 Delaville Le Roulx, July 29, 1789, BB 12, AC, Lorient; Maillot, August 1, 1789, JJ 7, AC, Toul; Creuzé-Latouche, *Journal des Etats généraux*, pp. 165–66. *See also* Durand, June 29, 1789, carton 5–56, Archives diocésaines de Cahors.

20 Jacques-Athanase de Lombard-Taradeau, 'Lettres (1789–91),' ed. L. Honoré, *Le Var historique et géographique*, 2 (1925–27), pp. 245, 247, 261, 274–75, 324.

21 Ferrières, *Correspondance*, August 6, 1789; Claude-Jean-Baptiste Garron de la Bévière to his wife, August 5, 1789, 1 Mi 1, Archives Départementales de l'Ain.

22 Guillaume Gontier de Biran to the Municipality of Bergerac, retrospective letter of May 22, 1790, carton 1, Archives Communales de Bergerac, Fonds Faugère; Emmanuel Barbotin, *Lettres de l'abbé Barbotin*, ed. A. Aulard (Paris, 1910), August 23 and 29, 1789; Gauville, *Journal*, pp. 16–20.

23 Périsse-Duluc, September 17, 1789, MS. 5430, BM, Lyon.

24 Périsse-Duluc, September 17, 1789, MS, 5430, BM, Lyon.

25 Virieu, September 1, 1789, Archives of the Château de Viennois. See also the analysis of Theodore Vernier to the Municipality of Lons-le-Saunier, August 30, 1789, 'Lettres de Vernier,' Archives Communales de Bletterans (non-classé).

26 Lombard-Taradeau, 'Lettres (1789–91),' 271; Louis-Prosper Lofficiel, 'Lettres de Lofficiel,' ed. M. Leroux-Cesbron, *La nouvelle revue rétrospective*, 7 (1897): 111; Périsse-Duluc, September 2, 1789, MS 5430, BM, Lyon.

27 Virieu, October 12 and 16, 1789 Archives of the Château de Viennois; Jean-de-Dieu Boisgelin de Cucé to Comtesse de Gramont, October 6, 1789, AN, M 788; Gontier de Biran, October 12, 1789, carton 1, Archives Communales de Bergerac, Fond Faugère.

28 Boisgelin de Cucé, undated, *ca.* mid-November 1789, *pièce* 141, AN, M 788.

29 Boisgelin de Cucé, November 3, 1789; also November 7 and 23, AN, M 788.

30 Thibaudeau to Faulcon, undated but probably early January 1791; printed in Faulcon, *Correspondance*, 141.

31 Visme, December 7, 1789, 'Journal des Etats généraux.' The vote was 453 for the Right and 443 for the Left. See *AP*, 10, pp. 414–15.

32 Guillaume-Benoît Couderc, 'Lettres de Guillaume-Benoît Couderc (1781–92),' ed. M. O. Monod, *Revue d'histoire de Lyon*, p. 420; T. Lindet, *Correspondance de Thomas Lindet pendant la Constituante et la Législative (1789–92)*, ed. A. Montier (Paris 1889), p. 38; Delaville Le Roulx, January 18, 1790, BB 13, AC, Lorient; Duquesnoy, *Journal*, 2, pp. 196–97, 269. See also Faulcon, *Correspondance*, 2, p. 140–41; Ménard de la Groye, January 1, 1790, 10 J 122, AD, Sarthe; and Goupilleau, January 11, 1790, Collection Dugast-Matifeux, no. 98, BM, Nantes.

33 Louis-Marie de La Revellière-Lépeaux, *Mémoires*, 3 vols. (Paris, 1895), 1, p. 85.

34 Quoted in G. Walter, *Histoire des Jacobins*, (Paris, 1946), pp. 93–94.

35 Lindet, *Correspondance*, p. 38.

36 Lindet, *Correspondance*, November 22, 1790, p. 247.

17

The origins of the civil war in the Vendée

CLAUDE PETITFRÈRE

When France declared war on Austria, on 20 April 1792, it was not only in order to defend the Revolution from invasion but also to spread the ideas of liberty and sovereignty abroad, as the Convention's decree of 15 December 1792 would proclaim. Yet less than a year later, in March 1793, a great many people within the country rejected this same freedom and opted to join forces with those powers which, under English leadership, were launching an external attack upon the French Republic.

Of all the regions which rebelled in the name of King and Religion the west of France was the most significant on account of the intensity, duration and consequences of the conflict. To the north of the river Loire, both inside Brittany and upon its eastern borders, there were sporadic outbreaks of guerilla warfare, organized by small groups of militant opponents of the Revolution, called *chouannerie*. South of the Loire, in an area which embraced four departments (the Loire-Inférieure, Maine-et-Loire, Vendée and Deux-Sèvres – see Figure 17.1) and which is known as the Bocage – a zone of mixed woodland and pasture, as opposed to the open-field areas that surround it – rebellion occurred on a far more massive scale. There it involved the vast majority of the inhabitants, especially those living in the countryside, in a savage civil war which has been somewhat inappropriately named after just one of the departments concerned, *la guerre de Vendée*, or simply *La Vendée*.

The Vendean rebellion is one of the landmarks in the history of Revolutionary France. For almost a year, between March and December 1793, it threatened the very existence of the Republic which was being undermined inside the country at the same time as it was being attacked on every frontier. On 1 October Barère, a *montagnard* deputy in the Convention, declared from the rostrum: 'La Vendée . . . voilà le charbon politique, qui dévore le coeur de la République française; c'est là qu'il faut frapper.'[1] The Vendée was also significant because of its persistence, it was almost a revolt without end. The so-called *grande guerre* was terminated in December 1793 when republican troops crushed the Catholic and Royal Army at Le Mans and Savenay, but unrest continued until 1800 in the

Reprinted in full, except for notes and tables, from *French History*, 2 (1988), pp. 187–207.

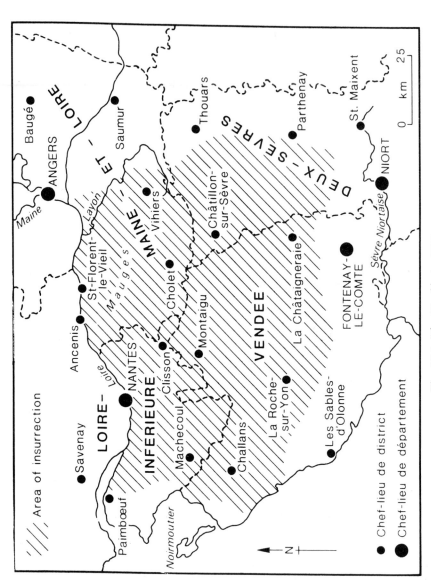

Fig. 17.1 The Vendée in 1793

form of guerilla warfare similar to *chouannerie*. There were also two minor rebellions in the nineteenth century: in 1815 when Napoleon returned from Elba; and in June 1832 when the duchesse de Berry, daughter-in-law of Charles X, made an abortive attempt to raise the Vendeans in favour of her son, the duc de Bordeaux.

The Vendée has lived on ever since, lodged firmly in the collective memory of the inhabitants of the Bocage and providing a feeling of unity, a kind of regional consciousness for men and women who were divided between three provinces (Brittany, Anjou and Poitou) under the *ancien régime*. It can be said that a new province, La Vendée, emerged from the civil war which was to be defined by an enduring loyalty to the ideas and parties of the right. To this day the Vendée continues to relive its past. After the First World War the rural exodus, demographic mobility and the passage of time all progressively eroded memories of the events of 1793 and the years that followed, to the point where it became necessary to create commemorative associations to keep the tradition alive. But the approach of the bicentenary of the French Revolution has served to stir up a passionate and often raucous debate between 'conservative' and 'progressive' historians concerning the level of repression which occurred during the final months of *la grande guerre*. Attention has been focused upon the beginning of 1794 when the 'infernal columns' of General Turreau swept through the Bocage in a merciless fashion. This robust controversy carries strong political overtones. For 'conservatives' it is a matter of discrediting the Revolution as a whole, above all the Republic, which is held responsible for the 'genocide' of French citizens (*le génocide franco-français*). For 'progressives', on the other hand, it is a question of playing down the massacres, and thus reducing the burden of Republican guilt, by insisting that they should be located in the monarchical tradition of firmly repressing all popular uprisings.

I

While it is the outcome of the insurrections in the west which is the most controversial issue at present it should not be forgotten that the problem of why the rebellion occurred in the first place has always greatly exercised historians. Many have shared the incomprehension of Barère, who spoke of 'the enigmatic Vendée', or of Michelet who, in 1847, wrote in his famous *Histoire de la Révolution française*: 'Au moment où le monde s'élance vers la France, se donne à elle, devient Français de coeur, un pays fait exception; il se recontre un peuple si étrangement aveugle et si bizarrement égaré qu'il arme contre la Révolution, sa mère, contre le salut du peuple, contre lui-même. Et, par un miracle du diable, cela se voit en

France; c'est une partie de la France qui donne ce spectacle: ce peuple
étrange est la Vendée.'[2]

Starting from the premise that the Revolution was made in order to
liberate the people, proponents of an historiographical tradition favourable to the Republic proved incapable of accepting that the Vendeans could
have risen up of their own accord. The insurrection could only have
stemmed from a conspiracy, from an 'infernal plot' hatched by priests
and nobles, as Richard and Choudieu, two representatives on mission from
the Convention, were already suggesting in Year II of the Republic.
According to this view the people of the Vendée were good and virtuous
but gullible and uneducated, far removed from the eighteenth-century
Enlightenment, and they allowed themselves to be more easily led astray
than others. The most outstanding statement of this interpretation is to be
found in the fine, scholarly works which appeared in the late nineteenth
century. Celestin Port's *La Vendée angevine*, for example, which was
published in 1888, viewed the uprising as a result of 'l'initiative violente
d'affidés aux aguets . . . à la conjuration incessante des gentilhommes,
des émigrés'.[3] Charles-Louis Chassin, editor of an eleven-volume collection of source materials entitled *Études documentaires sur la Vendée et la
chouannerie* (1892–1900), shared the same attitude. In the preface to this
huge undertaking Chassin laid bare his prejudices as he claimed to have
searched the archives for 'the key to royalist machinations'.[4] In the
twentieth century, books like those of Léon Dubreuil (*Histoire des insurrections de l'ouest*) and Gérard Walter (*La guerre de Vendée*) took up the
conspiracy thesis afresh.[5] Gérard Walter pointed to the simultaneous
outbreak of rebellion all over the Vendée, and wrote: 'On croirait difficile-
ment à une pure coincidence, à un simple jeu du hasard. On a plutôt
l'impression de se trouver en présence d'un commencement d'exécution de
l'offensive synchronisée, imaginée par la coalition antirévolutionnaire en
vue d'abattre la France républicaine.'[6]

At the start of the nineteenth century another historiographical tradition had already been established by royalist or generally conservative
historians who adopted an opposite stance to the Republicans, turning
the Vendée and *chouannerie* into a spontaneous, popular rebellion for God
and King. In other words, they saw the revolt as one which aimed at
restoring the politics and religion of an *ancien régime* that was nostalgically viewed as a kind of golden age. The most famous royalist history of
the Vendée was in fact penned by a survivor of the war, the marquise de la
Rochejaquelein. Her memoirs were published in 1815 and were intended to
refute the Republican interpretation: 'cette guerre n'a pas été, comme on
l'a dit, excitée par les nobles et par les prêtres . . . Il n'y a eu ni plan, ni
complots, ni secrètes intelligences. Tout le peuple s'est levé à la fois.'[7] This
interpretation was endlessly reiterated by a multitude of like-minded
historians throughout the nineteenth century (for example, in Jacques

Crétineau-Joly's *Histoire de la Vendée militaire* or the abbé Félix Deniau's *Histoire de la Vendée*) and so on into the twentieth (from Émile Gabory's *La Révolution et la Vendée*, to recent publications like P. Doré-Graslin's *Itinéraires de la Vendée militaire*).[8]

While these two historiographical currents are completely at odds with each other they none the less share a good deal of common ground. In the first place they are motivated by political objectives: for authors in both camps it is less a matter of understanding the rebellion than of justifying the conduct of royalists or republicans, the uprising or its repression. In each case a Manichaean dichotomy is imposed upon the reader and a struggle between Good and Evil is portrayed, with the former naturally to be found on the side which the historian is supporting. These opposing historiographical traditions also operate from the same basic premise: that of a particular way of life in the west and even the 'special characteristics' of its people, which would explain why their reactions were without parallel elsewhere in Revolutionary France. For proponents of the Republican interpretation these 'unique features' include lack of education, a propensity for superstition and deference towards superiors, seigneurs and parish priests. For defenders of the royalist position it is a matter of religious belief, self-sacrifice, loyalty and all the other Christian virtues which are held to belong exclusively to the Vendeans.

Historians went a long way towards solving the 'riddle' of the Vendée when, instead of restricting themselves to assertions of *idées reçues* like the ideological, moral, or psychological particularism of the people who inhabited the rebellious areas, they began to look for the material causes of such behaviour. They enquired to see if there was some correlation between extremely localized economic and social structures and the impact of reforms of the Revolutionary period upon them. A study published on the eve of the First World War, André Siegfried's *Tableau politique de la France de l'ouest sous la Troisième République*, clearly confronted the issue.[9] Having contrasted the right-wing affiliations of inhabitants of the granite regions of the west with the left-wing allegiance of those in the surrounding limestone areas, he wondered whether or not this apparent geological determinism masked a difference in land tenure, which constituted the real explanation for the divergent political options. The large estates that predominated in the Armorican massif could have inculcated a submissive attitude towards landowners and priests and hence a conservative vote, while the multiplicity of small properties in the open-field areas of the Parisian basin forged a spirit of independence that favoured democratic opinions. This interpretation is by no means a wholly convincing one because it does not hold true in other parts of France, like Normandy or the Limousin, and Siegfried himself was aware of its limitations. However, this book had the merit of attempting to relate the ideological dimension to economic and social factors. This approach was taken up again during the 1960s in three studies by Paul Bois, Marcel Faucheux and Charles Tilly, which have brought many new perspectives to bear upon the problem.

In his book *Paysans de l'ouest* which, in fact, only deals with the department of the Sarthe, Bois actually begins with a critique of Siegfried's *Tableau politique*.[10] Bois criticizes the latter for having produced a sociological rather than a historical treatment of the subject. He deliberately sets his own study in a longer-term context, searching in the past for 'la véritable explication du présent', that is to say, of the political bifurcation of the Sarthe into a right-wing west and a left-wing east. In his quest for the origins of this division Bois focused upon the Revolutionary period. The Bocage which covered the department in a uniform fashion housed two contrasting populations. To the west a rather prosperous and homogeneous peasantry lived on relatively fertile land. Peasant holdings remained very small but they were expanding while the seigneur was absent but respected. The bourgeois, on the other hand, was mistrusted; he 'n'apparaît dans les campagnes que pour . . . disputer la terre' and then, as the property owner, he collected rents. In eastern parts of the Sarthe, by contrast, the peasants were overpopulating a very infertile soil and they were much poorer than their western counterparts. Generally unable to purchase any land they were resigned to their situation and, unlike peasants to the west, they were not engaged in conflict with the bourgeoisie. Moreover, this eastern peasantry was more heterogeneous because, in order to survive, the poorest among them were obliged to take up weaving. It was via these weavers that urban influence penetrated the countryside. 'L'homme des villes n'apparaît pas ici, comme à l'ouest, en concurrent dans la lutte pour la terre, mais en associé pour l'écoulement de la production artisanale.'

The Revolution unleashed the western peasants' accumulated animosity towards the bourgeoisie. Village communities united in strength around their natural leaders, the parish priests, to oppose the bourgeois rather than the nobles, who had left the countryside and yet were still considered to be part of rural society. Moreover, to long-standing reasons for detesting the bourgeoisie the Revolution was to add new ones, which arose from numerous disappointments with its legislative measures. These occurred in the agricultural sphere, where the bourgeoisie secured the greater part of the national lands that were sold in western parts of the department; in respect of taxation, because direct taxes rose higher than under the *ancien régime*; in economic matters, as the *assignats* quickly lost their value and the price controls of September 1793 caused popular discontent; and finally in military terms, on account of conscription. All in all the Revolution was imposed by the town-dwellers, chiefly for the benefit of those 'alien elements' the bourgeois. Hence the peasant uprising was directed against them in the western half of the department.[11] Bois' study broke new ground in another way too. While deflecting attention away from ideological dimensions towards economic and social factors, as Siegfried's book had done earlier, it also inverted the traditional view by asserting that *chouans* in the Maine rebelled *against* the bourgeoisie rather than *for* the nobles and 'good' priests (those who had refused the oath of 1791).

The books by Faucheux and Tilly, which both appeared in 1964, were orientated in a similar direction. The former's *L'insurrection vendéenne de 1793* bore a sub-title (*Aspects économiques et sociaux*) that was sufficiently indicative of the author's approach.[12] For Faucheux, as for Bois, the popular classes were ranged against the bourgeoisie because the reforms implemented by the new regime had all favoured the latter and disappointed the former. There was, however, a fundamental difference of opinion between the two historians. Faucheux painted a very gloomy picture of the Vendean economy. According to him it was already suffering from structural defects when it was hit head-on by the crisis which accompanied the end of the *ancien régime*. As a result poverty reached an unacceptable level. In his view, therefore, the Vendée was a rebellion produced by hunger and suffering, an idea diametrically opposed to Bois' notion of *chouannerie* erupting in the most prosperous part of the Sarthe.

Tilly's book, though entitled *The Vendée*, was only concerned with southern Anjou, a small sector of the rebellious zone.[13] Tilly, an American sociologist, conducted a comparative study of the Mauges, the western part of this territory which rebelled against the Revolution, and the Val de Loire and the Saumurois which remained loyal. He applied the concept of 'urbanization' to the region, defining it as 'the set of broad social changes which has commonly accompanied the growth in size and influence of cities'.[14] Thus he designated all the combined activities which brought about the rise of the bourgeoisie, from administrative centralization to the creation of a national market. For Tilly the Revolution was an integral part of this well-advanced process of 'urbanization' in France, to which it gave a sharp impulsion. In western France the areas which rallied to the Revolution were those that have been most thoroughly urbanized for the longest period of time. Those which fought against it, on the other hand, corresponded with zones where urbanization was a recent phenomenon, in the throes of development to be sure but where its progress was extremely uneven. In southern Anjou the Mauges was in just this situation. Its village communitites were turned in upon themselves because they practised no more than subsistence agriculture. They were far removed from the market, unlike villages in the Val-Saumurois which sought commercial contacts in order to sell their wine, linen and hemp. In the Mauges, where great estates predominated, the absentee seigneur inspired a dutiful respect. It was his agent, the bourgeois, who attracted the resentment of tenant farmers. The existence of a mercantile bourgeoisie, in charge of the domestic manufacture of cloth and handkerchiefs from Cholet, deepened the antagonism between popular classes and wealthy non-nobles. By contrast, in the Val-Saumurois the bourgeois was not seen as an exploiter but as a necessary middleman for the distribution of crops. Local nobles, 'far from that distant domination of the lands which characterized their cousins in the neighbouring areas',[15] were rather less wealthy than in the Mauges and sometimes engaged as producers in direct competition with the peasants who, in this instance, were nearly always landowners. The Revolution thus reacted upon two rather different sorts of communities to produce opposite effects. In the Mauges it fulfilled the wishes of the bourgeoisie, without satisfying the peasants, whose long-standing hostility was exacerbated and burst into insurrection. Tilly consequently concurs with the interpretations of Bois and Faucheux in seeing the rebellions in the west as a war of the people against the bourgeoisie, a conflict generated by the negative impact of revolutionary reform upon a particular type of society.

It may be argued that none of the three books just reviewed succeeds in giving a general account of the causes of the Vendean revolt. Bois sees the weavers of the eastern Sarthe as upholders of the Republic, whereas in the vicinity of Cholet their counterparts were especially militant royalists. Faucheux emphasizes the role of poverty in the Vendée, yet in Anjou, the least affluent area, the Baugeois, remained loyal to the Revolution. Finally, Tilly rather exaggerates the economic isolation of the Vendée where agriculture was not wholly autarchic but sustained a flourishing cattle trade with the Parisian region. The three authors have none the less recorded important advances in academic research and have provided the starting-point for my own work. If the Vendée was not simply a crusade, as so many historians in the royalist tradition have claimed, if religious belief was not the only factor motivating the rebels and if, as Bois, Faucheux and Tilly maintain, material interests underpinned their ideology, then this should be reflected in the social composition of the Vendean factions. Yet the social origins of the insurgents are not known in any great detail. Tilly was correct when he wrote: 'who fought in the Vendée is apparently so obvious to most of its historians that they do not ask the question. Yet no one really knows . . . it is even generally agreed that a great many rustics, plus some noblemen and priests, marched in the rebel armies. Beyond this, there is not much accord.'[16]

II

An answer to this question has been found, at least for the Maine-et-Loire, a department which roughly corresponds to the former province of Anjou. Dossiers compiled by survivors of the civil war or their dependants in 1824 and 1825, in the hope of receiving a pension from the restored monarchy, have been conserved at the departmental archives. On this basis it has been possible to analyze details concerning 5484 Vendean rebels for the year 1793. These have been cross-checked for accuracy by making reference to other sources, such as lists of combatants and prisoners, which are much rarer but which have the advantage of being contemporary with the event.

Thus, armed with a representative sample of partisans on the royalist side – 'whites' as they were called after the colour of their flag – a comparison was made with a similarly representative sample of 'militants' from the other side, in other words supporters of the Revolution. It was not easy to select a criterion for selection, but in the end the National Volunteers of the years 1791 and 1792 were chosen. At that time the Constituent and then the Legislative Assembly appealed to the French people to sign up with battalions especially created to meet the threat of a counter-revolution led from abroad. The men who responded were for the most part enthusiastic supporters of the new regime. In Anjou, before the introduction of conscription prescribed by the law of 24 February 1793, they enlisted on a purely voluntary basis. The Vendean rebels detested these volunteers just as much as the National Guard in which they had served; both guardsmen and regular volunteers were conflated in the minds of their opponents and were collectively known as 'blues' from the colour of their uniforms. In this sample the primary concern is with political rather than military history and so the list does not merely include the men who actually enlisted in the first three battalions of volunteers from the Maine-et-Loire. Instead, all those who offered their services to save the *grande nation* were included, whether they were accepted by the authorities entrusted with the task of establishing these army units or not: *in toto* 4089 partisans of the Revolution.

A statistical analysis of these two samples of 'whites' and 'blues' enables one to pinpoint the geographical distribution of the two partisan tendencies in Anjou. The Vendean rebels were exclusively recruited from the western half of the Maine-et-Loire, in other words from the more primitive terrain of the Armorican massif which was typified by the Bocage, an area permeated with water-courses, pastures and woodland, its fields enclosed by hedges. By contrast the 'blues' emanated from all over the department but especially from the Loire valley and the eastern half of the department, an open-field area which formed part of the Parisian basin. A second discovery was that the rebels were nearly all country people. Although small towns in the Bocage, like Cholet, did participate in the uprising, in proportion to their population they furnished the Catholic and Royal Army with fewer recruits than the countryside. In the Mauges it can be said that the degree of involvement of communities in the insurrection was inversely proportional to the size of the population. Conversely the 'blues' were townsmen first and foremost. It is worth noting that the two main towns, Angers and Saumur, between them provided 43 per cent of the volunteer force. A type of political division had occurred which coincided with the distinction between town and country and Bocage and open-field (or 'plain' as the rebels called it).

This division is mirrored in the sharply contrasting social structures of the two samples. The sociological composition of the Catholic and Royal Army faithfully reflects the general profile of the population in the Bocage, with the exception of the *bonne bourgeoisie* (the upper strata of society beneath the nobility) who were scarcely in evidence and account for a mere 1.6 per cent of the rebel sample (*see* Table 17.1). Apart from the bourgeoisie every other social category in the Bocage participated strongly in the uprising. Setting aside the clergy, who were overwhelmingly in favour of the rebellion but were not actually involved in the fighting, and also nobles, who were mostly in the high command but whose numbers were small, it was the peasantry who formed the backbone of the army, with 62.8 per cent of the sample. Every element in the peasantry was well represented from middle-class tenant farmers (locally known as *métayers*) to small-holders (*closiers* or *bordiers*) and wage-earners (agricultural workers and domestic servants). But the Vendée was not just a peasants' revolt as has so often been maintained. Artisans and shopkeepers made up 34.5 per cent of the insurgents. Nearly 20 per cent exercised one of the traditional crafts which were to be found in every village, such as millers, butchers, joiners, carpenters, stone-masons, cobblers, blacksmiths, etc. The rest were weavers who worked at home, supplying the merchants of Cholet who were in practice the directors of this domestic industry, or *manufacture* as it was called. The weavers produced linen cloth and handkerchiefs, made from a mixture of linen and cotton, which were sold by the merchants in the Atlantic ports of Nantes, La Rochelle, or Bordeaux and then shipped to the United States and European colonies in the Americas.

Table 17.1 Social composition of 'Whites' and 'Blues' in Anjou

Socio-professional category	'Whites'		'Blues'	
	Total	%	Total	%
Bourgeois occupations (upper and middle bourgeoisie)	77	1.63	403	12.38
Artisan and shopkeeping professions (minus textile workers)	900	19.09	1,635	50.25
Textile trades	728	15.44	469	14.41
Agricultural occupations	2,962	62.82	663	20.38
Other professions	48	1.02	84	2.58
Total of recorded occupations	4,715	100.00	3,254	100.00

The composition of the 'blues (who were also called 'patriots') was completely different. While peasants predominated among the 'whites' they were underrepresented in the opposing camp where they formed only 20 per cent of the sample. The bulk of the volunteers in the Maine-et-Loire were artisans and shopkeepers from the large and small towns: they formed 65 per cent of the total. Finally, the most striking distinction was the important role played by the upper and middle bourgeoisie, who comprised more than 12 per cent of the 'blue' sample. Quite clearly the middle classes had opted for the Revolution.

The contrasting social profiles of 'whites' and 'blues' and their relatively circumscribed geographical recruitment leads one to infer that a struggle for material advantage lay hidden beneath the clash of ideologies. If the upper bourgeoisie, artisans and shopkeepers offered their services for the defence of the Revolution it was because they had derived some benefit from the new order. In economic terms, with the abolition of the trade guilds, monopolies and commercial restrictions which had restrained competition and retarded the development of capitalism under the *ancien régime*, they had acquired freedom of enterprise. Those among them who owned property recorded their satisfaction with the liberation of landed wealth from the seigneurial system and with the rural code of September–October 1791, which guaranteed landowners absolute control in farming their land, as well as the right to enclose it according to Physiocratic ideals. At the political level, meanwhile, the bourgeoisie took control of the departments, districts and towns. In a region where less than one-fifth of rural males were literate the urban notables were the main beneficiaries of local elections in which, until the summer of 1792, the poorest inhabitants (the 'passive' citizens) were not even given the vote. Indeed, the bourgeoisie rushed to fill the numerous posts which the reform of administration and justice brought in their wake and which were partly allocated by means of election.

Ideology also played a role, and the urban elites were clearly satisfied in this respect too. The principles of Liberty, Equality before the Law and National Sovereignty that the new regime put into effect – even to the extent of introducing the election of parish priests as part of the reform of the church – constituted an array of ideas that was thoroughly familiar to them. They had imbibed such ideas at secondary school and defended them in debate in the students' clubs and young men's associations which had sprung up on the eve of the Revolution. Consequently they not only found material satisfaction in the Revolution but they also felt that it belonged to them in intellectual terms; it was theirs.

Conversely, the Revolution appeared alien to people in the countryside, especially to those of the Bocage which had few big towns and was poorly connected by road with the outside world. The Revolution was imposed upon them by the bourgeois administrators of department and district, or by national guards from the larger and smaller towns. No doubt this would have proved acceptable if the reforms being implemented had met the expectations of people living in the countryside, but such hopes were soon dashed. Each social group nursed particular grievances against the new order, while other sources of discontent affected the inhabitants of the Bocage as a whole.

III

To begin with let us examine the disappointments of the peasants who formed the bulk of the insurgents in 1793. As their *cahiers de doléances* clearly reveal, what they had hoped for from the convocation of the Estates General was, above all, a substantial reduction in taxation. Under the *ancien régime* the Bocage was more heavily taxed than the lowland areas on its borders. (Perhaps this was because it was under-administered as the regional administrative centres, the headquarters of the intendancies, were situated outside or upon its periphery – Tours for Anjou and Rennes or Poitiers for the other provinces.) Yet this injustice was perpetuated and even aggravated during the early years of the Revolution. The *taille* was replaced by the land tax (*contribution foncière*), which was, in theory, intended to tap income from the soil in proportion to its extent. However, since the government needed money urgently there was no time to conduct a land survey which would have facilitated a more equitable distribution of the new tax. The base that had been employed in the past for the *taille* was used for the new imposition. Moreover, the rate at which the *contribution foncière* was levied increased continually between 1790 and 1792. Lastly, the laws of 1 December 1790 and 28 June 1791 allowed landowners to have the new tax paid by their tenants, whereas under the *ancien régime* it had been customary to divide taxes (whether *taille, capitation,* or *vingtièmes*) between landowners and tenant farmers. These fresh legislative measures were all the more severe for peasants in the Bocage because most of them were tenants whilst their counterparts on the surrounding plains were landowners.

The solitary satisfaction which the peasants obtained in respect of taxation was the suppression of the *gabelle*. Yet this only affected those who farmed in Anjou, where the *gabelle* was imposed, since Poitou and Brittany had been exempt from this tax. Even so the Angevins were obliged to agitate in order to obtain the suspension of the salt tax by the local authorities, while they awaited its legal abolition. This was only decreed by the National Assembly on 21 March 1790, on an extremely unfavourable basis since two-thirds of the *gabelle* was added to the *taille* in the form of a supplement for the current year.

The peasants had not only paid taxes to the king, they were also obliged to pay tithes to the church and seigneurial dues as well. The Revolution abolished both, but not completely. Tithes were only effectively suppressed in the case of landowning peasants: according to the law of 10 December 1790 tenants and share-croppers were required to pay their landlords the equivalent of the former tithe in cash. This was known as 'neo-tithing'. Consequently for tenant farmers, in other words for the mass of the peasantry in the Bocage, the burden remained unaltered; only its recipient had changed. As for seigneurial dues, it should be remembered that deputies in the National Assembly had voted for abolition in principle on the night of 4 August 1789, but at the same time it was decided that dues which were levied on property, those which remunerated the seigneur, would have to be redeemed. In the event it was only in the summer of 1792 that seigneurial dues were abolished without compensation. Even this further measure was incomplete where tenant farmers were concerned because the decree of 25 August 1792 allowed landlords to include the equivalent of former dues in the rents they charged. The solution adopted for phasing out tithes was therefore also employed with regard to seigneurial dues, once again to the benefit of landlords.

In these circumstances it is easy to understand why agrarian reform was much more popular in areas of widespread peasant landownership than in the Bocage, where the majority were only tenant farmers. This is a point which has recently been emphasized by two Canadian historians, T. J. A. Le Goff and Donald Sutherland.[17] The latter, who has studied the department of the Ille-et-Vilaine, argues that the geography of *chouannerie* more or less coincided with areas of substantial bourgeois landowning. These bourgeois were, moreover, the main target of the insurgents. In the heart of Brittany, where the incidence of taxation was relatively light (neither *taille* nor *gabelle* were levied there) and where seigneurial impositions were not especially onerous, the main issue was the payment of ground rent. This caused a great deal of anxiety during the closing years of the *ancien régime* on account of the growing gap between agricultural incomes and rapidly inflating rents. The question remains as to why the *chouans* spared the properties of nobles and clergymen from attack. Sutherland reckons that this was because they were considered to be an integral part of the rural community. The *seigneurie*, in particular, remained a vigorous institution, offering many services to the peasants (for example, by placing at their disposal a system of justice which dealt with a multitude of disputes between individuals, like family matters, and so perpetuated the image of the seigneur as arbitrator and defender of the weak). The importance of landlord-tenant relations should not, however, be exaggerated among the factors which produced rebellion in western France. In the Vendée all types of peasant rose up, from landowners to agricultural labourers and household servants. Yet the bias of the Revolutionary assemblies in favour of landholders was, without any doubt, a major source of discontent in a region where tenant farmers constituted the most widespread category of peasant.

Was there not an opportunity for the peasantry to increase their landownership with the sale of church property? In the event these sales, effected for the most part in 1791, were another reason for disappointment among the peasants, because the property was sold by auction and they were unable to purchase much of it. In the district of Cholet, for example, peasants did not succeed in acquiring more than 9 per cent in value of what was sold, compared to over 23 per cent for the nobility and, above all, the 56 per cent which went to the upper bourgeoisie. Bois maintained that such disappointment was one of the main reasons for bitterness towards the new regime on the part of his *Paysans de l'ouest*. Arguably this factor needs to be kept in proportion because on the plains surrounding the Bocage the peasants also lost out, though to a slightly lesser extent than in the Mauges: they were able to buy 21 per cent of the land sold in the district of Saumur and 25 per cent in the district of Vihiers.

Another social group which participated heavily in the revolt, the weavers from the Cholet *manufacture*, also had good reason to feel aggrieved. Their handkerchiefs were selling badly at the beginning of the Revolution and production was collapsing. The main reason for this seems to have been the free trade treaty which France signed with England in 1786 and which flooded the French market with British products that were cheaper to buy owing to the technological superiority of their producers. Unemployment hit the weavers extremely hard and they already constituted the poorest section of the rural community, even when work had been available. With the crisis worsening their lot the weavers were prepared to take violent action. They were often identified as ringleaders in disturbances which occurred during the early years of the Revolution and in 1793 they rose up *en masse*. The situation in the Sarthe described by Bois is not at all applicable in this instance. Yet it is hardly surprising to find these weavers following the white flag because their employers, the merchants, were the mainstay of the 'patriotic' contingent in the area. 'Ce sont', wrote the municipal administration at Cholet, 'les seuls qui sont toujours bien montrés et sur lesquels on puisse toujours bien compter.'[18] Now, as a result of the economic crisis, these merchants ordered fewer and fewer goods from the weavers and it was they who were blamed for the consequent unemployment and poverty; it was but a short step from such social conflict to political and then military confrontation.

Small retailers and artisans who were not involved in the production of textiles did not harbour the same grievances against the commercial bourgeoisie as did the weavers. They were independent workers (at least if they were master craftsmen) who sold their produce on the local market and had no need for the merchants as middlemen. Yet they were affected by the impoverishment of their customers, the peasants and weavers.

Besides, as a small group in the village community they could not easily avoid taking sides with the party of the majority. Like most of the upper bourgeoisie, they either had to support the insurgents or move into areas which remained loyal to the Republic. In order to understand the outlook of those shopkeepers and artisans who participated in the rebellion, while their counterparts in the large towns formed the basis of the revolutionary faction, it is therefore necessary to take account of what might be termed 'social pressure'. In the heart of the Bocage, submerged in a mass of peasants hostile to the Revolution, they joined them in rebellion; in peripheral areas, where opinion was divided between 'whites' and 'blues', they split between the two camps; on the plains to the east and in the major towns, where their customers were mostly bourgeois and where revolutionary ideas predominated, they opted, overwhelmingly for the new order.

To this list of sectional grievances must be added those which affected the rural population of the Bocage as a whole. During the *ancien régime*, as has been noted, the area was under-administered. This shortcoming was not rectified by the Constituent Assembly: none of the *chefs-lieux* of the new departments (Nantes, Angers, Fontenay-le-Comte and Niort) was situated inside the rebellious zone. But more serious still was the undermining of the parish, which acted both as an administrative unit and as the framework for community life. Under the *ancien régime* each parish in the Bocage had retained an individual character; it formed a community that was united around church and priest. The *curé* was not only a shepherd to his flock but performed secular functions too. He was in charge of the parish registers, ran the school if there was one, distributed alms, sometimes cared for the sick and had a hand in the choice of midwives. He often acted as a testamentary executor and, since he was a member of the small, privileged elite with a modicum of education, he acted as spokesman in front of magistrates and administrators. However, the Revolution sought to transfer many of the parish priest's tasks to new administrative units, the municipal councils, thereby overturning customary practice as well as wounding local pride. Besides, the new municipalities were fewer in quantity than the old parishes which, while remaining ecclesiastical units, were themselves reduced in number. In a region where the population was so thinly spread each tiny village had constituted a single parish but, in order to save money, the Civil Constitution of the Clergy attempted to align parish boundaries with those of the municipalities: in towns and villages with less than 6000 inhabitants only one church was to be left in being. The authorities thus proceeded to suppress roughly a quarter of the parishes in the Bocage and sometimes rather more; in the district of La Roche-sur-Yon 19 out of 52 were abolished, no less than 36 per cent. This regrouping of parishes made everyday life more difficult since in order to take part in worship it often became necessary to travel some distance along roads that were virtually impassable, especially in winter. It also entailed the closure of churches, which deeply shocked the local inhabitants. They watched in sorrow and anger as bells were dismantled from belfries, statues were removed from their pedestals, sacred urns were taken from the shrines and parish registers were withdrawn from the presbyteries, to be transferred to a neighbouring church that was viewed as alien and something of a rival. It was as if the heart was being torn from the community and its past erased.

In addition to this, the Vendean rebels witnessed an attempt to remove practically all of their parish priests. Since virtually every *curé* and *vicaire* in the Bocage refused to swear the oath of allegiance to the Civil Constitution of the Clergy, which was required by the law of 26 December 1790, the district authorities tried to replace these 'refractories' with 'constitutional' priests from other areas. Almost everywhere, throughout 1791, inhabitants gathered together to oppose the installation of these new clergymen who were referred to as 'intruders'. It was often necessary to install them forcibly but, as soon as the national guards departed, the inhabitants obliged the 'intruder' to leave. To this grievance, which was of a clerical nature since it related to the organization of the church, should be added a purely religious one. Heeding the words of refractory priests, the inhabitants of the Bocage considered the 'intruders' to be bad priests, heretics with whom association would lead to eternal damnation.

To fully comprehend the depth of religious discontent would involve measuring the level of piety in the Bocage and then comparing it with the plains that supported the Revolution. In the eighteenth century were people more religiously inclined in areas which were destined to rebel than elsewhere? This is a possibility but it has not been convincingly demonstrated. We should not endow the Vendée of the *ancien régime* with the characteristics it was to exhibit in the nineteenth century, after the triumph of religion and clericalism that inevitably stemmed from the struggle against the Revolution. Yet, while it is difficult to quantify religious faith, some idea of its essence can be obtained. Catholicism may have taken a different shape in the Bocage from the one it had assumed on the plains. Such an hypothesis has recently been formulated by Timothy Tackett. He argues that by the end of the *ancien régime* western France was a sort of reservoir for traditional Catholicism, heavily impregnated with Tridentine ideology, whereas regions in the centre of France had been won over to a more 'democratic' concept of religion under the influence of the Enlightenment. According to Tackett, priests in the Bocage were better off and thicker on the ground, factors which enabled them to create a 'mini-society' within each parish. To a greater extent than elsewhere they embodied the Counter-Reformation spirit of the seminaries which they transmitted to their parishioners. By contrast in central France, where the number of priests was fewer, it was secular ideology bearing the imprint of the *philosophes* which prevailed and produced the novel concept of the 'citizen-priest'. The clergy in western France were, moreover, in a much better position to influence the rural community because they were frequently recruited from the peasantry, while priests in the centre of France were drawn from the urban middle classes.

In Tackett's view, Catholicism in central France came very close to the concept articulated in the Civil Constitution of the Clergy. In those areas priests and their flocks saw the reform as no more than an administrative overhaul of the church. Conversely, the Civil Constitution was completely alien to the outlook of clergy in western France who viewed it as a 'Protestant' heresy. The unfavourable impact of its implementation in the Vendée was exacerbated by the enthusiasm with which it was applied by bourgeois administrators. They were heavily influenced by the Enlightenment and sought radical change in religious matters, as the general *cahiers* of the third estate show. In these documents the abolition of tithes, religious vows and chapters was sought, along with the sale of church property and the election of parish priests and bishops – demands which were all included in the Civil Constitution. For Tackett it was the hostility of this 'progressive' bourgeoisie to the unseemly religious zeal of a 'backward' rural world which was the major cause of conflict.

What are we to make of the thesis advanced by Tackett? It is an attractive one, but it does need to be verified by means of detailed study at the local level. Yet, whatever the origins of religious discontent its role in unleashing the Vendean rebellion is quite evident. It was inspiration of this sort to which the rebels themselves most often laid claim. Religious belief not only gave them a basic justification for waging war, it also constituted an ideological bond capable of uniting insurgents who had other reasons for revolt, which often varied from group to group. Moreover, religion was ideally suited to encourage a sense of sacrifice. By cloaking barely acceptable hatreds in an aura of sanctity it provided a laudable motive for fighting, killing and dying.

IV

The shortcomings of the religious policy espoused by the Constituent Assembly, exacerbated by the lack of understanding and intolerance of the local authorities, were undoubtedly the most important cause of the Vendean rebellion. Yet there were others. The main error in traditional explanations of the rebellion in western France – both those which invoke a conspiracy and those which posit a spontaneous uprising for God and King – has been their claim to have provided a unique solution to the riddle. But human behaviour is always more complex. The revolt of the Vendée originated in an accumulation of grievances, in the gradual build-up of disappointments. Disturbances broke out in the Bocage at the outset of the Revolution (this has been established for Anjou where there was rioting against the *gabelle*), they multiplied in 1791, the year when the Civil Constitution of the Clergy was implemented, and they continued to worsen during the year that followed. In February 1793 a final blunder by the central government, which decided to conscript soldiers and send them to the frontiers, was sufficient to turn these sporadic disturbances into a general uprising. The point of no return had been reached: rather than journey far away to die in the service of a hated regime it was better to stay and fight at home. There is no doubt that none of these blows to the quality of everyday life would, on their own, have been capable of engendering a revolt on the scale of the Vendée. But together they produced a concatenation of grievances which unleashed a civil war all the more easily because the Revolution appeared to attack religious beliefs as well as material interests.

Behind all these hated reforms the inhabitants saw the exploitation and injustice of the 'new masters'. This was how they referred to the rich bourgeois who had benefited from the Revolution by buying up church property and monopolizing posts in the administration, judiciary and army. Whatever the more deep-seated reasons for their revolt, whether they were peasants who had been offended by unjust taxation or frustrated in their quest for land, whether they were unemployed weavers, or just simple parishioners defending their priest and their concept of religion, the Vendean rebels all had the same enemy in common: the bourgeois, as landlord or merchant, as administrator or 'constitutional' clergyman and also as national guardsman, that new type of soldier who fought his own people and imposed reform in a brutal fashion. The civil war in the Vendée thus sometimes took on the appearance of a 'class struggle' against the beneficiaries of the new regime, organized by those who had been, or who felt they had been, rejected by the Revolution. It is easy to understand why these losers allied themselves with those who had been deprived of privilege or power – the parish priests and seigneurs – in as much as they considered the former to be their natural leaders and the latter the natural defenders of the community, military specialists no less. In the present state of our knowledge it seems that the Vendée can no longer be held to be an incomprehensible rebellion, as 'the work of the devil', in Michelet's words. The indignant exclamation of this great historian arose from an interpretation of the Revolution that is now outdated. Michelet thought that the Revolution as a whole had been made for the benefit of the people, in which case popular rebellion in the Vendée appeared perverse. But, as has now been recognized for some time, the Revolution was a bourgeois revolution rather than a popular one. Agrarian reform in particular operated to the advantage of rich property-owners rather than in the interests of poor tenant farmers.

It remains to enquire why the whole of rural France did not rise up in revolt. Why was rebellion confined to the Vendée, or more generally to the Bocage of western France? In the first place it is important to stress that this statement is not entirely correct. There were plenty of small-scale Vendées and a more serious uprising in the southern Massif Central, which involved the departments of the Haute-Loire, the Lozère and the Aveyron, though it is true that all these revolts were speedily suppressed. In the event only the Bocage of the southern Armorican massif was to experience a mass rebellion; even Brittany itself contained patriotic enclaves within the zones of *chouannerie*. In order to explain the uniqueness of the civil war in the Vendée the weak response of the 'blues' must be considered paramount. The Bocage was practically devoid of troops since the larger towns, which were well endowed with regular soldiers and national guards, were all situated outside the area. The situation was completely different in Brittany. If Brittany experienced no more than *chouannerie* it was doubtless largely due to the fact that it possessed a substantial network of towns with the capital, Rennes, occupying a central position. But the uniqueness of the Vendean rebellion also seems to have been linked to specific factors in the Bocage: not the inscrutable and peculiar characteristics of its inhabitants, which have so often been adduced, but a cluster of singular elements in its economic, social and cultural make-up. It was typified by dispersed habitation, a low level of peasant landownership, a particular form of parish community and perhaps also a specific religious outlook, as Tackett has argued. Taken individually these factors were to be found in other parts of France, but together they created a unique situation in the Vendée. In undertaking reform, the Revolutionary assemblies made the mistake of considering France as a unified whole and thus they took no account of the great variety of local conditions. This was the consequence of the rationalism and universalism which had been derived from the Enlightenment. It is not surprising that reforms applied in a uniform fashion to regions with divergent economic, social and cultural structures should have produced contradictory results. In the Vendée these reforms generated a whole range of grievances and finally a general rebellion, while elsewhere they managed to satisfy a majority of the inhabitants and thus provided a basis of support for the new regime.

Notes

1 Cited in C. Petitfrère, *La Vendée et les Vendéens* (1981), pp. 40–1
2 J. Michelet, *Histoire de la Révolution française* (1952), i. p. 1141.
3 C. Port, *La Vendée angevine* (1888), i. p. xxiii–xxiv.
4 C.-L. Chassin, *La préparation de la guerre de Vendée. 1789–1793* (1892), i. p. v.

5 L. Dubreuil, *Histoire des insurrections de l'ouest* (2 vols, 1929), and G. Walter, *La guerre de Vendée* (1953).

6 Alter, *La guerre de Vendée*, p. 52.

7 *Mémoires de Madame la Marquise de La Rochejaquelein, écrits par elle-même, rédigés par M. le baron de Barante* (Bordeaux, 1815). The quotation is taken from the sixth edition (1848), pp. 98–9.

8 J. Crétineau-Joly, *Histoire de la Vendée militaire* (2 vols, 1843); F. Deniau, *Histoire de la Vendée d'après des documents nouveaux et inédits* (6 vols, Angers, 1843); E. Gabory, *La Révolution et la Vendée* (1925); and P. Doré-Graslin, *Itinéraires de la Vendée militaire* (1979).

9 A. Siegfried, *Tableau politique de la France de l'ouest sous la Troisième République* (1913).

10 P. Bois, *Paysans de l'ouest* (Le Mans, 1960).

11 P. Bois, *Paysans de l'ouest*, pp. 572–4.

12 M. Faucheux, *L'insurrection vendéenne de 1793* (1964).

13 C. Tilly, *The Vendée: a sociological analysis of the counterrevolution of 1793* (Cambridge, Mass., 1964).

14 Tilly, *The Vendée: a sociological analysis of the counterrevolution of 1793.* p. 10

15 Tilly, *The Vendée: a sociological analysis of the counterrevolution of 1793*, p. 131.

16 Tilly, *The Vendée*, p. 321.

17 T. J. A. Le Goff, *Vannes and its region. A study of town and country in eighteenth-century France* (Oxford, 1981), and D. Sutherland, *The Chouans. The social origins of popular Counter-Revolution in Upper Brittany* (Oxford, 1982).

18 Cited in C. Petitfrère, *Les Vendéens d'Anjou 1793* (1981), p. 357.

18

Federalism

ALAN FORREST

Federalism was less a coherent ideology than a polemical device, the creation of a bitter and concerted campaign of political denigration. In the summer of 1793, when the word first entered the everyday vocabulary of the French Revolution, there were few who were ready to lay claim to it. It was used almost entirely as a term of abuse by those who wished to belittle their opponents or to cast doubt upon their political credentials. To the critics of federalism, its central characteristic was a willingness to sacrifice national unity for selfish gain, to break up the political integrity of France in the interests of individual cities or regions. It was depicted as the

Reprinted in full, except for notes, from C. Lucas, ed. *The French Revolution and the Creation of Modern Political Culture*. Volume II: *The Political Culture of the French Revolution* (Oxford, Pergamon Press, 1988), pp. 309–27.

obvious antithesis of nationalism, and the Jacobins who most enthusiastically embraced the ideology of the nation were quick to exploit the opportunity which this provided. By 1793 Revolutionary nationalism had become increasingly intolerant of local initiative, increasingly determined to impose national unity from the centre, increasingly insistent that French alone could be the language of liberty and that others – Bretons, Basques, Flemings, Corsicans – must recognize the cultural and political superiority of France. In this context it was tempting to see federalism as yet another manifestation of localism, as yet another bid by the regions to throw off the control of the centre. The fact that France was embroiled in foreign war only seemed to make these criticisms more pertinent and more damning.

Given the widespread tendency to equate the national interest with that of the Revolution, it was perhaps inevitable that Jacobin political discourse should have developed in this way. Yet in 1789 and 1790 local liberties had been fiercely upheld, with the municipal revolution offering encouragement to enterprise and initiative from city councillors and regional pressure-groups. Michael Sydenham is right to emphasize the quite dramatic change in outlook which had taken place. 'The fact is,' he writes, 'that in the late summer of 1792, probably in mid-September, the word "federal," which had hitherto signified patriotic unity, became a term of political opprobrium and proscription.'[1] The local federations which had been so prominent in the French provinces in 1790 had disappeared, and with them much of the spontaneity of that first glad morning of Revolution in provincial cities. In 1790, for example, Bordeaux and Toulouse could celebrate together their patriotic foresight in putting down royalism in Montauban; two years later any such celebration would have been regarded with intense suspicion as a symbolic assertion of local difference. The *fête de la fédération* had changed in nature, to become a public and symbolic reassertion of the importance of the nation – and, by implication, of political centralism. And already in 1792 the sections of Paris were warning of the threat which right-wing opinion in the departments could pose to republican unity:

Des directoires de départements coalisés osent se constituer arbitres entre l'Assemblée Nationale et le roi. Ils forment une espèce de Chambre haute éparse au sein de l'Empire: quelques-uns même usurpent l'autorité législatrice; et, par l'effet d'une ignorance profonde, en déclamant contre les républicains, ils semblent vouloir organiser la France en républicque fédérative. C'est au nom du roi qu'ils allument les divisions intestines.[2]

Nor was this suspicion restricted to the capital. In the Gard, where Rabaut Saint-Etienne proposed the creation of a 'fédération armée des départements méridionaux' to defend themselves against the threat of foreign invasion, his initiative was vitriolically denounced by those who felt that it was damagingly divisive. In September 1792 Danton went so far as to deny the validity of any local attachments or departmental loyalties in Revolutionary politics. He was not himself a Parisian, he told the Convention; he had been born in a department and returned there from time to time with the greatest of pleasure. But, he warned, 'aucun de nous n'appartient à tel ou tel département, il appartient à la France entière.' [3] Already the identification was being drawn between departmental politics and the destruction of national unity, an identification which would make deadly propaganda against the federalist authorities during the following summer.

The full impact of that propaganda was not lost on contemporaries. A number of departments teetered on the brink of federalism, wooed by their neighbours to support their acts of rebellion, deterred only by the knowledge that their support would be misconstrued, their political deviation crucified. The case of the Drôme is particularly instructive, a department whose geographic position in the Rhône valley left it exposed to the siren-like appeals of Marseille and Lyon. There can be little doubt that the anger expressed in Valence at the spread of 'anarchy' in the capital was politically potent. It was exactly the sort of sentiment which pushed other localities into open rebellion. But the authorities in the Drôme, with what turned out to be great foresight, allowed themselves to be persuaded by their Jacobin *procureur*, Payan, who warned against hasty and impolitic action. Payan, it is clear, believed devoutly in the essential rightness of his cause; he was in fact fighting a desperate and successful rearguard battle against pro-Girondin and anti-Parisian forces which threatened to engulf the department. His tactics, however, had less to do with ideology than with simple self-preservation. It would, he suggested, be unwise to appear to slander the people of Paris by accusing them of reducing the government to a state of anarchy. An address too critical of Paris could lead to damaging repercussions and even to reprisals. For 'sous des dehors patriotiques cette adresse pouvait donner lieu à des interprétations perfides qui compromettroient l'esprit républicain . . . qu'il était aussi injuste qu'impolitique de présenter comme une faction dangereuse à la liberté les Représentants du peuple et les autorités constituées de Paris . . . qu'il ne fallait pas surtout sembler vouloir désigner comme anarchistes les plus énergiques deffenseurs de la liberté . . . qu'il était encore impolitique d'appeler par des sarcasmes contre Paris la division entre cette cité et les départements de la République.'[4] He went so far as to suggest that the people of Paris might themselves be the best judges of the political troubles that beset the capital, a proposition which the Valentinois, unlike their counterparts in many other provincial cities, seemed prepared to accept. They were wise to do so, since within a few weeks their reaction to events in the capital would have become the touchstone of political reliability, the yardstick by which their loyalty to the Revolutionary state would come to be judged. The least suspicion of deviationism, of wishing to unite local opinion behind a provincial city or a regional club, might lead to denunciation, and denunciation to punishment. Nor was it an issue that can be understood in terms of Left and Right, of extremists and moderates. When the *hébertiste* club in Lille wanted to rally support from surrounding societies in the early months of Year II, it was deterred by the fear that such action might be construed as 'federalism.'

In other words, by the end of 1793 the Jacobin image of federalism had gained a wide constituency; and it has tended, in a somewhat diulted form, to enjoy widespread credence among historians. In part this can be ascribed to the vigorous Jacobin propaganda offensive which followed the spate of revolts in the summer months; in part to the active involvement of the club network in local towns and villages; but principally to the savagery of the repression that rained down on those who were in any way implicated in so-called federalist activity. Accusations of federalism were not confined to the major provincial cities like Marseille or Bordeaux or Caen, nor to the ringleaders of the revolts against the Convention. In departments like the Gard and the Vaucluse small towns and villages were heavily implicated, and the repressive energies of the *Commission Populaire d'Orange* were focused on the eradication of the heresy from south-eastern society. Repression could have an educative as well as a purely policing aspect. This does not mean, of course, that those towns and cities which rebelled against Paris during the summer of 1793 were necessarily dedicated to achieving clear federalist goals, or that the local judges and councillors who took part in the movement would recognise the aims which the courts and the government ascribed to them. Indeed, practically to a man, they rejected any charge of federalism as being totally without foundation. They might be in revolt against the abuses and extravagances of Parisian politics, but they were not, they insisted, trying to break up the unity of the country or to establish separate regional administrations. In all the major centres of revolt, the leaders would seem to have been unanimous in rejecting any federal form of government for France. They continually emphasized the scrupulous legality of their demands. As the *Comité Général des 32 Sections de Marseille* phrased it in May 1783, Marseille had no quarrel with the law of the land. 'On y prêche l'amour de la Patrie et de la Liberté, le respect des Lois, la nécessité de l'ordre, le besoin de s'unir et de s'aimer . . .'[5] There was nothing, they felt, in their language or their actions that could be interpreted as destructive of national unity. The case was put even more pressingly by two advocates of rebellion, Hallot and Fonveille, in their address to the Department of the Drôme. They urged general insurrection as the only answer to France's woes, but not a 'federalist' insurrection. It was a distinction, they insisted, which would be clearly drawn:

Ils vous parlent de fédéralisme; ils vous disent que nos démarches ne
tendent qu'à établir le fédéralisme dans la République; citoyens, il
n'est pas un seul d'entre vous dont les lumières ne soient suffisantes
pour juger l'imposture de cette accusation ou le vide de son application.

Que vous proposons-nous? est-ce de morceler la République, de
vous aggréger à une section du peuple français, pour vous isoler de
l'intérêt commun et procurer dans l'état plusieurs centres de puissance, d'action, de mouvement? A ces traits seulement reconnoissons
le fédéralisme.

Au contraire, nous voulons que tous les Français, soumis aux mêmes
lois, animés des mêmes principes, unis d'une même lien, dirigés vers
un même but, fondent par leur toute-puissance, par l'exercice indivisible de leur souveraineté, un gouvernement libre nécessairement un,
nécessairement homogène, la république une et indivisible.[6]

There is no reason to question the sincerity of Hallot and Fonvielle or to
quibble with their admirably lucid reasoning. Like most of the other
federalist leaders they considered themselves to be loyal republicans and
were horrified by the charges of counter-revolution which were laid against
them. They were also committed constitutionalists who saw in the Constitution the guarantee of liberty and of equality before the law which was
the birthright of every citizen. And there is little or nothing to suggest that
they preferred an American style of constitution, with its federal structure
and intense suspicion of centralized power, to that with which France had
been endowed. Indeed, as good provincial bourgeois, they often seemed
quite obsessed by constitutional niceties, arguing that the status quo must
be preserved and casting a critical eye on the more extreme revolutionary
initiatives emanating from Paris. They could with some justice claim that it
was not they, but the Paris Jacobins, who were in breach of the Revolution's laws, and they rejected any claim that they were putting national
unity at risk. In the same address to the people of the Drôme the case for
federalism was persuasively laid out. Resistance to oppression, claimed
Hallot and Fonvielle, made common action indispensable, and if that
action was to be classed as federalism, then it was the citizen's constitutional right to stand up to an oppressor which provided its justification.
'Fédérons-nous, citoyens de la Drôme,' they pleaded, 'fédérez-vous avec
tous les Français, et voyons ce que diront les factieux lorsque la France
entière n'aura qu'un centre d'unité, et se sera fédérée pour ne forme qu'un
tout indivisible.'[7] Their declared aim, and that of federalist municipalities
throughout France, was that of saving and defending the Republic, not of
putting the national interest at risk.

If that is true, it may legitimately be asked why the federalist revolt
aroused such heated passions among the Jacobins and in the population at

large. In ideological terms the threat which it posed might seem to have been slight. Few, even at the time, took seriously the possibility of a splintered sovereignty, with the federalist cities acting as the focal points for regionalist movements. Of the leading Girondins only Buzot and Barbaroux toyed briefly with the ideas of political regionalism and sought to restore part of their lost power to the French provinces. If Madame Roland is to be believed, for instance, Barbaroux was attracted by the idea of an independent 'République du Midi,' of a federal structure whereby Marseille and the south might break away from Paris and from the unacceptable face of sans-culotte politics. But the evidence for the existence of a significant secessionist movement is unconvincing. Of the cities which raised the standard of revolt in the summer of 1793, only Marseille could muster much backing from the small towns and villages of its hinterland. Lyon lacked any significant level of support among the countrymen of the Forez and the Bresse, where the very name of Lyon still conjured up images of royalism and counter-revolution. Bordeaux, which might have seemed well placed economically to exploit its ties with the rural communities of the south-west, achieved only mediocre results: of 559 communes in the Gironde, some 130 accepted to follow the *Commission Populaire* down the road to rebellion. Only Marseille was in the happy position of being able to command respect and loyalty from the people of Provence, among whom it enjoyed an enviable reputation for revolutionary integrity. The Marseillais had worked hard to build up their following. In 1791 and 1792 they had sent out *pèlerinages* to villages throughout the region, winning them over to support of the city's initiatives; they had intervened against the Chiffonistes in Arles and against moderate factions in Avignon; above all, they had marched to Paris in response to Barbaroux's call and had penned the battle song of the Republic, the Marseillaise. But, significantly, few of the communes which accepted to follow Marseille's lead – and they were many in the Var, Vaucluse and Bouches-du-Rhône – were won over by Barbaroux's federalist dream. The fear of secession, of the gradual break-up of the Republic, was wholly unreal, the result of Jacobin scaremongering and of the political paranoia which characterized that precarious summer.

In contrast, the political threat posed by the federalist revolt was real enough. No government could with equanimity stand by and allow the major cities of France to withdraw their recognition and reclaim their share of national sovereignty. More particularly, no government could be expected to tolerate a series of urban revolts at a time when the frontiers were under threat from foreign armies and when internal communication was so vital to provision French forces. The civil war in the west could only increase the sense of national malaise, and the fear was always present that the federalist cities would join forces with the Vendeans against Paris. Toulon's treason in handing over the navy and the port installations to the English and the Spanish fleets merely served to underline the scale of the danger which threatened. The rebel cities were, of course, keenly aware of the degree to which their actions could be represented as assaults on French interests, as deliberate acts of sabotage to undermine the security of the *patrie*. They knew how their revolts would be interpreted in Paris, yet they had little choice about timing, since, even if the links between federalism and the Girondins are somewhat tenuous, the original impetus to revolt often followed closely on the revolution of May 31 and the arrest of the Girondin leadership in the Convention. And though they took great care not to identify their cause with those of royalists or counter-revolutionaries, their efforts were doomed to failure. Refractory priests and *émigré* nobles were attracted by the existence of political havens where the writ of revoutionary government did not run. The presence of General Précy at the head of the Lyonnais army, and the involvement of a sizeable number of *ci-devants* among the officer corps, could not but add to Lyon's uncertain reputation in republican circles. Nor did the federalist cities win much favour by distancing themselves from the Vendean rebels. The Bordelais, it is true, kept their troops in the Vendée, fighting in the Republican armies against the *Blancs*. But Lyon refused to provide supplies for troops passing down the Rhône valley on their way to join the *Armée d'Italie*; and violence frequently flared between government soldiers and the partisans of the federalist cities. As a result, federalism was already cursed with an unpatriotic image, even before the propaganda disaster that was Toulon. With the French armies still struggling on the frontiers, it was unavoidable that the federalist cities would be tainted by accusations of counter-revolution and of treason.

These charges were the more difficult to refute in that the essence of federalism was so very elusive. If it was not a coherent ideology, why did it have such a widespread appeal in the French provinces? How widespread, indeed, was the threat which it posed? Who was and who was not 'federalist' during the summer of 1793? The answers to such questions are perhaps less clearcut than might be expected. If the figures published by the federalist centres themselves could be believed, then the movement was deeply implanted throughout the *hexagone*. Pamphlets and handbills printed in Bordeaux, Marseille and Caen all spoke of sixty, or sixty-six or sixty-nine departments ready to take up arms against the 'usurpateurs' in the capital. The principal Girondin politicians also believed in the validity of these figures and earnestly repeated them in their memoirs. And a generation of historians, in the mould of Henri Wallon, took up the cry. But in reality these claims amounted to very little. All the principal centres of the revolt, desperately anxious to justify themselves in the eyes of others and to gain some semblance of support that would lessen their isolation and feelings of vulnerability, sent out *commissaires* to convert others to their cause. From Caen they went to the major centres of

Normandy and Brittany; from Lyon to Burgundy and the Rhône valley; from Bordeaux to the Charentes and to the departments of the south-west; from Marseille to the towns and villages of Provence. They were often warmly received by their neighbours, whom they regaled with their fears of Jacobin oppression and their optimistic declarations of intent; in many cases they came away blessed with the good wishes of their hosts and with greetings that conveyed encouragement. But they should have treated such greetings with circumspection. The fact that a department or municipality pronounced a few encouraging words to two men obviously devout in their political protestations was not a promise of practical assistance, and the same departments whose support was so gratefully reported in the federalist cities would rarely agree to tolerate the passage of a federalist army across their territory or to provide any of its own men as reinforcements for the cause. As the Bordelais discovered to their cost, others – like the administrations of the Haute-Vienne and the Corrèze – were less interested in the dream of insurrection than they were concerned to guarantee their own safety, with the result that fraternal greetings could soon turn to disclaimers and recrimination. The number of departments which actively involved themselves in the movement, as Paul Hanson has revealed in his thesis, was strictly limited. At most forty-nine were moved to protest about the proscription of the Girondins in the days following June 2, as against the thirty-two which rushed to approve the Jacobins' action. And of these forty-nine, only thirteen continued to resist after a few days. Seven were in the north-west of the country, in Brittany and Normandy (the Calvados, Côtes-du-Nord, Eure, Finistère, Ille-et-Vilaine, Mayenne and Morbihan); the Rhône-et-Loire was followed by the Ain and the Jura; the south-east was represented by the Bouches-du-Rhône and the Gard; to be followed shortly afterwards by the Var; and the Gironde stood alone against the national government in the south-west. Elsewhere opposition did not pose any serious threat to the Convention's authority, consisting of little more than short-lived protests about the arrest of their deputies and self-righteous squawks about the dangers of anarchy in the capital.

But in those areas where the revolt took root, the political threat to Paris was clear enough. Propagandist missions sought to destroy the confidence of the people in their own government. The Lyonnais, for example, rushed to offer protection to any town or district which might feel threatened by the Jacobin menace. 'Si les brigands vous menacent, vous nous verrez accourir à votre secours avec un zèle égal à votre énergie. Nous avons tous le même intérêt; tous le même besoin: l'intérêt de nous unir, le besoin de l'ordre.'[8] The various popular commissions usually went rather further, denying the writ of the national government in the territories over which they had control. Some went so far as to propose that government be withdrawn from Paris altogether, given the threat to public order which the Parisian sections were deemed to constitute. On June 19, for instance, the *Commission Populaire* in the Gironde took up an idea that already enjoyed a certain mode in the federalist cities and invited all those of like mind to send a delegation to a new central assembly at Bourges 'pour y concerter les moyens d'exécuter avec accord, et d'une manière uniforme, les mesures adoptées par les départements.'[9] What they were proposing was nothing less than the establishment of an alternative national government at a central spot which would be removed from the political intemperance of Paris. Even more alarming was the fact that the federalist authorities generally backed up their threat with force, raising departmental battalions, ostensibly to defend themselves against attack, but also with the declared intention of marching on Paris to restore the integrity – and the authority – of the Convention. In practice such military ambitions were thwarted by poor organization, fear, and public indifference. Recruitment, coming so soon after the *levée des 300,000*, proved sluggish, and the battalions were seriously undersubscribed. Desertion was as serious a problem for the federalist leaders as it was for government generals, and it took threats of draconian punishment to bully soldiers into their units. Their effectiveness in the field was, in the event, very limited: Bordeaux's *force départementale*, for example, got no further than Langon on its long march to Paris before dispersing in drunken disorder. But the symbolic threat for the Convention and for national unity should not be underplayed. Lyon did raise an armed force of 6400 men, a force which could be used for offensive as well as defensive purposes. Troops from Marseille and Nîmes did plan a joint military operation in the corridor of the Rhône valley before being dispersed at Pont Saint-Esprit. A federalist army from the north-west did engage Republican soldiers in battle at Brécourt. Both for French Republicans and for their enemies abroad, the federalist revolt was a serious blow to the image of 'la République une et indivisible.'

Yet the federalist leaders insisted that they were not counter-revolutionaries, that their commitment was to the Republic and to the constitution. If allegations of 'federalism' must be dismissed as the language of factionalism, then so must the charge that they were closet royalists, providing behind their constitutional facade an opportunity for the agents of the King to build a bridgehead on French soil. Despite the hope which the revolts aroused in *émigré* communities in Turin and Coblentz, there is no evidence to suggest that the federalist leaders had monarchist leanings. Many of them, indeed, had had long political careers in revolutionary politics in their respective cities, their involvement on the municipal councils dating back to 1789 or 1790. They might be conservative revolutionaries – in the Orne some of them had regarded the Tenth of August as a serious lapse into unconstitutional behaviour – but their commitment to the Revolution cannot be called into doubt. In most instances the revolt centres on the popular sections; in one case – Caen – it was the Jacobin

Club itself which took the first steps toward insurrection. Even in Lyon, where Précy and his royalist associates held so much military authority, political power did not pass out of the hands of the republican politicians who controlled the sectional movement and the *Commission Populaire* of the Rhône-et-Loire. And Précy himself was a liberal monarchist who cannot be seen as a mere agent of the émigrés and who had no formal correspondence with the princes during the period of the siege. What is more, in the voluminous declarations of faith produced by the rebels, there is no hint of an appeal to monarchical reaction. On June 2 the sections of Lyon proclaimed their loyalty to the Republic to anyone who would listen: 'Toutes les sections de la Cité vous jurent, et à la République entière, de défendre jusqu'à la mort, l'unité, l'indivisibilité de la République, le respect des personnes et des propriétés, la soumission entière à la loi, aux autorités constituées, aux décrets émanés des représentants du peuple . . .'[10] A speech printed and circulated by one of the leading federalist sections in Toulon made the point even more strongly: they were dreaming of a more perfect form of republicanism. 'Le gouvernement républicain est sans contredit le meilleur, dit J. J. Rousseau, mais, pour en jouir, il faudroit être des anges. Hé bien, citoyens, devenons vertueux et nous en jouirons, car dans ce sens ange et homme vertueux sont synonimes.'[11] Despite their clear differences with the government in Paris, they remained committed to the principles underpinning republican government. In the vast majority of cases they even allowed a vote to be taken on the new Constitution.

If the federalist cities refrained from criticising republican institutions, they were relatively free with their criticism of Paris and its citizens. Indeed, it is tempting to see anti-Parisian sentiment as a major element in their politics, given the violence of their language toward the capital. The Lyonnais, in common with other federalist cities, bitterly resented the prominent role which Paris was able to play in national politics, and quickly concluded that the Parisians had abused that role. They should follow Lyon's example by showing respect for the laws; they should cease to oppress those around them; they should liberate the Convention from the pernicious influence of their popular movement. In short, Paris was 'cette cité orgueilleuse qui a trop longtemps abusé de son pouvoir et de son influence dangereuse.'[12] It was a popular image. Even the radicals in Toulon had denounced Parisian influence and Parisian ambition in January 1793, when they had – somewhat ironically – proposed that a battalion be raised to march on Paris to liberate the Convention. From time to time the resentment which Paris evoked in the provinces became politicized, and that resentment could lead to extreme and injudicious threats from provincial politicians. Isnard achieved instant notoriety, and did much to undermine the Girondin cause, by his rash declaration, 'au nom de la France entière,' that 'Paris serait anéanti.'[13] But he was not alone. In Toulouse, where federalism proved a short-lived phenomenon, Arbanière urged open rebellion, in his rather picturesque phrase, 'afin que les eaux de la Garonne, du Gers, de l'Aude, du Tarn, du Lot, de la Corrèze, de l'Ariège, de l'Hérault, de la Durance et du Rhône forment un torrent pour engloutir cette monstrueuse ville de Paris.'[14] The anger of provincial leaders was sometimes fuelled by economic grievance, by the feeling that the national government had abandoned their local industries to their fate or had destroyed a local source of wealth or trade. Jealousies were increased by the contrast between the subsidised bread in the capital and the inflated prices which local people were forced to pay. In the Calvados, for instance, there was widespread suspicion that the Parisians had manipulated the Maximum for their own selfish purposes: here, in Mathiez's phrase, 'le fédéralisme des subsistances doubla le fédéralisme politique.'[15] But in this respect the Calvados may be something of an exception. More generally, economic grievances added weight to federalist propaganda, but were rarely central to the revolts themselves. At root, it was not Paris that was under attack, but the kind of politics which Paris represented.

Indeed, the extent of anti-Parisian feeling in provincial towns can easily be exaggerated. It is true that federalist spokesmen often talked of the need for political decisions to be taken locally and gloried in a sense of their own identity. In the south especially, the language of the parish pump had an instant and powerful appeal. But localism was not a guarantee that a community would turn against Paris or reject the national revolution. In Toulouse, where local chauvinism ran high, the federalist revolt was marked by a predictably particularist mentality, but this expressed itself in the rejection of links with all outsiders, including the federalist centres of Bordeaux and Marseille, and arguably had the effect of reducing the city's insurrection to utter impotence. For many French communities the rivalries which rankled most deeply were the local ones, between towns and cities which saw one another as competitors for the same spoils and the same trade, rather than between provincial opinion and that of a distant capital. Traditional rivalries died hard, and they had in many cases been exacerbated by the administrative lottery of 1790 when departmental and district responsibilities had been fought over and the allocation of tribunals and justices of the peace determined. Mutual ill-feeling was greatest between local rivals, like Albi and Castres, Bordeaux and Libourne, Saint-Flour and Aurillac. This lack of local unity became very obvious during the federalist revolts themselves, for it was rare to find an entire department united behind its *chef-lieu*. The Jacobins could usually play on such animosities to find a counterweight to the main city, a town that would be eager to distance itself from the revolt and act as a launching-pad for government retaliation. Thus in the Bouches-du-Rhône they found ready support in Aubagne, in the Gironde in La Réole. In the Jura they could play off Dôle against Lons-le-Saunier, in the Orne Domfront against Alençon. More locally still, Salon and Martigues, near-neighbours who had fought bitterly over the award of a district in 1790, continued to fight on opposite sides during the federalist upheavals in the south-east. As Donald Sutherland has emphasized, 'it is only partly correct to describe the federalist movement as "provincial" since Paris did retain large islands of loyalty throughout the Republic which were later used as bases for repression.'[16]

A close examination of the attacks made against Paris shows that the target was seldom the city or its inhabitants *en bloc*, but rather the extremists whom it was believed to harbour. Everywhere the charges were the same, that the Revolution was being distorted and would eventually be destroyed by the 'malveillants,' the 'anarchists,' the 'gens sans aveu' of the Paris popular movement. These anarchists are seldom defined. But repeatedly, even monotonously, they are accused of taking over the sectional movement in the capital and of seeking to control the Montagnard 'faction' in the Convention. The Jacobin deputies were reduced in their propaganda to the rather unflattering role of mouthpieces for the anarchists in the streets and the popular *faubourgs*. Deputies sent on missions to the provinces were similarly stripped of any opinions of their own, becoming in their turn the creatures of the most bloodthirsty Parisian *sans-culottes*. All were condemned as 'hommes de sang,' symbolized by Robespierre and more particularly by the hated figure of Marat. The Montagne, indeed, was increasingly seen as a helpless puppet in the hands of the Paris Commune, and no advice or news emanating from the Convention or from the Jacobin Club was awarded any credence. When Paris informed the federalist cities that the Convention could debate freely, this was dismissed as the predictable 'sophismes' of the 'anarchistes.'[17] The assessment of the Section de la Grande Côte, on the Croix Rousse in Lyon, was in this regard highly typical. The Convention, said the Section, could not be free, for the simple reason that it was engulfed by Parisian anarchy:

> La section n'a pu s'empêcher de voir que la Convention Nationale est opprimée par les tribunes qui par des huées, des cris, des hurlements, forçent au silence les deputés patriotes . . . qu'elle est opprimée par la Commune de Paris plus puissante qu'elle et qui s'est permis l'infraction de plusieurs décrets, notamment de ceux relatifs à la liberté de la presse.[18]

The departments of the north-west – the Calvados, Ille-et-Vilaine and Eure – attempted to rally their neighbours to the anti-jacobin cause by stirring up fury against what they termed the 'usurpateurs' of the capital. The Parisians, they declared, must be punished for their crimes, 'pour avoir commis les vols et les assassinats de septembre; pour avoir, à cette époque à jamais exécrable, demandé l'établissement d'un Triumvirat; forcé l'élection d'un Marat et de ses vils complices; et dès les premiers jours de l'Assemblée Conventionnelle, préparé son avilissement et provoqué sa dissolution.'[19] All the federalist departments attacked Paris in these terms, seeing the Paris popular movement as the natural enemy of the political stability which they craved, and accusing the Commune of denying them their most basic constitutional rights. It was this perception which explained their insistence on the need for departmental armies and which lay behind their desire to move the Convention to the safety of a provincial town. It was this view, too, which pushed them to make their most dangerously immoderate demands. The Breton departments, for instance, wanted the Commune to be immediately purged and all state subsidy to the *sans-culottes* to be ended; they further asked that there be established in Paris as many communal authorities as there were judicial divisions. They wanted nothing less than the total destruction of the *sans-culottes' power base.*

This concern to root out the worst abuses of Parisian radicalism meant that the federalist cities could appear very negative in their attitude to others and highly tentative in the reforms which they proposed. They rushed to express their outrage at the harm being done by 'malveillants'; they dreamed somewhat nostalgically of a return to constitutionalism; they spoke of a world where the Convention would be freed from illegitimate pressures and where all eighty-three departments could enjoy a measure of real equality without fear of domination from the capital. They never tired of denouncing extremism in others, and stressed the importance of increased vigilance to defend the interests of 'public safety.' To this end, federalism was an intensely confrontational movement, concerned less with the definition of political principle than with the eradication of abuse. All Lyonnais, claimed the sections on June 2, had become brothers together, in that they united in combatting their common enemies – 'l'anarchie, le royalisme, la féodalité, le despotisme, tous les monstres, enfin, qui voudroient soulever leurs têtes hideuses et qu'ils ont juré d'écraser.'[20] It might seem a formidable enterprise, but it was a task of policing, of *épuration*, rather than of pursuing a positive political programme. Where the political ideals were taken up or incorporated into anti-jacobin propaganda, they generally emanated from Girondin politicians whose manifestos and appeals had made some impact. Buzot, for instance, won considerable favour with his emphasis on the importance of constitutional propriety and his insistence that the 1791 constitution had provided an admirable political balance; for him, the political schism dated from the September Massacres in Paris and the Jacobins' refusal to condemn the *septembriseurs*. In particular, departmental and municipal authorities clutched at the words of their own deputies who had raised their voices in alarm at supposed Jacobin plots and outrages. Vergniaud had alarmed his Bordeaux constituents when he had written, 'sous le couteau,' on May 5, that persecution awaited them all: 'Si vous demeurez dans l'apathie, tendez vos bras; les fers sont préparés et le crime règne.'[21] Barbaroux made a very similar impact in the urban centres of the Midi. And a highly polemical pamphlet published by Birotteau, the deputy from the Pyrénées-orientales, enjoyed considerable vogue in federalist cities. They responded to his bloodcurdling images of Jacobin anarchy, warmed to their assigned role as the champions of liberty, and saw justification for their rebellion in his chilling description of the tyranny that was being prepared: 'Les poignards étaient prêts, les rôles des bourreaux distribués, le prix du crime payé d'avance.'[22]

But if the federalist leaders quoted the words of Girondin politicians and took comfort from their support, it would be wrong to see federalism as a 'Girondin' movement. The overthrow of the Girondins in the Convention on May 31–June 2 is too often taken as the starting-point for any analysis of federalism, and it is too easily assumed that the series of provincial revolts which took place in the ensuing days must necessarily be directly related to political events in the capital. The picture looks beguilingly simple. A large provincial city with moderate representation in the Convention revolts against Jacobin tyranny on hearing in the early days of June that their parliamentary institutions had been defiled and their members arrested. The bonds of personal loyalty to their deputies lie at the root of the revolt, combined with a class solidarity between the Girondins in Paris and the moderate bourgeoisie of the French provinces. This is the image of federalism classically described at the end of last century by Henri Wallon, a historian for whom the federalists were heroes to be lionized and the Girondins the doyens among Revolutionary democrats:

> Défenseurs résolus de l'inviolabilité de la représentation nationale, ce sont eux que l'on accusera d'avoir voulu diviser la France; et le mot qui exprime l'union de leurs efforts dans la pensée patriotique de maintenir intacts les droits du peuple souverain sera le titre de leur condamnation.'[23]

Though a substantial literature now exists to belie this image, it is still to be found in even the most recent general discussions of federalism. Of course there was some link between events in the capital and the defiant mood in the provinces during the summer of 1793; it would be foolish to suggest otherwise. News of the Jacobin *coup* was met with incomprehension and anger in many towns and cities. But, except perhaps in Bordeaux, from where such a large part of the Girondin delegation hailed, the personal ties should not be exaggerated or the impact of national politics overstated. In some of the most notable instances of insurrection, the federalist revolt had, as we have seen, actually preceded the Jacobin seizure of power in Paris. The events of May 31 must therefore be put more clearly in their true context, as a spur to revolt in communities where there was already a grievance against Jacobins, as confirmation to those who had already risen against their local Jacobin town bosses that their initiatives had been timely and necessary. In Lyon, for instance, the *Commission Populaire* protested in the most explicit terms against the violation of the Convention, 'victime d'une faction scélérate.'[24] It hardened their attitudes and strengthened their resolve. But it cannot explain the initial impulse to federalism.

Federalism was a local movement born out of local circumstance. That is the message which is made resoundingly clear in the increasing number of studies devoted to the individual rebellions of the summer of 1793. The revolts generally began as movements of the towns' sections, often linked to the elites of the municipal councils, and they had their roots in the politics and the social climate of the communities themselves. They might be impatient for a new constitution; they might be outraged by reports of the extravagant and threatening behaviour of the Parisian sections; they might be kept abreast of Paris politics by their local deputies. But again and again we find that the insurrection was less against Parisian enemies than against local ones, that the revolts were aimed at Jacobin excesses at home rather than at the Club in Paris. Thus Albert Goodwin identifies political events in and around Caen as holding the key to the insurrection in Normandy; in Lyon the sectional revolt was aimed at Chalier and his municipal administration, not at national figures like Robespierre or Marat; and in Toulon, as Malcolm Crook makes clear, federalism had its roots in years of acrimonious faction-fighting. The withdrawal of recognition from the Convention, he writes, 'was the consequence rather than the cause of a municipal revolution at Toulon which replaced one local faction with its bitter enemy.'[25] If this is true – and it seems to be corroborated by virtually every local study so far produced – then federalism can be understood only in terms of local issues and local power struggles. The national situation was never more than tangential, despite the propaganda of the federalist authorities, who increasingly borrowed the language and imagery of the Girondin–Montagnard struggle to justify their defiance. In a country where regional differences remained paramount and where the nation-state was a recent creation, politics retained its distinct local dimension. Clubs and sections in Lyon and Marseille were in no sense carbon copies of their Parisian namesakes. By emphasizing what was different in each local situation the historian can hope to offer some explanation of what may appear the most puzzling aspect of federalism – the divergence and autonomy of the responses which were evoked. Why, for instance, was the movement so weak in Toulouse when Bordeaux and Marseille were engulfed by anti-jacobin sentiment? Why were major commercial cities like Nantes and Dijon apparently exempt from their influence? Why did the movement sweep some departments but not others?

Why, finally, within a single region, were there such startling differences between the reactions of individual towns and villages? These are questions which cannot be adequately answered in terms of a single, national political discourse.

Economic interests may go some way to provide an explanation, but again they do not tell the whole story. In trading ports and industrial cities the Revolution often did seem to place economic well-being in jeopardy, and the ravages of war and emigration made themselves felt. A feeling that their local economy was being made to suffer for Paris's political goals could help to focus opposition and could serve to unite very different social groups behind the federalist banner. This helps explain, for instance, the militancy of many Lyon silkworkers in the anti-jacobin cause, or the support of the Bordeaux sections for a movement led by the merchant and professional interests of the City. Bordeaux, it is true, is one city where it is tempting to see federalism as a bourgeois movement, since representatives of the legal and commercial fraternities did hold many of the leading positions on the departmental and municipal councils, on the *Commission Populaire*, in the more conservative sections, and in the command of the *force départementale*. The leaders of the sectional movement, like Section Simoneau, represented the commercial interest of the Bordeaux waterfront and urged action to defend the values of trade and enterprise. So in Nîmes the leading activists, and those who served as presidents, secretaries and *commissaires* of the sections, represented a clear commercial and professional interest. In Marseille, where the sections contained a strong representation of the city's commercial elite, the Central Committee of the sections defended trade and capitalism in the most explicit terms. In a printed address to the people of Toulon in May 1793 it angrily rejected criticisms of egotism and cupidity:

> On accuse le commerce. Et qui nourrit aujourd'hui Marseille et les Départemens, si ce n'est le Comité de subsistance? Qui fournit annuellement à la France l'immense quantité de bled nécessaire à sa consommation? qui garnit vos arsénaux, vous donne des matelots et des ouvriers, anime et fait mouvoir six millions de bras, si ce n'est le commerce?[26]

Even if the richest merchants in these cities were rarely present in person on the federalist bodies, their interests were consistently represented by the lesser merchants, by younger brothers, by their clerks and *commis*. Federalism and economic interest were both in specific local contexts interwoven, and an economic interpretation of the movement can never be entirely dismissed. But it would be rash to try to build a simple class model of the revolts on such impressionistic observations. In most of the larger cities federalism was essentially a movement of the sections, and the sections were in no sense committed to the maintenance of narrow trading or professional interests. In Lyon, for instance, it may be true that the militant Section de la Croisette contained some of the most coherent spokesmen of the rich merchant elites of the city; but others of the federalist sections were dominated by artisans and silkworkers. It is difficult to find any coherent social explanation for their enthusiastic espousal of the revolt.

The conclusion is inescapable that federalism was a political movement, not a social one, and a political movement that evolved from revolutionary rather than counter-revolutionary traditions. If the federalist authorities were unanimous in their 'anti-jacobinism,' the focus of their anger was less the Jacobin government in Paris than local Jacobin militants who were adjudged to have abused power in their towns and cities or to have posed an intolerable threat to the security of life and property. Their language might be the language of Robespierre and Marat; but their bloodcurdling threats and their cannibalistic promises were particular to the Midi or to the valley of the Rhône. Federalism was in the vast majority of cases a movement of republicans, of men fearful for the gains they had made, angry that their Revolution was being deformed and undermined by their political opponents. It had its roots in local schisms and conflicts which could be just as acrimonious as any in the capital. In Lyon and Marseille the revolt took the form of risings by the sectional assemblies against Jacobin municipalities which had had a chance to demonstrate their intolerance of opposition during several months of contentious city administration. In Toulon, where federalism was in no way blunted by being delayed, it was again the conduct of the local Jacobins which inspired insurrection. By the summer of 1793 they might have seemed moderate and reasonable to the extent that it was they who tried to cool the enthusiasms of their allies in the clubs; but it was not forgotten that they had during the previous year been merciless in rooting out all political opposition in the city, nor that, the previous October, they had closed down the eight sections of Toulon rather than accept the fact of political pluralism. And even where Jacobins were not actually in power, their opponents lived in constant fear of their violence and their intrigues. Their widespread hatred of Marat – and it is interesting that it was Marat rather than Robespierre who was the constant butt of their abuse – stemmed from the violence of his verbal outbursts and from the fear that local Jacobin militants were being encouraged by his example to forgo constitutional methods and turn instead to anarchy. In the eyes of many local republicans the Jacobin clubs had become the principal source of political dissension in their local communities. This in turn caused widespread bitterness, a bitterness which was to prove a fruitful breeding-ground for insurrection.

Federalism, in other words, can be seen as a response to the excesses and provocations of others. It is to be found in communities where there were intense political divisions and rivalries, where the initial unanimity about the aims and methods to be followed had been shattered, where the political innocence of the early months of the Revolution had been destroyed. Where harmonious relations continued to exist among Republicans, on the other hand, in communes without internecine strife between clubs and sections, there was rarely any suggestion of support for insurrection. To understand the nature of federalism, therefore it is necessary to study the development of political behaviour in the community since the beginning of the Revolution, as it is here that the seeds of later turbulence were sown. Did a town enjoy a substantial period of relative harmony, with all the major interest groups devoted to the cause of reform? Were issues like religion and recruitment already causing deep political dissension in 1791 and 1792? Was consensus sacrificed in the early months with the appearance of royalist lobbies or through the terror tactics of individual *patriotes*? In the Midi, especially, moderation was difficult to maintain in a climate where the level of politicisation was high and where violence, both of deed and of language, was widespread. In Nîmes such divisions go back to the *Bagarre* in 1790 and to the deep hatreds between Catholics and Protestants which vitiated any idea of a peaceful revolution in the town. In Avignon and the Comtat the destructive excesses of Jourdan Coupe-Têtes ensured that local politics would remain permanently riddled with factionalism. Everywhere in the south the strong penetration of clubs and societies guaranteed that even the most mundane of local initiatives risked becoming politicized, with a consequent increase in denunciation and mutual intolerance. Violence, too, has its dialectic, and federalism, stripped of its ideological pretensions, can be seen as an essential part of that dialectic within the local community.

In the larger cities the federalist revolt always managed to retain a certain veneer of ideology. The world of pamphlets and political newspapers, of petitions and counter-petitions from clubs, municipalities, societies and sections, ensured that it was enshrined in a political vocabulary which gave it a degree of respectability. Like their mentors in the Convention, Barbaroux and Isnard, Boyer-Fonfrède and Vergniaud, the leaders of the major urban revolts were highly literate and well-versed in the art of propaganda. But federalism was not confined to the greater urban centres. In the south-east, where the club movement was most deeply rooted and where even moderately-sized villages might expect to have their own society affiliated to the Jacobins, federalism spread rapidly out from the main towns of Marseille and Aix to engulf a considerable part of the rural hinterland. And here, in the villages of Provence and the former Comtat, the character of the movement appears in all its stark simplicity. Here there is little pretence to an understanding of national issues, beyond a crude renunciation of 'anarchie' or of 'maratisme.' Villagers accustomed to follow and to respect the Revolution as it was practised in Marseille – and the Marseillais were always solicitous in informing them of their latest initiatives – turned to support of the federalist revolt less out of ideological conviction than out of loyalty to the men who had educated them in revolution over the previous months. Marseille was now instructing them to help destroy Parisian anarchy, and the leaders of villages like Vénasque had no hesitation in accepting that they were the true revolutionaries, engaged in the noble task of destroying 'un complot horrible' hatched in the Paris *faubourgs*. Without further question they closed their club and formed a section, assured that this was the most appropriate action to prevent the destruction of their revolution. In the words of Jean-Andéol Coste, accused of urging other young men in his village of Camaret to join the federalist force to march on the Convention, he was only doing what he believed to be right, since 'la fière cité de Marseille doit être toujours notre modèle et notre boussole.'[27] Political philosophies were the concern of people more sophisticated than themselves. In the confused world of Revolutionary politics the best that villages could do was to follow those whom they presumed to understand things best.

In this climate political divisions merged easily into personal conflicts, principle into a desire for revenge. Pleas to the Marseille army to help restore 'le bon ordre' were often accompanied by more precise demands – that they free the village from an egalitarian mayor, or from the influence of extreme Jacobins, or from the terror exercised by local patriots. Just as the Lyonnais were far more interested in purging their municipal politics and executing Chalier than in any national issues, so at village level the needs of the federalist leaders were often brutally simple. At Malaucène, for instance, the sectional leaders openly rejoiced at the murder of several village patriots, the men by whom they had been thwarted and threatened over a period of years. At Mormoiron the arrival of the Marseillais was greeted with rapture by villagers who were looking forward to a bloodbath. Joseph Saurel, one of the leading opponents of the local club, gloated publicly that 'les Marseillais allaient arriver avec une guillotine et que les patriotes y passeraient.'[28] The desire for vengeance was never far from the village agenda. Family and clan loyalties helped cement political divisions as sons and wives used the excuse of the federalist revolt to avenge past wrongs to their relatives. And there were plenty of wrongs, real or imaginary, to enflame opinion. French troops at the time of the annexation, National Guards in the years since, patriot armies under Jourdan, all had been callous, brutal, or merely insensitive in their dealings with the village people. Religion had been insulted, carts requisitioned, livestock stolen, besides the arrests and persecutions which family honour demanded should be avenged. All these figure among the reasons given for their anti-jacobin involvement by the men and women arrested in 1793 in the villages of the Vaucluse. What was lacking was any clear awareness of what federalism was, other than the opportunity to express their deeply held dislike for the patriot faction in their midst. In some places it would seem that former royalists and those who had opposed the annexation of the Comtat back in 1790 now hitched their star to the federalist cause. Elsewhere it was a sort of catch-all of measures symbolic of their rejection of Jacobinism. At Grillon, for instance, a village with longstanding factional divisions, the declared aims of the federalists were 'de fermer la sociéte populaire, de brûler la tribune, d'établir des sections, d'arracher l'arbre de la liberté, de destituer la municipalité et le juge de paix.'[29] But in virtually every case where violence of this sort was perpetrated, there is clear evidence that federalism was in no sense an independent and free-standing political movement. It was merely the latest in a long series of factional feuds within the village.

That is not to imply that federalism should be written off as a political nullity, as an irrelevance in any study of the essential character of Revolutionary France. It might even be said to have represented very accurately the nature and the aspirations of the Revolution in the French provinces, where questions of honour and family and village tradition counted for far more than abstract concepts like liberty and equality. It was for this very reason, indeed, that the Jacobins saw it as presenting a unique challenge to their maintenance of office and to their centralist vision of the Revolutionary state. Federalism was, it is true, ideologically rather feeble, lacking the political or sociological rigour which the political scientist is entitled to demand of a serious political movement. But it made a strong appeal to local loyalites and played on a widely-held gut resentment of the bully-boy tactics which so often characterized Jacobin militants in towns and villages. Where factionalism already ran deep, where local politics had lost any pretence at unanimity or at a spirit of co-operation, there federalism would find ready support. Hence, perhaps, the contrast between those towns and cities which became deeply embroiled in revolt during the summer of 1793 and those – like Rouen, or Dijon, or Nantes – where that turbulent period elicited only the most muted of responses. By the same reasoning it might be assumed that to local people the conduct of their elected representatives during the Federalist revolt would hardly have constituted a crime, as the Jacobins and their tribunals insisted, far less a conscious act of counter-revolution. In the short term, of course, they were excluded from office and forced into exile, if they were lucky enough to escape appearing before one of the terrorist courts or revolutionary commissions. But in the longer term many of them were to return to positions of influence under the Thermidoreans and the Directory. At national level Sieyès, and with him the Convention, were to repudiate the Revolution of May 31 and restore those who had participated in acts of opposition to it to their rightful place in the body politic. Locally many of the former federalists returned to high office, apparently undeterred by their experiences during the Terror. This should occasion little surprise. These men were, after all, literate, politically aware, socially respected –

the kind of representatives to whom provincial Frenchmen would naturally turn for leadership in municipal affairs. They were the natural spokesmen of that political class which had been created in the provinces by the municipal revolution of 1790. And they were seen to be what they in fact were, good republicans intent on making their corner of the Republic more efficient and prosperous, men of moderation who resented, as did so many of their fellow citizens, the increasingly harsh and divisive invective emanating from Paris. After 1795 the charge of 'federalism' left no stain on their reputations. It had always been a smear, a term of political abuse beloved of their opponents, and now these opponents were in their turn discredited. Indeed, by 1795 it retained little of its meaning, and none of its political force. Those who had been tarred with the federalist brush two years earlier were now restored to their functions; federalism had given way quite effortlessly to respectable, often rather conservative, provincial repubicanism.

Notes

1 M. J. Syndenham, 'The Republican revolt of 1793 – a plea for less localized studies.' *French Historical Studies* 12 (1981), p. 124.
2 J. M. Roberts and R. C. Cobb (ed.), *French Revolution Documents* (Oxford, 1966), 1, p. 509.
3 H. Morse Stephens, *Orators of the French Revolution* (Oxford, 1892), 2, p. 177.
4 Arch. Dép. Drôme, L44, Directoire du Département de la Drôme, minute of May 27, 1793.
5 Arch. Mun. Toulon, L2–1–5, Comité-Général des 32 Sections de Marseille, 'Adresse aux citoyens de Toulon,' May 1793.
6 Arch. Nat. AF^{II} 43, 'Adresse de citoyens Hallot, député de la Gironde, et Fontvielle, député des Bouches-du-Rhône, à leurs frères du Département de la Drôme,' pp. 8–9.
7 Arch. Nat. AF^{II} 43, 'Adresse de citoyens Hallot, député de la Gironde, et Fontvielle, député des Bouches-du-Rhône, à leurs frères du Département de la Drôme,' p. 9.
8 Arch. Dép. Rhône, 1L375, 'Adresse de 32 sections de la ville de Lyon aux habitants des campagnes,' adopted by the Lyon sections in June 1793.
9 Arch. Dép. Gironde, 12L36, Commission Populaire de la Gironde, minute of June 19, 1793.
10 Arch. Dép. Rhône, 1L375, 'Les sections de la ville de Lyon aux habitants du Département et de toutes les municipalités voisines.'
11 Arch. Mun. Toulon, L 2–I–4, 'Discours prononcé dans la Section no. 8 par le Citoyen Badeigts-Laborde, membre de ladite Section.'
12 Arch. Dép. Rhône, 1L375, 'Adresse des autorités constituées du District et de la ville de Barcelonnette,' 25 June, 1793.
13 J. M. Roberts and J. Hardman (ed.), *French Revolution Documents* (Oxford, 1973), vol. 2, p. 67.
14 M. Lyons, *Révolution et Terreur à Toulouse* (Toulouse, 1980), p. 67.

15 H. Calvet, 'Subsistances et fédéralisme,' *Annales historiques de la Révolution Française* 8 (1931), p. 230.

16 D. Sutherland, *France, 1789–1815: Revolution and Counter-Revolution* (London, 1985), pp. 175–76.

17 Arch. Nat. AF^{II}43, 'Adresse des citoyens Hallot et Fonvielle à leurs frères du Departement de la Drôme,' p. 10.

18 Arch. Dép. Rhône, 1L375, minute of Section de la Grande Côte, June 9, 1793.

19 Arch. Mun. Toulon, L2–I–6, 'Assemblée centrale de résistance à l'oppression – déclaration à la France entière' (1793).

20 Arch. Dép. Rhône, 1L375, 'Les Sections de la ville de Lyon aux habitants du Département et de toutes les municipalités voisines,' June 2, 1793.

21 P. Bernadau, *Histoire de Bordeaux* (Bordeaux, 1839), pp. 428–29.

22 Arch. Dép. Rhône, 1L375, 'J.B. Birotteau, député à la Convention par le Département des Pyrénées-orientales, aux François.'

23 H. Wallon, *La Revolution du 31 mai et le fédéralisme en 1793* 2 vols. (Paris, 1886), 1, p. ii.

24 Arch. Dép. Rhône, 1L375, adresse des Lyonnais à la Convention Nationale 'et au peuple français.'

25 M. H. Crook, 'Federalism and the French Revolution: the revolt in Toulon in 1793', *History* 65 (1980), p. 384.

26 Arch. Mun. Toulon, L2–I–5, 'Comité-Général des 32 sections de Marseille, aux citoyens de Toulon,' May 1793.

27 Arch. Dép. Vaucluse, 8L26, commune de Camaret, dossier Jean-Andéol Coste.

28 Arch. Dép. Vaucluse, 8L39, commune de Mormoiron, dossier Joseph Saurel.

29 Arch. Dép. Vaucluse, 8L25, commune de Grillon, interrogations.

19

Saint-Just: the military commissar

NORMAN HAMPSON

Alsace, at the end of the eighteenth century, was quite unlike any other part of France. It had been annexed comparatively recently, during the previous century, and the monarchy had respected its local identity. A French province from the administrative point of view, socially, culturally and economically it remained part of a German world where nationality was a matter of feeling rather than political allegiance. Before the Revolution it was separated from the rest of France by a customs barrier, and its main trade routes were along and across the Rhine. The overwhelming mass of the population spoke German or Alsatian and could not understand French. In the one city of importance, Strasbourg, the social and intellectual elite could also speak French, but they had often been educated

Reprinted in full, execpt for notes, from N. Hampson, *Saint-Just* (Oxford, Basil Blackwell, 1991), pp. 140–60.

in Germany. Protestantism had been tolerated by the monarchy in Alsace, but since it was not recognized in the rest of France, the Protestant pastors in Strasbourg had been to school and university abroad. This was also true of many Catholics. [Euloge] Schneider, who was to emerge as an extremist during the autumn of 1793, was an Austrian who had been professor of Greek at the university of Bonn before he was appointed episcopal vicar at Strasbourg. Even the bilingual leaders of Strasbourg society, whilst they might share in the national enthusiasm for the revolution, did so with a difference and retained a strong sense of their peculiar local identity. They felt somewhat apart from Frenchmen who came from what they called 'the interior'. Alsace was also unique in the importance of its Jewish population. The men of 1789 believed that part of their mission was to incorporate Jews into French society by granting them full civic rights. Earlier discrimination had tended to confine them to commerce and banking, and their role as suppliers of capital had not always endeared them to their debtors. Class tensions in Alsace were therefore liable to be exacerbated by popular anti-semitism. As revolutionary governments became more radical, they became more suspicious of the affluent, and more inclined to identify themselves with urban artisans. Where Alsace was concerned this meant, for the most part, people who could barely understand French. The Jacobin Club at Strasbourg conducted its sessions in both French and German.

The impact of the Revolution on this idiosyncratic society was both complex and difficult for men from the 'interior' to appreciate. Alsace could not respond like the rest of the country to the new conception of France as an integrated national communty. To the majority of the rural population, isolated by the linguistic barrier, the Revolution was an essentially alien movement. When the revolutionaries reorganized the Church they provoked a good deal of local hostility. In the Bas-Rhin 90 per cent of the clergy refused to take the oath to the new religious settlement and forfeited their livings. In the only other part of France where there was a similar general rejecton of the Civil Constitution of the Clergy – the Vendée – the sequel had been armed revolt against the republic. As early as 1791 there were signs of serious disaffection in the rural areas of Alsace where the population was inclined to sympathize with royalism and with its cardinal-archbishop, Rohan, who declined to take the oath to the Civil Constitution, abandoned his palace in Strasbourg and withdrew to that part of his diocese that lay beyond the Rhine.

Strasbourg itself was rather more responsive to the new message. The Revolution was initially welcomed by the urban elite, which saw it as an essentially political movement. Such people at first dominated the local Jacobin Club which, like most such clubs in the rest of France, was well-heeled, well-mannered and moderate in its politics. After the king's flight in 1791 things changed, and the club passed under the control of men of a more radical temper. They also tended to be less local. With the threat of war in 1791 and war itself a year later, Strasbourg acquired a new significance as a base on the frontier, and army officers – from the interior – assumed a new importance within the Jacobin Club. This probably accentuated a trend, also present in the Vendée, for urban radicalism and rural conservatism to exacerbate each other as fear reinforced conviction on both sides. The Strasbourg Jacobins were exceptional in calling for a republic in 1791 and demanding war as early as January 1792.

When the outbreak of war brought the overthrow of the monarchy Strasbourg went through a particularly stormy year. Alarmed at the way things were going, the moderates created their own club. When he heard of the Parisian insurrection of 10 August 1792 the mayor closed down the Jacobins. During the local elections that autumn the members of the Jacobin Club were eliminated from the municipal government and retained only three seats on the administration of the department. This situation was reversed by visiting Montagnard representatives on mission, who purged the administration and installed one of their local supporters as mayor, despite opposition from the Sections, or political wards, which reflected grass-roots opinion. When the representatives moved on, the Sections reasserted themselves, only to have their own nominees for municipal office dismissed by the department. As in other provincial cities in the spring of 1793, there was an essentially local conflict between urban radicals, who relied on support from visiting deputies from Paris, and the Sections, who resented this interference from outside. Such local particularism was especially strong in Alsace. Each side looked for support in high places, and since the protectors of the local radicals were Montagnard deputies, their opponents tended to identify themselves with the Girondins. When, after the Parisian coup d'état of 2 June 1793, the Girondins tried to organize a national revolt against Paris, this raised understandable doubts about the loyalties of the disaffected local authorities.

The situation was particularly grave in Alsace, since German-speaking opponents of the Montagnards were thought likely to sympathize with the Austrian and Prussian armies immediately to the north of them in the Palatinate and just across the Rhine. Whether or not the local authorities were actually prepared to welcome the allied armies, suspicious Frenchmen, unfamiliar with local politics and unable to understand what the people around them were saying, were bound to see themselves as a kind of beleaguered garrison, defending a stronghold with a civilian population whose heart was not in the fight. In October 1793, before Saint-Just arrived, other representatives on mission purged the administration of the department yet again, set up a *comité de surveillance* drawn from all the local authorities and gave the criminal court 'revolutionary' powers, which allowed it to dispense with some judicial formalities and to judge without appeal.

What made the situation even more dangerous than that in the Vendée was the proximity of enemy troops. During the autumn of 1793 the Committee of Public Safety had managed to recover some ground in Belgium, but only by depleting the armies on the eastern front. In the face of pressure from the Austrian and Prussian forces, the gains made in the previous year were abandoned, France was invaded, her frontier fortresses taken or besieged, and by late October an Austrian army had penetrated almost as far as Strasbourg itself. Thirty or forty miles to the westward the Prussians threatened to outflank the Army of the Rhine and to invade Lorraine. In September the Committee of Public Safety undertook a wholesale purge of the army commanders, who were blamed for the unsuccessful campaigns of the summer. The Moselle Army, facing the Prussians, were entrusted to Hoche who, at twenty-five, was even younger than Saint-Just. Pichegru, who was given command of the Rhine Army, was regarded as an experienced veteran. He was thirty-two. Both generals were men of humble origin who had risen through the ranks. They owed everything to the Revolution, they had proved their ability and they were ambitious to make a name for themselves, but they had no experience of high command and they were in charge of troops demoralized by defeat and facing a winter campaign for which they were desperately short of equipment and supplies. The War Minister, when he decided to make Pichegru senior to Hoche, told him that he was to assume supreme command if the two armies linked up. Unfortunately he did not tell this to Hoche, but this was of no immediate consequence whilst the French armies faced different opponents on separate fronts.

In mid-October the Committee of Public Safety decided to send Saint-Just and Le Bas of the Committee of General Security to the Rhine Army. There was not exactly a shortage of political commissars on the eastern front, where there were already four attached to each of the two French armies of the Rhine and Moselle. Two more were despatched to the Rhine Army only ten days before Saint-Just and Le Bas. The latter were perhaps in a special position since – unlike all the others – they sat on the two most powerful committees of the Assembly but this, in itself, gave them no officially superior status. Their powers were defined as 'extraordinary' but since those of their colleagues were 'unlimited' this scarcely clarified the situation. Quite apart from this hierarchical problem, the plethora of deputies in a military area threatened to repeat what had happened in the Vendée, where the representatives on mission had endorsed the professional rivalries of 'their' generals.

Philippe Le Bas was a few years older than Saint-Just, but not yet thirty. For a Montagnard, he was an unusually modest man. He wrote to his father that it was not his practice to intervene in debates when others had already made his points for him, and he had not thought it worth his while to publish his speech on the appropriate punishment for Louis XVI. He was, however, no nonentity and, unlike Saint-Just, he had already been on one mission to the front. A native of the Pas-de-Calais, he knew the Robespierres. He was one of the little circle that gathered at the house of Duplay, where Robespierre lived, and a few weeks before setting out for Alsace he had married Duplay's youngest daughter, Elisabeth. The question naturally arises of how far Saint-Just was personally responsible for the decisions that went out over the names of himself and Le Bas, and it is insoluble. Perhaps it does not matter very much, since the two men seem to have thought along very similar lines. Le Bas wrote to his wife, towards the beginning of their mission, 'I like and respect him more and more every day. . . The most perfect agreement and constant harmony have prevailed between us.' In July 1794 he was virtually to commit suicide when he insisted on taking his place alongside the proscribed Saint-Just. When he and another deputy had been sent to the Army of the North during the summer, they inaugurated their mission with a proclamation denouncing absenteeism and blaming indiscipline on the officers. They arrested generals and sent officers before the revolutionary tribunal. This set the pattern for what was to happen in Alsace, although the language of the proclamations there had a new crispness that came unmistakably from Saint-Just. When Le Bas wrote to the Committee of Public Safety or to Robespierre, Saint-Just sometimes added a postscript. It is reasonable to assume that they acted in concert, although Saint-Just probably played the leading part. When they returned to Alsace in December, after a brief visit to Paris, accompanied by Le Bas's wife and sister, it was Saint-Just, rather than Elisabeth's husband, who dictated the terms on which the women would be allowed to go. To avoid a wearisome repetition of 'Saint-Just and Le Bas', I intend to follow the practice of most historians, when describing the mission to Alsace, of referring to the former alone, but the reader should bear in mind that both men were involved.

The essential object of the mission was to reverse the military situation, save Strasbourg and drive the Austrians and Prussians out of France before winter put an end to campaigning. This meant that the first objective of the two deputies was to pull the Rhine Army together by restoring discipline and reviving its morale. Their initial proclamation promised precisely that.

> We have arrived and we swear in the name of the army that the enemy will be conquered. If there are amongst you traitors or men indifferent to the people's cause, we bring the sword that shall strike them. Soldiers! We have come to avenge you and to give you leaders who will conduct you to victory. We are resolved to seek out merit, to reward and promote it and to track down every crime, whoever may have committed it.

This may have gone down well with the troops but it probably made rather a different impression on the other deputies in the area by its assumption that everything had to be done from scratch and that it would be done by the two newcomers.

Saint-Just appreciated that morale-building was something of an exercise in public relations. This gave him a good opportunity to indulge his penchant for epigrammatic language and flamboyant gesture. Periodic proclamations assured the army of victory and hurled defiance at the enemy. He replied to a Prussian request for a parley, 'All that the Republic accepts from its enemies and sends back to them is lead.' Fine words did not blind him to the need for the buttering of parsnips. His interventions to ensure the wellbeing of the soldiers suggested that the deputies were thinking primarily of the rank and file and were not inclined to equate the army with its staff officers. As we shall see, he took extraordinary measures to ensure that the troops had boots, shirts and cloaks for the winter campaign. The wounded were to be given comfortable beds in the houses of the more prosperous citizens of Strasbourg. Such general measures were reinforced by well publicized examples of both reward and punishment. Individual soldiers were given horses and arms to reward distinguished conduct. When some of them expressed apprehension about what was happening to their farms in their absence, Saint-Just wrote to the local authorities of the men concerned requesting them to make sure that the land was cultivated at the public expense. When the unfortunate Méquignet, however, requested permission to leave the army and return to Poitiers to look after his fortune of 40,000 livres, Saint-Just had him publicly cashiered and imprisoned for the duration of the war.[1] He intended to generate the impression that nothing could escape his notice, that merit would always be sure of its reward, and its opposite of punishment. His order to Dièche, the general in command of the town garrison, 'Send the gunner who brought this to the clothing store and arrest the clerk who said that he had no time to serve him', was enough to raise a cheer in any army.

Although he did not follow his own advice to representatives at the front to sleep under canvas, Saint-Just did not spare himself. He was on the move all the time, and when the French armies took the offensive he was in the thick of things, proving himself to be as fearless as any of the troops. This was convincingly attested by the deputy, Baudot, who was attached to the Moselle Army. 'I too have been with the armies and seen him in action – and I never saw anything like it. My testimony cannot be suspected for I certainly have no liking for him'.[2]

Saint-Just's determination to show his solicitude for the troops was not prompted by any concern for his popularity. He made it clear to all involved, generals, administrators, local Jacobins, private soldiers – and to his colleagues from the Convention – that he considered himself to be in charge and that his will was law. This was how he envisaged 'revolutionary' action: the suspension of time-wasting formalities in favour of instantaneous action directed by the man in command. As he wrote to Robespierre, 'People make too many laws and too few examples'.

In an attempt to restore some discipline to the defeated army, all ranks were confined to camp and officers told that they would be held responsible if their men succumbed to the temptations of nearby Strasbourg. Dièche was ordered to tell the man in charge of the military hospital that he had twenty-four hours in which to stop admitting malingerers. Three days later the same director, the senior surgeon and chief medical officer all had half of their salary stopped for a month to punish them for the insanitary conditions in their hospital. Any officer found in Strasbourg was to be disciplined, as the unfortunate captain who asked Saint-Just the way to the theatre discovered to his cost. Soldiers trying to enter the city hidden in carts and wagons were to be shot.

As Le Bas explained in a letter to his wife, he and Saint-Just were trying to give the impression that they had eyes everywhere and that any infraction of their rules would be promptly discovered and punished. 'At the moment when he is least expecting it, a general finds us paying him a visit and demanding an account of his conduct.' They followed their usual practice of seizing on specific examples and giving them maximum publicity. A lieutenant was told to explain why one private had been passed over and another, without the requisite period of service, promoted corporal in his place. This sort of thing probably kept everyone in authority on his toes, but it must have meant that the men in command had to devote a good deal of their time to matters of administrative detail. The commander-in-chief, Pichegru, received four requests in a day for information about such matters as the disposal of twenty-three horses. Dièche was reprimanded for failing to reply to five similar enquiries. How far this led to obsession with minutiae and reluctance to assume responsibility on the part of those in command it is impossible to say.

In accordance with the principles of 'revolutionary' action, the powers of the military court were strengthened, and its jurisdiction extended to civilians. Saint-Just preferred this tribunal to the civilian court that his fellow-representatives had elevated to revolutionary status. What he wanted was swift and dramatic actions that would impress and intimidate. This meant making examples. Faced with complaints about the quality of the bread baked for the army, he ordered the military prosecutor to hold an inquiry and to 'make an example on the spot'. There was an obvious danger here that frightened subordinates would demonstrate their zeal by finding scapegoats and paying more attention to the number of their victims than to their guilt. One general was dismissed and then reinstated the next day when it was discovered that he had been blamed for something done by someone else. Saint-Just sent Pichegru's chief of staff before the revolutionary tribunal and then reinstated him when Pichegru complained. He was prepared to listen to other people and to change his mind when challenged by men he trusted, but someone had to have the courage to confront him and he himself was perhaps more concerned with the effect of his 'examples' than with the guilt of those he accused. The military court had ten men shot with the maximum publicity, in front of the army: one general, two colonels, one captain, three NCOs, one private, a man from the army administration and a war contractor. Saint-Just was not a terrorist like those of his colleagues in other areas who engaged in mass executions, but the man who had once been unable to forgive Rousseau for his acceptance of the death penalty had no inhibitions about enforcing it in the name of the Revolution.

Saint-Just saw one of his main functions as ensuring that the troops got the supplies and equipment they needed if they were to take the offensive. His direct line to Carnot allowed him to dispel the latter's comfortable illusion that there were 100,000 men available for action in Alsace, and to persuade the Committee of Public Safety to send reinforcements to the eastern front. Taking a comprehensive view of his 'extraordinary' powers, he threatened the administrators of eight neighbouring departments with the revolutionary tribunal if they did not immediately comply with requisitions of food imposed on them in August. During the autumn of 1793 other representatives on mission, encouraged by the revolutionary government to act on their own initiative, often imposed requisitions and taxes on their own authority but none of them acted on the same scale as Saint-Just. The richer citizens of Strasbourg were ordered to raise 9,000,000 livres and to supply 5,000 boots and 15,000 shirts, besides providing 2,000 beds for wounded soldiers. Although his area of responsibility was officially confined to the Rhine Army, he imposed another levy of 5,000,000 livres on Nancy without consulting his colleagues in Lorraine. The money was initially described as a voluntary subscription, then it became a forced loan, and it was eventually made clear that none of it would be repaid. Of Strasbourg's nine million, six were allocated to the army, one for improving the fortifications of the town, and the remaining two for the relief of the civilian population. At Nancy the army was to get 90 per cent of the money raised. True to his preoccupation with inflation, Saint-Just claimed that he was going to reduce prices by restricting the amount of capital in circulation, but since he proposed to spend the money as soon as he had raised it, this did not look very realistic.

On the whole, Saint-Just and Le Bas left strategy to the generals, confining their own activity to providing the armies with the resources, both moral and material, that they needed for victory. Saint-Just seems to have envisaged the main French offensive as coming from 'his' Rhine Army, with Hoche and the Moselle Army in support. Carnot, however, preferred an outflanking movement by Hoche, aiming at the Rhine, in order to threaten the communications of the Austrian forces before Strasbourg. A general offensive began on 11 November. Pichegru made little headway and it was Hoche who drove the enemy back. Ignoring his instructions to advance eastwards and take the Austrians in the rear, he headed north-east, apparently making for the Palatinate, only to be bloodily repulsed at Kaiserslautern. He then fell back, abandoning some of the territory that he had just gained. In early December Saint-Just and Le Bas made a hurried visit to Paris, presumably to discuss the situation with Carnot. Rather surprisingly, none of them seemed disposed to blame Hoche, even though he had refused to communicate his plans to Saint-Just on grounds of military secrecy. Later that month the French armies resumed the attack. This time Hoche headed eastwards, the Austrians were outflanked, the allied armies driven out of France and the repubican armies advanced into Germany. Understandably enough, since it was the Moselle Army that had played the greater part in the victory, the deputies attached to that army, Baudot and Lacoste, put Hoche in supreme command. Hoche naturally accepted this, since he was unaware that the War Minister had reserved the post for Pichegru. The latter offered his resignation, and the disagreement cannot have improved relations between Baudot and Lacoste on the one hand and Saint-Just and Le Bas on the other. One should not make too much of this, however. What mattered was the victory.

What one makes of Saint-Just's contribution to the success of the French armies is likely to be determined by one's sympathy or antipathy towards the man himself, since the verdict rests on intuition rather than on proof. Some of his achievements were more impressive on paper than in actual fact. Despite his threats, much of the extraordinary taxation was never paid, most of the money raised was never spent, and the residue was taken over by the Treasury in the spring of 1794. The assessments seem to have been arbitrary, even by revolutionary standards: a Turkheim banker had his contribution reduced on appeal from 160,000 to 30,000 livres. In other words, the effect of the forced 'loan' was moral rather than material, although that was probably not how it appeared to the major contributors. The requisition of boots and clothing, on the other hand, was much more effective, bringing in 17,000 boots and over 20,000 shirts in Strasbourg alone. The effect of this on an ill-equipped army, fighting in winter weather, must have been very considerable. Saint-Just's admirers have presented him as the saviour of Alsace, but it is worth remembering that the main military contribution came from Hoche and the Moselle Army. Although his mission was officially to the Rhine Army, Saint-Just had also helped to provide Hoche with reinforcements of men and sup-plies. He had stood by him after the check at Kaiserslautern and he is entitled to some of the credit for Hoche's success. It would be going too far, however, to regard the French victory as the direct consequence of Saint-Just's 'revolutionary' initiatives in Strasbourg. His incessant interference in the management of Pichegru's army may have had something to do with its comparatively modest performance. These are matters that historians are free to debate at leisure. From the point of view of the Committee of Public Safety, what mattered was that French troops, who had looked like losing Strasbourg in October, had driven the enemy out of France by the end of the year. When it came to allocating the credit for this very satisfactory state of affairs, the committee would have a natural tendency to attribute the main share to its own men, Carnot and Saint-Just. It had sent Saint-Just out to do a job and it looked as though he had done it very well indeed.

Where military matters were concerned – and they were what counted most – it is not difficult to argue that his eventual success was itself the justification for the means that he chose to employ. In civilian politics such clear-cut results were unobtainable. The deputies in Alsace were the prisoners of a situation that they had not created and could not entirely control. They may have convinced themselves that they had found the correct solution to their problems, but whatever they did was liable to create as many difficulties as it resolved. There *were* counter-revolution-aries and enemy agents about, who had to be detected and eliminated, besides loyal repubicans who disagreed with each other about what should be done, and it was not always possible to distinguish the one from the other. Underlying everything else were tensions between Alsatians and the men from the interior. Whatever path Saint-Just tried to hack through this jungle, it was probably impossible for anyone, especially for an outsider, to avoid losing his bearings and interpreting the tangled situation in terms of what he wanted to believe.

From the start Saint-Just tended to rely on the army – in other words, on men from the interior – to implement his policies. He neglected the local criminal court in favour of the military tribunal, even where civilians were concerned. He tended to disregard the various agencies of local government – department, district and municipality – and to use as his intermediary the military governor of Strasbourg, Dièche, who was not a local man. To begin with, like the other representatives on mission, he turned for advice about local politics to the Jacobin Club, inviting it to let him have its views on the competence and reliability of Dièche, the administrators of the department and the staff officers of the National Guard at Strasbourg. Unlike his colleagues, Mallarmé and Lacoste, who liked to give their republican rhetoric an airing in the club, Saint-Just and Le Bas do not appear to have attended its meetings. They kept their distance and communicated with it by letter. Although they asked the club for its opinion, they did not pay much attention to it: the club denounced Dièche as drunken and incapable, but this did not shake the deputies' confidence in him.

What seems to have turned Saint-Just against the local men was the –

probably false – report of a plot by all the administrative bodies to betray Strasbourg to the Austrians. Before one is in too much of a hurry to condemn his credulity one has to remember that the nephew of the Austrian commander-in-chief was picked up in the city and fourteen local people were arrested at a meeting with the Austrian chief of intelligence, who escaped. The deputies might well write to the Committee of Public Safety. 'We have earned the right to be suspicious.' What followed was probably a mistake, but they were in no position to take risks. They purged the entire administration at all levels. All but three members of the department were arrested, together with the district and the entire municipality, apart from the mayor. Men who had been presidents or secretaries of the Sections at the time of the coup d'état against the Girondins were also imprisoned. Two of Saint-Just's colleagues, Guyardin and Milhaud, arrested the staff officers of the National Guard, while Dièche seized its commanding officer. This was to make a clean sweep of men who may have belonged to a particular faction but were also seen by the Alsatians as their own people. The purge extended beyond Strasbourg itself, to include the municipal officers of Neuf-Brisach and Saverne and the departmental administration of the Meurthe, who were scarely within the jurisdiction of men who had been sent to the Rhine Army. Saint-Just complained to the *comité de surveillance* at Strasbourg that there were 'thousands' of suspects at large in the city and it had arrested none of them.

This was too much even for Dièche and Monet, the mayor of Strasbourg, even though neither was a local man. When each of them protested Monet was put firmly in his place: 'We are not here to fraternize with the authorities but to judge them.' He took the hint, henceforth did what he was told and became one of Saint-Just's trusted agents. The Jacobin Club seems to have been less willing to accept the elimination of people who owed their offices to local election, and there was little further contact between the club and the deputies until they purged it in December. From his own point of view, Saint-Just behaved with revolutionary rectitude. He did not send men for trial unless he believed that there was credible evidence against them. He regarded the dismissal of the local officials as a necessary precaution and, in accordance with the Law of Suspects, such men were merely to be detained and not put on trial. He gave orders that, once safely transferred to the interior, they were to be humanely treated, and it was not his fault if they were actually held incommunicado. What he did was understandable enough, in the critical circumstances, but it was bound to alienate local opinion which, in turn, reinforced his suspicions of all Alsatians.

These feelings were shared by Gateau, whom he had summoned to help him. In a letter to their mutual friend, Daubigny, Gateau denounced the 'fanaticism, indolence and Germanic stupidity' of the local population. This had become the general opinion of the men from the interior. Monet who, although mayor of Strasbourg, came from Savoy, agreed that Alsace could be regenerated only by people from other parts of France. Dièche – from the Rouergue – concurred that 'heads more German than French' needed 'vigour and terror'. Baudot and Lacoste went even further. When, at the end of the year, there was a mass exodus from northern Alsace of the frightened civilian population, fleeing with the retreating allied armies, they made the helpful suggestion that the government should seize this opportunity to colonize the area with men from other parts of France. 'The only thing to do is to guillotine a quarter of the inhabitants of these parts and keep only those who have taken an active part in the Revolution.' By comparison with some of his colleagues, Saint-Just was not merely a moderate but a humanitarian. Nevertheless he noted in his diary that it would be a good idea to change the names of all the towns and villages in Alsace and call them after French soldiers. He invited the Alsaciennes to abandon their famous costume and head-dress, as a symbol of both Germanism and Catholicism. At the end of his mission he set aside 600,000 livres from the 2,000,000 previously allocated to the poor, for the establishment of a French-language school in every village. Like a good deal else that he did, this was a gesture rather than a policy: francophone teachers were hard to find and not a single school was actually opened.

In conformity with his poor view of the local population, Saint-Just therefore ordered the Strasbourg Jacobins to write to the clubs in seven neighbouring departments, inviting them to send missionaries to Alsace to regenerate the local population. About fifty militants responded to the call, and the process of selection ensured that they would not be men of a modest or self-effacing stamp. Their leader was Schneider, the former professor of Greek at Bonn and episcopal vicar at Strasbourg, who was currently acting as public prosecutor to the revolutionary tribunal. This was the old civilian court, not the military tribunal favoured by Saint-Just, who does not seem to have had much direct contact with Schneider. Calling themselves the *Propagande*, Schneider's men roved over the Bas-Rhin, decked out in uniforms that they created for themselves, trailing their cavalry sabres and accompanied by a military escort. Saint-Just seems to have put paid to attempts to raise a local 'revolutionary' army, but that was probably because he did not trust the Alsatians. Schneider's band was a revolutionary army in all but name. It sent suspects for trial before the revolutionary tribunal, imposed special taxes on the rich, requisitioned supplies and inflicted heavy penalties on traders who disregarded price controls. One unfortunate was fined 3,000 livres for charging too much for a couple of lettuces. By the standards of the time, Schneider's men were not particularly bloody, but they were still responsible for the execution of thirty-one men. As befitted extremists in the autumn of 1793, they took an active part in the assault on religion that swept the country in November.

On the 20th Schneider himself was one of those who abjured the priest-hood at the Festival of Reason in Strasbourg cathedral. Dechristianization was not universally popular with the local radicals, especially when it came to destroying the monuments to 'superstition' in their own cathedral.

Saint-Just was not directly involved in any of these activities, but he must have been well aware of what was going on and he allowed it to happen. He was not the kind of man to tolerate activities of which he disapproved. He himself signed an order for the destruction of the statues outside the cathedral, and there is no convincing evidence to suggest that he dissociated himself from the attack on religion. Schneider's style was different from his own but Saint-Just had been responsible for the creation of the *Propagande*, and its activities were very similar to what he himself was doing.

Early in December Saint-Just and Le Bas paid their brief visit to Paris, where they must have been surprised by the change in the political climate. The Committee of Public Safety had come to realize the danger of anarchy as a result of the do-it-yourself enthusiasm of local extremists, whose excesses threatened to produce chaos and to provoke revolt. A law voted on 4 December put the machinery of the Terror under the control of the two governing committees. Representatives on mission were henceforth prohibited from raising taxes of their own, and local revolutionary armies were dissolved. Robespierre had already declared war on dechristianiza-tion. This was not merely a matter of saying that the extremists were going too far. In the feverish atmosphere of 1793, whatever was unorthodox was suspected of being intentionally counter-revolutionary, and orthodoxy was coming to be defined as acceptance of the policies of the Committee of Public Safety. For Robespierre dechristianization, which had been actively promoted by Proli and his quartet, was not merely vulgar and offensive to his deep-rooted deism. He saw it as an attempt by foreigners and enemy agents to divide the country and set the revolutionaries at each other's throats, under the disguise of innocent revolutionary enthusiasm. Saint-Just had been away from Paris politics for a long time. What was going on – or what was believed to be going on – was not something that one could discover from reading the newspapers. When Robespierre presumably briefed him about what was 'really' happening he was in no position to check this from his own observations, and he himself was, in any case, equally prone to sniff counter-revolution in every whiff of dissent.

He returned to Alsace in a new frame of mind. The histrionic Schneider, Austrian priest turned dechristianizer, corresponded very well to the kind of man whom Robespierre regarded as the latest and most dangerous enemy of the Revolution. Schneider himself provided Saint-Just with the pretext he needed, by making a flamboyant entry into Strasbourg with a coach and six, accompanied by his new wife, a wealthy heiress, said by Schneider's enemies to be the latest of his requisitions. Within twenty-four hours of his return to Alsace, Saint-Just had him arrested, exposed on the scaffold alongside the guillotine and sent off to Paris for trial by the revolutionary tribunal. Saint-Just was later to denounce him as a counter-revolutionary, and he was executed in the spring of 1794. The other members of the *Propagande* could consider themselves lucky to be sent back to their homes without being prosecuted.

This initiated the third phase in Saint-Just's Alsatian policy. He had begun by trying to work with the local people but come to distrust them. Then he imported missionaries from the interior, only to come to the conclusion that they were no more reliable. All that remained was to enforce the government's policies by men who could be relied on to carry out orders. That meant, in the first instance, Dièche and Monet. The department was purged once again, and also the Jacobin Club. Henceforth it transacted its business in French only, which must have cut it off from the local artisans. The new *comité de surveillance* did not include a single local man. The revolutionary tribunal began prosecuting Schneider's agents as enthusiastically as it had formerly disposed of their victims. Saint-Just himself was later to complain, in a famous phrase, that the Revolution was 'frozen'. He never understood that this was the inevitable result of a situation in which safety was to be sought only in blind obedience to whatever happened to be the orthodoxy of the moment.

He was able to dispose of the local population more or less as he wished, but he did not have the same authority over the other deputies who were in Alsace on missions similar to his own. How he got on with them would affect future relations in the assembly when they had all returned to Paris. From the start he made it clear to the Committee of Public Safety that he considered the others to be in the way, urging his colleagues to recall them and arguing that two, or at most four, were enough in Strasbourg. The committee duly reduced the numbers to four with each army but also dispatched one of its members, Hérault de Séchelles, to Alsace on a mission of his own. On arrival Hérault suggested opening up a correspondence with Saint-Just and Le Bas. The latter commented, rather oddly, in a letter to Robespierre, 'We are astonished.' He went on to complain that the representatives on mission who had failed to prevent the advance of the Austrians ought to have been recalled. Saint-Just added a cryptic postscript: 'Confidence has no value any longer when one shares it with the corrupt.' This is usually taken to be a reference to Hérault, who had been denounced by Fabre d'Eglantine, in Saint-Just's presence, but it could have been aimed at the other deputies as well. Whatever it meant, it was scarcely a prelude to good relations.

From the start Saint-Just and Le Bas considered themselves to be in a class apart. 'In accordance with the nature of our mission we considered it our duty to act in isolation.' That was not how the others saw it, and they resented Saint-Just's assumption that his membership of the Committee of

Public Safety endowed him with superior status. One must not make too much of this. The others did occasionally correspond with Saint-Just and he was prepared, on occasion, to take their advice. When Milhaud and Guyardin assured him that a *procureur-général* of Saverne whom he had dismissed was an excellent citizen, Saint-Just reinstated him. There was, however, bound to be friction when deputies with ill-defined powers and areas of jurisdiction got in each other's way, especially when two of them behaved as though they thought themselves to be speaking in the name of the revolutionary government. Saint-Just had no inhibitions about dispatching orders to areas far from Strasbourg. When he purged the administrators at Nancy, Faure, who was on mission there, reinstated some of them. Baudot and Lacoste, who had not had a chance to learn about the changed atmosphere in Paris, were understandably shocked by Saint-Just's abrupt turning against Schneider, which he did not bother to explain to them. They complained about Schneider's 'persecution' and protested again when Saint-Just went on to purge the administration of the department without consulting them.

These discontents surfaced briefly in the Assembly on 29 December, just before Saint-Just's return to Paris. Hérault complained that he was being criticized for his extremism in Alsace. He knew that he had been denounced for his contacts with Proli, who was now wanted as an alleged counter-revolutionary, and demanded an opportunity to clear his name. Hérault was followed by Mallarmé, who had been recalled from Alsace, and Simon. Mallarmé claimed that Saint-Just and Le Bas had been mistaken when they ordered the trial of the administrators of the Meurthe, who had been appointed by the deputies Milhaud and Soubrany. According to Mallarmé the men concerned had been falsely denounced by rogues whom they were about to expose. Simon followed this up by saying that Saint-Just and Le Bas had made the same mistake at Strasbourg. There too they had been taken in by false accusations against worthy officials who had been appointed by other deputies. The assembly referred both matters to the two governing committees, who could have had no idea of the merits of these charges and counter-charges. Neither Mallarmé nor Simon questioned Saint-Just's motives, but that was only moderately reassuring. By the end of 1793 to suggest that a man had made a mistake was the first step towards implying that it was done for a purpose. Like over-zealous psychiatrists, the deputies were inclined to ask themselves why the patient had chosen to allow himself to become ill.

Saint-Just's mission to the Rhine Army can therefore be rated a military success. That was what mattered most at the time. On the basis of *post hoc ergo propter hoc* he deserved the credit for the reversal of the military situation. His colleagues on the committee would not forget that, at a time when it was under fire and owed its survival to its military achievements. He had shown himself to be a man of energy and courage.

When confronted with logistic problems he could get things done by methods whose success legitimized whatever was arbitrary or unorthodox. This was what he understood by 'revolutionary' government. Where politics was concerned the situation was different and he could not hope for the same kind of results. Revolutionary government aspired to enlist the spontaneous enthusiasm of the population as a whole for policies with which 'the people' could identify. That was not going to happen in Alsace. Saint-Just had perhaps better reasons than most unsuccessful politicians for believing that it was not his fault. In many respects Alsace *was* foreign. It was also an exposed frontier outpost where the government could not afford to take any risks. If purging administrators meant forfeiting local support, that was a price that had to be paid. He was perhaps more at fault in giving his tacit approval to Schneider and his band, in the belief that Alsace could be regenerated by a different kind of popular movement, imposed from the outside. His subsequent volte-face suggested that safety was to be found only in obedience.

If regeneration seemed as far off as ever, that was because unworthy agents had betrayed 'the people'. But perhaps Alsatians were not really 'people' in the same way as the French. Until they had been re-educated – in French – they would have to be ruled by men who knew what was best for them, men like Dièche and Monet, who could be relied on to do what they were told. If Saint-Just came to the conclusion that this was the lesson of his mission to the Rhine Army, that would be in acordance with what we know of his temperament, his convictions and the position in which he found himself. He had probably not yet asked himself the awkward question of what to do if the situation in Alsace were to be repeated in the rest of France. Perhaps Frenchmen were not the real people either, until they had been re-educated.

Notes

1 A. Soboul, 'Sur la mission de Saint-Just à l'armée du Rhin', *Annales historiques de la révolution française*, 136–7 (1954), pp. 221–2. This article reprints decrees and proclamations, in Saint-Just's hand, relating to the first part of his mission to the Rhine Army.
2 M. A. Baudot, *Notes historiques sur la Convention nationale, le Directoire, l'Empire et l'exil des votants* (Geneva, 1974), p. 166.

20

The 9 Thermidor: motives and effects

MARTYN LYONS

For generations of French historians, and for generations of syllabus-setters in English universities, the French Revolution ended on 9 Thermidor of the Year II. French history then went through an embarrassing hiatus, only to resume again with Bonaparte's seizure of power on 18 Brumaire VIII. It is not my purpose here to try to fill this gap, but merely to suggest that in regarding 9 Thermidor as the end of the Revolution, we have taken for granted an interpretation of the Revolution which has perhaps overstated the role of Robespierre and the Terror. The elements of continuity which link the various stages of the history of the First Republic need re-emphasizing.

Orthodox French historiography has seen 9 Thermidor as a break in the history of the Republic which inaugurated a reaction against the Revolution. It has portrayed 9 Thermidor as the victory of a group of unscrupulous, corrupt, and even unpatriotic men, concerned only to save their own skins. The Thermidoreans were pygmies trying to revive the conspiracy of the Titans. For Robespierre himself, they were 'une ligue de fripons qui lutte contre la vertu publique'.[1] For Buchez and Roux, the significance of 9 Thermidor could be summarized as the triumph of mediocrity over genius. For Mathiez, too, the struggle against Robespierre was a personal one, led by corrupt individuals, united only by a desire to save their heads from the guillotine.

On the other hand, Furet and Richet have challenged the prevailing orthodoxy, and implicitly revised the status of 9 Thermidor. They suggest that by the time of the Terror, the main gains of the Revolution had been achieved. The Constituent Assembly and the Girondins had fulfilled the reforming impulses of the eighteenth century. They describe the Terror as the 'dérapage de la Révolution'[2] – that is to say, the Revolution went into a skid, or, in naval terms, it was dragging its anchor. Furet and Richet imply that the Terror was an irrelevant parenthesis, brought about by purely accidental factors.

Such an interpretation, it is suggested, has serious defects. One can only regard the Terror as a temporary distortion of the Revolution if one ignores the role played by direct popular action in the revolutionary successes of 1789; and if one regards the war, and civil war, which

Reprinted in full, except for notes, from *European Studies Review*, 15 (1975), pp. 123–46.

contributed so much to the Terror, as complete accidents. The Terror was necessary to secure the gains of the Revolution against the threat from within and from without.

Nevertheless, Furet and Richet may be right in viewing 9 Thermidor as the date when the Republic was brought back into the mainstream of liberalism which was the main characteristic of the Revolution (and indeed of Jacobinism, too). Clive Church seems to concur with this view in a recent essay when he describes the Directory as 'a board of executors for the revolutionary settlement'.[3] The Thermidorean régime continued both Robespierrist attitudes to the lower classes, and the middle-class constitutionalism of the Constituent Assembly. It is best seen, therefore, as a continuation of revolutionary traditions, rather than as a reaction against all the Revolution stood for.

The historiographical battle still rages. Furet has alleged that orthodox historians had a distorted view of the Terror because they saw it too much as a precedent for Bolshevism and the 1917 Revolution. The cudgels have been taken up by Claude Mazauric, one spokesman for the Communist interpretation of the Revolution, and a preacher of what Furet calls 'la vulgate mazaurico-soboulienne'. Mazauric even accuses Furet and Richet of being unpatriotic. To attack Jacobin history, he claims, is to reveal one's anti-national bias. Furet was clearly 'ashamed' of this episode of French history. This paper implicitly takes the view that there was nothing shameful about the Revolution of 9 Thermidor.

Since Mathiez, the history of the Revolution has concentrated too heavily on the role of Robespierre, and thereby thrown into obscurity the work of the *Comité de Sûreté Générale*, although the wide police powers of this committee made it a vital part of the machinery of the Terror. After the Convention had ordered the arrest and imprisonment of the Robespierrists on 9 Thermidor, the Paris Commune released them, and Robespierre was eventually taken to the *Hôtel de Ville*. The members of the *Comité de Sûreté Générale* then played a leading role in persuading the Convention to outlaw the Robespierrists, and in appointing Barras to lead the Convention's troops against the Commune.

By concentrating on the members of the *Comité de Sûreté Générale*, this paper will try to rectify the traditional impression of the Thermidoreans. It will suggest that some of them, at least, acted out of logical and reasonable motives. No serious attempt has really been made to explain these motives: for the Thermidoreans have too often been assumed to have simply reacted to the promptings of their guilty consciences, and to irrational, personal prejudices against Robespierre.

I shall try to show that the opposition of the *Comité de Sûreté Générale* was not purely negative, and that it was based on reasons of policy, not simply on personal resentment. In particular, differences in religious policy will be stressed as the main ideological conflict in the *coup* of 9 Thermidor.

Finally, the paper will emphasize the degree to which 9 Thermidor, seen so often as the work of reactionaries, was interpreted by the *Comité de Sûreté Générale* and by its main authors as a revolution of the Left.

I

After Robespierre's supporters had rescued him from the Luxembourg, the Convention and the Paris Commune fought for the support of the Paris sections. Hanriot, commander of the National Guard, had been arrested, but the rebel Commune succeeded in liberating him from the headquarters of the *Comité de Sûreté Générale*. Hanriot, however, failed to put military pressure on the Convention, and support for the Commune ebbed away. When the forces of the Convention penetrated the *Hôtel de Ville*, they met little opposition.

By 3.00 a.m. on 10 Thermidor, the *Place de Grève* was littered with the human débris of the Revolutionary Government. In the *Hôtel de Ville*, Philippe Lebas had shot himself in the head; Augustin Robespierre, who had thrown himself from a top storey window, had broken his thigh; Couthon, a cripple, had either fallen or thrown himself from his wheelchair down the stone staircase of the *Hôtel de Ville*, where he lay with a gaping wound to the forehead. The giant Coffinhal, enraged by the failure of the Commune, which he attributed to the drunken incompetence of Hanriot, seized Hanriot, and threw him bodily out of a third floor window of the *Hôtel de Ville*, Hanriot lay half-dead in an interior courtyard, undiscovered for another twelve hours. Coffinhal himself escaped, but after hiding for five days among the débris and faecal matter on the *Ile des Cygnes*, returned starving to Paris, and was arrested. St Just gave himself up stoically, and sat under guard in the *Hôtel de Brionne*, now a broken man. Robespierre the elder, who had attempted to blow his brains out but succeeded only in breaking a jaw, lay in great pain, but apparently conscious, on the great table of the *Comité de Salut Public*, where curious *sans-culottes* taunted him mercilessly, asking 'Ne v'la-t-il pas un beau roi?', 'Sire, votre majesté souffre?'[4]

How had the leadership of the Revolutionary Goverment been brought to this scene of death and destruction? The events of 9 Thermidor did not constitute a spontaneous popular uprising in rejection of the revolutionary bureaucracy, but rather a *coup* from above. The most striking aspect of 9 Thermidor is precisely the lack of popular intervention, the inertia of the Paris sections, and ultimately, the loyalty of their leaders to the existing government. Soboul found that only ten out of forty-eight revolutionary committees of the Paris sections persisted in their support for Robespierre long enough to compromise themselves. Rudé and Soboul have related this apathy to the publication of a new Wage Maximum by the Commune of

Paris, on 5 Thermidor, which meant an actual reduction in wages in many trades. When the Commune challenged the authority of the Convention, and National Guardsmen began to assemble outside the *Hôtel de Ville*, many *sectionnaires* assumed at first that the crowds were discontented workers demonstrating *against* the Commune.

The events of 9 Thermidor cannot be explained without taking into account the passivity of the sections of Paris, but they were the culmination of essentially parliamentary struggles. They were conceived and carried out by a minority of Montagnard deputies, including those of the *Comité de Sûreté Générale*, whose strategy was not popular rebellion, but intrigue in the corridors of the Convention itself.

The 9 Thermidor must be placed in the background of a France in which revolutionary initiative had been crushed, in which the unanimity enforced by an increasingly remote government was becoming an empty ritual, and in which the controlled economy and attacks on traditional religion offended the susceptibilities of the rural population. The claim that the war demanded extreme measures lost its justification after [the battle of] Fleurus opened up Belgium to the Republican armies. Within the government itself, Robespierre was resented not so much for his personal ascendancy, which was never complete, but for his apparent hold over the country, and above all for his dictatorial pretensions. In the early days of Messidor, an emergency meeting of the Committees of Public Safety and General Security was held, at which St Just criticized anarchy in the departments, and the usurpation of authority by the *Représentants en mission*. He concluded by recommending the dictatorship of one man, Robespierre. The latter, with feigned reluctance, agreed to assume the heavy responsibilities of such a difficult task, but found that only Couthon, Lebas and David supported the proposal.

II

The Montagnards not only resented Robespierre; they feared him. It is not easy to imagine the atmosphere of fear and tension which enveloped the intense political activity of the month and a half which preceded the *coup* of Thermidor. The record of the debates in the Convention and the Jacobin club reveal only intermittent glimpses of this anxiety. For the main political activity of these weeks occurred outside the debating chambers, in cafés, private apartments, and in the corridors of the Convention. Our main sources for the activities and conspiracies of the deputies remain private memoirs. Because of their retrospective and self-justificatory nature, they present obvious pitfalls, but they alone can illuminate the machinations of the dissident Montagnards who engineered 9 Thermidor.

For Mathiez, these men formed 'une opposition souterraine qui avait la peur pour mobile et pour ciment.[5] Their fear of assassination was a very real one, however. Not only had Marat and Lepeletier suffered this unwelcome form of martyrdom, but in Prairial Amiral had attempted to shoot Collot d'Herbois, and Cécile Renault had been forestalled in her attempt on the life of Robespierre.

Most of all, however, the deputies were afraid of themselves, suspicious of Robespierre's intentions, and, predicting that they would be the next victims of the guillotine, prepared to take desperate measures to forestall their own arrest. No deputy dared go out unarmed. All carried a pair of pistols, or, more discreetly, a dagger like Tallien, or, if they had not entirely lost the habits of a *grand seigneur*, a sword-stick like Amar. Robespierre never left his house unless accompanied by a bodyguard, usually composed of the jury of the Revolutionary Tribunal. The public prosecutor, Fouquier-Tinville, afraid that his victims' relatives would one day take their revenge, also took this precaution, and is reported to have lived in a virtual state of siege during Prairial and Messidor. Even when they did go out, the deputies knew that they were unlikely to shake off the shadows which darkened their every movement. Robespierre's spy followed Thuriot and Bourdon de l'Oise during Messidor, and Tallien, too, was followed. According to one acquaintance, Fouché slept at a different address every night to escape arrest. Vadier, President of the *Comité de Sûreté Générale*, put his own spy Taschereau on Robespierre, but Taschereau betrayed him, preferring to report to Robespierre on Vadier's movements.

It was only a matter of time before a crisis exploded to dissipate this intolerable atmosphere of mutual suspicion, and fear of proscription, which had paralysed the Jacobin leadership. A few impetuous deputies urged an early solution. During the procession at the Fête of the Supreme Being, Lecointre de Versailles threatened to kill Robespierre. He and a group of nine deputies planned to propose the arrest of Robespierre, and, if the proposal was defeated, to assassinate him in the Convention. Completely independently, Bourdon de l'Oise made his own plans. Shortly after the debate on the law of 22 Prairial, he left his will with his lawyer, and told him he intended to put Robespierre to death with a bloodstained sword which had seen service at the fall of the Bastille. There were any number of aspirants ready to play Cassius to Robespierre's Caesar, but for the moment, wiser heads urged prudence. Vadier and Lindet, for example, persuaded Lecointre to wait for a more favourable moment. The façade of unanimity concealed a seething hatred. The pastoral slopes of the Mountain covered a volcano which was about to erupt.

There is little doubt that the Revolution of 9 Thermidor was a revolution in self-defence against impending proscription. The Montagnards' suspicions were justified, and their instinct of self-preservation fully comprehensible. It is clear from the debates on the law of 22 Prairial that Montagnard deputies were afraid of a new purge even at this date. The law, which reorganized the Revolutionary Tribunal and its procedures, was objectionable to moderates because it dispensed with defence witnesses, and paved the way for the trials of the prison conspiracies in Messidor. But Bourdon de l'Oise saw in the law a deeper significance for the deputies themselves. On 23 Prairial he insisted that the law should contain a guarantee that no deputy could be sent before the Revolutionary Tribunal without the Convention's approval. Although Robespierre defeated Lecointre's suggestion for an indefinite adjournment, neither he nor Couthon fully succeeded in allaying fears that the *Comité de Salut Public* intended to use the law to eliminate dissident *Conventionnels*.

The law of 22 Prairial thus encouraged rumours of a proscription of Montagnards – rumours on which Fouché, among others, was not slow to capitalize. There are further indications that such was indeed Robespierre's intention. According to Barère, the *Comité de Salut Public* was presented with a list of eighteen deputies, who had exceeded their mandate, and exercised a culpable tyranny over the departments to which they had been sent *en mission*. Only lack of concrete evidence, or his own legalistic scruples, prevented Robespierre from making this public. It was perhaps Robespierre's failure to convince the *Comité de Salut Public* of the necessity for this measure which led him to abandon the committee, and to cultivate the support of the Jacobin club. Robespierre's mistake was not to name his enemies on 8 Thermidor, when he might still have been able to rely on the deputies of the Centre. His reticence did not reassure those who feared they would be included in such an accusation, and convinced them of the need to take the initiative on the ninth.

The Montagnards, therefore, had cause to distrust Robespierre. Their natural urge to protect themselves was in some cases coloured by personal motives. For Tallien, for example, it was important to rescue his mistress from prison. Although many of the future Thermidoreans may be accused of corruption, Robespierre by no means had a monopoly of virtue. Even he could hardly accuse a man like Vadier, with his much-vaunted 'soixante ans de vertu', of dining sumptuously, keeping mistresses and accepting bribes. It is time, however, to raise the conflicts of Thermidor from the level of personal prejudices and petty antagonisms.

III

The motives which turned these frightened Montagnards into future Thermidoreans must now be examined. Was there, for instance, a prepared plan of action against Robespierre? It did not seem so to the uninitiated deputies of the Plain, 'les crapauds du Marais'. For the deputy Thibaudeau,

Le neuf thermidor, la grande majorité de la Convention ne s'attendait point à ce qui arriva. Ce fut comme un coup de tonnerre. Il n'y avait plus de raison ce jour-là pour attaquer Robespierre, ni par conséquent pour espérer la fin de sa tyrannie . . . Y eut'il une conjuration réelle contre lui? Quels furent les conjurés? C'est ce qu'on n'a jamais bien su.[6]

From the records of the debates of 9 and 10 Thermidor, from the list of deputies whose arrest was ordered by the Commune on 9 Thermidor, and from the evidence of memoirs, pamphlets and reminiscences, four main groups can be distinguished among the Thermidoreans: ex-Dantonists, *Représentants en mission* returning from the provinces, the *Comité de Sûreté Générale*, and finally, the *Comité de Salut Public* itself.

The contribution of the ex-Hébertists, however, is impossible to establish, It is impossible to identify the Hébertists as a political group with coherent political aims, unless we take at face value Fouquier-Tinville's attempts to identify *Hébertism* with atheism, and the so-called Hébertists with a *complot militaire*. The future Thermidoreans in the *Comité de Sûreté Générale* did not hesitate to arrest suspected accomplices of Hébert. The *canonniers* of the Parisian *armée révolutionnaire* were still an important political force, but the Montagnard opposition seems to have regarded them as hostile and dangerous.

The first focus of opposition, then, came from the ex-followers of Danton, like Lecointre de Versailles, Thuriot, Legendre and Bourdon de l'Oise, who was their real parliamentary spokesman at this time. It was Thuriot who shouted above the clamour on the 9 Thermidor: 'Tais-toi, bourreau! le sang de Danton te coule dans la bouche, il t'étouffe!'[7] For these Thermidoreans of the right, the 9 Thermidor represented Danton's posthumous revenge. At the same time, their opposition crystallized around important issues: the defence of the *Conventionnels* against arbitrary arrest and summary trial, the injustices of the law of 22 Prairial, and, above all, they demanded the reform of the Revolutionary Tribunal.

The second group of dissident Montagnards, the *Représentants en mission*, also felt threatened by Robespierre. Unlike the Dantonists, however, they had sinned not by moderation, but by extremism. Barère lists some of the men against whom the *Comité de Salut Public* was invited to take action. They include Tallien, Fréron, Barras, Alquier, and Dubois-Crancé. The *Comité de Salut Public* reproached these men for the savagery of their repression of the federalist revolt, crushed by Tallien in Bordeaux, Barras and Fréron in Provence, Dubois-Crancé and Fouché in Lyon. Their severity was thought to add unnecessarily to the régime's enemies, and to provide the foreign powers with a stronger case for their hostility towards France.

Mass executions, the delegation of power to *commissions ambulantes*, revolutionary taxation, and the creation of private revolutionary armies all worried the central government. Suspicions of corruption also clouded the records of certain deputies like Tallien, Barras, Fréron and Rovère. At the same time, however, two clear issues can be discerned in the opposition of these deputies to Robespierre. The first was the question of decentralization. The point for Robespierre was not simply that these men returned from the provinces enriched with wealth extorted from suspects, or embezzled from the property of *émigrés*. What was at stake was the difficulty experienced by the government in controlling even those *Représentants* whose private morality was unquestioned – a difficulty aggravated when these deputies were as far away as Marseille or Toulon. The *Comité de Salut Public* had no option but to recall the wayward deputies, attempt to enforce the law of 14 Frimaire, and to resort to a system of private espionage. Gouly, for example, was sent to report on the activities of Javogues in the remote mountain fastnesses of the department of the Loire. Julien was sent to spy on Carrier in Brittany (he recommended his immediate recall), before moving on to Bordeaux. For Robespierre, the *Représentants* who carried out their personal policies in the departments were a threat to the unity and centralization which were essential to the success of the Revolution. These men challenged not only Robespierre personally, but his whole conception of revolutionary discipline.

The religious issue also divided the *Représentants* and Robespierre. Several *Représentants* were among the chief protagonists of the dechristianization campaign in the provinces. In the opinion of Mathiez, the religious issue was used merely as an excuse to defeat Robespierre, who was aiming not at the re-establishment of Catholicism, but at a rallying of all Republican forces under the banner of the Supreme Being. There is evidence to show, however, that both sides took the issue more seriously than this.

The main grievance against Fouché, for instance, was his atheism. He had alienated the government by his violent attacks on traditional Catholicism, and by his motto, 'La mort est un sommeil éternel', which he had inscribed on gravestones in cemeteries which he passed. He was suspect, too, in his association with Chaumette, ex-*procureur* of the Paris Commune, proscribed as an Hébertist, and, by implication, a dechristianizer. This theme appeared again in Robespierre's speech of 8 Thermidor, which he described as his 'testament'. 'Non, Chaumette, non, Fouché', he asserted, 'la mort n'est pas un sommeil éternel'.[8]

The violent secularization recomended by men like Fouché, Mallarmé, and Dartigoeyte in the departments threatened the government's formula of 'la liberté des cultes'. For Robespierre, as for all Rousseauists, the denial of the immortality of the soul was philosophically unacceptable. More important, crude attacks on traditional peasant beliefs were politically dangerous. Some kind of civil religion was for Robespierre a guarantee of social order, while atheism seemed to him the doctrine of a decadent aristocracy. The closure of churches, and the worship of the Goddess of Reason could not therefore be tolerated. Thus a number of deputies were ready to vote for the arrest of Robespierre on 9 Thermidor out of a fundamental disagreement over the government's policy of centralization, and its opposition to dechristianization.

Robespierre's opponents could thus find common ground on which to unite against him. For tactical reasons, the *Comité de Sûreté Générale* gave the renegade *Représentants* its protection. According to Vadier, 'le comité avait tout fait en faveur de Talien, Fouché et autres, pour détourner l'effet des dénonciations portées contre eux, par la raison qu'ils étaient poursuivis par Robespierre'.[9] Sénart, the agent of the committee, detested what he called 'représentocratie', and his hatred of Tallien in particular makes his evidence difficult to assess. He stresses that the *Comité de Sûreté Générale* deliberately overlooked the crimes of dissident Montagnards, in order to present a united front against Robespierre.

IV

The issues of centralization and religion were the subject of disputes between the *Comité de Salut Public* and the *Comité de Sûreté Générale*. Before analysing the conflicts which arose between them, the members of the latter committee must first be identified, for by no means all were critical of Robespierre.

Two members of the *Comité de Sûreté Générale* in fact identified themselves as Robespierrists. Philippe Lebas shared missions with St Just to the armies of the Rhine and the Nord, and married the daughter of Duplay, Robespierre's landlord. The least pretentious of the Robespierrist group, he was also, because of his moderation and his loyalty, the most sympathetic. On 9 Thermidor, he was arrested with Robespierre, St Just and Couthon at his own request. Nor did David share his colleagues' reservations about Robespierre. His main responsibilities during the Terror lay not in the *Comité de Sûreté Générale*, but in the organization of Fêtes, and the celebration of revolutionary cults. David's reputation as a painter should not blind historians to his total lack of political courage and defective judgement. On 8 Thermidor, he had promised to 'drink the hemlock' with Robespierre. Immediately regretting this the following day, he stayed away from the Convention on the advice of Barère, and having taken an emetic, pleaded illness.[10]

Several other members of the committee can be ignored for our purpose. Joseph Lebon was absent in Arras, and his compatriot and enemy Gouffroy had resigned after the Jacobins had condemned his journal *Rougyff*. Panis, a friend of the Desmoulins family, had also retired from the committee in Nivôse after the arrest of his brother-in-law Santerre. Of their colleagues, not all were totally committed to the *coup* of 9 Thermidor. Jagot and Lavicomterie, for example, were too frightened to appear in the Convention on that day, and in consequence were expelled from the committee.

The following remarks therefore concern principally the regular membership of the *Comité de Sûreté Générale*, and those who, together with the rump of the *Comité de Salut Public*, assumed the leaderhip of the Convention on 9 Thermidor: Vadier, Amar, Voulland, Moise Bayle, Elie Lacoste, Dubarran, Louis du Bas-Rhin, and Philippe Rühl.

Like the other groups of deputies mentioned, these men resented Robespierre's dictatorial pretensions. Robespierre withdrew from the *Comité de Salut Pubic* in Messidor, perhaps because he was now isolated in the committee, and his appeals for a new purge had been rejected. His latest biographer has pointed out Robespierre's tendency to retreat into solitude before an impending crisis. This time his withdrawal from the committee merely encouraged rumours that he was manipulating the government from behind the scenes – rumours which were reinforced by reports that dossiers were brought to his lodgings secretly every day.

It is true that the Convention was responsible for renewing the powers of the *Comité de Salut Public*, but so strong was the fear of arrest and proscription that this had become a formality. Robespierre's authority lay first in the Jacobin club, where he did not have unanimous support, but where the expulsion of Fouché in Messidor testified to his dominant influence. With Payan as *agent national*, Robespierre could rely on the Commune of Paris. Thirdly, with Hanriot in command, the National Guard of the capital was assumed to be Robespierrist. (As it happened, the events of 9 Thermidor demonstrated that Hanriot was a liability, and that the loyalty of the National Guard was divided.) Not only did Robespierre control the Jacobin club, the Commune of Paris, and the National Guard, but he appeared to control the Revolutionary Tribunal, by appointing as jurors his personal followers, Delaunay, Didier, Châtelet, Girard, Laviron, his landlord's cousin, and Loyer, his grocer.

Furthermore, a series of incidents provoked complaints from the *Comité de Sûreté Générale* that the *Comité de Salut Public* was encroaching on its legitimate authority. Robespierre and St Just reproached Amar for the inadequacy of his report on the India Company scandal. He had failed to relate evidence of financial fraud to a wider context of political conspiracy. The *Comité de Sûreté Générale* had not been consulted on the presentation of the law of 22 Prairial. The *Comité de Salut Public* accused it of being slow to act on denunciations of suspects submitted to it. Robespierre criticized Vadier's law of 21 Messidor, which authorized the release of imprisoned agricultural workers, in order to alleviate the shortage of manpower at harvest-time. By confiding these releases to the local revolutionary committees, Vadier undermined Robespierre's attempts to make the *Comité de Salut Public* solely responsible for the release of suspects. One fact emerges from this exchange of mutual recriminations: they reflected not merely personal antipathies within the revolutionary leadership, but also resistance on the part of the *Comité de Sûreté Générale* to growing demands for centralization by the *Comité de Salut Public*. St Just, in his uncompleted speech of 9 Thermidor, declared that the government was not divided, but dispersed. He went on to accuse the *Comité de Sûreté Générale* of a lack of rigour, and to acknowledge but refute its fears of centralization:

> Quel plan d'indulgence, grand Dieu! que celui de vouloir la perte d'hommes innocents! Le Comité de Sûreté Générale a été environné de prestiges pour être amené à ce but. Sa bonne foi n'a point compris la langue qui lui parlait un dessein si funeste; on le flattait, on lui insinuait qu'on visait à le dépouiller de son autorité.[11]

As far as the *Comité de Sûreté Générale* was concerned, however, the rival committee had already begun to reduce its authority. The government's reports on the Hébertists (23 Ventôse), and on the Dantonists (11 Germinal), had been entrusted to St Just. On 27 Germinal, the *Comité de Salut Public* established its own *bureau de police*, which was responsible, more than any other single factor, for embittering relations between the two committees. For the *Comité de Sûreté Générale*, this body, under the supervision of the Robespierrist Lejeune, was a threat to its own police authority. It was seen as an instrument of Robespierre's personal will, and the creation as a gesture of no confidence in the *Comité de Sûreté Générale*.

Ording has shown that the *Comité de Sûreté Générale* still dealt with the bulk of police dossiers, and has deduced that the fears of the police committee were therefore unjustified. However, it was its potential authority which was resented, and the interpretation of the *Comité de Sûreté Générale* was not entirely erroneous. Members of the *Comité de Salut Public* admitted signing orders without discussion, and often without reading them, and so it was possible for Robespierre or St Just to exercise a personal control over the *bureau de police*, in spite of the theoretical collective responsibility of the *Comité de Salut Public* as a whole.

Serious conflicts certainly arose, and when Robespierre stopped referring business to the *Comité de Sûreté Générale* after 24 Floréal, there was always a possibility that the two committees might enforce contradictory policies. Such conflicts cannot all be attributed to the obtuseness of the *Comité de Sûreté Générale*, as Ording perhaps implied. The arrest of the entire revolutionary committee of the *section de l'Indivisibilité*, for reasons which are not altogether clear, was attributed to Robespierre. One of its members, Henry Bodson, described this arrest as one of the main causes of hostility to Robespierre on 9 Thermidor. Another suspect,

Pierre Chatelain, was the victim of this rivalry. Arrested in autumn, 1793, he was released by the *Comité de Sûreté Générale* in Frimaire, but imprisoned again by the *Comité de Salut Public* in Messidor. The *Comité de Sûreté Générale* again freed him in Thermidor, and it appeared, significantly, that his offence had been to prevent spectators from shouting 'Vive Robespierre!' at the Fête of the Supreme Being.[12] Taken individually, such cases seem perhaps trivial, but they accumulated to form a considerable source of grievance.

These grievances aggravated a fundamental difference of approach to police work on the part of the two government committees. The *Comité de Sûreté Générale* realised that the most accessible information about royalist and counter-revolutionary circles came from within those circles, from royalists, counter-revolutionaries, and their intimates themselves. Hence the committee enlisted, by blackmail if necessary, a network of informers, who were often invaluable, but whose political loyalty to the Republic was not above suspicion. Ferrières-Sauveboeuf, an ex-noble, gave the authorities information about the inmates of La Force, and then of Pélagie, in the hope of avoiding execution and obtaining his release. He also claimed personal knowledge of the baron de Batz, and the elusive duc de Châtelet. Dossonville, another agent of the committee, knew so much inside information about every government of France up to the 1820s, that they were all forced either to imprison or employ him. Although probably always a royalist, he provided the government with vauable information, specializing in discovering forgers of revolutionary paper currency. Sénart, too, who masterminded the arrest of Catherine Théot, was not approved by the *Comité de Salut Public*. It is not wholly true to say, like Ording, that the arrest of Sénart was the work of the *Comité de Sûreté Générale* itself. It was only agreed after a long discussion, at which this committee took his defence.

Robespierre objected to the morality of employing agents who were not devoted Republicans. Effective spies, however, could not afford to be incorruptible. They were obliged to offer and accept bribes, and in Dossonville's case, to seduce the wives of suspects, in order to infiltrate subversive groups. These methods, however, were anathema to the over-scrupulous Robespierre. A note found among his papers, outlining the formation of the ideal political police organization, suggests how little he understood of the realities of secret police work. This paper declared that

> Un patriote sans probité est un monstre exécrable, en qui l'on ne peut avoir de confiance solide et un patriote sans lumières est capable, par un zèle indiscret, d'opérer un grand mal, au lieu de l'éviter . . . Tout délateur enfin qui n'agit que par motif d'intérêt, dans l'espoir d'une récompense, est un faux Républicain.[13]

The author of this plan is anonymous; he would have received short shrift from the *Comité de Sûreté Générale*. On 8 Thermidor, Robespierre referred again to the political police, when he castigated 'L'excessive perversité des agens subalternes d'une autorité respectable constituée dans votre sein'.[14] Vadier came to the defence of the *Comité de Sûreté Générale*, arguing that it exercised a very strict control over its agents.

The religious issue was another important point of conflict between Robespierre and the *Comité de Sûreté Générale*. Several members of the police committee held extreme anti-clerical views. Lavicomterie, for example, was the author of *Crimes des Papes depuis St Pierre jusqu'à Pie VI*. Philippe Rühl had shattered the famous relic, *La Sainte Ampoule*, in the presence of a vast crowd in front of Rheims cathedral, and thrown its contents to the wind. Vadier, too, had told the Convention, 'Vous n'aurez la tranquillité que lorsqu'il n'y aura plus de prêtres sur la territoire de la République'.[15] This was hardly compatible with Robespierre's instruction to Dumont: 'Il faut punir les prêtres séditieux et inciviques, mais non proscrire ouvertement le titre de prêtre en soi'.[16]

Since 18 Floréal, Vadier and Amar had opposed Robespierre's recognition of the existence of God, and of the immortality of the soul. The Fête of the Supreme Being on 20 Prairial suggested to the *Comité de Sûreté Générale* that Robespierre now favoured a policy of appeasement towards Catholicism. They resented his role as the 'new Pontiff', but, above all, they feared that a policy of reconciliation would lead to a resurgence of counter-revolutionary clerical activity. Courtois later asserted that Robespierre was trying to win support on the Right of the Convention. Vadier reacted by threatening to guillotine a hundred of his 'crapauds du Marais'.

The conflict found its clearest expression in Vadier's report on Catherine Théot, delivered on 27 Prairial, which, by thowing religion into ridicule, attempted to ruin Robespierre's policy of conciliation, and prepared the crisis of 9 Thermidor. Catherine Théot herself was a visionary whose messianic prophecies had already earned her a period of imprisonment in the Bastille in 1779, and had brought her to the notice of Chaumette in 1793. Credulous peasants, the sick, and army recruits afraid of death in battle, all came to her house in the *rue Contrescarpe* to hear expositions of the Gospels, and predictions that the imminent fall of Anti-Christ, and the humbling of the Great Ones, would soon usher in an era of peace and the end of oppression. She herself, 'La Mère de Dieu', claimed to be the medium of this transformation. The group's absurd initiation ceremonies were easy targets for Vadier's ironic barbs, but his claim that Théot was being manipulated by Orléanists and clerics was a little more serious.

The report was received with sardonic laughter in the Convention, and, apparently, in the Jacobin club. Behind the sarcasm, however, lay a serious purpose. The report was an attack on religion, an attempt to link it with the counter-revolution, and a personal attack on Robespierre. For one of Théot's patrons, the ex-Constituant Dom Gerle, possessed a *certificat de civisme* supported by Robespierre. Finally, on 9 Thermidor, Vadier 'revealed' that Théot had written a letter to Robespierre informing him that, according to the prophecies of Ezekiel, he was the new Messiah.

The importance of the report must not be over-estimated. Robespierre succeeded in preventing the case going before the Revolutionary Tribunal, on the grounds that he wanted the case further investigated. But this argument may simply have been a tactical move. Vadier had produced a masterpiece of propaganda, describing an innocent and ridiculous gathering manipulated by sinister, counter-revolutionary figures. The affair must also be seen in the context of widespread occultist practices investigated by the *Comité de Sûreté Générale* in Avignon, Compiège and elsewhere. Vadier had wounded Robespierre where he was most vulnerable, by undermining his *amour propre*, and had successfully threatened his credibility as the High Priest of the cult of the Supreme Being. Vadier had ensured that the prophecies of the 'Mère de Dieu' would not be fulfilled, and that, in his own words, 'L'oeuf que la poule couve n'aura pas de germe'.[17]

Religious questions lay at the heart of the Montagnard opposition to Robespierre, and were not merely an excuse for that opposition. Catholicism, and its alternatives – the revolutionary calendar, the Civil Constitution, the worship of the Supreme Being – formed, after all, the most important cultural issue of the Revolution. It is perhaps worth noting that there was a minority of Protestants in the *Comité de Sûreté Générale*: Moise Bayle's family had emigrated to Switzerland after the Revocation of the Edict of Nantes; Rühl's father was a pastor in Strasbourg; Henri Voulland was a Calvinist, and had been associated with the pastor Rabaut St Etienne in the Constituent Assembly. I do not wish to resurrect the myth that attacks on Catholicism were the work of Protestants, Jansenists, Freemasons and other messengers of Satan. The *Comité de Sûreté Générale* gave Protestants no special protection. Amar, for example, prepared a dossier on the *parti Protestant* and its links with federalism. Many Protestant suspects were arrested, some specifically accused of *fanatisme*. Several members of the committee, however, came from areas where strong religious feeling of any kind might be dangerously divisive: Voulland from the Gard, Louis and Rühl from the Bas-Rhin, Vadier from the Ariège, all areas with important Protestant communities. These men had direct local experience of religious strife, which may have inspired their hatred of all kinds of religious fanaticism.

It is remarkable, too, how many of Robespierre's enemies came from the Midi. Bayle was from Marseille, Vadier and Barère from the Pyrenees, Amar from Grenoble, Voulland from Uzès, Jagot from the Ain, Lacoste from the Dordogne, and Dubarran from the Gers. The *Représentants en mission* already mentioned, like Tallien, Fréron, Barras and Rovère, returned to Paris from the southern cities of Marseille, Bordeaux, Avignon and Toulon. The southern origins of these Thermidoreans is in striking contrast to the predominantly northern Robespierrists (the Auvergnat Couthon provides the exception). This is of more than academic interest. Robespierre, who had never been south of the Loire, had no experience of the situation in the Midi. He did not know the strength of popular Catholicism in the South-West, or of counter-revolutionary Royalism in Marseille, except at second hand. For the Thermidoreans, Robespierre's policy of religious conciliation was a surrender in the face of the enormous strength of the counter-revolution in the Midi. Some of them, in their turn, under-estimated the damage that dechristianizaton was causing the Republic, and this misjudgement prevented the left-wing Montagnards from imposing their extreme views on post-Thermidorean France. In their opinion, however, Robespierre did not realize that vigorous measures against the clergy were essential to the defence of the Republic in the Ariège, the Gers, and the Gard. He refused to heed Vadier's warning of 27 Prairial:

> N'est-ce pas au fanatisme qu'on doit les troubles de Nîmes et de Montauban, de la Lozère et d'Avignon, d'Arles et du camp de Jalès? Citoyens, ce n'est jamais qu'au nom du ciel que la guerre civile a pris naissance, et que la superstition a ensanglanté la terre.[18]

The White Terror in the Gard and the Ariège, the activities of the *Compagnie de Jésus* in the Rhône valley, were to bear out these fears. For the Thermidoreans, Robespierre was guilty of under-estimating the strength of the enemy in the south.

V

The opposition of the fourth group of Robespierre's adversaries, those within the *Comité de Salut Public*, is already well-documented. There is little point in rehearsing here the details of Billaud's doom-laden silence in committee, Carnot's military differences with St Just, criticism of Collot's mission to Lyon, or Barère's vacillations.

A serious attempt was made to weaken Robespierre, when the government agreed to send six companies of *canonniers* away from Paris to the *Armée du Nord*. This move, which reduced the authority of Hanriot and the National Guard, formed the basis of the compromise of the 4 and 5 Thermidor. In return for this concession by St Just, Barère and his colleagues agreed to accelerate the enforcement of the Ventôse decrees, which envisaged the liquidation of the property of suspects for the payment of poor relief to the indigent. Even at this late stage, therefore, the dissidents within the government were willing to co-operate with Robespierre, and a letter by Voulland to his constituents on 8 Thermidor expressed optimism about the unity of the government.

Robespierre was responsible for the failure of the compromise. He did not believe in the sincerity of the negotiators, and perhaps felt abandoned by St Just. The improvement achieved by the intermediaries, St Just and Barère, was quickly nullified by Robespierre's speech of 8 Thermidor, which called for a purge of government committees. Philippe Rühl relates how the two committees were subjected to a withering attack by Robespierre, who accused the *Comité de Sûreté Générale* of not taking action against certain of the renegade *Représentants en mission*. He tells, too, how Couthon lured the members of the *Comité de Sûreté Générale* to a meeting on 9 Thermidor to discuss the case of Dubois-Crancé, in order to prevent them from attending the session of the Convention, where St Just was beginning his final, interrupted speech on the government committees. Barère, too, explained to his confidant Vilate,

> Ce Robespierre est insatiable; parce qu'on ne fait pas tout ce qu'il voudrait, il faut qu'il rompe la glace avec nous. S'il nous parlait de Thuriot, Guffroy, Rovère, Lecointre, Panis, Cambon, de ce Monestier, qui a vexé toute ma famille, et de toute la séquelle Dantoniste, nous nous entendrions; qu'il demande encore Tallien, Bourdon de l'Oise, Fréron, Legendre, à la bonne heure;. . . mais Duval, mais Audouin, mais Léonard Bourdon, Vadier, Voulland, il est impossible d'y consentir.[19]

If Robespierre had been content, then, with purging the Mountain of Dantonists, he might have found support within the government. But by demanding the heads of several *Représantants en mission*, as well as attacking the *Comité de Sûreté Générale*, he alienated moderate support, and prepared 9 Thermidor.

VI

The 9 Thermidor, identified by many historians with political reaction and the advent of a bourgeois Republic, thus in part owed its origins to the extreme left wing of the Convention. For a while the moderates feared the severity of the Terror, the *Comité de Sûreté Générale* felt that Robespierre was not severe enough. It was these men, together with Robespierre's opponents in the *Comité de Salut Public*, who organized the defeat of the Commune on 9 Thermidor, with Voulland proposing Barras as the leader of the forces of the Convention, and outlawing the supporters of Robespierre. Robespierre's call for religious conciliation had angered them, and the vigorous measures taken in the provinces to suppress counter-revolution provided a constant source of disputes. In a sense therefore, the coup of 9 Thermidor was a revolution of the Left.

Neither Barère, Billaud, Collot or the members of the *Comité de Sûreté*

Générale imagined that the overthrow of Robespierre would necessarily mean the end of the Terror. When, on 11 Thermidor, Barère proposed a new list of jurors for the Revolutionary Tribunal, there was no question of replacing the public prosecutor Fouquier-Tinville. He presented the names of Bernard de Saintes and Duval as new members of the *Comité de Salut Public*, candidatures which did not indicate that a relaxation of the Terror would follow. The Thermidoreans of the left enjoyed a brief period of power. In some provinces, dechristianization reached climax only after 9 Thermidor. In other words, it was not immediately clear that, as a price of its alliance, the Centre would demand an end to political repression.

It will no doubt be objected, in the tradition of Babeuf and Buonarroti, that the Thermidoreans were irresponsible, and that they are to blame for not realizing that Robespierre was essential to the success of the Revolution. Such an objection calls for several remarks. In the first place, Babeuf himself supported the Thermidoreans, and for a time welcomed the overthrow of Robespierre. Neither he nor the other Thermidoreans of the left could see into the future and this is not the place for a discussion of the failures of the return to parliamentary government. The Thermidoreans of the left miscalculated the damage caused by extreme policies like dechristianization, and they failed to interpret popular support for Danton at his trial as a plea for the relaxation of the Terror. They perhaps did not appreciate enough the extent to which military victories had diminished the need for repression. Some of them, like Barras, Fréron and Tallien perhaps did realize this, and performed a prompt *volte-face* after Thermidor. For the other Thermidoreans of the left, however, the Thermidorean régime of the Year 3 became a perversion of their original intentions.

Secondly, there is a very real sense in which the régimes of Thermidor and the Directory were conceived as much in the original spirit of the Revolution as the régime of the Year 2. For in spite of their class nature, and in spite of the White Terror, they achieved important victories over royalism, inaugurated considerable administrative reforms, and consummated the advance of the bourgeoisie, who had always provided the leaders and main beneficiaries of the Revolution.

Thirdly, it is unreasonable to accuse the Thermidoreans alone of bringing the Revolution to a close, because in a sense, it was already 'glacée'. If the régimes which followed tried to strike a delicate balance between Right and Left, then this had been prefigured by the fall of the Hébertists and Robespierre's own attacks on the *citras* and the *ultras*. If the popular risings of Germinal and Prairial Year 3 were abortive, it was partly because the Robespierrist Terror had already decapitated their potential leadership. If there was no popular movement in support of Robespierre on 9 Thermidor, it was because the advance of bureaucratic centralization had crushed revolutionary initiative in the grassroots of the sections. All this was not the work of the Thermidoreans: it was achieved by the Jacobin régime as a whole.

It does not appear, as Mathiez thought, that the opposition to Robespierre's social policies was the main source of grievance against him. As we have seen, the Thermidoreans were prepared to compromise over this. The Ventôse decrees play no part in the debates of 9 Thermidor; they are entirely absent from the justifications of persecuted Jacobins after Thermidor. The evidence therefore suggests that this was a peripheral issue. It was peripheral, after all, to the Terror, which was necessary not to promote a social revolution, but to defend the liberal gains of the Revolution against the menace of foreign invasion and civil war.

Although personal antipathies no doubt played their part in the pre-Thermidorean political struggles, serious differences of policy also existed which transcended trivial personal enmities. The Thermidoreans acted in legitimate self-defence, anticipating a purge and the guillotine.

The *Comité de Sûreté Générale* objected to Robespierre's policy of religious appeasement. For its members, the Supreme Being was not the answer to the Vendean rebels, and their counterparts in the Ariège, the Lozère and the South-East. The committee resented Robespierre's criticism of its police methods, and it reacted against creeping centralization, and Robespierre's dictatorial pretensions. They resisted the over-concentration of power in the hands of one man and one body. They reacted against the excesses of a long tradition in French politics, of which the Communist Party and the U.D.R. [Union for the Defence of the Republic, *ed.*] are the modern heirs. For the 9 Thermidor represented the end of a dictatorship, and the return to parliamentary government. The *Conventionnels*, for so long intimidated either by the people of Paris, or by their own executive organs, now re-asserted themselves. Collot d'Herbois told the Convention on 9 Thermidor, surrounded by the guns of the Commune, 'Voici l'instant de mourir pour la patrie et de la sauver'. The response was immediate: 'Aux armes! Vivre libres ou mourir!'[20] One deputy recalled that 'Si jamais j'ai cru mourir, c'était bien dans ce moment.'[21] One should therefore not be surprised if the *Conventionnels* looked back on 9 Thermidor as their finest hour.

Notes

1 Robespierre, *Discours et rapports à la Convention*, ed. Bouloiseau (Paris, 1965), p. 306.
2 F. Furet and D. Richet, *La Révolution* (2 vols., Paris, 1965), i, pp. 170–3.
3 C. H. Church, 'In search of the Directory', in *French Government and Society, 1500–1850: essays in memory of A. Cobban*, ed. J. F. Bosher (London, 1973), 279. This still leaves us to define *which* revolutionary settlement? If contem-

poraries had agreed on this, the troubled life of the Directory might have been happier and longer.

4 Anon., *Faits receuillis aux derniers instants de Robespierre et de sa faction du 9 au 10 thermidor* (Paris, year 2).

5 A. Mathiez, *La Révolution française* 3 vols. (Paris, 1927), vol. 3, pp. 195–6.

6 A. C. Thibaudeau, *Mémoires sur la Convention et le Directoire* 2 vols. (Paris, 1824), vol. 1, pp. 82 and 87.

7 Barras, *Mémoires*, ed. G. Duruy (Paris, 1895), p. 186, although Aulard attributes the remark to Garnier de l'Aube in his *Histoire politique de la Révolution française, 1789–1804* (Paris, 1926), p. 498.

8 Robespierre, *Discours*, op. cit., p. 292.

9 Sénart, *Révélations puisées dans les cartons des comités de salut public et de sûreté générale*, ed. A. Dumesnil (Paris, 1824), p. 151.

10 A. Kuscinski, *Dictionnaire des Conventionnels* (Paris, 1919).

11 St Just, *Discours commencé par St Just à la séance du 9 Thermidor* (Paris, year 2), pp. 4–5.

12 AN F$_7$.4643, doss. 3, Pierre Chatelain.

13 AN F$_7$.4433, plaq. 2, no. 43, *papiers trouvés chez Robespierre*: 'Observations soumises aux lumières patriotiques et démocratiquement républicaines du C.S.P.'.

14 Buchez and Roux, *Histoire parlementaire de la Révolution française* (Paris, 1837), vol. 33, pp. 406–48.

15 Buchez and Roux, op. cit., vol. 33, p. 164.

16 Letter to Dumont, 6 Brumaire year 2, in *Correspondance de Maximilien et Augustin Robespierre*, ed. G. Michon (Paris, 1926).

17 cit. Vilate, *Les Mystères de la Mère de Dieu dévoilées* (Paris, year 3).

18 M.-G.-A. Vadier, *Rapport et décret présentés à la C.N. au nom des comités de s.g. et de s.p.*, (Paris, year 2), p. 4.

19 Vilate, *Causes secrètes de la Révolution du 9 au 10 thermidor* (Paris, year 3).

20 *Journal de Perlet*, no. 674, 11 Thermidor, year 2.

21 Durand de Maillane, *Histoire de la C.N.* (Paris, 1825) p. 201.

THE CROWD, TERROR AND COUNTER-TERROR

Presentation

This section is intended to introduce students to the more problematic phenomena of the Revolution. As such, the contributors retrace some of the ground covered in the previous section, but from an analytical perspective. The behaviour of the crowd, the emergence of Terror as a system of power and the institutionalization of political violence are themes which seemed relatively uncontroversial a generation ago. Today, they provoke intense and introspective debate among historians – an indication that the older explanations no longer provide a sufficient account of the issues under consideration.

In truth, however, there is more at stake than this. The view which we take of the actions of the crowd, of the Terror, of the descent into collective savagery, is apt to colour our assessment of the Revolution as a whole. Was terror and political violence systemic, or a one-off product of intractable circumstance? Where should we locate the terrorist mentality? In the behavioural reflexes of the Revolutionary crowd, perhaps, or in the minds of deputies engrossed in the task of regeneration? Depending on the answers to questions of this type, we can 'model' the Revolution in various ways. The French Revolution was violent and incipiently totalitarian in its politics from Day One. On the contrary, it is divisible into two 'phases': a liberal, humanitarian and reforming first act, followed by a struggle for survival which generated a dictatorship and the curtailment of individual liberties. Alternatively, we might wish to conceptualize the Revolution in terms of social 'layers': that is to say a violent and proto-terrorist populace whose interventionism in politics progressively detached legislators and administrators from the ideals of the Enlightenment. If a scenario based on fracture is selected, a further question arises: is it safe to continue thinking about Revolutionary political culture in unitary terms?

Since the traditional wisdom on these matters only receives passing mention in the pages that follow, it may be worth restating the position. In the days before discourse analysis came to the aid of historical research, historians tended to believe what contemporary actors said about themselves and the episodes in which they participated. Contemporary opinion judged the uprising against the king on August 10, 1792 to have marked a critical turning-point in the cycle of Revolution, indeed a 'second Revolution'. The events of that summer concluded the most fertile phase of parliamentary reform and ushered on to the stage the familiar impedimenta of Terror: the organized crowd, violence directed against those deemed guilty of political 'crimes', and the first institutions of public vigilance. Thereafter, a frankly illiberal regime took shape which swiftly eroded the cultural and political gap between bourgeois and plebeian Revolutionaries. The chief reason for this development was the need to take the people into partnership in order to defend the Revolution from its domestic and foreign enemies. Indeed, it was the war effort (both internal and external) that sanctioned the Terror,

[handwritten: dictatorship was in yr. 2.]

conceived now as a system of government as well as a weapon of state violence against those unable to meet exacting criteria of citizenship. *[handwritten margin: Beliefs of Scholars up 2 1970s]*

Here we have the verdict of the majority of scholars as it stood until the 1970s. This viewpoint was shared even by putative revisionist historians. In 1965, François Furet and Denis Richet had yet to discover the thread of predestination in Revolutionary political culture. 'Far from representing an inescapable model of revolution', they argued, 'the dictatorship of the Year Two bore the hallmarks of the contingent and exceptional, the signs of distress.'[1] Thus, while revisionism was starting to make headway on other fronts, the dichotomies of Revolutionary politics and their explanatory underpinnings survived intact. Not so today, as several of the Readings in this section bear witness. They show how pressure to re-examine the darker, fratricidal dimension of the Revolution has built up from several directions. For a start, it is possible to detect a societal shift away from the phenomenon of radical Revolution. Modern historians, unlike their immediate predecessors of the 1950s and 1960s, display a lack of sympathy for the dilemmas confronting the Montagnard dictatorship in 1793–4. No doubt this impatience reflects the discredit heaped upon neo-jacobin and Marxist accounts of the French Revolution in recent years. Once the focus of a thousand doctoral dissertations, the embattled politics of the Year Two no longer inspire researchers. The 'game of analogies'[2] (that is the comparison of 1789 and 1917) now attracts only those who are interested in the pathology of political violence. *[handwritten margin: Diffs of more recent interpretation]*

However, the exercise in reassessment of the Terror and its organs has also been driven by the arrival on the scene of new methodologies. In the 1980s scholars who had become impatient with the neatness of arguments rooted in circumstance, started to employ linguistic theory in a search for the specifically ideological origins of the Terror. Political philosophy and the rediscovery of relevant writings in the works of several nineteenth and twentieth-century thinkers hastened this process. More recently the analytical techniques of cultural anthropology have greatly enriched our understanding of the crowd and the corollary phenomenon of violence in a Revolutionary context. What kind of picture is beginning to emerge in consequence? A more complex one, without doubt. For it is important to point out that the 'thesis of circumstance' (applied both to the Terror and to Revolutionary politics in general) has been sidestepped rather than overturned. François Furet now seeks to uncouple the Terror from the imperative of public safety (Reading 22), but many scholars still adhere to this scenario as the best available explanation. On the other hand, research into crowd behaviour shows signs of making rapid progress, now that it has been released from the rather static categories imposed by Albert Soboul and George Rudé a generation ago. Building on the early work of Georges Lefebvre, Colin Lucas demonstrates just how contingent and ambivalent were the actions, and rhetoric, of the so-called Revolutionary crowd (Reading 21). *[handwritten margin: NEW METHODOLOGIES; linguistic theory; cultural anthropology; circumstance sidestepped not overturned]*

Yet it is political philosophy and discourse theory, in a heady mixture, that currently make the running. The refusal of compromise, coercion – and therefore violence – were endemic to Revolutionary political culture, it is suggested.

Consequently the temptation of the Terror solution was there right from the beginning, and it was almost inevitable that the Revolutionaries would succumb. This conclusion is reached on the basis of an analysis of 'Rousseauian' ideology: its obsession with regeneration, its voluntarism and its total acceptance of the thesis of sovereignty of the people. All of the Revolutionaries were in thrall to this ideology, claims Furet; and in due course it produced not only the mechanisms of the Terror but the inflated and multipurpose language of popular 'absolutism' which Bronislaw Baczko unravels to such good effect (Reading 24). The net result of this line of argument, as will be noted, is instantly to telescope an experience of Revolution conceived hitherto in terms of 'phases' and 'layers'. The liberal phase of the Revolution (1789–92) receives short shrift indeed, its political restraint and reforming endeavours either overlooked or denied. Not surprisingly, therefore, the pursuit of the Terror to its supposed ideological origins has prompted a number of objections, especially now that the history of the early Revolution is in the process of being rewritten (Reading 16). Nonetheless, if we were to confine our attention to the period of the Terror proper, many scholars would agree (albeit reluctantly) that reductionist arguments based on circumstance no longer suffice to capture the sheer enormity of the phenomenon.

Colin Lucas specializes in disentangling closely related phenomena without recourse to *a priori* assumptions, and his essay extends our knowledge in several ways.[3] First he offers a corrective to the once solid, but now rather fragile, research on the crowd carried out by the previous generation. If we are really to grasp how the crowd fitted into the political culture of the Revolution, we must study it in the round. That is to say in its ecological environment, and not as some kind of disembodied chorus to *sans-culottes* politics. The Revolutionary crowd, properly speaking, was not born overnight: it evolved tentatively and contingently. The same holds for the several other species of 'purposive' crowds such as the female gatherings studied by Olwen Hufton (Reading 15), of course. Whatever the yardstick chosen – organizational capacity, targeting of enemies, political awareness, discourse – the crowd emerges as a richly protean phenomenon. Indeed, Lucas refuses to disconnect crowd behaviour during the Revolution from its *ancien-régime* roots, hesitating to argue for any durable shift in mentality. Even its rhetoric needs to be decoded with care, he believes, for what appears at first sight to be evidence of a significant rupture may simply denote a transposition of older loyalties. Some consideration of the gender patterning of crowd actions would undoubtedly strengthen and extend these arguments. For there now exists parallel research on crowd mobilizations in the 1770s which tackles the gender issue and in so doing detects another thread of continuity linking the old regime to the new.[4]

As the remarks made earlier hinted, François Furet's contribution should be read less as a narrative account of the Terror than as a question-raising argument with other historians. In fact, his piece is sketchy and unnuanced as a description of the Terror. Although he joins with Norman Hampson (Reading 19) in drawing attention to the role performed by the *représentants-en-mission*, for example, he tends to overplay the activities of the Paris *armée révolutionnaire*. The law of 22 Prairial Year Two which dramatically escalated the body-count of the Revolutionary Tribunal is rightly highlighted (as crucial to his argument), but that of 14 Frimaire (crucial to an understanding of the modalities of repression outside Paris) is not mentioned at all. However, it is the interrogation of the 'givens' of Revolutionary historiography that counts in this instance. Furet readily concedes that the Terror – as an apparatus of power – only came into being gradually, and that the argument from circumstance is still useful in this regard. Yet he insists that the Terror – as a political idea – had an ancestry stretching back to the start of the Revolution. The question therefore resolves into one of measuring and assessing a complex interaction, and it is his contention that the chronology, duration and scope of the Terror are in the final analysis most effectively explained in ideological terms.

If the terrorist reflex is to be counted a characteristic feature of Revolutionary mentality, the unappetizing career of Nicolas Guénot – as related by Richard Cobb (and Claude Hohl) – would fit the bill nicely. Guénot was a terrorist-in-waiting, so to speak – a splinter off Lucas's crowd, fashioned into a dutiful cog of Revolutionary Government. His life story brings the Terror down to earth, but at the same time it raises a question. Where should we place a man like Guénot in the overall pattern of experiences during the Year Two? Cobb paints with words; he creates a vivid and compelling picture of careerism, of casual violence institutionalized, of a world turned upside-down; but he hesitates to claim typicality for his subject. Ultimately Guénot's biography is just that – his life story – and we must extract from it what we can. Through this lens we glimpse many of the themes of big city living in the eighteenth century: escape from failure and provincial claustrophobia, the banality of violence, survival on the margins of power, how to turn public events to private advantage, and so forth. Perhaps Guénot was typical of *some* militants for *some* of his painfully long career. He was certainly typical of most of the footsoldiers of the Revolutionary crowd, in as much as we do not actually know what he thought about the great events that raised him up only to cast him down.

Nicolas Guénot had been in political disgrace for several months when the coup against Robespierre and his supporters in the Committees took place. Consequently his exit from the Terror was eased (initially at any rate) by his 'victim' status. However, most of the architects, upholders and accomplices of the Terror could claim no such alibi. This is the point made by Bronislaw Baczko in the reading which concludes this section. Thermidor was an event – swift and bloody – whereas escape from the Terror was bound to be a protracted and agonizing business. In the days and weeks following Thermidor, the Revolutionaries had to decide how far to retreat and in which direction, this while many of the institutions, most of the personnel, and the entire rhetorical edifice of the Terror were still in place. Public opinion looked to the Convention and its newly purged Committees for a lead, but pressures at the base (notably the clamour for a release of suspects) made stabilization hard to achieve. Baczko explores the subsequent disintegration and descent into a politics of vengeance from every angle; however, the extract reproduced here is drawn from the first part of his argument. In it he describes and illustrates the extraordinarily tenacious language of the Terror which moulded imaginations and policed behaviour at every level. For several pregnant weeks after the coup, this 'controlled unanimity' served to freeze the political situation, but then language lost its grip and reality pushed to the surface once more.

Notes

1 F. Furet and D. Richet, *La Révolution française* (2 vols., Paris, Réalités-Hachette, 1965; English translation London, Weidenfeld and Nicolson, 1970), i, p. 295.
2 *See* M. Vovelle, '1789–1917: The Game of Analogies', in K. M. Baker, ed. *The French Revolution and the Creation of Modern Political Culture*, Volume IV: *The Terror* (Oxford, Pergamon Press, 1994), pp. 349–78.
3 In this context, see also C. Lucas, 'Revolutionary Violence, the People and the Terror', in Baker, *The French Revolution and the Creation of Modern Political Culture*, volume iv: *The Terror*, pp. 57–79.
4 *See* C. A. Bouton, *The Flour War: Gender, Class and Community in Late Ancien Régime French Society* (Pennsylvania State University Press, 1993).

21
The crowd and politics

COLIN LUCAS

I

There is termerity in discussing a subject already burdened with the weight of several generations of historians, sociologists, and psychologists – 'impudence' was the word that came to Richard Cobb's mind at the thought of reconsidering the riots and *journées* of revolutionary Paris. More than temerity, it would be folly to pretend to encompass in one paper a phenomenon so diverse in its forms and manifestations. The purpose here is limited to a discussion of the political function of the crowd in the Revolution. The paper seeks first to emphasize some of the elements of continuity between the Ancien Régime and the Revolution. It is necessary, therefore, to examine with care the Ancien Régime crowd. On this basis, it

Reprinted in full, except for notes, from C. Lucas, ed. *The French Revolution and the Creation of Modern Political Culture*. Volume II: *The Political Culture of the Revolution* (Oxford, Pergamon Press, 1988), pp. 259–85.

may be possible to underscore some original characteristics of crowd behaviour fostered by the Revolution. Finally, the paper discusses some of the ways in which the revolutionaries tried to cope with the crowd. In sum, the intention here is to sketch how the crowd is part of the political culture of the Revolution.

There was not of course just one crowd, no more in the French Revolution than in any other period of history. The simple aggregation of human beings in a single place – perhaps going about their business as in a market or gathered to stare at some incident – is only a crowd in the purely descriptive sense of a density of people. Even when a gathering of people ceases to be or from the outset is not a passive agglomerate of individuals, an active crowd takes distinct forms and behaves in distinct ways. It is common to distinguish between, for example, festive crowds, audience crowds, panic crowds, and aggressive crowds. Each is distinguished from the other partly by occasion and context and partly by behaviour. Possibly, what distinguishes most clearly the crowd from an aggregate of human beings is a shared sense of purpose in being assembled together with some sense that this purpose is achieved collectively, either by acting collectively or else simply by being gathered together. This is what we may term the 'purposive' crowd. Certainly, individuals gathered at a market have for the most part the similar purpose of buying goods; but it is only when they become aware that such goods can only be obtained in a satisfactory manner by collective action that they become a purposive crowd. This is what distinguishes a market dispute watched by large numbers of people from a market riot. The participants in festive crowds, audience crowds and so on all share a common sense of why they are there and an understanding that their being there together collectively has a different meaning from accomplishing the same act individually.

It is a self-evidence to note that the purposive crowds of the Ancien Régime were equally present during the Revolution. No historian would question the essential continuity between the *émotions* and *séditions* of the Ancien Régime (albeit the relatively tranquil eighteenth century) and the turbulences of the decade 1789–99. It is evident in the market riots and *taxations populaires*; it is evident in the crowds' frequent recourse to rituals that differ little from those of the sixteenth or seventeenth centuries. There are strong echoes of earlier peasant wars in the rural disturbances of the Revolution, from the *jacqueries* of its earlier years to the endemic turbulence of its later years – we see the same methods of action, the same targets, often the same geography, and even frequently the same leading figures whom Yves-Marie Bercé identifies as 'troublemakers' in earlier times (nobles, priests, mayors, veteran soldiers, and craftsmen). Credulity, myth, rumour, panic fear, notions of hoarding, speculation and plot were as potent movers of popular wrath before 1789 as they

were after. The tolling of the *tocsin* mobilizing a local population against
the troops of counter-revolution or against the republican soldiery, against
brigands or against *gendarmes*; the mobilizing capacity of supposed
written documents, such as 'les ordres du roi' invoked in peasant disturbances in 1789 or the 'missive écrite en lettres d'or' alluded to in southern
religious disturbances in 1795–96; the importance of women in food riots,
the role of young unmarried men in collective disturbance, the habit of
placing women and young children in the front line of an aggressive crowd
– none of these characteristics (and many more) of crowd behaviour in the
Revolution was new. This is not to suggest that patterns of crowd behaviour in the late eighteenth century merely reproduced those of the early
modern period. But it is to stress that they were still strongly anchored in
the habits of earlier times analysed by historians of both France and
England.

   Those historians who have addressed the question of the crowd in the
Revolution directly have not of course ignored some elements of continuity.
Yet, whilst acknowledging the indispensable destructive power of the
crowd and emphasizing the importance of quite traditional economic
issues as mobilizers of the crowd, they have tended to concentrate on a
single phenomenon – the 'revolutionary crowd'. Such an approach is
epitomised by George Rudé who, under the title of *The Crowd in the
French Revolution*, is in fact concerned only with the revolutionary crowd
of the great Paris *journées*. Rudé, indeed, elsewhere explicitly rejects all
forms of crowd other than the 'aggressive' crowd as being significant in
this context. For Rudé, the aggressive crowd is coterminous with the
political crowd. As far as the revolutionary crowd is concerned, the
definition is largely that of a crowd aware of the political issues of the
Revolution and consciously intervening to act upon them.

   It does not diminish the importance of Rudé's work if we emphasize
how fuzzy his definitions are in some respects. For one thing, they depend
upon a particular definition (and a very modern definition at that) of what
is political. Rudé accords only a cursory glance at pre-revolutionary eighteenth-century movements: he concedes only a kind of rudimentary political quality to Parisian disturbances around the Parlement and considers
rural disturbances to be entirely marked by 'political innocence'. Such an
approach comes dangerously close to identifying 'political' with an awareness of and commentary on high politics. Moreover, within the Revolution
itself, Rudé's definition of the revolutionary crowd is confined in practice
to popular collective action in the sense of radicalising the Revolution
(despite a rather awkward chapter on Vendémiaire, concerned perhaps
above all to show how popular opinion supported the Convention). This
is curiously at once both an elastic and restrictive definition. On the one
hand, it leads Rudé to include a discussion of the Champ-de-Mars which
was not a crowd of the same order as the others he chooses: the report of

the *commissaires* of the Municipality stated categorically that 'il y avait des groupes de monde, mais sans foule décidée'.[2] On the other hand, it leads him to exclude entirely (except for Vendémiaire) crowd actions which clearly display an awareness of the political issues of the Revolution and a conscious intervention to act upon it, but which do not operate in the sense of radicalizing it – for example, the anti-jacobin crowds at Lyon and Marseille in 1793 or the various popular resistances to the Revolution such as *chouannerie*, some aspects of the White Terror, religious riots, etc. The assumption here is a value judgment about what is 'revolutionary', which denies validity to any other form of crowd action even when it can be classed as 'political' in Rudé's own usage of the word.

These premises betray a further ambiguity. It is axiomatic that the crowd as a collective actor in the Revolution antedated the appearance of the *sans-culotte* movement. Yet, while we should acknowledge that the Parisian popular movement was born out of the lessons learned by Parisian crowd action, its relationship with the crowd is in fact ambiguous, an ambiguity which Soboul's study does little to relieve. Rudé tends to equate *sans-culotte* with the crowd. Yet, it is perhaps too simple to propose that the political consciousness of these radical militants, revolutionary in the sense of propounding permanent change through action upon the structures of power, directly expressed in articulate form a consciousness possessed by the crowd. Clearly, there was a relationship between *sansculottisme* and the crowd; equally clearly, a new political consciousness, or at least a consciousness modified in its terms, came to inhabit the crowd during the events of the early Revolution. Yet, precisely what that relationship was and, indeed, just how revolutionary the crowd was are questions that bear much closer analysis – closer than this paper has space for.

If we turn back to Georges Lefebvre's earlier study of revolutionary crowds, we find a discussion that is in some ways more sophisticated. Lefebvre is, for example, less restrictive in his definition of the crowd. He is ready to include a wider range of crowds as worthy of attention and he discusses different types of market riot and rural distrubance as well as the *journées*. Furthermore, he elaborates a concept of 'la mutation brusque de l'agrégat en un rassemblement révolutionnaire',[3] an idea recently reformulated by Jacques Beauchard as the transition from the 'atomized crowd' via the 'crowd in fusion' to the 'organized crowd'.[4] Furthermore, Lefebvre posits that this mutation is the product of some external event 'qui réveille les sentiments affectifs'. This is valuable because it stresses the importance of examining other types of crowd as actors in revolution as well as the classically defined political crowd. It is valuable also because it stresses that all crowds are potentially interveners in the process of revolution. It is valuable finally because it directs our attention to this moment of metamorphosis, in particular to the manner in which exterior events act upon 'les sentiments affectifs' and to the degree of transformation involved.

Does, as in Kafka's 'Metamorphosis', the consciousness remain basically the same within the transformed exterior or does the consciousness change also?

The notion of 'les sentiments affectifs' introduces a further stimulating point in Lefebvre's analysis. The existence of a crowd supposes, he argues, the prior existence of a collective mentality. On entering the 'aggregate', the individual escapes from the pressure of the small social groups which provide the context of his daily life and becomes available 'aux idées et sentiments qui sont le propre de collectivités plus étendues dont il fait également partie'. It is clear that Lefebvre is in fact thinking of the availability to notions of 'the nation' or to more general social interests such as those of the poor. As we shall see shortly, it is possible to read this in a different way.

However, at this point, Lefebvre's argument begins to deviate. At root, his definition of the revolutionary crowd is the same as that of Rudé – acting in the sense of protecting and radicalising the Revolution. By prior collective mentality Lefebvre essentially means the growth of political consciousness and even if, in an aside, he admits that it feeds off popular memory, 'sur une tradition très ancienne', he discusses it in terms of the political education offered by the elections and the cahiers, the events of June–July 1789, and so on. For Lefebvre, as for Rudé, the purposive crowd in the Revolution is the one that assembles for a revolutionary purpose; its purest expression must be the Parisian section demonstrations of 1793. For Lefebvre also, 1789 is a rupture in the history of popular behaviour.

It is by taking another look at the pre-revolutionary crowd that we may redirect Lefebvre's analysis and understand the crowd's transposition into the revolutionary environment.

II

It is possible to argue that a prime feature of the Ancien Régime purposive crowd was its ability to act as a representative. I do not mean to advance that all crowds in all situations inescapably had a representative function. But, as an extension of its collective character, the crowd easily acquired the function of representing the community whose members composed it. It did not represent the community in a formal or direct way. This representation was more emblematic or virtual than direct. Not all the members of the community usually entered any particular crowd and it did not implement a policy debated and determined by the community, though some forms of rural contestation both before and during the Revolution could come close to that. Nonetheless, by its public and collective character, the crowd established and fed off a rapport with those members of the community who observed it without participating directly in it. One can cite many examples of this – the prevalence of youth groups in disturbances, exclusive by definition yet so clearly representative of collective community attitudes in practice; or else, market disturbances to which, as Steven Kaplan has noted, local officials so frequently conceded some tacit legitimacy; or else, the recurrent presence of figures from outside the *menu peuple*. Indeed, spectators were not merely an inescapable but rather, an indispensable part of crowd action. Spectators were an audience crowd alongside the acting crowd; indeed, it is frequently difficult to distinguish the two on the ground. Spectators were rarely indifferent to the actions of the crowd. At times, they verged on participation – the classic example is the scene at the Bastille on July 14 where, according to one observer, there was gathered 'une foule innombrable de citoyens, la plupart par le seul mouvement de la curiosité' and when, as the victorious crowd surged back up the rue Saint-Antoine with its prisoners, a 'nombre inconcevable des femmes, des enfants, des vieillards . . . semblaient s'élancer des fenêtres des maisons en criant: *Les voilà, les gueux! on les tient!*'.[5] More usually, they observed and commented. Of course, the crowd frequently overstepped at some point the limit of community acceptability. All that it did cannot, therefore, be deemed to be a community endorsed gesture. But, it is equally clear that the crowd frequently achieved and usually claimed a representative status, just as it is clear that spectators were usually aware of the claim to which they either acquiesced tacitly or openly or else which at some point they began to reject, often intervening either directly or indirectly to check or reprove actions.

The characteristic localism of the eighteenth-century crowd also reinforced this representative quality. Localism is self-evident in disturbances in villages or small towns. But, even where geographically wider movements were involved, the separate identity of groups from different communities appears to have been maintained. To take examples from the Revolution itself, it is clear that in the anti-seigneurial attacks which could move crowds over a radius of ten or more miles groups from individual villages tended to remain distinct within the multitude. As the crowd passed each village, the inhabitants of that village were incited to join in with a cry addressed collectively 'il faut que les gens de . . . se joignent à nous'; witnesses in subsequent judicial enquiries frequently described such crowds simply by listing the villages from which they were composed.[6] Similarly, the predominant localism is visible in the anti-jacobin disturbances in the Midi in 1795 and 1797 when a crowd from a particular village or small town travelled to murder someone from its own community whilst leaving other victims untouched for the crowds to come from their own particular community. Such a pattern was not confined to small localities. Urban disturbances in provincial towns during the Revolution frequently involved definable *quartiers*, whether as the locality of a riot or as an attack by one on another. One can cite among the many examples, the pattern of disturbances affecting La Carreterie and La Fusterie at Avignon, or the Plan d'Olivier and Le Boutonnet at Montpellier, or the different *quartier* identities of the *chiffonistes* and the *monnaidiers* at Arles. Even when one can attach socio-economic characteristics to such a pattern, they are far from being the only or indeed the dominant factor.

As for Paris, despite the fluidity of the population both socially and geographically noted by Daniel Roche, one can still discern the same feature. David Garrioch has recently demonstrated convincingly the primacy of neighbourhood in Parisian sociability. Crowd action was remarkably limited topographically inside the city, even during the Revolution. Leaving aside market riots, one can see this for example in the riots over child kidnapping in 1750. Despite the multitude of disturbances and the wide diffusion of the rumour at their source, the incidents were localized and separate; the participants seem to have been people living close to each incident. Similarly, the disturbances of August–September 1788 were closely confined to the area around the Parlement, principally the Place Dauphine and the Pont-Neuf. Only very late in the events was the crowd drawn out towards the Porte-Saint-Martin and the Faubourg Saint-Germain for purposes which will be discussed shortly. Although the evidence is scanty, it seems here again that the crowd was composed predominantly of people from the neighbourhood – the few arrested were from the vicinity or from just across the river; the best contemporary account gives it that character and describes a clear example of the rapport between the crowd and the spectators, between those in the street and those in the houses and shops giving out onto it. Similarly, in the Réveillon riot in the Faubourg Saint-Antoine, few people from outside the immediate vicinity intervened. Even the Bastille crowd was heavily localized: 70 per cent of the 'Vainqueurs de la Bastille' resided in the Faubourg Saint-Antoine. Although this event did draw participants from a wider area, the inhabitants of the Faubourg Saint-Antoine and the Fabourg Saint-Marcel remained quite distinct entities, each providing itself with its own leader (the *brasseurs* Santerre and Acloque). Indeed, it is significant that in the confusion of the early moments people from the Faubourg Saint-Antoine should have been able to recognize Elie and to know that, as an 'officier de fortune' in the Régiment de la Reine, he would know what to do; it is equally significant that Elie, understanding that he would also have to direct people who did not know him, immediately returned home to put on his uniform. These two faubourgs continued throughout the Revolution to have a separate crowd identity, Saint-Antoine even developing its own spokesman in the person of Gonchon. But, though less visible, one may reasonably expect other quarters to have retained at least elements of a similar identity. Certainly, the section demonstrations of 1793 were by their very essence quarter-based. The instinct to distinguish oneself by group appartenance was a prevalent one. For instance, when in July 1791 the Cordeliers Club tried to organize a mass demonstration-march from the Bastille to the Champ-de-Mars under one banner, the other clubs all insisted on marching each under its own banner; similarly, the works preparing the Champ-de-Mars for the Fête de la Fédération in 1790 was not a mass effort 'toutes classes confondues' but rather one in which each trade remained distinct, each displaying its own banner.

One can argue, therefore, that the eighteenth-century crowd enjoyed a particular, functional relationship with its community and that it remained characteristically rooted in locality and neighbourhood. Even in the urban context and even in the great events of the Revolution, a large crowd should probably be seen as characteristically an agglomeration of crowds rather than as a single mass.

It is important to define more closely this community which, we suggest, the eighteenth-century crowd represented and to which it related. Community must not be understood as merely a neighbourhood defined topographically, although this is an indispensable element. It contains also a notion of collective awareness, an awareness of belonging to a collectivity which provides the context for one's social existence or rather sociability. Social differentiation and individual ranking are not abolished but they are placed within the coherence of a wider collectivity. It is a constituent of identity and a referent of behaviour. The community represents a context of existence and a guide to living in society. Thus, if community has a physical sense of neighbourhood proximity, it also has a moral sense of collective norms of conduct, as it were a moral proximity of shared assumptions about the relationship between the individual and the group. It is well-known that the all-embracing form of community visible in the early modern period was subject to considerable stress and defections by the time of the later Ancien Régime. Elite groups no longer participated in the festive manifestations of collective culture; elite culture and popular culture were diverging as were the value systems they articulated; it was much more rare to find people from outside the world of workshop, street trade, and *menu peuple* in the crowd; property owners seem more uncomprehending and more quickly frightened of the crowd. The community, in the sense we have adopted, was far advanced in the process of becoming defined in terms of social structure, of becoming the popular community; in turn, the values it embodied were becoming what historians like to term 'traditional' as opposed to 'modern'. However, if we take Paris as the place where traditional solidarities can be supposed to have decayed the most, the community remained at the end of the Ancien Régime of paramount importance to the mass of ordinary people, even if the quarters were less distinctively inward-looking and parochial than they had been a hundred years earlier. Arlette Farge and David Garrioch give multiple examples of the way in which the individual appealed to the community, measured his or her place and reputation by reference to it. The community was a defence and a tribunal which, by regulating itself, perpetuated itself.

Nonetheless, the divorce between the popular community and elites was not complete. Before 1789, the bourgeois and professional man in Paris and other cities was still caught in the web of community and to some extent still acquiesced in it. As Daniel Roche emphasizes, fear and under-standing, sympathy even, were perfectly compatible reactions in contem-porary observers. The elites were capable of virtually colluding in some sorts of disturbance, for example grain riots. The crowd in turn called upon them to participate, for instance in the way in which crowds enrolled half-consenting local figures of standing in their action – partly, at least, in order to restate the community identity. Indeed, during the Revolution, elite groups were quite capable of speaking to the crowd in the language of the popular community, as they did in the religious disturbances or during the Thermidorian Reaction. Yet, such figures could only manipulate the crowd if they adopted that language. The crowd was not moved by deference – not just any noble could lead peasants in the *chouannerie* simply by reflex of ancient superiority. The standard contemporary official interpretation of riot in terms of outside agents and leaders from a higher social class was as unsound for the Revolution as it was for the Ancien Régime. The crowd tended to throw up its own leaders and these leaders could change as the direction of an event changed. Maillard's leadership was born in the Bastille crowd; that of Hulin did not long survive his attempt to save victims of that crowd. Indeed, a classic example is provided by the attack on the Invalides: the governor 'vint lui-même, fit ouvrir la grille et parla au peuple. On l'écoutait assez; un seul homme réclama, et dit que tout délai était un péril nouveau, et dans l'instant la foule se précipita dans l'Hôtel.'[7]

It is not at all surprising, therefore, to find people from socially diverse backgrounds in the crowds analysed by George Rudé. This was natural enough. Yet, the social relationship across the indeterminate cleavage in the community was very ambiguous and well expressed around the crowd. Joseph Charron's contemporary articulation of collective behaviour in Paris at the end of the Ancien Régime into 'peuple, public, populace, canaille' was an awkward contemporary attempt to render the complex reality of the evolving relationship.[8] What Charron's account of the events of August–September 1788 does show very clearly is the ambiguity sur-rounding the crowd. He notes that 'la classe mitoyenne' enjoyed the noisy turbulence of ordinary street effervescence and was perfectly ready to flip a coin to a street urchin, knowing that it would be used to buy fireworks and bangers. He shows that many householders around the Place Dauphine were ready to set lights in their windows in some kind of complicity with the street crowd but that a few refused, 'voulant se singulariser, ou ignorant les convenances'. The crowd returned the next evening to break the windows of the recalcitrant. 'Convenances' clearly implied a tacitly recognized legitimacy of the crowd and a proper colluding solidarity; yet, the outright refusal of some to collude was a symptom of the growing detachment of the 'classe mitoyenne'; in turn, the reaction of the crowd reflected its instinct to enforce an inclusive community. However, once the festive aspect present in almost every Ancien Régime popular crowd got out of hand, the 'classe mitoyenne' took fright and endorsed the intervention of the *guet*. However, the *guet* behaved in a heavy-handed manner, provoking pitched battles, the burning of guard houses, and finally government mobilization of the *gardes françaises*. At this point, the property owners ('le public' in Charron's terms) intervened to defuse the situation. 'Le public sentit qu'il était important de ne pas se rassembler, et la populace . . . se retira sans murmurer.' Thus, this 'public' was clearly still able to assert its community membership and to persuade the crowd; yet, once again, it could only do so provided it did not cut across the crowd's own perceptions and values, for Charron points out that the crowd dispersed because it 'respectait (la garde française) avec laquelle elle n'avait jamais en rien à démêler'. Indeed, the 'populace' continued its hostility to the *guet*, culminating in another pitched battle. This left 'le public indigné . . . et les honnêtes gens dans l'inquiétude'. When, finally, the *guet* assaulted a group engaged in perfectly innocent conversation, 'au récit de ces actes d'inhumanité, tous les honnêtes gens se soulevèrent et demandèrent vengeance'.

In sum, Charron portrays a complex relationship of both tension and collusion between the crowd and the social groups on the edge of the community that the crowd represented. More than that, he reveals how these social groups accorded the crowd a certain legitimacy which did not arise, in this case, out of some sense that the crowd was serving a grander political design of the elites. However, the ambiguity of this relationship was to be laid bare in the Revolution. We may argue that the Revolution hastened the process of separation of elites from the popular community, from its claims and its values. The crowd's action in the Revolution may be seen as instrumental in accelerating the alienation of the propertied classes.

The crowd was peculiarly fit to be the organ of popular representation precisely because, whilst retaining its local, rooted quality, it stood outside the formal structures of the community. It abolished the hierarchies and relationships in the society of the neighbourhood and asserted the commonality of the members of the community in their undifferentiated membership of the crowd. The crowd was in a sense the community temporarily reformed. It was perhaps as close as one could get to the philosophers' ideal of society in the state of nature. It released its members from their established condition, it granted them relative anonymity, and it assembled them in a new association outside, on the street and in the squares. In order to exist, the crowd necessarily had to be outside (or, on occasion, the space provided by some large public hall). But, this location was essential in another sense: it confirmed the crowd's character as the community reformed for it involved the voluntary occupation of public space, a space not confined and defined by a particular activity but, rather, neutral by its undefined and common occupancy by many different activities and individuals. Indeed, the crowd disliked being confined and thus defined: if it entered a closed space in pursuit of a victim, it nearly always took him outside to deal with him, even if this merely involved throwing him out of the window. It is striking that the crowd at the Hôtel-de-Ville on July 14 took all its victims outside, none being killed inside; similarly, the prison massacres of 1795 (as distinct from murders by a few men) all involved extraction of the victims and their death outside. On the contrary, the crowd was always suspicious of enclosed, hidden spaces: one need only remember the fears of the July 14 crowd about the cellars of the Bastille and hidden subterranean passages or else the origins of the September Massacres.

The crowd articulated what the members of the community had in common. It transcended the particular interests of corporate bodies, trades, workshops, and so on, let alone individuals, and it could thus express a value system that underpinned popular attitudes. The crowd simplified conscious attitudes, it emphasized the common ground of values and codes of conduct which formed the mental base of popular social attitudes. It put a premium on the assumed and culturally instinctive bases of conduct rather than on rationalized attitudes to complex facts of a changing world. The consciousness of the crowd was, therefore, always likely to be more 'traditional' and more coherently simple than that of individuals. If we are looking for Lefebvre's 'sentiments affectifs', for the 'idées et sentiments qui sont le propre de collectivités plus étendues dont (l'individu) fait également partie', for the collective mentality which pre-exists the crowd, then it is here that we must look. It is this liberation of the traditional reflex that poses the principal problem in the crowd's transposition into the revolutionary environment and informs the whole question of its relationship to revolutionary politics.

The crowd, then, was the means through which the 'peuple' expressed its collective identity and its values. The crowd was the means through which it regulated its relationship with authority and the conduct of public affairs. The crowd was the means through which it asserted and defended its place in society. Finally, the crowd was also the means through which it was able to enforce its collective values upon deviant members within its own community. In a very direct sense, therefore, the representative and regulatory crowd was the natural organ of the people. Its members were too weak to have a significant action as individuals in regard to authority – whether state, social or economic authority – but collectively they could express their judgment and defend their interests. In this sense, the crowd invaded the public space not just physically, but also morally and politically.

The most direct and obvious expression of this function was the crowd's application of the moral economy in the market place, as defined by E. P. Thompson and demonstrated in the French context by Steven Kaplan and William Reddy among others. For us here, the significant point is that the crowd represented the community for it stated and acted upon its right to enforce the moral economy and to reprove, call to order, and even punish authority which failed to fulfil its obligations. This was perceived as a legitimate act both by the crowd and many of those who observed it in the Ancien Régime. However, this pattern is also visible in a wide spectrum of other relationships with authority. The eighteenth-century crowd acted against agents of government on a whole range of issues in exactly the same terms. The people were not passive acceptors of authority nor were they in a state of permanent rejection and hostility to it. Both David Garrioch and Arlette Farge demonstrate how quick Parisians were to have recourse to the *commissaires de police* in matters as diverse as domestic dispute, commercial dishonesty or disorderly behaviour. Public authority had a function in ordering the community which its members recognized as necessary, even though there were compelling unstated rules governing an individual's appeal to public authority especially in smaller societies. Yet, at the same time, people were equally quick to resist and reprove initiatives which stepped outside what was deemed to be legitimate and necessary action. The limits on authority were anchored in a popular system of values which authority could at times override by force, but which the community guarded through the crowd. Just as the community policed its own members by a savant dosage of derision, *charivari*, physical assault and even death, so it policed its policers by much the same methods. Rather than the law courts, it was the crowd which was the eighteenth-century answer to the ancient question *Quis custodet custodes?* Accounts of eighteenth-century 'émotions' make it clear time and again that it was the behaviour, real or suspected, of agents of authority which was the outside event which mobilized the crowd, the key to Lefebvre's 'mutation brusque'. We need refer only to the examples we have already used: in the 1750 kidnapping riots, it was the rumour that police agents were responsible that brought the crowds out and it was exclusively they who were attacked; similarly, the August–September 1788 gatherings only degenerated into riot when the *guet* attacked the crowd to which the crowd responded by attacking the guard posts, whereas it left the *garde française* alone because it had not thus misbehaved, at least until the very end of the events; on July 14, the sequence of events at the Bastille is important because the crowd did not attack until it was itself fired upon and the reproach levelled against those who were massacred was that 'on les disait canonniers, on disait qu'ils avaient tiré sur le peuple'.[9] For his part Charron, the chronicler of the August–September disturbances, was quite clear that there were rules about how to handle the crowd:

> Ce n'est pas le nombre d'hommes qui impose au public . . . ; c'est la bonne contenance des soldats, c'est l'ordre, et surtout la modération de leurs mouvemens . . . . Les gardes françaises se sont trouvés dans la malheureuse nécessité d'employer la force; sans que cependant il en eût à serrer aussi ces malheureux, de manière à ce qu'ils ne puissent échapper; car la justice qui frappe doit être encore justice. Elle change de nom, lorsqu'elle ne laisse à ceux qu'elle châtie que le désespoir et la mort.[10]

Clearly, there was more here than a simple tactical precept and, as we have seen, equally clearly the 'public' agreed with him.

The crowd observed, commented, judged. It was inescapable, therefore, that the crowd's action should contain a discourse of justice. This was a function of its sense of the legitimacy of its action. The perception of the people exercising justice was profoundly anchored in Ancien Régime popular perceptions. This was why the crowd had recourse so frequently to acts which echoed or parodied state justice. Hence, the propensity of crowds to hang unpopular figures in effigy; hence, the habit of the Parisian crowd of going to the Place de Grève, not just as a necessary large open space but as the site of public executions. The crowd could make mistakes, but it does not appear that the eighteenth-century mob was characteristically blind. Choice rather than accident is the answer to the question posed by any historian of eighteenth-century violence as to why this individual rather than another fell victim. The victim of a crowd was usually someone who was known to have infringed the rules or, more rarely, someone whose known previous behaviour made it likely that he had. It seems rare indeed that someone fell victim by mere virtue of his social position or public post. This feature is visible as much during the Revolution as before it. To cite at random, peasant crowds attacked only selected seigneurs and there were untouched châteaux in every troubled area; in 1791 and 1792, there were dozens of nobles in châteaux round Lyon and in the central Rhône valley indulging in unwise talk and maintaining unsavoury friendships, yet Guillin du Montet and the marquis de Bésignan were singled out for mass attack precisely because they had a long history of tyrannical abuse of the peasantry, compounded by intemperate behaviour at the moment of the riot; the disturbances of the 1795 White Terror in the south are simply incomprehensible without analysing the selective nature of the crowd action.

Even if we limit our remarks to the Ancien Régime for the moment, the exercise of justice is an act of power, an attribute of majesty. By exercising justice, by deliberately endowing it in many cases with the forms of the execution of royal justice, by exercising it in public and often in the very site of royal justice, the crowd was in fact laying claim to some portion of public power and erecting its own codes alongside those of the state. This is of course to overstate the matter by developing unduly implications which were certainly unperceived by the Ancien Régime crowd. The relationship between the crowd and public power was more complex and, until the Revolution, amounted at the most to a kind of coexistence. In absolutist theory, the Crown alone occupied the public space and it ruled over individuals who owed it unquestioning obedience. In practice, however, this public space was constantly invaded by the population in the shape of the crowd, which exercised definable functions of regulation and disapproval. In this sense, the crowd was political under the Ancien Régime, even if its action rarely surpassed a very localized and itemized reproach which did not constitute a direct threat to state power. Through the crowd, the people regulated, checked, and ultimately limited (albeit loosely) the exercise of state power in matters which affected directly the detail of their lives.

We may extend this notion of space a little further. Just as the royal state controlled the public space of power, so it controlled the physical public space of highways, streets, and squares. If the crowd invaded the public space, it was trespassing in both political and physical terms. This physical space was marked by a geography of public power: in Paris, the Place de Grève, the houses of the *commissaires*, the Hôtel de Ville, the hotel of the *commandant de guet* and that of the *prévôt des marchands*, the prisons, the *octroi* houses, the Palais, the Châtelet, the Bastille – and the pattern was repeated in any provincial centre. The crowd went out of its way to obey this geography, parading its effigies to the appropriate public building, dragging the broken bodies of *archers* and *mouches* to the house of a *commissaire*, carrying the debris of guard posts to the Place de Grève. At the same time, as the crowd receded from the public space, so the power of the state flowed back into this double physical and political space, epitomized by the reappearance of *archers* and police agents, by the judicial enquiries, the arrests, the trials and the public punishment. The relationship was fluctuating and to some extent ritualized, in which the crowd could establish no lasting hold on either physical or political space. This was partly because of the temporary, evanescent nature of the crowd itself; but it was also because the crowd, as representative of the community, sought only to regulate and not to substitute itself. It was a relationship recognized by both sides. The crowd did regulate itself both in the specificity of its choice of victim and by attempting to prevent actions which infringed its own codes. For its part, the repression of the state, for all its spectacular quality, was measured and highly ritualized. Both sides knew they had to respect and fear each other. And each side wrapped up the relationship in a mutual discourse of goodness: the popular assertion of the goodness of the king, on the one side, and the royal assertion of the goodness of the people, on the other.

In this context, the appearance of the Palais-Royal as a focus is significant. In 1780, the duc d'Orléans ceded the palace to his son (the future regicide), who opened the gardens to the general public. However, this was a privileged area which the police could not enter. It became, therefore, for Parisians a public space outside the state, a space that could be entered and occupied permanently. At the same time, a host of cafés opened up under the arcades where the politically active elite critics of the regime met. The Palais-Royal became a junction point between the much newer political action of the educated speechifiers in the cafés round the edge and the much older political action of the crowd swarming in the central gardens. It was this fusion that Arthur Young described in 1789 in his portrayal of the coffee-houses which are 'not only crowded within, but other expectant crowds are at the doors and windows, listening *à gorge déployée* to certain orators, who from chairs or tables harangue each his little audience'.[11]

We must note one final incarnation of the crowd in the public space under the Ancien Régime. This is what Arlette Farge has recently termed the 'crowd assembled' ('la foule conviée').[12] This was the crowd which assembled to witness the great public acts of state power – processions, *entrées*, public functions of officials from *gouverneurs* down to municipal councils and, above all, executions. Here, the crowd was invited into the public space, once again as a representative, to bear witness by its presence to the display of public power and, by its acquiescence, to restate the submission of the subjects. In practice, of course, the crowd was being solicited as much as convoked; it was a participant as well as a witness. Royal authority needed the stylized adherence of the crowd before which it paraded its majesty. The parade had no sense without its public and without the public's acquiescence. Yet, the line between acquiescence and approval was fine and both permitted their opposite – rejection and disapproval. The crowd, therefore, had the possibility of breaking out of the stylized role assigned to it and of commenting and hence regulating. The authorities were acutely aware of this potential and observed the reactions of the crowd attentively. The crowd did indeed comment. It could express approval by cheers and good humour: but even that could be a hostile act if the approval was for some person or institution of which the royal government disapproved. It could remain indifferent and silent, hostile therefore to the act it was called upon to approve. It could jeer and boo, resort to verbal and eventually physical violence. The crowd assembled was a necessary but dangerous public for the state.

Therefore, whether noisy or silent, the crowd was a definable actor in the play of Ancien Régime politics. It was a critical public that existed before the elite critics of the Ancien Régime broke out of the private world of salons and academies. Some authors have characterized this crowd as 'prepolitical' or effecting 'primitive political gestures'.[13] This is really to use the politics of the Revolution as the touchstone. Yet, it does raise the question of how the politics of the crowd adapted to the revolutionary context and to what degree they were transformed. The contention here is that there is a direct continuity between the functions of the prerevolutionary crowd and its functions in the Revolution, between the kind of value system the crowd articulated before 1789 and its development thereafter.

III

As far as Paris is concerned, the disturbances of August–September 1788 were the last to be framed almost exclusively in the classic terms we have described. This is true not only in their development as a reaction to repressive behaviour by agents of authority and in their recourse to the ritual execution of the effigies of authority figures held guilty; it is true also in their relationship to the Parlement, whose dismissal provided the original context of the gatherings and whose return in September amidst cheering crowds constituted the last act of these events. It is as well not to overemphasize the significance of the crowd's affection for the Parlement, to anticipate its meaning in the light of 1789. On the one hand, crowd support for the Parlement was an old phenomenon, dating from beyond the Jansenist controversy to the Fronde; on the other, the crowd's chants of 'Vive le Parlement' on its return were accompanied by cries of 'Le Procès à Dubois' (the *commandant du guet*), thereby revealing the centre of its preoccupations and, perhaps, the main sense that it now accorded to the return of the law court. Nonetheless, there was one other note. Charron emphasizes the wide unanimity in the reaction to the news of Necker's recall: 'c'est le Peuple qui conçut d'heureuses espérances du retour de M. NECKER; c'est le Public qui par ses témoignages de confiance fit remonter les effets à la bourse; c'est la Populace qui portait son portrait en triomphe au bout des longs bâtons qu'elle avait pris sur les ports; et c'est la Canaille qui faisait crier aux passans: *Vive M. Necker*'.[14] Beneath the accustomed rituals, the crowd was displaying not merely a knowledge of the broad lines of high politics (normal enough in Paris) but also a sense that one particular policy in government was in its interests.

Quite how popular consciousness developed to this point must be a matter for more extensive discussion than space allows here. As far as the Revolution is concerned, George Rudé is certainly correct to identify the process as an interplay of 'inherent' and 'derived' ideas, although his sense of 'inherent' ideas is quite different from the one here. In terms of background, one of the most stimulating suggestions is that of Steven Kaplan who sees the effect of the free grain trade experiments of the 1760s and 1770s and the decade of grain riots that accompanied them to have been to instil the notion that, beyond the traditionally identified hoarders and speculators, it was the government – indeed, the King himself – which was deliberately acting against the people and violating its fundamental responsibilities. Certainly, in 1788, Charron found quite absurd the notion that people did not know what was going on; in his view, even if they had not been instructed by elite debates, they clearly understood that economic conditions were the consequence of government policy – 'qu'on ne croye pas que des intelligences grossières soient sans énergie quand elles se communiquent . . . Si (la populace) a raisonné son mécontentement, si ses inquiétudes étaient fondées, elle a donc dû prendre part aux événemens'.[15]

We can see here one way at least in which a profound shift in consciousness was being prepared. It was a shift towards identifying popular interests as being in opposition not simply to acts of individual authority figures infringing the community's rules, but to the government itself. It prepared popular consciousness to make choices about government and to identify itself with the Tiers-Etat. It was in this ground that were rooted those agencies of revolutionary education normally cited by historians – pamphlets, orators, the elections, the cahiers, the assemblies for petitioning in June and July 1789, and so on. Yet, the impact of elections and assemblies in 1789 on popular opinion is not straightforward. If it is true that the Crown was inviting the population into the public space of politics, it was trying to do so in a restrictive and controlled manner. Above all, an electoral assembly was not well-suited in form or content to popular reflexes, while the poorer sections were excluded from much of the process and, in the towns, at best atomized into corporative assemblies which emphasized sectional rather [than] community interest. In 1789, and beyond, the crowd provided a far more potent education as it acted out its traditional functions of expressing a sense of injustice and of providing the instrument for regulation and for obtaining redress. Certainly, even in the earliest moments of the Revolution, the crowd revealed a remarkably rapid evolution. In September 1788, it still personalized its comment in the cry of *Vive M. Necker*; in the Réveillon riot (April 1789) it added to that shout the abstract slogan of *Vive le Tiers Etat*. Yet, the very traditionalism of the Réveillon riot both in its conduct and in its central meaning (after all, Réveillon and Henriot were being reproached for infringing community norms) pose the probably unresolvable question of what the crowd meant by the Third Estate. To what extent did it then, or indeed ever, mean to represent by this term (and subsequently 'the nation') anything more than the community and its values – a predominantly traditional perception vaguely informed by a sense of its wider applicability culled from and invested in language supplied by the elite revolutionaries? Even for the sans-culottes, Bill Sewell's suggestive pages reveal that the important changes wrought by the Revolution in their attitude to labour and trade identity served to emphasize 'their collective loyalty to a moral community' and to leave untouched 'the moral collectivism of the prerevolutionary corporate mentality'.[16] If, as Sewell says, that moral community had by 1793 become the one and indivisible republic, how substantively different were the perceived attributes of that republic from those that popular assumptions deemed necessary to good order and fair dealing in the prerevolutionary society?

The events of July 1789 illustrate many of these themes. Even leaving aside the question of prices which were such a powerful mobiliser, there was much about these events that was entirely traditional.[17] The response to the dismissal of Necker was the predictable one of parading his bust and that of Orléans (thought to have been exiled also) and forcing people to doff their hats. It was the Royal-Allemand's firing on this crowd which began the disturbances just as, as we have noted, it was firing from the Bastille that sparked the assault. Certainly, the power of Necker's dismissal to produce the crowd reaction is further evidence of the evolution of consciousness which we have discussed, whilst the similar effect of the troop movements shows the actualization of the latent sense that the royal government was hostile to the popular interest. Yet, the crowd's punitive action was in the traditional mode of attacks on specified individuals in retribution for specific conduct. We have already mentioned the deaths of de Launay and soldiers taken at the Bastille. It is equally clear in the case of de Flesselles, who had promised weapons but produced a chest full of old linen, who wrote a damagingly sybilline note to de Launay, and whose whole public conduct during the troubles was visibly suspect. Both Foulon and his son-in-law Berthier were accused in classic terms of starving the people – Foulon was ritually decorated with a necklace of nettles and a bunch of thistles 'pour le punir d'avoir voulu faire manger du foin au peuple' and, as for Berthier, 'on apportait du mauvais pain, et le peuple attribuait à M. Berthier tous ses malheurs'. Furthermore, the deaths of Foulon and Berthier in particular were very carefully presented as acts of justice: in Foulon's case, the crowd in the Hôtel-de-Ville insisted on having an ad hoc court of lawyers set up there and then to try him and he was placed on a low stool before the council table – obviously, the *sellette* of a regular court – until the crowd got impatient. And, as we have said, they (like de Flesselles) were taken out of the Hôtel-de-Ville to the Place de Grève just as were the condemned criminals of the Ancien Régime.

The crowd action in July was essentially reactive. It was engendered by panic fear and its motive was fundamentally self-defence. One cannot discern in the crowd, as distinct from the electors and their allies in the National Assembly, any demand for the withdrawal of the troops or any programmatic statements about sovereignty and the relationship between

National Assembly power and royal power. If we mean by 'revolutionary' the design of effecting a permanent change through the reorganization of power as distinct from remedying an immediate grievance perceived in isolation or punishing an individual in authority, then the July crowd does not appear revolutionary. The consequence of its action were, of course, profoundly revolutionary. By acting in the sense of the National Assembly, it brought to fruition a permanent reorganization of power. But that is not the same thing as having that end in mind. By reacting against the royal troops in a more extended but nonetheless essentially similar version of a time-honoured gesture, it helped to expel an already retreating royal power from the public space. But that does not mean that the crowd did not assume that royal power would flow back into that space in the normal course of events.

However, beneath the conventional quality of these gestures, there did lie important new implications in the crowd's action in July. The crowd invaded public space in the double sense which we defined earlier. But it did not encounter constituted royal power as in earlier times: royal power was in dissolution and, with the defection of the *gardes françaises*, the crowd encountered only the physical geography of Ancien Régime power and isolated agents of a dying authority. Instead, it encountered the electors, emerging and claiming power within these very events. The interplay between the crowd and the electors around the remnants of Ancien Régime officialdom and the constitution of a new authority was extremely complex, a phenomenon of simultaneous fusion and separation. Early in these events, de Flesselles 'ne voulut exercer d'autorité que celle qui lui serait donnée par les habitans de la capitale; et par acclamation tout ce qui était là le nomma président (du bureau de ville)'. It is debatable exactly which 'peuple' he had in mind: most likely the electors, but the scene took place at the Hôtel-de-Ville in front of 'la multitude qui s'y trouvait assemblée' and it was the crowd which had demanded that de Flesselles be called to the Hôtel-de-Ville. The nomination of Bailly as mayor and Lafayette as commander of the *milice* on July 15 was even more visibly a mass affair involving both electors and the crowd. Part of the legitimacy of the new authority in the capital therefore undoubtedly derived from its acceptability to the crowd. This was an important step.

This mixture of fusion and separation is even more evident in the other events at the Hôtel-de-Ville. Throughout the crisis (including the murders of Foulon and Berthier on July 22), the crowd was the compelling presence in the Hôtel-de-Ville. For a time, the crowd abolished the distinction between its occupation of the public space of power, outside in the square, and the interior seat of government authority. It had rendered the hidden area of power permeable, for the crowd inside was but the extension of the crowd gathered outside. Indeed, it demonstrated its fury when the committee withdrew to another room behind closed doors, saying that 'ils travaillaient là en secret, et hors de la présence des citoyens, pour les trahir'. Furthermore, the extraordinary popular triumph accorded to Elie after the fall of the Bastille (he was brought to the Hôtel-de-Ville, put up on the council table, crowned like some Roman Emperor surrounded by prisoners and by the silver, flag and great register of the Bastille) was a direct statement of popular power within the very seat of constituted authority.

Yet, at the same time, occupying the interior seat of power clearly constrained the crowd's behaviour. It retained a sense of limits on its ability to act, an indefinable sense that within the Hôtel-de-Ville a legitimacy other than that of the crowd held sway. This is visible in the events surrounding the death of Foulon. The crowd in the Hôtel-de-Ville demanded justice. However, it was persuaded by Bailly's argument, based in the assumptions of the elites' revolution, that Foulon had to be judged by due legal process which it was essential to maintain in order to protect the innocent even though, he conceded, there was a prima facie case against Foulon. The crowd refused to wait for referral to the ordinary courts and tried to force the electors to appoint a court. Yet, it was still ready to accept the electors' legalistic point that they had no power to appoint judges. At this juncture, the crowd tried to constitute a court itself. However, it did not choose men from its own ranks, but rather elite figures with a public function: two curés, an *échevin* and a former *échevin*, a *juge-auditeur* and even, under the pressure of the electors, a *procureur du roi* and a *greffier*. It was only with the procrastination of these figures that the crowd reverted to its traditional behaviour and above all to its traditional space of action by taking Foulon outside onto the Place de Grève.

The Foulon incident clearly demonstrated the limits on the revolutionary nature of the July crowd. However strong the discourse of justice in its action, it could not escape the notion that justice was normally a function of state, properly exercised in its forms and by the social elites. The function of the crowd was still to enforce that responsibility upon them and, if they failed or refused to assume it in a particular case, to substitute its own justice in its own forms for that case. There was not here any attempt to effect a permanent substitution, nor indeed any real consciousness that the fount of justice lay in the people. Notwithstanding this argument, however, the experience of July 14 was undoubtedly significant in actualizing shifts in popular perceptions. For one thing, if justice is an attribute of majesty, so too is pardon. Whereas the Ancien Régime crowd had often shouted for pardon on the Place de Grève, it had never obtained it; here, in the famous scene where Elie pleaded for the lives of prisoners at the Hôtel-de-Ville, it exercised that right. The revolutionary notion of the majesty of the people was given here a popular connotation which elite revolutionaries probably did not mean by the phrase. More important, no one reflecting later upon July could fail to understand that the crowd's action had effected permanent change. Bailly, who basically thought that these great changes had already been achieved by the National Assembly, nonetheless acknowledged that this was only understood by the legislators and 'les esprits éclairés' – 'La Bastille, prise et rasée, parlait à tout le monde'.

To what extent did crowd behaviour in the subsequent few years continue to display these same patterns? To what extent did it develop the transformations and resolve the ambiguities we have noted in the July crisis? It is of course easy to emphasize the continuities. Some of the examples we have used in our discussion of the Ancien Régime crowd already make the point. Even in Paris, the sugar riots of January 1792 and the soap riots of 1793 did not transcend at all the character and discourse of the most traditional price disturbances. Moreover, the nature of the punitive reaction and the rituals of popular justice remained much the same. One has only to think of the September Massacres with their deliberate institution of popular tribunals, although these massacres do point to other features as we shall see. One principal source of the crowd's attack in September 1792 was still the perception that constituted author-ity was failing in its obligation. Exactly the same pattern can be seen in the contemporaneous murder of Gérard at Lorient – murdered only after the crowd had failed to persuade the municipality to deal with him and then murdered in the classic fashion on the town square followed by a ritual parade of his dismembered parts.

One of the major problems in evaluating the development and trans-formation of crowd action is the appearance of organized crowds, assembled for some purpose of revolutionary politics under the direction of militants. As Michel Vovelle has emphasized, the organized crowd of this nature was a phenomenon distinct from the spontaneous crowd of the early Revolution. The political education of the popular militants who directed and focused such crowds took place in the clubs and sections even more than in the street. In practice, it is extremely difficult to identify the authentic voice of the crowd behind the spokesmen and the petitions claiming to present its case. We have posited that the crowd liberated the traditional reflex; it is likely therefore that the crowd was always less precise in its perception of the meaning of its actions and of the words of its spokesmen. Yet, this does not preclude important transformations in its action and above all in its political function.

It is clear, in the first place, that the crowd swiftly articulated a perception that the 'peuple' in the social sense of the popular classes was coterminous with the 'peuple'/'nation'. Even in a provincial town like Nogent-le-Rotrou a price-fixing crowd could cry 'Vive la Nation! Le blé va dimminuer!'[18] Equally, crowds were very quickly able to identify as enemies categories of people defined in terms of the politics of the Revolution, especially émigrés and non-juror priests. To cite at random, a crowd stopping grain at Choisy-au-Bec feared that this grain was on its way to émigrés; at Lorient, Gérard had been suspected of shipping arms to the émigrés; the September Massacres rested upon a particular perception of non-juror priests. The ability of the crowd to adduce and act upon such motives constituted a significant extension of its behaviour. Similarly, the electrifying effect of the war crises of 1792 and 1793 was profoundly different from the superficially similar defensive reflex in July 1789. Even if we consider only the theme of justice and regulation, it is evident that the definition of what sort of behaviour constituted infringement of the norms had undergone a dramatic extension. It was these kinds of transformations in the perceptions of the spontaneous crowd that gave elaboration to the traditional reflex that we have defined and moved beyond it. They laid the foundation for the crowd's availability to section organizers in the set pieces of 1793, for, as we have said, the crowd was not easily manipulated by outsiders whose exhortations did not coincide with its own canons.

Nonetheless, these transformations were not as clear-cut as they might appear. Significant though it must be that the crowd could articulate a condemnation of general categories of enemies, it is not evident that it acted in consequence. We have already used examples from the Revolution to show the personalized nature of reproach. The September Massacres provide another case in point. Although the mobilizing factors and the definitions of enemy were of the evolved type, the crowd clearly took pains – and in some cases, lengthy pains – to distinguish between individuals, liberating some and killing others. Certainly, the fact that the only sentence was death distinguishes this event from the very varied structure of punishment available to the Ancien Régime crowd (and visible in the much more traditional events of the White Terror of 1795 in the south) and this serves to emphasize how much the crowd had come to see counter-revolution as a heinous crime against the community. Yet, at the same time, a substantial number of those killed were ordinary criminals. This was not the accidental product of the blind mob. The element of deliberate selection applied in these cases too. Moreover, this happened elsewhere – for example, the crowd which murdered counter-revolutionaries at Aix-en-Provence in early 1793 also strung up a couple of thieves and a rapist, while in 1797 at Lyon, a byword for political massacre, the crowd murdered three thieves deemed inadequately sentenced and shortly after drowned a *chauffeur* in the Saône. The fact is that the crowd did not clearly distinguish between counter-revolutionary crime and crime *tout court* in a scale of values still anchored in the pre-revolutionary mentality. Even if some of the Suisses captured at the Tuileries on August 10, 1792 were massacred on the spot, the crowd also dragged many of them the not inconsiderable distance to the Place de Grève to execute them there.

However, the most important of all the transformations in the action of the crowd was the emergence of a clear sense that, in order to obtain redress of grievance, it had to go beyond agents of authority to put pressure on the seat of power. As we have seen, this sense was present in only the most confused form in July 1789. In October 1789, it was already very much more visible. Whatever the indefinable role of agitators, this was certainly a spontaneous crowd event. It was a traditional crowd movement in its preoccupation with bread, in the prominence of women in a disturbance over bread, in its perception of the King's role as the provider of bread, and in the crowd's forcing Maillard to lead it to do what it wanted to do. But it was new in its specific invasion of both seats of the source of government – the royal palace and the Assembly – rather than merely the seat of municipal government. It was new in its deliberate securing of the person of the King as a permanent, political solution to a perennial problem rather than the temporary solution provided by a *taxation populaire* and by the punishment of some delinquent local agent of authority. In these terms, it is October rather than July which appears the more significant event in shaping the revolutionary crowd.

Of course, October did not achieve an immediate and complete transformation in crowd habits. It still resorted to *taxations* and attacks on traditional objects of fury; even in 1793, it still put pressure more readily on the city government than on the Convention. Nonetheless, the lesson of October prepared and was reinforced by that of August 10, 1792. August 10 was the first really organized *journée*. It was promoted by radical politicians and the politicised *fédérés* from outside Paris played a prominent part. As such, the intentions of the Parisian 'peuple' around this event are not perhaps entirely easy to read. It was once again the firing of the troops on the crowd that provoked it to storm the palace. It is remarkable that the crowd in the September Massacres made no serious attempt to go near the Temple; nor was there any crowd intervention in the Convention's debates on the King; the crowd watched the King's execution in absolute silence, only breaking into cheers when his head was held aloft. The King's death, arguably one of the most revolutionary acts of the whole period, was accomplished without the intervention of the crowd (even as the 'crowd assembled' its behaviour was ambiguous and its approval *post hoc*): rather, it was the last episode in the struggle between the power of the elites and monarchical power.

The problem of assessing the true relationship between the crowd and organized political action even in 1793, its most potent year, is well illustrated by the Parisian disturbances of March 9–10, 1793 which saw both the breaking of the Girondin presses and what is usually presented as an attempted insurrection against the Convention under the aegis of a number of clubs. In fact, quite distinct elements were involved. On the one hand, the previous days saw substantial popular agitation when workers from different trades prepared to gather in considerable numbers in order to demand a reduction in the price of foodstuffs as well as talk that 'à n'en point douter . . . , vendredi prochain, on devrait se porter à la halle'. On the other hand, it was volunteer soldiers (possibly no more than fifty of them) who broke the presses and it was again volunteer soldiers and *fédérés* who paraded menacingly through the Convention. The talk about the sovereign people and the need to act was all in some section assemblies and clubs and it was aimed at the *fédérés* and volunteers.[19] Nonetheless, there were great demonstrations around the Convention in 1793. Despite their organized quality, these were entirely within the logic of the action developed by the spontaneous crowd. The crowd may not have followed the ramifications of sovereignty involved when one of its spokesmen said (to pick up a phrase from June 1792) 'le peuple est là; il attend dans le silence une réponse digne de sa souveraineté'.[20] It may not have understood in detail Enragé and militant sans-culotte ideas about the regeneration of society, permanent economic regulation and direct democracy. But it surely did understand at least that the seat of government could be invaded and that the holders of state power could be pressured into adopting measures that ensured more than temporary solutions to popular problems. To this degree, the Parisian crowd was by now revolutionary.

The proof of this is to be found not so much in the organized crowd of 1793, as in the spontaneous crowd, deprived of its leaders, in Germinal and Prairial Year III. In the face of appalling hardship, it resorted not to the traditional methods of *taxation* and attacks on suspected hoarders, nor even to pressurizing the municipal authorities; it turned directly to invading the Convention and its cry of 'Du pain et la Constitution de 93' explicitly linked a whole permanent organization of power to the resolution of its problem. Yet, at the same time, the Germinal and Prairial Days also demonstrate the limits on the crowd's capacity for revolutionary action. In practice, once it had invaded the Convention, it did not really know what to do with the power it had gained. It depended entirely upon the rump of radical deputies taking charge and providing it with detailed measures to enforce. It had no real concept of revolutionary substitution; it had no sense that its own power could somehow be permanent, only that the Convention could be forced to enact favourable measures whose permanence was guaranteed mostly by a naive view of the binding character of a constitution. In this respect, the crowd had not moved far beyond July 1789. Although temporarily overawed in 1795, the Convention was no longer constrained by the double jeopardy of invasion and provincial insurrection as it had been in 1793.

IV

In order to complete our discussion of the crowd in the political culture of the Revolution, we need finally to examine briefly the attitude of the revolutionary elites to it. During the arduous transition from the Ancien Régime to the Revolution, the crowd and the elites coexisted uneasily in the public space of power vacated by the monarchical state. At moments, groups committed to the revolution of the National Assembly were prepared to call upon the street. Thus, for example, when news of the *séance royale* arrived at Lyon, members of the *Cercle des Terreaux* on the balcony of their club incited a riot among 'le peuple et une partie des jeunes gens de la bourgeoisie' in the street below who, after forcing illuminations and maltreating the *prévôt des marchands*, ended up by destroying the *barrières*.[21] In fact, such a direct appeal was extremely rare and the *Cercle des Terreaux* had probably not measured the likely consequence of its enthusiasm. Certainly, the good bourgeoisie of Lyon quickly brought out the *milice bourgeoise* to control the disturbances and several weeks later marched out to repress quite brutally the rural disturbances of the region. Indeed, one of the principal 'revolutionary' consequences of crowd action in mid-1789 was to stimulate the crystallization of the bourgeois revolutionary authority with the creation of new municipal governments and national guards with the purpose of controlling the crowd. Even in Paris, it is quite clear that the prime motive of the electors was the question of public order more than Necker and the royal troops. As early as July 11, they were petitioning the National Assembly for a *garde bourgeoise* on the grounds that the presence of the troops was provoking 'émotions populaires'; as we have seen, they authorized the taking of arms in large part because of the armed crowds already in the streets and they instructed electors to go 'aux postes des citoyens armés, pour les prier de superséder, au nom de la patrie, à toute espèce d'attroupement et voie de fait'; the first act of the permanent committee was to organize the milice and to forbid crowds. For Bailly, there were no two ways about it – 'les électeurs, par leur courage et leur activité, ont sauvé la ville de Paris', and he did not mean from royal counter-revolution.[22]

For a short while, the crowd and the revolutionaries stood side by side in the arena vacated by the royal state. What better illustration than an incident on July 15 described by Bailly? A long procession wound from the Tuileries towards the Hôtel-de-Ville, comprising the *guet*, the *gardes françaises*, officials of the *prévôté*, electors, members of the National Assembly, the *milice parisienne*, under the gaze of a large, cheering crowd – in other words, it was both a demonstration in quite traditional form of the fusion of old and new agents of authority under the control of the new revolutionary power and also a claim for recognition and endorsement by the crowd assembled. Suddenly, the procession encountered 'une espèce de pompe triomphale' in which a *garde-française* crowned with laurel was being escorted in a cart by another large cheering crowd. The first procession joined in the plaudits of the second without ever quite knowing who the man was. By later 1789, however, the revolutionary authorities had largely completed their occupation of the public space of politics and they had inherited the functions of the Ancien Régime state. The enactment of Martial Law in the aftermath of the October Days enshrined the contradiction between the legal revolution of the elites and the crowd.

Inheriting the functions of state power, it is hardly surprising that the new authorities should also have inherited much of the Ancien Régime's relationship with the crowd. Yet, here too, there were significant transformations. Of course, eighteenth-century men of property feared both the crowd and monarchical power; they tended to fear the latter more than the former until the last decade of the century when fear of the crowd came to dominate. In France, the crowd's behaviour in 1789 appalled the more conservative even among moderate reformers – Mallet du Pan exclaimed in the *Mercure de France* 'Les Huns, les Hérules, les Vandales, et les Goths ne viendront ni du nord, ni de la mer Noire, ils sont au milieu de nous'; the abbé Morellet confessed that 'dès ce moment (le 14 juillet) je fus saisi de crainte à la vue de cette grande puissance jusque-là desarmée . . . puissance aveugle et sans freins'.[23] By 1792, such attitudes had spread to less obviously conservative figures: Thomas Lindet wrote in March 1792 from Normandy under the impact of *taxation* riots 'Nous voilà en état de guerre. . . . Verneuil a ouvert ses portes à l'ennemi'.[24] This eighteenth-century vision of the crowd as ignorant, dangerous, uncontrollable, actuated by murderous passions, had by 1795 overwhelmed any more sophisticated perceptions in the minds of the propertied advocates of the legal revolution.

Before then, however, such simplifications were by no means the rule. However much propertied revolutionaries would have liked to expel the crowd from the public space of politics, this was really not possible, even in the Ancien Régime mode of limiting it to spasmodic appearances. It was not just that the course of the Revolution gave it repeated opportunities and stimulants to act. It was more that, on the one hand, even moderate revolutionaries had to accommodate the fact that in 1789 the crowd had been instrumental in preserving the Revolution and, on the other, radical revolutionaries in particular understood that it could play that role again. Beyond that, their own discourse on sovereignty prevented the revolutionaries from having precisely the same relationship with the crowd as had had the old monarchical state. The word 'peuple' was extraordinarily ambiguous because of its double meaning: Thouret pointed this out at the very beginning in the debate of June 15, 1789 on what to call the Third Estate when he rejected Mirabeau's suggestion of 'représentans du peuple français' on the grounds that despite 'l'acception noble et générale du mot *peuple*, cette expression, si on la prenait dans le sens qui la limite à une classe infinie, blessait la dignité, et alors, ainsi restreinte, elle aurait pu en désigner non le tiers-état entier, mais la partie non éclairée'.[25] The difficulties in maintaining the distinction were immediately apparent: on July 16, whilst Mirabeau was rebutting Mounier's opposition to a call to dismiss the ministry with the phrase 'vous oubliez que ce peuple, à qui vous opposez les limites des trois pouvoirs, est la source de tous les pouvoirs', Moreau de Saint-Méry (president of the electors) was pointing to the enormous cheering crowd witnessing the King's visit to Paris, saying 'Et voilà, Sire, ce peuple qu'on a osé calomnier'.[26] Even if the exercise of political functions was reserved to active citizens until 1792, all individuals by virtue of their rights were participants in sovereignty. There was always the nagging point that the crowd did somehow claim a legitimacy and those who increasingly came to organize this crowd certainly made that claim. It was no casual shift of language that transformed Gonchon, who first appeared before the National Assembly as 'l'orateur du Faubourg Saint-Antoine', into 'l'orateur du peuple'.[27]

Various strategies beyond simple physical containment were available. One early example was the regulation of the right of petition by the decree of May 10, 1791 which, confining it to individual signed petitions, sought to atomize the crowd. Another strategy was the National Guard. Although until the Fall of the Monarchy it was reserved to active citizens, it overlapped in its lower ranks with the social stratum out of which much of the crowd came. When all adult males entered in 1792, it was recruited from the same population as the crowd. Like the crowd, the Guard took its members out of their daily context and gave them a collective identity. But, it also organized them in a hierarchy dominated, even past 1792 by men of some substance, and put them in the service of public authority. It was, then, the antithesis of the crowd; it was in a sense the crowd organized to control the crowd. Yet, the ambivalence of its nature was demonstrated time and again by its refusal to repress the crowd and by its involvement in Parisian *journées*.

The most elaborate strategy was to develop the Ancien Régime device of the 'crowd assembled'. Mona Ozouf has demonstrated the richness, diversity and pervasiveness of the revolutionary festival which flowered from the great Fête de la Fédération of 1790 on. The revolutionaries developed the notion of 'crowd assembled' far beyond anything that the Ancien Régime had envisaged. The *fête* incorporated the crowd into the revolutionary political process whilst sterilizing it. The popular collective instinct was harnessed: the crowd was assigned a function; it was instructed in the meaning which the revolutionaries gave to the Revolution; it was taught revolutionary good behaviour, so to speak. Nonetheless, the 'crowd assembled' still retained in one important respect the function it had had under the Ancien Régime. The 'passion de l'espace ouvert'[28] that characterized the revolutionary *fête* was not simply an echo of popular habits; it was a deliberate assertion of the state's occupation of the double physical and political public space. The crowd was still being called upon to endorse the power of the state. The crowd could, therefore, still withhold acquiescence as it had done in the past: the inhabitants of the Faubourg Saint-Marcel, for example, simply refused to turn up to the festival in memory of Simoneau, the murdered mayor of Etampes, in 1792. The revolutionaries needed this endorsement even more urgently than did the monarchy. Public executions also were still a statement of power and a demand for acquiescence as they had been before the Revolution. Indeed, the revolutionaries sought to make this even more explicit and to educate the crowd out of the confusion between ordinary criminality and counter-revolution, which reduced the significance of endorsement, by separating the two types of execution: executions of criminals remained on the Place de Grève and political executions hovered between the Place du Carousel and the Place de la Révolution until they were moved to the Barrière du Trône Renversée in Prairial Year II. The government still paid close attention to the reactions of the crowd at executions: one can positively hear the sigh of relief in the police reports on the execution of Hébert and the acclamations at the death of Robespierre were widely commented upon. Indeed, the removal of the guillotine to a remoter corner of Paris in face of the growing lassitude of the public was a sure sign that the Montagnard government was losing endorsement, or, as Saint-Just put it, 'la Révolution est glacée'. It was a significant symbol of the Thermidorians' desire to criminalize the radical Revolution that the guillotine returned to the Place de Grève from Thermidor Year II to Prairial Year III.

These examples from the Montagnard period demonstrate that the jacobins had no less of a problem in relating to the crowd than did their revolutionary predecessors. Whatever their plans for the 'peuple' and its place in revolutionary politics, the spontaneous crowd did not figure among them. The Jacobin Club reaction to the sugar riots of January 1792 was to call to order the 'citoyennes de Paris, qui pour du sucre, (violent) les droits les plus sacrés de la propriété'.[29] In this respect, radicals shared the basic premise of more moderate revolutionaries; their manner of accommodating the crowd was but an elaboration of the perspective of the moderates. Since one could not avoid either the presence of the crowd or the contribution it made to the Revolution, the solution to the problem was to distinguish between crowd actions, to appropriate some of them to the revolutionaries' cause by defining them as good, and relegating the rest as misguided, criminal, the product of manipulation by enemies of the good cause, or merely infantile. In this way, the revolutionaries were able to carry forward the definition favoured by the Ancien Régime that violent crowds were the product of ill-intentioned leaders; they were thus able to accept their own fear of the crowd, whilst at the same time rationalizing the inescapable fact of crowd violence by lauding it whenever it appeared to operate in the sense of the Revolution as it was defined by any particular revolutionary group. One early example of this process was the invention of the *Vainqueurs de la Bastille*. We have noted the ambivalent attitude of the revolutionary elites to the July crowd. By instituting the *Vainqueurs de la Bastille* with its formal designation of individual heroes after an enquiry, its pensions and its medals, the National Assembly appropriated the act, disassembled the crowd into heroic individuals, sanctified their action, and thus rendered it safe.

Robespierre's commentary on the insurrection of August 10 shows how radicals could develop this approach. Robespierre made the classic distinction between the crowd as the majestic instrument of sovereignty and the crowd as an irresponsible unruly destroyer:

> En 1789, le peuple de Paris se leva tumultuairement pour repousser les attaques de la cour, pour s'affranchir de l'ancien despotisme, plutôt que pour conquérir la liberté, dont l'idée étoit encore confuse, et les principes inconnus. Toutes les passions concoururent alors à l'insurrection . . . En 1792, il s'est levé, avec un sang-froid imposant, pour venger les lois fondamentales de sa liberté violée, pour faire rentrer dans le devoir tous les tyrans qui conspiroient contre lui . . . Il a exercé sa souveraineté reconnue et déployé sa puissance et sa justice, pour assurer son salut et son bonheur. . . . La manière solennelle, dont il a procédé à ce grand acte, fut aussi sublime, que ses motifs et que son objet . . . Ce n'étoit point une émeute sans objet, excitée par quelques brouillons, ce n'étoit point une conjuration ensevelie dans les ténèbres; on délibéroit au grand jour, en présence de la nation; le jour et le plan de l'insurrection furent indiqués par des affiches. C'étoit le peuple entier qui usoit de ses droits.[30]

The message is clear: this was an orderly, open, mature political act without 1789's frightening qualities and absolutely without relation to the riotous crowd as commonly defined. It was therefore a safe, welcome, legitimate act, an act of justice. This text provides an indispensable commentary upon Robespierre's oft-quoted private notes from mid-1793, where he wrote 'les dangers intérieurs viennent des bourgeois; pour vaincre les bourgeois, il faut rallier le peuple . . . Il faut que l'insurrection actuelle continue . . . il faut que le peuple s'allie à la Convention et que la Convention se serve du peuple'.[31] For Robespierre, the only good crowd was an organized crowd, directed towards specific revolutionary goals under the leadership of the radical elites in the Convention. However, the experience of 1793 revealed how unreliable even the organized crowd was. The inception of the Terror was the final appropriation of the crowd, the substitution of state violence for crowd violence. As Danton said, 'soyons terribles pour dispenser le peuple de l'être'.[32]

The Germinal and Prairial Days proved to the Thermidorians and the propertied inheritors of the Ancien Régime state power whom they represented that the legal revolution could not coexist with the crowd. Further, they proved that there was no need to accommodate the crowd. Despite the transformations we have tried to analyse, the crowd had failed as an instrument of popular intervention in and regulation of the elites' exercise of power. The era of the property owners' unadulterated fear of the 'classes dangereuses' and their complete exclusion from politics by a repressive state had begun. The experience of the crowd in the Revolution had provoked the final defection of the bourgeoisie from a culture based in notions of community. In this domain, the rupture with the eighteenth century began in 1795, not in 1789. As for the crowd, it fell back immediately into the highly traditional forms of market riot, the protection of community norms, the itemised reproach of individual infringements, and resistance to the innovating state that litter the provincial history of the Directory. This was the prelude to the long drawn-out agony of traditional popular protest, lit only by the brief flares of the early 1830s and the turn of the mid-century.

Notes

1 G. Rudé, *The Crowd in History* (London 1964), pp. 19–32, 47–50.
2 A. Mathiez, *Le Club des Cordeliers pendant la Crise de Varennes* (Paris 1910), p. 140.
3 G. Lefebvre, 'Foules Révolutionnaires' in *Etudes sur la Révolution Française* (Paris, 1963), p. 373.
4 J. Beauchard, La Puissance des Foules (Paris, 1985), pp. 89–103.
5 J. Flammermont (ed.), *La Journée du 14 Juillet 1789: Fragment des Mémoires inédits de L-G Pitra* (Paris, 1892), pp. 13 & 22.
6 A good example may be seen in the enquiry into the 1792 disturbances in the southern Drôme (Arch. Dép. Drôme L 196).
7 *Mémoires de Bailly*, 3 vols. (Paris, 1821–2), 1, pp. 373–4.
8 J. Charron, *Lettre ou Mémoire historique sur les troubles populaires de Paris en août et septembre 1788* (Londres, 1788). See also J. Kaplow, *The Names of Kings* (New York, 1972), p. 158.
9 Bailly, 1, p. 84.
10 Charron, *op. cit.*
11 A. Young, *Travels in France*, ed. C. Maxwell (Cambridge, 1950).
12 A. Farge, *La Vie fragile* (Paris, 1986), pp. 201–58.
13 Kaplow, *op. cit.*, p. 153; S. Kaplan, *Bread, Politics and Political Economy in the Reign of Louis XV*, 2 vols. (The Hague, 1976), 1, p. 194.
14 Charron, *op. cit.*
15 Charron, *op. cit.*

16 W. H. Sewell, *Work and Revolution in France* (Cambridge, 1980), pp. 92–113.

17 The analysis of the events of July 1789 in the following pages is based on the account given by Bailly (vols. 1 and 2).

18 A. Mathiez, *La Vie chère et le Mouvement social sous la Terreur* (Paris, 1927), p. 103.

19 A-M. Boursier, 'L'Emeute Parisienne du 10 Mars 1793' *Ann. hist. de la Rév. fr.* 1972, pp. 204–230.

20 M. Reinhard, *La Chute de la Royauté* (Paris, 1969), p. 323.

21 A. Brette, 'Journal de l'émotion de Lyon (29 Juin–5 Juillet 1789)', *La Révolution Française* 33 (1897), pp. 556–563.

22 Bailly, especially 1, p. 348.

23 *Mercure de France*, August 8, 1789; *Mémoires de l'abbé Morellet sur le dix-huitième siècle et la Révolution*, 2 vols. (Paris, 1821), 2, p. 4.

24 A. Montier (ed.), *Correspondance de Thomas Lindet pendant la Constituante et la Législative* (Paris, 1899), p. 337.

25 Quoted by Bailly, 1, p. 148.

26 Bailly, 2, p. 37; *Discours de M. Moreau du Saint-Méry, président de MM. les Electeurs, au Roi* (n.d.)

27 V. Fournel, *Le patriote Palloy; L'Orateur du peuple, Gonchon* (Paris, 1892).

28 M. Ozouf, *La Fête Révolutionnaire 1789–1799* (Paris, 1976), p. 151.

29 Mathiez, *Vie Chère*, pp. 46–8.

30 *Le Défenseur de la Constitution*, number 12.

31 *Papiers inédits trouvés chez Robespierre . . . supprimés ou omis par Courtois*, 3 vols. (Paris, 1828), 2, pp. 13–16.

32 Buchez et Roux, *Histoire parlementaire de la Révolution Française*, 40 vols., (Paris, 1834–38), 25, p. 56.

22
Terror

FRANÇOIS FURET

On September 5, 1793, the Convention made 'the Terror' the order of the day. By this action it signalled its intention to organize, systematize, and accelerate repression of the Republic's domestic adversaries and to ensure quick punishment of 'all traitors'. But this blunt and candid declaration, this inaugural vote of the Terror, came in unusual circumstances. That morning, the sans-culottes had invaded the Assembly demanding both bread and the guillotine – the guillotine in order to have bread. What they wanted, and what they would obtain a few days later, was a 'revolutionary army' of the interior, intended to strike terror in the hearts

Reprinted in full from F. Furet and M. Ozouf, eds. *A Critical Dictionary of the French Revolution* (Cambridge, Mass. and London, Belknap Press of Harvard University Press, 1989), pp. 137–50.

of hoarders and enemies of the Republic with the aid of a terrifying machine that would be part of its standard equipment, 'the fatal instrument that with one blow cuts short both conspiracies and the lives of their authors'. Shortly thereafter, a delegation of Jacobins offered a version of the same rhetoric less directly concerned with bread: those to be guillotined were 'traitors'. It was in order to give official satisfaction to the Paris militants that the Committee of Public Safety declared the Terror to be the order of the day.

The circumstances surrounding this celebrated vote indicate that before becoming a set of repressive institutions used by the Republic to liquidate its adversaries and establish its domination on a basis of fear, the Terror was a demand based on political convictions or beliefs, a characteristic feature of the mentality of revolutionary activism.

As such, it predated the dictatorship of Year II, the Republic, and the war with Europe. It had existed since the early summer of 1789, along with the related idea that the Revolution was threatened by an aristocratic plot that only prompt measures could thwart. The popular violence that engulfed Paris on July 14 was an early consequence of the partly economic, partly political logic that characterized the actions of the Paris crowd; the murder of the minister Foullon de Doué on July 22, followed by the murder of his son-in-law Bertier de Sauvigny, the intendant of Paris, was a summary punishment that temporarily quieted the obsession with grain hoarding and the Versailles plot. In September the terrorist idea found in *L'ami du peuple* and its publisher Marat its newspaper and its champion. The man whom the people of Paris led back to their city on October 6 was less a king than a hostage: in the return of 'the baker, the baker's wife, and the baker's boy' the people saw a guarantee that Paris would henceforth be supplied with food as well as an assurance that they would at last be able to monitor the king's activities and the manoeuvres of the queen and the royal entourage.

This general, systematic suspicion was inextricably associated with a persistent overestimation of the degree to which the enemy's strategy was deliberate and his resources were limitless. The plot drew substance from the idea of the enemy's omnipotence, which only the people could thwart. In its crudest form this image existed among the lower orders of the urban population, but it was also present in the minds of many deputies, since it was rooted in the new political culture: just as the Revolution was the reversal whereby the people reappropriated a power previously alienated to the king and to God, the political universe that it inaugurated was populated solely by wills, so that henceforth nothing remained outside human control. The new realm of power was occupied entirely by the people, which through its actions had reclaimed inalienable rights. Yet the people continued to be menaced by an anti-power, which like the nation was abstract, omnipresent, and all-enveloping, but which was hidden where the nation was public, individual where the nation was universal, and harmful where the nation was good. This anti-power was thus the negative, the inverse, the anti-principle of the nation. Such was the fantastic nature of revolutionary society's discourse on power, and it made the aristocratic plot one of the central figures of the revolutionary mentality. It was almost infinitely malleable, apt at interpreting every circumstance, and sustained most of all by ambiguities in the royal attitude.

Traces of the obsession with a plot can also be found, in less caricatural form than with Marat or the Cordeliers, in the words of deputies of the Constituent Assembly, where even at this early date the Assembly encouraged the notion that in case of public emergency it might be necessary to limit human rights. Consider, for example, the February 1790 debate on the right to emigrate: Mesdames, the aunts of Louis XVI, had been arrested on their way to Rome by local authorities in Burgundy. This led to a debate in the Assembly, ultimately resolved in favour of Mesdames by invoking the rights of man, but tested by a strong contrary case that invoked the national emergency. In the following year, the king's flight to Varennes and return to Paris publicly demonstrated the royal family's true sentiments; this minor plot – ill conceived and ill executed – was construed by revolutionary opinion as proof of the great plot, universal, omnipresent, and omnipotent. The Revolution had really already ceased to have a true constitutional king, despite the temporary fiction of an 'abduction'. Yet it made of this vanquished, captive, but reinstated monarch a formidable enemy, soon supported by all the kings of Europe.

The war raised both the stakes and the fears. It erased the line between opposition and treason once and for all. It turned nobles and refractory priests into enemies of the fatherland. It quickly dissolved what was left of the royal fiction after the Varennes episode, but not even the fall of the king on August 10 diminished the perceived threat to the Revolution from the conspiracy of external enemies and domestic traitors. On the contrary, the six weeks that separated the fall of the Tuileries from the meeting of the Convention on September 20 marked the entry of the Terror into revolutionary politics.

But the Terror was not yet the policy of the Revolution. For the Legislative Assembly was now only a caretaker regime, and real power had passed to the victors of August 10: the Paris Commune, composed of the former Insurrectional Committee, rounded out through carefully contrived elections to a complement of nearly three hundred members representing the cream of Parisian militancy. Under pressure from the Commune the Legislative Assembly voted on August 17 to establish a special tribunal and declared refractory priests to be criminals. Under the Commune's direct authority the Paris sections organized themselves as surveillance committees, conducting searches and making arrests. The punishment of the 'guilty' was the order of the day. By the end of August the bad news from the frontiers heightened the siege mentality and the obsession with punishment, which were responsible for the massacre of prisoners by mobs in Paris between September 2 and September 6.

This baleful episode illustrates the psychological and political mechanism of the Terror. The victims were mostly common law prisoners (nearly three-quarters of the more than a thousand killed), while the murderers were the victors of August 10: shopkeepers, artisans, national guards, *fédérés*, motivated by their obsession with treason. No orders, no identifiable instructions, came from above. The press poured oil on the fire, and the idea of liquidating traitors was of course an old refrain of Marat's, but the crowd needed no visible leader to conduct a slaughter arranged to look like a rough parody of justice. Danton, the minister of justice, did not intervene, and even the Girondin Roland wrote on September 3: 'Yesterday was a day over whose events a veil should probably be thrown'. A few weeks later, the September massacres would become a theme in the political battle between Girondins and Montagnards. At the time, however, the politicians of the Revolution endured the event as one accepts the inevitable.

In fact, the Terror was gradually established as a repressive system organized from above and institutionalized during the year 1793, as the Montagnards turned to activists in the Paris sections for support in taking control of the Revolution. The question whether the king's trial and execution formed the prelude to or even the first act of the Terror is not easy to answer. One may agree with Kant that the answer should be 'yes' if one sees the death of Louis XVI as an illegal violation of the constitutional contract by the Convention. Or one may answer 'no', along with Michelet, if one views the trial as the solemn affirmation of the new sovereignty of the people, incompatible with the old sovereignty of the king. The fact remains that the judgment and execution of Louis XVI were extensively and minutely debated and did not entail creation of emergency institutions.

However firm their legal underpinnings, the king's trial and execution did nevertheless signal a key political victory for the Mountain. Since September the Girondins had been banking on relaxation of repressive and coercive measures. The Montagnards relied on their alliance with militants in the sections and on the implementation of a terrorist policy. January 21 was a great symbolic victory for that strategy. In the spring, Dumouriez's military failures (followed by his defection to the enemy), the start of the Vendée war, and economic difficulties in Paris made it possible to move further in the direction of such a policy.

On March 11 the Convention established a Revolutionary Tribunal; on March 21 it set up the Committees of Surveillance, responsible at the local level for keeping an eye on 'suspects', a category largely left to the committees' judgment; on March 28 laws against émigrés were codified and strengthened, depriving those who emigrated of their property and providing for the death penalty if they returned to France. The philosophy behind these measures was well summarized by Danton, who had in mind the September massacres: 'Let us be terrible in order to dispense the people from being so'. The expulsion of the Girondins from the Convention on June 2 hastened the evolution towards terror by offering, in response to sans-culotte demands, an additional – and important – reward. Both domestic and foreign situations at the beginning of the summer justified a dictatorship by the committees and the dispatch of representatives with extraordinary powers to the rebellious provinces and the armies – measures outside common law. But once again it was the invasion of the Assembly by sectional militants on September 5 that placed the Terror on the agenda.

The Terror was from that point on a system of government, or rather, an essential part, the arm, of the revolutionary government. Its administrative structure was simple. At the top were the two committees, especially the Committee of General Security, whose responsibilities included surveillance and police. At the grass roots was a vast network of local revolutionary committees responsible for identifying and arresting 'suspects' and issuing certificates of civism. These were complementary tasks, since any grounds for not issuing such a certificate were also grounds for declaring a person 'suspect', that is, an enemy of the regime or merely a potential adversary, a fence-sitter. A wave of denunciation took advantage of this incitement by public authority. 'Suspects' were judged by special courts; the principal one was the Revolutionary Tribunal in Paris, created in March 1793 and reorganized in September to accelerate its operations. Divided into four sections, two of which functioned simultaneously, it comprised sixteen examining magistrates, a jury of sixty, and a public prosecutor with a staff of assistants, all named by the Convention on nomination by the two committees. The subordination of the court to political power was thus a matter of principle: trial was quick and judges lacked independence; deliberations were hasty and in fact limited to three days by an October decree intended to hamper the defence of the Girondin deputies. The autonomy of the Tribunal consisted in its power to free certain of the accused. Otherwise the stakes were life or death, for it was not long before judgments were reduced to just two: acquittal or execution. Verdicts were rendered by majority vote after secret deliberation, but in the March decree it was stipulated that judges 'state their opinions out loud'. Michelet and later Louis Blanc commented: 'The Terror was in this phrase more than in the whole project'.

But the Terror was not contained in any one institution, no matter how symbolic. It was also a ubiquitous means of government, through which the revolutionary dictatorship of Paris would make its iron hand felt everywhere, in the provinces and in the armies. It was exercised by way of 'the revolutionary army' created in September, a great reserve of activists under the authority of the sans-culotte Ronsin, a political gendarmerie that, keeping one eye on hoarders and the other on the notorious 'suspects', represented the Paris sections in every town and village in the Republic. Its chief operative was the *représentant en mission*, designated by the Convention and the Committee of Public Safety to organize the victory of the Revolution on the frontiers and exterminate the enemies of the Republic in the regions in revolt against or at war with Paris. He had full powers to establish special courts or courts-martial to hasten the work of repression, not to mention the even more expeditious justice meted out in the forms of mass executions, as in Lyons and the Vendée. The Terror thus operated through a motley fabric of improvised institutions; special courts modelled after the one in Paris were established in Arras, Cambrai, Brest, Rochefort, and Toulouse in the winter of 1793–94. But most of the organs of repression were 'extraordinary commissions', civilian or military, created ad hoc in the civil war zones and rendering judgments from which there was no appeal. It was not until the spring of 1794 that the Revolutionary Tribunal of Paris began asserting its jurisdiction over an increasing number of cases of counterrevolutionary crime. The laws of 27 Germinal (April 16) and 19 Floréal (May 8) capped this development by granting the Paris tribunal exclusive jurisdiction.

This spring of 1794 – a year after the creation of the Tribunal – was also the time of the administrative institutionalization of the Terror through the dreadful law of 22 Prairial (June 10), the draft of which is in Couthon's hand. A majority of the personnel serving the Tribunal were replaced, beginning with the public ministry, which had been headed from the beginning by Fouquier-Tinville. The novelty of the law lay in its redefinition of the mission and lethal omnipotence of the redoubtable court. Its fourth article stated that the Tribunal 'is instituted to punish the enemies of the people'. More political than juridical, this definition prefaced procedures that were more expeditious than judicial. The text eliminated the *instruction*, or preliminary investigation (article 12), and permitted charges to be brought merely on the basis of denunciations (article 9); it deprived the accused of the assistance of an attorney (article 16) and transformed the hearing into a mere formality by eliminating the examination of witnesses. Article 13 stated: 'If material evidence exists independent of the testimony of witnesses, the witnesses will not be heard'. Robespierre, who presided over the session of 22 Prairial, mounted the Assembly rostrum to defend his loyal Couthon against those few members of the Convention who were frightened by the nature of this revolutionary justice: 'We shall brave the perfidious insinuations of excessive severity with which some have sought to attack measures prescribed by the public interest. This severity is redoubtable only to conspirators, only to enemies of liberty'.

The law of 22 Prairial was rescinded in the wake of 9 Thermidor. Deprived of its political source of energy and detested by public opinion, the Revolutionary Tribunal ceased its activities. Though later reorganized, it had permanently lost the quasi-legitimacy and frightful utility it had derived for sixteen months from the idea of a government of exception, with terror the order of the day.

From this rise and fall arises a new set of questions, which have less to do with the institutions of revolutionary Terror than with their role and consequences. It is best to begin once again with Paris and with what information we have about the Revolutionary Tribunal. Examination of the monthly summaries of its activities from its inception to the fall of Robespierre reveals that between March and September of 1793 the Tribunal's work was curtailed, though already its verdicts were limited to either death or acquittal: five to fifteen death sentences were handed down each month, compared with a far greater number of acquittals. The number of 'cases' rose sharply in October, that is, just after the measures that followed the sans-culotte *journée* of September 5 – measures that made Terror the order of the day, established the Law of Suspects, and reorganized the Tribunal and replaced its personnel. Actually it was in September that the number of judges was raised from five to sixteen and the number of jurors from twelve to sixty. The personnel of the March 10 tribunal had been completely replaced, with hardly anyone left in place other than the public prosecutor Fouquier-Tinville and his two lieutenants. Control by the two committees had come to be exercised at will. The figures reveal what a spur these changes were to repression: 193 accused went to the guillotine in the final two months of autumn and through early January. Among these 'counterrevolutionaries' were not only Marie Antoinette, Madame Elisabeth, the duc de Biron (who was ex-general of the Armies of the Republic), and the former duc d'Orléans (who in vain had taken up the new name Philippe-Egalité), but also all the Girondins arrested or declared suspect since springtime, with Brissot and Vergniaud leading the way, followed by the remains of what had been the Feuillant group along with Bailly and Barnave. The guillotine exorcised the Revolution's past at the same time as it felled the Ancien Régime.

During the autumn the Tribunal was already judging more than a hundred suspects per month, but still acquitting more than half of them. Then, in March, as the prisons filled with suspects and the number of accused to be tried continued to increase, the proportion of death penalties rose, and this change was soon followed by a dizzying rise in the actual number of trials. The causes of the two phenomena were different. The first had to do with the sharpening of factional struggle in the first few months of 1794 and the radicalization of conflicts for power, which led in the end to the guillotine first for the Hébertists and later for the Dantonists (late March–early April): death became the universal sanction for political conflict. The second was, in essence at any rate, the result of the previously mentioned decree of 27 Germinal, carried on a motion by Saint-Just, which centralized revolutionary justice in Paris. This evolution culminated in the law of 22 Prairial, which completed the mechanism of the judicial Terror; nearly 700 judgments were handed down in Prairial and nearly 1000 in Messidor (June 21–July 21), and together these judgments resulted in close to 800 executions. The Paris prisons were overpopulated; they housed over 8000 'suspects' at the beginning of Thermidor. Only the fall of Robespierre on the ninth (July 27) halted the endless procession of tumbrils that historians have baptized the 'Great Terror'.

This summary of the results of the Terror in Paris, based on data from the Revolutionary Tribunal, may usefully be compared with a statistical study, published in 1935 by the American historian Donald Greer, of victims of the Terror nationwide. Confirming two earlier works, Greer arrives at a figure of 16,600 victims executed after being sentenced to death by a revolutionary court of justice (including, as we have just seen, 2625 in Paris). The number of arrests from March 1793 to the end of July 1794 was far higher, probably close to a half-million: this figure gives some idea of the shock caused by a repressive wave of these dimensions. It also indicates that there were not only acquittals but also, occasionally, penalties other than the death sentence, as well as 'suspects' who languished in prison until 9 Thermidor without being tried. The Terror's victims came from all levels of society, with each conflict producing its own characteristic shadings: more peasants in the Vendée, more bourgeois in Paris, Lyons, and Nîmes. In proportion to their relatively small numbers, the upper classes and clergy were comparatively hard-hit.

Greer's chronological graph of executions nationwide shows low or very low figures during the spring and summer of 1793, exactly as in Paris. But what followed was different: the number of death sentences peaks sharply in December 1793 and January 1794, with nearly 3500 executions in each of these two months. The tragic curve drops below 1000 from February to May and then climbs again in June and July until 9 Thermidor. The difference between these figures and those from the Revolutionary Tribunal in Paris is thus concentrated in the middle of the period, in the months of December and January, when the Terror was at its height in the provinces. This chronology suggests a first comprehensive interpretation.

If we can agree that the Terror began in March 1793 with the creation of the Revolutionary Tribunal and the first measures of public safety, then its least bloody period – indeed not very bloody at all – was the spring and summer of 1793. This was also the Republic's most critical period. The Prussians and Austrians took Condé, Valenciennes, and Mainz in July, and the domestic situation was catastrophic, with the federalist revolt, the victorious Vendean peasants, and the royalist insurgents in control of Lyons, Marseilles, and Toulon, to say nothing of the Paris sections' threats to the Convention. By contrast, when the number of death sentences and executions began to rise sharply in October, the Republic had been saved on the northern frontier by the battles of Hondschoote (September 8) and Wattignies (October 16). Lyons was retaken on October 9, and the Grand Army of the Vendean peasants was defeated at Cholet on October 17. Made the order of the day on September 5, the Terror, when viewed in relation to the war, both foreign and civil, seems to have been a belated response to a situation that had already begun to improve. The diagnosis is still more obvious if we take into consideration the fact that executions reached a peak in December and January and then resumed with even greater ferocity in the spring under Robespierre's personal dictatorship, at a time when the Revolution faced no more threats at home and the armies of the Republic were taking the offensive on the borders; the law of Prairial and the 'Great Terror' have lost any semblance of a connection with public safety.

This paradox can be understood with the aid of two examples, which help us to move beyond the abstraction of a chronological curve of executions. The situation under the Terror varied considerably in different localities and regions. In Greer's data, more than half the executions took place in the thirteen départements of western France, and twenty percent in the Rhône valley. Characteristic are the case of Lyons and the repression in the Vendée.

In Lyons class warfare superimposed its effects on the consequences of political struggle. The conflict between the Mountain and the Gironde was embedded in social antagonism between the lower classes and the rich. The crusade of the poor found its Savonarola in the Piedmontese merchant Chalier, who defected to serve the working people in their struggle against the merchant city. The workers lost the mayorality to a Girondin in November 1792, but the Jacobins held a majority in the Municipal Council and ultimately, in March 1793, obliged the council to approve one of Chalier's men. On May 29 the Girondins (on the eve of their elimination in Paris) took their revenge, thanks to an insurrection triggered by the levying of a special tax. The city quickly passed from the enemies of the Paris dictatorship into the hands of the royalists, who ruled throughout the summer; but it was retaken by troops of the Convention on October 9.

It now became an 'Emancipated City', symbolically rescued from its accursed past and destined to endure a partial razing, limited to the 'houses of the rich'. Couthon, the city's conqueror, carried out a relatively moderate repression in October. But in November he was replaced by Collot d'Herbois and Fouché, who proceeded with numerous hasty trials and summary executions. Levelling of the large residences along the quays of the Saône got under way. Several thousand suspects were guillotined, shot, or cut down en masse by firing squads. The terror lasted until March 1794.

The history of the revolutionary Terror in the Vendée obeyed the same logic and the same chronology. Again it was a case of putting down an insurrection, the most serious that the Revolution had had to confront. And as in Lyons repression not only came after the victory but actually reached a peak several months later. The Vendée rebellion actually began in March 1793, and reports of its victories resounded throughout the spring and early autumn. But it quickly subsided beginning in mid-October, when the peasant army was crushed at Cholet and moved north of the Loire in the hope of joining an English fleet at Granville, until what troops remained were destroyed in December in the battles of Le Mans and Savenay. But the revolutionary Terror – which is to be distinguished from atrocities and massacres committed in the heat of battle – raged from January to March 1794.

For if the war was pitiless on both sides, what began afterwards was of a different nature: it was a massive repression organized from above on orders of the Convention with the intention of destroying not only the rebels but the population, farms, crops, villages, and anything else that had served the 'brigands' as shelter. For such a task the guillotine was no longer sufficient, and in December Carrier resorted to mass drownings in the Loire. But it was in January that an idea proposed by Barère began to be put into effect: 'To destroy the Vendée'. The Republican troops divided into several columns, each with its own itinerary, with explicit orders to burn all homes and murder their inhabitants, women and children included. This dreadful operation continued until May, and its sad toll must be added to the strict costs of the war: the territory known as the 'military Vendée' (comprising parts of Loire-Inférieure, Maine-et-Loire, Vendée, and Deux-Sèvres) lost twenty per cent of its housing and a substantial percentage of its population.

Numerical estimates of the loss of human life have remained a subject of polemic. It is impossible to be as precise as one would like for two sets of reasons. In the absence of specific sources, historians must resort to comparisons between prior and subsequent population estimates. The documents, moreover, do not permit a breakdown of the three different types of mortality: persons killed in battle (on both sides), persons killed in terrorist repression (whether condemned by a court or simply massacred), and reduced birth rates and increased death rates in the years following the war. Hence it is impossible to give a precise estimate of the number of victims of the Terror in the Vendée. Nevertheless, taken together, the actions of Carrier in Nantes and of Turreau's infernal columns were responsible for deaths numbering in the tens of thousands.

This figure, by far the largest item in the final count of victims of the Terror, is left out of Donald Greer's statistics, based primarily on capital sentences. It must be added in round numbers to the total, which it increases considerably.

The legacy of the Terror poisoned all subsequent revolutionary history and, beyond that, all political life in nineteenth-century France. Throughout the Thermidorian period the Terror lurked about the fringes of the political scene. The royalists used it to forge a weapon of revenge, an instrument for settling local scores in areas where the population leaned toward their camp and Republican troops were thinly scattered, as in the Rhône valley. The republicans would have liked to forget the Terror and root the new institutions of the Year III in the law; Benjamin Constant and Madame de Staël worked feverishly between 9 Thermidor and 18 Brumaire to exorcise the ghost of the guillotine that haunted the Republic, but to no avail. Thermidor revived the royalist menace and counterrevolutionary violence, and the Directory was unable to adhere to the legal election dates stipulated by the Constitution. In September 1797 Augereau's army laid siege to Paris at the behest of the director Barras in order to save the Republic from a royalist parliamentary majority. The coup d'état of 18 Fructidor (September 5) was the signal for a new series of 'public safety' measures in which deportation to Guiana replaced the scaffold, with refractory priests paying the heavy price. The nation's revolutionary education proceeded on course, and the civil and military putsch of 18–19 Brumaire (9–10 November 1799) capped it off by establishing a regime 'that completed the Terror by replacing permanent revolution with permanent war' (Marx, *The Holy Family*).

In the nineteenth century memories of the Terror imparted a peculiar bitterness to civil struggle, while at the same time adding further passion to the great conflict between Ancien Régime and Revolution. By associating the advent of democracy with a bloody dictatorship, it supplied counterrevolutionaries with arguments and liberals with fears. It embarrassed or divided republicans and isolated socialists. In postrevolutionary France the monarchy was suspect because of the Ancien Régime, but the Republic was unable to cleanse its image of the blood spilled in its name. When it finally triumphed in the 1870s, it was because the republicans had conquered their own demons and presented a pacified version of their great ancestors from which the spectre of the guillotine had been exorcised. It was not until the twentieth century, with the injection of bolshevism and the development of a communist extreme left, that a cult of the Terror, associated with that of Robespierre, was established on grounds of revolutionary necessity, where for half a century it flourished in the shadow of the Soviet example.

Thus, there exists a history of the history of the Terror, associated with the vicissitudes of French political history over the past two hundred years. But that history can also be written in a less chronological mode by attempting to reconstitute the various types of interpretation to which the Terror has been subjected.

The most common strategy is to relate the Terror to circumstances external to the Revolution; we are told, then, that the Terror was merely the product of the tragic situation in which the Republic found itself in 1793 and was a terrible yet necessary instrument of public safety. Surrounded by enemies foreign and domestic, the Convention allegedly had no choice but to rely on fear of the guillotine to mobilize men and resources. We find this interpretation being advanced by the Thermidorians in the period immediately following Robespierre's fall, and it was destined to enjoy a brilliant future, for it can also be found in most French public school texts for reasons that are easy to understand: it has the advantage of offering to the ultimately victorious republican tradition a Revolution exonerated of guilt for the terrorist episode, responsibility for which is shifted to its adversaries. That is why this interpretation is favoured by many who consider themselves heirs of 1789, for it is a way of escaping the dilemma of contradiction or denial.

The 'circumstantial' thesis is often associated with another idea, according to which the Terror coincides with a period during which social strata other than the cultivated bourgeoisie were gaining access to power: specifically, the class of urban artisans and tradesmen from which the sans-culotte activists were recruited and which Mignet, for example, setting the tone for liberal historiography, dubbed the 'plebs' or the 'multitude' to distinguish them from the bourgeoisie of 1789. Thus circumstances presumably brought to the fore a second revolution, which lacks the historical dignity of the first because it was neither bourgeois nor liberal; its necessity was merely circumstantial, that is, subordinate to the principal course of the event, which continued to be defined by the principle of 1789 and the rise of the bourgeoisie. But the plebeian nature of this episode makes it possible to understand how the Terror was also the product of elementary political reflexes, at once egalitarian and punitive, triggered by military reverses and internal insurrections. The Ancien Régime had not known how to educate its people, and for this it paid a heavy price at the moment of its downfall.

It is not difficult to find elements of historical reality to support interpretations of this type. The Terror did in fact develop in the course of the Revolution at a time of foreign and domestic danger and out of obsession with 'aristocratic' treason and an 'aristocratic plot'. It continually justified itself in these terms as indispensable to the salvation of the fatherland. It was 'placed on the order of the day' and exercised in the name of the state and the Republic only under pressure from sans-culotte militants. The Paris prison massacres of September 1792 showed the extremes to which the punitive passions of the people might go. A year later, it was in part to channel those passions that the Convention and the Committees turned the Terror into a banner of government.

Nevertheless, neither the circumstances nor the political attitudes of the *petit peuple* are enough to account for the phenomenon. The 'circumstances', too, have a chronology. The risks for the Revolution were greatest at the beginning and in the middle of the summer of 1793, at a time when the activity of the Revolutionary Tribunal was relatively minimal. By contrast, the Terror intensified with the improvement of the situation and the victories, starting in October. It reached a peak during the winter, in a Lyons that had been vanquished for several months and in a defeated Vendée that had to be put to the torch, as well as in countless other places where there were violent clashes as a result of initiatives on the part of local militants or envoys of the Convention. There was indeed a connection between the civil war and the Terror, but it was not that the Terror was an instrument for ending a war; it followed and actually prolonged rather than shortened the war. One cannot credit it with patriotic devotion without falling into inconsistency, because to do so would be to assume – incorrectly, by the way – the existence of a counter-revolutionary France. Nor can one credit it with saving the fatherland or maintaining the Republic, since it came after the victory. 'The Great Terror', wrote the republican Quinet as long ago as 1867, 'nearly everywhere revealed itself after the victories. Can we maintain that it caused them? Can we argue that, in our systems, effect precedes cause?' (*Critique de la Révolution*).

The explanation involving the role of popular attitudes accounts for only some of the facts. It is indeed true, as we have seen, that the pressure to establish a terrorist dictatorship came chiefly from sans-culotte militants. But it is not a simple matter to establish a dividing line between the 'people' and the political elites, between 'popular' culture and 'high' culture. What about Marat, for example, who may be considered one of the purest ideologues of the Terror? To which group did he belong? This demi-savant, who since 1789 had been denouncing the aristocratic plot and tirelessly calling for scaffolds to be erected, straddled both 'cultures'. The same can be said of Hébert and the Hébertists, who extended his influence in Paris and played so important a role in the republican repression in Vendée. In fact, in 1793 terrorist discourse was in the mouths of nearly all the leaders of the Revolution, including those who had no special relation to sans-culotte activism, the legists and bourgeois of the committees and the Convention. Barère's demand in the summer of 1793 for the total destruction of the Vendée is enough to make clear the grip of terrorist fanaticism on all the Montagnard deputies.

Of course this call for widespread extermination grew out of the civil war, even if that was not its only cause. But, as Mona Ozouf has demonstrated, from the autumn of 1793 to the spring of 1794 the case for the necessity of the Terror abandoned the circumstantial grounds of the war in favor of a more fundamental justification: nothing less than the Revolution itself. After the end of March and the liquidation of the Hébertists, which put an end to the bloody escalation of what remained of sans-culottism, the Terror, by this point the exclusive instrument of the Robespierrist clan, had ceased to be a matter for learned and sometimes philosophical rationalization. It was less a part of the arsenal of victory than of an ambition for regeneration.

Nor was the climate any longer that of a besieged city, since the frontiers had been liberated and the civil war extinguished. The most obvious use of the guillotine was no longer the extermination of avowed enemies but rather that of 'factions': the Hébertists followed by the Dantonists. The Terror raged all the more fiercely because the Robespierrist group had no further support either on its left, among the activists, or on its right, in public opinion; it was a government of fear, which Robespierre portrayed in theory as a government of virtue. Conceived in order to exterminate aristocracy, the Terror ended as a means of subduing wrongdoers and combatting crime. From now on it coincided with and was inseparable from the Revolution, because there was no other way of someday moulding a republic of citizens.

Hence the Terror cannot be reduced to circumstances, whether the emergency situation or pressure from the *petit peuple*, surrounding its birth. Not that circumstances played no role; obviously they provided an environment in which ideology developed and allowed terrorist institutions to be gradually put in place. But this ideology, present in the Revolution of 1789, predated the circumstances and enjoyed an independent existence, which was associated with the nature of French revolutionary culture through several sets of ideas.

The first of these ideas was of man's regeneration, in which respect the Revolution was akin to a religious annunciation but in a secularized mode. The actors in the events actually conceived of their own history as an emancipation of man in general. The issue was not to reform French society but to reinstitute the social pact on the basis of man's free will; France represented only the first act of this decisive development. This truly philosophical ambition was unusual, however, in that it was constantly caught up in the test of actual history, as though the truth of a religious promise had been left to empirical verification by the facts. In the gap between facts and promise was born the idea of a regeneration, to reduce the distance between the Revolution and its ambition, which it could not renounce without ceasing to be itself. If the Republic of free citizens was not yet possible, it was because men, perverted by their past history, were wicked; by means of the Terror, the Revolution – a history without precedent, entirely new – would make a new man.

Another idea said roughly the same thing, or arrived at the same result: that politics could do anything. The revolutionary universe was a universe populated by wills, entirely animated by the conflict between good intentions and evil plans; no action was ever uncertain, no power ever innocent. As first Hegel and later Marx recognized, the French Revolution was the theatre in which the voluntarism of modern politics revealed itself in all its purity. The event remained ever faithful to its original idea, according to which the social contract could be instituted only by free wills. This attribution of unlimited powers to political action opened a vast field to radicalization of conflicts and to militant fanaticism. Henceforth each individual could arrogate to himself what had once been a divine monopoly, that of creating the human world, with the ambition of recreating it. If he then found obstacles standing in his way, he attributed them to the perversity of adverse wills rather than to the opacity of things: the Terror's sole purpose was to do away with those adversaries.

In the end, the Revolution put the people in the place of the king. In order to restore to the social order the truth and justice ignored by the Ancien Régime, it returned the people to its rightful place, usurped for so long by the king: the place of sovereign. What the Revolution, following Rousseau, called the general will was radically different from monarchical power in the manner of its formation yet identical to it in the extent of its jurisdiction. The absolute sovereignty of the king presaged the sovereignty of democracy. Wholly obsessed with legitimacy, having thrown off divine guidance without establishing reciprocal checks and balances in the American manner, the Revolution was unwilling to set limits to public authority. It had lived since 1789 on the idea of a new absolute – and indivisible – sovereignty, which excluded pluralism of representation because it assumed the unity of the nation. Since that unity did not exist – and Girondin federalism showed that factions continued to plot in the shadows – the function of the Terror, as well as of purging elections, was invariably to establish it. As early as 1795, in the discussion of the Constitution of Year III, Sieyès would blame the Terror on the Revolution's errors regarding the concept of sovereignty (speech of 2 Thermidor); somewhat later this idea was adapted and systematized by Madame de Staël, Benjamin Constant, and finally Guizot.

This explanation of the Terror is not incompatible with a more sociological type of interpretation, which incidentally can also be found in the work of Constant and Staël. An enthralling chapter of the latter's *Considérations sur la Révolution française* (book 3, chap. 15) in fact suggests that the Ancien Régime bequeathed to posterity not only its conception of sovereignty but also the harshness of its social relations. Aristocratic society, composed of castes created by the monarchy and fiercely jealous of their privileges, left the embers of its violence to the Revolution, which fanned them into conflagration: 'Because the various classes of society had almost no relations among themselves in France, their mutual antipathy was stronger . . . In no country were nobles as much strangers to the rest of the nation. When they touched the second class, it was only to give offence . . . The same scene was repeated from rank to rank; the irritability of a very sensitive nation inclined each person to jealousy toward his neighbor, toward his superior, toward his master; and all individuals not content to dominate humiliated one another.' In part, therefore, the 'Terror' may have stemmed from an egalitarian fanaticism born of an inegalitarian pathology in the old society. For there is no reason not to think that in the genesis of the bloody dictatorship of Year II, Ancien Régime and Revolution combined their effects.

23
The rise and fall of a provincial terrorist
RICHARD COBB

Terrorists were not born overnight, and as the average age of the committed militant was from 30 to 45, the key to his commitment must be sought, when such evidence exists about people not given to writing up their personal recollections, in a life of hardship, deprivation, and brutality during the decade preceding the revolutionary outbreak. In other words, it is necessary to extend to the humbler levels of society the benefits of the 'long view', exploited with great success by such talented biographers as Marcel Reinhard or Leo Gershoy, in their studies of Carnot and Barère. After so many years devoted to the investigation of 'social structures', it would be reasonable to insist upon the urgency of returning to the more conventional biographical approach, while, of course, still taking into account the collective assumptions of a trade, of a certain province, or of a given town or quarter, when attempting to assess the motivations of revolutionary militancy.

There is an admirable illustration of this theme in [the] biography of a middle-ranking terrorist, previously only known to history as the subordinate agent of the Committee of General Security who had carried out the arrest of André Chénier.[1] . . . Nicolas Guénot, in fact, offers an almost ideal case history of the emergence of a terrorist mentality and of the progressive commitment, in individual terms, to the politics of violence. It so happened that he plumped for the Jacobin Terror; he might equally well

Reprinted, with minor abridgements, from R. C. Cobb, *Reactions to the French Revolution* (Oxford, Oxford University Press, 1972), pp. 75–94.

have become a member of a royalist murder gang, a *sabreur* in the service of Christ & King. The important thing about him was that his place of birth, his trade, the terrible hardships that he had suffered in the fifteen years before the outbreak of the revolutionary crisis had predestined him to the politics of intransigence and vengeance. For Guénot, as for so many archetypal terrorist militants, the Revolution, and more especially the exceptional circumstances of 1793 and the year II, afforded the opportunity to get even with a cruel society and to take it out on his former exploiters: in this case, the rich and powerful timber merchants of the valleys of the Yonne and the Cure, on the edge of the lakes and forests of the brutal and wild Morvan.

Guénot was born in April 1754 – four years earlier than Robespierre – in the small *bourg* of Voutenay, in the Yonne (Upper Burgundy), a place numbering a little over three hundred inhabitants at the beginning of the century, on the Cure, a few miles south of the great timber port of Vermenton. He was the second son, and had a younger brother and a sister. He died in May 1832, aged 78, probably as the result of the cholera epidemic that swept France, England, Italy, and Russia in the course of that and the two following years. In his quite exceptional longevity, he was no doubt untypical of the average terrorist militant, a great many of whom were never even to see the Restoration; but it was only in this respect that he was untypical of the common run of the more enthusiastic acolytes of terror and repression, delation, and denunciation.

His life too might be taken as an illustration of that theme so much favoured by eighteenth-century novelists, so strongly condemned by the physiocrats: *la montée à Paris, les dangers de la ville*, the corrupting influence of the capital of luxury and vice. Only ten years earlier, *Monsieur Nicolas*[2] the printer's apprentice from nearby Auxerre – had come up to Paris, on the *coche d'eau*, to seek out his fortune. Guénot, too, it might be said, likewise became contaminated, though he had never had the chance that Restif had had of a well-to-do, patriarchal family background, an education with the Jansenists of Bicêtre, the constant care for his welfare of an elder brother who was a priest, and a network of family relationships provided for him when he first went to Auxerre. His father was a river-worker, like most of the inhabitants of this large village situated in the thick woodlands of the southern tip of the Yonne, [and] Guénot himself was naturally, inevitably, drawn to the trade of *flotteur* – the men, mostly from the Morvan and the Avallonnais, who floated the *trains de bois* down the Cure and the Yonne, into the Seine at Montereau, thence to the wood ports of Paris at Charenton and quai du Louvre. Like most dangerous trades – the men often had to wade up to their necks, in icy and fast-flowing waters, in order to retrieve runaway logs that had broken away from the rafts – the *flotteurs* constituted an intensely proud corporation, famous for their solidarity and feared for their readiness to brawl. They were ruthlessly exploited and ill-paid by the timber merchants. No trade could have been more readily orientated towards Paris, the *flotteurs* sometimes doing the journey a dozen or twenty times a year. Many of them stayed in the capital, whether in winter employment when the river traffic was interrupted till the March floods had subsided, or, in a desperate endeavour to escape from the servitude of the river altogether, in some other following, inland from the quays, but always within striking distance of them, as if the river even then exercised over them some sort of fascination, as a lifeline connecting them with a hard, rough childhood, with home and origin, and with their visible reminder, the *coche d'eau*, which brought up to Paris its daily contingent of Bourguignons and Bourguignonnes, of Morvandiaux and Morvandielles, as if indeed they preferred the proximity of known exploiters, of the timber merchants, to that of complete strangers plying trades that had no connection with the river.

Guénot made his first journey to Paris on a *train de bois*, at 17, in 1771. But he had had the independence – or perhaps the good sense – for Voutenay could offer him nothing better than this dangerous and physically demanding trade – to stay on in the capital, working, as far as one can make out, first of all on the quays of the timber port of the Louvre, as a docker or a porter – he was clearly a man of enormous physical strength, as indeed the *flotteurs* and the *gens de rivière* had to be – but before long, he moved slightly inland, to the vicinity of the Halle au bled, that is still within reach of the river world, its inns and its wild personnel. He was engaged for a time as a temporary *cocher de fiacre* [cab-driver, *ed.*], and though he did not possess a *patente*, which was required from the *Lieutenant criminel* to exercise this important trade – for the *cochers* were liable to come by a great deal of random information that might be of interest to the Government, whether it was a matter of abducting a girl to the discreet house of a man of high connections, of transporting stolen goods, or of getting out of the city, to a safe hiding-place, any person who needed to escape the attentions of the authorities with a maximum of speed and discretion – he seems to have established, in the course of the first half of the 1770s some useful connections with the police, as well as with the underworld. It was difficult to be a *cocher* without being both a part time informer and an occasional auxiliary of the underworld. Both connections were well worth keeping up for a man without means, and with only the minimum of education – Guénot could in fact read and write, but his spelling needs to be read out loud for his prose to be understandable – anxious to make his way in the world; and, unlike many other Bourguignons who had come up to the capital, he possessed no relatives in the city.

At 21, in 1775, he enlisted in the *Gardes Françaises* – a choice that tells us a lot about the young man, for they were about the most brutal, violent, and undisciplined regiment of the old army. They were intensely proud of their ability to kill, rapidly and silently, in defence of their regimental honour; and they were consequently very dangerous people to drink with, even more dangerous people to take on in a round of toasts or in a series of bets. As the result of a very long stay in Paris – they were attached to palace service in Versailles – they had come to establish close links both with the underworld and with the police. It was generally understood that the lowest sort of prostitutes reverted to them by right – the next grade belonged, by a similar understanding – to the better-placed informers. So, for the second time, Guénot was moving in an underworld of uncertain frontiers, but in which the police, the soldiery, and the criminal could meet on their own terms. In the course of seven years' service – all of it apparently spent in Paris – he was almost constantly in trouble with the magistrates and the *commissaires*, mostly for assault and for other acts of violence committed both on civilians and on soldiers of other corps in the course of week-end dances or in cafés. He was also court martialled more than once for indiscipline and insolence and, on one occasion, for having attacked an N.C.O. (who had apparently provoked him, for otherwise he would have been punished far more severely – he got away with a flogging). He was in and out of prison throughout his service; and in one of the brawls in which he was involved and in which sabres were drawn, he was severely wounded in the left arm, the use of which he never fully recovered. At 29, in 1783, after the peace, he was dishonourably discharged, and found himself, for the first time, *sur le pavé de Paris*. He was either expelled, or threatened with Bicêtre; or he may even have made the decision to return to Voutenay.

In any case, he went back there in 1783. But, with an arm almost entirely out of action, he could not go back to his original trade. For a few months, he acted as a farm labourer in the employment of his younger brother, who had made a success of his *vignoble*. But this must have been intolerably humiliating to the former *Garde Française*; and he was soon dismissed by his brother, after a further assault. In 1784, he took to the woods and was never seen without his rifle, clutched in his valid arm. He was now homeless, sleeping at night in huts of stolen logs, thatch and straw, roaming the woods by day and living off random poaching and the theft of wood. By 1785, he was once more in trouble, this time with the *maréchaussée*, following an assault on a farmer whom he suspected of having denounced him for poaching and whom he had shot at; he was also accused of having attempted to set fire to his farm. He was in prison in Vermenton for some time, had become an object of fear to most of his compatriots, including the members of his own family – he was by now the eldest, his brother having died in infancy.

It is not known when he returned to Paris. But he had had enough of Voutenay. All we know is that he was back in the capital at the beginning of 1789, and that he was once more exercising the trade of *cocher de fiacre*, this time with a proper *patente*. He had, it seems, also re-established useful contacts with *les mouches* – that myriad of informers employed by the *Lieutenant de Police* – and was almost certainly himself putting in occasional and appreciated work in this capacity. At this stage, public catastrophe and private fortune blended, in this particular instance to give to this man's mediocre, unprepossessing, and generally unsuccessful career the impetus and acceleration of outside events.

If he had not been born in the 1750s, Guénot would no doubt have been of little interest to the social historian. He was no exception to the general run of the *flotteurs* of the Avallonnais and the Morvan, among the most truly savage people in France – urban witnesses earlier in the century, at about the time of Guénot's birth – had described these rivermen as Hottentots, and it is true that the much-vaunted Enlightenment would not have meant very much to people who looked to the river for their living. Voutenay was an exceptionally brutal community, in which the timber merchants exploited to the full an abundant local labour force of landless rivermen, for as long as they were strong enough to carry out their herculean task. (They might be good for fifteen years or so, from the time of their first employment at adolescence – fifteen or sixteen – if, in the meantime, they had had the good fortune not to have been drowned or permanently maimed, or had not died of consumption or of some other disease of the lungs to which their watery calling naturally exposed them, especially at the time of the great spring floodwater, after the long interruption of the winter months, when the logs could go hurtling towards Paris – a period naturally favoured by the wood merchants, as prices would then be almost as high as in the late autumn.) There was not much future for the retired *flotteur* unless, like Restif's sober cousins, he could become a minor entrepreneur in his own right, in charge of the *trains de bois* for the profit of a company.

But Guénot was a man to whom the Revolution came almost exactly at the right moment, considering his age and his condition, as an opportunity to better himself, as well as a last chance to escape from a life previously marked by consistent failure. It is, of course, easy to blame him for his own misfortunes. Yet it is difficult to see how a more patient, more docile man could have bettered himself, at the level at which he had been forced to live. His violence was as much the result of rage and frustration at an unjust order of things, as a product of temperament and a result of long periods of heavy drinking in braggart military company. So the Revolution came as his big, unique chance. And, up and down the country, there must have been tens of thousands of men like him, of whom we know little or nothing. His military experience served him at last in enabling him to cut some sort of a figure in the quarter in which he had set up; he had had the good sense, for a man with a past that could be embarrassing, on returning to Paris, to establish residence in a District that he had not formerly inhabited, so that his escapades in the *Gardes Françaises* could be conveniently forgotten, while his value as an instructor to the newly constituted *garde nationale* would gain him a certain prestige among his new neighbours. Former N.C.O's and soldiers were among the chief beneficiaries of the early years of the Revolution and, indeed, of the Revolution as a whole. Only actors stood to profit so much from the violent hiatus in society.

His new residence, perhaps not untypically, was near the Palais-Royal, in what was to become the Section de la Butte-des-Moulins, or Section de la Montagne. Guénot was thus near the principal centres of gambling, prostitution, and receiving. By 1791, he had been promoted to the position of unofficial auxiliary to the *commissaire de police* of that District. The same year, along with another *cocher de fiacre* and a laundryman, he was rewarded by the municipal authorities for having uncovered and denounced a group of counterfeiters, associated with a counter-revolutionary, the sieur de Coligny; but the significant fact about this incident was that he warned some members of the gang of their impending arrest, so that they were able to make their escape. It seems probable that he may have had a share in their profits. In June 1792, he briefly entered the prison service, as turnkey in Sainte-Pélagie, while at the same time acting as a regular informer. After the September Massacres, we find him helping the *commissaire* of the place Vendôme, with particular responsibility for the lodging-houses, numerous in a quarter contiguous to the Palais-Royal. This was a further opportunity for him to exploit his specialized knowledge of the personnel of prostitution, and no doubt brought further profits. At about the same period, he carried out an unauthorised house search in the Section de la Halle au Bled, and was momentarily suspended from his rather vague functions in the neighbouring Section.

Early in 1793, he was transferred to the service of the *commissaire* of the Section des Piques – still near the Palais-Royal, which seems to have been his loadstar – and with special responsibility for the surveillance of the prostitutes, lodging-house keepers, speculators, deserters, and runaway noblemen – a profitable combination in its potentialities for graft. In February, he was involved in the uncovering of a gang of receivers, led by an old-clothes' merchant who had been attached to the administration of the Mont-de-Piété. As on a previous occasion, Guénot was accused of having given some members of the gang, including its chief, the tip, so that the most important were able to escape. One of his colleagues was sentenced, as a result of this act of collusion, to twelve years in the galleys, but Guénot was acquitted by a Paris criminal court; he seems at this time to have enjoyed the protection of the *Commune*.

He was now given a roving commission to keep an eye on the *garnis*, the Mont-de-Piété, and prostitution – the trinity of escape, receiving, and vice.

He was also once more carrying out house searches, armed with a pistol and a sabre and wearing an official sash. In March–April 1793, his beat was extended to include the Champs-Élysées; this brought him in a more extensive clientèle of conjurers, magicians, jugglers, sword-swallowers, tight-rope walkers, palmists, artificial savages, and hucksters, who plied in the booths and tents that thrived in this frontier zone of the capital, in the gardens and undergrowth off the wide avenues – a paradise for pickpockets and a trap for the gaping provincial.

By the autumn of 1793, he had graduated further to the position of accredited agent of the *comité de surveillance du Département de Paris*, carrying out on its behalf repressive missions and arrests in the neighbourhood of Paris. But his greatest opportunity came at the end of that year – he was then 39 – when he began to be employed as a full-time agent of the Committee of General Security, while still retaining his rather ill-defined post in the Section des Piques – the double award of a persistent and zealous informer. It was in this capacity that, on 17 Ventôse year II [7 March 1794], he carried out the arrest of André Chénier, in Auteuil, perhaps his principal claim to fame with most historians, but not the most significant event in his career as a terrorist.

More characteristic was his denunciation of a group of timber merchants from his own village, whom he chanced upon in a café near the Seine and whom he had the great satisfaction both of denouncing, as having evaded the *maximum*, and subsequently arresting. Among his other catches in the course of the spring and early summer of 1794 were Vergennes, several members of the Loménie de Brienne family, and the baron de Grimaldi – quite a distinguished bag, in fact. While on these repressive missions in the District de Sens, in his own Department, he also arrested several timber merchants and large farmers. He was also to be involved in one of the most controversial missions, to the village of Viarmes, in the bitterly quarrelsome District de Gonesse.

There is no doubt that he immensely enjoyed this opportunity to turn the tables on his class enemies, as well as the exercise of power, even at this modest, purely executive level (Guénot was in fact rather more than a mere *porteur d'ordre* who carried out arrest warrants, for he was sufficiently in the confidence of the police Committee to initiate arrests at his own discretion). We can see him entering houses in the course of a night search, armed with pistol and sabre, and proudly displaying his badge of office, and girt with a tricolour ribbon, in an effort to emulate the prestigious *Représentants en mission*. When he delivered a warrant, he accompanied his action with a crude commentary, deriving great satisfaction from blood curdling threats against the rich. Meanwhile, his ill-spelt letters flowed in unabated to the Committees and to Fouquier[-Tinville]. He enjoyed the Terror, had reached the high spot of his career at 40, was in it for what he could get out of it, and had the further satisfaction no doubt of feeling that the enemies of the Republic were also his own. Many of those whom he arrested he had known before the Revolution. He was undoubtedly partly motivated by considerations of vengeance; but, in view of his subsequent career, this is not a reason to doubt his sincerity as a terrorist. He certainly used the Terror to carry out his own private war against the rich; but some at least of these may well have sinned against *la sainte loi du maximum*. He was to have a very long time to reflect on his rôle as a terrorist; for his iron constitution played on him the cruel trick of keeping him alive for another thirty-eight years.

However, in Floréal year II [April–May 1794], he appears to have been dismissed, on a charge of embezzlement, in one of those extremely complicated affairs, involving the threat of arrest as a form of blackmail that so often deepens the history of the Terror. In any case, he seems to have fallen foul of Le Bas, the *robespierriste* member of the police Committee and, one might think, a dangerous person to quarrel with at this stage. He kept away from the Committee for the rest of the summer and even failed to draw his full pay. His disgrace was bound to have come about sooner or later; but, as far as Guénot was concerned, it had happened at a most fortunate time and through the agency of just the right person. He was still in disgrace, possibly even in prison, at the time of 9 Thermidor, a circumstance that enabled him to pass as a *victime des triumvirs*, as well as of Le Bas and Duplay, thus securing his full clearance early in the year III and preserving him from the more bitter effects of the Thermidorian reaction. After being formally acquitted on the embezzlement charge, in Frimaire year III [Nov.–Dec. 1794], he seems to have been reinstated in the police, though in what capacity it is not clear. It is suggested that he took part in the *journée* of 12 Germinal, and, both for this reason and as a result of his terrorist activities, he was denounced by his Section, after the Prairial Days; the *assemblée générale* called both for his disarmament and his arrest. Guénot was too much of a marked man to have escaped lightly on this occasion, and, unlike many ex-terrorists, he was not immediately released as a result of the amnesty of Brumaire year IV [Oct.–Nov. 1795]. Towards the end of the month, his wife petitioned the Minister of Justice in his favour. The Minister, while referring the matter to the *juge de paix* of the Section de la place Vendôme, wrote in the margin of the petition that Guénot was to be held in prison pending criminal proceedings. We do not know what the outcome of these may have been; but he was undoubtedly released by the beginning of the year V. There are few references to him during the next five years. Throughout the rest of the Directory, he appears to have carried out rather obscure duties as an *inspecteur de police*, while maintaining fruitful connections with the underworld, then at the height of its manifold activities. A man with a semi-criminal past and with at least one foot inside the Paris police system would probably have little to fear in a period when the collusion that always exists between the police and their clientèle was unusually close and effective; and Guénot, it may be recalled, already had some experience in dealing both with counterfeiters, prostitutes, receivers, and returned *émigrés*, all high priorities with the *Bureau Central* of the Directory years.

In this respect at least his career is unrepresentative of that of most middle-ranking terrorists who, especially in provincial France, found themselves exposed, during the years 1795 to 1799, though with varying fortunes during that chaotic period – many of them, for instance, returned briefly, to public office, in 1797, generally to be evicted once more a year later – to the full effects of the White Terror in the southeast and of the appropriately named Counter-Terror everywhere else. Guénot was in fact probably saved by his connections with the criminal world. He was above all lucky in being able to stay on in Paris, where any ex-terrorist could be reasonably safe and where he had not carried out his more dramatic repressive missions. He continued to enjoy protection from the police authorities and was possibly employed, in a subordinate position, by the newly-formed *Ministère de la Police générale*.

His luck ran out, however, in 1800, when he was dismissed, following a further charge of embezzlement. Soon after being caught begging near the Palais-Royal, he was confined to Bicêtre as a vagrant; and, in 1801, a police order sent him back to Voutenay, *en résidence surveillée*. This was the cruellest fate that could befall any ex-terrorist who had ever been active on the local scene; in the conditions of 1795 to 1800, such an order was often to send the victim to an absolutely certain lynching. Guénot was at least fortunate that this had not happened to him six years sooner. Even as it was, no homecoming could have been more dreadful, for, in the course of the previous seven years, much of his activities as a terrorist, especially in the Yonne, had filtered back to his compatriots; there was a natural river grapevine between Paris and Voutenay, and no Department could have been better informed about the affairs of the capital than the Yonne, with, of course, the Seine-et-Oise and the Seine-et-Marne, equally closely linked to Paris by road and river. This was why, in the course of the nineteenth century, the Yonne was so often the first to feel the *contre-coup* of the violent events of Parisian *journées*, though no doubt, the P.L.M. [railway, *ed.*] having bypassed the river valley, to take in Montbard and Dijon, this was less true after the 1850s.

The Napoleonic municipality was dominated by *notables* and headed by one of the leading timber merchants, the *maire*, Bourgeois. The leading local ex-terrorist was, embarrassingly, a *notaire*, who had undergone a fraudulent bankruptcy – something, in fact, right out of the Thermidorian case book. Guénot was guaranteed poor company. Harried by the almost universal loathing of the villagers, the poorer of whom had no doubt been jealous of Guénot's undoubted successes on the Paris scene – village communities do not easily forgive those of their members who go away and send back good reports – Guénot once more took to the woods, where he lived, on and off, for the next two years, clad in skins and stinking rags, his feet wrapped in sacking, leading out a hermit-like existence in a hide-out made of branches and ferns, suffering agonies in the bitterly cold winters of Burgundy, from his old wound, a prisoner of the heartless horrors of rural poverty and from the very real and constant terror that Bourgeois, his friends, and the Napoleonic *garde nationale* exercised over the whole community, sending regular reports to the Prefect, the Sub-Prefect, and the Minister of Police, on the subject of seditious remarks, drunkenness, village brawls, poaching, vagrancy, and any other threat to the established order. (Voutenay was no exception, in this respect, to the sort of administrative terror that was the common lot of French rural *communes* under the Imperial régime – a terror all the more pitiless in that it was invariably exercised by the well-to-do against the very poor.) It was not misanthropy alone, then, that induced Guénot to keep to the sheltering cover of the woods during the daytime. He knew that he could expect no mercy from Bourgeois. At night, he ventured out of his woodland retreat to the edge of the village, where some charitable soul – a poor carpenter, who had occupied minor office during the Terror – in this brutal and vindictive rural community, was in the habit of putting out food for him outside his cottage.

On one such occasion, on 30 December 1802, emboldened perhaps by previous impunity and driven from his hut by the intensity of the cold, Guénot accepted the hospitality of his well-wisher, whose cottage was on the very edge of the forest. At dawn, his presence having been reported by the eager spies of the *maire*, who had been waiting for months for just such an opportunity to settle accounts with *l'homme des bois*, he was ambushed in the cottage by a company of the *garde nationale*, commanded by Bourgeois himself, as he was about to return to the forest, with a basket of food and a bottle of wine. He managed to climb into the attic, as the men broke down the door of the single room, closing the trap-door after him, and hurling insults through it at his tormentors; but later, the *maire* having secured the help of a carpenter, he climbed out through a sky-light and emerged in full view of the baying rustics, on the roof, holding on to a chimney with his valid arm, and shouting barely distinguishable impreca-tions at his hunters (in the course of his time in the forest, he seems to have forgotten how to form coherent sentences) who had surrounded the cottage. Encouraged by Bourgeois, five members of the force took repeated shots at him, one from his kitchen, resting his rifle on the sink and exclaiming joyfully to his wife, each time he scored a direct hit: *je l'ai touché, je l'ai touché, j'ai touché le corbeau.* He received at least a dozen wounds, and after an hour and a half of random firing, bleeding copiously, he released his grip from the chimney and fell from the roof to the ground, breaking a leg and several ribs, and, while lying on the ground, daring his enemies to finish him off. He was, however, saved from certain lynching by the providential arrival of a *gendarme*, whom he knew and who was not from Voutenay. Guénot appealed to him to take him in charge; the *maire* claimed that he was quite well enough to walk the ten miles to the nearest prison, at Vermenton. But the *gendarme* obtained a cart and had him carried there. After a few days in Vermenton, he was transferred to Auxerre, convicted of vagrancy, and sentenced to the galleys. He was, therefore, escorted, on foot, to Rouen, where the *chaîne* was being formed for Rochefort. The garrison commander, a general, however – evidently a man who did not quite come up to the standard of callousness expected of the Napoleonic civilian official – decided that a semi-cripple, scarcely able to walk, deprived of the use of an arm, and weakened by loss of blood and by the long journey on foot from Burgundy to Upper Normandy, would never be able to reach Rochefort and would not be much use in the galleys even if, by some miracle, he did. He, therefore, ordered that he be sent back, by public transport, to Voutenay.

He was back in the village in March 1803. Shortly after, in a final and pathetic attempt to escape from his dreadful environment, he nevertheless took to the roads again, begging on his way, to reach Pithiviers, where he had a niece, who promptly turned him over to the *gendarmes*. He was once more escorted back to Voutenay, on an administrative order from the Prefect of the Yonne. This was his third, and final, return to his unloved and unlovely birthplace. He then resumed his existence as *un homme des bois*, devoting what energies he had left – and he must have been a prodigiously strong man, both physically and morally – to persistent efforts to bring his would-be assassins to justice. There was no justice for poor men in Napoleonic France; however, he did encounter some measure of success with the public prosecutor of Avallon, who ordered criminal proceedings to be started against the *maire* and his accomplices. Higher authority would have none of this – Napoleonic officials put authority before justice – the proceedings were quashed and the prosecutor blamed for his untimely zeal; shortly afterwards, he was removed. It had taken the combined efforts of the Minister of Police and the Prefect, in a series of urgent representations to the *Grand Juge*, to bring a halt to the wheels of justice.

As far as Guénot was concerned, the White Terror was to continue for the next eleven years, under a régime for which it has been claimed that it brought internal peace and order to France. Increasingly embittered and isolated, half mad and now well on into his 50s, addressing himself to the birds and the trees, muttering curses and obscenities, his hide-out perceptible half a mile off from the stink of excrement, and throwing stones at the village children when they taunted him: *père Guénot, père Guénot, tu ne nous fais pas peur, hou! hou!* imitating the hoot of an owl.

Like other ex-terrorists, he welcomed the Restoration as an opportunity at least to get even with his tormentors. The flow of his semi-literate denunciations once more began, addressed this time to [duc de] Decazes, whom he assured of his devotion to the Bourbon house, a house which he had loyally served in the *Gardes Françaises* – he did not mention the manner in which he had left that corps; he may even have been sincere in these expressions of devotion, for his persecutors had all loyally served the Empire. The letters and petitions continued through 1816 and 1817. But they remained unanswered; the *gendarmerie royale*, as had been the *gendarmerie impériale*, was even instructed to keep an eye on the wild man of the woods, as he ploughed through the undergrowth, in his Crusoe-like clothing, clutching with his valid arm the only friend he had left: his inseparable rifle. At this stage we lose sight of him. His iron constitution and perhaps, too, an open-air existence preserved him throughout the two Restoration reigns; his death is recorded, at the age of 78, in May 1832. He had married at some stage of the Revolution, and, by 1795, had five children; but these he abandoned in Paris on his enforced return to Voutenay. He never saw them again; during the Empire, he occasionally consorted, at nightfall with one or two village artisans, possibly as eccentric as himself, perhaps, too, like himself, former terrorists, though in a less exalted, local sphere.

There is no doubt that Guénot enjoyed the Terror. But it is difficult to know what he thought of the Revolution, for such a man does not confine his thoughts to memoirs. It is likely that Robespierre, Virtue, and the Supreme Being passed him by. What recollections would he have of the year II, his *annus mirabilis*? Probably, in his utter isolation in the woods, his mind became confused, so that he could no longer distinguish the year II from what went before or what came after. But there is no doubt about his courage, about the intensity of some rudimentary convictions, even if they were derived largely from hatred and from the desire for vengeance. He was almost pathologically violent; but so were his fellow-villagers. Balzac's *Les Paysans*, the author reminds us, came from the Avallonnais. It was his extreme good fortune that the strange chances of the Revolution should have enabled him to put his private violence to public use. There were no doubt many more terrorists like him, though less discoverable (the historian is well served with Guénot, for it is possible to follow much of his career, especially under the Empire, through the judicial records, a happy archival accident, though hardly so for the chief personage concerned), and certainly less corrupt, than he.

This harrowing story of rural brutality and nastiness is perhaps most indicative of the emergence of a terrorist vocation. But it also illustrates, horribly, the persistence of the polarisations of the revolutionary period, of how these too grew from those of the older order, and the everlasting memories of rural vengeance.

It is, too, a commentary on the much-played theme of *la montée à Paris*

– a commentary all the more striking in that Guénot, like Restif and Restif's characters, reached the capital by the *coche d'eau*. But poor Guénot was no Dick Whittington; in lieu of a cat, he had to make do with the beasts with whom he shared the forest and whom he sometimes ate: stoats, weasels, foxes, adders, rabbits, and badgers – and, in his case, *la montée* was followed by a bitter return, *une descente aux enfers*, the cruelty and the sheer length of which was too great a punishment even for a man who, briefly, had shown himself singularly merciless, harsh, vengeful, and unscrupulous in the pursuit of his enemies. It is not a pretty tale, but it illustrates perhaps better than anything that has been written over the last twenty years or more, the whole history of the Revolution, through the life and experiences of one man, and a man who had never read Jean-Jacques or anything else very much other than the catechism and, later no doubt, the *Père Duchesne* (the *Grandes Colères*, if not the *Grandes Joies*, of which would have been very much his style; Hébert knew his Guénots). [Claude] Hohl's book is a startling contribution to the neglected, but so important, history of mentalities. Guénot is the Terrorist Re-discovered and Re-created.

Of course, one must not make too much of Guénot as a sort of archetype. We know a great deal about his life before, during, and after the Revolution, because he was seldom out of court and was on the criminal fringe. It would be too easy to write off most forms of revolutionary commitment to the baser instincts, to envy, malice, and cruelty, as well as to the desire to make material gain out of an exceptional situation rich in opportunities for graft and for other forms of profit in kind (for it seems likely that Guénot, like most informers and policemen, may have forced prostitutes to supply him with their dangerous services *gratis*). It is an unfortunate accident of history that we are likely only to be fully informed about that minority of terrorists that, for one reason or another, had come up against the law and had been involved in litigation and subjected to various forms of administrative *surveillance*. One is well informed, for instance, about the prerevolutionary career of Jean-Marie Lapalus, one of [*représentant-en-mission*] Javogues' principal agents;[3] but one is not so well served on the subject of his master. There is nothing in Javogues' career in the ten years before the Revolution that would give any hint of the intensity of his intransigence, of his violence, and of his temerity as a *proconsul*. Perhaps the year II created Javogues in a new image; certainly, after his recall, he seems to have subsided into obscure mildness; and, even when the object of frequent denunciation during the Thermidorian reaction, he appears to have kept strangely quiet, as if he had spent all his energy, all his violence and all his enthusiasm in the course of a few chaotic, noisy months, displaying himself, like an angry comet, to his bewildered compatriots. But his death represented a return to what one would expect of him. [*Représentant*] Carrier, as we are so often told, was a great lover of children and had been regarded, in his native Cantal, as a shy, retiring, mild, and gentle person. In this respect, Marcel Reinhard's life of Carnot and [the] biography of the unattractive Cochon, the second Mirister of Police, have more to offer on this subject of the contrast between the quietude, the mildness, and the drab predictability of a provincial career in the fifteen or twenty years before the Revolution, and the vigour of repressive activity in the course of a mission in the year II.

In a way, [Hohl's] *Guénot* is such a good book because it is good almost by accident, by default. The author does not always realize just what a gold mine he has dug out, he is unwilling to obtrude on a personality sufficiently remarkable as a study in his own right, and perhaps we should be grateful to him for having been hesitant to bring out the pointers. But it is also clear that he is not always aware of the value of his short book as an example of the exploration of a personal case history and its application to our general understanding of the history of the Terror and the Counter-Terror. He clearly thinks of his subject as a semi-monster, and he frequently chides him for his cruelty, his violence, and his thirst for vengeance. Perhaps he does not, in the end, sufficiently relate the violence of the man to that of his background; and, in this respect, he is both less generous and less perceptive than Babeuf when, horrified by the lynchings of the first few days of the Revolution, by the sickening spectacle of the sudden tribalism displayed by the hitherto mild, peaceable, ironic Parisians, he reflected that the common people had been brought up in a bad, brutal school and that popular violence had derived much from the impunity of the violence, the provocativeness, and the sheer insolence of *les Grands*, in their relations with the lower orders, and, more especially, with their womenfolk, as well as from the savagery of a Government that did not hesitate to employ terror against the rural law-breaker. When first in Paris, in 1759, as a young printer's apprentice, Restif goes for a walk, with a girl on his arm, along the still untended, semi-wild avenues off the Champs-Élysées. After a time, he is caught up with by two elegant young men in silk jackets and carrying swords, who begin to walk at the same level as the couple, stopping when they do, keeping pace with them, jostling the young man and his girl, closing in more and more on Restif, persistently jogging his arm, tripping him with their feet, to the insistent accompaniment of the phrase: *que faut-il pour fâcher Monsieur?* The young Bourguignon looks stolidly ahead, refusing to be provoked. After a few more yards of this scene, with the four still walking abreast, one of the young men, after placing a swagger stick in some dirt on the road, holds it up to Restif's nose: *et ça, est-ce que ça va fâcher Monsieur?* Restif has had enough; breaking away from the girl, he picks up a piece of building material – a plank or a long piece of wood, lying by the path – and sets about the pair with it, to such effect that his aggressors, after a thorough trouncing, take to their heels. But the scene has been observed, and, immediately, the apprentice is set upon by a group of big Picard servants, in livery. At the same time, a horseman of the *maréchaussée*, riding by, pulls in his horse. The two young men, returning to the scene, ask him to take Restif in charge. He is soon brought before the *commissaire* of Chaillot and is about to be confined, before appearing in front of a magistrate, when the poor girl breaks down and starts weeping. The young men, perhaps moved, and anxious to make at least a token display of gallantry, tell the *commissaire* that the whole thing had been a joke and that they wish to withdraw the charge; they then take their leave, followed by the servants. The *commissaire* tells Restif that he has been fortunate, asking at the same time if he had recognized the livery of the servants; the apprentice, a newcomer to the capital, states that he has not. *C'est la livrée des d'Orléans*, comments the *commissaire*. Restif was to recall the incident in 1784, when he was writing that section of *Monsieur Nicolas* that dealt with his early life in Paris. 'Such is the tyranny of les Grands,' he then observes. But, ten years later, when he was completing the printing of this vast book, and having experienced the year II, he went on to add: '*La tyrannie des petits, des jaloux, des incapables, est pis encore . . .*' A great many people of all ranks had had similar experiences in the years before the Revolution, and had no doubt remembered them as vividly as Restif had this characteristic display of provocative and totally gratuitous insolence, nearly thirty years after it had occurred. This was, after all, the reality of life – or one of the realities of life – in *ancien régime* France. Guénot, too, was the product of a society, of a place, and of a trade. He did not need to have experienced the insolence of *les Grands*. It would have been surprising had he been anything other than violent, rancorous, and uncouth.

Notes

1 Claude Hohl, *Un agent du Comité de sûreté générale: Nicolas Guénot. Contribution à l'Histoire de la Terreur* (Commission d'Histoire économique et sociale de la Révolution française, Mémoires et Documents, XXII, Paris, Bibliothèque Nationale, 1968).
2 See N.-E. Restif de la Bretonne, *Monsieur Nicolas* (16 vols., Paris, 1797) [autobiographical account].
3 Colin Lucas, 'La brève carrière du terroriste de Jean-Marie Lapalus', *Annales historiques de la Révolution française*, no. 194, October–December 1968.

24

The end of Year Two

BRONISLAW BACZKO

On 24 Fructidor, Year II, forty-five days after 9 Thermidor and ten days before the end of Year II, during a stormy debate in which the divisions tearing the Convention apart were let loose, Merlin de Thionville, having attacked the 'terrorists', those 'knights of the guillotine', formulated three essential problems for the Republic, problems to which the Convention should give unequivocal replies: *Where have we come from? Where are we? Where are we going?* These questions were of capital importance; at a deep level they ran through the entire political debate. The Committee of Public Safety took these questions up on its own account and gave its own response. On a symbolic date, the day of the fourth *sans-culottide*,[1] which closed Year II, Robert Lindet, in a long speech, presented, in the name of the Committee, a sort of report on the state of the nation. This report, accepted by the Convention, was not, however, to put an end to its divisions; Lindet's replies, supposed to constitute the 'rallying point' and to restore lost unity, turned out to be provisional; they would be very swiftly challenged and overtaken.

The dramatisation of these questions plainly marks the feeling of being at a turning point, where the past, the present and the future can no longer be clearly distinguished, as if the period of Revolution had lost that magnificent transparency, glorified throughout Year II. At the end of this year, even the past had become opaque. The Committee of Public Safety was expected to give a twin evaluation of the route taken since the 'revolution of 9 Thermidor' and also of the more distant past of 'the terror' and the 'tyranny' from which this 'happy revolution' had delivered the Republic. As for the present, this was even more confused. The questions put by Merlin revealed that 9 Thermidor constituted a point of no return, but that the problem of ending the Terror was far from settled. On 10 Thermidor, the Convention triumphantly announced the victory of its 'revolution'; with the fall of the 'tyrant' and his acolytes the Republic had been saved and its oppression ended. At the end of Year II the established fact was clear: *ending the Terror* was not an *act* but a *process*, tense and with an uncertain issue. The Terror was not brought to an end by the fall of Robespierre; it was a road to be discovered and travelled.

The experience was unprecedented. It is well known that the political

Reprinted, in abridged form, from B. Baczko, *Ending the Terror: the French Revolution after Robespierre* (Cambridge, Cambridge University Press, 1994), pp. 33–42.

history of the Revolution possesses this particular interest of offering, within a relatively short period of time, the experiences of several regimes and political situations: a constitutional monarchy, the Terror, a republic founded on a representative and property-owning system, a dictatorship by plebiscite, etc. It is the same for the *emergence from the Terror*, a particularly complex experience. Begun on 9 Thermidor, this experience had to be worked out within a framework – political and symbolic, institutional and social – that was born of the Terror and modelled by it. Also, a number of questions inevitably had to be faced. What was to be done with the heritage bequeathed by the period of the Terror? What should be kept, and according to what criteria, of this political heritage, which emerged from the Terror as well as from the Republic, and even from the Revolution? What was to be done with the many consequences of the Terror, beginning with the gaols which overflowed with 'suspects' awaiting trial? How to dismantle both the institutions and the political and administrative personnel, who were products of the Terror, trained, to serve it and ensure its functioning? How to define the political arena that would follow the Terror? These were complex questions since ending the Terror had been accomplished by a political power and by people who had been agents of the Terror, who had actively and vigorously put it in place. The 'revolution of 9 Thermidor' had therefore to be thought of at one and the same time as a *break* in the history of the Revolution and as the pledge of its *continuity*. Beyond the Terror, the Revolution would thus affirm its allegiance to itself and its founding principles. The connection between the break and the continuity was not to be placed only in the political and collective field; it was also lived in tension individually by each person.

To insist on the unprecedented and complex character of this particularly political experience is all the more necessary in that the details and originality of the Thermidorean period are too often neglected by historiography. There is a 'Jacobin' tradition of revolutionary historiography according to which the heroic period of the Revolution, symbolised by Year II, the year of the *sans-culottes*, of the Jacobins, of the Mountain, of the pure and hard revolutionary *élan*, is on 9 Thermidor irremediably broken. Afterwards, everything else would be 'reaction' and, to put it briefly, the vain and heroic combat of the last *sans-culottes* and the last Montagnards, defending the stirring heritage of Year II against the 'reactionaries'. As if the 'last Montagnards' and the 'last Jacobins' were not themselves 'Thermidoreans': not only did they approve of and praise the benefits of the 'revolution of 9 Thermidor', but they also took part, after their fashion, in the experience, along with the other 'reactionaries', of *emerging from the Terror. . . .*

Only *fifty-six days* separate the fifth *sans-culottide* which closed Year II from 9 Thermidor of the same year. A very short period but one which was especially crowded, rich in new political events and phenomena. A political change was already under way but the die was far from being cast. The political actors occupied a largely open space. We have chosen the end of Year II precisely in order to conclude the chronology and to attempt an analysis of the road covered since 9 Thermidor. This choice is certainly arbitrary. The date is symbolic: Year II, according to the revolutionary calendar and not revolutionary legend, came to a painful end at the moment when the political actors themselves felt the need to reply to the questions: *where are we coming from? where are we? where are we going?* It is therefore a suitable date for the historian to take up these same questions, concentrating particularly on the concepts and values, on the representations and symbols, in the field of experience and on the horizon of expectations, of a people, of its representatives, of the historic shock it received.

'Where are we coming from?'

On 9 Thermidor, the revolution brought about by the Convention was contested by no one. No one defended Robespierre, or the triumvirs, nor had any doubts about their crimes and their treacherous schemes. In this sense, all the popular societies, all the constituted authorities, all the armies, in a word, all of France awoke on 10 Thermidor anti-Robespierrist, even 'Thermidorean'. This unanimity has struck historians. Michelet refers to the days after 9 Thermidor as so many days of general joy and relief; this description of rediscovered unanimity seems to recapitulate the account of the *fête de la Fédération* of 1790, itself a symbol of unity and revolutionary hope. But examined more closely, this admirable unanimity, which took over on the day after 9 Thermidor, is seen to be quite disturbing: it has difficulty in hiding an extremely complicated reality.

The unanimous approval of 9 Thermidor is expressed nowhere better than in more than seven hundred formal addresses of congratulations which, after the 'fall of the tyrant', flowed into the Convention from the entire country, from the constituted authorities, from the popular societies, from the armies. (During the sessions of the Assembly only a portion of these addresses were read out, often they were merely summarized, by receiving an 'honourable mention', in the *Bulletin*.) These texts were carefully calligraphed, most of the time on the good quality paper reserved for special occasions; reading them is particularly instructive, despite the monotony of their grandiloquence – or rather, *just because* of this monotony.

Take, by way of example, the address of the popular society of Granville-la-Victoire sent to the Convention on 15 Thermidor (the text was read at the bar of the Convention on the 22nd and received an honourable mention):

A new Cromwell desires to raise himself upon the debris of the National Convention; active vigilance sees through his schemes; prudence disconcerts them; a firmness worthy of the first Romans has the audacious conspirator arrested with his cowardly accomplices; their heads, destined for infamy, fall ingloriously under the avenging sword of the law which strikes without remission all offenders; the Republic is saved. Thanks be to Thee, Supreme Being who watches over the destinies of France; and you, virtuous representatives of a sovereign and free people, whatever your difficult labours, may love of the *patrie* keep you at your posts where trust has placed you and which you fill so worthily.

These are the wishes of the popular society of Granville, which also swears an oath of living free or dying, of combatting all tyrants and of denouncing all traitors. Long live the Republic! Long live the Convention!

The reconstituted popular society of *sans-culottes* of the commune of Montpellier sent its address on 16 Thermidor; it was to be presented to the Convention on the 26th:

Citizen-representatives! Ever since the people elected you and entrusted you with the sublime mandate that you have been able to fulfil, you have advanced steadily to the conquest of liberty and equality. You have shown yourselves to be great and worthy of the people in all the important events which have put the *patrie* in danger. But there have never been circumstances like these, about which we come to express our feelings; a new Catiline, an insolent dominator of the people and its representatives, having for a long time misled public opinion, which was deceived by his artful seductions, finally dared to cast aside the mask and give you the choice between submission to his will or death. You did not hesitate. Surrounded by the satellites of the tyrant you pronounced his condemnation, and when you were threatened by the personal dangers gathering over your heads, you responded with this sublime saying, this expression of unanimous devotion: we shall all die here for liberty. Thanks be to you!

The agricultural and revolutionary society made up of the *sans-culottes* of the twenty-two communes of the canton of Aurillac reported its emotions during the session of 17 Thermidor like this:

The great news brought yesterday by the mail gave rise to an extraordinary meeting. A member read it out; at the account of the

despicable conspiracy of Robespierre, all members of the society were
seized with horror and indignation; but then what joy, what consol-
ing calm took hold of all our souls, when the news followed that the
traitors had already suffered the fate that their crimes deserved; what
admiration for the virtuous people of Paris, for the forty-eight
sections who were able to resist the despicable seductions of these
scoundrels.

The popular society of Inzières experienced similar feelings:

At the news that we received of the treacherous plots which the
infamous Robespierre and his accomplices planned in order to
establish his illusory reign, we shuddered with horror. But immediately, learning of the firmness and wisdom that the Convention
employed and deployed at this moment so dangerous for itself and
the state, we cried out: Long live the Republic and may all her
enemies perish for ever! May their infamous memory be doomed
to universal execration from all peoples of the earth!

To finish, let us quote the address of the popular society of Montauban
which inclined towards the Jacobins (the address was read at the [Paris]
Society of Jacobins on 26 Thermidor):

Behold then Robespierre, this tiger corrupted by the taste of blood,
above all by the blood which circulates for liberty, *Behold him
vanished in the twinkling of an eye* from the place where the scoundrel came to gorge himself. He has vanished to bear his head under
the avenging sword of the Republic. Republicans will no longer suffer
the bitterness of hearing his machiavellian accents point out everywhere, in the most innocent groups of men, conspirators, intriguers,
traitors. Ah! Thanks be unto those who did in fact conspire and
intrigue against him and his guilty conspirators. They did not betray
the Republic, those who had hatched the plot which unmasked and
destroyed him; they . . . have raised public recognition to its highest
pitch.

Nearly all the addresses use the same clichés, combine the same rhetorical elements; they resemble each other so closely that they give the
impression of being inspired by a common model. They outdo each other
in the denunciation of Robespierre. 'New Catiline', 'modern Cromwell':
these epithets keep returning throughout the hundreds of pages. At times,
others are added: 'monster vomited up by the crime that desired a throne
to dominate the Republic and put the French in irons' (popular society of
Charolles); 'a monster, a double-dealer, hidden protector of the Republic's
enemies' (municipality of Grave-Libre); 'the hypocrite, the infamous, the
crafty' (popular society of Segonzac); 'offspring of the hermaphrodite race

of new Cromwells' (*section* of the Panthéon); 'a monster unparalleled in the high points of history' (3rd battalion of the Nièvre); 'reckless pygmy' (the *sans-culottes* of Ernée, *département* of Mayence). One also finds, in fact quite sporadically, the echo of the rumour of Robespierre-the-king ('Robespierre, this scoundrel . . . who had formed the appalling plan of re-establishing royalty in France in order to take possession of the throne', protested the popular society of Anse).

The addresses also outdo each other in glorification of the Convention and its admirable courage, worthy of the ancient Romans, in the face of the terrible dangers that threaten it: 'Citizen-representatives! We end by admiring your energy, this courage, this masculine boldness which distinguish you among the most pressing dangers. Ever firm at your post, continue to brave the dagger of the seditious, the traitors, the ambitious' (popular society of Pont-sur-Rhône). 'Remain at your post! May the universe that gazes upon you learn that the French people owes you both its salvation and its happiness' (the popular society, the constituted authorities, and all the people of Charli-sur-Marne). 'To the National Convention sitting on top of the holy Mountain, glorious Mountain, divine Mountain, holy and sublime Mountain, keep watching over the liberty of the people and hurl avenging thunderbolts against its enemies, receive our congratulations and our enthusiasm. Yet once more your energy, your courage, your wisdom and your firmness have saved the *patrie*' (society of the defenders of the republican Constitution, Vic-la-Montagne).

Not a single doubt, not a single reservation appears to trouble the enthusiasm with which these addresses overflow and below which figure sometimes hundreds of signatures.

However, these congratulations from the provinces, especially from little communes, reached the Convention en masse between 16 and 20 Thermidor and kept flowing in throughout the month of Fructidor. This time-lag was not due to political hesitations; we have noted that several addresses stress that their sending was decided 'on the spur of the moment', as soon as the news from Paris arrived. But the news travelled slowly, at best at the speed of a horse; it was still necessary to call the meeting, agree on the text, have it written down and sent to Paris. The slow pace of communication also explains the fact that in the files where the secretaries of the Convention arranged the correspondence, one finds, between two addresses congratulating the 'fathers of the *patrie*' for having defeated 'the monster, the despicable tyrant', other congratulations:

Remain at your post, unyielding Montagnards! All your decrees, bearing the stamp of Justice, announce to the astonished universe that all the virtues which are the order of the day preside over your government. The hearts of the citizens feel themselves attacked by the blow struck at Collot d'Herbois, by the ventures of the *assassins*

employed by Pitt against the sacred person of Robespierre (popular
society of Caudecoste, district of Valence).

If the society of Sollès [*département* of the Var] has not let you hear
its voice again, or rather if it has not offered you the just tribute of
homage that you more and more deserve, this is because, filled with
horror and indignation at the assassination aimed at two of your
number, Collot d'Herbois and Robespierre, it has lost its power of
speech. Today, now that the sword of the law has fallen upon the
heads of the assassins, now that Collot d'Herbois and Robespierre
are revenged and these infamous parricides can no longer make us
fear for our lives, our voice is more eager than ever to congratulate
you on your unshakeable firmness.

These addresses, which arrived towards the end of Thermidor, had been
carefully filed, but they were not presented to the Convention in order that
it might grant them an honourable mention . . . The assassination of the
'sacred person of Robespierre' to which they refer is not, of course, 10
Thermidor, but the confused story of Cécile Renault, a young girl of
twenty, who was found carrying a small knife as she tried to approach
Robespierre. Accused of having intended to make an attempt on his life,
she was condemned to death and led to the scaffold, on 29 Prairial, dressed
in the red shirt of parricides. The addresses, expressions of unanimous
indignation and enthusiasm, reached Paris after too long a delay; but the
clichés employed were largely reusable for condemnation of the 'new
Catiline'.

The repeated use of the same epithets – 'new Catiline', 'new Cromwell'
– in the hundreds of addresses does not cease to amaze. The addresses, as
we have seen, often bear hundreds of signatures. Many of these are written
awkwardly and with difficulty by hands which are not used to holding a
pen; one finds, at times, crosses instead of signatures and to some
addresses are joined long lists of citizens who 'being unlettered have asked
that the secretaries sign for them' (popular society of Orange, 18 Thermidor). The presence of these illiterate or semi-illiterate people at meetings
of popular societies shows, to be sure, the access of new social classes to
politics during the Revolution, and especially in Year II. But were they so
well-versed in ancient history, did they all know who the 'old Catiline'
was? Had the 'black legend' of Cromwell really experienced such a wide
circulation that his name came spontaneously to the mind of illiterates for
the purpose of condemning the 'new tyrant' defeated in Paris? And what
are we to think of these adolescents of fifteen years of age from the
company of Young Republicans of the commune of Angoulême who, so
spontaneously, expressed their emotions in these terms: 'How the Mountain was great in these terrifying moments! Yes, the universe shall learn

that it is above all conspiracies! Fathers of the *Patrie*, you are immortalized, you have deserved well of the human race! Remain in your place until all the scoundrels, all the tyrants, the Catilines, the Cromwells, the dictators, the triumvirs, are destroyed?'

These addresses reveal more than the spontaneous feelings of their compilers and signatories. Their very language points to the *conditions that make possible* the expression of the lofty unanimity they advertise. The clichés and stereotypes suggest a common model followed by all these addresses. This model is, moreover, quite easy to find; it is, as a matter of fact, the appeals of the Convention as well as the reports of its sessions which transmit these clichés and evidently constitute the primary source of inspiration. *The addresses speak the 'wooden language' of Year II*, the same, with a few more epithets, which had been employed to celebrate the preservation of the integrity of the 'sacred person of Robespierre'. Whatever the amount of real relief at the announcement of the 'fall of the tyrant', the addresses testify to the uniformity of language brought about by the Terror, to the unanimity commanded from above, to the conformism and opportunism acquired and internalised as political behaviour during the Terror. Those who drafted and signed these addresses were the same people who had already condemned federalism, the 'foul conspiracies' of Danton or the 'base Hébert'. (Moreover, some of the addresses draw the parallel between this 'new conspiracy' and the other older ones . . .) They had learnt well that faced with 'conspiracies' unmasked in Paris it was very risky to express any doubts; to take sides with the victors was the most elementary prudence. The monopoly of information and the stranglehold of central power over public opinion left it only one area of expression, that of increasingly extravagant rhetoric, of praise and blame.

It is, moreover, striking that the addresses presented the 'terrifying conspiracy' as a distant affair which had been acted out in Paris. After the execution of the 'triumvirs' the danger was over; the unanimous people gathered round the Convention, its 'rallying point'; the Revolution had gained a victory, the greatest (it is always the last victory which is the greatest, and the last conspiracy which is the most 'horrible'); the 'fathers of the Nation' remained in place. The people of Paris had once again been worthy of their country. The addresses passed over in silence the hesitations of the Parisian *sections*, which were, however, mentioned by Barère in his report. There were very few addresses which took the risk of stepping out of the limits outlined by the messages of the Convention and, more particularly, of denouncing Robespierre's local accomplices. Even, in this case, it was only a question of members of the Convention already 'unmasked', like Lebon at Arras, or Couthon at Clermont-Ferrand. Only once, in the Commune-Affranchie (formerly Lyon), did the popular society join to its address (bearing some 700 signatures) which recorded satisfaction at the dissipation of the 'new liberticide storm', an extract from the minutes of its meeting expressing a certain anxiety: 'What is important to avoid, is that the aristocracy should profit from our divisions. Today already [14 Thermidor] a number of strange figures were walking about our streets and their looks were sinister . . . That is true! cried the whole Assembly.'

Quite involuntarily, these addresses of allegiance pay homage, via the clichés, to Robespierre. In fact, they sometimes evoke the enormous prestige which he enjoyed. But, of course, they express indignation against this 'hypocrite' who has succeeded with incredible skilfulness to wear the mask of the virtuous and incorruptible patriot, and, consequently, to deceive the people who trusted in him. 'Our love for these men, whom we regarded as the firm pillars of the Republic, is changed into deep horror at the news of their conspiracy a thousand and thousand times too bold' (popular society of Guéret, *département* of the Creuse, 14 Thermidor). 'A short time ago all republicans would have shed torrents of tears on the tomb of a man who is today recognized as more criminal than the Cromwells, the Catilines, the Neros, and who has surpassed by his crimes, discovered in an instant, all the monsters whom nature had brought forth for the misfortune of nations' (citizens of Traignac-la-Montagne, *département* of the Corrèze).

What, on the day after 9 Thermidor, had become of the 'terrorists', the fervent supporters of Robespierre? There is no reason to think they fell silent; their voices merged with others in the uproar of popular societies and local administrations, of political activists who convened the meetings, drew up the addresses, etc. To be indignant at their opportunism would be too easy (moreover, a short while after the sending of these addresses there would be no shortage of denunciations on the spot, in their own communes). This opportunism and this uniformity of behaviour and language are also one of the faces of the Terror. The addresses of congratulations sent to the Convention show up a characteristic of the period which opened on 9 Thermidor, and which we have already mentioned: the ending of the Terror begins with a language, with political behaviour and social imaginations moulded during the Terror and bequeathed by it. The disintegration of this controlled unanimity, the laying bare of the conflicts and hatred accumulated during the Terror but which had remained stifled by it, this was a condition for ending the Terror as well as its inevitable result.

Note

1 *sans-culottide*. Since each of the twelve months of the revolutionary calendar lasted thirty days, five more days (six in a leap year) were required to make up the difference. These were named in honour of the *sans-culottes* and were observed as national festivals and holidays.

Glossary of Readers

Over the years a number of Readers devoted to the secondary literature on the French Revolution have appeared. Several of these compilations provide a useful supplement to the material contained in the present volume. Details, together with a digest of contents, are given below.

E. M. Acomb and M. L. Brown, eds. *French Society and Culture since the Old Regime* (New York, Holt, Rinehart and Winston Inc., 1966).

J. R. Censer, ed. *The French Revolution and Intellectual History* (Chicago, The Dorsey Press, 1989).

R. Forster and O. Ranum, eds. *Rural Society in France: Selections from the Annales, Economies, Societies, Civilisations* (Baltimore and London, The Johns Hopkins University Press, 1977).

R. W. Greenlaw, ed. *The Economic Origins of the French Revolution: Poverty or Prosperity?* (Boston, Mass., D. C. Heath and Company, 1958).

D. Johnson, ed. *French Society and Revolution* (Cambridge, Cambridge University Press, 1976).

F. A. Kafker and J. M. Laux, eds. *The French Revolution: Conflicting Interpretations* (Malabar, Fl., R. E. Krieger Publishing Company, 3rd edition, 1983).

J. Kaplow, ed. *New Perspectives on the French Revolution: Readings in Historical Sociology* (New York, Wiley, 1965).

D. LaCapra and S. L. Kaplan, eds. *Modern European Intellectual History: Reappraisals and New Perspectives* (Ithaca and London, Cornell University Press, 1982).

Digest of Contents

Godechot, Jacques, 'An Orthodox Critique of Cobban's *Social Interpretation*', **Greenlaw (1975)**, pp. 130–39.

Halévi, Ran, 'The Constituent Revolution and Its Ambiguities', **Censer**, pp. 139–51.

Hufton, Olwen, 'Women in Revolution, 1789–1796', **Johnson**, pp. 148–66.

Hunt, Lynn, 'Hercules and the Radical Image in the French Revolution', **Censer**, pp. 166–85.

Kaplow, Jeffry, Shapiro, Gilbert and Eisenstein, L., 'Class in the French Revolution: a Discussion', **Greenlaw (1975)**, pp. 223–50.

Labrousse, C. Ernest, 'The Crisis in the French Economy at the End of the Old Regime', **Greenlaw (1958)**, pp. 59–72.

Labrousse, C. Ernest, 'The Evolution of Peasant Society in France from the Eighteenth Century to the Present', **Acomb and Brown**, pp. 43–64.

Le Goff, Timothy J. and Sutherland, Donald M., 'The Revolution and the Rural Community in Eighteenth-Century Brittany', **Johnson**, pp. 29–52.

Lefebvre, Georges, 'The French Revolution and the Peasants', **Greenlaw (1958)**, pp. 73–83.

Lefebvre, Georges, 'The Place of the Revolution in the Agrarian History of France', **Forster and Ranum**, pp. 31–49.

Lewis, Gywnne, 'The White Terror of 1815 in the Department of the Gard', **Johnson**, pp. 286–313.

Lucas, Colin, 'Nobles, Bourgeois and the Origins of the French Revolution', **Censer**, pp. 3–25 and **Johnson**, pp. 88–131.

Mathiez, Albert, 'The Breakdown of the Ancien Régime', **Greenlaw (1958)**, pp. 30–32.

Mazauric, Claude, 'The French Revolution – a Bourgeois Revolution', **Greenlaw (1975)**, pp. 30–58.

Michelet, Jules, 'Famine in the Eighteenth Century', **Greenlaw (1958)**, pp. 1–4.

Mitchell, Harvey, 'Resistance to the Revolution in Western France', **Johnson**, pp. 248–85.

Ozouf, Mona, 'Space and Time in the Festivals of the French Revolution', **Censer**, pp. 186–200.

Popkin, Jeremy, 'The Prerevolutionary Origins of Political Journalism', **Censer**, pp. 110–34.

Reinhard, Marcel, 'Demography, the Economy, and the French Revolution', **Acomb and Brown**, pp. 19–42.

Rudé, George, 'The Outbreak of the French Revolution', **Greenlaw (1975)**, pp. 3–16.

Sée, Henri, 'The Peasants and Agriculture', **Greenlaw (1958)**, pp. 49–58.

Soboul, Albert, 'The Social and Economic Character of the French Revolution: its Relevance in the Modern World', **Greenlaw (1975)**, pp. 16–30.

Tackett, Timothy, 'The Meaning of the Oath', **Censer**, pp. 152–65.

Taine, Hyppolyte, A., 'The People', **Greenlaw (1958)**, pp. 16–23.

Taylor, George V., 'Capitalism and the Origins of the French Revolution', **Greenlaw** (1975), pp. 150–59.

Tocqueville, Alexis de, 'Feudalism in Eighteenth-Century France', **Greenlaw** (1958), pp. 5–15.

Van Kley, Dale, 'Church, State and the Ideological Origins of the French Revolution: The Debate Over the General Assembly of the Gallican Clergy in 1765', **Censer**, pp. 94–109.

Index